Innovations in Supply Chain Management for Information Systems:
Novel Approaches

John Wang
Montclair State University, USA

BUSINESS SCIENCE REFERENCE

Hershey · New York

Director of Editorial Content:	Kristin Klinger
Senior Managing Editor:	Jamie Snavely
Assistant Managing Editor:	Michael Brehm
Publishing Assistant:	Sean Woznicki
Typesetter:	Sean Woznicki, Mike Killian
Cover Design:	Lisa Tosheff
Printed at:	Yurchak Printing Inc.

Published in the United States of America by
Business Science Reference (an imprint of IGI Global)
701 E. Chocolate Avenue
Hershey PA 17033
Tel: 717-533-8845
Fax: 717-533-8661
E-mail: cust@igi-global.com
Web site: http://www.igi-global.com/reference

Library of Congress Cataloging-in-Publication Data

Innovations in supply chain management for information systems : novel approaches / John Wang, editor.
    p. cm.
  Includes bibliographical references and index.
  Summary: "This book presents exemplary research on the interface between information across the supply chains"-- Provided by publisher.

  ISBN 978-1-60566-974-8 (hardcover) -- ISBN 978-1-60566-975-5 (ebook) 1.
Business logistics. 2. Technological innovations. 3. Information technology.
I. Wang, John, 1955- II. Title.

  HD38.5.I54 2010
  658.5'036--dc22

                          2009032775

British Cataloguing in Publication Data
A Cataloguing in Publication record for this book is available from the British Library.

All work contributed to this book is new, previously-unpublished material. The views expressed in this book are those of the authors, but not necessarily of the publisher.

Editorial Advisory Board

Table of Contents

Detailed Table of Contents

In the current dynamic, competitive business environment, customers expect to see products they purchase to be shipped on the date it is promised. However, accurate calculation of promised ship date by suppliers can only be obtained at expense of corporate IT systems that provide accurate availability data. Our study indicates that refresh frequency of availability data in IT system substantially impacts accuracy of the ship date that is promised to customer. The value of customer service level corresponding to accuracy of promised ship date needs to be estimated against the costs of having necessary IT system. The estimation requires a simulation model of availability management process. In this paper, we describe how to model and simulate the availability management process, and quantify the customer service level resulting from various availability refresh rate.

Chapter 2

In this chapter we discuss rough-cut cost estimation in a capacitated made-to-order environment. We develop models that analyze the effects of shop workload, machine loading, and outsourcing decisions on product unit cost estimation. A comparative study of five alternative rough-cut cost estimation methods is presented. An activity based cost estimation model, which takes into account stochastic process characteristics as well as setup time, machine failures and product yields, was developed. The activity based cost estimation was found to perform better than the traditional cost estimation. We found that by taking into account the capacity and stochastic nature of the parameters, the cost estimation accuracy is improved significantly.

Chapter 3

Radio Frequency Identification (RFID) is believed to change how supply chains operate today. While RFID's promise for improved inventory visibility and automation in inventory management is making many supply chain players hopeful for increased sales and reduced operating costs, these benefits do come at a cost and involve risks. This paper presents a financial returns analysis that captures RFID's costs and benefits, and quantifies the financial risks of implementing RFID for various business sizes and products with different unit profits to understand when RFID makes business sense. More precisely, the returns analysis is performed using an econometric model to understand how break-even sales volumes, unit profits, tag prices, return on investment, and risks vary between a manufacturer and a retailer in a supply chain. The results are extended to multi-product cases as well. A sensitivity analysis is also performed to understand the returns in pessimistic and optimistic scenarios.

Chapter 4

Knowing consumers' shopping paths is an essential part of successful retailing. Good space management requires accurate data about consumer behavior. Traditionally, these data have been collected through, for example, panel interviews, camera tracking, and in-store observation. Their nature is more or less subjective. Modern technology makes it possible to use more objective methods, such as wireless local area network (WLAN) and radio frequency identification (RFID). In this article we examine the possibilities WLAN provides information systems studies. The empirical data is collected from a large DIY (do-it-yourself) store. The results show that WLAN has great potential for accurate and objective data collection processes and modeling data in retailing.

Chapter 5

Radio frequency identification (RFID) has generated vast amounts of interest in the supply chain, logistics, and the manufacturing area. RFID can be used to significantly improve the efficiency of business processes by providing automatic data identification and capture. Enormous data would be collected as items leave a trail of data while moving through different locations. Some important challenges such as false read, data overload, real-time acquisition of data, data security, and privacy must be dealt with. Good quality data is needed because business decisions depend on these data. Other important issues are that business processes must change drastically as a result of implementing RFID, and data must be shared between suppliers and retailers. The main objective of this article is focused on data management challenges of RFID, and it provides potential solutions for each identified risk.

The purpose of this chapter is to enhance our understanding of how web-based applications and complementary resources can work together to create competitive advantages in supply chains. This chapter is organized as follows. First, this chapter introduces the theoretical background of complementary resources. Then, it moves on to report a preliminary result of secondary data analysis that explores the role of complementary resources to the development of web-enabled supply chains. Lastly, this chapter reports a case study that focuses on identifying: 1) the complementary resources that influence the successful implementation of web-based applications for supply chain management, and 2) the degree to which certain types of complementary resources function to support the successful implementation of web-based applications.

Historically, the growth of the beef industry has been hampered by the various entities (breeders, cow-calf producers, stockers, backgrounders, processors, etc..) within the beef industry's supply chain. The primary obstacles to growth are the large number of participants in the upstream side of the supply chain and the lack of coordination between them. Over the last decade significant advances have been made in information and communication technologies. Many new companies have been founded to promote these technical advances. This research looks at both the upstream and downstream participants to determine the degree to which information technologies are currently being utilized and the degree to which these new technologies have driven performance improvements in the beef industry's supply chain. We find through our survey that, by and large, the beef industry does not use information technologies to their benefit and that the US beef supply chain is not yet strategically poised to enable the use of these technologies.

Endowed with abundant supply of raw materials and low labor cost Asian countries have become the world's largest exporters of apparel products for the past few decades. In 2007, the value of Asian suppliers' total apparel exports to the world amounted to US$ 165 billion which represented 52% of the world's total apparel exports. The gravity trade model is utilized with an exploration at the aggregate level. Analyzing the data for fourteen exporting countries and their sixteen importing partners from 2000 to 2007, the country-specific, economic, social factors, in additional to logistics performance are analyzed statistically to identify the major determinants that have influenced the apparel trading of Asian countries to the EU-15, and American markets. Taking the robustness advantage of the gravity model, the analytical results indicate strong support for the model with parameters including GDP, per capita GDP, population size, female employment, value added factors and logistics performance. All these show statistically significance and positive effects. In contrast, distance, real exchange rates and wages have negative impacts on apparel trading. An important finding is that new variables, namely exporting countries' logistics performance can derive competitive advantage, otherwise, it erects a trade barrier in its own right in apparel exports.

Chapter 9

Kwok Hung Lau, Royal Melbourne Institute of Technology University, Australia
Wun Leong Ma, Royal Melbourne Institute of Technology University, Australia

As a result of globalization, supply chains of many large business organizations nowadays tend to cover wider geographic areas spanning across different countries and continents. The growth in length and complexity gradually replaces the traditional linear supply chains with extended supply networks comprising not only suppliers, manufacturers, distributors, and end customers, but also service providers. With the increasing use of third-party logistics (3PL) providers by international firms seeking integrated logistics services, many global 3PL providers are forming partnerships with large corporations to take care of the latter's logistics operations in different regions. The selection of the right 3PL provider for alliance is therefore paramount to the success of global supply chain management. This chapter investigates the significance of this subject and proposes a supplementary framework for evaluation of 3PL providers as global logistics partners for international firms. Using resource-based view theory and competencies hierarchy as theoretical underpinnings, the framework focuses on the core competencies of 3PL providers and their abilities to attain economies of scale helping users achieve their outsourcing objectives.

Chapter 10

Heekyung An, Shimadzu Corporation, Japan

Considering the implications of EU environmental laws such as REACH (registration, evaluation, authorization, and restriction of chemicals) and EuP (directive on eco-design of energy-using products) as well as RoHS (restrictions of the use of certain hazardous substances in electrical and electronic equipment) Directive, they have been acquired to advance GSCM (green supply chain management) more and more. The aim of this article is to introduce the construction of GSCM system that improves collaborative relationships between an EEE manufacturer and its suppliers. The study is conducted in three steps. Firstly, the four elements, which are necessities to form collaborative relationships between an EEE manufacturer and its suppliers, are described. Secondly, the condition and construction of GSCM system including the four elements is proposed. Finally, we presented the method that the GSCM system is constructed as a practicable tool in the initial stage by a case study held in Shimadzu Corporation.

Hsiu-Chia Ko, National Sun Yat-Sen University, Taiwan
Fan-Chuan Tseng, National Sun Yat-Sen University, Taiwan
Chun-Po Yin, National Sun Yat-Sen University, Taiwan
Li-Chun Huang, National Sun Yat-Sen University, Taiwan

This study investigated user satisfaction when a new interorganizational information system (green supply chain management system; GSCMS) was introduced to a supplier by a leader in the Taiwan electronic industry. GSCMS providers, according to the requirements of the supplier network leader, trained the representatives of suppliers. All suppliers of two sample vendors (manufacturers of electronic products) were surveyed. Five putative influencing factors were considered: perceived usefulness, perceived ease of use, training, computer anxiety, and computer self-efficacy. We find four factors significantly affect user satisfaction. The results show that the training provided by focal vendors will influence the satisfaction of users. Next, the anxiety and uncertainty experienced by users decreases when they acquire more knowledge about the operation of the new GSCMS. Finally, user satisfaction can be increased by designing the functions and interfaces of a GSCMS in accordance with the user perceptions of usefulness and ease of use, moreover, implications and suggestions are also discussed.

Ruiliang Yan, Virginia State University, USA
Sanjoy Ghose, University of Wisconsin - Milwaukee, USA

With the rapid development of the Internet, many retailers and individuals nowadays use this technology to engage in direct e-retailing sales. In this article, we investigate the value of demand-forecast information sharing in a manufacturer-e-retailer supply chain. The value of market information depends not only on its accuracy, but also on the e-retailer's market power and the product's Web compatibility. We develop a theoretical approach to examine the value of information sharing for the manufacturer and the e-retailer first, and then we further check to see how information sharing is moderated by the e-retailer's market share and the product's e-market-base demand. Our results suggest that under some conditions, both the manufacturer and the e-retailer can be better off from information sharing. Especially when the e-retailer's market share is larger and the product's e-market-base demand is higher, information sharing is more valuable for the supply chain players. Using our analysis findings, we indicate marketing strategies that the manufacturer and the e-retailer may want to adopt.

Iraj Mahdavi, Mazandaran University of Science and Technology, Iran
Shima Mohebbi, K.N.Toosi University of Technology, Iran
Namjae Cho, Hanyang University, Korea
Mohammad Mahdi Paydar, Mazandaran University of Science and Technology, Iran
Nezam Mahdavi-Amiri, Sharif University of Technology, Iran

Functional relationship between supplier and buyer in an open market place leads to investigate the role of both quantifiable and non-quantifiable parameters in coordination mechanism with the aim of achieving higher performance in supply chain activities. Here, we develop a supply chain model and a new agent to analyze and simulate the players' behavior in the network. A cooperative game theory framework is utilized between buyer and supplier in order to increase the supply chain performance. The study is supported by presenting SC Net Optimizer as a tool for implementing the proposed coordination mechanism and evaluates the performance of the chain by simulation using stochastic Petri nets (SPNs). The model provides a more realistic optimization process by taking into consideration the dynamic information flow in an uncertainty environment.

Chapter 14

Research on international subcontracting has been policy-oriented and industry-focused. There is a lack of understanding of the phenomenon from strategic management and international business perspectives. This article conceptualizes international subcontracting as a type of relational contract formed by buyers and suppliers from different countries, aiming to facilitate the sourcing of products or components with buyer-specific requirements. It builds a transaction cost model for studying the strategic choice of international subcontracting as an intermediate governance structure, sitting between arm's length outsourcing arrangement and vertically integrated multinational enterprises (MNEs). A set of propositions are developed to aid future empirical research and to provide managers with some guidelines for organizing supply chain across borders. The model also allows managers to examine the complex nature of a range of subcontracting relationships and identify the specific mechanisms that can be used to preserve and manage the dyadic principal-subcontractor exchanges.

Chapter 15

Streamlining information flows across the physical supply chain is crucial for successful supply chain management. This study examines different structures of e-networks (i.e., virtual supply chains linked via electronic information and communication technologies) and their maximum capabilities to gain e-network benefits. Further, this research explores four levels of e-network integration based on a 2x2 e-network technology and transaction integration matrix. Of the four levels, an e-network with high e-technology/high e-transaction integration appears to be most desirable for the companies that aspire to achieve the maximum benefits from their IT investments. Finally, this study identifies three alternative transformation paths toward a powerful high e-technology/high e-transaction integration network and discusses strategic implications of selecting those paths, in terms of e-network structures, availability of financial and technical resources, supply chain members' collaborative planning, e-security mechanisms, and supply chain size.

Supply chains can be disrupted at both local and global levels. Just-In-Time (JIT) companies should be particularly interested in managing supply chain failure risk as they often have very little inventory to buffer themselves when their upstream supply chain fails. We develop previous research further and present a strategic framework to manage supply chain failure in JIT supply chains. We identify two dimensions along which the risks of failure can be categorized: location and unpredictability. We go on to identify strategies which companies can use either before (proactive) or after (reactive) the failure to manage supply chain failure. We support our framework with examples of actual responses to supply chain failures in JIT companies. It is also hoped that our strategic framework will be validated empirically in the future leading to specific guidance for managers.

The term 'supply chain management' has become common in the business world, which can be understood from the positive results of research in the area, particularly in supply chain optimization. Transportation is a frontier in achieving the objectives of the supply chain. Thrust is also given to optimization problems in transportation. The fixed-charge transportation problem is an extension of the transportation problem that includes a fixed cost, along with a variable cost that is proportional to the amount shipped. This article approaches the problem with another meta-heuristics known as the Nelder and Mead methodology to save the computational time with little iteration and obtain better results with the help of a program in C++.

Preface

SUPPLY CHAIN MANAGEMENT AND INFORMATION SYSTEMS: EVOLUTION, CURRENT STATE AND FUTURE TRENDS

Introduction

SCM (Supply Chain Management) is an integrative function, with primary responsibilities for linking major business functions and business processes within and across companies, into a cohesive and high-performing business model. It drives the coordination of processes and activities across areas of marketing, sales, product design, finance and information technology (Simchi-Levi, Kaminsky, & Simchi-Levi, 2008; Eltantawy, Giunipero, & Handfield, 2006). Information systems are an important enabler of effective SCM, since with the advent of e-business, if there is no effective web-based information system in place, there is essentially no business. Any company, though, can benefit from the successful implementation of SCM using different information systems options, including *enterprise resource planning* (ERP) and *decision support systems* (DSS) that are aimed towards assisting the different functional areas in a supply chain.

Folinas, Manthou, Sigala, & Vlachopoulou (2004) proposed that, "SCM in the new business era is considered as a medium for achieving short-term economic benefits and gaining long-term competitive advantages" (p.1). As Svensson (2007) noticed and confirmed by Ranjan & Sahay (2008), starting in the early 1990s the use of the SCM increased significantly as more and more companies began to recognize and appreciate its benefits. Businesses were now able to more carefully track their sales and order their merchandise according to the customers' preferences which lowered their costs of holding unnecessary inventory, and stocking only the items that were actually demanded by the customers. This is critical, since companies today face intense competition from existing rival and new players, and must continue to find new revenue opportunities and continually increase efficiencies.

SCM has become a topic of increased interest among companies of all sizes and specialties. Companies realize that in order to compete in the global marketplace and survive, they must rely on the most effective supply chains. The effective implementation of SCM involves a network of complex webs of independent, but interdependent, organizations which can communicate with each other (Simchi-Levi, Kaminsky, & Simchi-Levi, 2008; Christopher, 2005; Metzer, DeWitt, & Keebler, 2001). SCM builds upon a framework of logistical flows of products and information through a business. With the use of SCM, the whole becomes greater than the sum of the individual parts; however it does require proper management, cooperation, and trust among those involved in the network.

SCM has evolved from operating in an isolated environment, adopting advanced systems such as *enterprise resources planning* (ERP) systems to creating a network where suppliers and customers collaborate in order to extract and share knowledge and value. Many statements have been made to describe the current situation of SCM. SCM remains a high priority for manufacturers as a way to improve margins and retain and increase market share, and the principles of SCM involve responsiveness, reliability, resilience, and the use of effective relationships (Christopher, 2005; Simatupang & Sridharan, 2008). Ballou (2007) stated that the goal of SCM is to deal with the issues of customer satisfaction, inventory management, and flexibility.

According to Bozarth and Handfield (2006), there are three major developments that have bought SCM to the forefront of manager's attention. Those are electronic commerce, increasing competition & globalization, and relationship management. Littleson (2007) argued that in the past, managers tried to forecast demand, but today and in the future this practice has been replaced by effectively responding to demand. Other scholars (Ranjan & Sahay, 2008; Ferrer, Hyland, & Soosay, 2008) agree with this theory since in such a dynamic market, where consumers' behaviors and patterns are virtually impossible to forecast, it is better to employ tools that would help the businesses to respond to demand much quicker.

Economic instability in the U.S. and abroad is affecting a wide range of businesses. Therefore, SCM and IS are solid solutions for companies looking to do more with less. Without SCM, an organization is vulnerable to various risks if it cannot flexibly react to market changes -- overproduction and underconsumption, increased demand, changes in consumers' trends, and decrease in demand due to substitute products and competitors, etc. With the effective use of SCM, a company can adjust its output to the market -- prevent excessive equipment and inventory, reduce inventory costs, and be able to shorten its delivery time while at the same time increasing production to answer market needs in a shorter time frame.

Evolution

Much of the SCM literature has suggested frameworks for identifying and analyzing the evolution of SCM. Some analysts, such as Muzumdar and Balachandran (2001) and Ballou (2007), support a three-stage evolutionary process, while others such as Folinas et al. (2004) prefer a four-stage evolutionary process. Macmillan Group (2003) reflected a specific approach to the phenomenon of SCM, and created chronological dates to indicate SCM development. The evolution of supply chains has moved from the functions of logistics and physical distribution to focus on integration, time reduction and more streamlined processes. The integrated activities involved buyer and supplier relationships, and also purchasing and marketing strategies. The success of these activities relies on a corporate ability to develop the firm's internal and external linkages.

Ballou (2007) supported Macmillan Group (2003)'s idea. He divided SCM into 3 periods; past, present and future. He suggested that SCM was founded on the maintenance and transportation of military facilities and materials. People started trading one cost for another; however, there was logistic fragmentation which led to conflicts among those responsible for logistics activities. Physical distribution and logistics were used by both marketing and production areas, but they gave a little concern for issues of product flow. Later on, people started to embrace SCM in business. The flow of goods in the entire supply chain required the coordination of demand and supply from many institutions all the way to ultimate consumers. People focused more on the integration of SCM, rather than on logistics and physical distribution. Finally, he indicated that SCM and logistics would move toward globalization, free trade and outsourcing.

In keeping with Muzumdar and Balachandran (2001), SCM is becoming a mix between centralized planning and decentralized performance. This approach divided SCM into three stages; departmentalized or functional supply chain management, transformation into integrated supply chain management, and transformation to value networks. At the beginning, the attempts of executive managers to centralize supply chain planning were ineffective due to the lack of standardization of business information, poor data integrity and analysis support, and disparate technology systems. Later on, corporate managers utilized *business process reengineering* (BPR) to align their organizations. Many companies used advanced technologies such as *enterprise resource planning* (ERP) systems to lower the costs of computing and increase the penetration of enterprise. This led to an increase in the effectiveness of integrated and centralized supply chain planning processes. In the late 1980s, Wal-Mart made *point of sale* (POS) information available to its suppliers, deployed *electronic data interchange* (EDI) and rigorously enforced more frequent replenishment of its inventory with direct shipments to stores (Devendra & Owen, 2007). The Internet has also changed the way of companies do business. Integrated and centralized supply chain planning has become more effective and widespread and it will generate more customers for the firm. The sharing of information around product seasonality, promotional events, and new product launches between buyers and sellers will further enhance the trend, and increase the associated benefits of higher customer service levels and lower supply chain costs.

Besides using time sequences, some analysts use business processes to identify SCM evolution. Folinas et al. (2004) divided SCM into four types: *core logistics activities efficiency, co-ordination of internal organizational processes, inter-enterprise business exchange* and the *establishment of dynamic networks between virtual organizations*. SCM became more than a database process but rather a *decision support system* that helped managers to make decision effectively. Also, collaboration and coordination were additional and new changes that had taken place within the SCM process (Fawcett, Mannan, & McCarter, 2008; Pramatari, 2007). The change from single decision making into collaboration is essential in today's business world.

Future Trends

Increased globalization, free trade, and outsourcing have a resulted in a tremendous shift in the movement and consumption of goods and supply chain process. This trend required managing supply chain activities including material sourcing, production scheduling, and the physical distribution system and information flows (Benyoucef & Jain, 2008; Bovet and Martha, 2003); therefore, successful management of supply chains will give management a competitive advantage. However, Ballous (2007) argued that SCM should shift away from the contemporary view that SCM is a new frontier for demand generation-competitive weapon towards a new emphasis on designing and operating the supply chain to generate more profit for a company. In today's global economic crisis, Bovet (2008) stated that uncertain economic times can bring great opportunity for supply chain managers if they operate and think like global economists.

Sustainable Supply Chain

A paramount issue in SCM is sustainability. The Earth, probably the largest universal SCM, needs tremendous help given its current environmental woes. While environmental risks and pollution can disrupt supply chains to the extent of annihilating modern civilization, many leading organizations of the world are presenting evidence of a critical link between improved environmental performance and financial gains. As a result, business has an opportunity to not only save the world, but also to ensure its own profitability (Wang, 2008).

The objective of a sustainable supply chain is to recognize the environmental impacts of goods and processes, starting from the extraction of raw materials to the use of goods produced, all the way through to the final disposal of those goods. One goal of sustainability is, for example, to reduce resource use and waste generation, while at the same time moving away from one-time use and product disposal. The typical additions to this more efficient supply chain involving recycling, re-use and remanufacturing.

There are many interpretations of what "sustainability" refers to in SCM. In Carter & Rogers's words (2008), "The term sustainability, which increasingly refers to an integration of social, environmental, and economic responsibilities, has begun to appear in the literature of business disciplines such as management and operations" (p.361). This is commonly called the triple bottom line; sustainable supply chain management (SSCM) or green supply chain management (GSCM) is the strategic, transparent integration and achievement of an organization's social, environmental, and economic goals through the systemic coordination of key inter-organizational business processes for improving the long-term economic performance of the individual company and its supply chains. GSCM is based on integrating environment thinking into the part of SCM. It includes product design, material sourcing and selection, the manufacturing process, delivery of a final product to the customers, and the end-of-life management of a product (Srivastara, 2007). Other scholars (Sarkis, 2003; Dubler-Smith, 2005; Klassen & Vachon, 2006) also agree that GSCM emphasizes environmentally friendly practices, like source reduction, recycling, material substitution, reuse of materials, waste disposal, refurbishing, and repair.

An important social factor refers to a company's culture, core values, and ethics. In other words, it is how well a company pursues avenues of improving the community along with creating and delivering socially responsible products and services. These social factors influence the decisions made relating to environmental factors. These environmental factors include such choices as packaging materials, suppliers, logistics, etc. All of these have impacts on the carbon footprint of a company. Going green is one of the goals of, as well as the future of SCM. In line with Robinson & Witcox (2008), "The general perception of survey respondents is that 'green' holds more opportunity than risk. Seventy-one percent of executives view sustainability, green, and carbon-related issues as a source of brand/reputation opportunity. Similarly, sixty-three percent see these areas are presenting the opportunity for significant growth" (p. 62). The reason for such a heightened focus is that consumers are now buying with the consideration of the environmental impact from products and services. This brings about a new ideology of companies reviewing their supplier's SCM and making decisions based on sustainability. As the future of business is sustainability, new partnerships are being made between suppliers and companies with these principles of environmental factors and sustainability. These put a new face on the global competitive landscape with going green at the core.

Clearly, the economic factor is the firm's bottom line and should be transparent to shareholders. This allows companies to grow by improving profits, creating jobs, increasing the customer base, reducing costs, and promoting long-term competitiveness. The implementation is transparent in that going "green" has the element of reducing energy cost in utility bills or transportation costs, along with reducing package waste and hazardous materials from production. These items directly affect the bottom line, and are important since traditional competition differentiators have become broadly similar across many suppliers. One way, in which companies can differentiate themselves, reduce costs and improve service, is to consider the environmental, social as well as economic factors relating to their supply chain, thus building comparative advantage. Re-evaluating a company's supply chain, from purchasing, planning, and managing the use of materials to shipping and distributing final products, with an emphasis on improving environmental and social performance, has had real benefits.

Improving sustainability allows companies to create new products, cut costs, avoid long-term ills and give them an edge over less-sustainable companies. To move from a superficial level of support to a profound commitment, companies need to incorporate socially responsible values into their supply chains. Svenson (2007) argued that it is not enough to simply match supply and demand, the points of consumption, and origin first-order (non-renewable and non-recycled resources) supply chains to support SSCM, but must extend to second and n-order (non-renewable and non- recycled resources) supply chains in the future. There are potential economic advantages of intersections of economic, with social and or environmental performance. Consistent with Carter & Rogers (2008), companies that proactively address environmental and social concerns can influence government regulations, achieving reduced costs and shorter lead times. The proportion of environmental and social initiatives which result in enhanced economic performance cannot be ignored.

Comm & Mathaisel (2008) noticed a perfect example of sustainability. Since 1980, Wal-Mart has been using computers to track inventories. Wal-Mart's discount retailer position required tight controls on supplier management, for economic survival. Wal-Mart practices tough negotiations in terms of supplier pricing and delivery, and supplier contracts are solely placed on the merits of supplier efficiency. Some contracts are written with yearly pricing reductions, forcing suppliers to be more productive, and those that have met the standards have had sustainable success.

A dimension that must not be overlooked is SCM for *sustainable products,* which is "comprehending all kinds of products that have or aim at an improved environment and social quality, which can be related back to the already mentioned implementation of environmental and social standards" (Seuring & Muller, 2008, p. 1705). An example of this is today's cleaning products. Windex has a new concentrated, small container, refillable container. Consumers can refill the previously purchased Windex container with a new refill concentrate and then just add water to dilute the substance. This saves in many ways. Plastic containers are reused, which reduces material, energy and waste in the product life cycle. Consumers enjoy the same product standards and also the added benefit of improving the environment.

As indicated by McDaniel and Fiksel (2000), a company needs to incorporate environmental management as an integrated part of an entire organization. Therefore, it can monitor how the change is implemented and maintained while realizing its benefits. The payback includes major cost reductions and increased profitability, realized through the avoidance of purchasing hazardous materials as inputs which harm the environment as well as preventing the storage or disposal of process wastes which increase costs. This results in another cost reduction based on a decrease in publicity and potential liability risks.

Mahler (2007) proposed that "The best companies view sustainability not only as a chance to contribute to social goals, but also as a powerful source of competitive advantage" (p. 59). GSCM helps the businesses to actually reduce the costs through the environmental practices. Reusing and repairing materials instead of replacing them with new ones itself saves a lot of money that would otherwise be unnecessarily spent. A study by Sheu, Chou and Hu (2005) proved this theory through their findings. Using a linear multi-objective programming model these authors realized that the implementation of the GSCM increased the net profits by about 21%. Such growth and improvement suggests that every company in the future should follow the practices of GSCM. Also, Ko, Tseng, Yin, & Huang (2008) investigated the factors influencing suppliers' satisfaction of green supply chain management systems in Taiwan.

Service-Oriented Architecture (SOA)

Next-generation platforms incorporating Service-Oriented Architecture (SOA) and Radio Frequency Identification (RFID) deserve attention. Perceived as a key to interoperability and flexibility for future on-demand business applications, SOA is business-oriented, with an integrated end-to-end process view that focuses on integrated data (Sankar & Rau, 2006). It is built on an open architecture that uses standards such as Web services and protocols such as *simple object access protocol* (SOAP) and *extensible markup language* (XML).

SOA is a Web based support system that enables the sharing of data and information among users in a supply chain. SOA frees businesses from being limited by their systems through the creation of a platform that enables custom innovations and flexibility to change. The SOA system breaks up functionality into small individual components that are stored in a library or service repository. The components are then brought together using a set of business process workflow statements, where each process block in the workflow is a functional component of service (Aimi & Finley, 2007). SOA is the latest industry approach to IT integration. SOA allows businesses to plug in new services or upgrade existing services with relative ease to address new business requirements while providing the option of making services accessible through different channels without eliminating or complicating existing applications, preserving existing IT infrastructure.

New supply chain challenges come from increased data volumes that will continue to grow exponentially as more products, network configurations, customer details, and user preferences require management. Although all this data can give greater control to the business and make the supply chain information workers more productive, users also risk drowning in data if applications cannot synthesize and deliver the right data, at the right time, and in the right format. Automation in supply chain is needed with SOA concepts. SOA aims to enhance business services efficiency. As enterprises continue to exploit the opportunities provided by the Internet, Web services are becoming a new form of enterprise computing that is becoming more important both within and between enterprises. What's more, products are becoming more complex as customers demand sophisticated features, new services, and a greater number of choices. The increased rate of change is shrinking product life cycles and forcing supply chains to become more dynamic and diversified.

Simchi-Levi et al. (2008) found that SOA is the architecture adopted by all the major business software vendors as the basis for their development tools and platforms. Additionally, it is also widely used by systems integrators to develop custom applications. SOA provides new opportunities and challenges for SCM due to a business process execution language that makes maintenance much simpler and easier to learn. The use of *business process management* (BPM) to develop a top down approach to both application development and the composition of integrated, reusable components make them easy to use and maintain. Using SOA, companies can define their business processes and benefit from separating business logic from applications.

The evolution of SOA has enabled significant opportunities for companies to expand their existing SCM solutions, without making large scale upgrades. Zeng, Liu, & Zhen (2008) observed, "The service-oriented architecture (SOA) approach has attracted the most promising technology strategy for meeting the business imperative to increase agility while lowering total operating costs" (p. 364). Actually, SOA is a transparent aspect of sustainability. Providing a customizable interface that allows companies to continuously improve on their business applications without the additional technology costs associated with system upgrades. Smith (2008) reported that Flextronics used SOA to integrate acquired Soletron in more than 60 locations, 60 systems that supported more than 100 midsize and large sites in 30 countries across four continents without any service disruptions. SOA can be a useful aspect of almost any business.

Nadhan (2004) outlined eight key challenges companies face when implementing a SOA, namely *service identification, location, domain definition, packaging, orchestration, routing, governance,* and *messaging standards adoption* which required careful planning. Granebring and Revay (2007) explained why adopting new developments like service-oriented business intelligence (SOBI) will help daily decision support in the retail trade. SOBI, which is a mix of SOA and Business intelligence (BI), can solve integration problems in an enterprise. Kim and Lim (2007) also proposed that a new SOA approach using Web services for service delivery domain in the area of telecommunication *Operations Support System* (OSS), can help achieved business agility rapidly in today changing market circumstances.

Radio Frequency Identification (RFID)

Radio Frequency Identification (RFID) is an electromagnetic proximity and data transaction technology that has become increasingly important in improving the efficiency and optimization of SCM. RFID provides a way, using microchip-based tags, to identify individual items and distinguish them from each other, in turn tracking their location and movement. Supply chains commonly experience limited visibility, which can hinder progress. The emerging technology behind RFID enables dramatic improvements in visibility, which reduces uncertainty and the need for extra inventory buffers. The tags used are either active or passive; Active tags transmit information to receiving stations, while passive tags are read by scanners as they move through a supply chain. As Roberts (2006) claimed, "RFID was first conceived in 1948 and has taken many years for the technology to mature to the point where it is sufficiently affordable and reliable for widespread use" (p. 19).

RFID allows tagged items to be read by scanners without contact or a direct line of sight. The areas of theft protection and security are growing, and applications of RFID are being worked on due to the increased need for solutions. RFID has the potential of being applied everywhere, and regardless of its usage application, RFID provides broader efficiency and operational improvements over traditional processes. RFID is revolutionizing supply chains and offers a more efficient means of communication between suppliers and their partners, since scanning can be done at greater distances, and at greater speeds, than with previous technologies. It therefore enables customers to have more readily available the desired products where they are sought. The retail sector has been one of the main drivers of RFID adoption, led by Wal-Mart, Best Buy and DHL, and RFID technology ensures information can be efficiently collected, tracked, shared, and managed in a real time manner resulting in cost savings for companies (Sengupta & Sethi, 2007; Li & Ding, 2007).

A key advantage of RFID is that it is a system using non-contact, non-line of sight means to improve SCM, including replenishment in retail stores. Heinrich (2005) reported that a one time savings of about 5% of total system inventory can be achieved through RFID. "The savings is achieved by reducing order cycle time and improving visibility, which leads to better forecasts…reduction in order cycle time yields a reduction in both cycle stock and safety stock…" (p. 215). Manufacturers can also benefit from RFID through better inventory visibility, labor efficiency, and improved fulfillment. RFID can reduce the efforts requested for cycle counting, bar code scanning, and manual inventory tasks, and help provide benefits including reduced shrinkage, improved dock and truck utilization, and the ability to more accurately trace products movements are additional benefits.

The use of RFID is not without its challenges. Smith (2005) claimed that the problems facing the implementation of RFID include costs, failure rate, interference, security and privacy issues. Early adopters face higher initial cost, and late adopters face the cost of losing market share. Spekman and Sweeney (2006) believed some of the challenges facing RFID are due to lack of experience and expertise related to the physics of RFID. Examples of these concerns are demonstrated in the possibility of RFID tags to track banknotes (Angell & Kitzmann, 2006) and in the proposal to use bracelets with an embedded RFID tag to detect human activity (Smith, Fishkin, Bing, Philipose, Rea, Roy, & Sundara-Rajan, 2005). Yu (2007) argued that RFID still faces issues like reliability, interference from noise, and high implementation costs. Muir (2007) found that libraries using RFID can result in violations of patron privacy. Fenn and Raskino (2008) discovered that the technology itself is challenging, in that deploying two sets of equipment in the chips and readers and then modifying the data systems and workflows to work with it is not a simple task. RFID also cannot travel through metals and liquids, which could hinder information flow. RFID technology currently has no industry standardization, so standards should be put in place in the future to make tags and readers compatible regardless of the manufacturer. Viehland & Wong (2007) contended that lack of skilled professionalism might slow the development of RFID. Linking RFID with GPS will also enable users to pinpoint the exact location of their items, rather than giving a status update. The main threat is identified in five ways by Krotov & Junglas (2008) which could prove to be a threat to civil liberties and privacy. Those are *hidden placement of tags*, *unique identifiers for all objects worldwide*, *massive data aggregation*, *hidden readers*, and *individual tracking and profiling*.

RFID definitely has the potential to be placed into various objects to store and track information; therefore the objects are smarter and more useful. In addition, these new applications of RFID will be the base for new business opportunities (Puffenbarger, Teer, & Kruck, 2008; Bottani & Rizzi, 2007).

Firms that employ and make investments in RFID are likely to achieve significant strategic and operational advantages. At a minimum, it is expected that RFID can improve the governance of organizational processes due to enhanced inter-organizational integration and information sharing. This results in the assumption that RFID investments are associated with improved future benefit stream and consequently enhanced market value (Jeong, Lu, 2008). Fenn & Raskino (2008) even stated that, "a forced innovation becomes an opportunity" (p. 13). If manufacturers are forced to use RFID technology, the opportunities could be limitless.

RFID technology will no doubt continue to grow. It is one of the single most important features for improving the management of supply chains. RFID helps to optimize supply chains and allow them to function more effectively. Krotov and Junglas (2008) suggested that when looking at the future the development of RFID branches off in two different ways - there is the object orientated approach on the one side and then you have the visionary approach on the other. Other scholars do not try to differentiate between different approaches. Özelkan and Galambosi (2008) presented a financial return analysis that captures RFID's costs and benefits, and quantifies the financial risks of implementing RFID to better understand when RFID makes business sense. RFID technology and the underlying standards are readily available and mature enough to support production level pilots. RFID will have a substantial and positive impact on supply-chain performance, as it will improve operating margins, speed the flow of inventory, and improve supply-chain service levels. RFID-enabled supply chains will outperform their competitors with regard to operating cost and excellence of execution.

Conclusion

This preface reviews the history and evolution of SCM and information systems. The future of SCM continues to driven and affected by the topics discussed in this paper. Several trends in SCM are discussed, including the integration of IT throughout the supply chain, the attention placed on enterprises, supply chain relationships, the growing importance of sustainability, and reverse logistics. As a current trend, we found that the supply chain path from crude oil to the consumer is interactive and dynamic. Fluctuations in gas prices can push up or down the supply and demand chain. The effective use of SCM extends the organization beyond its walls to cover the whole entire chain starting from material suppliers, to end consumers, providing knowledge and analysis on the entire process of the movement of goods. As such, effective SCM influences all participants of the chain and includes many companies in the process.

Going "green" has had a substantial impact, and is one of the core principles of sustainability. Rising fuel costs and global warming have driven the need to find renewable sources of energy, along with environmentally friendly products and services. The companies of today and tomorrow are making supplier decisions based on the influence of sustainability as an important factor. Suppliers who cannot meet the expectations of sustainability find themselves falling short, thereby passing opportunities on to the next supplier. New alliances are being formed through the sustainability process, and SSCM help companies to view sustainability not only as an opportunity to contribute to social goals, but also to be leveraged as a powerful source of competitive advantage.

SOA is driving value by providing a customizable interface that allows companies to continuously improve on their business applications without the additional technology costs associated with system upgrades. SOA offers a way to deal with the challenges and improve supply chain performance. Companies are driven to introduce better and cheaper products more frequently because of rising consumer influence and global competition. New applications of RFID continue to be developed and refined, and the potential of RFID helps companies maximize their sales and profits. Finally, with all the benefits associated with future trends of SCM, there are also costs in terms of implementation, integration, privacy, security and interference. Although some ethical issues arise with the tracking of goods and buyers, the future of RFID technology is promising. Once appropriate and meaningful industry standards are set, the opportunities can be limitless.

John Wang
Editor

REFERENCES

Aimi, G., & Finley, I. (2007). SOA: The new value driver. *SCM Review*, 12-14.

Angell, I., & Kitzmann, J. (2006). RFID and the end of cash? *Communications of the ACM, 49*(12), 90-96.

Ballou, R. (2007). The evolution and future of logistics and supply chain management. *European Business Review, 19*(4), 1-10 & 341-347.

Benyoucef, L., & Jain, V. (2008). Managing long supply chain networks: Some emerging issues and challenge. *Journal of Manufacturing Technology Management, 19*(4), 469-496.

Bottani, E., & Rizzi, A. (2007). Economical assessment of the impact of RFID technology and EPC System on the fast-moving consumer goods supply chain. *International Journal of Production Economics, 112*, 548-569.

Bovet, D. (2008). The supply chain manager as global economist. *Supply Chain Management Review, 12*(6), 1-3.

Bovet, D., & Martha, J. (2003). *Supply chain hidden profits.* Hoboken, NJ: John Wiley Corporation.

Bozarth, C., & Handfield, R.B. (2006). *Introduction to operations and supply chain management.* Upper River Saddle River, NJ: Pearson Education Inc.

Carter, C.R., & Rogers, D.S. (2008). A framework of sustainable supply chain management: moving toward new theory. *International Journal of Physical Distribution and Logistics Management, 38*(5), 360-387.

Christopher, M. (2005). *Logistics & SCM: Creating value – adding networks* (3rd ed.). Prentice Hall Financial Times.

Comm, C., & Mathaisel, D. (2008). Sustaining higher education using Wal-Mart's best supply chain management practices. *International Journal of Sustainability in Higher Education, 9*(2), 183-189.

Devendra, M., & Owen, P.H. (2007). The death of time and distance: A holistic approach to supply chain management. *Graziadio Business Report, 10*(1), 1-2.

Dubler-Smith, D.C. (2005). The green imperative. *Soap, Perfumery, and Cosmetics, 78*(8), 24-26.

Eltantawy, R., Giunipero, L., & Handfield, R. (2006). Supply management's evolution: key skill sets for the supply manager of the future. *International Journal of Operations & Production Management, 26*(7), 822-844.

Fawcett, S., Mannan, G., & McCarter, M. (2008). Benefits, barriers and bridges to effective supply chain management. *Supply Chain Management: An International Journal, 13*(1), 35-48.

Fenn, J., & Raskino, M. (2008). *How to choose the right innovation at the right time.* Boston: Harvard Business Press.

Ferrer, M., Hyland, P., Soosay, C. (2008). Supply chain collaboration: Capabilities for continuous innovation. *Supply Chain Management: An International Journal, 13*(2), 160-169.

Folinas, D., Manthou, V., Sigala, M., & Vlachopoulou, M. (2004). E-volution of a supply chain: Cases and best practices. *Internet Research, 14*(4), 1-19.

Granebring, A., & Revay, P. (2007). Service-oriented architecture is driver for daily decision support. *Kybernets, 36*(5), 622-632.

Heinrich, C. (2005). *RFID and beyond.* Indiana: Wiley Publishing Inc.

Jeong, B., & Lu, Y. (2008). The impact of RFID investment announcements on the market value of the firm. *Journal of Theoretical and Applied Electronic Commerce Research, 3*(1), 41-54.

Kim, J.W., & Lim, K.J. (2007). An approach to service-oriented architecture using web service and BPM in the telecom-OSS domain, *Internet Research, 17*(1), 99-107.

Klassen, R., & Vachon, S. (2006). Extending green practices across the supply chain. *International Journal of Operations & Production Management, 26*(7), 795-821.

Ko, H.C., Tseng, F.C, Yin, C.P., Huang, L.C. (2008). The factors influence suppliers satisfaction of green supply chain management systems in Taiwan. *International Journal of Information Systems and Supply Chain Management, 1*(1), 66-79.

Krotov, V., Junglas, I. (2008). RFID as a disruptive innovation. *Journal of Theoretical and Applied Electronic Commerce Research, 3*(2), 44-59.

Li, Y., & Ding, X. (2007). Protecting RFID communications in supply chains. *Proceedings of the 2nd ACM Symposium on Information, Computer and Communications Security, Singapore* (pp. 234-241). New York: ACM Press.

Littleson, R. (2007). *Supply chain trends: What's in, what's out.* Retrieved January 14, 2009 from www.manufacturing.net

Macmillan Group. (2003). *Chronological dates.* Retrieved December 7, 2008, from http://www.develop.emacmillan.com/iitd/material/DirectFreeAccessHPage/SCM/ch1_ChronologicalDates.asp#

Mahler, D. (2007). The sustainable supply chain. *Supply Chain Management Review, 11*(8), 59.

McDaniel, J. S., & Fiksel, J. (2000). *The lean and green supply chain: A practical guide for materials managers and supply chain managers to reduce costs and improve environmental performance.* Washington, D.C.: U.S. Environmental Protection Agency, Office of Pollution Prevention and Toxics.

Metzer, J.T., DeWitt, W., & Keebler, J.S. (2001). Defining supply chain management. *Journal of Business Logistics, 22*(2), 1-25.

Muir, S. (2007). RFID security concerns. *Library Hi Tech, 25*(1), 90-98.

Muzumdar, M., & Balachandran, N. (2001). The supply chain evolution. *AspenTech, 11*(1), 1-4.

Nadhan, E.G. (2004). Service oriented architecture: Implementation challenges. *The Architecture Journal, 2*(1), 50-55.

Pramatari, K. (2007). Collaborative supply chain practices and evolving technological approaches. *Supply Chain Management: An International Journal, 12*(3), 210-220.

Puffenbarger, E., Teer, F., & Kruck, S. (2008). RFID: New technology on the horizon for it majors. *International Journal of Business Data Communications and Networking, 4*(1), 64-80.

Ranjan, J., & Sahay, B. (2008). Real time business intelligence in supply chain analytics. *Information Management & Computer Security, 16*(1), 28-48.

Roberts, C.M (2006). Radio frequency identification. *Computers & Security, 25*(1), 18-26.

Robinson, D.R., & Wilcox, S. (2008). The greening of supply chains. *Supply Chain Management Review, 12*(7), 61-66.

Sankar, C. S., & Rau, K-H. (2006). *Implementation strategies for SAP R/3 in a multinational organization: Lessons from a real-world case study.* Hershey, PA: CyberTech Publishing.

Sarkis, J. (2003). A strategic decision framework for green supply chain management. *Journal of Cleaner Production, 11*(1), 397-409.

Sengupta, A., & Sethi, V. (2007). The promise of RFID technologies. *Communications of the AIS, 20*(56), 957-994.

Seuring, S., & Muller, M. (2008). *From a literature review to a conceptual framework for sustainable supply chain management. Journal of Cleaner Production, 16*(15), 1699-1710.

Sheu, J., Chou, Y., & Hu, C. (2005). An integrated logistics operational model for green supply chain management. *Transportation Research, 41*(2), 287-313.

Simatupang, T., & Sridharan, R. (2008). Design for supply chain collaboration. *Business Process Management Journal, 14*(3), 401-418.

Simchi-Levi, D., Kaminsky, S., & Simchi-Levi, E. (2008). *Designing and managing the supply chain* (3rd ed.). McGraw Hill.

Smith, A. (2005). Exploring RFID technology and its impact on business system. *Informational Management & Computer Security, 13*(1), 16-28.

Smith, R. (2008). *Flextronics' SOA success a hit for customers, partners. InformationWeek 500: How They Did It - Customer Intimacy* (p. 98).

Smith, J., Fishkin, K., Bing, J., Philipose, M., Rea, A., Roy, S., & Sundara-Rajan, K. (2005). RFID based techniques for human activity detection. *Communications of the ACM, 48*(9), 39-44.

Spekman, R.E., & Sweeney, P.J. (2006). RFID: From concept to implementation. *International Journal of Physical Distribution & Logistics Management Year, 36*(10), 730-747.

Srivastara, S. (2007). Green supply-chain management: A state-of-the-art literature review. *International Journal of Management Reviews, 9*(1), 53-80.

Stephenson, S., & Sage, A. (2007). *Architecting for* enterprise resource planning. In *Information Knowledge Systems Management*. George Mason University, Fairfax, VA.

Svenson, G. (2007). Aspects of sustainable supply chain management (SSCM): Conceptual framework and empirical example. *Supply Chain Management: An International Journal, 12*(4), 226-266.

Tanowitz, M., & Rutchik D. (2008). Squeezing opportunity out of higher fuel costs. *Supply Chain Management Review, 9*(1), 1-4.

Viehland, D., Wong, A. (2007). The future of radio frequency identification. *Journal of Theoretical and Applied Electronic Commerce Research, 2*(2), 74-84.

Wang, J. (2008). Sustainable supply chain and the next-generation platforms. *International Journal of Information Systems and Supply Chain Management, 1*(1), i-iv.

Yu, S.C. (2007). RFID implementation and benefits in libraries. *The Electronic Library, 25*(1), 54-64.

Zeng, H.J., Liu, W.L., & Zhen, K. Y. (2008). Supply chain simulation: collaborative design system based on SOA – a case study in logistics industry. In *Proceedings of World Academy of Science, Engineering and Technology (*PWASET), *29*, 364-367.

Chapter 1
Modeling Accuracy of Promised Ship Date and IT Costs in a Supply Chain

Young M. Lee
IBM T.J. Watson Research Center, USA

ABSTRACT

In the current dynamic, competitive business environment, customers expect to see products they purchase to be shipped on the date it is promised. However, accurate calculation of promised ship date by suppliers can only be obtained at expense of corporate IT systems that provide accurate availability data. Our study indicates that refresh frequency of availability data in IT system substantially impacts accuracy of the ship date that is promised to customer. The value of customer service level corresponding to accuracy of promised ship date needs to be estimated against the costs of having necessary IT system. The estimation requires a simulation model of availability management process. In this paper, we describe how to model and simulate the availability management process, and quantify the customer service level resulting from various availability refresh rate.

INTRODUCTION

Being able to promise customers the desirable shipment (or delivery) date and fulfilling the orders as promised are important aspects of customer service in a supply chain. With the recent surge and widespread use of e-commerce, shoppers can now easily assess and compare customer service quality in addition to quality of goods and price among different vendors. This creates a very competitive business environment, thus making customer service a critical factor for success and survival of many companies. Competitive pressures are forcing companies to constantly look for ways to improve customer services by evaluating and redesigning supply chain processes. The Availability Management Process (AMP), also called Available-to-Promise (ATP) process, is a key supply chain process that impacts customer service since it determines customer promised ship (or delivery) dates, the accuracy of the promised ship date, order scheduling delay and order fulfillment rate as well as inventory level.

DOI: 10.4018/978-1-60566-974-8.ch001

It is possible for suppliers to have accurate promised ship date; however, it may require a high IT expense. In an ideal e-business environment, when a customer order is scheduled and a ship date is computed and promised to the customer, the availability of the product should exist when it is time to fulfill the order. However, in reality the availability data that are used for the scheduling the orders are not real time availability (physical availability), but they are availability information stored in an IT system (system availability). The availability data in the IT system (static view of availability) are typically refreshed (synchronized with real time availability) only periodically since it is very expensive to update the database in real time. Due to this potentially inaccurate view of the availability, some orders can't be shipped on the promised ship date. Therefore, for certain customer orders, products are shipped later than the promised ship date resulting in customer dissatisfaction. The accuracy of promised ship date can improve with high capacity computer hardware and software and improve the customer service; however, it would also cost substantially high IT expense. Therefore, one of key decisions in order fulfillment process is to properly balance IT system (e.g., IT expense) and accuracy of promised ship date. In this work, we study how availability fresh rate (IT system) impacts customer service level. The simulation model we develop helps making critical business decision on refresh rate of availability, and adequate investment in IT system.

Availability management involves generating an availability outlook, scheduling customer orders against the availability outlook, and fulfilling the orders. The generation of *availability outlook* is the push-side of the availability management process, and it allocates availability into ATP (Available-to-Promise) quantities based on various product and demand characteristics and planning time periods. *Order Scheduling* is the pull-side of the availability management process, and it matches the customer orders against the availability outlook, determines when customer orders can be shipped, and communicates the promised ship date to customers. *Order fulfillment* is executing the shipment of the order at the time of promised ship date. Even if an order is scheduled for shipment for a certain date based on the outlook of availability, the resources that are required to ship the product on the promised ship date may not be actually available when the ship date comes. A key role for effective availability management process is to coordinate and balance the push-side and pull-side of ATP, and to have adequate Information System (IS) capabilities so that a desirable and accurate ship date is promised to customers, and products are actually shipped on the promised date.

AMP or ATP process has been described in several research papers. Ball et al. (2004) gave an overview of the push-side (Availability Planning) and pull-side (Availability Promising) of ATP with examples from Toshiba, Dell and Maxtor Corporation. They stressed the importance of coordinating the push and pull-side of availability management for supply chain performance by making good use of available resources. Although ATP functions have been available in several commercial ERP and supply chain software solutions such as SAP's APO, i2's Rhythm, Oracle's ATP Server and Manugistics' SCPO modules etc. for several years (see Ball et al. 2004 for details), those ATP tools are mostly fast database search engines that schedule customer orders without any sophisticated quantitative methods. Research on the quantitative side of ATP is still at an early stage, and there are only a limited number of analytic models developed in supporting ATP.

For the push-side of ATP, Ervolina and Dietrich (2000) developed an optimization model as the resource allocation tool, and described how the model is used for a complex Configured-to-Order (CTO) environment of the IBM Server business. They also stress how the push-side (Availability Promising) and pull-side (Availability Planning) have to work together for the overall availability management performance.

For the pull-side of ATP, Chen et al. (2002) developed a Mixed-Integer Programming (MIP) optimization model for a process where order promising and fulfillment are handled in a pre-defined batching interval. Their model determines the committed order quantity for customer orders that arrive with requested delivery dates by si-multaneously considering material availability, production capacity as well as material compat-ibility constraints. They also studied how the batching interval affects supply chain performance under different degrees of resource availability. Moses et al. (2004) also developed a model that computes optimal promised ship date considering not only availability but also other order-specific characteristics and existing commitments to the previous scheduled orders. Pan et al. (2004) de-veloped a heuristics-based order promising model but with an e-commerce environment in mind. They modeled a process where customer orders arrive via Internet and earliest possible shipment dates are computed in real-time that are promised to customers.

All the previous work described above deal with either push-side of ATP or pull-side of ATP with an assumption that accurate inventory data are available in real time. However, in reality the inventory data not always accurate, and even if the optimal ATP tools are in place, order fulfill-ment performance would be less than perfect. The perfect fulfilment performance can be approached only if there exists Information Technology (IT) in the availability management process making available accurate inventory data in real time. In this paper, we describe an availability management simulation tool that estimates the accuracy of ship date commitment at the presence of imperfect, but realistic, IT environment, which results in inaccurate view of available inventory.

Determination of promised ship date is based on availability (inventory) information kept in a computer system (system inventory), which is assumed to be accurate. In actuality, the system inventory and the actual inventory (physical in-ventory) are synchronized only occasionally due to various reasons such as IT costs for the data re-fresh, inventory shrinkage, transactional errors and incorrect product identification. The error between the system inventory and the physical inventory could accumulate over time and is not corrected until the refresh of availability (synchronization of inventory), which takes place only periodically (for example, once a day, or a few times a day) since it is expensive to generate a new snapshot of availability that is consistent throughout vari-ous corporate business systems including ERP (Enterprise Resource Planning) system. In fact, inventory inaccuracy has been identified as a lead-ing cause for operational inefficiency in supply chain management. A recent study (DeHoratius and Raman, 2008) shows that the value of the inventory reflected by these inaccurate records amounts for 28% of the total value of the on-hand inventory of a leading retailer in the U.S.

There have been studies on impact of inven-tory inaccuracy on supply chain performance, including Iglehard and Morley (1972), Wayman (1995), Krajewski et al. (1987) and Brown et al. (2001). More recently, Kang and Koh (2002) simulated the effect of inventory shrinkage (thus inaccuracy) in an inventory replenishment system with an (s, S) policy. Kang and Gershwin (2004) and Kök and Shang (2004) developed methods to compensate for the inventory inaccuracy in replenishment. Fleisch and Tellkamp (2005) ana-lyzed the impact of various causes of inventory discrepancy between the physical and the infor-mation system inventory on the performance of a retail supply chain based on a simulation model. Lee at al. (2009) discussed one way to improve the inventory accuracy through RFID in supply chain, and quantified the improvement using a simulation model. This work also studies the impact of inventory inaccuracy, but focuses on the impact of inventory accuracy resulting from inventory database refresh on the accuracy on ship date commitment through a discrete-event simulation modeling approach.

Discrete-event simulation has been around for many years in simulating Supply Chain Management (SCM) processes to evaluate its effectiveness. McClellan (1992) used simulation to study the effect of Master Production Scheduling (MPS) method, variability of demand/supplier response on customer services, order cycle and inventory. Hieta (1998) analyzed the effect of alternative product structures, alternative inventory and production control methods on inventory and customer service performance. Bagchi et al. (1998) evaluated the design and operation of SCM using simulation and optimization, analyzed SCM issues such as site location, replenishment policies, manufacturing policies, transportation policies, stocking levels, lead time and customer services. Yee (2002) analyzed the impact of automobile model variety and option mix on primary supply chain performance metrics such as customer wait time, condition mismatch and part usage. Lee et al. (2004, 2008) simulated the impact of RFID on supply chain performance through improvement of inventory accuracy. However, there hasn't been any simulation modeling work that analyzes the impact of IT system on the supply chain performance. The development of simulation model for supply chain such as availability management process can be time-consuming. We hope that the simulation modeling framework we describe in this paper can be easily adapted to simulate various availability management situations in many business environments. The simulation framework has been used at IBM for several years, and has played a critical role in making strategic business decisions that impacted customer services and profitability in IBM.

The rest of chapter is organized as follows. In the next section, we describe the availability management process. In the following section, we describe how ship date promising is modeled simulated in various availability refresh frequency. Then, we describe simulation experiments done for IBM's server business, its impacts and results. Finally, we provide concluding remarks.

AVAILABILITY MANAGEMENT PROCESS

The availability management typically consists of three main tasks: (1) generating availability outlook, (2) scheduling customer orders against the availability outlook, and (3) fulfilling the orders. The process described here is based on IBM's hardware businesses, but general characteristics would be common for many other businesses. For certain business, customer orders arrive without any advance notice, requesting earliest possible fulfillment of the orders, usually in a few days. For some other businesses, on the other hand, customers place orders in advance of their actual needs, often a few months in advance. Typically, this kind of customers place the orders as early as 3 months before the requested delivery (due) dates, and early delivery and payment are not expected. Many buyers in this environment purchase products based on careful financial planning, and they typically know when they want to receive the products and make payment.

The generation of *availability outlook*, is the push-side of the availability management process, and it pre-allocates ATP quantities, and prepares searchable availability database that are used in promising shipment of future customer orders. For certain business, an availability outlook is generated by daily buckets, and the availability planning horizon goes out to a few weeks into the future. For some other businesses, an availability outlook is allocated by weekly buckets, and the availability is planned in much longer horizon, often a quarter (3 months) into the future. The ATP quantity is called *availability outlook* for this reason. The availability outlook is typically generated based on product type, demand classes, supply classes, and outlook time buckets. The product type can be finished goods

(FG) level for Make-to-Stock (MTS) business or components level for Make-to-Order (MTO) or Configured-to-Order (CTO) business. Demand classes can be geographic sales locations, sales channels, customer priority, sensitivity to delivery dates, profitability and demand quantity. Supply classes can be degree of constraints and value of products. Availability is pre-allocated into *availability outlook* bucket based on the dimension described above, and is rolled-forward daily or weekly. The availability outlook is determined based on availability of components, finished goods, WIP (Work-In-Process), MPS (master production schedule), supplier commitment, and production capacity/flexibility. When customer orders arrive, the availability outlook is searched in various ways according to scheduling polices to determine the shipment (delivery) date, which is then promised to customers.

Customer *order scheduling* is the pull-side of availability management, and it reacts to customer orders and determines shipment dates for the orders. Customer orders arrive with various specifications such as product types, the demand classes, customer classes and due dates. The order scheduler then searches through the availability outlook database, and identifies the availability that meets the specifications. The scheduling can also be done by an ATP engine that uses certain algorithm to optimize the schedules considering various resources, policies and constraints. The scheduler then reserves specific availability against each order, and decrements the availability according to the purchase quantity of the order. The ship dates of orders are determined from the time buckets where the availability reserved, and they is promised to customers. However, if the availability data are not accurate, incorrect ship dates might be determined and promised to customers. Depending on the business environment, various rules and policies are applied in this order scheduling process. Examples include first-come-first-served policy, customer priority-based scheduling, and revenue (or profit)-based

scheduling etc. In a constrained environment, certain ceiling can also be imposed to make sure the products are strategically allocated to various demand classes.

Order fulfillment is executing the shipment of the product at the time of promised ship date. Even if an order is scheduled with a specific promised ship date based on the availability outlook, the availability (ATP quantity) may not actually exist when the ship date comes. One reason for the inaccurate ship date is due to the capability of IT system that supports the availability management process. The order scheduling is done based on the availability outlook data in an IT system, which is typically refreshed periodically since it can be very expensive to update the database in real time and it can take substantial amount of time. The availability information kept in the IT system (system availability) is not always synchronized with the actual availability (physical availability). As the synchronization (refresh) frequency increases, the accuracy of promised ship date also increases; however, the resulting IT cost would also go up because high capacity of computer hardware and software may be required to be able to refresh the availability data in certain frequency. Due to the potentially inaccurate view of availability, unrealistic ship dates can be promised to customers. Therefore, for certain customer orders the necessary ATP quantities may not be available when the promised ship dates arrive, thus creating dissatisfied customers. The impact of IT on the fulfillment is discussed in detail in the later section. A key role for effective availability management process is to coordinate and balance the push-side and pull-side of ATP as well as IT resources so that customer service target is met while corresponding IT cost stays within budget.

SIMULATION OF SHIP DATE PROMISING

In this section, we describe the availability management simulation model that we develop to analyze the relationship between accuracy of promised ship date and IT costs. The model simultaneously simulates the three components of availability management process; generating availability outlook, scheduling customer orders and fulfilling the orders, as well as the effect of other dynamics such as customer shopping traffic, uncertainty of order size, customer preferences of product features, demand forecast, inventory policies, sourcing policies, supply planning policies, manufacturing lead time etc. The simulation model provides important statistical information on promised ship date, accuracy of the ship dates determination, scheduling delay, fulfillment rate as well as inventory level.

Modeling of Availability Outlook

Availability outlook (also called availability quantity) is modeled by multi-dimensional data array which represents various attributes of availability such as product type, demand class, supply class and planning period. The product type can be either finished goods or components depending on whether the business is MTO or CTO. As a simple example, for a process where there are two attributes of availability (product type and time period), the availability outlook is represented by 2-dimensional data array shown as cylinders in the Figure 1. The availability outlook is time-dependent; e.g., there is availability quantity for the current period (t=1), and there is availability quantity for future periods (t=2, 3, ...) as more availability quantity is expected to be available through production or procurement in future dates. The availability time periods can be daily buckets or weekly buckets depending on business environment. For example, in the Figure 1, quantity 3 of component 1 is available in the current day, and 5

more are expected to be available a day after, and 10 more are expected be available for day 3 and so on. The availability outlook can be determined from demand forecast and supply contracts etc., but it can also be computed by push-side ATP optimization tool. The availability outlook is used in computing the ship date of customer requests and orders. The availability quantity changes as a result of many events in the business.

Simulation of Ship Date Promising

The Figure 1 shows an example of how the ship date calculation is simulated in this work. Customer orders or ATP requests arrive in certain stochastic interval, usually modeled as a Poisson process. Each order has one or more line items, and each line item has one or more quantities. The order quantities can be modeled with probability distribution functions, which can be derived based on historic data. The line items and quantities are determined as the order is generated in the order generation event (details described in the next section). For each line item, certain components are selected as the building blocks of the product using a distribution function representing customer preference of component features. For example, in the Figure 1, the line item #3 of the order # 231, requires components 1, 3 and 4, one unit each.

For the orders that are requested to be fulfilled as early as possible, the simulation model looks for specified quantity of a chosen component starting from the first time period to the latter time periods until the availability of all the quantity is identified. In this example, the time periods (buckets) are in days. For the component #1, the requested quantity of 10 is identified in the first 3 days; 3 in day 1 (t=1), 5 in day 2 (t=2), and 2 in day 3 (t=3). Therefore, for the line item#3, the required quantity of component 1 is available by the third day. A similar search is carried out for component #3, which is available on the first day, and for component #4, which is available by the

Figure 1. Simulation of order scheduling and ship date calculation for as early as possible orders

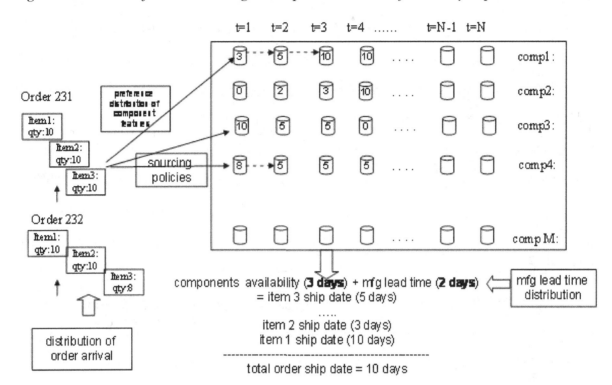

second day. Therefore, the component availability of line item#3 of the order#231 is the 3rd day. In this example, let's assume that the availability calculated for the line item#1 is 8th day, and that of the line item#2 is 1st day. When all the components are available, the product is assembled or manufactured, which takes a certain amount of time. The manufacturing lead time can be a fixed number of days or it can be described with a distribution function. The lead time to ship date is then calculated by adding the manufacturing (assembly) lead time to the availability lead time. Assuming that the manufacturing lead time for this example is 2 days, the partial ship date for item#1 is 10th day, for item#2 is 3rd day, and for the item#3 is 5th day, if the customer is willing to receive partial shipments. And the total order ship date is 10th day from the date of order or request. Therefore, the promised ship date for the order #231 is simulated to be 10 days from the order date for this example. When this order

is scheduled, availability quantities are reserved (e.g, the availability is decremented) for the order. Typically, for each order, availability is reserved from the latest possible availability bucket so that the availability in earlier time bucket can be used for generating favorable ship date for future orders. In this example as shown in the Figure 1, quantity of 10 for component 1 is reserved in t=3, and quantity of 10 for component 3 is reserved in t=3. However, for component 4, quantity of 5 is reserved for t=1, and another 5 is reserved t=2 instead of quantity 8 being reserved of for t=1 and 2 for t=2 because having availability of 3 at t=1 is more valuable than the availability of 3 at t=2 for scheduling and fulfilling future orders. Scheduling logic can vary based on the business rules and policies. Scheduling can also be carried out by a pull-side ATP optimization engine that optimizes order scheduling simultaneously considering inventory costs, backlog cost and customer service impact etc.

Figure 2. Simulation of order promising and ship date calculation for advance orders

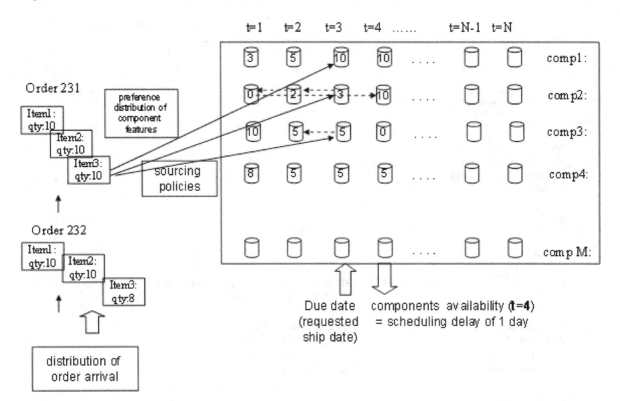

For the orders with advance due dates, the simulation model looks for specified quantity of a chosen component starting from the time period of due date (requested ship date), searches backward into the earlier time periods, and then forward to later time periods until the availability of all quantity is identified as shown in the Figure 2. For this example, the item 3 of the order #231 requires for the quantity of 10 of component #1, #2 and #3. However, in this case the order comes with requested ship date of t=3, say 3 days from the time of order. For component #1, the simulation model finds the availability of 10 on t=3, and reserves the availability. For component 2, it finds quantity of 3 on t=3, then it searches backward to find 2 more quantity on t=2 and then moves forward to find 5 more on t=4. But, in this case the simulation reserves availability quantity of 10 all on t=4 making availability quantity intact for t=2 and t=3 for future orders. For component

3, the simulation model finds availability of 5 on t=2 and t=3 each, and reserves them. In this case the overall availability date is t=4, a day after the due date. Therefore, the promised ship date for the order is simulated to be t=4, a day past the requested ship date.

Simulation of Event Generation

In this work, *availability outlook* changes as a result of four events; (1) demand event, (2) supply event (3) roll-forward event, and (4) data refresh event as shown in Figure 3. Each event changes the *availability outlook*; the demand event decrements the availability, the supply event increments the availability, the data refresh event refreshes the availability and the roll-forward event shifts the availability as explained in the next section. The data refresh event is the one that refreshes (synchronizes) system availability data. The events can be gener-

Figure 3. Multiple events that effect availability

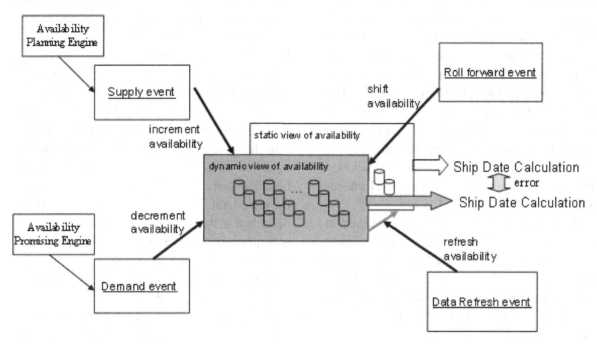

ated independently using probability distribution functions or fixed intervals. The model can be easily extended to include more events depending on the supply chain environment being modeled.

The demand event is the pull-side of availability management, and it includes order scheduling and fulfillment. The demand event is triggered when customer orders are generated, and it decrements the availability outlook (quantity) when it schedules customer orders. Customer orders are generated in certain stochastic interval, usually as a Poisson process. At the time of the order generation, each order is assigned with one or more attributes such as quantity, product type, demand class, supply class and due dates.

This assignment of attributes can be modeled with probability distribution functions based on historic sales data or expected business in the future. When an order is scheduled, specific availability quantities are searched in the availability outlook, which are then reserved for the order and are decremented from the availability outlook. The reservation (consumption) of specific

availability can be decided by the various policies and rules, such the sourcing policy, scheduling polices and fulfillment policies. The reservation of availability outlook can also be determined by *availability promising engines* that were described earlier. An ATP engine can be connected to the simulation model and communicates the optimal ATP reservation quantities it computes to the simulation model.

The supply event is the push-side of availability management, and it generates availability through schedules of production and procurement of components. The supply event is triggered in certain interval, e.g., weekly or monthly, and it increments the *availability outlook*. As finished products or building block components are reserved when customer orders are scheduled and fulfilled, additional availability is added to the availability outlook through production or procurement. This activity, supply event, is planned in advance of expected demand, e.g., months, weeks or days before the availability are actually needed in order to accommodate lead time for production and procurement. As a result of the supply planning, the availability outlook is updated and replenished. The replenishment quantity is typically determined based on the forecast of customer demand. The frequency and size of the replenishment are also decided by various replenishment policies. The allocation of availability outlook can also be determined by availability planning engines, some of which have been described previously. These ATP engines can be connected to the simulation model and communicate the optimal ATP allocation to the simulation model.

As simulation clock moves from a time bucket to another, the availability of products or components that have not been consumed are carried forward to an earlier time bucket. For example, at the end of the first day, the availability quantity of 2nd day moves to the availability quantity of 1st day, and that of 3rd day becomes that of 2nd day etc. Also, the availability quantity that is not consumed on the 1st day stays on the same day, assuming it is non-perishable. The roll-forward event can be triggered in a fixed interval, e.g., daily or weekly, depending on the business environment.

There are two instances of availability outlook; one representing the availability quantity at real time (dynamic view of availability, or physical availability), and another representing availability recorded in the availability database (static view of availability, or system availability). The system availability is the one that is used for scheduling of customer orders, and it not always accurate. The system availability is synchronized with physical availability only periodically because it is expensive to have IT architecture and capacities that allow real time synchronization. This synchronization between physical availability and system availability is modeled in the data refresh event. For example, the static view of availability is refreshed in every few minutes, every hour, or even every few days.

The discrepancy between the physical availability (dynamic view of availability) and the system availability (static view of availability) causes inaccurate ship date calculation. In our simulation model, ship dates are computed using both dynamic and static view of the availability, as shown in the Figure 3, and the magnitude and frequencies of ship date inaccuracy are estimated. The accuracy of promised ship date is an important indication of customer service level. The data refresh event can be modeled as fixed interval event or randomly generated event described by a distribution function. The analysis on how the refresh rate impacts the ship date accuracy is described in the following section.

Figure 4 shows a simplified overview of availability simulation model we developed. Here, the rectangles represent various tasks (and events), circles represent availability outlook, and the arrows represent the movement of process artifact (customer orders in this case). Generation of orders (or on-line shopping) is modeled in the first rectangle on the left side of the Figure 4, and general availability of products, features and prices are also available for customers here. An order then proceeds to the next task where a specific product is configured from the availability of components. A ship date is also determined here in the availability check (shop) task, which accesses the IT system that contains availability outlook data. If the customer is satisfied with a ship date, an order moves to next step, the availability check (buy) task, and is submitted. A promised ship date is calculated again here using the availability outlook data and order scheduling policies. A submitted order goes through the order processing task in the back office and order fulfillment process, where the model simulates the availability being consumed. The tasks specified as rectangles in Figure 4 can have certain processing time. They can also require certain resources such as an IT server, a part of whose resource is tied up in processing orders.

Figure 4. A sample availability management simulation model

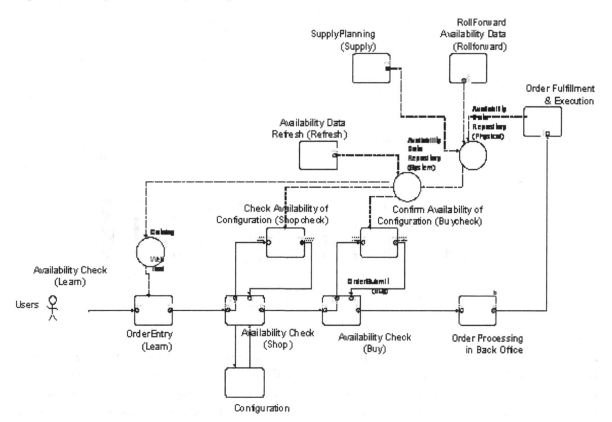

SIMULATION EXPERIMENTS AND RESULT

The analysis for the accuracy of promised ship date and availability refresh rate described here is based on an actual business case for an IBM's computer hardware business. For the business, ship dates are determined and promised to customers during the customers' shopping process at "web-speed". Customers make decisions on purchase based on the promised ship dates in addition to other criteria such as price and quality of goods. Once orders are placed, customers expect the products to be delivered on the promised dates. Often, keeping the promised ship date is more important than the promised ship date itself. Therefore, accuracy of promised ship date is very closely related to customer service.

In this business case, we used the availability simulation model to evaluate how the frequency of availability data refresh affects the accuracy of ship date information given to customers. The time bucket for availability outlook for this example is weekly; e.g, ship date is promised in weekly unit. Figure 5 shows a simulated ship date error profile for 3 months period for a product and for a demand class when the frequency of availability data refresh is once a day. The figure shows that there are quite a few occurrences of the ship date errors, whose magnitude are mostly 1 week. The simulation result shows that the magnitude of the ship date error increases to 2 weeks toward the end of the quarter.

Figure 6 compares ship date errors for four refresh frequencies, for customer orders arriving with three different demand classes for a specific business setting of the IBM hardware business.

Figure 5. Ship date error for DM class 1 with once a day refresh

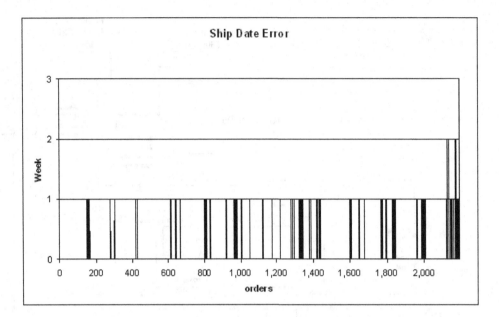

Figure 7 also summarizes the simulation results. In average, the ship date error went down to 1.4% from 3.2% as the refresh frequency increases from once a day to four times a day. However, the ship date error does not decrease substantially as the refresh rate increases beyond 3 times a day. This indicates that it is not worthwhile to improve IT system to refresh the availability more than 3 times a day for this particular business setting.

Figure 8 shows a trade-off between ship date error and IT Costs for refreshing the availability outlook in an IT system. As it is shown, as the refresh rate increases from once a day to four times a day, the IT costs increase substantially from $1.2 million to $2.3 million due to required computer hardware and software capacities. Although the general relationship between ship date error and IT Costs are not a surprise, the quantification of the trade-off is the key information that business leaders need to have to make sound business decision on the availability management process. The right decision is the balancing the ship date error (customer service) and IT costs that are reasonable for a business at the time of analysis. The simulation results from this case study clearly

show that IT system that refreshes the availability influences the accuracy of ship date calculation when customer orders are processed. Simulation is a useful tool for determining the trade-off between IT costs and supply chain performance. For this particular business environment, once a day refresh was decided as a reasonable frequency.

The simulation models described above for the cases studies were all validated by examining the simulation outputs of the AS-IS cases with actual data from the business. After the validation of the AS-IS cases, simulation models of TO-BE cases were used for analysis.

CONCLUSION

We develop a simulation model to study how refresh frequency of availability data in corporate IT system impacts accuracy of the ship date that is promised to customer. Our study quantifies accuracy of promised ship date for various refresh frequencies of availability data in a supply chain setting. As the refresh frequency of availability data increases, the accuracy of promised ship date

Figure 6. Ship date error for 3 various refresh frequencies

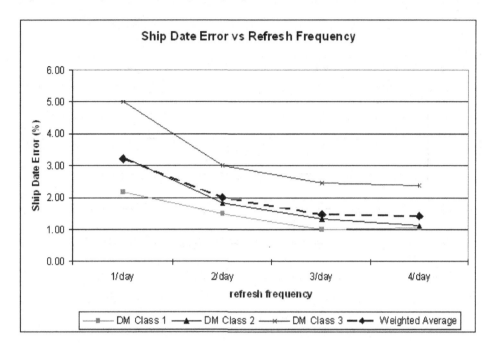

improves too; however, a high refresh rate of the data can require expensive IT system and is not practical for suppliers. Therefore, it is important to appropriately balance customer services resulting from the accuracy of promised ship date and IT costs resulting from IT system of computer hardware and software so that corporate goal for a customer service level within reasonable IT expenditure is met. Simulation has been proven to be a useful tool for the analysis. This work has helped business leaders in making informed decisions of balancing customer services and costs.

ACKNOWLEDGMENT

The author would like to thank Joseph DeMarco, and Daniel Peters of IBM Integrated Supply Chain (ISC) group for sharing their knowledge and experience in IBM's availability management processes and providing technical advices.

Figure 7. Ship date error summary for various refresh frequencies

Refresh Frequency	Ship Date Error			
	Once a day	Twice a day	3 Times a day	4 Times a day
DM Class 1	2.16%	1.51%	1.01%	1.04%
DM Class 2	3.25%	1.84%	1.33%	1.13%
DM Class 3	5.00%	3.00%	2.46%	2.39%
Weighted Average	**3.22%**	**2.00%**	**1.49%**	**1.42%**

Figure 8. Trade-off between ship date error and IT costs

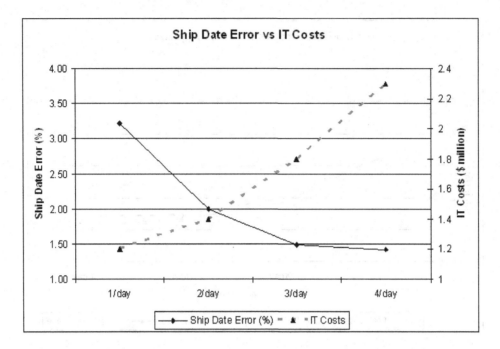

REFERENCES

Bagchi, S., Buckley, S., Ettl, E., & Lin, G. (1998). Experience using the IBM supply chain simulator. In D.J.Medeires, E.F.Watson, J.S. Carson, & M.S.Manivannan (Eds.), *Proceedings of the 1998 Winter Simulation Conference* (pp. 1387-1394).

Ball, M. O., Chen, C.-Y., & Zhao, Z.-Y. (2004). Available to promise. In D. Simchi-Levi, D. Wu, & Z.M. Shen (Eds.), *Handbook of Quantitative Analysis: Modeling in an-e-business era* (pp. 446-483). Kluwer.

Brown, K. L., Inman, A., & Calloway, J. A. (2001). Measuring the effect of inventory inaccuracy in MRP inventory and delivery performance. *Production Planning and Control, 12*(1), 46–57. doi:10.1080/09537280150203979

Chen, C.-Y., Zhao, Z.-Y., & Ball, M. O. (2002). A model for batch advanced available-to-promise. *Production and Operations Management, 11*(4), 424–440.

DeHoratius, N., & Raman, A. (2008). Inventory record inaccuracy: An empirical analysis. *Management Science, 54*(4), 627–641. doi:10.1287/mnsc.1070.0789

Ervolina, T., & Dietrich, B. (2001). Moving toward dynamic available to promise in supply chain management: Status and future research. In S. Gass, & A. Jones (Eds.). Preprints produced by R. H. Smith School of Business, U. of MD and Manufacturing Eng. Lab., NIST.

Fleisch, E., & Tellkamp, C. (2005). Inventory inaccuracy and supply chain performance: a simulation study of a retail supply chain. *International Journal of Production Economics, 95*(3), 373–385. doi:10.1016/j.ijpe.2004.02.003

Hieta, S. (1998). Supply chain simulation with LOGSIM-Simulator. In D.J.Medeires, E. F. Watson, J.S. Carson, & M.S. Manivannan. In *Proceedings of the 1998 Winter Simulation Conference* (pp. 323-326).

Iglehart, D. L., & Morey, R. C. (1972). Inventory systems with imperfect asset information. *Management Science, 18*(8), 388–394. doi:10.1287/mnsc.18.8.B388

Kang, Y., & Gershwin, S. (2004). *Information inaccuracy in inventory systems stock loss and stockout*. Joint MIT/INFORMS Symposium.

Kang, Y., & Koh, R. (2002). *Applications Research*. Research Report, Auto-ID Center, MIT.

Krajewski, L. J., King, B. E., Ritzman, L. P., & Wong, D. S. (1987). Kanban, MRP, and shaping the manufacturing environment. *Management Science, 33*(1), 39–57. doi:10.1287/mnsc.33.1.39

Lee, Y. M., Cheng, F., & Leung, Y. (2004). Exploring the impact of RFID on supply chain dynamics. In R.G.Ingalls, M.D. Rossetti, J.S. Smith, & B. A. Peters (Eds.), *Proceedings of the 2004 Winter Simulation Conference*. Retrieved from http://www.informs-sim.org/wsc04papers/147.pdf

Lee, Y. M., Cheng, F., & Leung, Y. (2009). A quantitative view on how RFID can improve inventory management in a supply chain. *International Journal of Logistics: Research and Applications, 12*(1), 23–43. doi:10.1080/13675560802141788

McClelland, M. (1992). Using simulation to facilitate analysis of manufacturing strategy. *Journal of Business Logistics, 13*(1), 215–237.

Moses, S., Grand, H., Gruenwald, L., & Pulat, S. (2004). Real-time due-date promising by build-to-order environments. *International Journal of Production Research, 42*, 4353–4375. doi:10.1080/00207540410001716462

Pan, Y., & Shi, L. (2004). Stochastic on-line model for shipment date quoting with on-line delivery gurantees. In R. G. Ingalls, M.D. Rossetti, J.S. Smith, & B.A. Peters (Eds.), *Proceedings of the 2004 Winter Simulation Conference*.

Wayman, W. A. (1995). Inventory accuracy through warehouse control. *Production and Inventory Management Journal, 36*(2), 17–21.

Yee, S.-T. (2002). Establishment of product offering and production leveling principles via supply chain simulation under order-to-delivery environment. In E. Yücesan, C.H. Chen, J.L. Snowdon, & J.M. Charnes (Eds.), *Proceedings of the 2002 Winter Simulation Conference* (pp. 1260-1268).

Chapter 2
Cost Estimation in a Capacitated Environment

Mark Eklin
Israel Institute of Technology, Israel

Yohanan Arzi
ORT Braude College, Israel

Avraham Shtub
Israel Institute of Technology, Technion City, Israel

ABSTRACT

In this chapter we discuss rough-cut cost estimation in a capacitated made-to-order environment. We develop models that analyze the effects of shop workload, machine loading, and outsourcing decisions on product unit cost estimation. A comparative study of five alternative rough-cut cost estimation methods is presented. An activity based cost estimation model, which takes into account stochastic process characteristics as well as setup time, machine failures and product yields, was developed. The activity based cost estimation was found to perform better than the traditional cost estimation. We found that by taking into account the capacity and stochastic nature of the parameters, the cost estimation accuracy is improved significantly.

INTRODUCTION

Nowadays, in the global competitive market, companies' prosperity is strongly dependent on their ability to accurately estimate product costs. This is especially true for firms operating in a make-to-order environment. For such firms, a small error in a price quote, resulting from erroneous product cost estimation, may make the difference between being awarded and losing a contract.

During the last decade, the relative weight of direct labor costs in manufacturing has dramatically diminished, while the relative weight of indirect costs has increased (Gunasekaran, Marri & Yusuf, 1999). Therefore, allocating indirect costs to products, without taking into account shop floor capacity, may lead to erroneous estimations. Despite this, most existing cost estimation models assume unlimited shop floor capacity. There are many such models in the literature. These models use information about the products, the materials and the production processes. Common approaches are:

DOI: 10.4018/978-1-60566-974-8.ch002

- Parametric cost estimation models that are based on:
  - Regression analysis (Cochran, 1976a, b; Ross, 2002).
  - Fuzzy logic (Jahan-Shahi, Shayan & Masood, 2001; Mason & Kahn, 1997).
  - Minimization of Euclidean distance between the estimated cost and its actual value (Dean, 1989).
  - Neural networks (Bode, 2000; Lin & Chang, 2002; Shtub & Versano, 1999; Smith & Mason, 1997).
- Bottom-up cost estimation models, in which the total cost is the sum of detailed components (Rad & Cioffi, 2004; Son, 1991; Stewart, 1982).
- Group technology cost estimation models that use the similarity between products from the same family (Geiger & Dilts, 1996; Jung, 2002; Ten Brinke, Lutters, Streppel & Kals, 2000).
- Hybrid cost estimation models that combine some of the models described above (Ben-Arieh, 2000; Sonmez, 2004).

Parametric, bottom-up, group technology and hybrid cost estimation models use only information about the product, the materials from which it is made, and the production processes required for its manufacture. None of the above cost estimation methods takes considers the available capacity on the shop floor. The assumption is that the available capacity is sufficient. However, in reality, one must deal with finite capacity and dynamic workloads, which may change over time.

Here we assumed that the total cost of the product is a function of the load on the shop floor (which is made up of the orders waiting to be manufactured or actually being manufactured in a certain time period). Specifically, we assumed that the cost of producing an order when the load is high is different from the cost of the same order when the load is low and most resources are idle.

It is our contention that ignoring the load on the available capacity distorts the product cost estimation and may lead to wrong decision-making.

In recent years, several researchers have suggested estimation models that consider limited capacity. However, in spite of the depth of these studies, most of these models focused on pricing and fit specific environments, such as monopolistic firms. These models were not general enough; they did not explain the relationship between the product costs and the workload. Banker et al. (2002) analyzed the issue of optimal product costing and pricing of a monopolistic firm that must commit, on a long-term basis, capacity resources. Falco, Nenni and Schiraldi (2001) developed a cost accounting model for line balancing, based on a plant's productive capacity analysis. They tested their model in a chemical-pharmaceutical plant. Balakrishnan and Sivaramakrishnan (2001) tried to estimate the economic loss of planning capacity on the basis of limited information and of delaying pricing until more precise information about demand becomes available.

Feldman and Shtub (2006) developed a detailed cost estimation model that performs capacity planning based on a detailed schedule of work orders assuming no outsourcing, no machine failures and no product defects.

Nevertheless, outsourcing cost is an important component of the total product cost. Firms use outsourcing to reduce costs or as a solution for limited capacity. Product cost depends on a make vs. buy decision. Cost trade-off is the main approach in a make vs. buy decision (Balakrishnan, 1994; Bassett, 1991; Ellis,1992, 1993; Levy & Sarnat, 1976; Meijboom, 1986; Padillo-Perez & Diaby, 1999; Poppo, 1998; Raunick & Fisher, 1972). In addition, strategic perspectives, such as competitive advantage and risk of dependence on suppliers, are also usually analyzed (Baines et al., 1999; McIvor et al., 1997; Venkatesan, 1992; Welch & Nayak, 1992).

There are several other areas, in addition to manufacturing, that deal with make vs. buy problems: Berman and Ashrafi (1993) and Helander et al. (1998) presented Integer Programming (IP) optimization models to facilitate make vs. buy decisions in component-based software development; Baker and Hubbard (2003) developed a model of asset ownership in trucking; Fowler (2004) discussed the issue of building components as opposed to buying in the development of new products and systems; Kurokawa (1997) examined key factors that affect make-or-buy decisions in research and development (R&D) settings—for instance, whether technology is developed in-house or acquired from external sources (e.g., through licensing or R&D contracts).

Traditionally, product manufacturing costs have been classified as: direct material, direct labor, or overhead. Traditional cost systems, also called volume based cost systems (VBC systems), trace overhead costs to the product by allocation bases. The most common allocation bases used in VBC systems are direct labor hours and machine hours. The amount of overhead allocated to a batch of products increases linearly with the volume produced. Therefore, it is assumed that direct labor hours increase in a linear fashion as the volume of output increases. This method is simple and easy to maintain, yet it could underestimate the true production cost and yield a less than accurate cost figure by using incorrect overhead rates.

Liggett et al. (1992) stated the underlying philosophy of Pareto analysis as follows: "Certain activities are carried out in the manufacture of products. Those activities consume a firm's resources, thereby creating costs. The products, in turn, consume activities. By determining the amount of resource (and the resulting cost) consumed by an activity and the amount of activity consumed in manufacturing a product, it is possible to directly trace manufacturing costs to products".

The first way in which ABC differs from traditional cost systems is that it is a two-stage procedure. In the first stage, it assigns all resource costs to the activities in activity centers based on resource drivers (O'Guin, 1991). Cooper (1998) defined the amount paid for a resource and assigned to an activity as a cost element. Novin (1992) argued that a cost pool does not have to contain only one activity. It can be classified into a few groups from a large number of activities. Regression analysis can be used in forming cost pools. In the second stage, costs are assigned to the products based on the product's consumption of the activities and the level of the activities in the ABC hierarchy (Novin, 1992; O'Guin, 1991). Cost drivers are used to assign the costs of activities to products. A cost driver can be any factor that causes costs to be incurred, such as number of machine setups, engineering change notices, and purchase orders. At least one cost driver is required for each activity. Use of more cost drivers may increase the accuracy of cost allocation.

Another unique feature of ABC is that its focus is on activities and the cost of these activities, rather than on products as in the traditional costing systems. This gives management the necessary information to identify opportunities for process improvements and cost reductions.

Sullivan (1992) listed the characteristics of the modern manufacturing environment, and stated that manufacturing companies become more information intensive, highly flexible and immediately responsive to the customer expectations in today's world. Due to the changing manufacturing environment, traditional cost accounting is rapidly disappearing. Traditional accounting systems were developed at a time when the percentage of direct labor cost was a large part of the total product cost. As the new technologies, such as the just-in-time philosophy, robotics and flexible manufacturing systems, were adopted, the direct labor component of production has decreased and overhead costs have increased. In today's manufacturing environment, direct labor accounts for only 10% of the costs, whereas material accounts for 55% and overhead 35%. As a result, product cost distortion occurs when allocating overhead

Figure 1. Research methodology

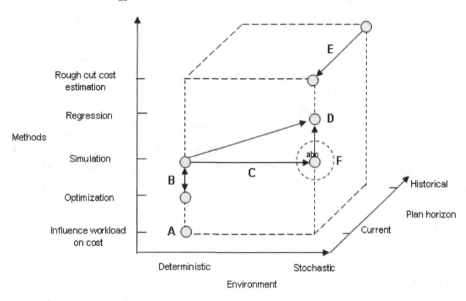

costs to the products arbitrarily on the basis of direct labor hours used by the products (Harsh, 1993). Cooper (1988) cited several situations that can cause distortions, such as production volume diversity, complexity diversity, material diversity and setup diversity.

RESEARCH METHODOLOGY

Firstly (see point A in Figure 1), a deterministic model for rough-cut cost estimation in a capacitated made-to-order environment was developed. This model was used to analyze the effect of shop workload, machine loading, and outsourcing decisions on the product unit cost estimation. The model estimates product unit costs, while taking into account the shop floor rough-cut capacity planning and by determining what to produce in the firm's shop and what to outsource. In order to reduce runtimes, a greedy heuristic algorithm was developed. A comparison of the proposed model with a model that takes into account precedence between operations and with traditional costing approach was conducted.

In the proposed model direct costs are allocated to products on the basis of their rough-cut planned schedule. Assigning a specific unit for production in regular rather than in extra hours decreases its product unit cost while increasing the unit cost of all other products. Hence, here we see that the product unit cost is affected directly by scheduling decisions. This is in opposition to traditional costing approaches.

After this (see point B in Figure 1), the existing cost estimation model for deterministic environments, which is based on marginal analysis—the difference between the total cost without the new order and the total cost with the new order—was improved. The proposed model is based on the integration of simulation and optimization. Data generated by the simulation were used in the optimization procedure that found good feasible solutions quickly. A computational study was performed to test different factors affecting the proposed model.

On the basis of the solution (see point C in Figure 1) that recommended the production volume of every product in each period, a cost estimation model that takes into account stochastic process and setup time, machine failures and yields of products was developed. The model integrates simulation with existing deterministic cost estimation models.

In next step (see point D in Figure 1), linear regression-based predictive models were generated for estimating the mean (MT) and the coefficient of variation (CV) of the total cost. In order to improve the CV predictive model, a neural network was used and tested; however, the neural network did not achieve an improvement in the CV prediction level.

Following this (see point E in Figure 1), in order to develop and to determine a practical tool, a comparative study of five alternative rough-cut cost estimation methods that can replace the simulation was done. Raw material and regular hour costs were the same for all methods; the real difference between the methods was in the way they estimated inventory holding, backorder and overtime costs. The five methods were:

- Rough-cut cost estimation method based on RCCP
- Rough-cut cost estimation method based on Time Unit Cost
- Rough-cut cost estimation method based on Snapshot Principle
- Rough-cut cost estimation method based on Bottleneck Analysis
- Rough-cut cost estimation method based on Smoothed Station

A cost estimation method, based on the forced idle time of the bottleneck workstation, was found to be outperform the others.

Finally (see point F in Figure 1), an activity based cost estimation model that takes into account stochastic process and setup time, machine failures and yields of products was developed. In opposition to the traditional cost allocation method, which assumes that indirect costs are caused equally by all the products, activity based costing seeks to identify cause and effect relationships to objectively

assign costs. The model integrates simulation with existing deterministic cost estimation models. It was shown, as expected, that the activity based cost estimation model performed better than the traditional cost system estimation model.

DETERMINISTIC MODEL FOR ROUGH-CUT COST ESTIMATION ASSUMING A TRADITIONAL (VOLUME BASED) COST SYSTEM

Major Assumptions

In this work, we developed a model that explains the relationship between product cost and workload. The model was based on the following assumptions:

- The firm is operating in a make-to-order environment.
- The planning horizon is fixed and known.
- The shop floor consists of several workstations.
- Each workstation consists of several capacitated machines of one or more types and is operated by at least one worker. The reliability of each machine is known.
- Machines of a specific type are assigned to a single workstation only.
- Workers who are assigned to regular shifts are paid for the entire shift, even if they are idle for part or the whole shift.
- Workers can be assigned to overtime, only when machines are scheduled to be busy.
- Workers get paid for extra hours even when the machine is unavailable.
- The shop produces several products. The total demand for each product for the planning horizon is known.
- The products are batched (e.g., by a planning system using lot-sizing rules). The number of units in each batch for the planning horizon is known.

- Any batch may be outsourced to subcontractors.
- Each product has a single production route. The production route consists of several operations. Each operation can be executed on a specific machine type.
- Setup time, between two successive batches, on a machine is sequence-independent.
- No late deliveries are allowed. Outsourcing is used to prevent late deliveries.

Model Formulation

Total Cost Calculations

In our approach, the company's total cost consisted of two components: the shop and the outsourcing costs. The various shop costs were organized hierarchically on three levels: machine level, workstation level and shop level. The costs related to the machine level were: machine operational costs, machine maintenance costs, machine insurance costs and tooling costs. The costs related to the workstation level were: direct labor costs (regular and extra hours) and workstation overhead costs. The costs related to the shop level were: material costs and various indirect costs such as building, computer systems, transportation, indirect labor and indirect materials.

The total shop cost was calculated bottom-up, from the machine level to the shop level. The cost of each level was the summation of all costs in the lower levels and all costs related to the specific level. Once the shop cost was calculated, the total cost was calculated by adding the outsourcing cost to the total shop cost.

Let t_{ik} and s_{ik} denote the run time per unit and the setup time per batch when processing operation i, $(I = 1,\ldots, I)$ on type k machines $(k = 1,\ldots,K)$, and n_{bm} the number of units in batch b, $(b = 1,\ldots, B)$ of product m. Y_{kmi} is the total yield of product m on a type k machine resulting from all losses of operation i and all its successive operations (percentages).

Further, let x_{imbk} be an integer decision variable indicating that operation i of product m of batch b, processed on a type k machine, is scheduled either for processing in the shop ($x_{imbk} = 1$) or for outsourcing ($x_{imbk} = 0$)). Then the scheduled capacity, $O_{km}^{machine}$, of a type k machine when processing product m is obtained by summing the setup times and total run times of all in-house operations required for processing the entire demand of product m on a type k machine.

$$O_{km}^{machine} = \sum_{b=1}^{B} \sum_{i=1}^{I} x_{imbk} \left(s_{ik} + \frac{n_{bm} t_{ik}}{Y_{kmi}} \right) \tag{1}$$

In Equation (1) we obtained the run time of an operation by multiplying the run time per unit, t_{ik}, by the number of units, n_{bm} and dividing it by the yield of the operation, Y_{kmi}.

The total scheduled capacity on a type k machine, $O_{km}^{machine}$, is obtained by adding up all the scheduled capacity on type k machines over all products:

$$O_{k}^{machine} = \sum_{m=1}^{M} O_{km}^{machine} \tag{2}$$

Let $R_{k}^{machine}$ denote the available capacity of the type k machines during regular work hours (after subtracting stoppages, failures and repair time). $O_{k}^{machine,R}$ hours should be scheduled for production during regular hours and $O_{k}^{machine,R} = \min \left(O_{k}^{machine}, R_{k}^{machine} \right)$, and $O_{k}^{machine,E}$ hours for production during overtime, $O_{k}^{machine,E} = \max(0, O_{k}^{machine} - O_{k}^{machine,R})$.

Let c_{k}^{O} and c_{k}^{MT} denote the operational and maintenance costs per work hour related to a type k machine, and c_{ik}^{T} the tooling costs per product unit related to operation i processed on a type k machine. Also let c_{k}^{I} denote the insurance costs for a type k machine per work day. Then, a type k machine's total cost (not including workstation overheads), $C_{k}^{machine}$, is defined as the sum of total in-house operational, maintenance, tooling and insurance costs for processing the total demand of all products on a type k machine:

$$C_k^{machine} = \sum_{b=1}^{B}\sum_{m=1}^{M}\sum_{i=1}^{I} x_{imbk}\frac{n_{bm}\left(t_{ik}\left(c_k^O + c_k^{MT}\right) + c_{ik}^T\right)}{Y_{kmi}} + c_k^I q_k T$$

(3)

where T denotes the planning horizon in days, n_{bm} the number of units in batch b of product m, and q_k the number of machines of type k.

In Equation 3 above, the following parameters were considered:

- The operational (or maintenance) cost of an operation is a product of: operational (or maintenance) cost per work hour, c_k^O (or c_k^{MT}), operation run time per unit, t_{ik}, and the number of units, n_{bm}, divided by the yield of the operation, Y_{kmi}.
- The tooling cost is a product of the tooling cost per unit, c_{ik}^T, and the number of units divided by the yield.
- The insurance cost for type k machines is a product of the insurance costs of a type k machine per day c_k^I, the length of the planning horizon T, and the number of type k machines, q_k.

As noted above, we assume that in each workstation j, all the W_j allocated workers are being paid for the entire H regular hours per day during the entire planning horizon of T days. The total regular hour labor costs in workstation j is, therefore, $c_j^R T W_j H$, where c_j^R denotes regular hour direct labor cost per work hour.

Since workers can be assigned overtime on busy machines only, the cost of overtime for direct labor in workstation j is:

$$c_j^E W_j \left[\left(\sum_k O_{kj}^{machine,E}/A_k\right)\Big/\sum_k q_{kj}\right]$$

where c_j^E denotes the overtime direct labor cost per work hour, $O_{kj}^{machine,E}$ the scheduled overtime, A_k the expected availability of a type k machine

(in percentages) and q_{kj} the number of machines of type k in workstation j.

Besides machine costs and direct labor costs (regular and overtime), we assume, at the workstation level, additional constant overhead costs, $c_j^{constant}$ per day. By summing up all four components, we can obtain the total cost of workstation j, $C_j^{station}$:

$$C_j^{station} = \sum_{k=1}^{K} C_{kj}^{machine} + c_j^R T W_j H + c_j^E W_j$$

$$\left[\left(\sum_{k=1}^{K} O_{kj}^{machine,E}\Big/A_k\right)\Big/\sum_{k=1}^{K} q_{kj}\right] + c_j^{constant} T$$

(4)

For calculating the total cost of the entire shop, we have to add to the workstation costs: the direct material costs and other indirect costs such as building maintenance, computer systems operation, transportation, indirect workers and indirect materials. Let c_m^{DM} denote the direct material costs of a unit of product m, n_{bm} the number of units of product m in batch b, and c^S the total indirect costs per day. The total cost of the entire shop c^{in} is calculated by:

$$C^{in} = \sum_{j=1}^{J} C_j^{station} + \sum_{m=1}^{M}\sum_{b=1}^{B} n_{bm} c_m^{DM} + c^S T$$

(5)

Note that Equation (5) assumes that defective units are reworked. The total outsourcing cost is obtained by:

$$C^{out} = \sum_{k=1}^{K}\sum_{b=1}^{B}\sum_{m=1}^{M}\sum_{i=1}^{I}\left(1-x_{imbk}\right) n_{bm} c_{ik}^{out}$$

(6)

where c_{ik}^{out} denotes the cost of outsourcing operation i of product k.

Finally, the total cost C is obtained by summing up the in-house and outsourcing costs:

$$C = C^{in} + C^{out}$$

(7)

In order to calculate the total cost C, we need to set the values of the decision variable x_{imbk}, which indicates which operations to perform in the shop, ($x_{imbk}=1$) and which to outsource, ($x_{imbk}=0$). This can be done by solving the following integer programming model, which minimizes the total costs:

$$MinC \qquad (8)$$

s.t.

$$O_k^{machine} \le L_k^{machine} \qquad \forall k, \ k = 1,...,K \qquad (9)$$

$$x_{imbk} = (0,1) \qquad (10)$$

where $L_k^{machine}$ denotes the total available capacity of a type k machine (including expected machine unavailability) and $O_k^{machine}$ denotes the total scheduled capacity on a type k machine (formulated in Expression (2)). Constraint 9 assures the capacity limitation.

Product Unit Cost Calculations

The total scheduled capacity $O_{jm}^{station}$ required for processing product m on workstation is obtained by summing up the total scheduled capacity of this product on a type k machine over all machine types in the workstation. Hence,

$$O_{jm}^{station} = \sum_{k=1}^{K} O_{kjm}^{machine} \qquad (11)$$

where $O_{kjm}^{machine}$ denotes the scheduled capacity on the type k machines in workstation j for processing product m.

Similarly, the scheduled capacity required for processing product m in the entire shop, O_m is obtained from:

$$O_m = \sum_{j=1}^{J} O_{jm}^{station} \qquad (12)$$

Following equation (3), the cost of producing product m on a type k machine, $C_{kn}^{machine}$, is:

$$C_{km}^{machine} = \sum_{b=1}^{B}\sum_{i=1}^{I} x_{imbk} \frac{n_{bm}\left(t_{ik}\left(c_k^O + c_k^{MT}\right) + c_{ik}^T\right)}{Y_{kmi}} + c_k^I q_k T \frac{O_{km}^{machine}}{O_k^{machine}} \qquad (13)$$

Similarly, following Expressions (4) and (5), the marginal cost of product m at workstation j is:

$$MC_{jm}^{station} = \frac{O_{jm}^{station}}{\sum_{k=1}^{K} O_{kj}^{machine}}$$

$$\left\{ c_j^R T W_j H + c_j^E W_j \left[\left(\sum_{k=1}^{K} O_{kj}^{machine,E} / A_k \right) / \sum_{k=1}^{K} q_{kj} \right] + c_j^{constant} T \right\} \qquad (14)$$

and the marginal cost of product m at the shop level is:

$$MC_m = \sum_{b=1}^{B} n_{bm} c_m^{DM} + \frac{O_m}{\sum_k O_k^{machine}} c^S T \qquad (15)$$

Finally, product m unit cost is obtained by dividing the sum of machine, marginal station, marginal shop and outsourcing costs, by the demand d_m for product m. Hence,

$$C_m = \frac{\sum_{k=1}^{K} C_{km}^{machine} + \sum_{j=1}^{J} MC_{jm}^{station} + MC_m + \sum_{k=1}^{K}\sum_{b=}^{B}\sum_{i=1}^{I}\left(1 - x_{imbk}\right) n_{bm} C_{ik}^{out}}{d_m} \qquad (16)$$

and the average product unit cost over all products, $\bar{C}$, is obtained by dividing the total cost, C (Expression 7) by the total demand:

$$\bar{C} = C \left/ \sum_{m=1}^{M} d_m \right. \qquad (17)$$

MODEL ANALYSIS

In order to analyze the effect of workload (demand) on the product unit cost, $C_m(d_m)$, a specific product ($m = 1$) with demand $d_m \ge 0$ was considered, and a number of simplified assumptions were made (a more realistic situation, without these assumptions, was tested experimentally as described in the Experimentation:

- The demand for all other products $m \neq 1$ is constant.
- Changes in the demand for product *1* do not cause any change in the cost allocation of all other products.
- The ratio between the processing time of product *1* and free regular-hour capacity is an integer number, which is equal for all types of machines.
- The ratio between the processing time of product *1* and free extra-hour capacity is an integer number, which is equal for all types of machines.
- It is cheaper to produce a product in-shop (either during regular or overtime hours) than to outsource it.

Let d_1^a and $d_1^b > d_1^a$ be the maximal demand of product *1* that can be produced during regular hours (with no overtime or outsourcing), and during both regular and overtime hours (but with no outsourcing), respectively. Then:

a) $C_1\left(d_1^a\right)$ is the minimal product *1* unit cost for $0 < d_1 \pounds d_1^a$. For this range, as the demand increases, the constant costs and the direct labor costs (which in this situation are actually constant) are divided between more units, and therefore, the product unit cost is reduced.

b) $C_1\left(d_1^b\right)$ is the minimal product *1* unit cost for $d_1 \, {}^3 \, d_1^b$. When demand reaches the shop's available capacity, outsourcing is started and the product unit cost increases with demand. It is, however, assumed that producing during overtime is cheaper than outsourcing. Obviously, as the constant costs and outsourcing costs increase, the demand effect on product unit cost is greater.

c) For $d_1^a < d_1 < d_1^b$, the minimal unit cost depends on an expression $\left(\dfrac{F_1}{d_1^a} - E_1\right)$ so that:

$$
MinC_1(d_1) = \begin{cases} C_1\left(d_1^b\right) & \text{for } \dfrac{F_1}{d_1^a} > E_1 \\[2mm] \left[C_1\left(d_1^a\right), C\left(d_1^b\right)\right] & \text{for } \dfrac{F_1}{d_1^a} = E_1 \\[2mm] C_1\left(d_1^a\right) & \text{for } \dfrac{F_1}{d_1^a} < E_1 \end{cases}
$$

where F_1 is product *1*'s total cost when the demand is equal to d_1^a and E_1 is the cost for producing a unit during overtime hours, when demand is in the interval $d_1^a < d_1 < d_1^b$).

Proof: Let d_1^c be the demand of product *1*, where $d_1^a + g$, $g>0$. Then:

$$
C_1\left(d_1^a\right) - C_1\left(d_1^c\right) = \frac{F_1}{d_1^a} - \left(\frac{F_1 + gE_1}{d_1^a + g}\right) = \frac{gF_1}{d_1^a\left(d_1^a + g\right)}
$$

$$
- \frac{gE_1}{d_1^a + g} = \frac{g}{d_1^a + g}\left(\frac{F_1}{d_1^a} - E_1\right) \tag{18}
$$

From (18), it is easy to see that for any d_1^c in the interval $(d_1^a, \, d_1^b)$:

- If $\dfrac{F_1}{d_1^a} < E_1$, $C_1\left(d_1^a\right) < C_1\left(d_1^c\right) \Rightarrow C_1\left(d_1^a\right)$ is the minimum;
- If $\dfrac{F_1}{d_1^a} = E_1$, $C_1\left(d_1^a\right) = C_1\left(d_1^c\right) \Rightarrow$ all $C_1\left(d_1^c\right)$ values in the interval $d_1^a < d_1^c < d_1^b$ are equal;
- If $\dfrac{F_1}{d_1^a} > E_1$, $C_1\left(d_1^a\right) > C_1\left(d_1^c\right)$ and the difference between $C_1\left(d_1^a\right)$ and $C_1\left(d_1^c\right)$ increasing with $g \Rightarrow C_1\left(d_1^b\right)$ is the minimum.

Using the Model

A shop manager would use the model for pricing a job on a "rolling horizon" basis. The model's ability to calculate the unit cost of each product in the shop instantly makes it a tool for generating a new production plan (i.e., number of units of each product assigned to be produced in the shop) whenever one or more new jobs are added in the planning horizon.

In spite of the simplifying assumptions and the model's simplicity, it can be used by a shop manager for evaluating important rules of thumb: "Once you decide that for a specific product using overtime hours is more profitable than outsourcing – this decision will be correct for every time demand exceeds supply – so do your best to increase the reservoir of overtime hours in case of an increase in demand for the product".

Experimentation

In order to get some realistic insight on the effect of workload, shop size and product mix on the product unit cost, a simulation study was conducted.

Nine different basic shop configurations were tested. The nine configurations were different in their number of workstations (3, 6 or 9) and their number of products (4, 6, or 8). For each one of the nine basic configurations, five different sets of parameters were randomly determined. Consequently, a total of 45 different configurations were tested.

The five sets were determined by sampling the parameters from random distributions as follows:

- Number of machine types in each workstation: Uniform (1, 4);
- Number of machines of each type: Uniform (1, 3);
- Number of batches of each product: Uniform (1, 4);

- Number of operations for producing each product: Uniform (1, 9);
- Mean times between failures: Uniform (16, 60) [hours];
- Mean times to repair: Uniform (1, 4) [hours];
- Number of units in each batch: Uniform (10, 30).
- Processing times were firstly sampled randomly from Uniform (1, 5) distribution and then normalized to meet the desired work loads.
- Operation setup times: Uniform (1, 3) [hours];
- Yield of each operation: Uniform (0.8, 1);
- Ratio between overtime and regular work hour costs: Uniform (1.25, 1.4).
- Ratio between outsourcing and total shop cost for each operation: Uniform (1.1, 1.5).

All other parameters were set to be constant and identical to all the 45 configurations (values are available from the authors).

Ten workload levels were fitted to each of the 45 configurations. First, processing times were adjusted to a workload of about 1 (100% of the available capacity including extra hours). Then, nine other workload levels, ranging from 0.5 to 5, were set by multiplying the number of units in each batch by factors of [0.5, 0.6, 0.7, 0.8, 0.9, 2, 3, 4 and 5].

For each configuration, machines were loaded in accordance with the demand, processing routes and capacities. Obviously, operations were outsourced for workloads that were greater than 1 only. For these workload levels, x_{imbk} values were set optimally by solving the model in Equations (8)–(10). After loading, product unit costs were calculated as described in NAME OF THE SECTION.

Figure 2. Experimental runtime (seconds)

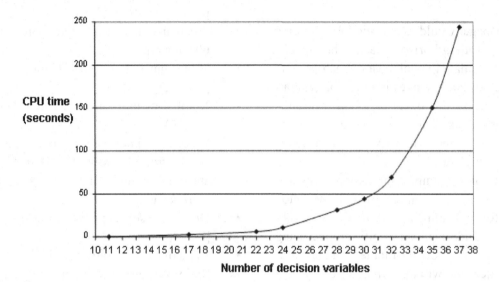

Model Implementation, Experimental Runtime and its Reduction

The model was implemented in ILOG OPL Studio™ (optimization software). All problem instances were run on a 900-MHz AMD Duron™ processor and 256 MB of RAM.

Experimental runtime for a sample replication of nine basic shop configurations was measured. Figure 2 presents the runtime as a function of the number of the decision variables, x_{imbk}. We can see that the runtime increased exponentially with the number of decision variables. So, it is very difficult to solve a real size problem in a reasonable amount of time. The reason is that for the proposed model we need to solve a nonlinear integer problem.

In order to reduce runtime, the problem can be modified without loss of optimality into a linear integer problem. Define $O_k^{machine,E}$ (the scheduled overtime hours) as a variable. Then the model becomes a linear one:

$$MinC \qquad (19)$$

s.t.

$$O_k^{machine} \leq THA_k q_k + O_k^{machine,E} \qquad \forall k, \quad k = 1,...,K \qquad (20)$$

$$O_k^{machine,E} \leq TEA_k q_k \qquad \forall k, \quad k = 1,...,K \qquad (21)$$

$$x_{imbk} = (0,1) \qquad (22)$$

$$O_k^{machine,E} \geq 0 \qquad \forall k, \quad k = 1,...,K \qquad (23)$$

where H and E denote the regular and overtime hours per day during the entire planning horizon of T days, respectively, $O_k^{machine}$ the total scheduled capacity on type k machines, (formulated in Expression (2)). Constraint (20) assures the capacity limitation. Constraint (21) defines the number of available overtime hours.

To reduce the runtime drastically, the following greedy heuristics is suggested:

- Step 1: Calculate, for each operation i of batch b that belongs to product m and is produced on a type k machine, the "In-

House Worthiness Measure", $IHWM_{imbk}$, as follows:

$$IHWM_{imbk} = \frac{Inhouse\ Variable\ Cost\ Ignoring\ Extra\ Hours}{Ousourcing\ Cost} =$$

$$= \frac{\left(n_{bm}\left(t_{ik}\left(c_k^O + c_k^{MT}\right) + c_{ik}^T\right)/Y_{kmi}\right)}{C_{ik}^{out}}$$

(24)

The smaller the $IHWM_{imbk}$, the bigger is the advantage of in-house production.

- Step 2: Sort all operations in ascending order according to the *IHWM*.
- Step 3: If the free capacity of machine type k is large enough – schedule the operation from the top of the sorted list for machine k, otherwise – outsource it.
- Step 4: Delete the operation from the list and go to Step 3.

Table 1 presents a list of operations, sorted by $IHWM_{imbk}$, for a typical example of a three-workstation-six-products configuration. The overtime vs. regular hour costs ratio is 1.25 and the indirect to direct costs ratio is 1.08. The workload level is 2 (200%). The total available capacity of each machine type and the scheduled capacity of each operation are also presented.

According to the *IHWM* heuristic, operations from the top of the list are generally produced in-house. The exception is the operation on a type 2 machine. The total available capacity of such machines (96 hours) is smaller than the scheduled capacity of the operation at the top of the list (124.71 hours), so this operation is outsourced. We can see, in this example, that the heuristic and the optimization results were the same.

For each of the 45 configurations, the following ratio was calculated, assuming that the workload level was 2 (200%):

$$\frac{Heuristic\ Total\ Cost - Optimal\ Total\ Cost}{Optimal\ Total\ Cost}$$

This ratio indicates the advantage of the optimization model on the *IHWM* heuristic. The average of the ratio, over all 45 configurations, was approximately 4%. Analysis of variance (ANOVA) was performed. For $\alpha=0.05$, the influence of the number of workstations or the number of products on these ratios was not significant. The conclusion is that the difference between the optimization model and the *IHWM* heuristic does not depend on the shop size.

Results

Figure 3 presents the results for the Table 1 example. We can see that the product unit cost was typically a concave function of the workload (which was approximately proportional to demand).

Results for workloads larger than 1 (when outsourcing takes place) showed that the product unit costs did not necessarily increase with the increase in the workload. For example, in Figure 3, the minimal unit cost for product 4 was obtained for a workload of 4 since product 2 and 3 were outsourced, which enabled product 4 to be processed during regular hours. Similarly, the minimal unit cost of product 1 was obtained for a workload of 5, since product 5 was outsourced. Hence, the product unit cost was affected by the current product mix in each planning horizon much more than by the product mix over the long-range.

Table 2 presents the x_{imbk}^{in} values for the "make or buy" problem for the Table 1 example. It shows that jobs are outsourced ("0" value) on workload levels 2, 3, 4 and 5 (greater than 100% workload).

Analysis of variance (ANOVA) was performed. For $\alpha =0.05$ the influence of the number of workstations or the number of products on these ratios was not significant. This shows that for the rough-cut deterministic model, the influence of the workload on the product unit cost does is unrelated to the shop size.

Table 1. Data for heuristic illustration (work load is 200%)

				Station 1		Station 2	Station 3	x_{imbk}	
				Machine Type 1	Machine Type 2	Machine Type 3	Machine Type 4		
Total Available Capacity (hours)				180.92	96	179.2	78.4	Heuristic	Optimal
Prod.	Batch.	Oper.	IHWM	Scheduled Capacity (hours)					
6	9	10	0.18	-	124.71	-	-	0	0
3	4	6	0.25	-	-	-	21.20	1	1
3	5	6	0.25	-	-	-	21.20	1	1
1	1	1	0.26	44.01	-	-	-	1	1
3	4	5	0.26	-	31.13	-	-	1	1
3	5	5	0.26	-	31.13	-	-	1	1
5	7	8	0.33	87.03	-	-	-	1	1
5	8	8	0.33	44.52	-	-	-	1	1
2	2	3	0.34	-	-	-	73.25	0	0
2	3	3	0.35	-	-	-	37.12	0	0
4	6	7	0.39	-	-	81.81	-	1	1
5	7	9	0.43	117.51	-	-	-	0	0
5	8	9	0.43	59.76	-	-	-	0	0
2	2	2	0.44	-	-	87.02	-	1	1
2	3	2	0.44	-	-	44.51	-	0	0
3	4	4	0.57	-	-	68.98	-	0	0
3	5	4	0.57	-	-	68.98	-	0	0

Figure 3. Product unit costs against workload levels

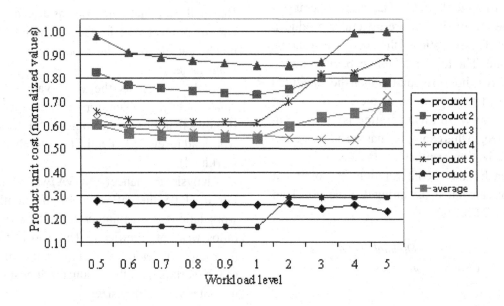

Table 2. Illustration of solution for the "make or buy" problem

Product	Batch	Operation	Work load level									
			0.5	0.6	0.7	0.8	0.9	1	2	3	4	5
1	1	1	1	1	1	1	1	1	1	1	1	1
2	2	2	1	1	1	1	1	1	1	0	0	0
2	2	3	1	1	1	1	1	1	0	0	0	0
2	3	2	1	1	1	1	1	1	0	0	0	1
2	3	3	1	1	1	1	1	1	0	0	0	0
3	4	4	1	1	1	1	1	1	0	0	0	0
3	4	5	1	1	1	1	1	1	1	1	0	0
3	4	6	1	1	1	1	1	1	1	1	0	0
3	5	4	1	1	1	1	1	1	0	0	0	0
3	5	5	1	1	1	1	1	1	1	1	1	1
3	5	6	1	1	1	1	1	1	1	1	1	1
4	6	7	1	1	1	1	1	1	1	1	1	0
5	7	8	1	1	1	1	1	1	1	0	0	0
5	7	9	1	1	1	1	1	1	0	0	0	0
5	8	8	1	1	1	1	1	1	1	1	1	0
5	8	9	1	1	1	1	1	1	0	0	0	0
6	9	10	1	1	1	1	1	1	0	0	0	0

For each of the 45 configurations, the ratio between the average (over all products) product unit costs for workloads of 0.5 and 1 was calculated. This ratio is an indicator of the degree of the affect of the workload on the product unit cost. Figure 4 presents these ratios for all 45 configurations.

The Proposed Model Compared to Traditional Costing Models

In traditional costing, the product cost does not depend on the workload. It is based on the ratio between the total cost of the historical period (without the direct material cost) and the scheduled capacity in hours, known as the cost per labor hour. Product cost is calculated as the sum of the direct material cost, the product of run time and cost per labor hour.

In Figure 5 the proposed model is compared to the traditional costing approach for the example in Table 1. The unit costs of products 3 and 6 and the average cost over all six products, calculated by the two methods, are presented. For the calculation of cost per labor hour we assumed that the historical period was the last planning horizon, that the workload in this period was 0.8 (80%) and that the product mix was similar to the product mix of the current planning horizon.

The traditional costing approach may underestimate (product 3) or overestimate (product 6) the unit cost.

Influence of Precedence between Operations on Cost Estimation

The assumption of the rough-cut deterministic model that there is no precedence between operations may lead to poor cost estimates. In this section we try to understand the influence of precedence between operations on cost estimation and suggest a way to correct the models' cost estimation.

Figure 4. Effect of workload on product unit cost in the 45 configurations

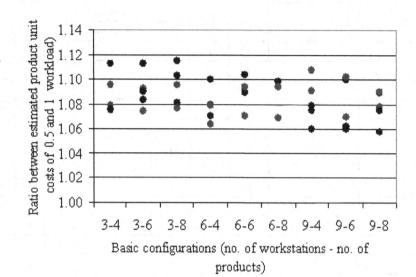

Figure 5. The proposed model compared to the traditional costing approach

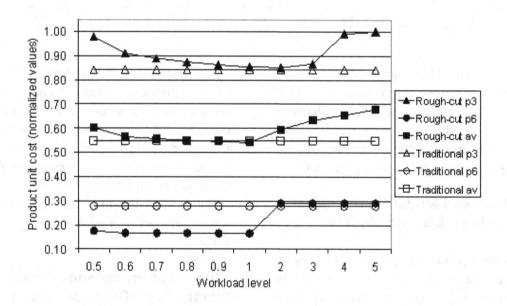

Table 3 presents the data of the Table 1, when the workload level is 1 (100%). Figure 6 displays the product Gantt chart. The Gantt chart consists of a set of four timelines, one for each machine type. The height of the timeline indicates the number of machines of the current machine type. For example, because there are two type 1 machines and only one of type 2, the height of the timeline of the type 1 machine is twice the size of the type 2 machine. In addition, the timeline of machine type 1 is separated into two sub-lines. We assumed that the workload

Table 3. Data for precedence models (workload is 100%)

				Station 1		Station 2	Station 3	x_{imbk}	
				Machine Type 1	Machine Type 2	Machine Type 3	Machine Type 4		
Total Available Capacity (hours)				180.92	96	179.2	78.4	Gantt Chart	Rough Cut
Prod.	Batch.	Oper.	IHWM	Scheduled Capacity (hours)					
1	1	1	0.26	22.51				1	1
2	2	2	0.44			44.51		1	1
2	2	3	0.34				37.12	0	1
2	3	2	0.44			23.26		1	1
2	3	3	0.35				19.06	0	1
3	4	4	0.57			34.99		1	1
3	4	5	0.26		16.57			1	1
3	4	6	0.25				11.10	0	1
3	5	4	0.57			34.99		1	1
3	5	5	0.26		16.57			1	1
3	5	6	0.25				11.10	0	1
4	6	7	0.39			41.40		1	1
5	7	8	0.33	44.52				1	1
5	7	9	0.43	59.76				1	1
5	8	8	0.33	23.26				1	1
5	8	9	0.43	30.88				1	1
6	9	10	0.18		62.86			1	1

Figure 6. Gantt chart before correlation

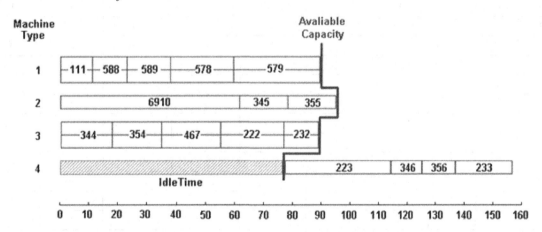

on machines of the same type is shared equally between the identical machines.

Each timeline indicates the status of a specific machine type over time. The ruled frame indicates a machine's forced idle time. The blank frame with numbers in it indicates operations. The number indicates product (m), batch (b) and operation (i), respectively. When two operations have the same product and batch numbers, the operation with the smaller number precedes the larger one. We assume that the dispatching rule is SPT.

We can see from the Gantt chart that machine type 4 operations: 223, 346, 356 and 233 must be outsourced, whereas the rough-cut model scheduled it for in-house production.

In order to improve the rough-cut model we proposed correcting the available capacity by subtracting the estimated forced idle time. Forced idle time may be estimated by the snapshot principle. This principle (Reiman & Wein, 1999) asserts that in a limiting time scale the vector of machines' idle time does not change during as a work order goes through the various stations in the shop. According to this principle we assumed that forced idle time of machine k during the planning horizon was equal to the forced idle time of the historical

period. To illustrate, we assumed that the historical period was the last planning horizon, and the forced idle time in this period on machine type 4 was 70 hours.

Table 4 presents data for the Table 3 example, with the available capacity of machine type 4 reduced by 70 hours—from 78.4 hours to 8.4 hours. In this case, the Gantt chart and the improved rough-cut model show the same results. Of course, accuracy of cost estimation strongly depends on the accuracy of the forced idle time estimation.

Figure 7 presents a comparison of the rough-cut model with the model that takes into account the precedence between operations for the example of Table 1. The unit costs of product 3, product 6 and the average cost over all six products, calculated by the two methods, are presented.

Table 4. Adjusted available capacity illustration (work load is 100%)

				Station 1		Station 2	Station 3	x_{imbk}	
				Machine Type 1	Machine Type 2	Machine Type 3	Machine Type 4		
Total Available Capacity (hours)				180.92	96	179.2	8.4	Gantt Chart	Rough Cut
Prod.	Bch.	Oper.	IHWM	Scheduled Capacity (hours)					
6	9	10	0.18		62.86			1	1
3	4	6	0.25				11.10	0	0
3	5	6	0.25				11.10	0	0
1	1	1	0.26	22.51				1	1
3	4	5	0.26		16.57			1	1
3	5	5	0.26		16.57			1	1
5	7	8	0.33	44.52				1	1
5	8	8	0.33	23.26				1	1
2	2	3	0.34				37.12	0	0
2	3	3	0.35				19.06	0	0
4	6	7	0.39			41.40		1	1
5	7	9	0.43	59.76				1	1
5	8	9	0.43	30.88				1	1
2	2	2	0.44			44.51		1	1
2	3	2	0.44			23.26		1	1
3	4	4	0.57			34.99		1	1
3	5	4	0.57			34.99		1	1

We can see that the difference in product 3's unit cost estimations was significantly larger than in product 6. This is because product 6 operations were not influenced by the available capacity correction. At very low and very high workloads, the difference between the two methods is not as large as for reasonable workloads. At very low workloads, in spite of the available capacity correction, the majority of the operations are still produced in-house. At very high workloads, the majority of the operations are outsourced, so that the available capacity correction does not influence the outsourcing decision.

STOCHASTIC MODEL FOR COST ESTIMATION ASSUMING AN ACTIVITY BASED COST SYSTEM

Major Assumptions

The following assumptions were made:

1) The processing and setup times are independent of the production period, sequence of operations and workload. The setup times are known constants when assuming a deterministic environment or random variables with known distributions (the means are equal to the constants from the deterministic environment) when assuming a stochastic environment.

2) Operation splitting is not allowed. An operation, which has started, is completed without interruption.

3) The machines are mutually independent and can be used simultaneously.

The parameters such as available work hours (regular and overtime), demand, the products' routes and costs are assumed to be constant and known in advance.

7) Production of each unit is performed within a single planning period.

Figure 7. Comparison between the rough-cut model and the model that takes into account precedence between operations

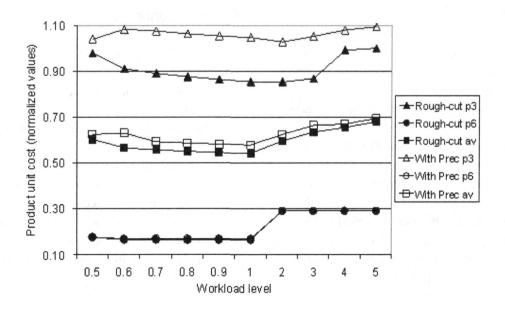

8) Workers stay in the shop for all regular hours but overtime stops as soon as all work is done.

9) There are no shortages of raw materials.

10) The capacity of the finished goods warehouse is unlimited.

11) Outsourcing is not allowed.

12) Capacity is limited and cannot be extended by purchasing new machines.

Notation

The following notation is used:

Indices

$t = 1,\dots T$: Index of periods in the planning horizon. T is the number of periods in the planning horizon

$i = 1,\dots N$: Index of product types. N is the number of product types

$j = 1,\dots M$: Index of machines. M is the number of machines.

$k = 1,\dots K$: Index of activities. K is the number of activities.

$l_k = 1,\dots L_k$: Index of cost drivers of activity k. L_k is the number of cost drivers of activity k.

Parameters

v_{it}: The variable cost for producing one unit of product i in period t assuming an infinite capacity

c_{it}: Inventory holding cost per unit of product i in period t

b_{it}: Backorder cost per unit of product i in period t

r_t: Regular labor cost per hour in period t

o_t: Overtime labor cost per hour in period t

d_{it}: Demand for product i in period t

a_{ij}: Processing time of a unit of product i on machine j (the mean when assuming a stochastic environment).

s_{ij}: Setup time of product i on machine j (the mean when assuming a stochastic environment).

$(wm)_t$: Total available regular work hours in period t

$(om)_t$: Total available overtime work hours in period t

I_{i0}: Initial inventory/backorder of product i

u_j: Total load on machine j

T_{jt}^I: Average forced idle time (between two operations) of machine j in period t

B_{jt}: The ratio between the forced idle time of machine j in period t and the average load on the shop floor

T_{ijt}^W: Product i's waiting time in queue before machine j in period t

A_{ijt}: The ratio between product i's waiting time in the queue before machine j in period t and the total load on machine j

L: Large positive number

$C_{max}(t)$: Makespan in period t

t_j^f: Mean time between failures for machine j

t_j^r: Mean time to repair for machine j

y_{ij}: Yield of product i at machine j

$C_{l_k i}$: Consumption of cost driver l of activity k per unit of product i

$CCD_{l_k i}$: Unit cost of cost driver l of activity k

Decision Variables

X_{it}: Number of units of product i produced in period t

I_{it}^+: Number of units of product i in inventory at the end of period t

I_{it}^-: Number of backorder units of product i at the end of period t

W_t: Number of regular hours used in period t. When the number of regular hours is constant, W_t is considered as a parameter equal to $(wm)_t$ and not as a decision variable.

O_t: Number of overtime hours used in period t

W_{it}: Number of regular hours used in period t on machine i

O_{it}: Number of overtime hours used in period t on machine i

I_{it}^{setup} : Indicator of setup time that takes value 1 when $X_{it} > 0$ and takes value 0 when $X_{it} = 0$

THE HEURISTIC MODEL OF FELDMAN AND SHTUB (2006) – MODEL A

Feldman and Shtub (2006) proposed an iterative heuristic model (Model A), which integrates a tactical level optimization model with a finite loading procedure.

The solution procedure comprises three phases. In the first phase, a linear programming (LP) model is solved. The solution is the recommended production volume of every product in each period that minimizes the total cost for the entire planning horizon. In the second phase, a scheduling procedure examines the solution's feasibility. The heuristic generates a non-delay schedule – i.e. a machine does not remain idle if it can start processing an operation. This procedure tests whether the resulting production volumes can be processed without violating the available capacity in each period. If the solution is feasible, it is adopted. Otherwise, if the scheduling procedure finds that due to operational constraints not all the required quantities can be processed, the procedure switches to the third phase. In the second phase, the maximal schedule length allowed in every period is this period's original capacity: $-(wm)_t + (om)_t$. In phase three, the capacity is adjusted, and the solution procedure starts anew from phase one. Capacity update affects the optimization phase (phase one) only, in the aim of reducing production. The iterative process stops when the model finds a feasible solution.

OPTIMIZATION INTEGRATED WITH SIMULATION – MODEL B

We propose an iterative heuristic model (Model B), which integrates a tactical level optimization model with simulation The proposed solution procedure consists of three phases. In Phase I, an improved linear programming (LP) model is solved. The solution is the recommended production volume of every product in each period that minimizes the total cost for the entire planning horizon. In the second phase, a simulation examines the feasibility of the solution. If the solution is feasible, it is adopted; otherwise, the procedure switches to Phase III. In Phase III, the machine idle time and the product waiting time coefficients are adjusted, and the solution procedure starts from Phase I. The iterative process stops when the model finds a feasible solution. Figure 8 shows a schematic diagram of Model B.

Phase I – The Optimization Model

Additional constraints were added in order to account for setup times and precedence constraints. The proposed aggregate planning model is:

$$\min \sum_{i=1}^{N}\sum_{t=1}^{T}\left(v_{it}X_{it} + c_{it}I_{it}^{+} + b_{it}I_{it}^{-}\right) + \sum_{t=1}^{T}\left(r_t W_t + o_t O_t\right)$$

$$(25)$$

s.t.

$$X_{it} + I_{i,t-1}^{+} - I_{i,t-1}^{-} - I_{it}^{+} + I_{it}^{-} = d_{it} \qquad \forall i, \forall t \qquad (26)$$

$$L \cdot I_{it}^{setup} \geq X_{it} \qquad \forall t, \forall i \qquad (27)$$

$$\sum_{i=1}^{N}\left(s_{ij}I_{it}^{setup} + a_{ij}X_{it}\right) + B_{jt}\frac{\sum_{k=1}^{M}\sum_{i=1}^{N}\left(s_{ik}I_{it}^{setup} + a_{ik}X_{it}\right)}{M\left((wm)_t + (om)_t\right)} \leq W_{tj} + O_{tj} \qquad \forall t, \forall j$$

$$(28)$$

$$\sum_{j=1}^{M}\left(s_{ij}I_{it}^{setup} + a_{ij}X_{it} + A_{ijt}\frac{\sum_{i=1}^{N}\left(s_{ij}I_{it}^{setup} + a_{ij}X_{it}\right)}{(wm)_t + (om)_t}\right)$$

Figure 8. The schematic heuristic model B

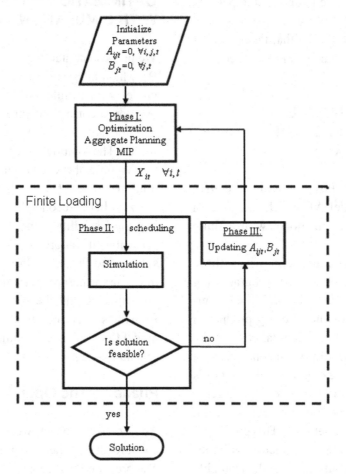

$\leq (wm)_t + (om)_t \quad \forall t, \forall i$ (29)

$W_t \leq (wm)_t \quad \forall t \; ; O_t \leq (om)_t \quad \forall t$

$W_{tj} \leq W_t$ (30)

$O_{tj} \leq O_t$ (31)

$I_{i0}^+, \; I_{i0}^- = const_i \quad \forall i; \; I_{it}^{setup} = (0, 1) \quad \forall i, \forall t \; ,$
$X_{it}, \; I_{it}^+, \; I_{it}^- \geq 0 \quad \forall i, \forall t; \; W_t, \; O_t \geq 0 \quad \forall t; \; W_{tj}, \; O_{tj} \geq 0 \quad \forall t, \forall j$

The objective function (26) is composed of the inventory holding cost, backorder cost, regular and overtime labor costs. The fixed costs are omitted from the objective function, as they are constants.

Constraint (26) balances the demand with the production volume and the changes in inventory. Constraint (27) sets 0 or 1 values to the setup variables, $I_{it}^{set \; up}$. Constraint (28) assures the capacity limitation by taking into account not only the processing time, but also the machine idle time. It was developed from:

$$\sum_{i=1}^{N} \left(s_{ij} I_{it}^{setup} + a_{ij} X_{it} \right) + T_{jt}^I \leq W_{tj} + O_{tj} \quad \forall t, \forall j \quad (32)$$

by defining the average idle time of the machines as a function of the load on the shop floor:

$$T_{jt}^I = B_{jt} \frac{\sum_{k=1}^{M} u_k}{M} = B_{jt} \frac{\sum_{k=1}^{M} \sum_{i=1}^{N} \left(s_{ik} I_{it}^{set \; up} + a_{ik} X_{it} \right)}{M \left((wm)_t + (om)_t \right)} \quad (33)$$

Constraint (29) assures a total production time limitation for each product, taking into consideration the total available regular and overtime hours in the period, which includes processing time and product waiting time in a queue before a machine. It was developed from:

$$\sum_{j=1}^{M}\left(s_{ij}I_{it}^{setup} + a_{ij}X_{it} + T_{ijt}^{W}\right) \leq \left(wm\right)_{t} + \left(om\right)_{t} \quad \forall t, \forall i \tag{34}$$

by defining the waiting time in a queue before a machine as a function of the machine load:

$$T_{ijt}^{W} = A_{ijt}u_{j} = A_{ijt}\frac{\sum_{i=1}^{N}\left(s_{ij}I_{it}^{setup} + a_{ij}X_{it}\right)}{\left(wm\right)_{t} + \left(om\right)_{t}} \tag{35}$$

Constraints (30) and (31) limit the number of regular and overtime hours used by machine i in period t, W_{tj} and O_{tj}, respectively.

The machine idle time coefficient B_{jt} and product waiting time coefficient A_{ijt} are initialized to 0 for each product, machine and period, and then recalculated in Phase II and updated in Phase III, until a feasible solution is obtained.

Phase II – Simulation

The production quantities for each product and each period, X_{it}, obtained from the aggregate planning model in Phase I, are inserted into the simulation in order to test whether their production violates the available capacity, $W_t + O_t$. Arena™ (simulation software) was used for executing the simulation. Two dispatching rules were considered: Shortest Processing Time (SPT) and Most Work Remaining (MWKR). Machine idle time coefficients $B_{jt} = \dfrac{T_{jt}^{I}M}{\sum_{k=1}^{M}u_{k}}$ and product waiting time coefficients $A_{ijt} = \dfrac{T_{ijt}^{W}}{u_{j}}$ were calculated for each product, machine and period.

Phase III – Capacity Update

If during Phase II, the solution obtained from the aggregate planning model is found unfeasible, then the machines' idle times and the product waiting time in the queue before the machines is estimated using the machine idle time coefficients $B_{jt} = \dfrac{T_{jt}^{I}M}{\sum_{k=1}^{M}u_{k}}$ and the product waiting time coefficients $A_{ijt} = \dfrac{T_{ijt}^{W}}{u_{j}}$. The two coefficients were derived from the simulation and applied to the optimization model of Phase I.

Cost Estimates

For both models (A and B), in order to estimate the cost of a new order, the total cost for the entire production plan is calculated twice – once with, and then, once without the new order. Thereafter, the cost of the new order is estimated by subtracting the total cost of the entire production plan without the new order from this with the new order.

OPTIMIZATION INTEGRATED WITH SIMULATION AND A COST ESTIMATE EXAMPLE

In this section we demonstrate how a feasible solution is obtained and how a new order's cost is estimated using Model B.

The example is based on a system that consists of three machines: M1, M2 and M3. There are three types of products that can be manufactured: P1, P2 and P3.

The planning horizon consists of five periods, each of a single day. The available capacity each day is expressed in regular and overtime work hours. There are eight regular and four overtime hours available each day. We first assumed that the company has initial demands, which represent

Table 5. Initial demand (units)

Product type	P1	P2	P3
Day 1	11	14	4
Day 2	13	18	4
Day 3	9	17	4
Day 4	10	17	4
Day 5	17	17	4
Total	60	83	20

Table 6. Products routing, processing times and setup times

	P1	P2	P3
Routing length (steps)	3	3	3
Routing (machine types)	M1-M2-M3	M1-M2-M2	M1-M2-M3
Processing times (min)	1, 3, 2	2, 4, 3	3, 5, 6
Setup times (min)	46, 40, 81	61, 54, 107	88, 186, 381

orders that the company has already accepted. The parts demanded for each period are described in Table 5.

The operation routing summary, processing times (min) and setup times (min) of the three product types are described in Table 6. The assumed dispatching rule is SPT.

The material, inventory and backorder costs were used as shown in Table 7. The labor costs used were US$ 28 for a regular work hour and US$ 36.40 for an overtime hour. Since this is a multi-period model with a finite planning horizon, we needed to account for 'the end of the planning horizon' phenomenon. For example, if the backorder cost of a product is lower than its variable manufacturing cost, the model's solution will be to pay the backorder fine and not to manufacture the product at all in the last period. Of course, this is not the case in the real world, where the number of periods is unlimited and the product will have to be manufactured eventually. We solved the problem by assigning a fairly high backorder cost in the last period – the fifth day in this example, so that only when the product cannot

be manufactured due to limited capacity reasons, the backorder costs were incurred.

The solution (production volumes), obtained after running the model for the initial demands (first stage), are presented in Table 8.

This solution is not feasible for Days 1, 2 and 3. Figure 9 displays the machine Gantt chart. The Gantt chart consists of a set of three timelines, one for each machine. Each timeline indicates the status of the resource over time. A blank frame with T_{ij}^I above it indicates forced idle times of machines j in period t. A squared frame, with two numbers – separated by a point – above it, indicates productive time. The number before the point indicates product type and the number after the point indicates a step in the route.

Figure 10 displays the product Gantt chart. The product Gantt chart consists of a set of three timelines, one for each product. Each timeline indicates the status of the product over time. A blank frame with T_{ijt}^W above it indicates product i waiting time in queue before machine j in period t. A squared frame with two numbers – separated by a point – above it, indicates productive time.

Table 7. Material, inventory and backorder costs

	P1	P2	P3
Material costs ($)	10	10	12
Inventory costs ($)	0.004	0.002	0.004
Backorder costs ($)	5	5	6
Backorder day 5 costs ($)	73	76	75

Table 8. Production volume for the initial demands (units) – Stage 1

Product type	P1	P2	P3
Day 1	60	14	4
Day 2	0	18	4
Day 3	0	17	4
Day 4	0	17	4
Day 5	0	17	4
Total	60	83	20

Figure 9. Machine Gantt chart – Stage 1

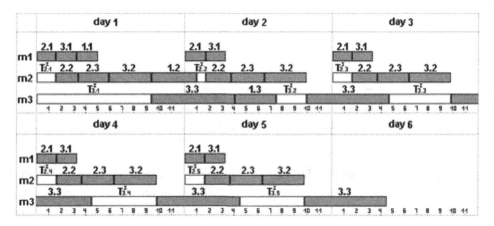

The number before the point indicates product and the number after the point indicates a step in the route. In order to emphasize the infeasibility of the suggested solution (Table 8), each lot (total demand for a product type in each day) is presented in Figure 10 relative to the day in which it was supposedly completing production. For example, according to Table 8, 60 units of P1 were supposedly completing production on Day 1. From Figure 10, it can be seen, that part of step 2 and step 3 of P1, must be delayed to Day 2. Hence, the Table 8 solution is not feasible.

Machine idle time coefficients $B_{jt} = \dfrac{T^I_{jt} M}{\displaystyle\sum_{k=1}^{M} u_k}$ and

product waiting time coefficients $A_{ijt} = \dfrac{T^W_{ijt}}{u_j}$ were

derived from the simulation and applied to the

optimization model.

Figure 10. Product Gantt chart – Stage 1

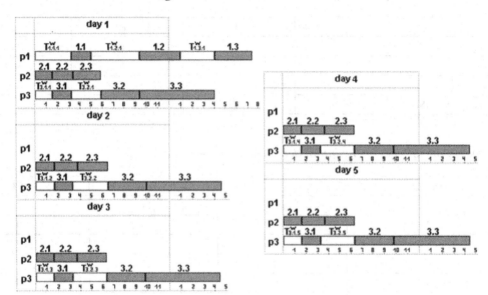

Table 9. Production volume for Stage 2 (units)

Product type	P1	P2	P3
Day 1	11	14	0
Day 2	13	18	0
Day 3	9	17	0
Day 4	10	17	0
Day 5	17	17	0
Total	60	83	0

The solution (production volume), obtained after updating idle time and product waiting time coefficients (second stage), is presented in Table 9.

In the second stage, the model found a feasible solution. The objective function value was US\$ 4,290. Figure 11 displays the machine Gantt chart, including the calculated forced idle times of machines, which were used to decrease available capacity in order to find a feasible solution. The machines' forced idle times are indicated by a ruled frame with T''^{I}_{ij} above it.

Figure 12 displays the product Gantt chart, including the calculated product waiting time in a queue before machines, which was used to decrease available capacity in order to find a feasible solution. The calculated product waiting time in queue before a machine is indicated by a ruled frame with T''^{W}_{ijt} above it.

Next we assumed that a new order proposal for three units of P3, which was due on Day 3, had arrived. The model was run for the initial demands in addition to the new order. The only change in the demand data with respect to Table 5 was an additional three units of P3 in period 3. After two stages, a feasible solution was found. According to the feasible solution, the additional three units of P3 were delayed beyond the planning horizon (Day 5), and therefore, the production volumes of this solution were the same as in Table 9.

Figure 11. Machine Gantt chart – Stage 2

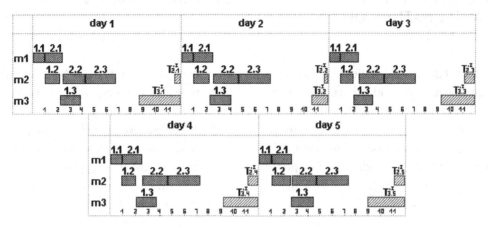

Figure 12. Product Gantt chart – Stage 3

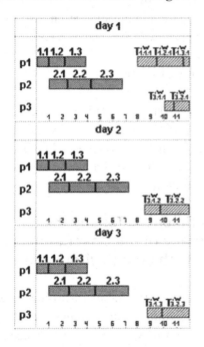

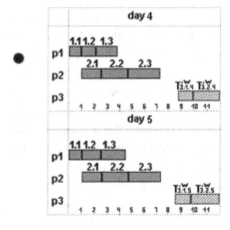

The objective function value obtained was US$ 4,551 as opposed to US$ 4,290 without the new order. Thus, the new order cost can be estimated as the difference between these two values: US$ 261. This cost estimation is different from the marginal cost associated with producing the new order, and does not deal with capacity limitations (the traditional method). The new order cost is only US$ 36. The difference between these values can be explained by the backorder costs incurred

after adding the new order to the shop. The big difference of US$ 261 resulting from the high backorder costs related to Day 5 (for technical reasons as explained earlier) is presented in Table 7. Replacing the fifth day's backorder costs with the regular backorder costs results in a cost of US$ 54 for the new order —which is still much higher than the cost estimate that ignored capacity limitations (US$ 36).

ADJUSTMENT FOR THE STOCHASTIC NATURE OF THE SHOP FLOOR

In order to adjust the cost estimates to a stochastic environment, the feasible production plan from the proposed procedure were inserted into the simulation. Setup and processing times were randomized based on the given distributions. A number (20 in the following experiment) of simulation replications were run, and the cost estimates were based on the average of these replications.

Stochastic Model for Cost Estimation with No Machine Failures and 100% Yields

The Experimental Designs

Two experiments were designed. The objective of the first experiment was to compare the total costs of the production plans derived from the proposed model (Model B) and the existing model (Model A) and between the CPU times required to run these two models. The objective of the second experiment was to compare the accuracy of the cost estimates for a new product in deterministic and stochastic environments, while using the two models (A and B). In both experiments the effect of changes in various factors on the results were checked. In order to achieve significant ANOVA (p-value < 0.05), following the estimation of variance on pilot runs, every treatment was replicated five times in both experiments.

Experiment I: Comparison between the Two Models

The experiment was aimed at comparing the objective function values and the CPU times of the two models.

Experimental Factors

Four factors were tested as follows:

- **product variety (P)**: Number of product types; two levels were considered: three and nine types of products.
- **Machine variety (M)**: Number of machine types; two levels were considered: three and nine machine types.
- **Routing length (N)**: Number of workstations in a production route; two levels were considered: three and nine workstations in a route.
- **Dispatching rule (R)**: The dispatching rule used in the simulation; two rules were considered: SPT and MWKR.

Number of Runs

A full factorial design led to 16 treatments in the experiment (two levels of P × two levels of M × two levels of L × two levels of R). Every treatment was replicated five times; thus there were a total of 80 runs.

Experiment II: Testing the Accuracy of the Cost Estimates in a Stochastic Environment

The experiment was aimed at testing the accuracy of the deterministic and stochastic cost estimates derived from Models A and B under a stochastic environment. In order to calculate a baseline for this comparison, 20 simulation replications were run for each treatment, and we estimated the "actual order's cost" as the average of these replications. For each run, a set of orders, already accepted for production, and a single new order were randomly generated. The models were implemented twice, first without the new order and second with the new order. Then, the cost of the new order was estimated as the difference between the total cost of the entire production plan without and with the new order. The dispatching rule used, in all the simulation runs, was MWKR.

Experimental Factors

The following seven factors were tested:

- **Product variety (P)**: Number of product types; two levels were considered: three and nine types of products.
- **Machine variety (M)**: Number of machine types; two levels were considered: three and nine machine types.
- **Routing length (N)**: Number of workstations in a production route; two levels were considered: three and nine workstations in a route.
- **Cost ratio (C)**: The ratio between backorder and variable production costs and between overtime and regular hour costs. The levels of (C) are: low ($o_t = 1.3r_t$, $b_{it} = 0.5v_{it}$) and high ($o_t = 2r_t$, $b_{it} = 1.5v_{it}$).
- **Demand index (D)**: Indicates the initial shop floor load. (D) is defined as:

$$D = \max_t \left(\frac{\max_j \sum_{i=1}^{N} \left(s_{ij} I_{it}^{setup} + a_{ij} d_{it} \right)}{W_t} \right).$$

Levels of (D) were either low (between 0.6 and 0.8) or high (between 1.2 and 1.4).

- **Distribution variance (V)** of setup and processing times. Two levels were considered: low (processing time $\sim U(0.85a_{ij}, 1.15a_{ij})$ setup time $\sim U(0.85s_{ij}, 1.15s_{ij})$) and high (processing time $\sim U(0.5a_{ij}, 1.5a_{ij})$, setup time $\sim U(0.5s_{ij}, 1.5s_{ij})$).
- **Optimization model (O)**. Two models were considered: Model A and Model B.

Number of Runs

A full factorial design led to 128 treatments in the experiment (two levels of P × two levels of M × two levels of L × two levels of C × two levels of D × two levels of V × two levels of O). Every treatment was replicated five times; thus there were a total of 640 runs.

Values of Constants for Both Experiments

In both experiments the number of periods in the planning horizon (T) was set to be five days and the total available regular and overtime hours in period t ($(wm)_t$ and $(om)_t$) were set as 8 and 4 hours, respectively.

Randomized Parameters for Both Experiments

The random variables for both experiments were generated randomly from the following uniform distributions:

- Machine types in a product's route: $U(0.5, M+0.5)$, rounded to the closest integer number.
- Mean processing time of one unit of product i on machine j (a_{ij}): $U(1, 6)$ minutes.
- Mean setup time of product i on machine j (s_{ij}): $U(10, 500)$ minutes.
- Demand for product i in period t (d_{it}): $U(5, 40)$; in Experiment II randomization was iterative until (D) was between 0.6 and 0.8 or between 1.2 and 1.4.
- Inventory holding cost per unit of product i in period t (c_{it}): $U(0.002, 0.004)$
- The variable cost for producing a unit of product i in period t under an infinite capacity environment (v_{it}): $U(8, 14)$ \$.
- Backorder cost per unit of product i in the last period, $t=5$ (b_{i5}): $U(60, 80)$ \$. The backorder cost per unit of product i (b_{it}) in

period $t{\neq}5$ is 0.5 v_{it} or 1.5 v_{it} depending on the value of (C).

- Regular labor cost per hour in period t (r_t): $U(15, 30)$ \$. The overtime labor cost per hour in period t, o_t is 1.3 r_t or 2 r_t depending on the value of the cost ratio (C)).

Models Implementation

Both models (A and B) were implemented in ILOG OPL Studio™ (optimization software) combined with Arena™ (simulation software). ILOG OPL Studio and Arena were connected by ODBC (Open DataBase Connectivity™) based on Microsoft Access™. Shop floor parameters (products, machines, routing) were generated by Microsoft Excel™. Figure 13 shows a schematic diagram of models implementation.

All problem instances were run on a 900-MHz AMD Duron™ processor and 256 MB of RAM.

RESULTS AND ANALYSIS

Results of Experiment I

Results of 80 runs were analyzed using the Wilcoxon test. A significant advantage of Model B in cost and in CPU time was found (p-value < 0.0001). Figure 14 presents a comparison between Models A and B in terms of the ratio: $\left(\dfrac{\text{Result Model } A - \text{Result Model } B}{\text{Result Model } B}\right)$ in the total cost of the entire production plan and in CPU time.

The significant factors and interactions found by the fixed effects ANOVA were (p-value < 0.05):

- **Interaction between product variety (V) and dispatching rule (R)** – for Model B, **cost** increased with increasing product variety when the dispatching rule was MWKR.

Figure 13. The schematic implementation of Models A and B

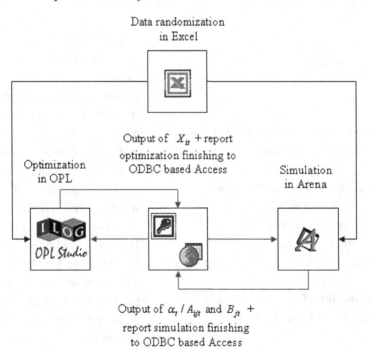

Data randomization in Excel

Optimization in OPL

Output of X_{it} + report optimization finishing to ODBC based Access

Simulation in Arena

Output of α_t / A_{ijt} and B_{jt} + report simulation finishing to ODBC based Access

- **Machine variety (V)** – Model B's advantage in **CPU time** increased with the increase in machine variety.
- **Dispatching rule (R)** – Model B's advantage in **CPU time** increased when the dispatching rule was MWKR.

Results of Experiment II

Results of 640 runs were analyzed by the Wilcoxon test. A significant advantage in the accuracy of the stochastic cost estimation over the deterministic approach was found (p-value < 0.0001). Figure 15 presents a comparison of the accuracy of the cost estimates. The cost estimation accuracy was calculated by the ratio:

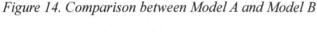

$\left(\dfrac{|\text{Result of cost estimation} - \text{Actual order's cost}|}{\text{Actual order's cost}} \right)$. In

order to calculate a baseline for this comparison, 20 simulation replications were run for each treatment, and we estimated the "actual order's cost" as the average of these replications. Figure

15 compares three cost estimation approaches: Capacitated Stochastic, Capacitated Deterministic and Traditional (cost estimation ignoring capacity limitations, workloads or other scheduling considerations).

The stochastic cost estimation has a significant advantage over the deterministic estimation. The advantage of the deterministic capacitated cost estimation over the traditional estimate was similar to the result of Feldman and Shtub (2006). The large difference from the baseline can be explained by the fact that we ignored backorder and overtime labor costs.

The significant factors found by the ANOVA fixed effects were (p-value < 0.05):

- **The interaction between product variety (P) and machine variety (M)** (Figure 16). The stochastic cost estimation's advantage increased with the increase in product variety, when machine variety was high.
- **The interaction between product variety (P), demand index (D) and distribution**

Figure 14. Comparison between Model A and Model B

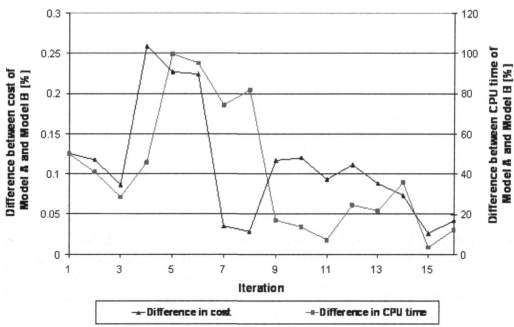

Figure 15. Comparison of stochastic, deterministic and traditional (unlimited capacity) cost estimations

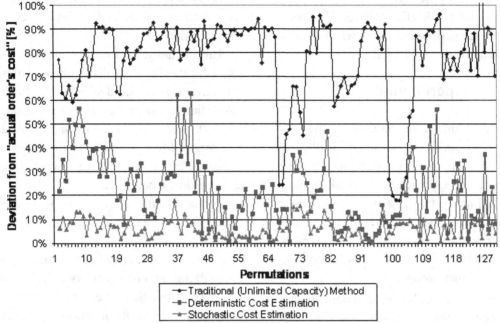

Figure 16. Interaction between product variety (P) and machine variety (M)

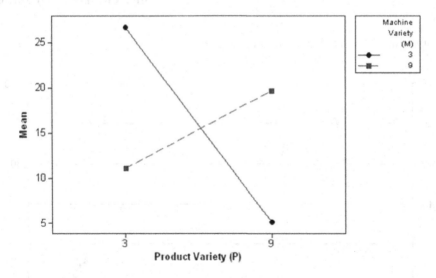

variance (V) (Figure 17). The stochastic cost estimation's advantage increased with the increase in product variety only when D was high and V was high.

• **The interaction between product variety (P), routing length (N) and cost ratio (C)** (Figure 18). The stochastic cost estimation's advantage increased with the

Figure 17. Interaction between product variety (P), demand index (D) and distribution variance (V)

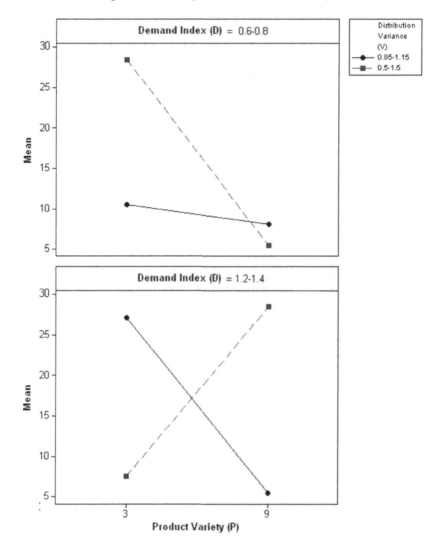

increase in product variety when routing length and cost ratio were both either high or low.

- **The interaction between optimization model (O), routing length (N) and cost ratio (C)** (Figure 19). The stochastic cost estimation's advantage generally increased when Model A was used. Only when routing length and cost ratio were both low, did the stochastic cost estimation's advantage decrease when the Model A was used.

ADJUSTMENTS FOR THE STOCHASTIC MACHINE FAILURES AND PRODUCT YIELDS

In this section the simulation-based model takes into account machine failures and product yields. As an input the simulation model received a feasible production plan, derived from either Model A or Model B (described earlier). Both models assume a deterministic environment. Other input for the simulation model are the parameters of the manufacturing system including the distributions of the random variables.

Figure 18. Interaction between product variety (P), routing length (N) and cost ratio (C)

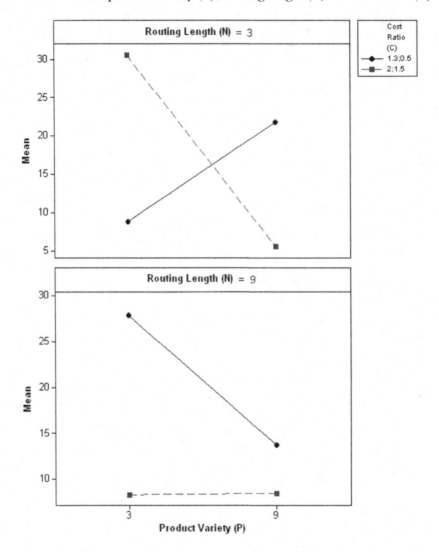

In order to estimate the total cost of the entire production plan, the simulation model was replicated (20 times in the current research) and for each replication, the total cost of the entire production plan was calculated. Then, the cost estimation of the entire production plan was derived from the average of the replications' results.

A Comparison between the Deterministic and Adjusted Stochastic Cost Estimations

We compared the accuracy of the cost estimates derived from the deterministic cost estimation models (Model A or B) to the accuracy of those derived from the stochastic simulation-based model, described in the previous section.

Figure 19. Interaction between optimization model (O), routing length (N) and cost ratio (C)

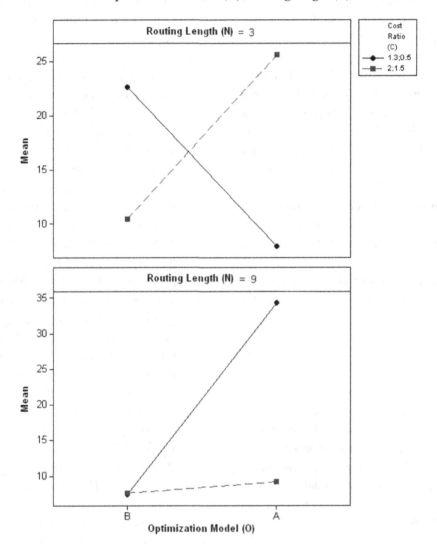

The Experimental Design

Experimental Factors

The following seven factors were tested:

- **Product and machine variety and routing length (P)**: Number of product types, machine types and workstations in a production route. Two levels were considered: three and nine product types, machine types and workstations in a production route.

- **Cost ratio (C)**: The ratio between backorder and variable production costs and between overtime and regular hour costs. The levels of (C) that were considered: low ($o_t = 1.3r_t$, $b_{it} = 1.5v_{it}$) and high ($o_t = 2r_t$, $b_{it} = 3v_{it}$).

- **Workload (L)**: The initial shop floor load; levels of (U) are low (between 0.4 and 0.5) and high (between 0.7 and 0.8).

- **Distribution variance of setup and processing times (VT)**. Two levels were considered: low (processing time $\sim U(0.85a_{ij}, 1.15a_{ij})$, setup time $\sim U(0.85s_{ij}, 1.15s_{ij})$) and high (processing time $\sim U(0.5a_{ij}, 1.5a_{ij})$, setup time $\sim U(0.5s_{ij}, 1.5s_{ij})$).

- **Distribution variance of time between failures and time to repair (VF).** Two levels were considered: low (time between failures $\sim U(0.85t_j^f, 1.15t_j^f)$, time to repair $\sim U(0.85t_j^r, 1.15t_j^r)$) and high (time between failures $\sim U(0.5t_j^f, 1.5t_j^f)$, time to repair $\sim U(0.5t_j^r, 1.5t_j^r)$).
- **Distribution variance of product yield (VY).** Two levels were considered: low (product yield $\sim$) and high (time between failures $\sim U(0.5y_{ij}, 1.5y_{ij})$).
- **Optimization model (O).** Two models were considered: Model A and Model B.

Number of Runs

A full factorial design of the seven experimental factors led to 128 treatments in the experiment. In order to achieve significant ANOVA (p-value<0.05), following estimation of variance on pilot runs, every treatment was replicated five times; thus there were a total of 640 simulations runs.

Constant Values

The number of periods in the planning horizon (T) was set to be five days and the total available regular and overtime hours in period t ($(wm)_t$ and $(om)_t$) were set to be eight and four hours per day, respectively. The dispatching rule used for operating the manufacturing system was Most Work Remaining (MWKR).

Sampled Parameters

The following values were generated randomly from the following uniform distributions:

- Machine types in a products' route: $U(0.5, M+0.5)$, rounded to the closest integer number.
- Mean processing time of a unit of product i on machine j in (a_{ij}): $U(1, 6)$ minutes.
- Mean setup time of product i on machine j in (s_{ij}): $U(10, 500)$ minutes.
- Demand for product i in period t (d_{it}): $U(5, 40)$; in the experiment, randomization was iterative until the workload (L) was between 0.4 and 0.5 or between 0.7 and 0.8.
- Inventory holding cost per unit of product i in period t (c_{it}): $U(0.002, 0.004)$\$.
- The variable cost for producing a unit of product i in period t under an infinite capacity environment (v_{it}): $U(8, 14)$\$.
- The backorder cost per unit of product i (b_{it}) in period $t \neq 5$ was 1.5 v_{it} or 3 v_{it}, depending on the value of the Cost Ratio (C). For the optimization models only, in order to force the shop to produce the maximal work volume within the 5 periods, we set the backorder cost per unit of product i in the last period, $t=5$ (b_{i5}) relatively high: $U(60, 80)$ \$.
- Regular labor cost per hour in period t: (r_t): $U(15, 30)$\$. The overtime labor cost per hour in period t, o_t, was 1.3 r_t or 2 r_t depending on the value (C).
- Mean time between failures for machine j (t_j^f): $U(12, 14)$ hours.
- Mean time to repair for machine j (t_j^r): $U(2, 3)$ hours.
- Yield of product i at machine j (y_{ij}): $U(95, 98)$ %.

Results and Analysis of Experiment

For each of the 640 simulation runs the new order cost was estimated by both the deterministic and the stochastic estimation models and the accuracy measure (absolute deviation from the 'actual' new order cost) was calculated. The results were analyzed using the Wilcoxon test. A significant advantage in the accuracy of the stochastic cost estimation model over the deterministic approaches was found with p-value<0.0001. For the deterministic approaches the average estimation accuracy was 29.1 percent with a standard deviation of 11.5 percent, while for the stochastic estimation, the average and the standard deviations were 5.3 and 3.0 percent, respectively. Figure 20 presents the significant improvement of the estimation derived from taking into account the stochastic nature of the manufacturing system (each point represents the average of 5 replications of each of the 128 treatments).

In order to compare between the deterministic and stochastic cost estimations, the following ratio was used:

$$\frac{|\text{Determenistic new order cost estimatiom- Actual new order cost}|}{|\text{Stochastic new order cost estimatiom- Actual new order cost}|}$$

When the deterministic and the stochastic cost estimations were equal, the ratio was equal to: 1. Values greater than 1 indicate an advantage

of the stochastic cost estimation over the deterministic one. In opposition, values less than 1 indicate an advantage of the deterministic cost estimation.

As a result of the fixed effects ANOVA, several significant effects (p-value<0.05) were found. Interaction plots of these effects are shown in Figures 21-24. In Figures 21-23 the vertical axis represents the mean of the abovementioned ratio. The significant effects were:

- **Distribution variance of time between failures (TBF) and time to repair (TTR).** Figure 21 shows that the stochastic cost estimation's advantage increased with the increase of the TBF and TTR.
- **The interaction between workload (L) and distribution variance of setup and processing times (VT).** Figure 22 shows that for high workloads, the stochastic cost estimation's advantage increased with the increase in the VT. In opposition, for low workloads the advantage of stochastic cost estimation decreases with the increase in this distribution.

Figure 20. Comparison of stochastic and deterministic cost estimations

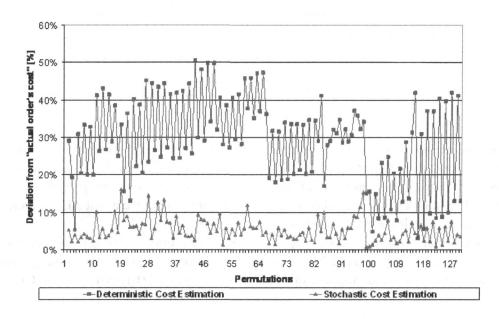

Figure 21. The effect of the distribution variance of TBF and TTR(VF)

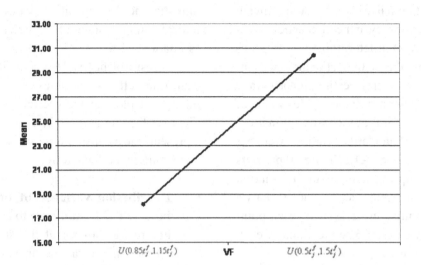

Figure 22. The interaction between workload (L) and distribution variance of setup and processing times (VT)

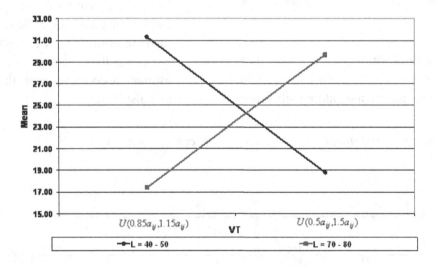

- **The interaction between product and machine variety and routing length (P) and the distribution variance of the product yield (VY).** Figure 23 shows that for a more complex manufacturing system (high level of P), the stochastic cost estimation's advantage increased with an increase in the distribution variance of the

product yield; for a simpler manufacturing system (low level of P), the stochastic cost estimation's advantage decreased with an increase in the distribution variance of the product yield.

- **The interaction between product and machine variety and routing length (P), workload (L) and cost ratio (C).** In Figure

Figure 23. Interaction between product and machine variety and routing length (P) and the distribution variance of product yield (VY)

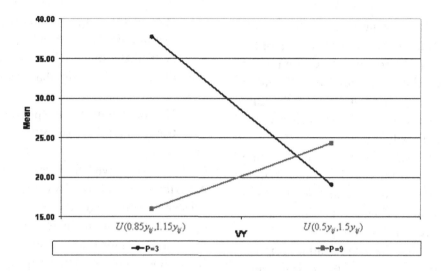

Figure 24. Interaction between product and machine variety and routing length (P), workload (L) and cost ratio (C)

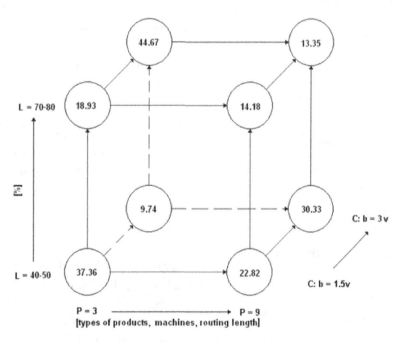

24, each circle indicates a single combination of P, L and C. The numbers within the circles are the average cost estimation accuracy of these combinations. Figure 24 shows that the stochastic cost estimation's advantage increases with the increase of workload when the cost ratio is high and product and machine variety and routing length are low.

THE PREDICTIVE MODEL BASED ON LINEAR REGRESSION

As previously defined, the objective of the current research was to develop a practical tool for estimating the total cost of a new order. Simulation studies are very time-consuming and difficult to perform and are, therefore, impractical for daily use. A fast rough-cut predictive model that can be implemented easily is needed.

Predictive models were used for estimating the mean (MT) and the coefficient of variation (CV) of the total cost of a production plan from the factors that were found to be significant in the previous section. For this purpose a linear regression, based on the data resulting from the simulation runs in the stochastic environments, was used. The simulated MT and CV were defined as independent variables, while the dependent variables were defined as follows:

- Deterministic total cost evaluation

$$TC_{det} = \sum_{i=1}^{N}\sum_{t=1}^{T}\left(v_{it}X_{it} + c_{it}I_{it}^{+} + b_{it}I_{it}^{-}\right) + \sum_{t=1}^{T}\left(r_{t}W_{t} + o_{t}O_{t}\right)$$

(36)

- Average workload (per machine, per day)

$$U_{t}^{a} = \frac{1}{M}\sum_{j=1}^{M}\frac{\sum_{i=1}^{N}s_{ij}I_{it}^{setup} + a_{ij}X_{it}}{(wm)_{t} + (om)_{t}}, \quad \forall t$$

(37)

- Standard deviation of workload (per machine, per day)

$$U_{t}^{sd} = \sqrt{\frac{M\sum_{j=1}^{M}\left(\frac{\sum_{i=1}^{N}\left(s_{ij}I_{it}^{setup} + a_{ij}X_{it}\right)}{(wm)_{t} + (om)_{t}}\right)^{2} - \left(\sum_{j=1}^{M}\frac{\sum_{i=1}^{N}\left(s_{ij}I_{it}^{setup} + a_{ij}X_{it}\right)}{(wm)_{t} + (om)_{t}}\right)^{2}}{M(M-1)}}, \forall t$$

(38)

- Average overtime labor cost: $\dfrac{\sum_{t=1}^{T} o_{t}}{T}$

- Average backorder cost: $\dfrac{\sum_{i=1}^{N}\sum_{t=1}^{T} b_{it}}{NT}$

- Half of the range of the processing time distribution (HT = 15 or 50)
- Half of the range of the machine failures (TBF and TTR) distributions (HF = 15 or 50).
- Half of the range of the product yields' distribution (HY = 15 or 50).

The data derived from the above described experiment included 1280 observations (640 runs and two total cost calculations for each run – with and without the new order). The data of 1024 observations (80% of total data) was used for the linear regression (training data set) and the remaining 256 observations (20% of data) were used for testing the resulting predictive model (testing data set).

Regression Results

The resulting predictive model for the stochastic estimation of the total cost was:

$$TC_{stoch} = 1.01 \cdot TC_{det} + 3.67 \cdot \sum_{t=1}^{T} o_{t}\Big/T + 3.34 \cdot \sum_{i=1}^{N}\sum_{t=1}^{T} b_{it}\Big/NT +$$
$$+981.59 \cdot U_{1}^{a} - 997.02 \cdot U_{1}^{sd} + 1337.73 \cdot U_{21}^{a} + 319.52 \cdot U_{2}^{sd} +$$
$$+475.54 \cdot U_{3}^{a} + 1257.69 \cdot U_{3}^{sd} - 1097.40 \cdot U_{4}^{a} + 2551.22 \cdot U_{4}^{sd} -$$
$$-523.14 \cdot U_{5}^{a} - 1359.66 \cdot U_{5}^{sd} + 4.61 \cdot HT + 1.5 \cdot HF -$$
$$-0.13 \cdot HY - 621.13$$

(39)

where TC_{stoch} is the predictive value for the mean total cost (MT). The residual analysis of the linear regression showed a statistical significance (p-value<0.0001) with $R^{2} \approx 1$ (Figure 25). Table 10 presents the significance analysis of the coefficients.

(A – regression results; T - data from simulation runs).

Similarly, an additional predictive model was derived for the coefficient of variations (CV) of

Figure 25. Adjusted correlation coefficient, R^2, of the training data based linear regression

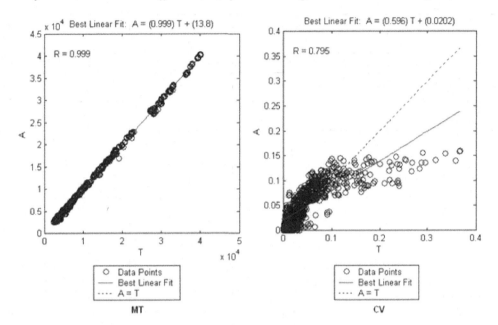

the total cost. This model was also significant statistically (p-value<0.0001) but with quite a low correlation coefficient $R^2 \approx 0.63$ (Figure 25).

The two predictive models, for MT and CV, were tested by linear regression on the basis of the testing data set. The correlation coefficients were similar to those of the training data set, $R^2 \approx 1$ for MT and $R^2 \approx 0.61$ for CV (Figure 26).

(A – regression results; T - data from simulation runs).

The cost of a new order is estimated, as explained above, by subtracting the total cost of the entire production plan without the new order from the cost with the new order. In order to examine the estimation accuracy of the regression-based predictive model, it was applied to the 128 runs of the testing data set; the estimation accuracy measure was calculated and the results were analyzed by the Wilcoxon test.

A significant (p-value<0.05) advantage in the accuracy of the regression-based cost estimation over the deterministic approach was found. For the regression-based cost estimation the average accuracy was 14.5 percent with a standard devia-

tion of 8.2 percent, while for the deterministic estimation, the average and the standard deviations were 23.4 and 11.5 percent, respectively.

Nevertheless, the simulation-based cost estimation was significantly (p-value<0.05) preferable over the regression-based estimation – an average estimation accuracy of 4.5 percent with a standard deviation of 2.9 percent for the simulation-based cost estimation. Figure 27 presents a comparison of the accuracy of the cost estimates.

A NEURAL NETWORK-BASED PREDICTIVE MODEL

In an effort to improve the predictive model, especially the one for CV, a Neural Network (NN) was implemented, using the same independent and dependent variables as the linear regression.

The NN was generated in MATLAB™. The network contained 17 neurons in an input layer, 17 neurons in a hidden layer (determined by trial and error), and a single neuron in an output layer. The input-output function between input

Table 10. Significance analysis of coefficients

Variables	Coefficients	Standard Error	t Stat	P-value
Intercept	-621.13	91.73	-6.77	0.00
TC_{det}	1.01	0.00	431.42	0.00
$\sum o_t / T$	3.67	1.86	1.98	0.05
$\sum \sum b_{it} / NT$	3.34	1.62	2.07	0.04
U_1^a	981.60	257.92	3.81	0.00
U_1^{sd}	-997.02	304.42	-3.28	0.00
U_2^a	1337.74	231.11	5.79	0.00
U_2^{sd}	319.52	337.75	0.95	0.34
U_3^a	475.54	280.48	1.70	0.09
U_3^{sd}	1257.69	333.59	3.77	0.00
U_4^a	-1097.40	269.52	-4.07	0.00
U_4^{sd}	2551.22	321.13	7.94	0.00
U_5^a	-523.14	250.28	-2.09	0.04
U_5^{sd}	-1359.66	371.01	-3.66	0.00
HT	4.62	0.59	7.83	0.00
HF	1.50	0.59	2.55	0.01
HY	-0.13	0.59	-0.22	0.82

and hidden layers was tan-sigmoid, and between hidden and output layers was linear. The training rule, determined also by trial and error, was the Levenberg-Marquardt Algorithm (Demuth & Beale, 2001).

Neural Network Results

The NN-based predictive model for CV achieved a dramatic improvement in the prediction level on the training data – $R^2 \approx 0.93$ and a negligible improvement on the testing data – $R^2 \approx 0.68$ (Figure 28). Hence, the NN did not result in any improvement over the linear regression-based predictive models.

(A – NN results; T - data from simulation runs).

A COMPARATIVE STUDY OF A ROUGH-CUT COST ESTIMATION IN A FINITE CAPACITY STOCHASTIC ENVIRONMENT

The current section introduces five alternatives to simulation that can be implemented easily. These alternatives, in addition to saving the time of developing and running simulations, are also

Figure 26. Adjusted correlation coefficient,R^2, of the testing data based linear regression

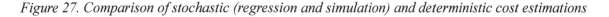

Figure 27. Comparison of stochastic (regression and simulation) and deterministic cost estimations

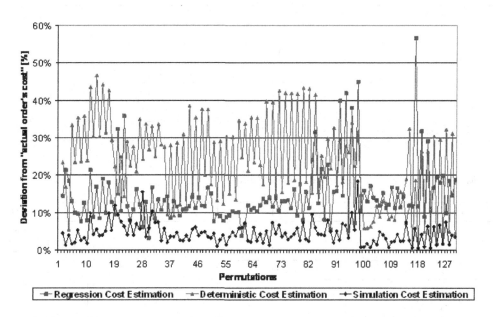

implemented in Microsoft Excel™. In opposition to ARENA™, Microsoft Excel™ is a readily available tool on most computers and most people are familiar with its use. A comparison study was carried out in order to determine the best cost estimation method across different shop configurations.

A Shop Floor Example

The following example serves as a basis for explanation of the techniques and methods that follow:

A shop floor consists of three machines: m1,

Figure 28. Adjusted correlation coefficient, R², of the NN-based cost estimation

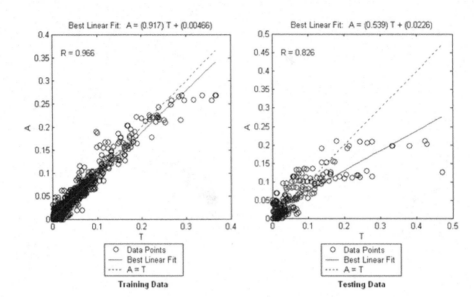

Table 11. Initial demand (units)

Product type	P1	P2	P3
Day 1	11	14	4
Day 2	13	18	4
Day 3	9	17	4
Day 4	10	17	4
Day 5	17	17	4
Total	60	83	20

Table 12. Daily demand including the new order (units)

Product type	P1	P2	P3
Day 1	11	14	4
Day 2	13	18	44
Day 3	9	17	4
Day 4	10	17	4
Day 5	17	17	4
Total	60	83	60

m2 and m3. Three types of products are manufactured on the machines: P1, P2 and P3. The planning horizon is five days. Daily available capacity is eight regular and four overtime work hours. The initial demand representing orders that the company has already accepted is presented in Table 11 (four units of product P3 on Day 1 are backorders from the historical to the current planning horizon).

A new order for 40 units of product P3, which

Table 13. Demand and production plan in the historical planning horizon (units)

Product type	P1	P2	P3
Day -4	0	63	0
Day -3	24	22	0
Day -2	19	21	0
Day -1	17	7	5
Day 0	0	17	4
Total	60	130	9

Table 14. Products routing, processing times and setup times

	P1	P2	P3
Routing length (number of steps)	3	3	3
Routing (machine types)	m1-m2-m3	m1-m2-m2	m1-m2-m3
Processing times (min)	1, 3, 2	2, 4, 3	3, 5, 6
Setup times (min)	46, 40, 81	61, 54, 107	88, 186, 381

Table 15. Material, inventory and backorder costs

	P1	P2	P3
Material costs ($)	10	10	12
Inventory costs ($)	0.004	0.002	0.004
Backorder costs ($)	5	5	6

is due on Day 2, has arrived. The task of the shop manager is to estimate the cost of these 40 units. The daily demand including the new order is presented in Table 12.

Assume that the production plan of the historical planning horizon, from period -4 to period 0, presented in Table 13, was equal to demand.

Also assume that dispatching rule SPT was used. Product routing, processing times (min) and setup times (min) of the three product types are presented in Table 14.

The material, inventory and backorder costs are summarized in Table 15, assuming US$ 28 for a regular work hour and US$ 36.40 for an overtime hour.

For simplicity, machine failure and product yields are ignored in this example.

Additional Assumptions

1) The production plan is feasible in terms of rough-cut capacity planning (RCCP).

Vollmann et al. (1997) described three approaches for RCCP. The first approach, "Capacity Planning using Overall Factors" (CPOF), is quickly computed but is insensitive to shifts in product mix. A second approach, "capacity bills", takes into account a changing product mix, but does not consider lead-time offsets. The third approach, "Resource Profile", takes lead-time offsets into account. Given that in the example the most products start and finish processing within a single work period, the Capacity Bills approach was adopted.

For example, the production plan in Table 12 is not feasible in terms of Assumption 1 and should be balanced (balancing techniques are presented in NAME OF SECTION). As we can see from Figure 29, on Day 2, machines m2 and m3 are overloaded. More work (12.9 hours and 12.5 hours, respectively) than the available capacity (12 hours) was scheduled.

2)   Data about the starting and finishing times for each job in historical planning horizon can be collected (with today's technology this can be done).

Figure 30 displays a machine Gantt chart that takes into account precedence between operations. Assumption 2 enabled us to generate such a Gantt chart. The chart consists of a set of three horizontal timelines, one for each machine. Each timeline indicates the status of the machines over time. A blank frame with T_{ij}^I above it indicates forced idle times of machines j in period t. A squared frame, with two numbers – separated by a point above it – indicates productive time. The number, left of the point, indicates product type and the number, right of the point, indicates a step in the route. According to Table 13, four

units of product P3 were supposed to have been completing production on Day 0. From Figure 30, it can be seen, that step 3 of product P3, must be delayed to Day 1.

Production Balancing

In order to balance a production plan with the limited capacity of each machine on the shop floor, two different techniques were used: Finite Loading (FL) and optimization.

Finite Loading (FL)

This is an aggregate production plan that was built by scheduling products according to due dates, one by one, from the beginning of the planning horizon, to its end – period-by-period – while filling up the machines' capacity in terms of RCCP. This procedure never overloads the machines.

In order to balance the production plan from Figure 29, using a finite loading procedure, the production plan on Day 2 on m2 and m3 had to be modified. This was done by reducing the quantities processed on m2 and M3. On Day 2 the quantity of P1 was reduced from 13 to 11, the quantity of P2 – 18 to 15 and the quantity of

Figure 29. RCCP chart with the new work order

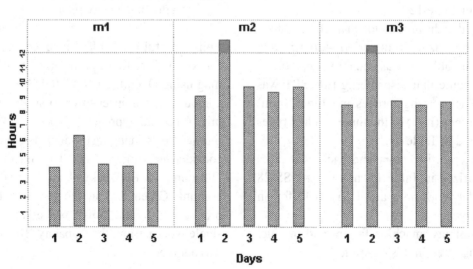

product P3 – from 44 to 37. The new production plan is presented in Table 16, and as we can see from Figure 31, it was a balanced and feasible production plan.

The total cost of the balanced production plan was US$ 3,683. In Table 17 we can see the components of the total cost.

Optimization

The solution in Figure 31 is feasible, but not necessarily optimal. An aggregate production plan that minimizes the total cost for the entire planning horizon was generated by an integer programming model. The model determined the number of units

of each product was to be processed in each production period in the planning horizon.

Table 18 and Figure 32 present the optimal solution for the example in Table 12 and Figure 29 (Backorder Day 5 costs are for product P1 –US$ 73, for product P2 –US$ 76 and for product P3 – US$ 75)

The total cost of the optimal production plan was US$ 3,531. Table 19 lists the components of the total cost.

As calculated above, the total cost of the balanced production plan without the new work order as result of optimization, according to RCCP, was US$ 2,814.

Figure 30. Gantt chart of the historical planning horizon

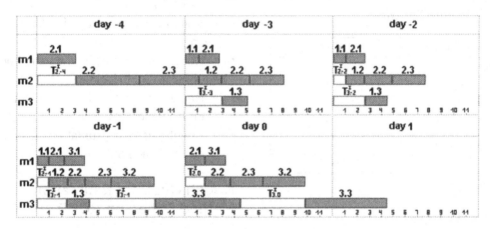

Table 16. Balanced and feasible production plan with the new work order based on a Finite Loading Procedure (units)

Product type	P1	P2	P3
Day 1	11	14	4
Day 2	11	15	37
Day 3	11	20	11
Day 4	10	17	4
Day 5	17	17	4
Total	60	83	60

Figure 31. RCCP chart with the new work order based on a Finite Loading Procedure

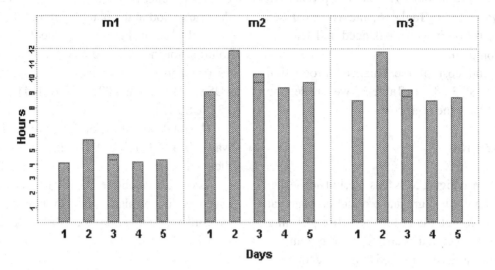

Table 17. The cost components of the balanced production plan with the new work order based on a Finite Loading Procedure

Component	Cost(US$)
Inventory Holding	0
Backorder	49
Overtime	364
Raw Material	2,150
Regular Time	1,120
Total	3,683

ROUGH-CUT COST ESTIMATION METHODS

This section presents five alternative rough-cut cost estimation methods for fast estimation of the cost of a new work order, while we use the techniques, described in NAME OF SECTION, for generating the aggregate production plan. Raw material and regular hour costs are the same for all methods; the real difference between the methods is in the way they estimate inventory holding, backorder and overtime costs. The five methods are:

- Rough-cut cost estimation method based on RCCP
- Rough-cut cost estimation method based on Time Unit Cost
- Rough-cut cost estimation method based on Snapshot Principle
- Rough-cut cost estimation method based on Bottleneck Analysis
- Rough-cut cost estimation method based on Smoothed Station

Rough Cut Cost Estimation Method Based on RCCP

The RCCP-based method calculates the cost of a new order on the basis of aggregate production plans derived from a commonly used RCCP procedure. Two production plans were generated – with and without the new work order. The total cost of each production plan was calculated by the cost function of Equation (1), taking into account variable production costs, backorder costs, overtime costs and inventory holding costs. Then, the cost of the new work order was estimated as the difference between the total costs of these two production plans.

Figure 32. RCCP chart with the new work order as a result of optimization

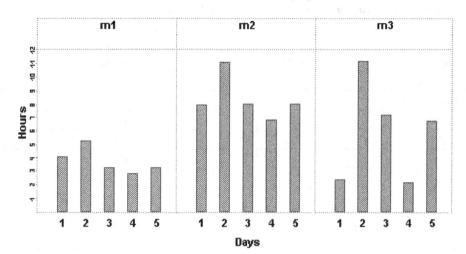

Table 18. Balanced production plan with the new work order as result of optimization (units)

Product type	P1	P2	P3
Day 1	33	25	0
Day 2	0	11	48
Day 3	0	13	8
Day 4	27	18	0
Day 5	0	16	4
Total	60	83	60

We now applied optimization as a balancing technique for the shop floor example. The estimated cost of the new order for 40 units of product P3 was the difference between the total cost of the optimal production plan with the new work order and the total cost of the optimal production plan without the new work order. From the example in NAME SECTION the estimated cost of the new order was: US$ 3,531 - US $2,814 = **US$ 717**.

Rough-Cut Cost Estimation Method Based on Time Unit Cost

This method calculates the average cost of a time unit on the basis of data from the past (from period $-(T-1)$ to period 0) by dividing the total cost by the total time (including setup time). The cost of

a new work order was estimated by the product of the expected production time (including setup time) of the new work order and the estimated "Time Unit Cost".

The time unit cost includes the inventory holding, backorder and overtime costs. The time unit cost, H, was calculated as follows:

$$H = \frac{\sum_{i=1}^{N} \sum_{t=-(T-1)}^{0} \left(c_{it} I_{it}^{+} + b_{it} I_{it}^{-} \right) + \sum_{t=-(T-1)}^{0} \left(o_{t} O_{t} \right)}{\sum_{i=1}^{N} \sum_{j=1}^{M} \sum_{t=-(T-1)}^{0} \left(s_{ij} I_{it}^{setup} + \frac{a_{ij} X_{it}}{y_{ij}} \right)} \quad (40)$$

This method assumed that the time unit cost of the historical planning horizon was a good estimation for the time unit cost of the current planning horizon. This time unit cost method

Table 19. The cost components of a balanced pro-duction plan with the new work order as aresult of optimization

Component	Cost(US$)
Inventory Holding	~0
Backorder	24
Overtime	237
Raw Material	2150
Regular Time	1120
Total	3,531

Table 21. Cost components of the production plan in Table 20

Component	Cost(US$)
Inventory Holding	0
Backorder	94
Overtime	447
Raw Material	2,008
Regular Time	1,120
Total	3,669

Table 20. Production plan according to the Gantt chart in Figure 30 (units)

Product type	P1	P2	P3
Day 1	0	55	0
Day 2	24	30	0
Day 3	19	21	0
Day 4	17	7	0
Day 5	0	17	5
Total	60	130	5

ignored the changes in the product mix in the two planning horizons and the differences in the capacity utilization.

Table 20 presents the production plan based on the Gantt chart in Figure 30 and Table 21 presents this plan's cost components.

The sum of inventory holding, backorder and overtime costs in the historical planning horizon was US$ 0 + US$ 94 + US$ 447 = US$ 541. The total time of scheduled work in the historical planning horizon was 76.3 hours. The hour cost was US$ 541/76.3 hours = US$ 7/hour.

It tool 9.33 hours to produce the 40 units of the new order. Raw material cost was 40 units * US$ 12 = US$ 480. The cost of the hours worked was 9.33 hours * US$ 7/hour = US$ 66. The total new order cost was: US$ 480 + US$ 66 = *US$ 546*.

'Forced Idle Time' Oriented Rough-Cut Cost Estimation Methods

In a stochastic environment, machines are subject to blockages and starvations. These cause forced idle time of machines and decrease their actual available capacity. Therefore, the classic RCCP methods need to be modified by reducing machine available capacity by the amount of forced machine idle time. The following three methods are used for estimating the forced idle time in order to improve the cost estimation of a new work order. All three methods use the basic RCCP model and adjust the machine available capacity.

Rough-Cut Cost Estimation Method Based on the SnapShot Principle

The Snapshot Principle (Foschini, (1980) asserts that the forced machine idle times do not change fast. According to this principle, we assumed that

Figure 33. RCCP chart with the new order according to the Snapshot Principle

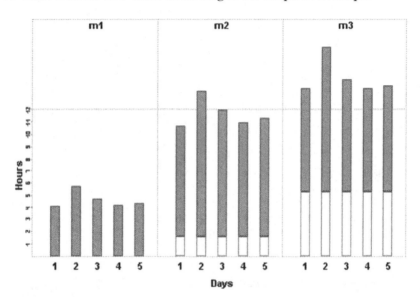

Table 22. Balanced production plan with the new work order as a result of optimization according to the Snapshot Principle (units)

Product type	P1	P2	P3
Day 1	0	32	4
Day 2	60	0	0
Day 3	0	17	4
Day 4	0	17	4
Day 5	0	17	4
Total	60	83	16

the forced idle time of a machine j in all periods in the planning horizon is constant and equal to the forced idle time of historical period 0. Hence:

$$T_{jt}^I = T_{j0}^I, \quad \forall j, \forall t = 1..T, \qquad (41)$$

where T_{j0}^I, the forced idle time of machine j in period 0 is known.

Figure 33 presents RCCP with the new order according to the Snapshot Principle. Estimates of forced idle times (1.6 hours on machine m2 and 5.2 hours on machine m3) were based on Day 0 of the Gantt chart on Figure 30. As we can see, the production plan is not balanced. We therefore

used optimization as a balancing technique. The optimum solution for the production plan from Figure 33 is presented in Table 22 and Figure 34. Table 23 presents the cost components of this plan.

Rough-Cut Cost Estimation Method Based on a Bottleneck Analysis

The bottleneck-based method assumed that the forced idle time in period t depended on the workload on the bottleneck machine. In Equation (12) the forced idle time of machine j in period t ($t = 1,....T$) was calculated as the product of the

Figure 34. RCCP chart with the new work order as a result of optimization according to the Snapshot Principle

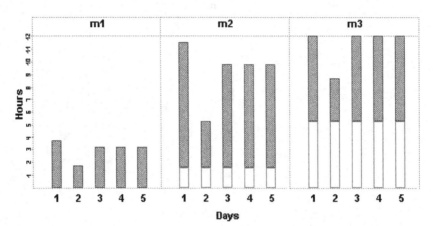

Table 23. Cost components of the balanced production plan with the new work order as a result of optimization according to the Snapshot Principle

Component	Cost(US$)
Inventory Holding	~0
Backorder	1,056
Overtime	598
Raw Material	2,150
Regular Time	1,120
Total	4,924

As calculated above, the total cost of the balanced production plan without the new work order as result of optimization according to the Snapshot Principle was US$ 3,484.

The estimated cost of the new order proposal for 40 units of product P3 was the difference between the total cost of the balanced planning with the new work order and the total cost of the balanced production plan without the new work order: US$ 4,924 - US$ 3,484 = **US$ 1,440**.

workload of the bottleneck machine in period t, and the average ratio (derived from past data) between the forced idle time of machine j and the workload of the bottleneck machine.

$$T_{jt}^l = \max_{j'} \left(\frac{\sum_{i=1}^N \left(s_{ij'} \cdot I_{it}^{setup} + \frac{a_{ij} \cdot X_{it}}{y_{ij'}} \right)}{\frac{t_{j'}^f}{t_{j'}^f + t_{j'}^r} \left(W_t + O_t \right)} \right) \bullet$$

$$\bullet \frac{1}{T} \sum_{t'=(T-1)}^0 \left(T_{jt'}^l \middle/ \max_{j'} \left(\frac{\sum_{i=1}^N \left(s_{ij'} \cdot I_{it'}^{setup} + \frac{a_{ij} \cdot X_{it'}}{y_{ij'}} \right)}{\frac{t_{j'}^f}{t_{j'}^f + t_{j'}^r} \left(W_{t'} + O_{t'} \right)} \right) \right) \quad \forall j, \forall t = 1..T$$

(42)

Table 24 presents the calculated forced idle time for a production plan with the new work order as result of optimization according to the bottleneck analysis.

Figure 35 presents RCCP with the new order according to the bottleneck analysis. As we can see, the production plan was not balanced. The optimum solution for the production plan from Figure 35 is presented in Table 25 and Figure 36. Table 26 presents the cost components of this plan.

As calculated above, the total cost of the balanced production plan without the new work order as a result of optimization according to the bottleneck analysis was US$ 3,050.

The estimated cost of new order proposal for 40 units of product P3 is the difference between the total cost of the balanced planning with the new work order and the total cost of the balanced production plan without the new work order: US$ 4,010 - US$ 3,050 = **US$ 960**.

Table 24. Calculated forced idle time for the production plan with the new work order as a result of optimization according to the bottleneck analysis

	Historical planning horizon					Current planning horizon		
	Idle time (Hours)		Bottleneck load	Idle time/ load		Bottleneck load with the new order	Calculated idle time (Hours)	
	m2	m3		m2	m3		m2	m3
Day 1	3.1	0.0	84%	3.7	0.0	66%	1.2	3.7
Day 2	0.0	3.0	59%	0.0	5.1	93%	1.7	5.2
Day 3	1.1	2.7	56%	1.9	4.8	66%	1.2	3.7
Day 4	1.0	7.7	73%	1.4	10.5	57%	1.1	3.2
Day 5	1.6	5.2	65%	2.3	7.8	67%	1.3	3.8
Average				1.9	5.6			

Figure 35. RCCP chart with the new order according to the bottleneck analysis

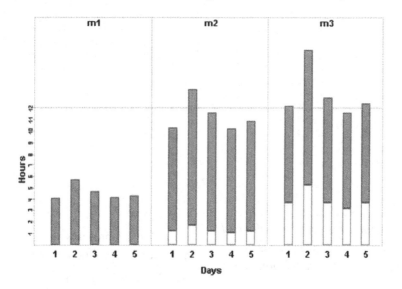

Rough-Cut Cost Estimation Method Based on a Smoothed Station Analysis

The smoothed station-based method was inspired by a balancing procedure for a mixed product assembly line under the constraint of shift duration. The objective of the balancing procedure, as shown in Thomopoulos (1970), is to minimize the fluctuation of assembly times required by each product at different stations during the shift. This objective function consists of the weighted sum of the products' deviations where a product deviation is the sum over all stations of the differences between the model processing time in a given station and its average processing time over all stations. We assumed that forced idle time in period t depended on this function. The smoothed station-based method also uses information from period $-(T-1)$ to period 0.

In Equation (13) the forced idle time of machine j in period t was calculated by the product between weighted sum of the products' deviations in period t, and the average ratio, over periods of

Table 25. Balanced production plan with the new work order as a result of optimization according to the bottleneck analysis (units)

Product type	P1	P2	P3
Day 1	0	26	19
Day 2	43	6	0
Day 3	0	17	19
Day 4	0	17	22
Day 5	17	17	0
Total	60	83	60

Figure 36. RCCP chart with the new work order as a result of optimization according to the bottleneck analysis

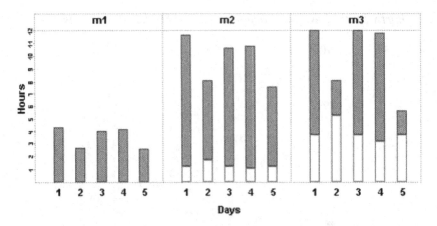

Table 26. Cost components of the balanced production plan with the new work order as a result of optimization according to the bottleneck analysis

Component	Cost(US$)
Inventory Holding	~0
Backorder	313
Overtime	427
Raw Material	2150
Regular Time	1120
Total	4,010

the historical planning horizon, between the forced idle time of machine *j* and the weighted sum of the products' deviations (see equation (43)).

Table 27 presents the calculated forced idle time for the production plan with the new work order as result of optimization according to a smoothed station analysis.

Figure 37 presents RCCP with the new order according to the smoothed station analysis. The production plan was not balanced. The optimum solution for the production plan from Figure 37 is presented in Table 28 and Figure 38. Table 29 presents the cost components of this plan.

As calculated above, the total cost of the balanced production plan without the new work order as a result of optimization according to bottleneck analysis is US$ 2,974.

The estimated cost of new order proposal for 40 units of product P3 is the difference between

Table 27. Calculated forced idle time for a production plan with the new work order as a result of optimization according to the smoothed station analysis

	Historical planning horizon					Current planning horizon		
	Idle time (Hours)		Weighted sum of the products' deviations	Idle time/ Weighted sum		Weighted sum of the products' deviations	Calculated idle time (Hours)	
	m2	m3		m2	m3		m2	m3
Day 1	3.1	0.0	11.7	0.27	0.00	10.7	1.2	3.2
Day 2	0.0	3.0	9.7	0.00	0.31	19.5	2.2	5.8
Day 3	1.1	2.7	9.2	0.12	0.29	13.6	1.5	4.1
Day 4	1.0	7.7	15.3	0.07	0.50	9.3	1.1	2.8
Day 5	1.6	5.2	13.5	0.12	0.39	13.3	1.5	4.0
Average				0.11	5.30			

Figure 37. RCCP chart with the new order according to the smoothed station analysis

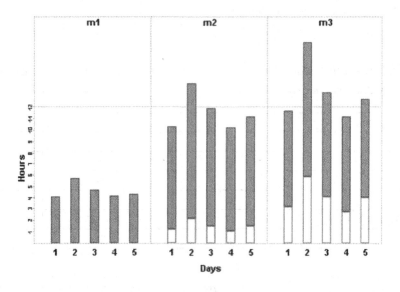

Equation (43).

$$T_{jt}^{I} = \sum_{j'=1}^{M}\sum_{i=1}^{N} \left| \frac{\sum_{i'=1}^{N}\left(s_{i'j'}I_{i't}^{setup} + \frac{a_{i'j'}X_{i't}}{y_{i'j'}}\right)}{N} - \left(s_{ij}I_{it}^{setup} + \frac{a_{ij}X_{it}}{y_{ij'}}\right)\right| \bullet$$

$$\bullet \frac{1}{T}\sum_{t'=(T-1)}^{0}\left(T_{jt'}^{I} / \sum_{j'=1}^{M}\sum_{i=1}^{N}\left|\frac{\sum_{i'=1}^{N}\left(s_{i'j'}I_{i't'}^{setup} + \frac{a_{i'j'}X_{i't'}}{y_{i'j'}}\right)}{N} - \left(s_{ij'}I_{it'}^{setup} + \frac{a_{ij}X_{it'}}{y_{ij'}}\right)\right|\right) \quad \forall j, \forall t = 1..T$$

the total cost of a balanced planning with the new work order and the total cost of the balanced production plan without the new work order: US$ 3,975 - US$ 2,974 = **US$ 1,001**.

ACTUAL ORDER'S COST CALCULATION

As a baseline for comparison of the accuracy of the different cost estimation methods we calculated the actual order's cost. The actual order's cost takes into account precedence between operations and the stochastic nature of the real problem. Simulation was used for this calculation. The simulation was implemented twice – with and without the new

order. The cost of the new order was estimated by the difference between the average total cost of the two production plans based on 20 simulation replications.

Figure 39 presents a detailed scheduling of the production plan with the new order. Tables 30 and 31 present finishing dates and the cost components of this plan.

The actual order's cost of the new order for 40 units of product P3 is the difference between the average of 20 replications with the new work order and the average of 20 replications without the new work order: US$ 4,221 - US$ 3,310 = **US$ 911**. (Table 32)

Table 28. Balanced production plan with the new work order as a result of optimization according to the smoothed station analysis (units)

Product type	P1	P2	P3
Day 1	0	25	24
Day 2	43	7	0
Day 3	0	17	15
Day 4	0	17	21
Day 5	17	17	0
Total	60	83	60

Figure 38. RCCP chart with the new work order as a result of optimization according to the smoothed station analysis

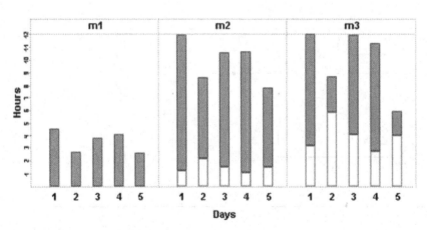

Additional Cost Estimation Methods

In this section, in addition to the five rough-cut cost estimation methods presented in Section NAME, we present two additional methods for cost estimation: cost estimation with simulation and traditional cost estimation.

Cost estimation with simulation is a-priori the best accurate method (in real life, because it is quite

Table 29. The cost components of the balanced production plan with the new work order as a result of optimization according to the smoothed station analysis

Component	Cost(US$)
Inventory Holding	~0
Backorder	277
Overtime	428
Raw Material	2,150
Regular Time	1,120
Total	3,975

Table 31. The cost components of the production plan with the new work order according to the Gantt chart

Component	Cost(US$)
Inventory Holding	~0
Backorder	360
Overtime	518
Raw Material	2,150
Regular Time	1,120
Total	4,149

Table 30. Finishing dates of the production plan with the new work order according to the Gantt chart (units)

Product type	P1	P2	P3
Day 1	33	25	0
Day 2	0	11	0
Day 3	0	13	48
Day 4	27	18	8
Day 5	0	16	0
Total	60	83	56

Figure 39. Gantt chart with the new work order

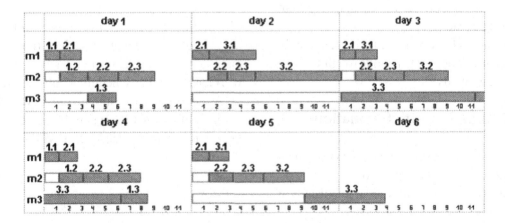

Table 32. Actual order's cost calculation based on 20 simulation replications

# of replications	Total cost without the new work order	Total cost with the new work order
1	3,333	4,400
2	3,283	4,016
3	3,173	4,385
4	3,303	4,076
5	3,153	4,055
6	3,324	4,139
7	3,304	4,060
8	3,303	4,188
9	3,409	4,093
10	3,335	4,383
11	3,383	4,204
12	3,316	4,043
13	3,312	4,060
14	3,430	4,423
15	3,165	4,542
16	3,420	4,069
17	3,302	4,584
18	3,285	4,163
19	3,350	4,430
20	3,305	4,101
Average	3,310	4,221

a good "copy" of processes on the shop floor, and in the laboratory environment, because the data generated by simulation repeats the method used to generate the data used as a baseline).

Traditional cost estimation is a-priori the worst accurate method because it only uses raw material costs to generate the estimate (without considering capacity).

These methods are presented in order to supply comparison approaches to the five rough-cut cost estimation methods.

Cost Estimation with Simulation

Table 33 presents another 20 simulation replications as a basis for cost estimation.

The cost estimate of a new order for 40 units of

product P3 is the difference between the average of 20 replications with the new work order and the average of 20 replications without the new work order: US$ 4,241 - US$ 3,337 = **US$ 904**.

Traditional Cost Estimation

The traditional cost estimation is calculated using the cost of a new order derived from the raw materials cost only, ignoring capacity limitations, workloads or other scheduling considerations.

A traditional cost estimate of a new order for 40 units of product P3 is simply the cost of raw materials: 40 units * US$ 12= **US$ 480**.

Table 33. Simulation replications as the basis for cost estimation

Total cost with the new work order	Total cost without the new work order	# of replications
4,625	3,286	21
4,556	3,385	22
4,421	3,176	23
4,023	3,307	24
4,095	3,363	25
4,129	3,380	26
4,412	3,381	27
4,098	3,312	28
4,170	3,295	29
4,104	3,163	30
4,423	3,411	31
4,061	3,317	32
4,388	3,459	33
4,306	3,335	34
4,091	3,314	35
4,136	3,414	36
4,043	3,381	37
4,508	3,416	38
4,072	3,316	39
4,160	3,328	40
4,241	3,337	Average

The Experimental Design

We now discuss our tests of the accuracy of the rough-cut cost estimation methods. Previous sections showed that the accuracy of cost estimation models is fairly robust to changes in the shop floor parameters. Therefore, in the current section, we concentrated on comparing the cost estimation methods and not on the impact of the shop floor parameters on the accuracy of the estimations.

Generation of Treatments

The seven shop floor parameters and their possible values were:

1. Initial shop floor load interval: low – 45%–55%; high – 80%–90%

2. The dispatching rule used in the simulation: Shortest Processing Time (SPT), Most WorK Remaining (MWKR)

3. Production plan balancing technique: Finite Loading; Optimization

4. Setup times, processing times, time between failures, time to repair and product yield are distributed uniformly with parameters: $0.85 \cdot average$, $1.15 \cdot average$; $0.50 \cdot average$, $1.50 \cdot average$

5. Number of workstations in a production route: 3, 9

6. Number of product types: 3, 9

7. Number of machine types: 3, 9

Thirty different treatments were generated by random sampling of the seven parameters. Equal probability (50%) for each of the two possible values was used. If a configuration of a new treatment was identical to one of the previous treatments, new values were sampled. Table 34 presents the configurations of the 30 treatments.

Experimental Description

For each treatment of the experiment, three sets of orders were randomly generated:

- Orders that were accepted for production

Table 34. Configuration of the treatments

# of machine types	# of product types	# of work stations in a route	Distribution of Stochastic Parameters	Production plan balancing technique	Dispatching Rule	Initial Shop Floor Load	#
3	3	3	Unif(0.85a,1.15a)	FL	MWKR	50	1
9	9	3	Unif(0.5a,1.5a)	FL	MWKR	90	2
3	9	9	Unif(0.5a,1.5a)	Opt	MWKR	50	3
3	9	3	Unif(0.85a,1.15a)	FL	MWKR	90	4
9	9	3	Unif(0.85a,1.15a)	Opt	MWKR	90	5
3	9	3	Unif(0.5a,1.5a)	FL	SPT	50	6
9	9	9	Unif(0.5a,1.5a)	Opt	SPT	90	7
3	3	9	Unif(0.85a,1.15a)	Opt	SPT	90	8
3	9	9	Unif(0.85a,1.15a)	Opt	MWKR	90	9
3	9	3	Unif(0.5a,1.5a)	Opt	SPT	90	10
9	3	9	Unif(0.5a,1.5a)	FL	SPT	50	11
9	9	9	Unif(0.85a,1.15a)	Opt	SPT	90	12
3	3	3	Unif(0.5a,1.5a)	FL	MWKR	50	13
9	3	3	Unif(0.5a,1.5a)	FL	MWKR	90	14
3	3	3	Unif(0.5a,1.5a)	FL	SPT	90	15
3	3	9	Unif(0.5a,1.5a)	Opt	MWKR	50	16
9	3	3	Unif(0.85a,1.15a)	FL	SPT	50	17
9	3	9	Unif(0.85a,1.15a)	Opt	MWKR	90	18
3	9	9	Unif(0.5a,1.5a)	FL	MWKR	50	19
9	9	9	Unif(0.85a,1.15a)	FL	SPT	90	20
3	3	9	Unif(0.85a,1.15a)	FL	SPT	50	21
3	3	3	Unif(0.85a,1.15a)	Opt	MWKR	50	22
9	3	9	Unif(0.85a,1.15a)	FL	MWKR	90	23
9	3	9	Unif(0.85a,1.15a)	Opt	SPT	50	24
9	3	9	Unif(0.5a,1.5a)	Opt	SPT	90	25
9	9	3	Unif(0.85a,1.15a)	FL	MWKR	50	26
9	3	3	Unif(0.5a,1.5a)	Opt	MWKR	90	27
3	9	3	Unif(0.85a,1.15a)	FL	SPT	50	28
3	9	3	Unif(0.85a,1.15a)	Opt	SPT	50	29
9	9	9	Unif(0.5a,1.5a)	Opt	MWKR	50	30

during a historical planning horizon (from period $-(T–1)$ to period 0).

- Orders that have already been accepted for production in the current planning horizon – from Day 1 to Day T.
- A single new order (whose cost is to be estimated).

Historical planning horizon data was inserted into a simulation model. By using simulation we generated a realization of the historical planning horizon (from period $-(T–1)$ to period 0) including the backorders from the historical to the current planning horizon.

The cost of the new order was estimated by implementing the five rough-cut cost estimation methods. As explained earlier, four of the methods (except time unit cost) were implemented twice – with and without the new order, and the cost of the new order was estimated by the difference between the total cost of the two production plans.

Each one of the five cost estimation methods was compared to a baseline, which was derived from 20 simulation replications of the current planning horizon, for each treatment. We calculated a measure named actual order's cost by averaging the cost of the new order resulting from all these 20 replications. The cost estimation accuracy of the kth treatment of method u ($u=1,,,,,7$: RCCP, Time Unit Cost, Snapshot, Bottleneck, Smoothed Station, Simulation and Traditional) was measured by two measures – the relative and the absolute relative deviation from actual order's cost, $D^{(uk)}$ and $AD^{(uk)}$, respectively. The measures are calculated as follows:

$$D^{(uk)} = \frac{Cost\ estimation^{(uk)} - Actual\ order's\ cost^{(uk)}}{Actual\ order's\ cost^{(uk)}}$$

(44)

and,

$$AD^{(uk)} = \frac{\left| Cost\ estimation^{(uk)} - Actual\ order's\ cost^{(uk)} \right|}{Actual\ order's\ cost^{(uk)}}$$

(45)

In addition to the five rough-cut cost estimation methods, two additional cost estimation methods, for each treatment, were applied: cost estimation with simulation and traditional cost estimation.

The number of periods in the planning horizon (T) was set to five days and the total available regular and overtime hours in period t ($(wm)_t$ and $(om)_t$) were set to eight and four hours, respectively.

The values for each treatment, for other shop floor parameters, were sampled randomly from uniform distribution with parameters as follows:

- Machine type: *(0.5, M+0.5)*; after sampling, the result was rounded to the closest integer number.
- Mean processing time of a unit of product i on machine j (a_{ij}): *(1, 6)* minutes.
- Mean setup time of product i on machine j (s_{ij}): (10, 500) minutes.
- Demand for product i in period t (d_{it}): (5, 40); randomization was iterative until the sampled initial shop floor workload interval was achieved.
- Inventory holding cost per unit of product i in period t (c_{it}): (0.04 v_{it}, 0.06 v_{it})\$.
- The variable cost for producing a unit of product i in period t under an infinite capacity environment (v_{it}): (8, 14)\$.
- Regular labor cost per hour in period t (r_t): (15, 30)\$.
- Mean time between failures for machine j (t_j^f): (12, 14) hours.
- Mean time to repair for machine j (t_j^r): (2, 3) hours.
- Yield of product i at machine j (y_{ij}): (95, 98) %.

In order to prevent a situation where we prefer to produce nothing and to pay backorder costs only, we set the backorder cost per unit of product i in the last period, $t=5$ (b_{i5}) to a relatively high value (for optimization only): $U(60, 80)$\$.

In order to understand the influence of the workload on the accuracy of the tested cost estimation methods, a sensitivity analysis was done for 15 workload levels: 10%, 20%, …, 150%. For each workload level, two replications were run.

The simulation model was run for the five days of the planning horizon.

Shop floor parameters were generated and cost estimations were calculated using Microsoft Excel™. Optimization was done using ILOG OPL Studio™ (optimization software) and the simulation was run by Arena™ (simulation software). All problem instances were run on a 900-MHz AMD Duron™ processor with 256 MB of RAM.

Results and Analysis

Results of the 30 treatments were analyzed by a t-test. A statistically significant advantage in the accuracy of the bottleneck-based rough-cut cost estimation method over the other rough-cut approaches was found (p-value < 0.05). Figure 40 presents a comparison between the absolute relative deviation from actual order's cost, $AD^{(uk)}$, values of the seven estimation methods – the five rough-cut methods: RCCP, Time Unit Cost, Snapshot, Bottleneck and Smoothed Station based rough-cut cost estimation methods, and the approaches for comparison: simulation and traditional.

Figure 41 presents a comparison between the relative deviations from actual order's cost", $D^{(uk)}$ and the values of the seven estimation methods.

The upper part of Table 35 presents the p-values of the differences in accuracy, for each pair of methods. The methods are listed in an ascending order of their $AD^{(uk)}$ values. Therefore, the table entries present the p-values of the advantage in terms of the accuracy of the methods listed in rows over those listed in columns.

The lower part of Table 35 presents the average, standard deviation, minimum value and maximum value of $AD^{(uk)}$ for each of the cost estimation methods.

Figure 40. Comparison between $AD^{(uk)}$ values of the tested cost estimation methods

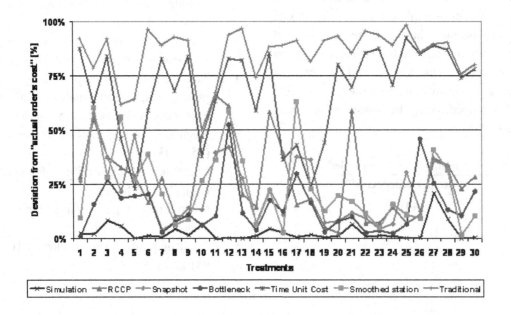

Table 35 shows the statistically significant superiority of the bottleneck method over the other non-simulation methods. There was no statistically significant difference between snapshot, smoothed station and RCCP. Time cost unit was statistically significantly less accurate than other methods, but better than traditional. From the lower part of Table 35 we can see that the behavior of the averages and standard deviations across the tested cost estimation methods was quite similar.

The differences in methods that led to differences in the observed results were:

• Time unit cost: ignored the changes in the product mix in the two planning horizons (historical and current) and the differences

Figure 41. Comparison between $D^{(uk)}$ values of the tested cost estimation methods

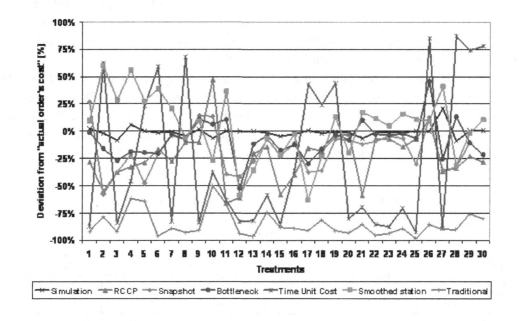

Table 35. Significant values of the advantage in absolute accuracy of each pair of methods

Method	Simula-tion	Bottleneck	Snapshot	Smoothed station	RCCP	Time unit cost	Traditional
Simulation	-	$9 \cdot 10^{-6}$	$3 \cdot 10^{-8}$	$2 \cdot 10^{-7}$	10^{-8}	$2 \cdot 10^{-17}$	$8 \cdot 10^{-26}$
Bottleneck	-	-	0.002	0.001	$4 \cdot 10^{-4}$	$2 \cdot 10^{-13}$	10^{-20}
Snapshot	-	-	-	0.224	0.054	10^{-10}	$4 \cdot 10^{-17}$
Smoothed station	-	-	-	-	0.159	$2 \cdot 10^{-9}$	$3 \cdot 10^{-15}$
RCCP	-	-	-	-	-	$6 \cdot 10^{-9}$	$2 \cdot 10^{-13}$
Time unit cost	-	-	-	-	-	-	$3 \cdot 10^{-6}$
Avg	3%	15%	22%	24%	27%	68%	85%
St. Dev.	4%	12%	15%	18%	19%	21%	12%
Min	0.1%	1%	4%	2%	3%	23%	50%
Max	21%	52%	58%	63%	66%	93%	98%

in the capacity utilization.

- RCCP: ignored precedence between operations; consequently, the result wrongly estimated overtime and backorders.
- Smoothed station: took precedence between operations into consideration by estimating forced idle time and changes in the product mix, but, according to the results, the weighted sum of the products' deviations was not a good enough estimator of the forced idle time.
- Snapshot: took precedence between operations into consideration by estimating forced idle time, but, according to the results, used too rough an assumption that the forced idle time of a machine j in all periods in the planning horizon would be constant.
- Bottleneck: took precedence between operations into consideration by estimating

forced idle time and differences in the capacity utilization. According to the results, the workload with bottleneck was quite a good estimator of the forced idle time.

Table 36 presents a comparison between the $D^{(uk)}$ values of the tested cost estimation methods. In the upper part of Table 36, 12 ranges of $D^{(uk)}$ were defined (from -50% and below to 50% and above in steps of 10%). The number of treatments in each range (from 30 possible) was counted. The lower part of Table 36 presents the average, standard deviation, range, minimum value and maximum value of $D^{(uk)}$ for each cost estimation method.

In Table 36, three ranges of $D^{(uk)}$ for bottleneck were considered: ±10%, ±20% and ±30%. The bottleneck results were less accurate for the first range – 40% (12 treatments from 30 possible were in the range ±10%), but were better for the second

Table 36. Comparison between $D^{(uk)}$ values of the tested cost estimation methods

Range of] values (%)	No of observations (out of 30)						
	Simulation	Bottleneck	Snapshot	Smoothed station	RCCP	Time unit cost	Traditional
-50 and below	0	1	1	2	5	16	30
-50 to -40	0	0	2	0	0	1	0
-40 to -30	0	0	7	2	5	2	0
-30 to -20	0	5	5	3	6	0	0
-20 to -10	0	8	3	1	7	0	0
-10 to 0	20	10	8	4	5	0	0
0 to 10	9	2	0	4	0	0	0
10 to 20	0	3	3	6	1	0	0
20 to 30	1	0	1	3	0	2	0
30 to 40	0	0	0	2	0	0	0
40 to 50	0	1	0	1	1	2	0
50 and above	0	0	0	2	0	7	0
Average	-1%	-8%	-18%	4%	-24%	-25%	-85%
Standard deviation	5%	17%	20%	30%	24%	68%	12%
Range	30%	98%	84%	123%	113%	180%	48%
Maximum	-9%	-52%	-58%	-63%	-66%	-93%	-98%
Minimum	21%	46%	26%	60%	47%	87%	-50%

range – 77% (23 treatments from 30 possible were in the range ±20%) and much better for the third range – 93% (28 treatments from 30 possible were in the range ±30%). Performances of other cost estimation methods were less accurate.

From Figure 41 and Table 36, we can see that in spite of its good average, smooth station are very unstable (the good average was the result of a trade-off between positive and negative values), as were RCCP and time unit cost. Bottleneck and snap shot gave quite good results – in spite of a bigger range; bottleneck had a better average and standard deviation than snap shot.

As we can observe in Figure 42, there was very high correlation between the bottleneck cost estimation and actual order's cost' – the coefficient of determination was equal to 0.983. Bottleneck underestimated actual order's cost a little – the slope was 1.058 and the bias was US$ 52.19 (for US$ 3,803 as the average order cost of 30 treatments – this is a small bias).

Figure 43 presents a sensitivity analysis of the workload influence (from 10% to 150% with steps of 10%) on the $AD^{(uk)}$ values of the seven estimation methods (RCCP, Time Unit Cost, Snapshot, Bottleneck and Smoothed Station, Simulation and Traditional).

Figure 44 and Table 37 present a sensitivity analysis of the workload influence (from 10% to 150% with steps of 10%) on the $D^{(uk)}$ values of the seven estimation methods (RCCP, Time Unit Cost, Snapshot, Bottleneck and Smoothed Station, Simulation and Traditional).

We can see that majority of models showed good results in a load range of 100% to 120%. The possible reasons for this are:

- Low flexibility in overtime (the majority of the models used maximum possible extra hours)
- Low flexibility in backorders (the majority of the models related to the entire new work order as a backorder).

Some models showed accurate estimates for specific loads:

- Smoothed station was very good at 60%, but extremely inaccurate at 70%

Figure 42. Correlation between bottleneck's cost estimation and that of actual order's cost

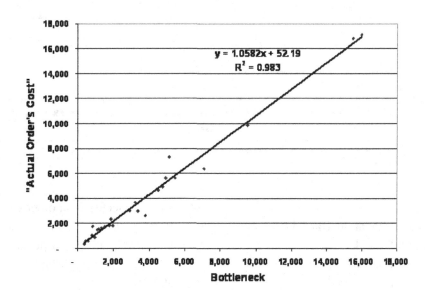

Figure 43. Sensitivity analysis of workload influence on AD^(uk) values

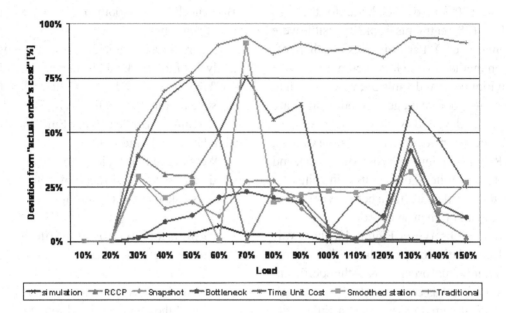

Figure 44. Sensitivity analysis of load influence on D^(uk) values

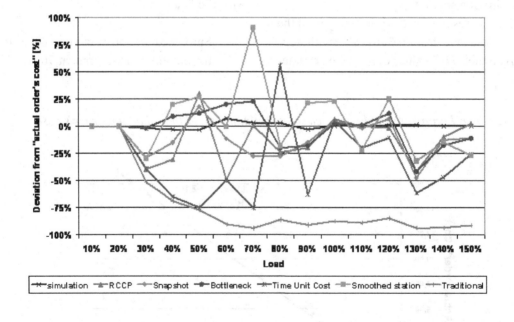

- RCCP was accurate at 70% and 110%, but inaccurate at 60% and 130%
- Time unit cost was very accurate at 100%, but inaccurate at other loads
- Snap shot was accurate from 100% to 120%

- and less accurate on other workloads
- Bottleneck was good at the majority of workloads; it was especially accurate at 30%, 100% and 110%; the worst case was at 130%.

Table 37. Detailed data of load influence on D$^{(uk)}$ values

Work loads	Method						
	Simu lation	Bottle neck	Snap shot	Smoo- thed station	RCCP	Time Unit Cost	Traditional
10%	0%	0%	0%	0%	0%	0%	0%
20%	0%	0%	0%	0%	0%	0%	0%
30%	-2%	-2%	-29%	-30%	-40%	-39%	-51%
40%	-3%	9%	-15%	20%	-31%	-65%	-69%
50%	-3%	12%	18%	27%	30%	-75%	-77%
60%	7%	20%	-11%	0%	-49%	-50%	-90%
70%	3%	23%	-28%	91%	0%	-75%	-94%
80%	3%	-20%	-28%	-18%	-24%	56%	-86%
90%	-3%	-18%	-15%	21%	-20%	-63%	-91%
100%	0%	3%	5%	23%	7%	5%	-87%
110%	0%	1%	-2%	-22%	0%	-20%	-89%
120%	1%	12%	7%	25%	-1%	-11%	-85%
130%	1%	-42%	-47%	-32%	-42%	-62%	-94%
140%	0%	-18%	-13%	-15%	-10%	-47%	-93%
150%	0%	-11%	-11%	-27%	2%	-26%	-91%

ADJUSTMENT OF AGGREGATE PLANNING MODEL TO ACTIVITY BASED COSTING (ABC)

In this section we change the objective function in order to use activity base costing.

Additional Assumptions

1) Each activity has a number of unique cost drivers.
2) Unit cost of each cost driver is known.
3) The fixed annual cost of each activity k is known.

The Objective Function Adjustment

The proposed objective function of the ABC optimization model is:

$$\min \sum_{i=1}^{N} \sum_{t=1}^{T} \left(\left(v_{it} + \sum_{k=1}^{K} \sum_{l_k=1}^{L_k} C_{l_k i} CCD_{l_k i} \right) X_{it} + c_{it} I_{it}^+ + b_{it} I_{it}^- \right.$$

$$\left. + \sum_{i=1}^{T} \left(r_t W_t + o_t O_t \right) \right) \quad (46)$$

In ABC, the fixed costs of the traditional cost system are represented as variable and fixed costs of activities. In objective function (12) we take into account the variable costs of activities. In the same way as in the traditional cost system, the fixed costs of activities are omitted from the objective function, since they are constants.

The Experimental Design

The experiment aimed to test the accuracy of the ABC model. The number of periods in the planning horizon (T) was set to five days and the total available regular and overtime hours in period t ($(wm)_t$ and $(om)_t$) were set to be eight and four hours, respectively.

For each run, two sets of orders were randomly generated:

- Orders already accepted for production in the current planning horizon from Day 1 to Day 5.
- A single new order.

The traditional cost system and the ABC models were implemented twice, first without the new order and second with the new order. Then, the cost of the new order was estimated as the difference between the total cost of the entire production plan with and without the new order.

In order to calculate a baseline for this comparison, 20 simulation replications of the ABC model were run, for each treatment, and we estimated the actual order's cost as the average of these replications. The cost estimation accuracy was calculated by the ratio:

$$\left(\frac{\left| \text{Result of cost estimation} - \text{Actual order's cost} \right|}{\text{Actual order's cost}} \right)$$

As we saw in earlier sections, either the difference in the accuracy of the cost estimation models was fairly robust to changes in the shop floor variables or the influence of these changes was non expectable. For this reason, an experiment, with only one experimental factor was conducted. We ran a predictive model that was used for estimation. Two levels were considered: a traditional cost system and the ABC model.

In order to achieve significant (p-value < 0.05) results, 30 replications were run. For each run two estimations were generated.

Other shop floor variables were generated randomly from the following distributions:

- Number of product types $\begin{cases} 3, & w.p.\ 0.5 \\ 9, & otherwise \end{cases}$

- Number of machine types $\begin{cases} 3, & w.p.\ 0.5 \\ 9, & otherwise \end{cases}$

- Number of workstations in a production route $\begin{cases} 3, & w.p.\ 0.5 \\ 9, & otherwise \end{cases}$

- Number of activities $\begin{cases} 1, & w.p.\ 1/3 \\ 2, & w.p.\ 1/3 \\ 3, & otherwise \end{cases}$

- Number of cost drivers per activity $\begin{cases} 1, & w.p.\ 1/3 \\ 2, & w.p.\ 1/3 \\ 3, & otherwise \end{cases}$

- Initial shop floor load $\begin{cases} 45\% - 55\%, & wp.\ 0.5 \\ 80\% - 90\%, & otherwise \end{cases}$

- Distribution of setup, processing times, time between failures, time to repair and product yield $\begin{cases} U(0.85 \cdot average, 1.15 \cdot average), & w.p.\ 0.5 \\ U(0.50 \cdot average, 1.50 \cdot average), & otherwise \end{cases}$

- The ratio between backorder and variable production costs and between overtime and regular hour costs $\begin{cases} o_t = 1.3r_t, & b_{it} = 0.5v_{it}, & w.p.\ 0.5 \\ o_t = 2.0r_t, & b_{it} = 1.5v_{it}, & otherwise \end{cases}$

- The dispatching rule used in the simulation $\begin{cases} SPT, & w.p.\ 0.5 \\ MWKR, & otherwise \end{cases}$

- Machine types in a product's route: $U(0.5, M+0.5)$, rounded to the closest integer number.

- Mean processing time of one unit of product i on machine j (a_{ij}): $U(1, 6)$ minutes.

- Mean setup time of product i on machine j (s_{ij}): $U(10, 500)$ minutes.

- Demand for product i in period t (d_{it}): $U(5, 40)$; randomization was iterative until the workload was between 45% and 55% or between 80% and 90%.

- Inventory holding cost per unit of product i in period t (c_{it}): $U(0.04\ v_{it}, 0.06\ v_{it})$ \$.

- The variable cost for producing a unit of product i in period t under an infinite capacity environment (v_{it}): $U(8, 14)$ \$.

- The backorder cost per unit of product i (b_{it}) in period $t \neq 5$ was $0.5\ v_{it}$ or $1.5\ v_{it}$ depending on the value of the cost ratio (C). In order to prevent situations where we would prefer to produce nothing and to pay backorder costs only, we set the backorder cost per unit of product i in the last period, $t=5$ (b_{i5}) relatively high (for optimization only): U(60, 80) \$.

- Regular labor cost per hour in period t (r_t): U(15, 30) \$. The overtime labor cost per hour in period t, o_t was $1.3r_t$ or $2r_t$ depending on the value of the cost ratio (C).
- Consumption of cost driver l of activity k per unit of product i (C_{ki}):U(0.05, 0.1).
- Unit cost of cost driver l of activity k (CCD_{lki}): U(5,40)\$.

Shop floor parameters (products, machines, routing) were generated and cost estimations were calculated using Microsoft Excel™. optimization was done using ILOG OPL Studio™ (optimization software) and simulation was run by Arena™ (simulation software). All problem instances were run on a 900-MHz AMD Duron™ processor with 256 MB of RAM.

Results and Analysis

Results of the 30 runs were analyzed by t-test. A significant advantage in the accuracy of the ABC cost estimation model over other rough-cut approaches was found (p-value < 0.05). Figure 5 presents a comparison of the accuracy of the cost estimates. The cost estimation accuracy was calculated by the ratio:

$$\left(\frac{|\text{Result of cost estimation} - \text{Actual order's cost}|}{\text{Actual order's cost}} \right)$$

In order to calculate a baseline for this comparison, 20 simulation replications were run, for each observation, and we estimated the actual order's cost as the average of these replications. Figure 45 compares two cost estimations approaches: the traditional cost system and ABC.

Activity based cost estimation was found to be significantly better than traditional cost system

estimation (p-value < 0.05). The reason for this is that ABC based cost estimation takes into account variable costs of activities.

Discussion and Conclusion

The research consisted of number of stages. In each stage we tried to relax part of the assumptions of previous stages:

- Precedence between operations and the stochastic nature of the shop floor (e.g., processing and setup times) were taken into account expanding the previously described deterministic rough-cut capacity planning model.
- In next stage additional stochastic parameters were taken into account: machine failures and product yields.
- Finally, factory overheads were allocated by activity based costing systems, as opposed to the traditional costing system.

It was demonstrated that with the relaxation of the assumptions and, as a result, by taking into account more complex environments, the accuracy of the cost estimation increased.

In parallel, additional efforts were directed to develop practical tools.

- A linear regression-based predictive model, which used deterministic cost estimation for estimating the cost in a stochastic environment was developed.
- Five alternatives to simulation, which can be implemented easily, were developed.

It was demonstrated that the proposed fast and easy-to-use models provided good estimates, but were less accurate than simulation. We suggest using simulation for important orders with large totals and/or high backorder costs, while for daily cost estimation the fast cost estimation models should be used.

Figure 45. Comparison of the traditional cost system and ABC cost estimation

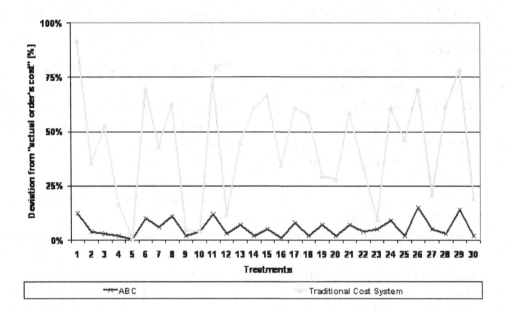

The effect of the shop workload, machine loading, and outsourcing decisions on the product unit cost estimate was analyzed. We demonstrated that in a made-to-order environment, the product unit cost is affected by the current product mix, the total shop workload, machine loading (including in-process batches) and outsourcing decisions. Since all these parameters change dramatically over time, product unit costs cannot be considered constant values, as traditionally accepted. Costing should be performed on a current basis, taking into account these factors.

The proposed costing model enables the estimation of the current product unit cost, taking into account all these aspects. The model estimates product unit costs on the basis of the shop floor's current status and the operations that are planned for production within a certain planning horizon. The model also recommends which operations to outsource if necessary.

In the proposed model direct costs are allocated to products on the basis of their rough-cut planned schedule. An assignment of a specific unit for production in regular rather than in extra hours

decreases its product unit cost while increasing the unit cost of all other products. Hence, the product unit cost is affected directly by scheduling decisions. This is in contradiction to traditional costing approaches.

Precedence between operations and the stochastic nature of the shop floor were taking into account. The existing cost estimation model in a deterministic environment was improved. The improvements are based on using simulation together with an optimization model. Information from the simulation is used in the optimization. These improvements increase both efficiency and effectiveness.

A cost estimation model that takes into account the capacity of the shop floor and the stochastic environment was developed. It was found that by taking into account the stochastic nature of parameters, such as processing and setup times, machine failures and product yields, the cost estimation accuracy was improved significantly. It was also found that the advantage of the stochastic cost estimation increases with the increase of the variances of the various random variables and the complexity of the manufacturing system.

A linear regression-based predictive model, which uses deterministic cost estimation for estimating the cost in stochastic environment, was developed. The derived predictive model is very promising for estimating the mean of the total cost but inadequate for estimating its coefficient of variance (CV). An attempt to improve the predictive model by using Neural Networks (NN) failed. No significant advantage was found for the NN-based estimations over the linear regression ones. Although the linear regression-based predictive model was inadequate for estimating the CV of the total cost, it still performed well for the mean of the total cost, and therefore, can be used for estimating the cost of a new order.

The cost estimations resulting from the linear regression-based predictive model were less accurate than the cost estimations derived from simulations, but still significantly better than the deterministic cost estimations. Moreover, the linear regression-based predictive model was found to be very easy to use. In order to implement this model in reality, a predictive model can be derived from historical data and updated from time to time. Therefore, a stochastic cost estimation based on regression may be used as a fast rough-cut predictive model that can be implemented quickly.

Five alternatives to simulation that can be implemented easily were. These alternatives, in addition to saving the time of developing and running simulations, are implementable in Microsoft Excel™. As opposed to ARENA™, Microsoft Excel™ is tool available on most computers and most people are familiar with its use. The accuracy of rough-cut prediction models, in comparison with simulation results, was examined across a wide range of shop configurations.

The bottleneck model was found to be better than the other tested models. Three other models yielded good results: smoothed station, snapshot and RCCP. The time unit cost model seems to be less accurate.

The reasons for bottleneck's advantage over the other methods are: (a) It takes into account precedence between operations by estimating the forced idle time and; (b) It takes into account differences in the capacity utilization on the bottleneck workstation. In contrast, the reasons for the disadvantage of the time unit cost model are: (a) It ignores the changes in the product mix in consecutive planning horizons (historical and current) and (b) It ignores the differences in the capacity utilization of historical and current planning horizons.

An activity based cost estimation model that takes into account the shop floor capacity and the stochastic environment was developed. The accuracy of the activity based cost estimation, in comparison to traditional cost system estimation, was examined across a wide range of shop configurations. The activity based cost estimation was found to be better than traditional cost system estimation.

Future research may focus on relaxing the assumptions of this work. A model that is capable of dealing with sequence dependent setup times, operation splitting, limited capacity of the finished goods warehouse and outsourcing may be more suitable for handling real-life problems. Also the job shop should be expanded to include more complex environments such as assembly lines or alternative routing. In addition, the influence of acceptance of current orders on the cost of future orders should be studied. The relation between the accuracy of the cost estimation and profitability as a function of pricing policy and customer characteristics should also be investigated.

ACKNOWLEDGMENT

This chapter is based on the following publications with permission from the publishers. The publishers retain the copyrights.

REFERENCES

Baines, T., Whitney, D., & Fine, C. (1999). Manufacturing technology sourcing practices in the USA. *International Journal of Production Research*, *37*(4), 939–956. doi:10.1080/002075499191616

Baker, G. P., & Hubbard, T. N. (2003). Make versus buy in trucking: Asset ownership, job design, and information. *The American Economic Review*, *93*(3), 551–572. doi:10.1257/000282803322156981

Balakrishnan, R., & Sivaramakrishnan, K. (2001). Sequential solutions to capacity-planning and pricing decisions. *Contemporary Accounting Research*, *18*(1), 1–26. doi:10.1506/Y6TG-1KQ9-12GV-L5YY

Balakrishnan, S. (1994). The dynamics of make-or-buy decisions. *European Journal of Operational Research*, *74*, 552–571. doi:10.1016/0377-2217(94)90231-3

Banker, R. D., Hwang, I., & Mishra, B. K. (2002). Product costing and pricing under long term capacity commitment. *Journal of Management Accounting*, *14*, 79–97. doi:10.2308/jmar.2002.14.1.79

Bassett, R. (1991). Make-or-buy decisions. *Management Accounting*, November, 58-59.

Ben-Arieh, D. (2000). Cost estimation system for machined parts. *International Journal of Production Research*, *38*(17), 4481–4494. doi:10.1080/00207540050205244

Berman, O., & Ashrafi, N. (1993). Optimization models for reliability of modular software systems. *IEEE Transactions on Software Engineering*, *19*(11), 1119–1123. doi:10.1109/32.256858

Bode, J. (2000). Neural networks for cost estimation: simulations and pilot application. *International Journal of Production Research*, *38*(6), 1231–1254. doi:10.1080/002075400188825

Cochran, E. B. (1976a). Using regression techniques in cost analysis - Part 1. *International Journal of Production Research*, *14*(4), 465–487. doi:10.1080/00207547608956619

Cochran, E. B. (1976b). Using regression techniques in cost analysis - Part 2. *International Journal of Production Research*, *14*(4), 489–511. doi:10.1080/00207547608956620

Cooper, R. (1988). The rise of activity-based costing - Part 2: What is an activity-based costing? *Journal of Cost Management*, *7*(4), 41–48.

Dean, E. B. (1989). Parametric cost estimating: A design function. *The Thirty-third Annual Meeting of the American Association of Cost Engineers*, San Diego, CA.

Eklin, M., Arzi, Y., & Shtub, A. (2008a). Rough-cut cost estimation in a capacitated environment. *International Journal of Information Systems and Supply Chain Management*, *1*(2), 19–39.

Eklin, M., Arzi, Y. & Shtub, A. (2008b). A comparative study of rough-cut cost estimation in a finite-capacity stochastic environment. *Accepted for publication in the International Journal of Revenue Management*.

Eklin, M., Arzi, Y., & Shtub, A. (2009). Model for cost estimation in a finite-capacity stochastic environment based on shop floor optimization combined with simulation. *European Journal of Operational Research*, *194*(1), 294–306. doi:10.1016/j.ejor.2007.11.048

Ellis, G. (1992). Make-or-buy: A simpler approach. *Management Accounting*, June, 22-23.

Ellis, G. (1993). Solving make-or-buy problems with linear programming. *Management Accounting*, November, 52-53.

Falco, M., Nenni, M. E., & Schiraldi, M. M. (2001). Development of a product-costing model oriented to productive capacity analysis. *The 4th SMESME International Conference*, Alborg, Denmark (pp. 180-187).

Feldman, P., & Shtub, A. (2006). A model for cost estimation in a finite-capacity environment. *International Journal of Production Research, 44*(2), 305–327. doi:10.1080/00207540500227646

Fowler, K. (2004). Build versus buy. *IEEE Instrumentation & Measurement Magazine, 7*(3), 67–73. doi:10.1109/MIM.2004.1337916

Geiger, T. S., & Dilts, D. M. (1996). Automated design-to-cost: Integrated costing into the design decision. *Computer Aided Design, 28*, 423–438. doi:10.1016/0010-4485(94)00030-1

Gunasekaran, A., Marri, H. B., & Yusuf, Y. Y. (1999). Application of activity-based costing: Some case experiences. *Managerial Auditing Journal, 14*(6), 286–293. doi:10.1108/02686909910280217

Harsh, M. F. (1993). *the impact of activity based costing on managerial decisions: an empirical analysis*. Ph.D. Dissertation, Virginia Polytechnic Institute & State University, Blacksburg, VA, USA.

Helander, M. E., Zhao, M., & Ohlsson, N. (1998). Planning models for software reliability and cost. *IEEE Transactions on Software Engineering, 24*(6), 420–434. doi:10.1109/32.689400

Jahan-Shahi, H., Shayan, E., & Masood, S. H. (2001). Multivalued fuzzy sets in cost/time estimation of flat plate processing. *International Journal of Advanced Manufacturing Technology, 17*, 751–759. doi:10.1007/s001700170121

Jung, J. Y. (2002). Manufacturing cost estimation for machined parts based on manufacturing features. *Journal of Intelligent Manufacturing, 13*(4), 227–238. doi:10.1023/A:1016092808320

Kurokawa, S. (1997). Make-or-buy decisions in R&D: Small technology based firms in the United States and Japan. *IEEE Transactions on Engineering Management, 44*(2), 124–134. doi:10.1109/17.584921

Levy, H., & Sarnat, M. (1976). The make-or-buy decision. *Journal of General Management, 4*(1), 46–50.

Liggett, H. R., Trevino, J., & Lavelle, J. P. (1992). Activity-based cost management systems in an advanced manufacturing environment. In H. R. Parsaei (Ed.), *Economic and financial justification of advanced manufacturing technologies*. New York: Elsevier Science Publishers.

Lin, Z. C., & Chang, D. Y. (2002). Cost-tolerance analysis model based on a neural networks method. *International Journal of Production Research, 40*(6), 1429–1452. doi:10.1080/00207540110116282

Mason, A.K. & Kahn, D.J. (1997). Estimating costs with fuzzy logic. *Association for the Advancement of Cost Engineering International Transactions*, EST.03.1-EST.03.6

McIvor, R.T., Humphreys, P.K. & McAleer, W.E. (1997). A strategic model for the formulation of an effective make-or-buy decision. *Management Decision, 32*)), 169-178.

Meijboom, B. R. (1986). A two-level planning procedure with respect to make-or-buy decisions, including cost allocations. *European Journal of Operational Research, 23*, 301–309. doi:10.1016/0377-2217(86)90296-1

Novin, A. M. (1992). Applying overhead: How to find the right bases and rates. *Management Accounting, 3*, 40–43.

O'Guin, M. C. (1991). *The complete guide to activity-based costing*. New Jersey: Prentice Hall.

Padillo-Perez, J. M., & Diaby, M. (1999). A multiple-criteria decision methodology for the make-or-buy problem. *International Journal of Production Research, 37*(14), 3203–3229. doi:10.1080/002075499190248

Poppo, L. (1998). Testing alternatives theories of the firm: Transaction cost, knowledge based and measurement explanations for make-or-buy decision in information services. *Strategic Management Journal, 19*(9), 853–877. doi:10.1002/(SICI)1097-0266(199809)19:9<853::AID-SMJ977>3.0.CO;2-B

Rad, P. F., & Cioffi, D. F. (2004). Work and resource breakdown structures for formalized bottom-up estimating. *Coastal Engineering, 46*(2), 31–37.

Raunick, D. A., & Fisher, A. G. (1972). A probabilistic make-buy model. *Journal of Purchasing, 8*(1), 63–80.

Reiman, M. I., & Wein, L. M. (1999). Heavy traffic analysis of polling systems in tandem. *Operations Research, 47*(4), 524–534. doi:10.1287/opre.47.4.524

Ross, R. B. (2002). *Regression analysis as a cost estimation model for unexploded ordnance clean-up at former military installations*.Master's thesis. Naval Postgraduate school Monterey CA.

Shtub, A., & Versano, R. (1999). Estimating the cost of steel pipe bending, a comparison between neural networks and regression analysis. *International Journal of Production Economics, 62*, 201–207. doi:10.1016/S0925-5273(98)00212-6

Smith, A. E., & Mason, A. K. (1997). Cost estimation predictive modeling: Regression versus neural network. *The Engineering Economist, 42*(2), 137–161. doi:10.1080/00137919708903174

Son, Y. K. (1991). Cost estimation model for advanced manufacturing systems. *International Journal of Production Research, 29*(3), 441–452. doi:10.1080/00207549108930081

Sonmez, R. (2004). Conceptual cost estimation of building projects with regression analysis and neural networks. *Canadian Journal of Civil Engineering, 31*(4), 677–683. doi:10.1139/l04-029

Stewart, R. D. (1982). *Cost Estimating*. New York: John Wiley & Sons, Inc.

Sullivan, W. G. (1992). A new paradigm for engineering economy. *The Engineering Economist, 36*(3), 187–200. doi:10.1080/00137919108903044

Ten Brinke, E., Lutters, E., Streppel, T., & Kals, H. J. J. (2000). Variant-based cost estimation based on information management. *International Journal of Production Research, 38*(17), 4467–4479. doi:10.1080/00207540050205235

Venkatesan, R. (1992). Strategic sourcing: to make or not to make. *Harvard Business Review*, (November-December): 98–107.

Vollmann, T. E., Berry, W. L., & Whybark, D. C. (1984). *Manufacturing planning and control systems*. Homewood, IL: Richard D. Irwin Inc.

Welch, J. A., & Nayak, P. R. (1992). Strategic sourcing: A progressive approach to the make-or-buy decision. *Academy of Management Executive, 6*(1), 23–31.

Chapter 3

Analysis of Financial Returns and Risks of Implementing RFID for Supply Chains

Ertunga C. Özelkan
The University of North Carolina at Charlotte, USA

Agnes Galambosi
The University of North Carolina at Charlotte, USA

ABSTRACT

Radio Frequency Identification (RFID) is believed to change how supply chains operate today. While RFID's promise for improved inventory visibility and automation in inventory management is making many supply chain players hopeful for increased sales and reduced operating costs, these benefits do come at a cost and involve risks. This paper presents a financial returns analysis that captures RFID's costs and benefits, and quantifies the financial risks of implementing RFID for various business sizes and products with different unit profits to understand when RFID makes business sense. More precisely, the returns analysis is performed using an econometric model to understand how break-even sales volumes, unit profits, tag prices, return on investment, and risks vary between a manufacturer and a retailer in a supply chain. The results are extended to multi-product cases as well. A sensitivity analysis is also performed to understand the returns in pessimistic and optimistic scenarios.

INTRODUCTION AND SCOPE

Efficient supply chain management is a crucial determinant of being a successful and profitable business. One possible way to achieve increased efficiencies in supply chains is through the use of Radio Frequency Identification (RFID), which can enhance the decision-making capability of information and decision support systems through accurate real-time data collection. RFID is the automatic identification and tracking of objects using radio frequency transmission. The objects can be practically anything such as cars, library books, toll tag devices, baggage at the airport, sponges used for surgical procedures, live animals, or even persons like hospital patients (Chao, Yang, & Jen, 2007; Al-Ali, Sajwani, A-Muhairi and Shahenn, 2007; Rivera, Mountain, Assumpcao, Williams, Cooper,

DOI: 10.4018/978-1-60566-974-8.ch003

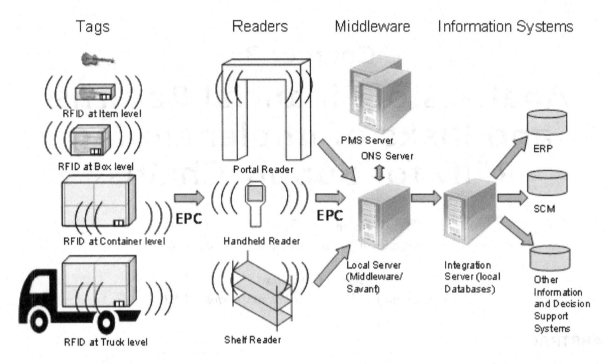

Lewis, Benson, Miragliotta, Marohn, Taylor, 2008). RFID tags store product information in an electronic product code (EPC). As illustrated in Figure 1, EPC from various RFID tags (that can be at item, box, container and truck level) is read via readers, and gets communicated to a middleware software (also known as Savant) which then identifies detailed information about the detected product from several database servers (known as the object naming service (ONS) and product markup service (PMS) servers). Next, the detailed product information gets communicated to local information system databases which in turn is fed into various enterprise resource planning (ERP) and supply chain management (SCM) applications for supporting planning and execution decisions. (The reader can refer to Terry (2004), Laran (2005) for more details on the information systems architecture and Wamba, Bedavid, Lefebvre, & Lefebvre (2006) for a description of a system architecture in a retail sector implementation.)

Although radio frequency technology has been known for a long time, the popularity of RFID is rising nowadays because of the decreasing price of the tags, advances in EPC standards development, and the mandated adoption of RFID by US Department of Defense and large retailers such as Wal-Mart, Target and TESCO for all of their top suppliers (Spekman and Sweeney II, 2006).

RFID Benefits

With recent advances, it seems that RFID deployment has a big potential to transform supply chain management as it automates identifying and tracking the items through the entire supply chain, and creating a virtual database that is attached to the product. As described earlier, this data can be fed into supply chain information systems to enhance supply chain visibility (as illustrated in Figure 1), and enable a better management of inventory by reducing inventory and shrinkage especially when shared between different supply chain players. How RFID can at least partially resolve the issue of shrinkage in the retail supply chain is mentioned in Huber and Michael (2007). They conducted some interviews from RFID vendors in Australia, and their results show that the perception of these vendors is that RFID collected data and their results show that it is possible to use RFID to minimize losses in the supply chain significantly. Also, De Kok, van Donselar and van Woensel (2008) perform a break-even analysis of RFID technology that focuses on inventory sensitive to shrinkage, and give some suggestions about the maximum amount of money a manager should actually invest in RFID.

As reported in Lee and Ozer (2007), in current supply chain management information systems the inventory records do not reflect the actual on-hand inventory. They state that this discrepancy "has a daunting effect on the resulting operating costs and revenue" (p.44), which they believe RFID technology has the potential to help with. Since "lost" goods in the supply chain are costing companies significant money (about 50 million Euros a day for European companies based on Atock, 2003), an RFID deployment can increase sales through reduction of out-of-stock items. Hardgrave, Waller, & Miller (2005) report a savings of 16 percent in out-of-stock items at RFID-enabled Wal-Mart stores. As Wal-Mart loses $1B in gross revenue due to out-of-stock conditions at store level, this 16 percent reduction in out-of-stock is quite significant (Spekman and Sweeney II, 2006). According to Sliwa (2003), Procter & Gamble estimates that about 14 percent of its products are out-of-stock at store level at any given moment. It is estimated that a 2% reduction could increase Procter & Gamble's revenue by $400 million. Similarly, Prater, Frazier, & Reyes (2005) report that Gillette can get 20% increase in sales compared to non-RFID tracked stores. As

Sarma (2004) states, studies of the global retail industry have shown that up to 65% of inventory records in retail environments are wrong. In addition, products are out-of-stock approximately 10% of the time, resulting in 4-5% lost sales that's worth about $100 billion annually. On the other hand, having too much inventory can result in billions of dollars of locked-up capital, high transportation costs, and other problems. RFID deployment can also decrease in-store and warehouse labor expenses, handle returnable items, make warranties traceable and product recalls efficient (Michael and McCathie, 2005). For improving demand-forecasting accuracy, Lapide (2004) highlights the potential benefits of an RFID implementation: capturing more accurate and timely shipment data and reducing the volatility of upstream demand. He also predicts the full impact of an RFID implementation to take effect within the next 7-10 years. Koroneos (2004) mentions a very useful application of RFID against drug counterfeiting. As reported by Philips Semiconductor (Philips, 2004), up to 7% of all drugs in the international supply chain may be counterfeit, and solutions based on RFID could save the industry $8 billion over the next few years alone. Based on US Department of Health and Human Services, Spekman and Sweeney II (2006) report this number as between $10-30 billion annually.

RFID Challenges and Concerns

While most analysts agree on RFID's potential beyond inventory management, the main challenges remain as cost, security and privacy, standards, information technology (IT) re-configuration and dealing with all the data collected. Consequently, there are still some skeptics about the benefits of RFID (see e.g. Sheffi, 2004; Angeles, 2005; Asif and Mandviwalla, 2005; Juels, 2006). As Sheffi (2004) states, RFID "is still not out of the fog of innovation" (p.9). Similarly, Venables (2005) declares that, although RFID technology offers significant potential benefits, it seems that it has delivered fewer benefits than expected. He states that until RFID is used comprehensively and integrated with existing technology, parallel systems will have to be used (i.e. both barcode and RFID tags), which means that IT needs to handle inputs in two formats with an enormous increase in the data captured and stored, thus making cost and complexity very high. He concludes that RFID technology seems to be a premature and unjustified investment. As Lee and Ozer (2007) state, "Being able to get more information faster and accurately by itself does not produce business values. It has to be used intelligently" (p.45). In this regard, there is still a need for the development of information systems that can make meaningful analysis based on RFID data (Terry, 2004). Data related issues are also discussed by Delen, Hardgrave and Sharda (2007) who analyze a case study using actual RFID data from a major retailer. These issues are related to false negative read (the reader fails to read the tag) and false positive read (the same tag is read by several readers) as well as the issue of dealing with the massive data that gets collected. Delen, Hardgrave and Sharda (2007) also conclude that the real business value of RFID lies in the data that is being collected as this information can be used for making better business decisions.

On the other hand, Hossain and Prybutok (2008) explore consumer acceptance of RFID technology. They conclude that "(1) higher perceived convenience of RFID technology leads to greater acceptance of this technology; (2) societal beliefs, value systems, norms, and/or behaviors influence the extent of consumer acceptance of RFID technology; and (3) higher perceived importance of and less willingness to sacrifice personal information security lead to lower intention to use RFID technology" (p.316.). White, Johnson and Wilson (2008) offer some insights of issues, approaches and benefits for supply chain managers who want to adopt RFID technology based on their survey of European supply chain managers.

An example of recently emerging security issues with RFID is described in the article "Is your cat infected with a computer virus?" by Rieback, Crispo and Tanenbaum (2006). They address the issue that data from RFID tags can make back-end software systems very vulnerable as they present the first self-replicating RFID virus that can compromise backend RFID middleware systems.

Since the cost of an RFID implementation is indeed one of the biggest issues, it requires a careful analysis. There are different kinds of costs involved: there are investment costs for the physical equipment (tags, readers, printers, network infrastructure, data collection software, "business" middleware software, labeling/automation equipment), for analytical resources, for systems integration, installation and communication (Deloitte, 2005). There are also recurring costs, (tags, tag application labor, training, support and system maintenance), and other costs (internal staff). The cost of individual tags is still not in the very low range, although it is decreasing. Pricing is usually based on volume, the amount of memory on the tag and the packaging of the tag (e.g whether it's encased in plastic or embedded in a label). For example, according to a 2005 September news release, Avery Dennison offers Generation 2 RFID tags for 7.9 cents, if order quantity is 1 million, which is so far the lowest price yet advertised in the industry (Avery, 2005).

Scope of this Study

Although RFID technology promises a better overall supply chain performance, the cost-benefit ratio could still be too high for a particular company's needs. As with any new technology, there is also some reluctance adopting this technology that has not demonstrated its full potential in practice, especially given the fact that many businesses invested a lot of money in barcodes. Currently, it seems that companies are reluctant to invest in RFID unless they are forced to do it.

Given all the potential benefits and skepticism about RFID, it is of general interest for the industry to understand when an RFID implementation makes a business case (Chao et al., 2007). Therefore, the purpose of this presented study is to analyze the effect of implementing RFID on the financial returns for different business scenarios. We also aim to analyze and quantify the risk associated with the RFID implementations, so a relatively simple model is proposed to quantify the returns and costs of an RFID implementation. The model is analyzed first analytically to derive managerial insights, and then through simulation to further investigate the RFID risk due to uncertainties related to RFID benefits and costs. Some of the specific research questions in this study can be listed as follows:

- When does RFID implementation make a business case?
- Can we create a decision model to compare "RFID" implementation decision with the as-is "no-RFID" case?
- How does the financial risk of an RFID implementation decision change with respect to the business size and the products?

The rest of the paper is organized as follows: after a brief literature review, we will introduce the model used. Then a computational analysis is presented. The final section includes a summary and conclusions.

LITERATURE REVIEW

Besides the literature cited in the Introduction section, here, we will provide a brief review of some of the RFID studies that are most related to the research presented here. The reader might want to refer to a recent paper by Chao et al. (2007) for a broader review of RFID literature as well as applications in different areas.

There are several cost and return on investment (ROI) analysis in the literature (see e.g. Fontanella, 2004; GMA, 2004; Hou and Huang, 2006). Fontanella (2004) discusses ROI of RFID investments conceptually indicating that implementations that synchronize the supply chain would have the most value-to-cost ratio but also the highest risk due to the maturity of the RFID technology and high dependency on external resources. Therefore, he recommends starting RFID implementations at a smaller scale. A study conducted by IBM and A.T. Kearney for the Grocery Manufacturers of America (GMA, 2004) presents a business case analysis for RFID implementation in the consumer packaged goods (CPG) industry, based on 24 business cases of large North American manufacturers with the majority of individual company sales exceeding $2 billion. Their analysis concludes that "very few CPG manufacturers -if any- can generate a positive return on investment for widespread EPC/RFID deployment at the pallet and case level with today's tag prices". Hou and Huang (2006) analyze RFID implementation decisions in the printing industry combining empirical data with a quantitative analysis about RFID implementation costs and benefits. They conclude their study by recommending an item level tagging in the printing industry. Vijayaraman and Osyk (2006) present the empirical results of a survey study that was conducted among the member organizations of the Warehousing Education and Research Council (WERC). Their findings indicate that WERC members are not yet ready to jump on the RFID bandwagon. Their survey shows that there are quite a few companies (especially manufacturers) who believe the ROI from RFID will be zero or less within a year of the RFID implementation. In a recent study, Wu and Chen (2007) have studied an RFID-enabled distribution center operation in Taiwan using simulation. They recommend usage of RFID tags at a case level. In their study they also provide a rudimentary cost-benefit analysis based on the simulation results in which they estimate that it would take about 6 years to break even with the RFID costs. On the other hand, Lee and Ozer (2007) claim that subjective assessment of the value of RFID by industry experts and conducting in-depth cases studies might create a credibility gap between the estimated and actual values and benefits of RFID. They offer to fill the credibility gap by using solid model analysis from a production and operations management point of view. They also point out that the potential of RFID is not only in logistics and inventory management but other areas such as manufacturing, after-sales service support and total product life cycle management, hence research in these directions should also be conducted. Ngai, Cheng, Lai, Chai, Choi and Sin (2007) analyze a case study of design and implementation of RFID in a Hong Kong aircraft company, including design, implementation and also lessons learned. This case study proves that RFID can improve asset visibility, operations, and reduce human errors. While their paper offers 13 lessons learned on strategic, management and operational level, their very first lesson on the strategic level is "to identify the advantages and return on investment", which is also the focus of the present paper.

The research presented herein extends previous RFID cost and ROI related studies and differs in several ways. Here, after developing a formal framework for the cost and benefit analysis of an RFID implementation, we develop conditions on unit profits, sales volumes and tag prices for RFID implementations to break even with the "as-is" situation without RFID. As far as we know, this type of formal analysis has not been carried out in existing studies. We show that unit profit to tag price ratio can be an important indicator of RFID implementation feasibility. Then, we perform a simulation analysis to analyze the net present value (NPV) of financial returns and to quantify RFID risks. While some simulation studies exist for identifying the operational impact of RFID, the analysis of RFID's financial risk using simulation

is rare. We model a hypothetical manufacturer and a retailer in an experimental design setting to reflect businesses of various sizes and different products.

MODELING ANALYSIS

In this section, a model is presented for analyzing the financial returns from RFID implementations. We consider a product manufacturer and a retailer in the supply chain. The main difference between the manufacturer and the retailer is that the manufacturer pays for the RFID tags and the retailer does not. On the other hand, both of these supply chain players incur all the fixed costs related to RFID. Since the retailer's problem will be a specific case of the manufacturer's, below, we will first present the model development for the manufacturer only, and then we will highlight the differences and implications for the retailer. Later in the Computational Experiments section, we will illustrate the impact of the RFID tag costs on both the manufacturer's and the retailer's RFID implementation decisions with various numerical examples. After introducing the notation, we will investigate properties of the expected returns and then we will provide a definition for RFID implementation risk. The notation and the formulation used in our model are described next:

Notation

T: planning period in years, where t is the index for years such that $t=1,...,T$

D_t: expected demand (sales volume) in year t, $t=1,...,T$ (without RFID)

$D_{RFID,t}$: RFID-adjusted expected demand (sales volume) in year t, $t=1,...,T$

l: % increase in sales benefits due to reduction in lost sales after RFID implementation

o: % unit profit benefits due to reduction in inventory and labor costs after RFID implementation

i: annual interest rate

$p_{t,Dt}$:   expected tag price in year t, which is volume-discounted based on the sales volume D_t, $t=1,...,T$

m_t: expected profit per unit (or unit profit) sold in year t, $t=1,...,T$ (without RFID)

$f_{D_{max}}$:   initial fixed costs of implementing RFID depending on the maximum anticipated sales volume capacity $D_{max} = max_t\{D_t\}$.

$s_{t,D_{max}}$:   maintenance and support costs of the RFID system in year t, depending on the maximum anticipated sales volume capacity $D_{max} = max_t\{D_t\}$, $t=1,...,T$.

$P_{RFID,t}$:   RFID-adjusted expected profit in year t, where $t=1,...,T$

Quantifying Expected Benefits of RFID

Assumption A. RFID implementation results in increased sales of l %.

As described in the introduction section, sales increase in Assumption A seems reasonable due to prevention of lost sales. Based on this the RFID-adjusted sales can be computed as $D_{RFID,t} = D_t(1+l)$.

Assumption B. RFID implementation results in increased unit profit of o %.

The increase in unit profits can be described mainly due to a reduction of operating costs resulting from labor savings, reduction of safety inventories due to more accurate inventory visibility, and decrease in shrinkage to name a few. Thus, based on this assumption and taking into account the RFID tag cost, the RFID-adjusted unit profit can be computed as $m_{RFID,t} = m_t(1+o) - p_{t,Dt}$.

Using the RFID-adjusted sales and unit profit and taking into account the annual maintenance cost for the RFID system, RFID-adjusted profit $P_{RFID,t}$ during year t is as follows:

$$P_{RFID,t} = D_{RFID,t}m_{RFID,t} - s_{t,D_{max}}$$

$$= D_t(1+l)[m_t(1+o) - p_{t,D_t}] - s_{t,D_{max}} \quad (1)$$

Accordingly, the NPV of financial returns from an RFID implementation can be computed as

$$NPV_{RFID} = -f_{D_{max}} + \sum_{t=1}^{T} P_{RFID,t}(1+i)^{-t} \quad (2)$$

One of our research objectives here is to identify those sales volume and unit profit combinations that make RFID implementation more attractive than not implementing RFID. We will refer to these strategies as "RFID" and "no-RFID" going forward. Based on equations (1) and (2), we can derive the benefits of an RFID strategy with respect to a no-RFID strategy as described below in the following proposition.

Proposition 1: *Let Δ_{RFID} denote the financial benefits from an RFID implementation. Based on Assumptions A and B, Δ_{RFID} can be quantified as*

$$\Delta_{RFID} = -f_{D_{max}} +$$

$$\sum_{t=1}^{T}\left(D_t\{m_t[(1+o)(1+l)-1] - (1+l)p_{t,D_t}\} - s_{t,D_{max}}\right)(1+i)^{-t} \quad (3)$$

The proof for all propositions and corollaries are discussed in the Appendix. Understanding of equation (3) is important to derive the conditions for viable RFID strategies. Some particular questions, which might be of interest are what unit profit levels, sales volumes and tag prices make RFID implementations justifiable. We will investigate some answers to these questions starting with the unit profits as described next.

Proposition 2: *Let m denote the average discounted unit profit for the RFID implementation defined as $m = \dfrac{\sum_{t=1}^{T} D_t m_t(1+i)^{-t}}{\sum_{t=1}^{T} D_t(1+l)^{-t}}$, then $NPV_{RFID} \geq NPV_{no\text{-}RFID}$ when*

$$m \geq \frac{f_{D_{max}} + \sum_{t=1}^{T}[D_t(1+l)p_{t,D_t} + s_{t,D_{max}}](1+i)^{-t}}{[(1+o)(1+l)-1]\sum_{t=1}^{T}D_t(1+i)^{-t}} \qquad (4)$$

Proposition 2 provides us clearly the required unit profit (m) values that make a business case for an RFID implementation. Implication of the relation in equation (4) is that $m_t \geq m$, $t = 1,...,T$ is a sufficient condition for justifying RFID implementations. As we will later illustrate numerically in the computational analysis section, it can be seen from the unit profit break-even threshold (right hand side of equation (4)) that as sales volumes decrease, RFID fixed costs become more important than RFID tag prices in determining the break-even unit profits. On a similar note, as sales volumes increase, importance of RFID tag prices increases for making RFID decisions. These observations are formally summarized in the following corollary.

Corollary 1: *As sales volumes decrease, RFID fixed costs become more important than RFID tag prices for making RFID decisions. The importance of RFID tag prices increase when sales volumes increase.*

The observation in Corollary 1 is quite important, since RFID fixed costs are often not as much emphasized in the industry as the RFID tag prices. However, one needs to note that as the RFID fixed and maintenance/support costs decrease in the future due to technological changes, the importance of fixed costs may diminish over time especially when sales volumes are very large. This may occur more quickly in the future under circumstances where large subcontractors bid to manage the RFID technology systems of multiple large companies (much like companies such as IBM and EDS bid to manage computing systems for large clients due to competitive advantages of economies of scale, lower costs and increased application of state of the art techniques and technologies). As expected, it can also be seen from equation (4) that an increase in fixed costs (both

initial and recurring) and tag prices negatively impact (increase) the required unit profit levels. On the other hand, an increase in profit benefits (o) and sales benefits (l) positively impact and decrease the required unit profit levels.

Similar to Proposition 2, condition for the required sales volumes can be driven under the assumption of constant sales volumes, as shown in the next proposition.

Proposition 3: *Let D denote the break-even sales volume for the RFID implementation, then* $NPV_{RFID} \geq NPV_{no-RFID}$ *when*

$$D \geq \frac{f_{D_{max}} + \sum_{t=1}^{T} s_{t,D_{max}}(1+i)^{-t}}{\sum_{t=1}^{T}\{[(1+o)(1+l)-1]m_t - (1+l)p_{t,D_t}\}(1+i)^{-t}} \qquad (5)$$

Equation (5) implies that $D_t \geq D$, $t = 1,...,T$ would be a sufficient condition for justifying RFID implementations. Note that for the right hand side of equation (5) to provide meaningful bounds on demand, the denominator in equation (5) should be positive. Negative value for the denominator indicates infeasibility of the RFID implementation decision. While the non-negativity is satisfied for a retailer (since tag prices are set to zero), for a manufacturer (or for the supply chain player who is paying for the RFID tags) this condition will need to be verified. In addition, we need to note that the right hand side of equation (5) in Proposition 3 has dependency on D, which requires an iterative solution to determine the break-even sales volume. For an iterative solution, the sales volume can be initiated for the first iteration with a small value to determine the fixed costs and tag prices, and then in the second iteration the sales volume D can be set to the value of the right hand side from the first iteration, and so on. Also, note that Propositions 3 does not always guarantee the existence of a break-even sale volume (D). Convergence of an iterative solution to a break-even point occurs when the denominator of equation (5) grows faster than the numerator with respect to the sales volume. In other words, this situation would occur when the relative growth of the RFID fixed costs $(RFC := f_D + \sum_{t=1}^{T} s_{t,D}(1+i)^{-t})$ with respect to the sales volume is lower compared to the growth of the "tag-price-adjusted profit" $(TPP := \sum_{t=1}^{T} D_t\{[(1+o)(1+l)-1]m_t - (1+l)p_{t,D}\}(1+i)^{-t})$. As we will show later in the numerical analysis section, when the unit profits increase and tag prices get lower due to quantity discounts, break-even sales volumes can be identified, and similarly, when unit profits are lower, break-even sales volumes might not be achieved. Based on these observations the following corollary is obtained.

Corollary 2: *When the relative growth of the RFC with respect to the sales volume is lower compared to the growth of the TPP, and the unit profit to tag price (UPTP) ratio satisfies the following relation*

$$\frac{m_t}{p_{t,D}} > \frac{(1+l)}{(1+o)(1+l)-1}, \quad \forall t, t = 1,...,T \tag{6}$$

then there exists a break-even sales volume D such that NPV_{RFID} ≥ NPV_{no-RFID}.

The UPTP ratio given in equation (6) provides a relatively simple rule of thumb for first pass feasibility check of RFID implementations. This relation also provides some managerial insights on how sales increase and margin increase impact the RFID decisions. Note that for the supply chain player who is not paying for the RFID tags (retailer) the UPTP condition is always satisfied, thus the only remaining condition to check is the relative growth of RFC versus the TPP. Similar to the break-even unit profits and sales volumes, break-even RFID tag prices can be obtained for the manufacturer as follows:

Proposition 4: *Let p denote the average discounted RFID tag price for the RFID implementation defined as* $p = \dfrac{\sum_{t=1}^{T} D_t p_{t,D_t}(1+i)^{-t}}{\sum_{t=1}^{T} D_t(1+i)^{-t}}$, *then NPV_{RFID}*

≥ NPV_{no-RFID} when

$$p \leq \frac{-f_{D_{max}} + \sum_{t=1}^{T}\left(D_t m_t[(1+o)(1+l)-1] - s_{t,D_{max}}\right)(1+i)^{-t}}{(1+l)\sum_{t=1}^{T} D_t(1+i)^{-t}} \tag{7}$$

An interesting result emerges from the comparison of UPTP ratio inequality in equation (6) with the break-even tag price inequality in equation (7). Using equation (6), we can obtain a different bound on the RFID tag prices and it can be shown that this UPTP-based bound is an upper bound on the break-even prices obtained from equation (7). This result is summarized in the following corollary.

Corollary 3: *Let $p_{UPTP} = m[1+o - (1+l)^{-1}]$ denote the UPTP-based price, where m is the discounted average unit profit defined as before. Then, p_{UPTP} is an upper bound on the break-even average discounted RFID tag price p such that p ≤ p_{UPTP}. Furthermore, p_{UPTP} becomes a relatively good estimator of p as sales volume and unit profit increase.*

Multiple Products Case

The results derived so far deal with the single product case (or a family of similar products) but extension of some of the results is possible for multiple products as well. Let's assume that there are K products, and k denotes the index for each product such that $k=1,...,K$. Accordingly, in order to reflect that the parameters described earlier may depend on the product itself, we can include the product dimension to each parameter. We can extend the results of Proposition 1 as follows:

Proposition 5: *For the multiple product case, financial benefits from an RFID implementation Δ_{RFID} can be quantified as:*

$$\Delta_{RFID} = -f_{D_{max}} +$$

$$\sum_{t=1}^{T}\left(\sum_{k=1}^{K} D_{k,t}\{m_{k,t}[(1+o_k)(1+l_k)-1] - (1+l_k)p_{k,t,D_{k,t}}\} - s_{t,D_{max}}\right)(1+i)^{-t} \tag{8}$$

A specific case for the multiple product case happens when unit profits, tag prices, sales increase benefits and profit margin increase benefits are constant across products. Based on Proposition 5, it is easy to see that this specific case can be analyzed in a similar way as the single product case where the sales volume can be set as the total sales volume for all products in each time period. In addition, the UPTP results in Corollary 2 for the single product case can be extended for the multiple products case as follows:

Proposition 6: Let Ω denote the set of all products such that $\Omega = \Omega_1 \cup \Omega_2$, where Ω_1 is a subset of products that is sufficient to justify the RFID fixed costs, then UPTP ratio is a sufficient condition to justify RFID for the products that fall into Ω_2.

Note that Proposition 6 implies that for a retailer who is not paying for the RFID tags, to achieve a break-even, justification of RFID fixed costs based on products in Ω_1 would be sufficient. One particular question of interest would be what that "minimal" subset of products consists of for justifying the RFID investments. As shown below, this "minimal" subset of products can be easily identified by evaluating the expected net profit per product over the planning horizon.

Proposition 7: Let E_k be the expected net profit per product over the planning horizon and $E_{[k]}$ are the ordered values such that $E_{[1]} \geq E_{[2]} \geq \ldots \geq E_{[J]} \geq \ldots \geq E_{[K]}$. Let $\Omega_{min} \subseteq \Omega$ be the minimal subset of products, then identifying Ω_{min}, is equivalent to identifying the first J products that at least break-even with the RFID fixed costs.

The other results given in Propositions 2, 3 and 4 do not easily generalize for the multiple product case. One straightforward extension of Proposition 2 can be derived under an additional assumption of constant unit profit across products. Similarly, Proposition 3 can be extended to multiple product case when sales volumes are constant across products and Proposition 4 can be extended to multiple product case with an ad-ditional assumption that tag prices are constant across products.

Quantifying ROI of RFID

While earlier we investigated returns from an RFID implementation, a related metric of interest may be the ROI, which shows the ratio of RFID benefits with respect to the RFID investments or costs. ROI can be quantified as stated in the following proposition:

Proposition 8: ROI of an RFID implementation can be quantified as

$$ROI_{RFID} = \frac{\Delta_{RFID}}{f_{D_{max}} + \sum_{t=1}^{T}\left(D_t(1+l)p_{t,D_t} + s_{t,D_{max}}\right)(1+i)^{-t}}$$

(9)

Note that since ROI_{RFID} is based on Δ_{RFID}, the break-even analysis results described earlier, it holds for ROI_{RFID} as well. In other words, the break-even points for unit profits, sales volumes and RFID tag prices in Propositions 2, 3 and 4 are also break-even points for the ROI_{RFID}. Another, perhaps less intuitive, insight can be driven related to the sensitivity of ROI_{RFID} with respect to sales volumes. As we show below in Proposition 9, the relative increase of ROI_{RFID} with respect to an increase in sales volume decreases as sales volumes become larger.

Proposition 9: Increase in ROI of an RFID implementation is decreasing in sales volumes.

The result in Proposition 9 is important as it shows that ROI from an RFID implementation increases insignificantly (almost flattening) as sales volumes become large. We will show that this is indeed the case numerically in the computational experiment section.

Quantifying Risk of RFID

Another research objective in this study is the assessment of financial risks associated with

RFID implementation decisions. As mentioned earlier in the literature review section, most of existing research on RFID focused on expected values but not on the risks. While the expected NPV analysis provides us a good starting point, it does not fully explain the risks involved with the RFID implementation decisions for different industry scenarios. Some of the traditional definitions of risk can be made based on deterministic or stochastic dominance and variability of outcomes (see e.g. Clemen and Reilly, 2004). The judgments resulting from these risk definitions are typically binary in nature such as either dominance or non-dominance, and lower or higher risk. On the other hand, instead of a binary comparison, a relative comparison of RFID and no-RFID outcomes might be desirable. Therefore an alternate definition of RFID implementation risk (which can be considered as the relative measure extension for stochastic dominance) can be defined as follows:

Definition 1 - Loss Probability (LP1): *Financial risk for RFID implementation decisions can be computed as the probability of the NPV benefits for the RFID Δ_{RFID} being less or equal to zero such that*

$$\mathrm{LP1}_{RFID} = P(\Delta_{RFID} \leq 0) = H(0) \qquad (10)$$

where $H(x)$ is the cumulative probability function for Δ_{RFID}.

Similarly, RFID implementation risk can also be defined based on ROI as follows:

Definition 2 - Loss Probability (LP2): *Financial risk for RFID implementation decisions can be computed as the probability of the ROI for the RFID ROI_{RFID} being less or equal to zero such that*

$$\mathrm{LP2}_{RFID} = P(ROI_{RFID} \leq 0) = G(0) \qquad (11)$$

where $G(x)$ is the cumulative probability function for ROI_{RFID}.

One challenge in evaluating LP is the identification of the distributions of Δ_{RFID} and ROI_{RFID}. Equations (1) and (8) provide good starting points but considering each element of the RFID system can have uncertainties, identification of the exact distribution analytically might not be possible. One approach that can be utilized for this purpose is simulation analysis as illustrated in the computational analysis section next.

COMPUTATIONAL ANALYSIS

In this section an analysis is done for a hypothetical manufacturer and a retailer. As indicated earlier, the main difference between the manufacturer and the retailer is that the manufacturer pays for the tag price and the retailer does not. Expected, pessimistic and optimistic RFID implementation scenarios were created for each supply chain player, based on possible RFID profit margin benefit, sales benefit, tag-price, and fixed costs. We assume that we are dealing with a single product or a family of similar products. The main reason for this assumption is that we would like to have a more controllable experimental analysis setting, and there is also lack of data for meaningful analysis for multiple products. For multiple product cases, it can be roughly assumed that the sales volume represents the total sales volume for all the products, and the unit profits can be considered as the average value for all the products. As it will be explained shortly, the baseline data for this analysis (such as the tag prices) is partially collected from an RFID vendor and it is partially based on previous studies reported in the literature. For each scenario, 90 business cases were analyzed in an experimental setting, which correspond to the combination of 10 sales volume scenarios and 9 unit profit scenarios (total scenarios analyzed = 540 = 2 players x 3 risk perception cases x 90 demand/unit profit combinations). The different factors and their corresponding experimental

Table 1. Factors and experimental levels for the computational analysis

Factors	Number of Levels	Levels
Supply Chain Player	2	Manufacturer, Retailer
Risk Perception	3	Pessimistic, Expected, Optimistic
Sales Volume	10	1000, 5000, 10000, 25000, 50000, 100000, 250000, 500000, 750000, and 1000000
Unit Profit	9	$0.50, $1, $2, $4, $8, $16, $32, $64, $128

levels in our analysis are summarized in Table 1. In order to drive further insights on the RFID decision problem, several analyses were conducted for each of these aforementioned cases including break-even analysis, UPTP ratio analysis, ROI analysis, and simulation and risk analysis. Before describing each analysis, the data and assumptions will be described in more detail next.

Data

Tag Prices

The current RFID tag prices for our study were obtained from the Righttag Inc. (www.righttag. com, January 2006) for Gen 2, Class 1 tags. The summary statistics for these tag prices are shown in Figure 1 for varying purchase quantities. There is quite a bit of speculation on future RFID tag prices. According to some experts (Vollmer, 2004, p.40), below 1 cent tags are expected to come out in about 5 to 10 years with the emergence of new RFID production technologies (e.g. for packaging RFID tags). Others believe that in 5 to 10 years 5 cent tags will be possible with the increased RFID tag demand, which would lead to the increase in production volumes. In a cost simulation study, Swamy and Sarma (2003) analyzed feasibility of low cost RFID systems. They simulated manufacturing and assembly processes to understand the feasibility of the 5-cent tag, assuming some manufacturing processes are changed and that large volumes are being manufactured. Their results show that assuming 300,000 wafer starts per year,

RFID tag costs can be as low as 4.49 cents using the traditional assembly process. They also found that line balancing and throughput improvements are the key drivers on the assembly side of tag manufacturing. Thus they conclude that even with existing technology it may be possible to achieve the 5 cents tag cost at a sufficiently high volume of tags. In fact, there have already been several press releases by RFID tag manufacturers such as Alien (2005) and Avery (2005) advertising about 12.9 and 7.9 cent tags for order quantities over 1 million, respectively. Therefore, we have assumed that over the next 10 years the prices will change between 1 to 10 cents depending on the volume of interest as shown in Figure 2. More specifically, the tag price is decremented by 1 cent for each sales volume level having (10 cents, 5 cents, ..., 1 cent) prices correspond to volumes of (1 thousand, 100 thousand, ..., 1 million) units, respectively. The tag prices between 2007 and 2016 were linearly interpolated between the current prices and the assumed future tag prices (Figure 3).

In the presented study, we made several assumptions to do a sensitivity analysis on the impact of tag prices on RFID implementations. First, we assumed that tag prices are uncertain and may vary between the minimum and maximum values as given in Figure 2. Second, we considered an expected, a pessimistic and an optimistic scenario for the tag prices as follows: a triangular distribution is assumed using the minimum and maximum tag prices. For the expected scenario, the mode of the triangular distribution is set as the median tag price. For the pessimistic scenario, the mode of the

Figure 2. Current tag prices (Source: Righttag Inc., www.righttag.com, January 2006)

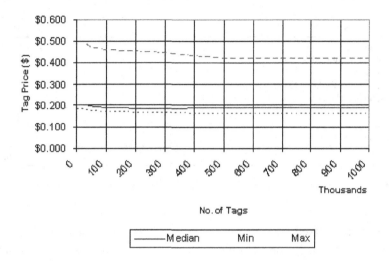

Figure 3. Assumed future tag prices

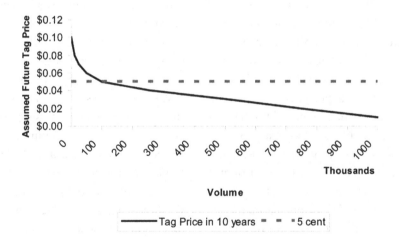

triangular distribution was set as the maximum tag price, and similarly, for the optimistic scenario, the mode of the triangular distribution was set as the minimum tag price.

Note that the use of triangular distribution is quite common in planning and decision analysis, especially when little is known about the distribution of a random variable, data is scarce and when the values are changing within a minimum and maximum values with a guess on the most likely

(modal) value (see e.g. Vose, 2000, p. 129, p. 273; Law and Kelton, 2000, p. 318, p. 386).

Fixed Costs

RFID systems consist of several components such as tag readers, printers/encoders, and middleware. The costs for the hardware and software as well as the internal and external consulting implementation efforts make the initial fixed costs. It is quite

Table 2. Hardware, software and external service costs of RFID, Source: Sirico (2005a and b)

Description	Total
One Thermal RFID Printer/encoder	$5,000
Two Dock Door Read Points, includes: • 3 x EPC compliant, multi-protocol reader • 8 x Bi-static 915MHz Antennas • 4 x Industrial Strength Enclosure for Dock Doors • Cables, UPS, Lights, Mounting Hardware, Ballards	$15,000
Hardware Total:	$20,000
RFID Middleware (varies by vendor):	$30,000
External Services:	$50,000
Total	**$100,000**

difficult to come up with a fixed cost estimate unless the scope is well defined. For example, questions such as number of sites and volumes can be important. A $100K estimate for a "slap and ship" solution is described in Sirico (2005a and b) as shown in Table 2. Sirico (2005a) mentions that this solution is good for volumes of up to 1000 units per day after which the system becomes a bottleneck. Here, we assumed 5-day working weeks, and approximately 4% system efficiency loss, yielding 250,000 units per year.

Sirico (2005a) also mentions that additionally five to seven people will be needed to support the implementation with 1 full time person and the rest of the people spending at least half of their time on the project. With these additional labor requirements, Sirico (2005a) estimates that the total cost comes to $500K to $750K. In addition, an annual maintenance and support for the RFID system will need to be considered as well, which Sirico (2005a) estimates as 10-15% of the external service costs of approximately $50K. Based on these data, we computed the initial and annual fixed costs for different volumes as shown in Figure 4. Note that based on this figure, while a sales volume of 250K would require an initial fixed cost of $500K to $750K, an additional sales volume of say, for example, one additional unit would require purchasing of an additional RFID system costing $1000K to $1500K. As

we will show later on, underutilization of the RFID system capacity may imply infeasibility of RFID implementations especially at low unit profits. A 10% yearly increase in annual fixed (operating) costs is assumed for our analysis to reflect expected increases in wages and external consulting fees.

In order to do a sensitivity and simulation analysis, expected, pessimistic and optimistic fixed cost scenarios were created using a triangular distribution in a similar way described above for the tag prices, where the support for the triangle is based on the minimum and the maximum expected fixed costs, and the mode is selected to be the mid-point (between the minimum and the maximum values), maximum, and minimum fixed cost values for the expected, pessimistic, and optimistic scenarios, respectively.

Increased Sale Benefit

Gruen, Corsten, & Bharadwaj (2002) estimate that approximately 50% of the out-of-stocks are resulting in lost sales. Therefore elimination of out of stock should help to increase sales. They estimate in the majority of the cases that out-of-stocks range between 5-10% with an average of 8.3%. Intel (2004) estimates the out-of-stocks as 8-12%. Figure 5 provides several benchmark estimates from different references on the mag-

Figure 4. Initial and annual fixed costs of an RFID implementation (based on Sirico, 2005a)

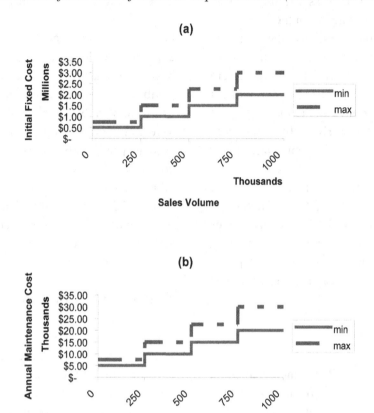

Figure 5. Increased Sales benefits due to elimination of out of stock based on different sources

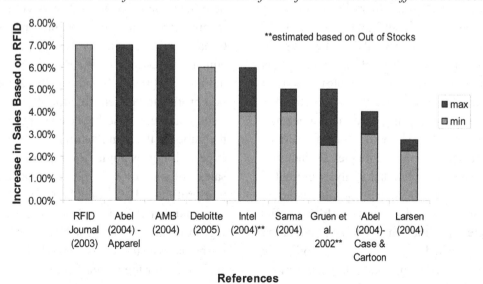

nitude of this sales increase as a result of RFID implementations. Estimates from these previous studies and RFID implementations indicate that the increased sales benefits have a wide uncertainty and will range between 2-7%, which we used here as a baseline for our numerical analysis. While it is not in our scope to investigate the validity of these sales benefits (similarly profit margin benefits), the reader can refer to Lee and Ozer (2007) for a critical review of some of the previously published RFID benefits. Again, in order to do a sensitivity and simulation analysis, a triangular distribution was assumed for the increased sales benefits, representing the expected case using a triangular distribution of (2%, 4.5%, 7%), pessimistic case as (2%, 2%, 7%), and the optimistic case as (2%, 7%, 7%).

Profit Margin Benefits

Other major benefits of an RFID implementation, such as inventory and labor reduction impact the costs, and accordingly, the profit margins. GMA (2004) provides a detailed analysis of the RFID benefits from increased sales due to reduction of out-of-stocks, inventory reduction, labor reduction and elimination of credits/claims. This study shows that the benefits vary drastically for different products. Based on this study, it can be estimated that on average, 36% of the total RFID benefits will result from elimination of out-of-stocks and 64% is due to the other factors that contribute to the profit margin. Based on these percentages we estimated a baseline interval for the profit margin benefits as 3.6% and 12.4%. We should note that GMA's (2004) analysis was primarily for the CPG industry. Therefore the computational analysis presented here will be more reflective of the CPG industry and other industries where similar RFID benefits are expected. For the sensitivity and simulation analysis, expected, pessimistic and optimistic cases were created using triangular distributions of (3.6%, 8%, 12.4%), (3.6%, 3.6%, 12.4%) and (3.6%, 12.4%, 12.4%), respectively.

Sales Volume and Unit Profit

For the subsequent analysis, we have taken an experimental design approach in which various business scenarios were created using different combinations of sales volumes and unit profits. More specifically, ten sales volumes were selected to reflect various company sizes and to coincide with the price-break points of the fixed and variable costs (where possible) as follows: 1000, 5000, 10000, 25000, 50000, 100000, 250000, 500000, 750000, and 1000000. Similarly, the unit profits were selected to reflect various products and industry sectors: $0.50, $1, $2, $4, $8, $16, $32, $64, $128.

Break-Even Analysis

In this section, a break-even analysis is conducted using the results of Section 3. Expected, pessimistic and optimistic scenarios were analyzed and compared. For the expected, pessimistic and optimistic cases, RFID tag prices, fixed costs, increased sales benefits and profit margin benefits were all set at their expected, pessimistic and optimistic values (as described in the Data section), respectively. For the expected case, the resulting break-even unit profits and sales volumes for a manufacturer and a retailer are presented in Figure 6, based on Propositions 2 and 3, assuming an annual interest rate of i=10%. While the results in Figures 6 (a) and (b) indicate that a break-even unit profit can be identified for all experimented sales volumes, these break-even points are not the same for the manufacturer and the retailer, as expected. For example, for a manufacturer with sales volumes of 1 million units a break-even unit profit of $4.42 would be required while the same number is $3.17 for a retailer. An interesting observation is that for lower sales volumes the break-even unit profits are relatively closer to each other for the manufacturer and the retailer, while this difference increases as the sales volumes increase. This result can be explained as follows:

although the retailer is not paying for the RFID tags, based on Proposition (2) (equation (4)) we see that as sales volumes decrease, RFID fixed costs become more important than RFID tag prices in determining the break-even unit profits for making RFID implementation decisions. The results also show that (as expected) low volume RFID implementations can be justified for products with high unit profits. For example, as seen in Figure 6 (a), for quantities of 1,000 units a break-even unit profit of $793.03 is required. We would like to note that in Figures 6 (a) and (b), the sales volumes of 250K, 500K, 750K and 1000K and the associated break-even unit profits correspond to fully utilized RFID systems (based on the RFID fixed costs and capacities described in Figure 4). When the RFID system is not fully utilized, the break-even unit profits naturally go up. For example, for the manufacturer, the break-even unit

profits for sales volumes of 250,001, 500,001, and 750,001 (where an additional RFID system investment would need to be made, yielding capacities of 500K, 750K and 1000K, respectively), the break-even unit profits are $7.66, $6.04, and $5.48, respectively. Thus due to the step function behavior of the RFID fixed costs, the break-even unit profits are not decreasing for higher sales volumes if the RFID system is under-utilized. While not shown in Figure 6 (b), similar observations for the retailer also apply.

Regarding the break-even sales volumes, the analysis indicates that a break-even sales volume does not exist for all unit profits. As shown in Figures 6 (c) and (d), for unit profits of $4 or less for the manufacturer, and $2 or less for the retailer, a break-even sales volume could not be identified. These findings are interesting and can be explained due to significant increase in RFC

Figure 6. Break-even unit profits and sales volumes for a manufacturer and a retailer for the expected case

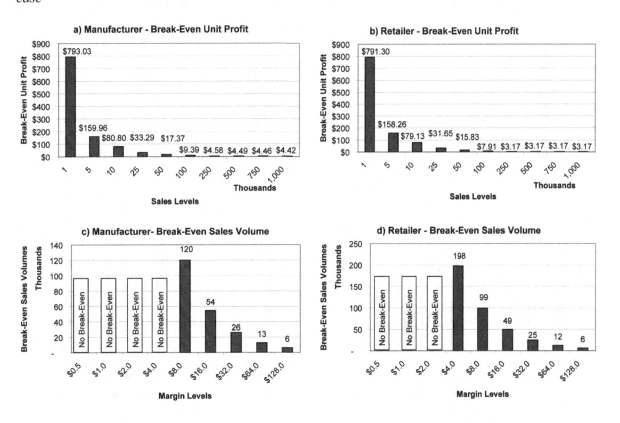

as compared to TPP as discussed in Corollary 2. Another observation worth mentioning is that as unit profits increase, the difference between the break-even sales volume of a manufacturer and a retailer decreases (in fact being identical here for a unit profit of $128 in Figures 6 (c) and (d)). This result can be explained based on Proposition 3. As can be seen from the denominator of the right hand-side of equation (5), as the unit profits increase, the tag prices become less significant in identifying the break-even sales volume values.

Sensitivity analysis results are shown in Figures 7 and 8 for the manufacturer and the retailer, respectively. As it can be seen, the interval of uncertainty is quite high comparing the pessimistic and the optimistic cases. For example, for a low volume manufacturer justifying RFID implementations for an annual sales volume of 1000 units would require a unit profit as low as $621.37 in the optimistic case, and as high as $1043.96 in

the pessimistic case. Similarly, for a high volume manufacturer justifying RFID implementations for an annual sales volume of 1M units would require a unit profit as low as $3.51 in the optimistic case, and as high as $6.15 in the pessimistic case. In both Figures 7 (c) and 8 (c), we see that for a pessimistic case, break-even sales volumes do not exist for unit profits of $4 or less. Similarly, optimistic case analysis in Figures 7 (d) and 8 (d) indicate that break-even sales volumes do not exist for unit profits of $2 or less.

Similarly, the break-even points and upper bounds for tag-prices were identified based on Proposition 4 and Corollary 3. The results for the expected case are shown in Figure 9. Some of the conclusions can be summarized as follows: when unit profits are very low (less than $2), it might not be possible to break even in tag-prices even when the sales volumes increase. This observation is in alignment with the previous break-even

Figure 7. Manufacturer's break-even unit profits/sales volumes for pessimistic and optimistic cases

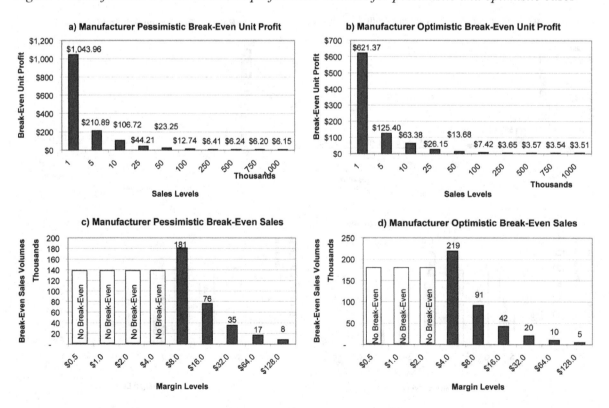

analysis presented in Figures 6-8. On the other hand, for the expected case, when tag-prices fall to $0.10 or below, the unit profit of $4 may break even at sales volumes of 250K, 500K, 750K and 1000K. Note that as explained earlier (see Figure 4 and related discussion), these sales volumes represent fully utilized RFID systems. When the RFID system is underutilized, for example say, at a unit profit of $8 and a sales volume of 260 K (when an investment for a maximum capacity of 500K is made), the break-even tag prices become negative indicating infeasibility of the RFID implementation. As expected, as unit profits and sales volumes increase, the break-even tag-prices increase as well. For example, for a product line with a unit profit of $128 and sales volumes of 250K and higher, an RFID implementation could be justified even when the RFID tag-prices are $14.45. Overall, the results indicate that there is no magic "5 cents" tag-price as widely accepted in the industry that would be sufficient to ad-

dress all business scenarios. We also computed the UPTP-based upper bound on break-even tag-prices based on Corollary 3, which are also shown in Figure 9. It is worth noting that the upper bound becomes tighter as the unit profits and sales volumes increase, indicating that for the corresponding industries and companies UPTP analysis would indeed give an initial feasibility sense on the RFID implementation.

Sensitivity results based on optimistic and pessimistic RFID costs and benefits that are partially shown in Figure 10 indicate again that there is significant uncertainty with respect to the break-even prices. For example, the pessimistic case indicates that for unit profits of $4, one might not have a break even sales volume.

ROI Analysis

In this section, an ROI analysis is presented for RFID implementation decisions based on the

Figure 8. Retailer's break-even unit profits/sales volumes for the pessimistic and optimistic cases

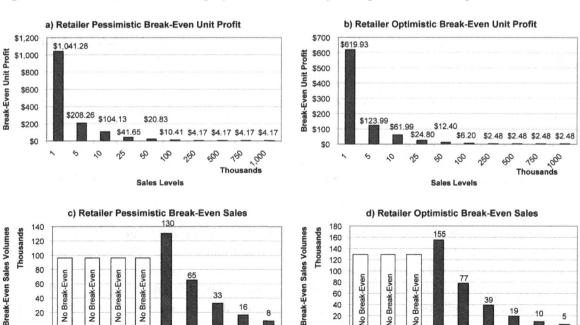

Figure 9. Manufacturer's break-even tag prices and UPTP upper bounds for the expected case

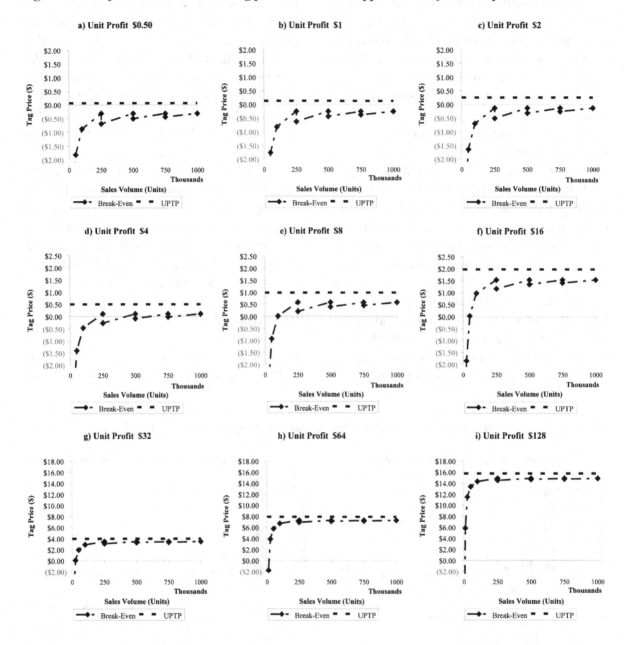

results presented in Proposition 8. The results are shown in Figure 11 for the manufacturer for the expected, optimistic and pessimistic cases. In general, the ROI results are in alignment with the break-even analysis, indicating that the manufacturer will expect to lose money for unit profits of $4 or less (except for the optimistic case with sales volumes of 250K, 500K, 750K, and 1000K, when

the RFID system is fully utilized). As unit profits increase and the sales volumes reach break-even quantities, ROI becomes positive as expected, but due to the step function behavior of the RFID fixed costs, low utilized RFID systems may result in negative ROI as in the case of unit profit of $8 with sales volumes of 250,001 and 500,001 under the pessimistic scenario (-24% and -4%,

Figure 10. Manufacturer's break-even tag prices and UPTP for the optimistic and pessimistic cases

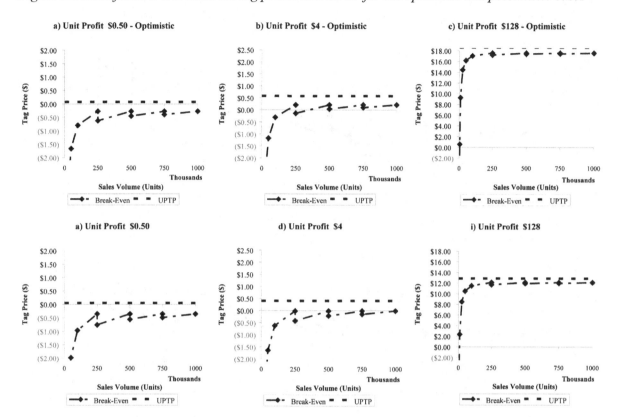

respectively). Other observation worth mentioning is that the slope of the ROI function flattens as sales volume goes up. This observation, which is also discussed in Proposition 9, is interesting since it seems that after a certain threshold the increase in returns from an RFID implementation is diminishing with respect to increases in sales volumes. Figure 11 indicates that this turning point of ROI occurs at sales volumes of 250 K. For sales volumes higher than 250K the ROI still increases but in relatively small increments. Another result from Figure 11 is that as unit profits increase, the ROI potential for RFID investments may increase significantly. For example for a unit profit of $8 and 250 K sales volume the pessimistic, expected, and optimistic ROI values are 25%, 75% and 119% respectively. The same numbers for a unit profit of $124 and 250 K sales volume are 1898%, 2695% and 3407%, respectively. The results indicate

that for large corporations with high unit profits and sales volumes, RFID costs can be recovered almost 19 to 34 times.

The results also indicate that underutilization of an RFID system can impact the resulting ROI significantly. For example, a manufacturer with a unit profit of $128, who made an investment for an RFID system capacity of 1M units, would have an ROI of 2793% for a fully utilized RFID system (with a sales volume of 1M units) in the expected risk case, versus 2222% for an under-utilization case with a sales volume of 750,001 units, which indicates a significant decrease in ROI of 20%. Similar observation is made for all cases of underutilization, but it seems that as RFID system capacity decreases, the impact of utilization on ROI is more significant. For example, again for a unit profit of $128, for RFID capacities of 500K and 750K, the manufacturer's ROI would

Figure 11. Manufacturer's ROI for the expected, optimistic and pessimistic cases

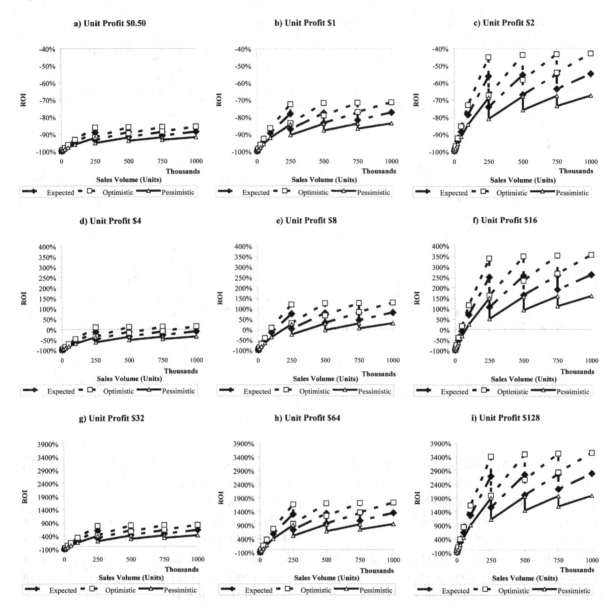

be reduced 28% and 44%, respectively for under-utilization cases. As the unit profits decrease, this ROI discrepancy between a fully utilized versus underutilized system becomes even larger. For example, for a unit profit of $16, the potential difference in ROI is 27%, 37%, and 58% for RFID implementations with capacity of 500K, 750K, and 1000K, respectively, for the expected case. The results indicate that, while optimistic case estimates of ROI reduction is less than the expected case, this reduction in ROI is amplified for the pessimistic cases, especially for lower unit profits, and for companies with lower sales volumes. For example, for a unit profit of $16, and for a RFID system with capacity of 500K, a 54% and 67% ROI reduction may occur for an underutilized system under optimistic and pessimistic cases, respectively. The same numbers

Figure 12. Retailer's ROI for the expected, optimistic and pessimistic cases

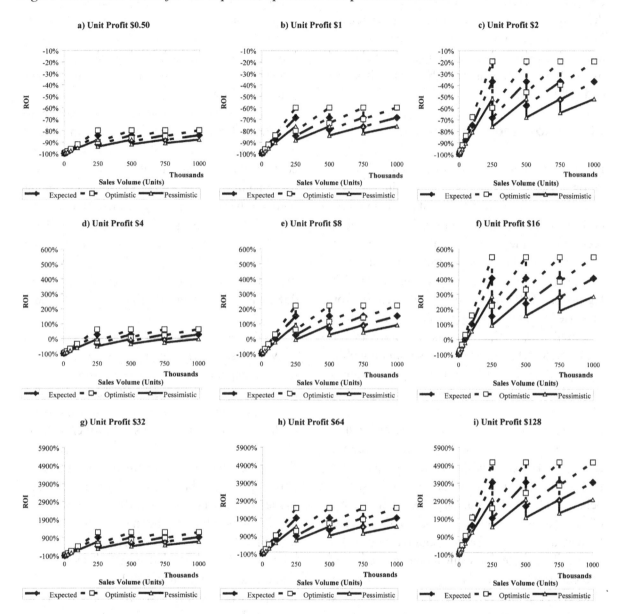

for an RFID system with a capacity of 1M units are 25% and 31%, respectively.

The ROI analysis for the retailer is shown in Figure 12. Similar observations for the manufacturer apply, except that the ROI is expected to further increase for the retailer, since RFID tag prices are paid by the manufacturer. For a unit profit of $8 and 250 K sales volume the pessimistic, expected, and optimistic ROI values are 92%,

153% and 223%, respectively. Similarly, the ROI for a unit profit of $124 and 250 K sales volume are 2973%, 3944% and 5062%, respectively. These ROI values for the retailer are 1.5-3.7 times more than the manufacturer's, which explains why manufacturers might be more skeptical than the retailers on RFID implementation decisions. In general, ROI ratio of retailers to the manufacturers seems to increase as unit profits are lower. As unit profits increase, the gap between the ROI of the retailer and manufacturer seems to decrease. For example, retailer to manufacturer ROI ratio average of all cases corresponding to a unit profit of $8 is 2.45, and the same number for a unit profit of $128 is 1.31.

Simulation and Risk Analysis

In this part of our analysis, a full factorial simulation experiment was conducted using the ten sales volume levels and nine unit profit levels as described earlier, thus resulting in 90 business scenarios. In the simulation all parameters and variables were taken as uncertain including the sales volumes, interest rate, unit profits, RFID tag prices, RFID fixed costs, RFID benefits for increased sales and margin benefits. A negative binomial distribution was assumed to reflect the discrete behavior of the sales volume with a standard deviation of 10% of the expected value. (Note that with this assumption on the magnitude of the standard deviation, the parameters of the negative binomial distribution can be estimated in a straightforward way (see e.g. Law and Kelton, 2000, p. 324)). A normal distribution was assigned to describe the unit profits and the interest rate behavior also with a standard deviation of 10% of the expected values. All distributions were truncated at zero not to allow negative values. We would like to note that while technically correct, avoidance of truncation is insignificant in our case since the probability of having negative values is almost zero (since it would require sampling values 10 standard deviations away from the expected value). Similarly, our standard deviation assumption establishes virtual bounds on the unit profits and interest rates since a +/-3 standard deviation from the expected value would mean a 99.73% confidence interval. Also while we used a negative binomial distribution for the sales volume, use of a normal distribution would yield similar results since the sales volumes considered here

are relatively large for a statistical analysis. As described in the data section earlier, for the other parameters related to the RFID costs and benefits, a triangular distribution is assumed to change the values within the minimum and maximum parameter values.

Each simulation was run for 1000 times for both "RFID" and "no-RFID" scenarios using the @Risk 4.5 decision analysis software (www.palisade.com). In general, the simulation results (shown for a manufacturer in Figure 13) are in agreement with the break-even analysis presented earlier. While for low margin products (unit profits of $0.5, $1, $2, $4) no break-even could be achieved, the break-even volumes steadily decrease for higher margin products yielding volumes of 100K, 50K, 25K, and 10K for unit profits of $16, $32, $64, and $128, respectively.

As discussed in Section 3, while the expected NPV analysis provides us a good starting point, it does not explain the risks involved with the RFID implementation decisions for different unit profits and sales volumes. Analysis of the distribution of each simulation output can shed further insights about the risk. As seen in Figure 13 from the NPV for the 5th and 95th percentiles, for quantities corresponding to break-even volumes and even higher, there is an overlap of RFID and no-RFID distributions, which can be an indicator of the risk of the RFID implementation decision.

Next, LP is computed based on Definitions 1 and 2 to understand the RFID risk. Since the results for LP1 and LP2 are very similar, LP1 is presented here in Figures 14 and 15 for a manufacturer and a retailer, respectively. As it can be seen from these figures, although break-even can be established for unit profits of $8 and higher for the manufacturer and for unit profits of $4 and higher, for the retailer based on an expected NPV analysis there can be a significant risk of implementing RFID for all unit profits when sales volumes are low. Also at break-even values a 50% risk is observed approximately. As in the previous

Figure 13. Simulation Results for the 5% and 95% percentile NPV values for RFID and no-RFID scenarios for a manufacturer for the expected case

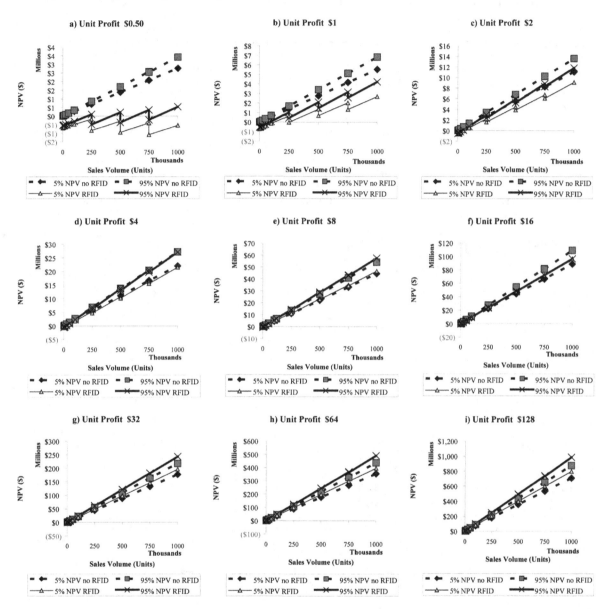

results, it can be observed that RFID implementations with underutilized RFID systems are prone to higher risk. For example, for a manufacturer with a unit profit of $8, while the fully utilized RFID system with a capacity of 250K units has a risk of approximately 4% for the pessimistic case, the same number is 99% for the underutilized RFID system with a capacity of 500K units. Even for

the optimistic case the corresponding risk for the same underutilized system is quite significant with a magnitude of approximately 37%.

To illustrate that RFID implementation risk is not completely eliminated with higher unit profits, we show several Δ_{RFID} distributions for a unit profit of $128 in Figure 16 for the manufacturer. As it can be verified, the LP for sales volumes

Figure 14. Manufacturer's risk (LP1) of RFID for expected, pessimistic and optimistic cases

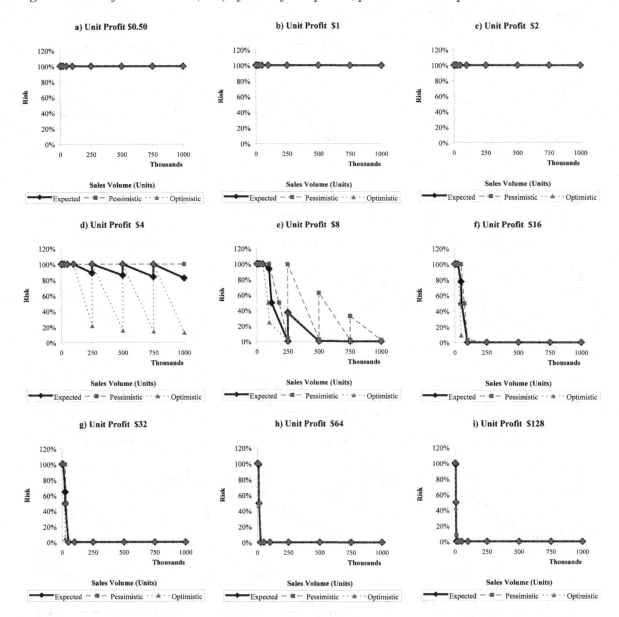

of 1000, 5000, 6450 (break-even quantity), and 10000 units are 100%, 87.85%, 61.08% and 0%, respectively.

SUMMARY AND CONCLUSION

While there are some concerns about RFID in terms of cost, security and privacy, standardiza-

tion and IT infrastructure, adoption of RFID has been gradually increasing as larger supply chain players such as Wal-Mart and Department of Defense mandate it in their supply chain. RFID implementation decisions require detailed understanding of the trade-offs between costs, benefits and risks. In this paper, we focused on quantifying the financial benefits and risks of RFID. A financial returns analysis is performed

Figure 15. Retailer's risk (LP1) of RFID for expected, pessimistic and optimistic cases

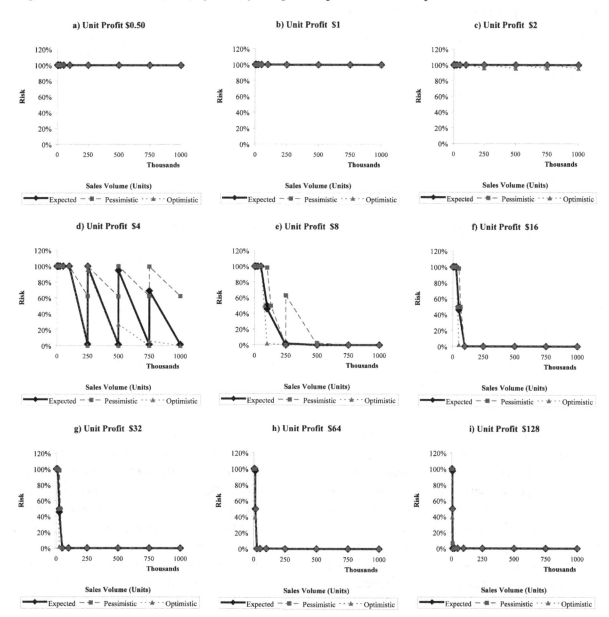

using an econometric model to understand how break-even sales volumes, unit profits, tag prices, ROI and risks vary for both a manufacturer and a retailer in a supply chain. The results are extended to multi-product cases. While the baseline data is benchmarked to existing studies, sensitivity analysis was also performed to understand the returns in pessimistic and optimistic scenarios.

Some of the main findings can be summarized as follows:

- UPTP (Unit Profit to Tag Price) ratio can be used as a first-cut feasibility check for the feasibility of RFID implementations. UPTP-based prices represent an upper bound for the break- even tag price. This

Figure 16. Δ_{RFID} distributions for deploying RFID technology and corresponding risk (LP1) for unit profit of $128 and for different sales volumes

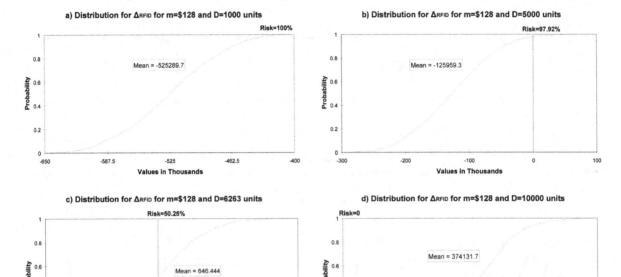

bound gets tighter as sales volumes and unit profits increase. For multi-product cases, UPTP ratio is a sufficient condition for RFID implementation feasibility once the fixed costs are covered by a subset of the products that yield high returns.

- The financial benefits and risks of an RFID implementation vary depending on the supply chain player, sales volumes, and unit profits: for lower sales volumes, the break-even unit profits are relatively closer to each other for the manufacturer and the retailer, while this difference increases as the sales volumes increase. A similar observation can be made for break-even sales volumes. For higher unit profits, the break-even sales volumes are relatively closer to each other for the manufacturer and the re-tailer, while this difference increases as the unit profits decrease. From a pessimistic

perspective, we identified that industries with unit profits of $4 or less might not be able justify RFID implementations. In the optimistic case the same applies for industries with unit profits of $2 or less. This is due to the fact that the RFID fixed costs seem to be increasing faster at low unit profits than the expected benefits of RFID as sales volumes increase.

- While many studies focus on RFID tag prices, RFID fixed costs also seem to play an important (perhaps more important) role in RFID implementation decisions. While the tag prices are decreasing as we speak, even assuming "no tag price burden" as in the case of a retailer, RFID investments might not be justified for low unit profits and low volume products. These results consequently show that the widely ac-cepted of "5 cent" tag being a justification threshold for RFID implementations might not hold.

- ROI analysis for RFID implementations shows that the slope of the ROI function flattens as sales volume go up, indicating that after a certain threshold (around 250 K units) the increase of returns from an RFID investment are diminishing with respect to the increase in sales volumes. As unit profits increase, ROI potential for RFID investments increase significantly. Ratio of the retailer's ROI to that of the manufacturer's seems to increase as unit profits are lower. On the flip side, as unit profits increase, the gap between the ROI of the retailer and manufacturer seems to decrease. We obtained a retailer to manufacturer ROI ratio average of 2.45 for all cases corresponding to a unit profit of $8, and the same ratio for a unit profit of $128 is 1.31.

- Risk analysis based on LP (loss probability) indicates that break-even points based on an expected value analysis only guarantee a 50% loss (approximately). Therefore to eliminate risk, adequate sales volumes (or unit profit) need to be maintained for each product. Similarly, pessimistic and optimistic analyses show a significant gap between expected NPV for an RFID implementation, indicating risks of RFID returns being uncertain as well.

- Underutilization of RFID system capacity impacts the financial returns from an RFID implementation adversely, resulting in an increase of the required break-even profit margins, a decrease in required break-even RFID tag prices, a decrease in ROI and an increase in financial risks. It seems that as RFID system capacity decreases, the impact of utilization on ROI is more significant. As the unit profits decrease, the ROI discrepancy between a fully utilized versus underutilized system becomes even larger. The results also indicate that, while

optimistic case estimates of ROI reduction is less than the expected case, this reduction in ROI is amplified for the pessimistic cases, especially for lower unit profits, and for companies with lower sales volumes. For all RFID implementation scenarios analyzed, we have seen a minimum of 20%, in average 57%, and maximum 386% ROI reduction for a manufacturer (the same values for a retailer are 25%, 55%, and 240%). The over 100% ROI decrease cases corresponding to lower unit profits ($4 and $8) indicates that feasible RFID implementation decisions may become infeasible (resulting in negative ROI) when the RFID system is underutilized.

In conclusion, we believe that while there are quite a few uncertainties related to RFID related benefits and future costs, the framework and results presented in this paper can provide a guidance to the industry in RFID implementation decisions. On the other hand, we also would like to highlight that for a specific implementation, the proposed simplified model for the quantification of the ROI of an RFID implementation should be enhanced based on the specific conditions of the implementation to capture different costs involved in an RFID system as well as other kind of anticipated effects from exploitation of RFID. We also believe that some of the future research may include empirical studies to identify RFID benefits in different industry segments more accurately. As recently mentioned in Lee and Ozer (2007), analytical models can be developed to quantify the true benefits of RFID. The data from these empirical and analytical studies in conjunction with the proposed ROI modeling framework will not only enable us understand each industry segment in more detail but also will increase the accuracy of our understanding on the expected ROI and risks of RFID. In addition, extension of the current analysis can be done to understand amortization of RFID investments. This may help companies, which often justify capital and technological expenditures based on amortizing costs over a period of years. While we investigated financial risks of RFID, yet another interesting research question would be quantifying other types of RFID risk such as privacy concerns, and how these different types of risks are perceived by different players in the supply chain.

ACKNOWLEDGMENT

We would like to thank the anonymous referees for their valuable feedback.

REFERENCES

Abel, P. (2004). *RFID benefits*. Paper presented at Productivity Conference Nashville, TN, p. 20, Retrieved from http://www.fmi.org/events/productivity/2004/Prod_CDROM/presentations/RFID_benefits.pdf

Al-Ali, A. S. A., Sajwani, F., Al-Muhairi, A., & Shahenn, E. (2007). Assessing the feasibility of using rfid technology in airports. In *1st Annual RFID Eurasia, Istanbul, Turkey*.

Alien, (2005). *Alien Technology Corporation announces 12.9 cent RFID Labels*. Retrieved from Available at URL: http://www.isminfo.com/RFID/PDFs/2005_09_13_Alien.pdf

Angeles, R. (2005). RFID technologies: Supply-chain applications and implementation issues. *Information Systems Management, 22*, 51–65. doi:10.1201/1078/44912.22.1.20051201/85739.7

Asif, Z., & Mandviwalla, M. (2005). Integrating the supply chain with RFID: A technical and business analysis. *Communications of the Association for Information Systems, 15*, 393–427.

Atock, C. (2003). Where is my stuff? *Manufacturing Engineering, 82*(2), 24–27. doi:10.1049/me:20030202

Avery, (2005). *Avery Dennison offers GEN 2 RFID inlays at lowest price industry*. Press Release. Retrieved from http://www.rfid.averydennison.com/pages/news/pdf/091905.pdf

Chao, C.-C., Yang, J.-M., & Jen, W.-Y. (2007). Determining technology trends and forecasts of RFID by a historical review and bibliometric analysis from 1991 to 2005. *Technovation, 27*, 268–279. doi:10.1016/j.technovation.2006.09.003

Clemen, R. T., & Reilly, T. (2004). *Making hard decisions with DecisionTools* (1st ed.). Duxbury Press.

Delen, D., Hardgrave, B. C., & Sharda, R. (2007). RFID for better supply-chain management through enhanced information visibility. *Production and Operations Management, 16*(5), 613–624.

Deloitte, (2005). Chips with everything. *Deloitte Consulting Consumer Business*. Retrieved from http://www.ebusinessassociation.org/ssi/events/presentations/ Chips%20with%20everything.pdf

Fontanella, J. (2004). Finding the ROI in RFID. *Supply Chain Management Review, 8*(1), 13–14.

GMA. (2004). A balanced perspective: EPC/RFID Implementation in the CPG Industry. *Grocery Manufacturers of America*. Retrieved from http://www.gmabrands.com/publications/docs/2005/BalancedPerspective.pdf

Gruen, T. W., Corsten, D. S., & Bharadwaj, S. (2002). *Retail out of stocks: A worldwide examination of extent, causes, and consumer responses*. Washington, D.C.: Grocery Manufacturers of America. Retrieved from http://www.gmabrands.com/publications/docs/RetOOS.pdf

Hardgrave, B., Waller, M., & Miller, R. (2005). *Does RFID Reduce Out of Stocks?* Sam Walton School of Business, RFID Research Center, University of Arkansas, Fayetteville, AR.

Hossain, M. M., & Prybutok, V. R. (2008). Consumer acceptance of RFID technology: An exploratory study. *IEEE Transactions on Engineering Management, 55*(2), 316–328. doi:10.1109/TEM.2008.919728

Hou, J.-L., & Huang, C.-H. (2006). Quantitative performance evaluation of RFID applications in the supply chain of the printing industry. *Industrial Management & Data Systems, 106*(1), 96–120. doi:10.1108/02635570610641013

Huber, N., & Michael, K. (2007). Vendor perceptions of how RFID can minimize product shrinkage in the retail supply chain. In *1st Annual RFID Eurasia, Istanbul, Turkey.*

Intel (2004, September). *EPC-RFID solutions that power the high-resolution supply chain.* Retrieved from http://www.intel.com/business/bss/solutions/blueprints /pdf/oatsystems.pdf

Journal, R. F. I. D. (2003, November 14). *Report: RFID benefits not equal.* Retrieved from http://www.rfidjournal.com/article/articleview/651/1/26/

Juels, A. (2006). RFID security and privacy: A research survey. *IEEE Journal on Selected Areas in Communications, 24*(2), 381–394. doi:10.1109/JSAC.2005.861395

Kok, A. G., Donselaar, K. H., & Woensel, T. (2008). A break-even analysis of RFID technology for inventory sensitive to shrinkage. *International Journal of Production Economics, 112*(2), 521–531. doi:10.1016/j.ijpe.2007.05.005

Koroneos, G. (2004). FDA opens door to RFID packaging. *Pharmaceutical Technology, 28*(12), 17.

Lapide, L. (2004). RFID: What's in it for the forecaster? *The Journal of Business Forecasting Methods & Systems, 23*(2), 16–20.

Laran (2005). *A basic introduction to RFID and its use in the supply chain* [White paper]. Retrieved from http://admin.laranrfid.com/media/files/WhitePaperRFID.pdf

Law, A. M., & Kelton, W. D. (2000). *Simulation modelling and analysis* (3rd ed.). McGraw Hill Higher Education.

Lee, H., & Ozer, O. (2007). Unlocking the value of RFID. *Production and Operations Management, 16*(1), 40–64.

Michael, K., & McCathie, L. (2005). The pros and cons of RFID in supply chain management. In *Proceedings of the Fourth International Conference on Mobile Business, July 11 - 13, 2005, Sydney Australia, Session 11D.*

Ngai, E. W. T., Cheng, T. C. E., Lai, K., Chai, P. Y. F., Choi, Y. S., & Sin, R. K. Y. (2007). Development of an RFID-based Traceability System. *Production and Operations Management, 16*(5), 554–568.

Philips. (2004). Item-Level visibility in the pharmaceutical supply chain: A comparison of HF and UHF RFID technologies. Philips Semiconductors TAGSYS Texas Instruments Inc, July 2004 [White paper]. Retrieved from http://www.ti.com/rfid/docs/manuals/whtPapers/jointPharma.pdf

Prater, E., Frazier, G., & Reyes, P. (2005). Future impacts of RFID on e-supply chains in grocery retailing. *Supply Chain Management, 10*(2), 134–145. doi:10.1108/13598540510589205

Rieback, M. R., Crispo, B., & Tanenbaum, A. S. (2006). Is your cat infected with a computer virus? *Fourth Annual IEEE International Conference on Pervasive Computing and Communications, Pisa, Italy.*

Rivera, N., Mountain, R., Assumpcao, L., Williams, A. A., Cooper, A. B., Lewis, D. L., et al. (2008). *ASSIST - Automated System for Surgical Instrument and Sponge Tracking*. 2008 IEEE International Conference on RFID, Las Vegas, Nevada.

Sarma, S. (2004). The RFID advantage. *Express Computer Online Magazine*. Retrieved from http://www.expresscomputeronline.com/20041129/technology06.shtml

Sheffi, Y. (2004). RFID and the innovation cycle. *The International Journal of Logistics Management*, *15*(1), 1–10. doi:10.1108/09574090410700194

Sirico, L. (2005a, July 7). *The cost of compliance*. Issue #36, July 7, 2005. Retrieved from http://mrrfid.com/index.php?itemid=4

Sirico, L. (2005b, August 3). *The cost of compliance II: The Details*. Issue #40. Retrieved from http://mrrfid.com/index.php?itemid=50

Sliwa, C. (2003). RFID tunes into supply chains. *Computerworld*, *37*(33), 23–26.

Spekman, R. E., & Sweeney, P. J. II. (2006). RFID: from concept to implementation. *International Journal of Physical Distribution & Logistics Management*, *36*(10), 736–754. doi:10.1108/09600030610714571

Stevenson, W. J. (2002). *Operations management* (7th ed.). Irwin/McGraw-Hill.

Swamy, G., & Sarma, S. (2003, February 1). *Manufacturing cost simulations for low cost RFID systems*. [Auto-ID Center White Paper]. Massachusetts Institute of Technology. Retrieved from http://peumans-pc.stanford.edu/research/monolithic-low-cost-rfid-tags/hidden/mit-autoid-wh017.pdf

Terry, L. (2004). Supply chain software gets ready for RFID. *Supply Chain Systems Magazine*, *24*(6), 18–20.

Venables, M. (2005). RFID - Don't believe the hype. *Manufacturing Engineering*, *84*(5), 8–9. doi:10.1049/me:20050502

Vijayaraman, B. S., & Osyk, B. A. (2006). An empirical study of RFID in the warehousing industry. *International Journal of Logistics Management*, *7*(1), 6–20. doi:10.1108/09574090610663400

Vollmer, D. (2004). RFID from compliance to competitive advantage. *Red Prairie Presentation to Productivity, Dallas, TX*. Retrieved from http://www.fmi.org/events/productivity/2005/exh_ed/presentations/Vollmer.pdf

Vose, D. (2000). *Risk analysis* (2nd ed.). Wiley.

Wamba, S. F., Bedavid, Y., Lefebvre, L. A., & Lefebvre, E. (2006). RFID technology and the EPC network as enablers of mobile business: A case study in a retail supply chain. *International Journal of Networking and Virtual Organizations*, *3*(4), 450–462. doi:10.1504/IJNVO.2006.011872

White, A., Johnson, M., & Wilson, H. (2008). RFID in the supply chain: lessons from European early adopters. *International Journal of Physical Distribution & Logistics Management*, *38*(2), 88–107. doi:10.1108/09600030810861189

Wu, Y.-C. J., & Chen, J.-X. (2007). RFID application in a CVS distribution center in Taiwan: A simulation study. *International Journal of Manufacturing Technology and Management*, *10*(1), 121–135. doi:10.1504/IJMTM.2007.011405

APPENDIX – PROOFS FOR PROPOSITIONS AND CORROLLARIES

Proof of Proposition 1: Representing $\text{NPV}_{\text{no-RFID}} = \sum_{t=1}^{T} D_t m_t (1+i)^{-t}$ and based on equations (1) and (2), it can be shown that $NPV_{RFID} = NPV_{no\text{-}RFID} + \Delta_{RFID}$.

Proof of Proposition 2: Based on Proposition 1 we know that the RFID benefits can be quantified as Δ_{RFID}. Substituting $\sum_{t=1}^{T} D_t m_t (1+i)^{-t} = m \sum_{t=1}^{T} D_t (1+i)^{-t}$ and manipulation of Δ_{RFID} such that $\Delta_{RFID} \geq 0$ yields the desired result.

$$\frac{f_{D_{\max}} + \sum_{t=1}^{T} [D_t (1+l) p_{t,D_t} + s_{t,D_{\max}}](1+i)^{-t}}{[(1+o)(1+l)-1]\sum_{t=1}^{T} D_t (1+i)^{-t}} = \frac{f_{D_{\max}} + \sum_{t=1}^{T} s_{t,D_{\max}} (1+i)^{-t}}{[(1+o)(1+l)-1]\sum_{t=1}^{T} D_t (1+i)^{-t}} + \frac{(1+l)}{[(1+o)(1+l)-1]} p$$

Let $p_{\min} = \min_t p_{t,D_t}$ and $p_{\max} = \max_t p_{t,D_t}$, then based on the definition of averages (weighted averages to be more precise) $p_{\min} \leq p \leq p_{\max}$ needs to hold for any sales volume D_t.

First, we note that as $D_t \to 0$, we have $\dfrac{f_{D_{\max}} + \sum_{t=1}^{T} s_{t,D_{\max}} (1+i)^{-t}}{[(1+o)(1+l)-1]\sum_{t=1}^{T} D_t (1+i)^{-t}} \to \infty$ (becoming large since even at low

demand values there is initial and recurring fixed costs), thus $\dfrac{f_{D_{\max}} + \sum_{t=1}^{T} s_{t,D_{\max}} (1+i)^{-t}}{[(1+o)(1+l)-1]\sum_{t=1}^{T} D_t (1+i)^{-t}} \gg \dfrac{(1+l)}{[(1+o)(1+l)-1]} p$

holds, indicating that RFID fixed costs become more important than the RFID tag-prices as sales volume decreases. For the second part of the proof, we will assume that RFID initial fixed costs and annual fixed costs increase by h_f and $h_{s,t}$ units, respectively, for every δ increase in sales volume, thus having a form as follows: $f_{D_{\max}} = h_f D'$ and $s_{t,D_{\max}} = h_{s,t} D'$, where $D' = \left\lceil \dfrac{D_{\max}}{\delta} \right\rceil \delta$ with $\lceil \ \rceil$ denoting the roundup operation indicating that the fixed costs are step functions. Let also $D_{\min} = \min_t D_t$. Now we can see that

$$\frac{D'[h_f + \sum_{t=1}^{T} h_{s,t} (1+i)^{-t}]}{[(1+o)(1+l)-1]D_{\min}\sum_{t=1}^{T} (1+i)^{-t}} \geq \frac{f_{D_{\max}} + \sum_{t=1}^{T} s_{t,D_{\max}} (1+i)^{-t}}{[(1+o)(1+l)-1]\sum_{t=1}^{T} D_t (1+i)^{-t}}$$

$$\geq \frac{D'[h_f + \sum_{t=1}^{T} h_{s,t} (1+i)^{-t}]}{[(1+o)(1+l)-1]D'\sum_{t=1}^{T} (1+i)^{-t}} = \frac{[h_f + \sum_{t=1}^{T} h_{s,t} (1+i)^{-t}]}{[(1+o)(1+l)-1]\sum_{t=1}^{T} (1+i)^{-t}}$$

Next note that as $D_{\min} \to \infty$ we have $D' \to D_{\min}$, thus

$$\frac{D'[h_f + \sum\limits_{t=1}^{T} h_{s,t}(1+i)^{-t}]}{[(1+o)(1+l)-1]D_{min}\sum\limits_{t=1}^{T}(1+i)^{-t}} \rightarrow \frac{[h_f + \sum\limits_{t=1}^{T} h_{s,t}(1+i)^{-t}]}{[(1+o)(1+l)-1]\sum\limits_{t=1}^{T}(1+i)^{-t}}$$

needs to hold, which in turn implies that:

$$\frac{f_{D_{max}} + \sum\limits_{t=1}^{T} s_{t,D_{max}}(1+i)^{-t}}{[(1+o)(1+l)-1]\sum\limits_{t=1}^{T} D_t(1+i)^{-t}} \rightarrow \frac{[h_f + \sum\limits_{t=1}^{T} h_{s,t}(1+i)^{-t}]}{[(1+o)(1+l)-1]\sum\limits_{t=1}^{T}(1+i)^{-t}}$$

Note that as D_t changes from small to large (or 0 to ∞), the expression $\dfrac{f_{D_{max}} + \sum\limits_{t=1}^{T} s_{t,D_{max}}(1+i)^{-t}}{[(1+o)(1+l)-1]\sum\limits_{t=1}^{T} D_t(1+i)^{-t}}$ decreases from large to small indicating that the contribution of $\dfrac{(1+l)}{[(1+o)(1+l)-1]}p$ thus the RFID tag prices become more important as sales volume increases.

Proof of Proposition 3: Similar to the proof of Proposition 2, substituting $D_t = D$, $t = 1,\ldots,T$ and setting $\Delta_{RFID} \geq 0$ yields the desired result.

Proof of Corollary 2: The proof follows from Proposition 3. Since $RFC > TPP$ at $D=0$, when the relative growth of the RFC with respect to the sales volume is lower compared to the growth of the TPP ($\partial RFC/\partial D < \partial TPP/\partial D$) holds, RFC and TPP intersect at, at least one break-even point (see e.g. Stevenson, 2002, p. 187 for related examples) Also analyzing the denominator of equation (5) as $(1+o)(1+l)-1]m_t - (1+l)p_{t,D} > 0$ yields the UPTP ratio.

Proof of Proposition 4: Similar to the proof of Proposition 2, substituting $\sum\limits_{t=1}^{T} D_t p_{t,D_t}(1+i)^{-t} = p\sum\limits_{t=1}^{T} D_t(1+i)^{-t}$ and setting $\Delta_{RFID} \geq 0$ yields the desired result.

Proof of Corollary 3: p_{UPTP} is obtained by rearranging the inequality in equation (6). Note that p_{UPTP} only considers TPP and omits the RFID fixed costs. Let

$$\varepsilon = \frac{f_{D_{max}} + \sum\limits_{t=1}^{T} s_{t,D_{max}}(1+i)^{-t}}{(1+l)\sum\limits_{t=1}^{T} D_t(1+i)^{-t}}$$

denote the maintenance cost components of the right hand side of expression (7). It is easy to see from equation (7) that the desired result is obtained as follows:

$$p \leq \frac{-f_{D_{\max}} + \sum_{t=1}^{T} \left(D_t m_t [(1+o)(1+l)-1] - s_{t,D_{\max}} \right)(1+i)^{-t}}{(1+l)\sum_{t=1}^{T} D_t (1+i)^{-t}}$$

$$= \frac{\sum_{t=1}^{T} \left(D_t m_t [(1+o)(1+l)-1] \right)(1+i)^{-t}}{(1+l)\sum_{t=1}^{T} D_t (1+i)^{-t}} - \frac{f_{D_{\max}} + \sum_{t=1}^{T} s_{t,D_{\max}} (1+i)^{-t}}{(1+l)\sum_{t=1}^{T} D_t (1+i)^{-t}}$$

$$= m[1+o-(1+l)^{-1}] - \varepsilon = p_{UPTP} - \varepsilon \leq p_{UPTP}$$

Now, let's analyze ε further by letting $f_{D_{\max}} = h_f D'$ and $s_{t,D_{\max}} = h_{s,t} D'$ as in the proof of Corollary 1, then we have

$$\frac{D'[h_f + \sum_{t=1}^{T} h_{s,t}(1+i)^{-t}]}{(1+l)D_{\min}\sum_{t=1}^{T}(1+i)^{-t}} \geq \varepsilon = \frac{f_{D_{\max}} + \sum_{t=1}^{T} s_{t,D_{\max}}(1+i)^{-t}}{(1+l)\sum_{t=1}^{T} D_t(1+i)^{-t}} \geq \frac{D'[h_f + \sum_{t=1}^{T} h_{s,t}(1+i)^{-t}]}{(1+l)D'\sum_{t=1}^{T}(1+i)^{-t}} = \frac{h_f + \sum_{t=1}^{T} h_{s,t}(1+i)^{-t}}{(1+l)\sum_{t=1}^{T}(1+i)^{-t}}$$

Next, we see that as $D_t \to \infty$, we expect to have $D_{\min} \to \infty$ and $D' \to D_{\min}$, thus yielding

$$\frac{D'[h_f + \sum_{t=1}^{T} h_{s,t}(1+i)^{-t}]}{(1+l)D_{\min}\sum_{t=1}^{T}(1+i)^{-t}} \to \frac{h_f + \sum_{t=1}^{T} h_{s,t}(1+i)^{-t}}{(1+l)\sum_{t=1}^{T}(1+i)^{-t}}, \text{ which gives } \varepsilon \to \frac{h_f + \sum_{t=1}^{T} h_{s,t}(1+i)^{-t}}{(1+l)\sum_{t=1}^{T}(1+i)^{-t}}$$

Thus, we see that when sales volumes are increasing (or constant) ε (the difference between p_{UPTP} and p) becomes a constant. Furthermore, as m_t becomes large, since p_{UPTP} thus p increase ε becomes relatively insignificant thus p_{UPTP} becomes a relatively good estimator for p.

Proof of Proposition 5: The proof is similar to that of Proposition 1.

Proof of Proposition 6: If Ω_1 is a subset of *products justifying the RFID fixed costs then*

$$\sum_{t=1}^{T} \left(\sum_{k \in \Omega_1} D_{k,t} \{ m_{k,t}[(1+o_k)(1+l_k)-1] - (1+l_k)p_{k,t,D_{k,t}} \} \right)(1+i)^{-t} \geq f_{D_{\max}} + \sum_{t=1}^{T} s_{t,D_{\max}}(1+i)^{-t}$$

should hold. Thus, for the rest of the products that belong to Ω_2 *the following is a sufficient condition for justifying an RFID implementation*

$$\sum_{t=1}^{T} \left(\sum_{k \in \Omega_2} D_{k,t} \{ m_{k,t}[(1+o_k)(1+l_k)-1] - (1+l_k)p_{k,t,D_{k,t}} \} \right)(1+i)^{-t} \geq 0$$

which in turn indicates that

$$m_{k,t}[(1+o_k)(1+l_k)-1] - (1+l_k)p_{k,t,D_{k,t}} \geq 0, \quad \forall k,t, k \in \Omega_2, t = 1,\ldots,T$$

would be sufficient. Rearranging the terms we obtain the UPTP ratio as follows

$$\frac{m_{k,t}}{p_{k,t,D_{k,t}}} > \frac{(1+l_k)}{(1+o_k)(1+l_k)-1}, \quad \forall k,t, k \in \Omega_2, t = 1,...,T$$

Proof of Proposition 7: Based on Proposition 5 we see that

$$E_k = \sum_{t=1}^{T} D_{k,t}\{m_{k,t}[(1+o_k)(1+l_k)-1]] - (1+l_k)p_{k,t,D_{k,t}}\}(1+i)^{-t}, \ k = 1,...,K$$

and accordingly, $\Omega_{\min}$ can be identified as

$$\Omega_{\min} = \left\{ k \in \{[1],[2],...,[J]\} \mid \sum_{j=1}^{J-1} E_{[j]} < f_{D_{\max}} + \sum_{t=1}^{T} s_{t,D_{\max}}(1+i)^{-t} \le \sum_{j=1}^{J} E_{[j]} \right\}$$

Proof of Proposition 8: As shown in Proposition 1, Δ_{RFID} shows *the returns from an RFID implementation. Cost of an RFID implementation consists of the initial and annual fixed costs and RFID tag cost as given by* $f_{D_{\max}} + \sum_{t=1}^{T}\left(D_t(1+l)p_{t,D_t} + s_{t,D_{\max}}\right)(1+i)^{-t}.$

Proof of Proposition 9: Using Δ_{RFID} from Proposition 1, we can re-write ROI_{RFID} as

$$ROI_{RFID} = \frac{\sum_{t=1}^{T} D_t m_t[(1+o)(1+l)-1](1+i)^{-t}}{f_{D_{\max}} + \sum_{t=1}^{T}\left(D_t(1+l)p_{t,D_t} + s_{t,D_{\max}}\right)(1+i)^{-t}} - 1$$

Next, by taking the partial derivative with respect to D_j we see that

$$\frac{\partial ROI_{RFID}}{\partial D_j} = \frac{m_j[(1+o)(1+l)-1](1+i)^{-j}}{Cost} - \frac{\sum_{t=1}^{T} D_t m_t[(1+o)(1+l)-1](1+i)^{-t}}{Cost^2}\frac{\partial Cost}{\partial D_j}$$

where $Cost = f_{D_{\max}} + \sum_{t=1}^{T}\left(D_t(1+l)p_{t,D_t} + s_{t,D_{\max}}\right)(1+i)^{-t}.$

Letting $f_{D_{\max}} = h_f D'$ and $s_{t,D_{\max}} = h_s D'$ as in the proof of Corollary 1, assuming that $\frac{\partial p_{j,D_j}}{\partial D_j} \to 0$ (which basically states that after a certain purchase volume the vendor cannot provide any more quantity discounts on RFID tags), and defining $p_{\min}$ as the minimum possible tag price as sales volumes increase, we see that as $D_j \to \infty$, $\frac{\partial Cost}{\partial D_j}$ does not grow ($\frac{\partial Cost}{\partial D_j} \to (1+l)p_{\min}$ since RFID fixed costs are step functions, indicating constancy within a certain sales volume interval). From here, we see that as the sales volumes increase, the denominators of all expressions defining $\frac{\partial ROI_{RFID}}{\partial D_j}$ grow faster than the numerators, therefore, as $D_j \to \infty$, the relationship $\lim_{D_j \to \infty} \frac{\partial ROI_{RFID}}{\partial D_j} = 0$ should hold.

Chapter 4
Collecting Consumer Behavior Data with WLAN

Patrik Skogster
Rovaniemi University of Applied Sciences, Finland

Varpu Uotila
Turku School of Economics, Finland

ABSTRACT

Knowing consumers' shopping paths is an essential part of successful retailing. Good space management requires accurate data about consumer behavior. Traditionally, these data have been collected through, for example, panel interviews, camera tracking, and in-store observation. Their nature is more or less subjective. Modern technology makes it possible to use more objective methods, such as wireless local area network (WLAN) and radio frequency identification (RFID). In this article we examine the possibilities WLAN provides information systems studies. The empirical data is collected from a large DIY (do-it-yourself) store. The results show that WLAN has great potential for accurate and objective data collection processes and modeling data in retailing.

INTRODUCTION

Most of the customer's in-store behavior is made in an unconscious state. Because of this, the customers are afterward unable to explain their purchase decisions in more detail. Most of the purchase decisions are made inside a store. The challenge of the retail business is to create an environment where the customer has a bilateral relation with the store, to optimize the customer's use of time, and to offer a buying experience that the consumer wants to renew later (Soars, 2003). The pleasure produced by the store environment is a significant reason for the extra time used by the consumer inside the store. In fact, in these occasions consumers spend more money than intended (Donovan, Rossiter, Marcoolyn, & Nesdale, 1994).

The purchasing behavior of a customer inside the store has been studied for several dozens of years. Various studies have been made on unplanned buying, store and product types, the demographic features of the consumer profiles, and the effect of the internal campaigns of the store. Also, the data-processing and decision-making processes, which take place in the store, have been researched. For example, Park, Iyer, and Smith (1989) studied how the time customer spends and his/her earlier knowledge of the store can affect the making of unplanned purchases. These can appear as failure in the making of planned purchases and changes in other purchasing behavior.

Consumers' buying behavior has been studied with in-store videos and interviews (Underhill, 1999). However, according to Larson, Bradlow, and Fader (2005), the results of these studies are limited to general recommendations, which only increase the convenience of the customers. Only a few studies, which contain really large data sets, have been conducted on the customers' complete shopping paths so far. This has not been possible earlier with traditional data collecting methods (Larson et al.; Sorensen, 2003).

From the retailers' point of view, space management is a significant factor in a successful store (Soars, 2003). A good store is one where the largest possible amount of products is in the sight of the largest possible amount of customers as long as possible. Also, the placement of the products must be realistic concerning logistic issues. As Underhill (1999) states, a good store is the kind where the products are placed along the customers' routes and sight in a way that makes the customer consider buying. Still, how can the retailer know where their customers really walk and spend their time?

The purpose of this study is to explore how information about customer traffic can be collected from a large DIY (do-it-yourself) store with the help of modern technology and how the collected data can be analyzed. The main focus is on collecting customer traffic data with the help of WLAN (wireless local area network) and analyz-

ing them with different models using geographical information systems (GIS). A similar study has not been done before within the DIY context and Scandinavian service industry. Therefore, this study contributes to different practical solutions but also to theoretical discussion.

The empirical data of the study have been collected in a large, modern DIY unit located in Scandinavia. The store belongs to a large DIY chain. The study has been limited to concern the store in question and its customers in August 2006.

LITERATURE REVIEW

The consumer buying behavior process inside the store has been studied for several dozens of years. There have been attempts to research it in many different ways. For example, Köhne, Totz, and Wehmeyer (2005) use conjoint analysis, a classical technique, to identify consumer preferences in multi-attribute decision making for designing a new context in sensitive services. They evaluate consumer behavior by using a fictitious example of location-based services in a touristic setting.

In this article, four different data collecting methods are briefly discussed: WLAN, radio frequency identification (RFID), camera tracking, and in-store observation. These methods can also be combined. Another possible technique for collecting data on consumer behavior in the store is interviewing the customers as they leave. This kind of memory-based technique can lead to high inaccuracy in the results. However, this technique makes it possible to collect a very inclusive picture of the customers' shopping experience (Phillips & Bradshaw, 1991). This collecting method is not studied in this article as it clearly deviates from the other methods. Also, Bluetooth technology can be mentioned as a method for collecting consumer behavior data.

People and machines can be tracked with wireless local area networks without any additional devices and by using the already existing wireless network. That is why the installing of this tracking system in the desired outdoor or indoor space can be very fast. The WLAN tracking system consists of the network and the tags, which are being tracked. This technology has been used among others in health care centers and both mine and tunnel construction (Martikainen, 2006).

RFID is a common name for technologies that use radio waves to identify individual products. RFID consists of a reader and tags. The tag contains a microchip and an antenna (Jones, Clarke-Hill, Shears, Comfort, & Hillier, 2004). RFID is thought of as the successor of the bar code because with RFID technology, individual products can be identified instead of product categories (Spekman & Sweeney, 2006). In addition to retail warehouses, RFID technology is used in the health care sector, libraries, and the travel sector to follow luggage (Juban & Wyld, 2004). RFID has also been used to track the shopping paths of customers in a store. Sorensen (2003) researched over 200,000 shopping paths in a supermarket. According to him, the number of the studied shopping paths in earlier studies has been a few hundred at its largest. He estimates being the first who has studied tens of thousands shopping paths in detail. In Sorensen's research, the customers' shopping trolley or basket was tracked with a small tag placed at the bottom of it. Also, Larson et al. (2005) used the RFID technology in their study. They studied the customer routes in an American grocery market. An RFID tag had been placed at the bottom of every shopping trolley and was located at intervals of 5 seconds. RFID readers had been placed throughout the store. In their study, 27,000 shopping paths were collected and every third route was analyzed. In the study, attention was not paid to the customer's actual purchases or to different sales tactics of the store. Larson et al. did valuable work, especially on changing the routes of different lengths to a comparable format. They analyzed the routes by a grouping algorithm developed by them. It made the handling of the large amount of spatial information possible quantitatively. The customer routes varied between 2 minutes and 2 hours. One customer could be located as many as 1,500 times.

By tracking the customer with a camera, the shopping paths can be studied with fair easiness (Dodd, Clarke, and Kirkup, 1998). With this information, the product categories and the customer rotation can be planned so that they are as optimal as possible for the consumer. At the same time, it can also be found out how long the customer stays in the store and which offers or other messages in the store he or she responds to. Phillips and Bradshaw (1991) wrote how in-store customer behavior has been mainly studied using manual recording techniques. With this technique, the customer can be tracked around a store. Also, product handling, verbal contact with the store staff, and display viewing can be added to the study. It is also almost impossible to get an inclusive picture of customer behavior throughout the whole store. However, the labor intensiveness makes the technique very time consuming and difficult to obtain large sample sizes.

In a standard camera tracking survey, the store is first inspected and the camera locations are selected. Trial photographs are taken to check each location. The optimum number of cameras is a compromise between having the smallest possible amount of cameras to minimize the amount of time spent analyzing the film and having enough cameras for the adequate coverage of the store. Each camera takes one photograph every minute. Analyzing the film is the most labor-intensive part in the camera tracking study (e.g., Kirkup & Carrigan, 2000; Newman, Yu, & Oulton, 2002).

It is possible to observe and to follow the customers also from inside the store while they are shopping. It is very uncommon that the customer notices that he or she is being watched. A template of the store layout, on which all entrance and exit areas, tills, gondolas, and special product displays have been marked, can be used in the observation and tracking. In addition, it is possible to

Table 1. Effects on the quality of the data when using different collecting methods

	subject of data collection	way of data collection
WLAN/RFID	can affect	does not affect
camera tracking	does not affect	can affect
in-store observation	does not affect unless the consumer notices the observer	can affect

add the specific product categories that are being researched. When the shopper enters the store, his or her shopping path is marked on an individual template to show where the customer stopped to look, to browse, or to purchase and so on. Also, the day of the week, time of the day, and length of the time spent in the store are all recorded with observable characteristics of the customer. In addition, time spent at a specific location or display in the store can be recorded. The individual tracking forms can be processed for evaluations by computer (M. Johnson, 1999).

The effects on the quality of the data set when using different collecting methods have been collected in Table 1. In Tables 1 and 2, WLAN and RFID are viewed as one collecting method because they have very similar features but clearly deviate from camera tracking and in-store observation.

When a local area network or RFID is used, the customer can behave abnormally because he or she knows that his or her route is being tracked. However, the collecting of the data set is performed by a technical device, which makes the collecting process itself objective. When camera surveillance is used, the customer does not know that he or she is being followed, but when the collected data are recorded from filmstrip to the computer, there is a possibility for researcher interpretation. For in-store observation, the data are most vulnerable. The customer can notice that he or she is being followed. This can lead to changes in behavior. Also, the observations made by the person conducting the collection are subjective.

The different collecting methods are best suitable in different situations. Determining the best collecting method depends on the objectives of the study in question. Features of the four different data collecting methods have been collected in Table 2.

Camera tracking and observation are best suitable when studying detailed consumer behavior. With these methods it is, for example, possible to find out which products the customer considers, between which choices he or she chooses from, which product he or she finally takes, and if he or she has interaction with the store staff. The disadvantage of both methods is the labor intensiveness, which causes large data sets quite impossible to collect. Also accurate shopping paths and customer traffic information is hard to obtain. Camera tracking and in-store observation are more suitable for tracking customer traffic in a small store and observing consumer shopping behavior in detail.

The sample size depends on the objectives of the study: The more specific the information that is wanted, the larger the sample size should be (Uusitalo, 1991). For a large sample size, the best data collecting method is either RFID or WLAN. Because of the technology, both of them make the collecting of large data sets possible. However, it is not possible to collect data concerning other behavior features besides the shopping paths, and technical disturbance and problems can occur.

When using WLAN and RFID, the tag can be attached to the shopping cart or basket or be given to the customer to carry. When the tag is being given to the customer, a very large sample size is more difficult to reach because of the labor intensiveness. When the tag is attached to the cart

Table 2. Features of different data collecting methods

	advantages	disadvantages
WLAN/RFID	– possibility to track the customer, shopping cart, or basket very accurately – possibility for a very large data set – collecting data requires very little or no workforce	– memory limitations when the collected data set is very large – possible technical disturbance and problems before and during the data collection – possible labor intensity when setting up the system – setting up the system can be expensive but the actual collecting of the data is not
camera tracking	– possible to study also other customer behavior features besides the shopping paths – an easy way to get a mediocre picture of the customer traffic	– labor intensive – large data sets almost impossible to collect and to analyze – accurate shopping paths almost impossible to find out especially in large stores
in-store observation	– possibility to study consumer behavior in detail	– labor intensive – large data sets almost impossible to collect and to analyze

or basket, no extra staff is needed and then very large sample sizes are possible. The placement of the tag affects what is measured in the study. When the tag is carried in the cart or basket, the whole path of the customer is not tracked. Only a quite good picture is obtained because the customer can leave the cart or basket at times when getting a product. When the customer carries the tag, a very precise picture of the customer's shopping path is obtained. Then the only limitation to the accuracy of the path is the location accuracy. The DIY store customer often moves in the store without a shopping cart or basket. If the tag would be attached to the carts and baskets, it might limit the number of the potential participants in the study.

WLAN and RFID are very similar as data collecting methods but quite dissimilar in their technical qualities. RFID is an identifying technology and not a location technology (Schwartz, 2004). WLAN as a data collecting system is easy to set up because the already existing wireless network can be used. When using RFID, readers must be put in the store as densely as possible for the tag to be recognized. For example, if the tag is to be recognized within a 2-meter radius, then the readers should be placed every two meters.

This is why RFID as a location technology is difficult to move from one place to another. It is more suitable to a store, where customers' shopping paths are monitored on a long-term. Then the system can be set up there permanently or at least for a long time.

In the literature there has also been discussion on the limitations of these consumer follow-ups. Virtual reality or videotape methods (e.g., Hui & Bateson, 1991) using conjoint choice experiments could manipulate environmental variables to determine the magnitude of the effects that changing tenants and environments have on consumer responses. Also, as Wakefield and Baker (1998) conclude, including two or more stores with different environmental aspects and/or a variety of characteristics would overcome the concern of limited site research.

The use of various spatiotemporal data (data with time and location elements) and information usually greatly improves decision making in many different fields (Christakos, Bogaert, & Serre, 2003). Examples can be found in Meeks and Dasgupta (2004). However, when using spatial and temporal information to improve decision making, attention must be paid to uncertainty and sensitivity issues (Crosetto & Tarantola, 2001).

Because the spatial data fusion process is by its origins a process that produces data assimilations, the challenges it is facing are largely related to the data handling process. Data integration processes, synchronous sampling, and common measurement standards are developed to optimize the consumer behavior data-fusion performance. This includes increasing both the data management process and data collection efficiency (e.g., Fischer & Ostwald, 2001; Rafanelli, 2003).

The collection of data and their availability can also be seen as a strategic matter. Roberts, Jones, and Frohling (2005) highlight the importance of making sense of networks that comprise many nodes and are animated by flows of resources and knowledge. The transfer of managerial practices and knowledge is essential to the functionality of these networks and resources. A survey made by Vanderhaegen and Muro (2005) reveals that almost all of the organizations (90%) making use of spatial data "experience problems with the availability, quality and use of spatial data." In general, the organizations using the widest range of data types experienced the greatest difficulties in using the data.

The quality of the spatial data is still only one of the many factors that must be taken into consideration within spatial data fusion. Clearly, the results of any spatial data fusion are only as good as the data on which it is based (R. G. Johnson, 2001). One approach to improve data quality is the imposition of constraints upon data entered into the database (Cockcroft, 1997). The proposal is that "better decisions can be made by accounting risks due to errors in spatial data" (Van Oort & Bregt, 2005).

METHODOLOGY

In this study, the data were collected with the help of WLAN. The features of WLAN as a data collection method are the tracking system's easy installation in a large store, the possibility

of collecting large data sets, the objectivity of the collecting method, the possibility to track customers with less than 1-meter accuracy, and the portability of the tracking system to other stores in the chain. There is also the possibility of disturbance and technical problems. WLAN is probably the newest technology used in tracking customers. It was chosen because it has some major advantages compared to other tracking methods and provides a valuable and useful tool for stores in retail.

The data set was collected by locating a tag carried by the shopping customer with the help of the wireless local area network. The data was collected in a modern DIY store in Scandinavia. The store of this study has more than 20 departments. There are four service points and an information desk in the store. There is also a small cafeteria located in connection with the main entrance. The store has a total of 5,100 square meters of selling space.

There were 30 tags in use in August 2006 during a time period of 2 weeks. Data were collected from 4 to 6 hours per day. The customer routes were located every day with variance between mornings and evenings so that after the collecting period, tracked shopping paths could be found from nearly all opening hours from different days of the week. The data were collected neither during the first opening hour of the morning nor during the last closing hour of the evening. The amount of customers during these times was so small that the results would not have been reliable. The sample size of the study was 866 (Table 3). An average of 72 shopping paths was located during 1 day. The store was open on weekdays from 7:00 in the morning to 8:00 in the evening. On Saturdays, the store was open from 9:00 a.m. to 3:00 p.m. The number of the tracked shopping paths per day varied between 60 and 93.

A scanning circuit located the tag at intervals of 10 seconds. The customer got the tag immediately in the entrance area of the shop. The customer was given instructions to keep the tag with him

Table 3. Located routes

Time		Week 1						Week 2						Σ
		Th	Fr	Sa	Mo	Tu	We	Th	Fr	Sa	Mo	Tu	We	
a.m.	8–9	0	10	0	0	5	0	11	0	0	10	0	5	41
	9–10	0	11	13	0	10	0	13	0	15	14	0	12	88
	10–11	0	11	16	0	15	0	17	0	17	18	0	22	116
	11–12	0	7	16	0	19	0	9	0	20	11	0	16	98
p.m.	0–1	0	11	18	0	12	0	17	0	9	8	0	15	90
	1–2	0	10	14	0	7	4	7	11	14	8	0	0	75
	2–3	0	0	5	10	0	14	0	16	1	0	14	0	60
	3–4	6	0	0	14	0	18	0	23	0	0	18	0	79
	4–5	20	0	0	15	0	9	0	15	0	0	14	0	73
	5–6	18	0	0	15	0	13	0	10	0	0	18	0	74
	6–7	25	0	0	10	0	11	0	18	0	0	8	0	72
	Σ	69	60	82	64	68	69	74	93	76	69	72	70	866

or her during the whole shopping trip and to give it to the nearest cash desk when leaving the store. If there were more people in the group, the same person had to carry the tag all the time. When the customer was given the tag, the identification number of the tag, the time, the gender and age of the customer, and the size of the group were recorded.

The customer was not asked directly any information; the figures are estimates of the recorder. The age was approximated in one of the four different groups. These groups were 18 to 30 years, 30 to 45 years, 45 to 60 years, and over 60 years. Seventy percent of the customers were men and thirty percent were women. Over half of the customers shopped alone, one third with one other person, and the rest in a bigger group. Forty percent of the customers were approximated being between 30 and 45 years old. About one third was between 45 and 60 years, and the rest were over 60 years or between 18 and 30 years old. The proportions of different types of customers varied a little depending on the time of the day and the day of the week.

The majority of the customers who participated in the study were men. In the total sample there were slightly over 30% of women and nearly 70% of men. The customers' age and gender share can be seen in Figure 1. The percentages in the different classes of pillars represent a relative share of the whole sample of the study.

The majority of the customers were between 30 and 45 years old. There were 40% of them. Less than one third of the customers were 45 to 60 years old. There were almost as much customers in the 18- to 30-year group than in the over-60-year group. Both represent approximately one eighth of the total population. The male customers' relative share is the biggest in the over-60-year-old customer group. However, there were a majority of male customers in all the age groups. The customers' ages are subjective estimates of the recorder. The majority of the customers who participated in the study were shopping alone. There were more than half of them. The shares of groups of different sizes of the total population can be seen in Figure 2.

About one third of the customers were shopping with one other person and 11% of the customers

Figure 1. Gender and age of the participants

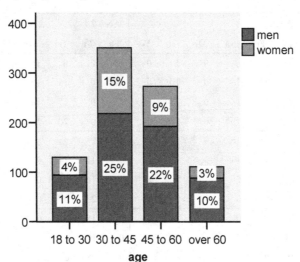

Figure 2. The size of groups

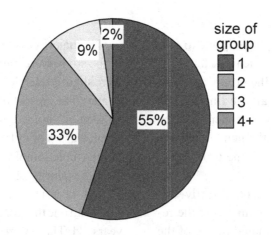

were shopping in groups of three or more people. There were no major variations in the group sizes during different times. Lone shoppers formed the majority at all times. The largest shares of lone shoppers were found on the weekdays in the mornings (between 8 a.m. and noon). A typical customer in this study was 30 to 45 years old, male, and shopping alone.

Taking the tag was totally voluntary. By taking the tag, the customer gave permission to track his or her shopping paths in the store. The majority of the customers to whom the tag was offered took it. On average, every fifth customer denied.

The number of customers to whom the tag was offered, the number of customers who refused, and their share can be seen in Table 4.

The number of the collected routes was compared with the amount of the cash transactions of the time in question (Table 5). The cash transactions describe the number of the groups better than the total amount of customers, but the tags were also distributed to groups instead of individual customers. It was approximated that on average, a fifth of the customers' routes were located. During the busiest days, more than 30% of the shopping

Table 4. Proportion of refusals

Time	Week 1						Week 2						
	Th	Fr	Sa	Mo	Tu	We	Th	Fr	Sa	Mo	Tu	We	Σ
Were offered the detector	79	79	107	80	85	90	99	110	100	88	82	83	1 082
Refused	10	19	25	16	17	21	25	17	24	19	10	13	216
Proportion of refusals (%)	12,7	24,1	23,4	20,0	20,0	23,3	25,3	15,5	24,0	21,6	12,2	15,7	20,0

Table 5. Proportion of cash transactions

Time	Week 1						Week 2					
	Th	Fr	Sa	Mo	Tu	We	Th	Fr	Sa	Mo	Tu	We
Proportion (%)	33	19	15	18	22	23	27	24	16	26	25	31

paths were tracked, and about 15% were tracked during the quietest days.

The numbers are only suggestive because they have been calculated from the same time period that the customers were given tags. In other words, the customers still had tags when the cash transactions were not being counted anymore. These numbers do not include the groups, which did not make purchases.

ANALYSIS

The whole sample of the study was analyzed by modeling with the help of spreadsheets (Microsoft Excel), statistical software (SPSS), and GIS software (MapInfo and ArcInfo). The GIS software was used especially in the illustrating process. The models represented here concentrate on studying the customer traffic as a whole instead of explaining individual shopping paths.

In the first model, all the locations are marked on the base plan of the store as pixels. This way, detailed data can be obtained about which parts of the store the customers visited. The location accuracy is at its best within a half a meter. The weakness of this pixel model is the fact that from the map it cannot be seen if there have been more locations in one pixel. The amount of the loca-

tions in smaller aisles especially cannot be easily verified from this kind of figure.

In the second model, the large square model, the base plan of the store is divided into 21 squares in the horizontal direction and into 11 squares in the vertical direction. Consequently, 219 different square locations were formed on the base plan; 182 of these squares included tracked customer locations. The rest of the 37 squares are located in areas that were inaccessible to the customers, in the cafeteria, or near the entrance doors. The area of one square is about 25 square meters in reality. The disadvantage of this model is the large size of the squares. This is why the same base plan has been added with the location points from the pixel model. Combining the large squares and the exact customer traffic locations, the whole figure gives a better overview of the customer traffic. The clear advantage of this model is that from the base plan, it is easy to see where the customers spend their time in the store.

The third and fourth models are similar to the large square model. In these models, the base plan is also divided into squares but the squares are smaller than in the second model. In the medium square model, the base plan of the store is divided into 42 squares in the horizontal direction and 23 squares in the vertical direction. Altogether, 906 squares are formed on the base plan from

Figure 3. Pixel model

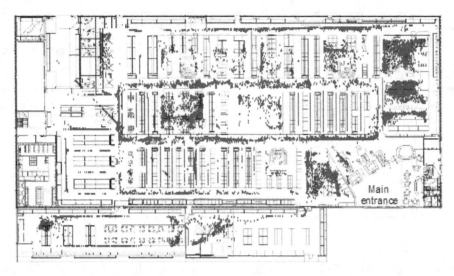

Figure 4. Large square model

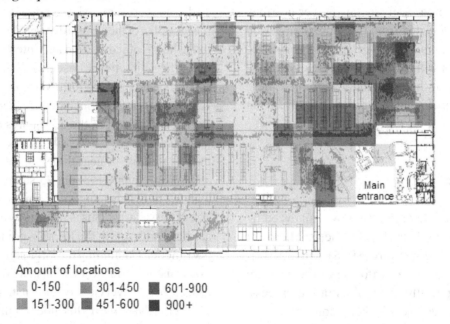

Amount of locations
▢ 0-150	▣ 301-450	▨ 601-900
▨ 151-300	▨ 451-600	▪ 900+

which 520 squares include tracked locations. The amount of squares without tracked locations is fairly large because, for example, large gondolas and other store furniture take up a whole square, making it inaccessible to the customers. The area of one square of the third model is approximately 6 square meters in reality. In the fourth model, the small square model, the used squares are the smallest. In the model, the base plan of the store is divided into 105 squares in the horizontal direction and 56 squares in the vertical direction, forming over 5,000 squares on the base plan. One square equals about 1 square meter in reality. Although the information provided by the picture is more accurate than in the second or third model, the picture seems to be, in a way, chaotic.

Figure 5. Medium square model

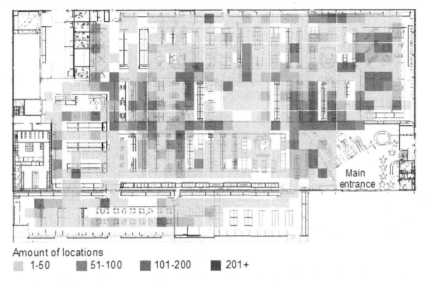

Amount of locations
1-50   51-100   101-200   201+

Figure 6. Small square model

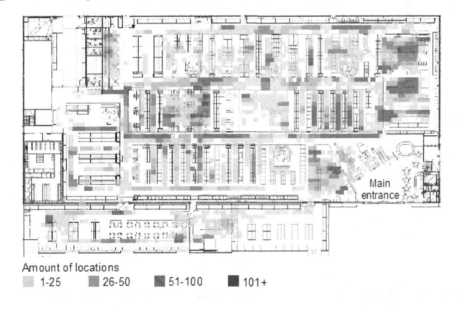

Amount of locations
1-25   26-50   51-100   101+

In Figures 7, 8, and 9, it can be seen how at the different times of day and on different weekdays the consumer behavior is not significantly different.

CONCLUSION AND DISCUSSION

The retailing industry needs objective information about consumer behavior. The cornerstone of the strategic planning processes are to give the right services and products in the right place at the right time. An excellent picture of customer traffic can be obtained when collecting data with

Figure 7. Example of consumer routes on Tuesday morning

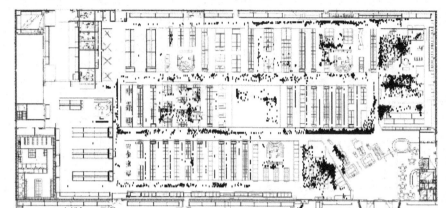

Figure 8. Example of consumer routes on Friday afternoon

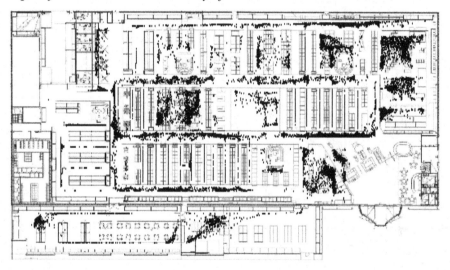

wireless local area networks and analyzing them with spreadsheets and geographical information systems. As seen in this study, it is possible to analyze the customer traffic data sets in several different ways.

The purpose of this article was to examine how information about customer traffic can be collected from a large DIY store with the help of modern technology and how the collected data can be analyzed. Consumer behavior research methods and processes must be capable of accept-

ing wide ranges of data types, accommodating natural-language extracted text reports, historical data, and various types of spatial information (maps, charts, images). Therefore, the processes must have learning abilities. These processes must develop adaptive and learning properties, using the operating process to add to the knowledge base while exhibiting sensitivity to unexpected or too-good-to-be-true situations that may indicate countermeasures or deceptive activities. The performance of the processes needs to be

Figure 9. Example of consumer routes on Saturday

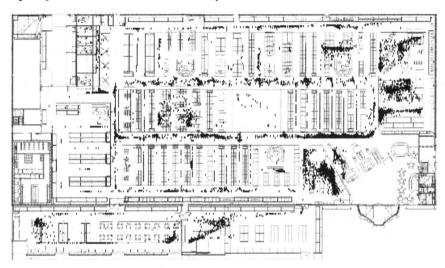

improved exponentially. When the amount of processed data increases and analysis becomes more complicated, efficient and linked data structures are required to handle the wide variety of data. Data volumes for global and even regional spatial databases will be measured in millions of terabits, and short access times are demanded for even broad searches. In this article, WLAN technology provided the technological platform. As a result, this technology provided an enormous amount of valuable data. The continued handling of this data was done mainly by GIS tools. The results can therefore be shown in several visual formats and more specific analysis can be done. Actually, only the researcher's imagination can limit further analysis. The data and tools do not create barriers.

When different consumer data collecting methods are used, the quality of the data can weaken in two different ways. When collecting the data, the customers may alter their behavior if they know that they are being tracked. The second possible weakness is caused by the data collector. Personal beliefs and attitudes can affect the observations. In other words, the observations are subjective.

The subjectivity can appear when observations are collected or when they are interpreted. Different models are best suited in different situations since they have their own advantages and disadvantages. By using only the pixel model, wrong conclusions can be drawn from the customer traffic. On the other hand, the weakness of the large square model is the fact that the used squares have a rather big size. Together, the pixel and the large square models give a good overview of the customer traffic. The medium square model and the small square model give more exact information about the customer traffic, but for an overview they are somewhat vague. They are more suitable when analyzing the different departments or sections of the store.

The results of this study can be applied to practical issues in many ways. First, it helps to allocate the right products near the routes that consumers prefer. Second, personnel workload can be rationalized with the help of the systems described. When the actual consumer route information is accompanied with data about the time of the day, a retailer can divide the available personnel resources to the most appropriate service desks during the day and the week. The practical implications can be applied directly to consumer behavior analysis, store management, and, for example, in the utilization of consumer hot spots—places that gather consumers' interest.

Theoretical implications are concentrated on the technology and methodology comparison. This article gives implications on the consumer behavior theories. The methodology tests theories in practice with a large sample size.

As with any single study, there are still a number of limitations in this article. First, caution must be used in extending the results of this research to other settings. While the research area was a single DIY store that was similar to many large DIY stores across Scandinavia in the store assortment, it must be remembered that all locations and stores are unique. There are no two identical surroundings and consumer profiles.

There may also have been factors influencing the tenant values that were not captured in the data, such as good or bad relationships with neighboring shops. Third, there might have been a "grass is greener" effect, meaning that shopping is more enjoyable outside the consumers' customary stores. When an individual consumer within a store context is away from home and enjoying the novelty of another store, it may make the consumer act out of the ordinary. In this study, the locations of the customers' permanent residences were not fully studied. In the area are numerous summer cottages and also a major highway passes the store. Therefore, it can be supposed that nonlocals performed a significant amount of the examined shopping paths.

It is important to note the limitations inherent in a limited site study. Because the differences in shopping location alternatives (i.e., by including surveys and/or follow-ups in several stores in the study) were not directly assessed, it is tenuous to conclude that consumer perceptions were not generalized. Given this limitation, future research examining the effect of changes on affective and behavioral responses should more precisely incorporate consumer behavior differences. For example, before and after studies (e.g., Downs & Haynes, 1984) could measure the impact of renovations and tenant additions.

Because the research area analyzing the consumer's behavior with modern technology is a very new field of research, there is only a small amount of previous research done and the relevant amount of source material is very limited. For example, a similar study has not been done before within the DIY context. Source material about processing the customer traffic data was especially almost impossible to find. Studies that have been made in the field of retail business have been clearly emphasized in the perishables business, but there is only a limited amount of material concerning the DIY trade. Therefore, this study gives new methodological viewpoints. This is also the main limitation of this study. More empirical data and analyses are definitely needed in order to achieve more reliability and validity.

Because in a DIY store a similar study has not been carried out earlier, very many technical problems had to be solved. The sample size of the study is so big that sufficient comprehensiveness has been reached to guarantee the validity and reliability of the study. Validity can be defined as the ability of a study to reflect the true state of affairs. In this study the shopping paths do not have large variance on different days of the week and times of the day. Therefore, the internal validity of this study is acceptable. Since the data were collected from only one DIY store, it is quite clear that the external validity needs to be enhanced through a comparative study in other representative DIY units.

The research design (quantitative, descriptive) and methodology (empirical follow-up, sampling, and literature review) allowed for neither comparisons between various research groups under controlled conditions, nor a longitudinal study. The study was conducted only during a 2-week period. The outcomes are almost entirely based on hard evidence rather than the perception of participants, for example, norm- or criterion-referenced tests.

Outcomes reported here, for example, changes in behavior, depend on narrow information about consumer masses in a certain geographical area (visitors in a certain DIY store) rather than on a representative sample providing deep knowledge of the behavior of certain consumers in the store. However, the amount of collected data gives justification to the results.

The technology used can also give an impact on the reliability and validity of the results. Arumugam, Doufexi, Nix, and Fletcher (2003) report the impact of Bluetooth interference on the WLAN system and vice versa. Modern mobile phones usually have Bluetooth capability, and their impact on the results of this study has not been measured.

In this study, attention has been paid to reliability during the whole research process. In the store, there are only a few areas in which there are no locations. These areas are the cash desk area and the outer corner on the side of the main entrance in the outer shop store. The missing locations can possibly be explained by the fact that the local area network has not covered the area in question. The second alternative to the missing locations is the fact that there have continuously been many active tags simultaneously side by side in the area. This has possibly caused disturbance to the location system. Therefore, attention should be paid also to technological issues. Larson et al. (2005) have developed a research frame and performed a study very similar to this one. The results of their study were generalized. Also in this study external validity comes true. In this study the sample size is big; this marks off the random results. Thanks to random sampling, the data of the study present the target population well. The data collecting method can be considered objective and the location exactness of the data collecting method sufficient for reliable information. Thus, it can be supposed that the results of the study are similar when repeated. In other words, the study can be considered as rather reliable.

REFERENCES

Arumugam, A. K., Doufexi, A., Nix, A. R., & Fletcher, P. N. (2003). An investigation of the coexistence of 802.11g WLAN and high data rate Bluetooth enabled consumer electronic devices in indoor home and office environments. *IEEE Transactions on Consumer Electronics, 49*(3), 587-596.

Christakos, G., Bogaert, P., & Serre, M. (2002). *Temporal GIS: Advanced functions for field-based applications.* Berlin, Germany: Springer.

Cockcroft, S. (1997). A taxonomy of spatial data integrity Constraints. *GeoInformatica, 1*(4), 327-343.

Crosetto, M., & Tarantola, S. (2001). Uncertainty and sensitivity analysis: Tools for GIS-based model implementation. *International Journal of Geographical Information Science, 15*(5), 415-437.

Dodd, C. A., Clarke, I., & Kirkup, M. H. (1998). Camera observations of customer behavior in fashion retailing: Methodological propositions. *International Journal of Retail & Distribution Management, 26*(8), 311-317.

Donovan, R. J., Rossiter, J. R., Marcoolyn, G., & Nesdale, A. (1994). Store atmosphere and purchasing behavior. *Journal of Retailing, 70*(3), 283-294.

Downs, P. E., & Haynes, J. B. (1984). Examining retail image before and after a repositioning strategy. *Journal of the Academy of Marketing Science, 12*, 1-24.

Fischer, G., & Ostwald, J. (2001). Knowledge management: Problems, promises, realities, and challenges. *IEEE Intelligent Systems, 16*(1), 60-72.

Ganesh, J. (2004). Managing customer preferences in a multi-channel environment using Web services. *International Journal of Retail & Distribution Management, 32*(2/3), 140-146.

Hui, M. K., & Bateson, J. E. (1991). Perceived control and consumer choice on the service experience. *Journal of Consumer Research, 18,* 174-185.

Johnson, M. (1999). From understanding consumer behavior to testing category strategies. *Journal of the Market Research Society, 41*(3), 259-288.

Johnson, R. G. (2001). *United States Imagery and Geospatial Information Service geospatial transition plan.* Bethesda, MD: National Imagery and Mapping Agency.

Jones, P., Clarke-Hill, C., Shears, P., Comfort, D., & Hillier, D. (2004). Radio frequency identification in the UK: Opportunities and challenges. *International Journal of Retail & Distribution Management, 32*(3), 164-171.

Juban, R. L., & Wyld, D. C. (2004). Would you like chips with that? Consumer perspectives of RFID. *Management Research News, 27*(11/12), 29-44.

Kirkup, M., & Carrigan, M. (2000). Video surveillance research in retailing: Ethical issues. *International Journal of Retail & Distribution Management, 28*(11), 470-480.

Köhne, F., Totz, C., & Wehmeyer, K. (2005). Consumer preferences for location-based service attributes: A conjoint analysis. *International Journal of Management and Decision Making, 6*(1), 16-32.

Larson, J. S., Bradlow, E. T., & Fader, P. S. (2005). An exploratory look at supermarket shopping paths. *International Journal of Research in Marketing, 22*(4), 395-414.

Martikainen, O. E. (2006). Complementarities creating substitutes: Possible paths towards 3G, WLAN/WiMAX and ad hoc networks. *Info, 8*(4), 21-32.

Meeks, W. L., & Dasgupta, S. (2004). Geospatial information utility: An estimation of the relevance of geospatial information to users. *Decision Support Systems, 38*(1), 47-63.

Newman, A. J., Yu, D. K. C., & Oulton, D. P. (2002). New insights into retail space and format planning from customer-tracking data. *Journal of Retailing and Consumer Services, 9,* 253-258.

Park, C. W., Iyer, E. S., & Smith, D. C. (1989). The effects of situational factors on in-store grocery shopping behavior: The role of store environment and time available for shopping. *The Journal of Consumer Research, 15*(4), 422-433.

Phillips, H. C., & Bradlow, R. P. (1991). Camera tracking: A new tool for market research and retail management. *Management Research News, 14*(4/5), 20-22.

Rafanelli, M. (2003). *Multidimensional databases: Problems and solutions.* London: Idea Group Publishing.

Roberts, S. M., Jones, J. P., & Frohling, O. (2005). NGOs and the globalization of managerialism: A research framework. *33*(11), 1845-1864.

Soars, B. (2003). What every retailer should know about the way into the shopper's head. *International Journal of Retail and Distribution Management, 31*(12), 628-637.

Sorensen, H. (2003). The science of shopping. *Marketing Research, 15*(3), 30-35.

Spekman, R. E., & Sweeney, P. J., II. (2006). RFID: From concept to implementation. *International Journal of Physical Distribution & Logistics Management, 36*(10), 736-754.

Underhill, P. (1999). *Why we buy: The science of shopping.* New York: Simon & Schuster.

Vanderhaegen, M., & Muro, E. (2005). Contribution of a European spatial data infrastructure to the effectiveness of EIA and SEA studies. *Environmental Impact Assessment Review, 25*(2), 123-142.

Van Oort, P. A. J., & Bregt, A. K. (2005). Do users ignore spatial data quality? A decision-theoretic perspective. *Risk Analysis, 25*(6), 1599-1610.

Wakefield, K. L., & Baker, J. (1998). Excitement at the mall: Determinants and effects on shopping response. *Journal of Retailing, 74*(4), 515-539.

Chapter 5
Facing the Challenges of RFID Data Management

Indranil Bose
University of Hong Kong, Hong Kong

Chun Wai Lam
University of Hong Kong, Hong Kong

ABSTRACT

Radio frequency identification (RFID) has generated vast amounts of interest in the supply chain, logistics, and the manufacturing area. RFID can be used to significantly improve the efficiency of business processes by providing automatic data identification and capture. Enormous data would be collected as items leave a trail of data while moving through different locations. Some important challenges such as false read, data overload, real-time acquisition of data, data security, and privacy must be dealt with. Good quality data is needed because business decisions depend on these data. Other important issues are that business processes must change drastically as a result of implementing RFID, and data must be shared between suppliers and retailers. The main objective of this article is focused on data management challenges of RFID, and it provides potential solutions for each identified risk.

INTRODUCTION

According to the definition provided by the *RFID Journal*, "radio frequency identification (RFID) is a generic term that is used to describe a system that transmits the identity of an object or person wirelessly in the form of a unique serial number, using radio waves. It's grouped under the broad category of automatic identification technolo-gies." RFID is much more advantageous than the barcode and other smart card technologies. When a large quantity of items are moved from one place to another place, the individual reading and processing of tags is time consuming when using barcode. RFID can deal with those items with the design and mapping of generic IDs of individual products. In Malaysia the government's commitment to drive the use of RFID has led to the successful adoption of chip-based credit cards. The Veterinary Services Department of Malaysia has decided to tag all 2.5 million livestock animals with economic value such as cattle, goat, and pigs by 2008 (Businessweek, 2007). It is expected that the RFID technology will grow very fast over the next three years. The global RFID market, which would include services, software, readers, and tags, will grow from $2.8 billion in 2006 to $8.1 billion by 2010 (The Economist, 2007).

RFID has a wide range of applications including warehouse resources management system (Chow, Choy, Lee, & Lau, 2006), integrated inventory management system (Saygin, 2007), retail management system (Sellitto, Burgess, & Hawking, 2007), real-time food traceability system (Connolly, 2007; Folinas, 2006; Kelepouris, 2007; Regattieri, Gamberi, & Manzini, 2007; Kempfer, 2007), product lifecycle management system (Harrison, McFarlane, Parlikad, & Wong, 2005; Parlikad & McFarlane, 2007), health care environment management system (Janz, Pitts, & Otondo, 2005), library resources management system (Yu, 2007), and shop-floor automation and factory information system (Qiu, 2007). Popular retailers like Wal-Mart, Gillette, Marks & Spencer, Tesco, Target, and Home Depot have already adopted the RFID technology. Using RFID data, Wal-Mart can predict the sales of a given item on a store-by-store basis and find out the reason why some products did not sell well. RFID allows Wal-Mart to sit down with its partners and plan how best to move products (Roberti, 2004). Gillette investigated the manner in which its tagged products were delivered from factory to customer store in its packaging and distribution center. Benefits reported by these stores appear to be directly related to the availability of the RFID data that are more accurate and timely than what was previously available, thereby allowing stock inventory to be better managed (Roberti, 2005a).

RFID data that is collected during the manufacturing process includes process start and finish time, product location, equipment location, labor location, equipment working status, stock keeping units (SKU), staff members' identities, and quantity of goods received. In retail industry, date of manufacture, product ingredients, temperature history, number of operation cycles, total time in operation, and details of maintenance would be recorded. Apart from the manufacturing and retail industry, RFID also plays an important role in the health care industry. Verichip is marketing its human-implantable RFID chip for medical use. The chip, which is the size of a grain of rice, can be injected into a person's arm. The pertinent medical records can be saved in the chip with a 16-digit code. Verichip expected the sales resulting from RFID chips to increase from $27.3 million in 2006 to $36 million in 2008 (Marcial, 2007).

Venture Development Corp. surveyed 100 chief technology officers and found that data management and monitoring was rated as one of the most important issues in the implementation of RFID systems (Li, Visich, Khumawala, & Zhang, 2006; O'Connor, 2004). Conventional systems, such as bar code printers and readers, are designed for human processing and are restricted to low transaction volumes. On the contrary, RFID can automate these processes and has the potential to generate much more data. RFID increases the volume of data substantially, as items leave a trail of data while moving through different locations. It is known that Wal-Mart's in-store RFID implementation will generate about 7.5 terabytes of RFID data a day. This overwhelming amount of data calls for newer and efficient data management approaches (Kasturi, 2005).

The reliability, quality, and management of the data must be sufficient because business decisions are made with these data. RFID technology entails risks with regard to data management, which can have an important influence on the result of implementing the technology. Another important issue is that business processes must change drastically as a result of implementing RFID because it is a completely new way of doing business. The main focus of this article would be to discuss the risks involved in data management and the solutions that can be adopted to lessen these risks.

RFID SYSTEM ARCHITECTURE

An RFID system consists of three main components, namely, tag, antenna, and reader. An RFID tag consists of a microchip attached to an antenna. Tags are either active or passive. Passive tags derive the power from the field generated by the reader. An RFID antenna is connected to the RFID reader. The antenna activates the RFID tag and transfers data by emitting wireless pulses. The RFID reader handles the communication between the information system and the RFID tag. The signals transfer to the host computer and pass through to the electronic product code (EPC) network. After that, the data is stored in the database server or other business application systems. There is an important tool called RFID middleware which consists of a set of software components that act as a bridge between the RFID system components (i.e., tags and readers) and the host application software. In other words, middleware tools are used to manage RFID data by routing it between tag/readers and the systems within the businesses. Middleware solutions filter duplicate, incomplete, and erroneous data that it receives. After digesting all data from the various sources, middleware forwards only the meaningful events to the enterprise systems. The tasks of the RFID middleware include data filtering, classification, data normalization, and aggregation of data transmitted between tags and readers for integration with the host application (Bhuptani & Moradpour, 2005; Goyal & Krishna, 2005; Shah, 2006). The detailed functions of the middleware are described in the following sections.

Data Filtering and Classification

Tag data needs to be cleansed to remove duplicate messages. Filtering and alerts may need to be raised based on certain predefined rules for data collection. Data filtering would mainly divide into low-level data and semantic data filtering. Low-level data filtering cleans the raw RFID data, and semantic data filtering extracts data on demand or interprets semantics from RFID data. The data classification can be done by the periodic batch program, which will pull all transaction data from the RFID application and dump it into a staging table in the middleware. A processor will periodically scan the staging table for any new transactions. This processor will match each record in the staging table with the history table. The purpose of this matching is to filter out duplicate transaction records and reduce network traffic (Goyal & Krishna, 2005). An example of data filtering and classification is the purchase order (PO) receiving process and advanced shipment notifications (ASNs). In an RFID supply chain, the transaction using the RFID will start with the supplier placing the tag on the pallet for the buyer. While the tagged pallet is stored in the warehouse, an ASN which contains the tag and pallet information would be sent to the buyer. The data will include shipment number, vendor name and location, number of containers, transaction date, quantity, and item description, and would be sent through the ASN to the buyer. When the pallets arrive at the receiving site, the reader at the dock will read the tag information. The data will be transmitted by the middleware for further identification and filtering. Then the filtered transaction will be classified according to tag ID, reader ID, location, and PO number, and will become a formal PO transaction (Goyal & Krishna, 2005).

Data Normalization

In the absence of standards, reader data formats and communication protocols for a host are usually proprietary. To function in a multi-vendor environment, the RFID middleware software is responsible for translating various reader data formats into a normalized format for easier integration at the host application level. The Physical Markup Language (PML), which is a standard technology based on the eXtensible Markup Language (XML), helps to transform and model the selected data (Folinas, 2006; Harrison et al., 2005; McMeekin et al., 2006). The host application receives processed and normalized data sent from the tag, via the reader and the RFID middleware software. The host application typically is a previously existing software system in an enterprise. Those systems can include a manufacturing execution system (MES), supply chain management (SCM) system, warehouse management system (WMS), and enterprise resource planning system (Bhuptani & Moradpour, 2005; Kleist, Chapman, Sakai, & Jarvis, 2004; Sellitto et al., 2007; Vijayaraman & Osky, 2006; Warden, 2005).

Data Integration

The RFID middleware can make it much easier to integrate retail data. Forecasts and orders become more accurate (Asif & Mandviwalla, 2005; RFID Journal, 2007). Collaborative planning, forecasting, and replenishment (CPFR), enterprise resource planning (ERP), warehouse management systems (WMS), and transportation management systems (TMS) allow companies to optimize forecasts, productions, and warehouse transportation. A combination of these systems with the RFID technology will result in more frequent and less costly data reads, thereby significantly enhancing their productivity (Twist, 2005). This would help to have the right product in the right place at the right time. Inventory is only needed for inappropriate information. RFID would provide better, faster, and more accurate information for allocation of resources and optimization of manufacturing process. High capital investment of RFID technology can be minimized through the backend integration of the enterprise applications. An enterprise application integration-based RFID middleware developed by Goyal and Krishna (2005) provided a two-way integration between an RFID application and any business application. The RFID integration mainly maintained a channel of communication between the business application and the RFID application. Also, the data needed to transfer and move from the RFID application to a schema, which will be used by the middleware to process and then submit for further processing to the business applications. Another important function of data integration is mapping of the classified data to the business application it should hit and interfacing the data to the business application in a format that is acceptable to that application.

Example of Middleware

Siemens RFID middleware, developed by the Integrated Data Systems Department of Siemens Corporate Research, is a good example of RFID middleware. Siemens RFID middleware enables semantic RFID data filtering and automatic data transformation, supports RFID object tracking and monitoring, and can be adapted to different RFID-enabled applications. The Siemens RFID middleware consists of event managers and a data server (Wang & Liu, 2005). Event managers are the front end of the system. These include reader adapter, filter, and writer. Reader adapter is the component that interacts with the RFID readers. A reader adapter can control the reading frequency and also receive data from the reader. The filter is the data filtering component to detect the duplicate and error data from raw RFID data. The writer would format the data with PML and send them to different targets.

After event managers filter and normalize the data, the data would be forwarded to the RFID data server, which includes the components of RFID data manager, RFID data store, product data store, and RFID data archive. RFID data manager is the key component of the RFID data server in an RFID data management system. It consists of three layers: semantic data processing layer, query layer, and decision-making layer. The semantic data processing layer provides high-level semantic data processing including automatic data transformation and semantic filtering. The query layer provides RFID object tracking and monitoring support. The decision-making layer provides low inventory alerts and trend analysis. The RFID data store stores RFID data for RFID object tracking, monitoring, decision making, and data retrieval. The product data store stores the static data such as product description and product model. In the RFID data archive, non-active data are archived into historical partitions. Finally, the RFID data server provides an application integration layer to integrate the system with other applications. Figure 1 shows the whole RFID system architecture and the corresponding RFID middleware system.

Figure 1. RFID system architecture and middleware system

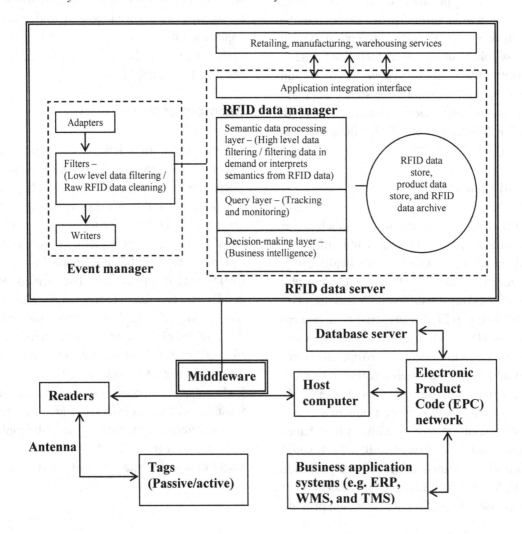

CHALLENGES AND SOLUTIONS

Before discussing the challenges of data management for RFID systems, the framework for data processing must be investigated. The framework consists of five stages for data flow, namely, data collection, data preprocessing, data analysis, data evaluation, and data integration and usage.

Data is a measurement of reality that may consist of measurements or observations. Those measurements or observations comprise numbers, words, or images. When the data becomes organized, it becomes information. Data collection, which refers to the process of preparing and collecting business data, usually takes place in the early stage of a project. A formal data collection process is necessary as it ensures that the data gathered is both well defined and accurate. Data preprocessing is the act of processing data before the syntactic analysis. Preprocessing is also used in data mining before data is filtered, analyzed, and a model is constructed. Data analysis is the act of transforming data with the aim of extracting useful information. During the process of analysis,

one or more models will be used. Data evaluation is the systematic determination of quality, merit, worth, and significance of data. Data integration is the act to allow the movement of data from one device or software to another. For example, RFID data could be transferred to an Enterprise Resources Planning system. Data integration allows companies to optimize forecasts, production, and warehouse transportations. Thus, these five stages are important in management of data for the RFID information system. Figure 2 shows the model of an RFID data management system.

Data Collection

Real-Time Acquisition of Data

Although accurate information can be obtained for all tagged parts close to real time for most of the supply chain systems, most current tools cannot handle the amount and the real-time aspects of those data (Ranky, 2006). The manufacturing companies track the number of pallets shipped out hourly and daily, and upload the informa-

Figure 2. The model of an RFID data management system

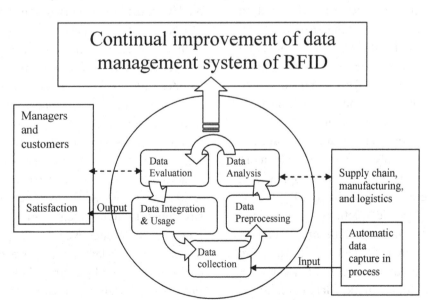

tion in batch mode, possibly every few hours or every shift. As RFID technologies become more ubiquitous, real-time transmission of data poses additional challenges in the ability of managers to process the information in a timely manner (Angeles, 2005). The challenge lies in processing such voluminous data and making timely decisions that are tied to the manufacturing execution systems (Saygin, 2007).

In the wireless manufacturing (WM) technology, RFID has played an important role in the collection and synchronization of the real-time field data from manufacturing workshops. It is crucial that the real-time shop-floor information visibility and traceability enable the implementation of just-in-time manufacturing to reduce the shop-floor work in process inventories and to smoothen their flows (Huang, Zhang, & Jiang, 2007).

In logistics management and supply chain management, the critical issues are to integrate the inventory, distribution, and sales data, and to make the integrated logistics information available to the organization in real time. The key point of logistic information integration is the real-time acquisition and recognition of distribution information. Compared to traditional approaches for logistics data capture and identification (e.g., bar code), RFID technology enables real-time automatic data capture, data identification, and information interchange; therefore, merchandise tracking, product sorting, and distribution data collection and analysis can be efficiently accomplished (Hou & Huang, 2006). As the RFID-enabled supply chain is able to get real-time information from all interfaces in the supply chain accurately and quickly, this facilitates aggregation of forecasts upstream into the supply chain and provides more accurate forecasts at the store and supplier level (Pagarkar, Natesan, & Prakash, 2005).

One of the feasible solutions is to develop operational data management architectures. Operational data management architectures are common in the financial industry. For example, trading systems collect market data in real time,

execute trading strategies heuristically, identify trading opportunities, and forward the results to traders for action (Palmer, 2004). Actually, different solutions have been proposed by different companies and researchers for the efficient tracking and monitoring of real-time data.

Chen, Chen, Chen, and Chang (2007) have proposed an RFID object tracking system which is able to track the data from an RFID-tagged object efficiently. Communication between RFID tags and RFID readers are performed by various RFID protocols according to different factory standards. While the RFID readers get the information stored in the RFID tags, the reader is responsible for generating a message and sending it to the backend system using the application layer protocol.

Sybase has suggested a real-time RFID solution which takes asset location data collected by AeroScout's Real Time Location System (RTLS). RTLS feeds that data to Sybase applications, which then aggregate and process the data and deliver it to mobile devices such as smart phones and PDAs (Collins, 2004).

False Read

RFID has the advantage that the RFID tags can be read without human intervention and without line of sight, and this enables bulk reading. However, if the data itself is inaccurate, RFID does not provide any value (Tellkamp, Angerer, Fleisch, & Corsten, 2005). False reads is the result of radio waves being distorted, deflected, absorbed, and interfered with (Angeles, 2005). Extreme temperature ranges, labeling standards, and packaging constraints are some of the potential causes affecting the radio waves transmission (Sellitto et al., 2007). As RFID systems are extremely susceptible to environmental noise, environmental factors such as reflective surfaces (e.g., swinging metal doors) or leaky protective devices (e.g., carrying cases with ill-fitting lids) can make the false read problem much worse by misdirecting

RFID signals. In other words, although an RFID reader obtains the data from the tag, it does not mean that the reading is part of the true data flow or business process. The false read problem in turn can significantly affect the reliability of reporting, decision support, and other information systems (Janz et al., 2005). Venture Development Corporation surveyed 100 chief technology officers, and the respondents indicated there are severe problems with RFID devices sending false reads or multiple reads of the same tag. It is also reported that a significant amount of noise and uncorrected data are often generated from an RFID-based system (Li et al., 2006).

Another false read problem concerns the inability of a reader to pick up data from every item on a pallet. Multiple tags are present in a reader's RF field and must be identified and tracked simultaneously. When more than one tag is present in the reader's range, tag collision can result in misreads or no reads. Since passive tags do not contain their own energy source, power consumption constraints are also imposed. In fact, the accuracy of some readers can fall below 90% (Asif & Mandviwalla, 2005). Moreover, the range of most readers drops drastically if the pallets have metal foil packaging or high water content because both these substances absorb radio waves. For example, the reader cannot read a tag behind a can of soda because the aluminum and the contents of the can block the signal transmission (Lin & Brown, 2006).

However, innovative solution strategies are being proposed to handle these problems. Efficient anti-collision algorithms are being developed, including time-division-multiple-access (TDMA), phase-jitter-modulation (PJM), and frequency and time-division-multiple-access (FTDMA). The anti-collision function requires cooperation between the tags and readers to minimize the risk of many tags responding all at one time (Asif & Mandviwalla, 2005). In some cases, the algorithm may be as simple as each tag waiting a random amount of time before responding to a reader's request (Bhuptani & Moradpour, 2005). Progress is also being made in attempts to produce more power-efficient chip design and efficient error-correcting-code (ECC) schemes. It is also critical that business rules are well defined so as to separate useful data from unwanted data (Evans, 2004). Lin and Brown (2006) suggested that the accuracy could be improved by reading pallets as they rotate during the packaging process. This allows the reader to get signals from the tags at different angles. Besides, readers must be properly installed and potential electromagnetic interference or barriers must be eliminated to ensure data accuracy.

Data Preprocessing

Data Explosion

RFID technology would increase the volume of data substantially, as items leave a trail of data while moving through different locations (Kanters, 2007; Vijayaraman & Osky, 2006). Firms that have tracked pallets and cases with RFID tags would show an increase of at least 30% in the data that needed to be processed (Angeles, 2005). The costs associated with storing RFID-generated data and the data-generating capabilities of RFID hardware and software would then increase (Janz et al., 2005; Lin & Brown, 2006). At the same time, more time will be needed to process the data (Lin & Brown, 2006). Database administrators need to be able to deal with the potential stress on the databases, both in terms of speed and volume involved in processing RFID applications. Angeles (2005) has estimated that tracking all items from production to point of sale for a manufacturing process would require 3,000 database transactions per second on the low end and upwards of 30,000 on the high end. If each product has 1,000 bytes of data associated with it, the RFID system would generate 10 terabytes of data per year. If the data is stored for five years, a 50-terabyte database will be needed.

For the food industry in the UK, food retailers will face the problem of inability to handle and make effective use of the data captured by RFID systems. Since the retail systems will collect a massive and continuous stream of real-time data, the storage and transmission of this data will impose severe strains on existing data management and storage structures and strategies (Jones, Clarke-Hill, Comfort, Hillier, & Shears, 2005). Besides, a field research conducted by Wal-Mart, the Auto-ID Center, and the key suppliers at Wal-Mart's pilot distribution center in Oklahoma resulted in the generation of 30 times more data, as products were tracked through the supply chain (Li et al., 2006).

One of the feasible solutions for the data explosion is the use of data warehouses. A data warehouse is adapted to store data extracted from different sources of a manufacturing process. The data such as process start time/finish time, equipment working status, equipment location, Stock Keeping Unit (SKU), staff members' identities, and quantity of goods received can be recorded and properly stored using a data warehouse. Moreover, the process information such as the process progress and staff members' responsibility would also be recorded (Chow, Choy, & Lee, 2007).

Data explosion could also be handled through pipeline processing. Once you have a Savant concentrator architecture in place, pipelines could be set up to handle the streams of data. Pipelines separate streams of EPC data to handle load and coordinate the data streams after they have been captured (Palmer, 2004). The Auto-ID Center at MIT developed a a software program named 'Savant' to manage the enormous amount of data expected to be generated by RFID readers. The filtering, collecting, and reporting layer , is essential in order to deploy large quantities of RFID tags and readers without overwhelming the network capacity (Asif & Mandviwalla, 2005; Harrison et al., 2005; Palmer, 2004).

Another possible solution is to determine the level of granularity for data collection. The granularity of data collection should be driven by business requirements and not by the technical limitations. It should be up to the business managers to define what constitutes a business event. The frequency of read or write events should be adjusted to the business needs (Evans, 2004). Only goods that need to be recalled such as fresh perishable produce or meat or high-value items such as expensive electronic gadgets or luxury designer goods may require a more detailed record of their movements through the purchase experience (Angeles, 2005). This will help to reduce the burden on the network and on data storage systems.

Data Analysis

Data Mining

After a vast amount of data is gathered from the activities along the supply chain, this data must be warehoused and mined to identify patterns that can lead to better control of the supply chain. The feasible solution is data mining. Data mining is a process that uses data analysis tools to discover relationships in data or potentially useful information that may be used to make valid predictions. Another objective of data mining is to discover hidden facts contained in databases.

Ngai, Cheng, Au, and Lai (2007) have proposed an RFID-integrated m-commerce framework for the container depot management support system (CDMSS). The data are gathered and stored in the data analysis module of the CDMSS for data mining. Useful business information are extracted from the data and this enables better decision making. Using online analytical processing (OLAP) technology with RFID technology, instant decisions can be made based on the data collected from the RFID-integrated m-commerce framework. Different popular data mining techniques such as discriminant analysis (DA), decision trees (DT), and artificial neural networks (ANNs) can be used to enhance the data analysis process.

Data Evaluation

Data Quality Assessment

Data obtained from the RFID readers only describe the events, activities, transactions, and numbers. Without organization of those numbers, they would not make much sense. Turban, Mclean, Wetherbe, Bolloju, and Davison (2002) have said:

Information is data that have been organized so that they have meaning and value to the recipient. The recipient interprets the meaning and draws conclusions and implications. Data processed by an application program represent a more specific use and a higher value added than simple retrieval from a database.

Actually, the data quality characteristics are rather subjective. Data quality attributes such as accuracy, completeness, timeliness, consistency, and relevancy can be intuitively defined by people. Accuracy represents data that is correct; completeness relates to an all-encompassing value allowing a task at hand to be addressed; the timeliness dimension reflects the creation and removal dates of the data; consistency ensures product quality standards; and relevancy is associated with how the data is used in a specific task. Only if all these data quality attributes are satisfied, then RFID will be beneficial for businesses.

Data Security and Privacy

RFID chips embedded in retail products without the knowledge of the customers who buy those products could remain in products for indefinite periods and so can be potentially traceable beyond the limited scope of their original purpose (Angeles, 2007). Use of RFID in supply chain applications before the point of sale is of no concern to consumers because there are no privacy implications. However, the use of RFID after the point of sale has privacy implications (Dobson & Todd, 2006). If the RFID tags are not removed or deactivated when the customer leaves a store, the customer can be monitored via the radio signals that continue to emit from their purchases.

Moreover, if the unique product information on an RFID tag is linked to some identifiable customer information, such as a credit card number, which may in turn offer access to further personal data such as address, income, and even the credit rating, then this allows the retailer to build up detailed profiles of their customers. This suggests that a widespread network of RFID receivers could be constantly observing, processing, and evaluating consumers' behaviors and purchases. There is the possibility that retailers may sell personalized data to other commercial organizations for illegal purposes (Jones, Clarke-Hill, Hillier, Shears, & Comfort, 2004). Finally, the linking of personal identification data with a unique product code would also mean that individuals would have the possibility of being physically stalked without their knowledge or consent (Jones et al., 2004).

Ayoade (2006) has proposed the Authentication Processing Framework (APF) to provide assurance to RFID users that the information stored in the tag is secure in the sense that only authenticated readers of the APF have access to the tag. The data received by the reader from the tag is encrypted, and this data can only be decrypted by using the decryption key from the APF. Moreover, for preventing the tags from being cloned, a heuristic Jigsaw encoding scheme is proposed. This simple scheme helps encrypt an EPC code into a pseudo-EPC code. The pseudo-EPC code looks like a random code, and an attacker is not able to reverse it into a valid EPC code in a short period of time. Attackers, even with same RFID reader, can only make cloned tags with these pseudo-EPCs. Such encryption is able to protect EPC data on passive RFID tags (Wong, Hui, & Chan, 2006).

Inventory control requires a radio signal strong enough to track inventory across a warehouse.

However, for contactless purchases of retail products, the signal that just extends a few inches from the card reader can be used. Each purchase is separately encoded. Identity thieves cannot steal radio signals and use data to make subsequent illicit purchases (Ward, 2007). Finally, deployment of RFID tag-embedded products must be accompanied by the effective enforcement of privacy legislation, voluntary self- and co-regulation, and codes of conduct (Reid, 2007).

Data Integration and Usage

RFID Data Integration with Existing Business Processes

Business processes must change drastically as a result of implementing RFID, so enterprises must

carefully consider RFID before implementing it. Methodology such as Analytic Hierarchy Process (AHP) can be used to assist organizations in judging if the RFID technology is suitable for them (Lin & Lin, 2007). The framework for evaluating RFID adoption is shown in Figure 3.

Companies interested in adopting RFID should reexamine how supply chain decisions are made. This will require a deep understanding of how RFID impacts supply chain dynamics. For example, as organizations migrate to RFID, they may have to consider an environment made up of both barcodes and RFID tags at the case or palette level (Brown & Russell, 2007). Systems integration is not just about sending the filtered data into the ERP systems. It requires solutions to help the end users understand the data, and link it with the systems and processes. Servers that

Figure 3. A framework for evaluation of RFID adoption

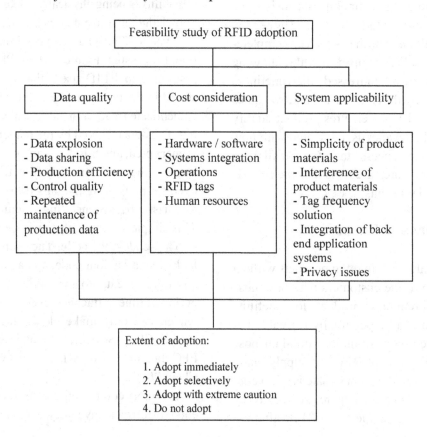

form the backbone of the information technology infrastructure for the company would require understanding of what is being collected from the edge devices in order to automate the analytical and feedback processes. Spieβ, Bornhövd, Lin, Haller, and Schaper (2007) suggested the Smart Item Infrastructure (SII), which provides the solution for RFID data integration with the business process automation. The business process bridging layer, one of the five layers of SII, describes the services to aggregate and transfer data from the RFID to business-relevant information, thereby reducing the amount of data being sent to the enterprise application systems.

Data Sharing

Retailers using RFID would be most interested in attaining faster processes, higher visibility of flows, and a decrease in errors and discrepancies, so that they can maximize the profit. Data sharing would be the key to this challenge. Sharing the data with suppliers would allow them to track shelf availability more accurately and reduce the chance of stockouts.

The first step in data sharing is the exchange of RFID raw data. The retailer provides feedback to the supplier on the status of the incoming delivery. After that, the exchange of RFID data within a business context should be implemented between partners. At this stage partners start using RFID to understand its business significance and identify achievable business benefits. Retailers and suppliers can benefit greatly from RFID, but RFID data sharing is a major process change which is needed to make the most out of it (RFID Journal, 2007). One of the examples for data sharing is sharing of EPC data of Target and Wal-Mart beginning with 13 manufacturers. The pilot represents a major advance toward the goal of using EPC data to track goods throughout the entire supply chain (Roberti, 2005b).

All the challenges in the management of RFID data and their corresponding potential solutions that are discussed in this section are summarized in Table 1.

FUTURE RESEARCH DIRECTIONS

Many new research questions can be posed from the listing of challenges and solutions for RFID data management. At present the problem of false read is a major issue for RFID tags. An important research question in this area is: what is the optimal amount of time the tag should be exposed to the reader so that the reading is accurate and at the same time the process of movement of the tagged item is not substantially delayed? Another important research idea that requires further exploration is: for a basket of items that are individually tagged, what should be the optimal sequence in which the tags should be read? Associated with the false read problem, is the difficult issue of detection of outliers in tag readings? How can an operations manager determine whether a reading is spurious. In addition to his or her intuition and domain knowledge, what mathematical and pattern matching techniques can be used to determine the correctness of the reading. When transporting a basket of different products from the distribution center to the retail outlet, numerous readings will be generated at different points of time. Decision rules must be developed for filtering this data. However, more research needs to be done to ascertain if those decision rules should be of a generic nature or if they should be dependant on the characteristics of the product. The filtered data on the tagged products is likely to be stored in a data warehouse that will receive such data from a number of points of data capture. What should be the most appropriate schema to be used in the data warehouse so as to maintain the integrity and concurrency of the temporal data arriving from multiple sources at different times? The data stored in the data warehouse needs to

Table 1. Challenges and proposed solutions for the management of RFID data

Challenges	Proposed Solutions
Real-time acquisition of data	• Operational data management architecture is needed. • RFID object tracking system that is able to keep maintenance and efficient tracking of the data from an RFID-tagged object is proposed. • A real-time RFID solution is suggested by Sybase.
False read	• Efficient anti-collision algorithms are being developed, including time-division-multiple-access, phase-jitter-modulation, and frequency and time-division-multiple-access. • Progress is made in attempts to produce more power-efficient chip designs and efficient error-correcting-code schemes. • The accuracy could be improved by reading pallets as they rotate during the packaging process. It allows the reader to get signals from the tags at different angles and obtain the best view. • Potential electromagnetic interference or barriers must be eliminated to ensure data accuracy.
Data explosion	• Data warehousing is adapted to store data extracted from different sources of a manufacturing process. • Pipelines could be set up to handle the streams of data. • The Auto-ID Center at MIT developed a software program named 'Savant' to manage the enormous amount of data expected to be generated by RFID readers. • The level of granularity for data collection must be determined.
Data mining	• An RFID-integrated m-commerce framework for the Container Depot Management Support System has been proposed. • Different popular data mining techniques such as discriminant analysis, decision trees, and artificial neural networks can be used.
Data security and privacy	• Authentication Processing Framework is proposed. • For preventing the tags from being cloned, a heuristic Jigsaw encoding scheme is proposed. • For contactless purchases of retail products, the signal that just extends a few inches from the card reader can be used.
Data integration with existing business processes	• An environment made up of both barcodes and RFID tags at the case or palette level should be considered. • Analytic Hierarchy Process can be used to assist organizations in judging if they are suitable to adapt the RFID system. • Smart Item Infrastructure, which provides the solution for the RFID data integration with the business process automation, is proposed.
Data sharing	• Exchange of RFID raw data. • RFID data within a business context should be shared between partners.

be of sufficient quality so that they can be of use subsequently. But existing metrics for assessment of data quality may not be sufficient for assessment of RFID-related data. More importantly, researchers will have to define different data quality metrics for different applications using RFID. For example, the data quality metrics used in retail outlets may be different from those used in the supply chain. The summarized data from the data warehouse will be amenable to data analysis. This raises a number of research questions in the area of data mining. What kind of patterns should analysts hope to discover from this data—clusters, sequences, association rules, or outliers? Will popular standalone methods of data mining like decision trees, neural networks, K-means clustering, and so forth be sufficient, or will there be a need to develop specialized or hybrid algorithms specially tailored to RFID data? Privacy issues related to RFID tags have been discussed in this article. But a generic approach that disables all tags after the point of sale may not always be appropriate. Some customers may be inclined to reveal the movements of some products of some marketing companies in return for monetary rewards, but not the movement of all products of all companies. Organizations will have to find a systematic way to do selective disablement of tags based on customers' preferences and will have to maintain a list of tags of particular products of some companies that are not disabled. Integration of the RFID information system with the enterprise information system is a major challenge in itself. However, researchers must answer whether a phased or a big-bang approach should be adopted for the implementation of the integration project, keeping in mind the physical and human resources of the organization. Finally, benefits of RFID can be achieved through sharing of data related to movement of items. However, all participants in the supply chain may not be willing to share business-critical data as that may lead to eroding their power and profit. Researchers must decide on the optimal dynamics of data revelation and sharing between the various parties.

CONCLUSION

In this article we have discussed the existing challenges for data management of RFID, and put forward several suggested solutions for the successful business implementation of RFID. For the false read problem, technical tests of specific cases must be performed to reduce the problems of tags collisions and absorption by packaging material. Apart from data filtering, business rules must be set up to govern data collection and storage. While RFID would generate a massive amount of data, the first step in a successful data management strategy is to ensure that only meaningful data is collected for the backend applications and data repositories. It is critical that there are well-defined business rules to separate duplicate or unwanted data from useful data. This will help in reducing the burden on the network and on data storage systems (Evans, 2004). When linking RFID technology to existing enterprise applications, the changes in infrastructure need to be done in a way that minimizes cost. Also, use

of RFID may lead to privacy issues, especially after the point of sale, and there is a need to handle this in a very careful manner, keeping in mind the preferences of the customers.

More and more companies are expected to implement RFID technology in the near future. Although RFID poses many challenges to current data management systems, this technology is much more advantageous than the barcode and other smart card technologies. Several potential solutions have been suggested to address the various challenges related to real-time acquisition of data, false read, data explosion, data mining, data security and privacy, data integration with existing business processes, and data sharing. Some specific research questions related to these challenges that need to be explored further have been listed in the previous section. In the future, it is foreseeable that data management will continue to remain a major concern for worldwide adoption of RFID.

REFERENCES

Angeles, R. (2007). An empirical study of the anticipated consumer response to RFID product item tagging. *Industrial Management & Data Systems, 107,* 461-483.

Angeles, R. (2005). RFID technologies: Supply-chain applications and implementation issues. *Information Systems Management, 22,* 51-65.

Asif, Z., & Mandviwalla, M. (2005). Integrating the supply chain with RFID: A technical and business analysis. *Communications of the Association for Information Systems, 15,* 393-427.

Ayoade, J. (2006). Security implications in RFID and authentication processing framework. *Computers & Security, 25,* 207-212.

Bhuptani, M., & Moradpour, S. (2005). *RFID field guide: Deploying radio frequency identification systems.* New York: Prentice Hall.

Brown, I., & Russell, J. (2007). Radio frequency identification technology: An exploratory study on adoption in the South African retail sector. *International Journal of Information Management.*

Businessweek. (2007, April 25). *Asia RFID market need gov't boost.* Retrieved from *http://www.businessweek.com/globalbiz/content/apr2007/gb20070425_369568.htm?chan=search*

Chen, J.L., Chen, M.C., Chen, C.W., & Chang, Y.C. (2007). Architecture design and performance evaluation of RFID object tracking systems. *Computer Communications.*

Chow, H.K.H., Choy, K.L., & Lee, W.B. (2007). A dynamic logistics process knowledge-based system—an RFID multi-agent approach. *Knowledge Based Systems, 20,* 357-372.

Chow, H.K.H., Choy, K.L., Lee, W.B., & Lau, K.C. (2006). Design of a RFID case-based resource management system for warehouse operations. *Expert System with Applications, 30,* 561-576.

Collins, J. (2004, August 23). *Sybase initiates RFID solution.* Retrieved from *http://www.rfidjournal.com/article/articleview/1093/1/1/*

Connolly, C. (2007). Sensor trends in processing and packaging of food and pharmaceuticals. *Sensor Review, 27,* 103-108.

Dobson, T., & Todd, E. (2006). Radio frequency identification technology. *Computer Law & Security Report, 22,* 313-315.

Evans, N.D. (2004, June 28). *Planning for RFID data.* Retrieved from *http://www.rfidjournal.com/article/articleview/1004/1/82/*

Folinas, D. (2006). Traceability data management for food chains. *British Food Journal, 108,* 622-633.

Goyal, K., & Krishna, D. (2005). *RFID middleware—integration to the entire supply chain.* RFID Journal White Paper.

Harrison, M., McFarlane, D., Parlikad, A.K., & Wong, C.Y. (2005). *Information management in the product lifecycle—the role of networked RFID.* Auto-ID Center White Paper.

Hou, J.L., & Huang, C.H. (2006). Quantitative performance evaluation of RFID applications in the supply chain of the printing industry. *Industrial Management & Data Systems, 106,* 96-120.

Huang, G.Q., Zhang, Y.F., & Jiang, P.Y. (2007). RFID-based wireless manufacturing for walking-worker assembly islands with fixed-position layouts. *Robotics and Computer-Integrated Manufacturing, 23,* 469-477.

Janz, B.D., Pitts, M.G., & Otondo, R.F. (2005). Information systems and health care II: Back to the future with RFID: Lessons learned—some old, some new. *Communications of the Association for Information Systems, 15,* 132-148.

Jones, P., Clarke-Hill, C., Comfort, D., Hillier, D., & Shears, P. (2005). Radio frequency identification and food retailing in the UK. *British Food Journal, 107,* 356-360.

Jones, P., Clarke-Hill, C., Hillier, D., Shears, P., & Comfort, D. (2004). Radio frequency identification in retailing and privacy and public policy issues. *Management Research News, 27,* 46-56.

Kanters, R.H.L. (2007). *Data management risks of radio frequency identification (RFID).* Unpublished Masters Thesis, Tiburg University, The Netherlands.

Kasturi, R. (2005). *Tapping the RFID data flood.* Retrieved from *http://www.intelligententerprise.com/showArticle.jhtml?articleID=163100818*

Kelepouris, T. (2007). RFID-enabled traceability in the food supply chain. *Industrial Management & Data Systems, 107,* 183-200.

Kempfer, L.M. (2007). A dollop of RFID. *Material Handling Management, 62,* 40-41.

Kleist, R.A., Chapman, T.A., Sakai, D.A., & Jarvis,

B.S. (2004). *RFID labeling: Smart labeling concepts & applications for the consumer packaged goods supply chain.* Printronix.

Li, S., Visich, F.K., Khumawala, B.M., & Zhang, C. (2006). Radio frequency identification technology: Applications, technical challenges and strategies. *Sensor Review, 26,* 193-202.

Lin, K., & Lin, C. (2007). Evaluating the decision to adopt RFID systems using analytic hierarchy process. *Journal of American Academy of Business, 11,* 72-78.

Lin, P.P., & Brown, K.F. (2006). Radio frequency identification and how to capitalize on it. *The CPA Journal, 76,* 34-37.

Marcial, G.G. (2007, May 28). *VeriChip is I.D.'d as a winner.* Retrieved from *http://www.businessweek.com/magazine/content/07_22/b4036093.htm?chan=search*

McMeekin, T.A., Baranyi, J., Bowman, J., Dalgaard, P., Kirk, M., Ross, T., Schmid, S., & Zwietering, M.H. (2006). Information systems in food safety management. *International Journal of Food Microbiology, 112,* 181-194.

Ngai, E.W.T., Cheng, T.C.E., Au, S., & Lai, K. (2007). Mobile commerce integrated with RFID technology in a container depot. *Decision Support Systems, 43,* 62-76.

O'Connor, M.C. (2007, January 8). *Michelin shrinks its e-tire pressure monitor.* Retrieved from *http://www.rfidjournal.com/article/articleview/2950/1/1/*

O'Connor, M.C. (2006a). *Warehouse management systems that handle RFID data.* Retrieved from *http://www.rfidjournal.com/magazine/article/2259*

O'Connor, M.C. (2006b, August 18). *Apparel & footwear summit attracts wide audience.* Retrieved from *http://www.rfidjournal.com/article/articleview/2599/1/1/*

O'Connor, M.C. (2004, November 30). *RFID users want clear data.* Retrieved from *www.rfidjournal.com/article/articleview/1232/1/1/*

Pagarkar, M., Natesan, M., & Prakash, B. (2005). *RFID in integrated order management systems: RFID, VMI and CPFR in integrated order management systems for retail supply chains.* RFID Journal White Paper.

Palmer, M. (2004, February 2). *Build an effective RFID architecture.* Retrieved from *http://www.rfidjournal.com/article/articleview/781/1/82/*

Parlikad, A.K., & McFarlane, D. (2007). RFID-based product information in end-of-life decision making. *Control Engineering Practice.*

Qiu, R.G. (2007). RFID-enabled automation in support of factory integration. *Robotics and Computer-Integrated Manufacturing.*

Ranky, P.G. (2006). An introduction to radio frequency identification (RFID) methods and solutions. *Assembly Automation, 26,* 28-33.

Reid, A.S. (2007). Is society smart enough to deal with smart cards? *Computer Law & Security Report, 23,* 53-61.

Regattieri, A., Gamberi, M., & Manzini, R. (2007). Traceability of food products: General framework and experimental evidence. *Journal of Food Engineering, 81,* 347-356.

RFID Journal. (2007, February). *EPC/RFID data sharing: Enter a new era of supply chain collaboration between retailers and suppliers.* Retrieved from *http://www.rfidjournal.com/whitepapers/download/209*

RFID Journal. (2003, September 22). *Tesco deploys class 1 EPC tags.* Retrieved from *http://www.rfidjournal.com/article/articleview/587/1/1/*

RFID Journal. (2002a, October 24). *CD tracking project deemed a hit.* Retrieved from *http://www.rfidjournal.com/article/articleview/98/1/1/*

RFID Journal. (2002b, June 24). *Learning from Prada*. Retrieved from *http://www.rfidjournal.com/article/view/425*

Roberti, M. (2005a, October 31). *The serendipity effect*. Retrieved from *http://www.rfidjournal.com/article/articleview/1960/1/2/*

Roberti, M. (2005b, October, 17). *Target, Wal-Mart share EPC data*. Retrieved from *http://www.rfidjournal.com/article/articleview/1928/1/1/*

Roberti, M. (2004, April 30). *Wal-Mart begins RFID rollout*. Retrieved from *http://www.rfidjournal.com/article/articleview/926/1/1*

Saygin, C. (2007). Adaptive inventory management using RFID data. *International Journal of Advanced Manufacturing Technology, 32,* 1045-1051.

Sellitto, C., Burgess, S., & Hawking, P. (2007). Information quality attributes associated with RFID-derived benefits in the retail supply chain. *International Journal of Retail & Distribution Management, 35,* 69-87.

Shah, S. (2006). *Semantics and Internet of things*. RFID Journal White Paper.

Spieß, P., Bornhövd, C., Lin, T., Haller, S., & Schaper, J. (2007). Going beyond auto-ID: A service-oriented smart items infrastructure. *Journal of Enterprise Information Management, 20,* 356-370.

Tellkamp, C., Angerer, A., Fleisch, E., & Corsten, D. (2005). *From pallet to shelf: Improving data quality in retail supply chains using RFID*. Auto ID Center White Paper.

The Economist. (2007, June 7). *Radio silence*. Retrieved from *http://www.economist.com/search/displaystory.cfm?story_id=9249278&CFID=15975447&CFTOKEN=95269337#top*

Turban, E., Mclean, E., Wetherbe, J., Bolloju, N., & Davison, R. (2002). *Information technology management: Transforming business in the digital economy*. New York: John Wiley & Sons.

Twist, D.C. (2005). The impact of radio frequency identification on supply chain facilities. *Journal of Facilities Management, 3,* 226-239.

Vijayaraman, B.S., & Osyk, B.A. (2006). An empirical study of RFID implementation in the warehousing industry. *International Journal of Logistics Management, 17,* 6-20.

Wang, F., & Liu, P. (2005). *Temporal management of RFID data* (pp. 1128-1139). Siemens Corporate Research.

Ward, M. (2007). The price of speed. *National Petroleum News, 99,* 28-32.

Warden, T. (2005). *The RFID software conundrum*. RFID Journal White Paper.

Wong, K.H.M., Hui, P.C.L., & Chan, A.C.K. (2006). Cryptography and authentication on RFID passive tags for apparel products. *Computers in Industry, 57,* 342-349.

Yu, S.C. (2007). RFID implementation and benefits in libraries. *The Electronic Library, 25,* 54-64.

This work was previously published in the International Journal of Information Systems and Supply Chain Management, Vol. 1, Issue 4, edited by J. Wang, pp. 1-19, copyright 2008 by IGI Publishing (an imprint of IGI Global).

Chapter 6

Complementary Resources, Web–Based Applications, and the Development of Web–Enabled Supply Chain:
A Case Study of Paint Supply Chain

Yootaek Lee
Babson College, USA

Jay Kim
Boston University, USA

Jeffery G. Miller
Boston University, USA

ABSTRACT

The purpose of this chapter is to enhance our understanding of how web-based applications and complementary resources can work together to create competitive advantages in supply chains. This chapter is organized as follows. First, this chapter introduces the theoretical background of complementary resources. Then, it moves on to report a preliminary result of secondary data analysis that explores the role of complementary resources to the development of web-enabled supply chains. Lastly, this chapter reports a case study that focuses on identifying: 1) the complementary resources that influence the successful implementation of web-based applications for supply chain management, and 2) the degree to which certain types of complementary resources function to support the successful implementation of web-based applications.

INTRODUCTION

The complexity of managing supply chain has increased and became an essential element to which firms need to pay extra attention due to the escalated expectation from customers and globalized supply network. As a result, the development of a supply chain which can effectively match supply and demand is not an option but is a necessity for firms

DOI: 10.4018/978-1-60566-974-8.ch006

to achieve competitiveness. With the emergence of Internet technology, firms begin to recognize web-based applications as an important medium for improving the effectiveness of matching supply and demand.

It was estimated that there were 97 million Internet users worldwide at the end of 1998 and the revenues from on-line businesses reached to $7.8 billion (International Data Corporation, 1999). These same sources predict that the number of estimated worldwide Internet user to be 1.4 billion by the end of 2008 and the projection for on-line business revenues (B2C and B2B) is $13.6 trillion by 2012 (International Data Corporation, 2008). These statistics reflect the increasing need of utilizing various web-based applications in developing competitive supply chains launched on Internet.

With the widespread adoption of web-based applications built on Internet infrastructure in managing supply chains, many studies report performance improvements in various areas such as cost reduction (e.g., Croom, 2000; Robinson et al., 2005), increased responsiveness (e.g. Frohlich and Westbrook, 2002; Auramo et al., 2005), and financial performance (Dehning, et al., 2007). Some studies also report that firms have created a competitive advantage by implementing web-based applications in supply chains (e.g., Alt, et al., 2001).

Nevertheless, not all firms appear to be leveraging the capability of web-based applications to the same extent. From a study of the savings achieved by using web-based applications in a specific case of buyer-designed machine parts, Emiliani and Stec (2002) report that the actual savings are less than expected. In addition, Lynagh et al (2002) report that 40% of firms in the logistics service industry that implemented web-based applications consider their web practices to be either "very ineffective" or "somewhat ineffective."

These inconsistent reports raise an important question. Why, in some cases, does the effort of implementing web-based applications seem to fail whereas, in other cases, it generates a competitive advantage? Resource-based theory provides a framework for augmenting our understanding of the effects of web-based applications on supply chain competitiveness. Resource-based theory emphasizes the role of heterogeneous resources and the capabilities of firms in explaining competitive advantage (Barney 1991; Peteraf, 1993), and has the potential of explaining the different results that have been reported.

According to resource-based theory, web-based applications *per se* are not a source of competitive advantage because they are readily available to all firms in a competitive factor market. Resource-based theory suggests that firms need to utilize resources and capabilities unique to them, so called 'complementary resources,' in order to gain competitive advantage from implementing information technologies (Clemons and Michael, 1991; Wade and Hulland, 2004).

Several studies have explored the role of complementary resources in the implementation of information technologies prior to the introduction of web-based applications (e.g., Neo, 1988; Hansen and Wernerfelt, 1989). However, little research has been done to provide insights into precisely how these resources are utilized to support the implementation of web-based applications in supply chains.

The contribution of this study is to enhance our understanding of how web-based applications and complementary resources can work together to create competitive advantages in supply chains. This chapter is organized as follows. First, this chapter will introduce the theoretical background of complementary resources. Second, this chapter reports a preliminary result of secondary data analysis that explores the role of complementary resources to the implementation of web-based applications in developing web-enabled supply chains. Lastly, this chapter reports an exploratory case study. The case study identifies the specific set of complementary resources and the degree to which certain types of complementary resources function to support the successful implementation of web-based applications in a paint supply chain.

THEORETICAL BACKGROUND

Resource-Based Theory

According to resource-based theory, firms hold heterogeneous resource-portfolios as a result of design, history, or luck, and this heterogeneity is responsible for explaining the differences in the financial returns of firms (Barney, 1991). However, the above-normal return that yields a so-called 'competitive advantage' (Porter, 1991) tends to vanish when competitors can readily acquire resources from a factor market. Accordingly, one of the main focuses of resource-based theory is how to increase the barriers to imitation, known as *'isolating mechanisms'*.

Resource-based theory suggests that firms need to develop firm-specific resource bundles by combining resources and capabilities in unique and inextricable ways (Dierickx and Cool, 1989). These resources that are inextricably combined into resource bundles, called complementary resources, provide a way to achieve and sustain competitive advantage (e.g., Black and Boal, 1994).

While resource-based theory has been widely accepted in various research areas, there has been a lack of consensus on the definition of resources. Some studies make a distinction between resources and capabilities, where resources refer to tangible, intangible, and human-related assets, and capabilities refer to a firm's ability to integrate and deploy resources (Grant, 1991; Ross et al., 1996). Others define resources more broadly by including assets, knowledge, capabilities, and processes (Scanchez et al., 1996; Wade and Hulland, 2004). Because the main purpose of this study is to identify various resources that influence the successful implementation of web-based applications, this study

adopts a more inclusive view of resources. Accordingly, and drawing on a recent study by Wade and Hulland (2004), this study defines resources as tangible assets (e.g., information technology, customer database), intangible assets (e.g., brand reputation, knowledge, culture), and capabilities that can transform inputs into outputs of greater worth (e.g., ability, process).

Complementary Resources

A number of studies have emphasized the role of complementary resources in explaining the relationship between information system implementation and firm performance (e.g., Clemons and Michael, 1991; Powell and Dent-Micallef, 1997; Power, 2005). According to the emerging resource-based theory, web-based applications can contribute to achieving competitive advantage only when firms can configure and utilize complementary resources in a way that cannot be easily identified and replicated by their competitors. This study defines *complementary resources* as assets and capabilities that, when utilized in conjunction with information technology, will create synergistic results (e.g., Black and Boal, 1994; Powell and Dent-Micallef, 1997).

Researchers have identified various complementary resources that are related to the implementation of new information technology. For example, several case studies propose that the utilization of qualitative organizational variables such as CEO commitment, an open culture, management vision, and consensus for the implementation of a new information technology influenced performance (e.g., Neo, 1988; Hansen and Wernerfelt, 1989; Powell, 1995). Some researchers argue that firm-specific IT training programs, skills, and tacit knowledge of employees may also serve as complementary resources that can leverage the value of new information technology, while others discuss supplier relationships, business process design, IT planning, and the structure of organizations (E.g. Keen, 1993; Hammer and Champy, 1993).

In their study examining the role of complementary resources in the implementation of information technology to create competitive advantage, Powell and Dent-Micallef (1997) synthesize the previous findings of potential complementary resources. However, these findings include only those complementary resources related to information technologies that were available prior to the introduction of web-based applications.

Based on the Ser-M model (Cho & Lee, 1998), Korea's Ministry of Commerce, Industry and Energy (MOCIE) has identified four main resources that support the implementation of web-based application in managing various activities in supply chains since 2002. The four resources are environment, IT resources & infra, process, and people.

Web-Based Applications in Supply Chains

Numerous effects of implementing web-based applications to support supply chain processes have been proposed in several studies, including purchasing (Emiliani and Stec, 2002; Boer et. al., 2002; Willcocks & Plant, 2003), production (e.g., Sarkis and Sundarraj, 2002), and distribution (Rao, 1999; Ellinger, et al., 2002). The expected benefits include reduced transaction costs in purchasing, reduced levels of inventory across a supply chain, a shortened production planning horizon, and increased potential for optimal distribution (Robinson, et al., 2005). However, researchers emphasize that firms need to evaluate current processes to determine if these processes need to be reengineered. Although researchers see the significant potential of web-based applications as enabling mechanisms, they also note that web-based applications may not be able to fix flawed processes.

The adoption of web-based applications has also been considered as part of a supply chain

strategy. Simchi-Levi and Simchi-Levi (2000) describe two extreme supply chain strategies, pull and push, and suggest that a hybrid strategy should be considered to best utilize the web-based applications in developing a competitive supply chain. Lee (2002) develops four different types of supply chain strategies and illustrates how the capability of web-based applications can be leveraged by each strategy. A recent study identifies four strategic groups, each one characterized by the adoption of the web-based applications in different areas, by using a discriminant analysis (Cagliano et. al., 2005).

Although researchers recognize the demand for integrating web-based applications with other resources, the discussion of that relationship has been limited and fragmented in a supply chain context. Therefore, this study first reports a preliminary result of a secondary data analysis to explore the role of complementary resources in developing web-enabled supply chains. Then, this study reports an in-depth case analysis to identify complementary resources to the implementation of web-based applications in developing competitive supply chains in a pain supply chain.

THE ROLE OF COMPLEMENTARY RESOURCES

The Secondary Data

In order to evaluate the utilization level of web-based applications in managing supply chains, Korea's Ministry of Commerce, Industry and Energy (MOCIE) has developed four main complementary resources to the successful implementation of web-enabled supply chains based on the Ser-M model (Cho & Lee, 1998). Then, MOCIE has collected survey data since 2002. The survey is conducted annually and collected data from 500 firms spread across 11 industries such as Finance, Telecom, Electronics, Automobile, Petrochemical, Distribution,

Table 1 Score Card for the Index

Construct	Weight
Environment (15%)	Customer (30%) Supplier (30%) Industry (20%) Policy & etc. (20%)
IT Resource & Infra (20%)	Computing & Networking (18%) Security & Risk Mgt. (17%) DB & System Integration (19%) IT staff & policy (22%)
Process * (35%)	Buy side Operations Sell side Support
People (30%)	CEO (44%) Executives (23%) Team (18%) Organization (15%)

*The weight for the components of process construct is adjusted for each industry

Construction, Transportation, Machinery, Steel and Textile/Apparel.

In this section, we present a preliminary descriptive analysis result of the data collected in 2002. Top 50 firms based on revenue are selected from each industry and 500 firms are responded in 2002. This extremely high response rate of 90.1% was due since the survey was requested and conducted by government organization.

As shown in Table 1, the survey questions include four resource constructs such as Environment, IT Resources & Infra, Process, and People. For each resource constructs, multiple components are developed to measure different dimensions of constructs. All variables were measured using Likert-type scales comprised of 7 items. Then, the weights of components, acquired from a Delphi method, are assigned in order to develop index scores.

A Preliminary Descriptive Analysis

The first column of Table 2 shows the number of firms by industry. The apparel industry holds the largest portion (12.4%) followed by finance (10.6%) and petrochemical industry (49%). The total scores in the last row of Table 2 show that the Environment resource has the highest index score (60.7) followed by IT & Infra (50.1), Process (49.2), and Human (48.3). As shown in Figure 1, the result indicates that respondents perceive that the Environment resource supports the development of web-based supply chains relatively at the higher level than other resources. On the other hand, firms need to develop or acquire more Human resource and Process resource to support the development of web-enabled supply chains.

Figure 2 represents the index scores of overall resource, shown in the last column of Table 2, by industry. As shown in Figure 2, Finance industry shows the highest index score of overall resource while apparel industry shows the lowest index score. This indicates that each industry shows a different level of support from complementary resources in developing web-enabled supply chains.

The data in Table 2 also shows that each industry has different index scores for each resource. For example, Apparel industry has relatively a high index score of Environment resource (51.9) while the index score of Process resource and Human resource are very low, 35.0 and 35.1 respectively.

Table 2. Web-enabled supply chain index score

	No of Firms	E-supply chain Index Score Env. IT & Infra Process Human Overall				
Industry	62 (12.4%)	51.9	40.6	35.0	35.1	38.7
Apparel	49 (9.8%)	59.8	49.8	52.5	54.1	53.5
Petrochemical	46 (9.2%)	54.8	44.7	46.9	41.5	46.0
Steel	40 (8.0%)	59.2	44.0	45.7	42.1	46.3
Machinery	41 (8.2%)	67.4	51.5	53.1	54.7	55.4
Electronics	45 (9.0%)	64.5	49.5	56.7	49.4	55.4
Automobile	48 (9.6%)	57.5	47.4	50.0	48.0	50.0
Construction	41 (8.2%)	61.4	50.3	48.7	50.5	51.5
Distribution	40 (8.0%)	59.6	47.1	46.4	45.9	48.4
Transportation	35 (7.0%)	67.6	64.1	50.4	58.0	58.0
Telecommunication	53 (10.6%)	68.2	65.0	58.6	56.6	60.7
Finance	**500**	**60.7**	**50.1**	**49.2**	**48.3**	**50.8**
Total						

Construction industry has a low index score of IT resource (47.4), but has a high index score of Environment resource. This analysis implies that each industry has different complementary resource portfolios that support the development of web-enabled supply chains.

The preliminary analysis of the secondary data collected by MOCIE indicates that different types of complementary resources can play different roles to the development of web-enabled supply chains at an industry level. The rest of this chapter will turn our attention to a firm level to acquire an in-depth understanding of what the actual complementary resources are and how they

work to support the development of web-enabled supply chain in a paint firm.

DESCRIPTION OF CASE STUDY METHODOLOGY

Methodology

This study performs exploratory case research and uses qualitative methodology. Given its exploratory nature, this study does not focus on generalizing the findings but rather on gaining in-depth insights into the complexity of resource

Figure 1. Index score by resource

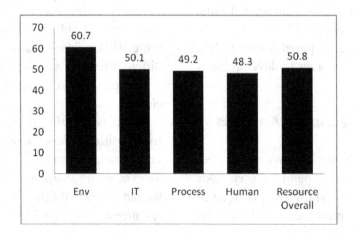

Figure 2. Resource overall index score by industry

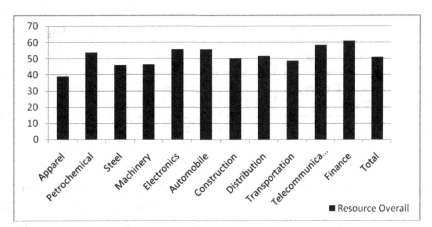

connectedness. Therefore, this study adopts a single case approach and follows the framework proposed by Eisenhardt (1989).

One important primary source with whom this researcher worked closely was a senior executive director who had spent more than 20 years in the company. Because of his broad and in-depth understanding of operations and the market conditions in the industry, this individual was selected with the objective of minimizing key-informant bias (Bagozzi and Philips, 1982). Moreover, the selection of this informant is consistent with the general recommendation regarding the most knowledgeable informant (Venkatraman and Grant, 1986). Other primary sources of data included site visits, face-to-face interviews, and electronic meetings.

Background of the Case Site

A manufacturer and distributor of paint products, the DP company was founded in 1945 and has maintained a leading position in technology and quality in the Korean paint industry, but has encountered a decrease in market share due to increased price competition in the market during the past ten years.

DP introduced a web-based application to support transactions with its independent dealers in 2001 in order to create a competitive advantage over competitors. Later, DP successfully implemented web-based applications to support various supply chain tasks ranging from purchasing indirect materials to providing customer services. DP made a significant investment in implementing web-based applications for its supply chain, and its market value as measured by stock price has increased continuously even though the market value of most major competitors has decreased during the same time period.

SUPPLY CHAIN MANAGEMENT AT DP

Overview of Conventional Supply Chain Management

Figure 3 describes the overall structure of DP's supply chain. DP acquires raw materials from suppliers and some finished goods from contract manufacturers.

The process of producing paint is characterized by many products, low volume, high setup cost, and batch processing. Recently, DP began to decentralize its production by increasing the proportion of OEM production. The logistics function is located in the main factory and

Figure 3. Overall supply chain structure of DP

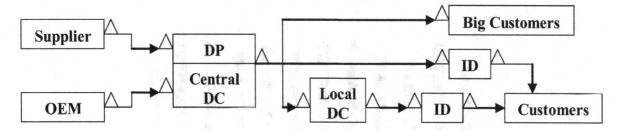

manages seven warehouses supporting local demands.

The main distribution channels for DP include Independent Dealers (IDs) and direct sales to large customers. In general, IDs deal with a selected brand product, based on exclusive contracts, and handle 67% of DP's total sales. DP also supplies professional painting companies, large organizations, and do-it-yourself (DIY) customers.

The challenges that DP sought to address by implementing web-based applications were related to increased price competition in the marketplace, the need to develop more direct relationships with large business customers, inefficiency in the ordering process, and the increased costs associated with handling small-volume orders.

Implementing Web-Based Applications in the Supply Chain

DP's CEO and management team evaluated the operations of the company's supply chain and decided to implement web-based applications in order to better support supply chain tasks. As shown in Figure 4, web-based applications were created to support three systems: material purchasing, dealer order processing, and customer order processing.

The web-based dealer order system (WDOS) was established with seven web-based applications to support the dealer order process. This system enables dealers to process orders on the web in less than one minute by looking up the item in the web catalog, placing the order, and receiving an order confirmation. Dealers who purchase products on credit can review their account balance and track the progress of orders through production to shipment.

More importantly, however, the system has provided "available-to-promise" (ATP) capability to dealers through web-based inquiries into the inventory status and production schedule, thus significantly reducing the dealers' uncertainty in managing their inventory. In addition, the sales representatives benefit by no longer having to collect orders from dealers, and can now concentrate on promoting product sales and providing technical support.

Second, to support customer order processing, a web-based customer order system (WCOS) was established with eight web-based applications as shown in Figure 4. This system enables customers to view products in the web catalog, place and track orders and find the closest dealer location, and get on-line technical support for the use of products. When DP receives a small-volume order from a customer, the system finds the closest dealer that has an auto-tinting system (ATS) and directs the order to that dealer. A third party logistic partner (3PL) picks up the product from the dealer's shop and delivers it to the customer. In 2001, the production of small-volume orders by ATS reached 34% of all small-volume orders, resulting in $432,000 in cost savings.

Third, DP established an upstream web-based procurement system (WPS) with three web-based

Figure 4.

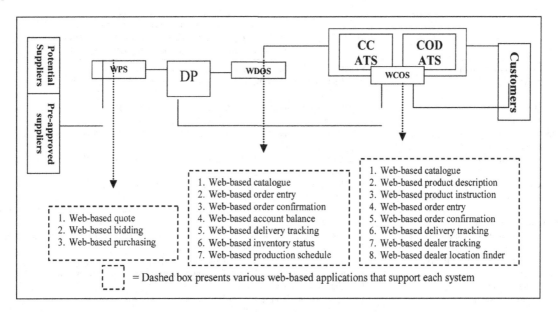

applications in order to purchase MRO and non-strategic materials, such as product containers and packaging. Through this system, DP publishes the required materials and quality specifications so that non-pre-approved suppliers can submit a quote on the web. DP can then check a potential supplier's credit and allow the supplier to participate in on-line bidding for MRO and reverse auctions.

THE IDENTIFICATION OF COMPLEMENTARY RESOURCES

The Process of Developing a Complementary Relationship Matrix

The purposes for creating this matrix were first to systematically determine which resources DP utilized for the successful implementation of web-based applications, and second to analyze the relative value of each complementary resource to a particular web-based application. The following steps were used to develop the matrix: 1) identify

an initial list of complementary resources, 2) receive key informant's adjustments to the list, 3) quantify the relative value of the complementary resources to each web-based application, and 4) consolidate the final results.

The data collected was ordered into worksheets as shown in Table 3. Each of the web-based applications is listed in the top row, the initial list of complementary resources supporting these applications is in the left column, and a brief description of how each complementary resource would support the implementation of a web-based application was entered in the right column.

Second, these completed worksheets were sent to the key informant at DP so that he could verify and screen the initial list of complementary resources, reducing it to the final list which would be examined in the rest of the study.

Third, in order to better understand the relationship between the complementary resources and web-based applications, their relative value was determined by assigning a weighted score for each resource as it was related to an application. The scores were coded as 1 (somewhat related), 2

Table 3.

	Web-based Customer Order System **(e-catalogue, Product Description, Product instruction, Order confirmation, Order** **tracking, Dealer location finder, Customer support)**
- Dealer owners workshop - COD owners training : - Brand Reputation - CEO's Commitment - Open Communication - Management Consensus - Strategic orientation of acquiring customer information for the CRM - Make-to-Order (MTO) - Strategic orientation of product focus - Strategic orientation of delivery service differentiation - Strategic orientation of shorter order lead time differentiation - Strategic orientation of ATP service differentiation - Co-Ownership Dealer (COD) - Auto Tinting System	Enables dealers to better respond to customer orders from WCOS Enables COD owners to better respond to customer orders from WCOS : Enables customer to place an order based on e-catalogue, description, and instruction without quality uncertainty of the product Enables DP to consider the Web implementation at the strategic level and efficiently develop the system Enables employees at DP to understand the value of implementingthe system and its potential benefit for the company Enables DP to efficiently reallocate the corporate resources needed to develop new capability without resistance Enables DP to design the WCOS to capture customer information for the order entry and on-line customer support Enables DP to design the WCOS to quickly transfer the customer order and enables the MTO-based system to run through ATS and dealers Enables DP to design and to run the WCOS for the right customer segment Enables DP to design the WCOS in a way to support reducing delivery time and differentiating the delivery service Enables DP to design the WCOS in a way to reduce customer order lead time Enables DP to design the WCOS to provide product availability and delivery time information to customers Enables DP to efficiently and effectively respond to customer orders through the WCOS Enables DP to respond to small-volume orders and reduce the delivery lead time for the order from WCOS by delivering the product from the closest ATS equipped dealer

(important), or 3 (critical) based on the researcher's knowledge of the company, experience, and judgment and are shown in Table 5.

Finally, the researcher developed the complementary relationship matrix presenting a final list of complementary resources and their relative value to each web-based application. In addition, the complementary resources were classified using categories found in the process of literature review (e.g., Grant, 1991; Barney, 1991; Keen, 1993). In further analysis, total scores representing the relative value for each resource and for each resource category were calculated (see Table 5).

Complementary Resources to the Implementation of Web-Based Applications

Through the process described above, 43 significant complementary resources were identified based on each resource's importance to the implementation or improvement of WCOS. For example, the complementary resource 'brand reputation' (row 3) was included because it enables customers to use WCOS without being concerned about product quality. In addition, because managing the supply chain encompasses diverse functional areas such as purchasing, manufacturing, and sales, the complementary resources: 'CEO's commitment' (row 4), 'communication' (row 5) and 'management consensus' (row 6) were considered to be important factors related to the successful implementation of web-based applications supporting WCOS.

Among the complementary resources related to the web-based customer order system (WCOS), the 'auto-tinting system (ATS)' and 'co-ownership dealer shop (COD)' play particularly important roles in making WCOS work efficiently. ATS is an automated paint production system. The operator at the dealer shop selects the product and color based on the customer order. Then,

Table 4. Identified complementary resources

Code	Complementary resources	Code	Complementary Resources
C1	Dealer owners workshop	C37	Capability of redesigning the person-to-person product description
C2	COD owners training	C38	Capability of redesigning paper-based quotes
C3	Sales personnel training	C39	Capability of redesigning paper-based bidding
C4	Purchasing personnel training	C40	Capability of reducing number of supplier meetings
C5	Technical support for WDOS	C41	Capability of redesigning face-to-face auctions
C6	Financial support for WDOS	C42	Capability of redesigning the paper based RFQ
C7	Price incentive for adopting WDOS	C43	Strategic orientation of purchasing admin. cost efficiency
:	CEO commitment	:	Direct purchasing from supplier to e-marketplace
C20	Objective information searching	C56	3PL deliver service from DP to dealer shop
C21	Management consensus	C57	3PL delivery service from the closest available shop to customer
C22	Recognition of external environment &	C58	Co-Ownership Dealer (COD)
C23	new IT innovation	C59	ATS
:	Capability of developing the customer	:	Color Matching Software
C33	order delivery process with 3PL partner	C69	3PL information sharing (order, machine production,
C34	Capability of developing on-line cus-	C70	and dealer location)
C35	tomer support process	C71	
C36	Capability of developing customer order		
	treatment process with dealer		
	Capability of developing customer prod-		
	uct return process		

the tinting machine automatically mixes the material to produce the required color. Although some competitors have installed auto-tinting systems with their dealers as well, they have not been able to match colors as well as DP, which developed its own color-matching software and machine based on thirty years of production data and experience.

A co-ownership dealer shop (COD) shares its ownership with DP in a strategic partnership. While the original owner runs the store, DP provides operation manuals, training programs, web-based dealer order system (WDOS) support, auto-tinting system (ATS) installation, and a guaranteed margin. Since most dealer shops are small businesses that often operate under severe financial burdens, the introduction of the COD program was considered to be a 'win-win' strategy for both DP and its dealership owners. These co-ownership dealer shops, equipped with ATS and WDOS, enable DP to respond to customer orders more effectively.

The strategic orientation of the complementary resources: 'delivery service differentiation', 'short order lead-time', 'product focus' and 'available-to-

promise (ATP)' are also recognized as important resources to the WCOS design. In addition, DP has aligned the 'make-to-order' (MTO) strategy for its architectural paint products and 'customer relationship management' (CRM) with the capability of acquiring immediate customer order information from WCOS. This alignment allows DP to improve service quality by fulfilling customer expectations while reducing finished goods inventories across the supply chain.

Using the same logic, the complementary resources related to the web-based procurement system (WPS) and the web-based dealer order system (WDOS) are identified. Although WDOS, WPS, and WCOS individually have 47, 29, and 49 complementary resources respectively, there are 71 relevant complementary resources in total because some complementary resources are related to two or more systems as shown in Table 4.

The Development of a Complementary Relationship Matrix

Table 5 is a simplified matrix representing the quantification of complementary relationships for

Table 5. A simplified complementary relationship matrix

Web-based SC Systems → Functions of each application / **Complementary Resources**	WPS Web-quote	WPS Web-bidding	WPS Web-purchasing	WDOS e-catalogue	WDOS Order entry	WDOS …	WDOS Inventory status	WDOS Production schedule	WDOS e-catalogue	WDOS Product description	WDOS Product instruction	WCOS Order entry	WCOS Order confirmation	WCOS Delivery tracking	WCOS Dealer location finding	WCOS Customer support	Resource-relatedness score	Resource Factors *(Resource relatedness score subtotal)*
(C2) COD owners training	2			1	1	…	1	1	1	1	1	1		1	1	1	15	Human resources (66)
(C4) Purchasing personnel training		2	2			…											6	
(C12) Reducing dealer resistance				2	2	…	2	2	3	3	3	3	3	3	3	3	38	Inter-org relationship (157)
…						…												
(C15) Color matching knowledge				3	3	…	3	3	3	3	3	3	3	3	3	3	45	Knowledge (80)
(C20) CEO commitment	2	2	2	2	2	…	2	2	2	2	2	2	2	2	2	2	36	Organizational (252)
(C49) Delivery service differentiation				3	3	…	3	3	2	2	2	3	1	3	1	2	29	Strategy (173)
(C59) Co-ownership dealer development				3	3	…	3	3	3	3	3	3	3	3	3	3	45	Structure (132)
(C35) Capability of developing customer order treatment process					3	…	1	1				3	3				12	Process (150)
(C63) MRP	2	2	2	3	1	…	2	2				3	1				18	Technology (275)
(C69) Auto tinting system (ATS)	2	2	2	2	2	…	2	2	3	3	3	3	3	3	3	3	38	
…						…												
Total	56	59	56	60	109	…	85	86	63	65	66	109	73	81	63	59	1291	
	57							77.3								72.4		

each resource as it relates to the implementation of web-based applications.

Table 5 shows the three web-based systems established by DP as headings in a row at the top of the matrix. The web-based applications that support each system are represented in columns beneath the system heading. The complementary resources that are related to each web-based application are represented in the rows of the matrix.

Each cell of the matrix represents a relative value, called the resource relatedness score (RRS), of a particular complementary resource to a particular web-based application. For example, as '(C2) COD owners training' is somewhat related to all of WDOS' and WCOS' sub-applications, the value given is a (1). On the other hand, '(C4) purchasing personal training' is importantly related (2) only to the applications of WPS. In some cases, a complementary resource is related to some applications but is given a different weight. For instance, '(C12) reducing dealer resistance to direct sales', is importantly related (2) to WDOS, critically related (3) to the WCOS, and not related to the WPS.

The total resource relatedness score (RRS) for each resource is shown at the end of each row. This score indicates the degree to which a particular resource is utilized to implement web-based applications. For further exploration, these resources were organized into eight potential factors drawn from the literature: human resources, inter-organizational relationships, knowledge, strategy, process, structure, organization, and technology (e.g., Keen, 1993; Powell, 1995; Powell and Dent-Micallef, 1997).

DISCUSSION

The Breadth of Complementary Resources

This study provides insight into the breadth of complementary resources that can be utilized to

implement web-based applications in order to develop a more competitive supply chain. Whereas previous efforts to identify complementary resources have focused primarily on resources within an organization, this study identifies a number of complementary resources that are related to inter-organizational factors such as 'built-in trust' among partners, 'reducing supplier and dealer resistance,' and diverse 'support programs' for supply chain partners. This finding agrees with the result of a recent study that suggests that the successful implementation of web-based applications for supply chain management depends not only on reducing internal barriers, but also on reducing external barriers and developing inter-organizational collaboration (Frohlich, 2002; Soliman and Janz, 2004).

Second, this study also adds "knowledge" to the list of complementary resources that need to be considered. Although knowledge assets are recognized as a unique and valuable resource in strategic planning (Prahalad and Hamel, 1990), little attention has been given to the importance of knowledge assets in the supply chain context. Indeed, DP's knowledge assets such as 'color matching skill' and 'product coding' are embedded in the development of web-based applications and play a critical role in leveraging the value of the auto tinting system (ATS). The addition of knowledge-based resources implies that implementing a web-based application is more than just replacing an existing information system. Rather, firms may be required to reconfigure existing resources and develop new resources by utilizing available tacit and explicit knowledge in order to leverage the capability of web-based applications.

Third, this study emphasized the importance of utilizing other technology resources in the implementation of web-based applications. As Alt et al. (2000) identified in their case study of 'The Swatch Group', the success of implementing web-based applications in managing Swatch's supply chain depended on the technology; in this case, the master database. DP also utilizes diverse technology resources in its successful implementation of web-based applications; specifically, its dealer information database, 3PL information system, and various MRP modules, such as master production scheduling, machine production data, and product balance on hand. While information technology itself has been viewed as a central resource that requires diverse complementary resources to gain competitive advantage, its role as a complementary resource has been frequently ignored. However, the results of this study suggest that a critical component in the successful implementation of web-based applications may be the integration of additional technology resources in such a way as to leverage web capabilities in order to attain a competitive advantage.

The Relative Importance of Each Complementary Resource

In addition to the breadth of complementary resources, this study shows through its analysis of resource relatedness scores (RRS) the degree to which a particular resource is utilized to implement various web-based applications. For example, as shown in Table 3, 'color matching knowledge' and 'co-ownership dealer development' show the highest RRS scores (45) of all the resources. This implies that DP utilized these resources more intensively than any other resources for the successful implementation of web-based applications. The total RRS of 'reducing dealer resistance to direct sales' and 'auto tinting system' shows the next highest RRS score (38) and implies that these resources are relatively less intensively utilized than the above two resources but more intensively utilized than the other resources.

Since firms may require different types of complementary resources depending on the competitive environment they face, the total RRS for each resource factor can provide a more general idea of what kinds of resource factors are utilized to implement web-based applications. Thus, we see in Table 3 that technology and organizational

factors are more intensively utilized than any other resource factors, followed by strategy, inter-organizational relationships, process, and structural factors.

The total RRS for each resource factor suggests that the implementation of web-based applications may not only be considered at the operational level but also at the strategic level (e.g., integrating MTO and differentiation strategy into the implementation of web-based applications) as well as at the structural level (e.g., development of co-ownership dealer and color center). In addition, DP utilized both internal factors (e.g., human resources and knowledge) and inter-organizational factors (e.g., reducing dealer resistance and built-in trust).

In sum, the complementary relationship matrix developed in this study provides a systematic tool for identifying complementary resources and analyzing the way resources are related to the implementation of web-based applications. A careful examination of this matrix may provide more advantages for planning the implementation of web-based applications. Whereas the Design Structure Matrix (DSM) (Eppinger, 2001) is focused on improving efficiency by reducing information exchanges and repetition of tasks, the complementary relationship matrix (CRM) is focused on improving effectiveness by recognizing complementary resources and their relatedness to the successful implementation of web-based applications.

Future Research Directions

As Black and Boal (1994) claimed in their exploration of paths to achieving sustainable advantage, "the list of ingredients from the recipe is not a cake. A cake requires the ingredients plus the relationships among them for a successful result." In the same way, this study has attempted to show how complementary resources and web-based applications relate to each other to create competitive advantages in a supply chain. Because the analysis of this research is based on a single case study, it is not aimed at a generalization of findings but is more focused on understanding various complementary resources that can influence the implementation of web-based applications. Therefore, there exist significant opportunities for future research.

First, more systematic research efforts are required to generalize the results of this study. For example, a multiple case study method is recommended to identify additional complementary resources and to verify the findings of this single case study. Based on the results of multiple cases studies, researchers could develop multi-item scales for each resource factor.

Second, future research is required to develop more systematic ways of understanding resources' relatedness. This study quantified the resource relatedness (i.e., critical, important, and related) based primarily on the researcher's experienced subjective judgment. However, more systematic methods require identifying not only the degree of resource relatedness but also the resource interactions in order to enhance our understanding of how complementary resources and web-based applications work together to create competitive advantage.

Third, the understanding of the underlying characteristics of complementary resources can help researchers to investigate various potential resource combinations to create competitive advantage. The analysis of the interaction among resources that have different characteristics may provide information about which combination of characteristics might produce the most sustainable competitive advantage.

Finally, further research needs to develop performance variables of web-enabled supply chains and investigates the relationship between complementary resources and the performance. The investigation of what complementary resource can explain the performance variance of firms can help us to better manage the resource development process and resource of implementation process.

REFERENCES

Auramo, J., Kauremaa, J., & Tanskanen, K. (2005). Benefits of IT in supply chain management: an explorative study of progressive companies. *International Journal of Physical Distribution & Logistics Management, 53*(2), 82–100. doi:10.1108/09600030510590282

Barney, J. B. (1991). Firm resources and sustained competitive advantage. *Journal of Management, 17*(1), 99–120. doi:10.1177/014920639101700108

Barratt, M., & Rosdahl, K. (2002). Exploring business-to-business market sites. *European Journal of Purchasing & Supply Management, 8*(2), 111–122. doi:10.1016/S0969-7012(01)00010-7

Black, J. A., & Boal, K. B. (1994). Strategic resources: traits, configurations, and paths to sustainable competitive advantage. *Strategic Management Journal, 15*, 131–148.

Boer, L. D., Harink, J., & Heijboer, G. (2002). A conceptual model for assessing the impact of electronic procurement. *European Journal of Purchasing & Supply Management, 8*, 25–33. doi:10.1016/S0969-7012(01)00015-6

Cagliano, R., Caniato, F., & Spina, G. (2005). E-business strategy: How companies are shaping their supply chain through the internet. *International Journal of Operations & Production Management, 25*(12), 1309–1327. doi:10.1108/01443570510633675

Cho, D., & Lee, D. (1998). A new paradigm in strategy theory: 'ser-M'. *Monash Mt. Eliza Business Review, 1*(2), 82–97.

Clemons, E. K., & Michael, M. C. (1991). Sustaining IT advantage: the role of structural differences. *MIS Quarterly, 15*(3), 275–293. doi:10.2307/249639

Croom, S. (2000). The impact of web-based procurement on the management of operating resources supply. *Journal of Supply Chain Management, 35*(1), 4–10. doi:10.1111/j.1745-493X.2000.tb00065.x

Dehning, B., Richardson, V. J., & Zmud, R. W. (2007). The financial performance effects of IT-based supply chain management systems in manufacturing firms. *Journal of Operations Management, 25*, 806–824. doi:10.1016/j.jom.2006.09.001

Dierickx, I., & Cool, K. (1989). Asset stock accumulation and sustainability of competitive advantage. *Management Science, 35*(12), 1504–1513. doi:10.1287/mnsc.35.12.1504

Ellinger, A. E., Lynch, D. F., & Hensen, J. D. (2002). Firm size, web site content, and financial performance in the transportation industry. *Industrial Marketing Management, 32*(3), 177–185. doi:10.1016/S0019-8501(02)00261-4

Emiliani, M. L., & Stec, D. F. (2002). Realizing savings from online reserve auctions. *An International Journal of Supply Chain Management, 7*(1), 12–23. doi:10.1108/13598540210414355

Essig, M., & Arnold, U. (2001). Electronic procurement in supply chain management: an information economics-based analysis of electronic markets. *The Journal of Supply Chain Management, 37*(4), 43–49. doi:10.1111/j.1745-493X.2001.tb00112.x

Frohlich, M. T., & Westbrook, R. (2002). Demand chain management in manufacturing and services: web-based integration, drivers and performance. *Journal of Operations Management, 20*(6), 729–745. doi:10.1016/S0272-6963(02)00037-2

Grant, R. (1991). The resource-based theory of competitive advantage. *California Management Review, 33*(3), 114–135.

Keen, P. (1993). Information technology and the management difference: A fusion map. *IBM Systems Journal, 32*, 17–39.

Lee, H. L. (2002). Aligning supply chain strategies with product uncertainties. *California Management Review, 44*(3), 105–119.

Lynagh, P. M., Murphy, P. R., Poist, R. F., & Grazer, W. F. (2001). Web-based informational practices of logistics service providers: An empirical assessment. *Transportation Journal, 40*, 34–45.

Peteraf, M. A. (1993). The cornerstones of competitive advantage: A resource-based view. *Strategic Management Journal, 14*, 179–191. doi:10.1002/smj.4250140303

Powell, T. C., & Dent-Micallef, A. (1997). Information technology as competitive advantage: the role of human, business, and technology resources. *Strategic Management Journal, 18*(5), 375–405. doi:10.1002/(SICI)1097-0266(199705)18:5<375::AID-SMJ876>3.0.CO;2-7

Power, D. (2005). Determinants of business-to-business e-commerce implementation and performance: A structural model. *Supply Chain Management, 10*(2), 96–113. doi:10.1108/13598540510589179

Rahman, Z. (2003). Internet-based supply chain management: using the Internet to revolutionize your business. *International Journal of Information Management, 23*, 493–505. doi:10.1016/j.ijinfomgt.2003.09.004

Rao, B. (1999). The Internet and the revolution in distribution: A cross-industry examination. *Technology in Society, 21*, 287–306. doi:10.1016/S0160-791X(99)00018-4

Robinson, E. P., Sahin, F., & Gao, L. (2005). The impact of e-replenishment strategy on make-to-order supply chain performance. *Decision Sciences*, *36*(1), 33–64. doi:10.1111/j.1540-5915.2005.00065.x

Sarkis, J., & Sundarraj, R. P. (2000). Factors for strategic evaluation of enterprise information technologies. *International Journal of Physical Distribution & Logistics Management*, *30*(3/4), 196–220. doi:10.1108/09600030010325966

Simchi-Levi, D., & Simchi-Levi, E. (2000). The dramatic impact of the impact on supply chain strategies. *ASCET* Vol. 2, Montgomery Research Inc.

Soliman, K. S., & Janz, B. D. (2004). An exploratory study to identify the critical factors affecting the decision to establish Internet-based inter-organizational information systems. *Information & Management*, *41*, 697–706. doi:10.1016/j.im.2003.06.001

Venkatraman, N., & Grant, J. H. (1986). Construct measurement in organizational strategy research: A critique and proposal. *Academy of Management Review*, *11*(1), 71–87. doi:10.2307/258332

Wade, M., & Hulland, J. (2004). The resource-based view and information systems research: Review, extension, and suggestions for future research. *MIS Quarterly*, *28*(1), 107–142.

Wernerfelt, B. (1984). A resource-based view of the firm. *Strategic Management Journal*, *5*(2), 171–180. doi:10.1002/smj.4250050207

Willcocks, L. P., & Plant, R. (2003). How corporations e-source: from business technology projects to value networks. *Information Systems Frontiers*, *5*(2), 175–193. doi:10.1023/A:1022601607218

Chapter 7

A Comparison of Information Technology in Supply Chains:
U.S. Beef Industry and U.S. Food Industry

George. N. Kenyon
Lamar University, USA

Brian. D. Neureuther
State University of New York at Plattsburgh, USA

ABSTRACT

Historically, the growth of the beef industry has been hampered by the various entities (breeders, cow-calf producers, stockers, backgrounders, processors, etc..) within the beef industry's supply chain. The primary obstacles to growth are the large number of participants in the upstream side of the supply chain and the lack of coordination between them. Over the last decade significant advances have been made in information and communication technologies. Many new companies have been founded to promote these technical advances. This research looks at both the upstream and downstream participants to determine the degree to which information technologies are currently being utilized and the degree to which these new technologies have driven performance improvements in the beef industry's supply chain. We find through our survey that, by and large, the beef industry does not use information technologies to their benefit and that the US beef supply chain is not yet strategically poised to enable the use of these technologies.

INTRODUCTION AND BACKGROUND

In a study of the U.S. beef industry and the use of information technology (IT) to enable the industry's supply chain, Neureuther and Kenyon (2008) found that the beef industry is not using IT to any significant advantage except in the area of information collection. They further found that IT could enhance supply chain performance and integration, but the supply chain is not yet strategically poised to do so. They attributed this to several reasons:

1. Beef in the U.S. is thought of as a commodity product
2. The U.S. beef industry lacks a common vision and industry goals.
3. The mentality of downstream partners in the supply chain constrains incentives and

DOI: 10.4018/978-1-60566-974-8.ch007

Table 1. Beef industry IT recommendations (Neureuther and Kenyon, 2008)

IT Usage
Increase the use of e-markets and e-commerce for auction houses in order to create visibility and reach, reduce transaction costs, and facilitate asset swap to achieve better utilization of key assets
Create tangible rewards for adherence to standards, such as contracts that require a higher price per pound for beef that meets an agreed upon level of supply and/or an agreed upon grade specification
The use of electronic data interchange (EDI) technologies (or even internet XML applications) to link animal record keeping information throughout the supply chain – from cow/calf producer to retailer – by individual animal
Begin enabling IT at the downstream partners and then pull usage to the upstream participants.
Infrastructure
Coordination mechanisms need to be matched to the market structure in order to improve value
Better communication of consumer demands needs to occur throughout the supply chain
Better education of the typical rancher of supply chain management benefits, especially in the areas of coordination, vertical integration, and IT usage is a must

information movement to upper levels in the supply chain.

4. In addition, auction houses have developed into information clearinghouses for much of the information in the supply chain and few are using e-markets or e-commerce tools.

5. Mistrust of internet usage dominates the industry where there is a feeling that small producers may be eliminated by adopting IT.

6. Current supply chain entities partners perceive little or no benefit to moving their processes online with respect to cost savings in procurement.

Based on these findings, they made several recommendations for the beef industry in the area of IT use in the supply chain and with respect to infrastructure changes that will need to occur in order to enable the use of IT. A synopsis of the recommendation is found in Table 1.

Given these conditions in the upstream portion of the Beef Industry's supply chain, it would make sense then, to look at the US beef industry and compare its readiness for the use of IT to that of other food industries. To this avail, this research will examine the use of IT in the food manufacturing industry, using the 2003-2007

Industry Week/MPI Census of US Manufacturers. Specifically, the research will examine the usage of using information technologies in food manufacturing supply chains by examining the impact of information technologies and supply chain performance measures. In the analysis, profitability, costs of goods sold, labor costs, material costs, and overhead costs will be analyzed with each of the technology platforms of MRP, MRPII, Demand Planning, EDI, online purchasing and online selling. The results will then be compared to the US beef industry.

OBJECTIVES

Even though a solid foundation of supply chain research exists (Chandra and Kumar, 2000; Levy and Grewal, 2000; Mentzer, Dewit, Keebler, Min, Nix, Smith and Zacharia, 2001; Lambert, Cooper, and Pagh, 1998; Langley and Holcomb, 1992; Min and Mentzer, 2000; Chandrashekar and Schary, 1999; Cooper, Lambert, and Pagh, 1997; and Croxton, Garcia-Dastugue, Lambert, and Rodgers, 2001) there is inconsistent evidence that any of the supply chain management research can be effectively integrated into industry practice or provide sustainable performance improvements (Moberg,

Speh, and Freese, 2003). Since it is estimated that poor coordination between the supply chain participants in the U.S. food industry is wasting $30 billion annually (Fisher, 1997), it becomes clear that an analysis of the supply chains in the food industry is of interest. It then becomes important to analyze the degree to which this industry is contributing to the waste. Salin (2000) conducted a study of the beef supply chains and the use of information technology in which three primary issues affecting the success of beef supply chains were discussed. She found that 1) technology and scale, 2) auctions, alliances, and competitiveness and 3) traditional relationships were significant issues in supply chain performance. The purpose of Salin's (2000) study was to use interviews from the beef sector to describe the information technologies used in this industry.

As an extension of Salin's (2000) work the goal of this research is to seek whether or not sustainable process improvements by supply chain integration has been realized in the US food industry. More specifically, the objective of the research is to assess the impact of internet technologies on the food industry's supply chain. In order to meet this objective, the following propositions are proposed:

1. The US food industry is not using information technology to any significant advantage (advantage can be cost reduction of information gathering or transactional).
2. Information technology enhances supply chain integration by use of the internet and other information technologies.

It is paramount that a good understanding of the US food manufacturer's chain is achieved in order to examine these propositions. To this avail, the research will give an in depth overview of the US food manufacture's supply chain by examining change drivers in the supply chain and current coordination strategies and information technology usage in the supply chain. Then, a survey of supply chain participants in the industry will be discussed and analyzed with respect to the above objectives and propositions, with conclusions and findings following.

LITERATURE REVIEW

Nitschke and O'Keefe (1997) suggest that consumer value is created not by individual firms but rather by business enterprises. They further suggest that the competitiveness of an enterprise is dependent upon both the competitiveness of the individual firms and the nature of the linkages between the firms in the supply chain. A key observation made by Nitschke and O'Keefe (1997) was that coordination mechanisms need to be matched appropriately to the market structure is order to improve value. As an example, auction systems traditionally used in commodity markets would not be appropriate for differentiated products and segmented market strategies. Coordination mechanisms are practices/tools that are intended to enable better communication of information, facilitate continuous improvement, speed up response time, improve product quality, and create closer relationships between customers and suppliers.

One method used to vertically integrate the food industry's supply chain has been the increasing use of contracts. Mighell and Jones (1963) have categorized contracts into three basic groups: market-specification contracts, production-management contracts, and resource-providing contracts. Market-specification contracts are those where the buyer provides a market for a seller's output, while the producer retains control over the production process. Production-management contracts are those where the buyer provides a market and can specify and/or monitor production practices or input usage. Romeo (2006) writes about several restaurant chains that are using contracts at the customer-retailer interface to buy beef at certain prices to hedge against price risks. Resource-providing contracts are defined as those where the buyer provides a market outlet, supervises production practices and supplies key inputs. They assume the greatest proportion of the risk, but may retain ownership of the product.

Narayanan and Raman (2004) have identified some limitations to contract-based solutions for supply chain improvements. First, outcome variables are highly correlated with the unobservable actions of other participants and are often difficult to isolate. Second, designing contracts to overcome actions that impact on the principal's welfare can be difficult when individuals within the supply chain are "risk-averse". Finally, attempts to mitigate actions that impact the individual's welfare with contract-based solutions can exacerbate the problems for the other party.

Vertical partnerships are defined as an arrangement between a buyer and seller to facilitate a mutually satisfying exchange over time, which leaves the operation and control of the two businesses substantially independent (Hughes, 1994). Fearne (1998) states that there are four key aspects to vertical partnerships: partnerships are entered into freely, partnerships must offer mutual benefits, these benefits occur overtime, and partners remain substantially independent. He also describes five benefits to vertical partnerships: improved market access, improved communications, higher profit margins, greater discipline, and higher barriers to entry.

Horizontal partnerships, such as producer co-operatives, have existed for centuries and generally have three key motives (Fearne, 1998), 1) meeting the volume requirements for major customers and increasing bargaining strength in their dealings with major buyers and sellers, 2) accelerating the pace and reducing the cost of penetrating new markets and 3) sharing the costs associated with developing new products and adopting new technologies.

The vast majority of the food supply chain entities do not participate in any of these mechanisms. Even with the development of these coordination mechanisms, problems still exist. Narayanan and Raman (2004) noted that resistance from key stakeholders could often be explained by their refusal to change old ways of doing things or by their inability to perceive the benefits of a proposed change. Lawrence (2006) pleads that the U.S. beef supply chain needs confidence in their products and needs every entity within the supply chain to have strong relationships. In addition, Euclides (2004) notes that the quality of the final product and the need to lower environmental risk are significant aspects of a holistic approach to the beef supply chain in Brazil. Given the failure of these mechanisms to improve the overall coordination of upstream participants in the beef industry's supply chain, how can better information flows drive future improvements?

INFORMATION TECHNOLOGY AND THE US FOOD INDUSTRY

Narayanan and Raman (2004) stated that changes in supply chain operations often included applications of information technology (IT). Peypoch (1998) discussed how the leveraging of cost-cutting benefits typically available with IT through the streamlining of activities and the utilization of this technology to create electronic communities (networks) drives closer relationships among competitors, suppliers, buyers, and sellers. Through the creation of electronic communities, the traditional barriers that exist between supply chain participants could be reduced. By using a multi-tiered structure that provides for different vertical and horizontal interactions, electronic communities can increase an organization's exposure, thus allowing a more orderly and efficient trading process. Peypoch (1998) further claimed that the potential results would lower the cost structure across an entire industry such that all participants would benefit.

Wise and Morrison (2000) state that future exchanges between supply chain participants (either product or information) would need to occur such that buyers and suppliers were able to form tighter relationships while still maintaining the reach and efficiency of internet commerce. In order for future e-commerce models to succeed in the long run, rewards must flow to both sellers and buyers. While the physical transfer of goods is the goal of all business transactions, the information that defines the transaction can be separated and exchanged electronically. It is this information that is frequently more valuable to companies than the underlying goods themselves (Wise and Morrison, 2000; Lewis and Talalayevsky, 1997; Lewis and Talalayevsky, 2004).

More recently, Choi, Tsai and Jones (2009) examined how a regional supermarket store chain in the retail food industry develops its enterprise network infrastructure to outperform its larger competitors. In this study, critical success factors for firms to build an effective enterprise network infrastructure are highlighted. It is suggested that IT planning in the retail food industry needs to be firmly tied to critical business goals. In addition, Mohtadi (2008) reviews the determinants of information sharing between retailers and their suppliers, in the food industry supply chain. He examines the behavior of food retailers in their adoption of information sharing with suppliers. He finds that retail firms with larger number of suppliers are more inclined to share, rather than to withhold, information. Further, García-Arca and Prado-Prado (2008) in analyzing two Spanish companies in the food sector discuss a methodology for the implementation of information systems; with emphasis on the logistics field.

Yao, Palmer, and Dresner (2007) studied electronically-enabled supply chains (ESCs) using data from a survey of 183 managers in the food industry. They found that top management support and external influences are both important determinants of ESC use in the food industry, that perceived benefits to customers, perceived benefits to suppliers, and perceived internally focused benefits, are all found to influence positively ESC

use and Third that distributors are more likely to perceive greater customer benefits from ESC use than are manufacturers and retailers. Finally, Frasquet, Cervera, and Gil (2008) studied the influence of customer orientation on the application of IT to the supply chain and of these on the development of channel relationships based on trust and commitment. A questionnaire-based personal survey was conducted among manufacturers. The found that that customer orientation affects the application of IT to logistics, and IT has a positive impact on manufacturer and supplier commitment to the relationship.

DATA COLLECTION

Using the data from the Census of Manufacturers Surveys of years 2003 through 2007, as conducted by the Manufacturers Performance Institute, the usage of information technology systems by US Food Manufacturers, NAICS 311, is analyzed. The IW/MPI Census of Manufacturers was conducted using an online questionnaire and a hard-copy questionnaire that was twice mailed from MPI to approximately 12,000 plant leaders (NAICS 31 through 33 levels). Responses are received by MPI, and then entered into a database, edited, and cleansed to ensure answers were plausible, where necessary. All respondent answers to the survey are anonymous. As an incentive, respondents were offered one-time access to a database of this year's findings and entered into a random drawing for monetary awards. The response rates for the years 2003 through 2007 totaled 3,550.

Though many of the respondents are invited to participate every year, the responses are anonymous. Therefore, there is no way of tracking a given respondent across several years. Bardhan, Whitaker and Mithas (2006) analyzed the Census of Manufacturers Surveys response rates and founded the survey to be representative of U.S Census data at the 3 digit NAICS code level.

Table 2. Breakout of IT system usage by NAICS Industry Group 311 respondents

Information Technology Applications	2003	2004	2005	2006	2007
ERP (Enterprise Resource Planning)	22.5%	17.1%	31.3%	26.7%	40.0%
ERP II (Enterprise Resource Planning)	7.5%	8.6%	0.0%	3.3%	5.0%
APS (Demand-Management/Forecasting)	22.5%	40.0%	25.0%	33.3%	40.0%
EDI (Electronic Data Interchange)	45.0%	48.6%	50.0%	30.0%	50.0%
OP (Online Purchasing)	30.0%	31.4%	31.3%	33.3%	35.0%
OS (Online Selling)	20.0%	14.3%	25.0%	23.3%	10.0%

Source: MPI Census of US Manufacturers Survey

A breakout of the respondents from the NAICS Industry Group 311 used in this analysis is shown in Table 2. The IT Systems used in the US food industry and which were examined for this study include Enterprise Resource Planning systems (ERP and ERP II), Demand Management and Forecasting systems, Electronic Data Interchange systems, Online Purchasing systems, and Online Selling systems. The percentages of users of these systems within the 311 Industry respondents are shown in Table 2.

In comparing the US food industry manufacturers to the US beef industry, it is recognized that upstream organizations within the beef industry supply chain (i.e.; Cow-Calf Producers, Stockers, and Order Buyers) are too small to afford these types of IT systems. It is proposed that if any of these systems prove to be beneficial to downstream organizations, that their usage could be extended upstream, improving communication, coordination, and synchronization of activities; thus improving the efficiency of the overall supply chain.

A brief description of the nature of the companies (processes types, product volume and mix structure, size as measured by the number of employees, and age of the plants) examined in this study in Tables 3 through 6 that follow.

Analysis of Data

Using the database information, an analysis of variance was conducted using the Proc Mixed procedure in SAS. The dependent variables of profitability, cost of goods sold, labor costs, material costs, and overhead costs were analyzed with respect to the IT systems identified earlier. These variables are key performance measures used in analyzing supply chains (Kenyon and Neureuther, 2008). The variable, *year*, was treated as an independent variable to account for any environmental factors that may be associated with a specific year. The 4-digit NAICS code variable was modeled as a random variable to account for differences between industry groups within the food manufacturing industry. Each of

Table 3. Breakout of processing types within the NAICS Industry Group 311 respondents

Process Types	2003	2004	2005	2006	2007
Discrete	7/17.5%	3/8.82%	2/13.33%	4/13.33%	2/10%
Continuous	24/60%	26/76.47%	9/60%	15/50%	14/70%
Mixed	9/22.5%	5/14.7%	4/26.67%	11/36.67%	4/20%

Source: MPI Census of US Manufacturers Survey

Table 4. Breakout of product volume and mix within the NAICS Industry Group 311 respondents

Product Volume and Mix	2003	2004	2005	2006	2007
High Volume/ High Mix	0	8/23.53%	3/20%	9/31.03%	11/55%
High Volume/ Low Mix	0	13/38.24%	5/33.33%	7/24.14%	6/30%
Low Volume/ High Mix	0	11/32.35%	7/46.67%	10/34.48%	1/5%
Low Volume/ Low Mix	0	2/5.88%	0	3/10.34	2/10%

Source: MPI Census of US Manufacturers Survey

Table 5. Breakout of Plant Size within the NAICS Industry Group 311 respondents

Plant Size	2003	2004	2005	2006	2007
<100 Employees	22/55%	15/42.86%	6/37.5%	11/36.67%	5/25%
100-249 Employees	13/32.5%	11/31.43%	5/31.25%	11/36.67%	5/25%
250-499 Employees	3/7.50%	4/11.43%	3/18.75%	4/13.33%	6/30%
500-1000 Employees	2/5%	4/11.43%	1/6.25%	2/6.67%	2/10%
>1000 Employees	0	1/2.86%	1/6.25%	2/6.67%	2/10%

Source: MPI Census of US Manufacturers Survey

the associated IT systems were treated as binary independent variables, with 1 indicating the IT system type is used by the organization and zero indicating it was not. Table 7 shows the number of respondents by NAICS and Year, along with their respective percentages, and Table 2 shown the percentage breakout of the IT usage within the NAICS 311 industry by years. An analysis on each of the dependent variables; profitability, cost of goods sold, labor costs, material costs, overhead costs, and degree of customer and supplier integration with dependent variables of year, NAICS code, and binary variables for each of the IT systems is conducted next.

Profitability

Plant profitability can be measured by the ratio of gross profits divided by net sales (Siegel and Shim, 1991; Williams, et. al., 2008). It is expected from literature that information technologies can facilitate greater efficiencies in the production and distribution processes, and with better forecasting and planning tools potentially promote more sells: thus, increasing revenues and decreases expenses. Based upon these assertions the following null hypotheses are proposed:

H1: Information Technology system will not improve plant profitability.

Table 6. Breakout of plant age within the NAICS Industry Group 311 respondents

Plant Size	2003	2004	2005	2006	2007
<5 Years	1/2.5%	2/5.71%	0	0	0
5-10 Years	4/10%	6/17.14%	2/12.5%	2/6.67%	1/5%
11-20 Years	4/10%	5/14.29%	2/12.5%	6/20%	5/25%
>20 Years	31/77.5%	22/62.86%	12/75%	22/73.33%	14/70%

Source: MPI Census of US Manufacturers Survey

Table 7. Breakout of NAICS Industry Group 311 – food manufacturers and processors

4 Digit NAICS Codes	2003	2004	2005	2006	2007	Total
3111 - Animal Food Mfg	1/2.5%	2/5.7%	1/6.3%	3/10.0%	0	7/5.0%
3112 - Grain & Oilseed Milling	1/2.5%	3/8.6%	0	1/3.3%	2/10.0%	7/5.0%
3113 - Sugar & Confectionery Product Mfg	3/7.5%	2/5.7%	1/6.3%	0	1/5.0%	7/5.0%
3114 - Fruit & Vegetable Preserving & Specialty Food Mfg	2/5.0%	4/11.4%	1/6.3%	3/10.0%	3/15.0%	13/9.2%
3115 - Dairy Product Mfg	7/17.5%	0	3/18.8%	5/16.7%	2/10.0%	17/12.1%
3116 - Animal Slaughtering & Processing	2/5.0%	5/14.3%	4/25.0%	4/13.3%	3/15.0%	18/12.8%
3117 - Seafood Product Preparation & Packaging	0	0	0	2/6.7%	0	2/1.4%
3118 - Bakeries & Tortilla Mfg	4/10.0%	1/2.9%	3/18.8%	4/13.3%	0	12/8.5%
3119 - Other Food Mfg	7/17.5%	6/17.1%	0	6/20.0%	8/40.0%	27/19.1%
Code not disclosed by respondents	13/32.5%	12/34.3%	0	2/6.7%	5.0%	31/22.0%
Total	27	23	13	28	19	110

Source: MPI Census of US Manufacturers Survey

$H1_a$: Enterprise Resource Planning systems will increase plant profitability.

$H1_b$: Enterprise Resource Planning II systems will increase plant profitability.

$H1_c$: Electronic Data Interchange systems will increase plant profitability.

$H1_d$: Forecasting/Demand Management systems will increase plant profitability.

$H1_e$: Online Purchasing systems will increase plant profitability.

$H1_f$: Online Selling systems will increase plant profitability.

Due to excessive skewness and kurtosis in the Profitability metric, a Log_{10} transformation was used. Table 8 shows the respective p-values of each year of the study. At the 0.05 level of significance, only the year 2004 was found to be marginally significant with respect to the model using ERP, APS, and EDI.

In the single variable models, only OS systems increased the plants profitability, and none of these systems were found to be significant at the 0.05 level, except for APS. It is generally accepted that good planning makes for good results, and that the foundations of good planning is accurate

and reliable forecasting. Thus, this finding tends to be opposite of what would be expected. There are two possibilities leading to this result; 1) the volatility of demands for products and services is low, making the expense of owning and operating an advanced forecasting /demand management system greater than the revenues associated with the increases accuracy in the planning, or 2) management has not effectively integrated the forecast results in their planning processes.

When the independent variables were analyzed in combinations, along with their possible interactions, similar results were found. In all of the models, none of the main affect variables were found to be significant, and the only interactive affects of significant were between EDI and OP, and APS and OP; see the ERP|EDI|APS|OP|OS model. When the non-significant variables and interactions were removed from the ERP|EDI|APS|OP|OS model, the only affect found to be significant was APS, and it again negatively affected profitability. Though there is evidence that APS significantly affect plant profitability, the effect is to decrease profitability. Based upon these finding, we must fail to reject the null hypothesis. The full statistical output can be found in Table A1 of Appendix A.

Table 8. Profitability analysis: The affect of year

	ERP	ERP II	APS	EDI	OP	OS	OP, & OS	APS, OP, & OS	ERP, OP, & OS	ERP II, OP, & OS	EDI, OP, & OS	ERP, APS, OP, & OS	ERP, EDI, APS, OP, & OS	ERP, EDI, APS, OP, & OS	ERP, EDI, APS, OP, & OS
Int.	<.0001	0.0680	<.0001	<.0001	<.0001	<.0001	<.0001	0.0209	0.0069	0.0927	<.0001	0.0428	0.0083	0.2210	0.0524
2003	0.2274	0.2854	0.1686	0.2347	0.2414	0.2499	0.2204	0.1383	0.2659	0.2443	0.2292	0.1802	0.2573	0.2435	0.1038
2004	0.0957	0.1612	0.0661	0.0964	0.1205	0.1071	0.1295	0.0749	0.1718	0.1827	0.1342	0.1210	0.1660	0.1996	0.0668
2005	0.6893	0.7264	0.6560	0.7345	0.6932	0.7673	0.6508	0.7603	0.6668	0.6405	0.6262	0.8087	0.5935	0.6139	0.6506
2006	0.1931	0.2014	0.1574	0.1813	0.2192	0.1755	0.1618	0.1950	0.2254	0.1644	0.1869	0.2233	0.2070	0.1900	0.1479
2007															

Cost of Goods Sold

In the MPI survey, the cost of goods sold (COGS) variable is reported as a percentage of revenues. Again, due to excessive skewness and kurtosis, the COGS variable was transformed using a Log_{10} transformation. The hypotheses testing the performance metric of cost of goods sold are as follow:

H2: Information Technology system will not improve the plant's cost of goods sold.

$H2_a$: Enterprise Resource Planning systems will increase the plant's cost of goods sold.

$H2_b$: Enterprise Resource Planning II systems will increase the plant's cost of goods sold.

$H2_c$: Electronic Data Interchange systems will increase the plant's cost of goods sold.

$H2_d$: Forecasting/Demand Management systems will increase the plant's cost of goods sold.

$H2_e$: Online Purchasing systems will increase the plant's cost of goods sold.

$H2_f$: Online Selling systems will increase the plant's cost of goods sold.

The resulting p-values for the affect of each year can be seen in Table 9.

In the single variable models, both ERP and OS systems tended to lower the plant's cost of goods sold, while only APS and OP systems were found to be significant at the 0.05 level. When the independent variables are analyzed in combinations, along with their possible interactions, similar results were found. None of the main affect variables were found to be significant in any of the models, and the only interactive affects found to be significant were between EDI and OP, and APS and OP; See the ERP|EDI|APS|OP|OS model. When the non-significant variables were removed from the ERP|EDI|APS|OP|OS model, only the main affect variable APS was still found to be significant; and it effect is to increase the

Table 9. Cost of goods sold analysis: The affect of year

	ERP	ERP II	APS	EDI	OP	OS	OP, OS	APS, OP, & OS	ERP, OP, & OS	ERP II, OP, & OS	EDI, OP, & OS	ERP, APS, OP, & OS	ERP, EDI, OP, & OS	ERP II, EDI, OP, & OS	ERP, EDI, APS, OP, & OS
Int.	<.0001	<.0001	<.0001	<.0001	<.0001	<.0001	<.0001	<.0001	<.0001	<.0001	<.0001	<.0001	<.0001	<.0001	<.0001
2003	0.9020	0.9354	0.9956	0.9563	0.9219	0.9520	0.9269	0.8652	0.8678	0.9445	0.9101	0.8810	0.8688	0.9236	0.3622
2004	0.5576	0.5151	0.3867	0.4654	0.5565	0.4894	0.5673	0.4148	0.6532	0.5742	0.5852	0.5933	0.6584	0.5722	0.2454
2005	0.9636	0.9010	0.8884	0.8947	0.8617	0.8966	0.8563	0.9642	0.9365	0.8629	0.8702	0.9890	0.9359	0.8728	0.9747
2006	0.7484	0.7764	0.7955	0.8265	0.6778	0.7457	0.7172	0.5906	0.6803	0.7164	0.6888	0.6710	0.6812	0.6883	0.8701
2007	.	.	.	.	.	.	.	.	.	.	.	.	.	.	.

plant's cost of goods sold. From these results there is evidence that both APS and OP significantly affect the plant's cost of goods sold. There is also evidence that ERP, EDI, and OS systems when used with other IT systems can significantly affect the plant's cost of goods sold. Unfortunately, the singular, and net interactive affects in all cases was to increase the plant's cost of goods sold. Thus, we again fail to reject the null hypothesis. The full statistical output can be found in Table A2 of Appendix A.

Labor Costs

In the MPI survey, labor costs were reported as a percentage of the cost of goods sold. Due to excessive skewness and kurtosis, the cost of labor variable was transformed using a Log_{10} transformation. The hypotheses testing the performance metric of labor costs are as follow:

H3: Information Technology system will not improve the plant's labor costs.

$H3_a$: Enterprise Resource Planning systems will increase the plant's labor costs.

$H3_b$: Enterprise Resource Planning II systems will increase the plant's labor costs.

$H3_c$: Electronic Data Interchange systems will increase the plant's labor costs.

$H3_d$: Forecasting/Demand Management systems will increase the plant's labor costs.

$H3_e$: Online Purchasing systems will increase the plant's labor costs.

$H3_f$: Online Selling systems will increase the plant's labor costs.

The p-value of each year in the study can be seen in Table 10, where it can be seen that none of the years were significant at the .05 level.

In the single variable models, only ERP, ERP II, and APS system showed evidence of lowering the plant's labor costs; and with the exception of EDI, none of these IT systems were found to be significant. When the independent variables are

Table 10. Labor costs analysis: The affect of year

	ERP	ERP II	APS	EDI	OP	OS	OP, OS	APS, OP, & OS	ERP, OP, & OS	ERP_II, OP, & OS	EDI, OP, & OS	ERP, APS, OP, & OS	ERP, EDI, OP, & OS	ERP_II, EDI, OP, & OS	ERP, EDI, APS, OP, & OS
Int.	<.0001	<.0001	<.0001	<.0001	<.0001	<.0001	<.0001	<.0001	<.0001	<.0001	<.0001	<.0001	<.0001	0.0020	<.0001
2003	0.3862	0.4494	0.4316	0.5494	0.4495	0.4316	0.4675	0.4235	0.2762	0.5132	0.5416	0.2601	0.3446	0.5865	0.3386
2004	0.7165	0.8363	0.7997	0.9325	0.7859	0.8330	0.8344	0.7785	0.6144	0.8043	0.9645	0.6053	0.7918	0.9049	0.8520
2005	0.6836	0.6333	0.6379	0.5230	0.5886	0.6596	0.5253	0.5058	0.5071	0.5289	0.5756	0.4895	0.5503	0.5704	0.5023
2006	0.4151	0.4535	0.4476	0.6859	0.4387	0.4080	0.4618	0.4583	0.2608	0.4567	0.4991	0.2960	0.3326	0.5033	0.4420
2007															

analyzed in combinations along with their possible interactions similar results were found. By automating the transmission of data to suppliers the work load on purchasing managers should be significantly reduced; allowing them to spend more time on other activities, and/or reducing staff. From these results, we fail to reject the null hypothesis. The full statistical output can be found in Table A3 of Appendix A.

Material Costs

In the MPI survey, the cost of materials was reported as a percentage of the cost of goods sold.

The hypotheses testing the performance metric of labor costs are as follow:

H4: Information Technology system will not improve the plant's material costs.

H4$_a$: Enterprise Resource Planning systems will increase the plant's material costs.

H4$_b$: Enterprise Resource Planning II systems will increase the plant's material costs.

H4$_c$: Electronic Data Interchange systems will increase the plant's material costs.

H4$_d$: Forecasting/Demand Management systems will increase the plant's material costs.

H4$_e$: Online Purchasing systems will increase the plant's material costs.

H4$_f$: Online Selling systems will increase the plant's material costs.

As can be seen in Table 11, the intercept was strongly significant at the 0.05 level in all models, and the year 2006 was found to be significant in one model and marginally significant most of the other models. In each year the estimate effect tended to decrease material costs, with the largest decreased effect in 2006.

In the single effect models, with the exception of ERP systems, all of the IT systems tended to lower the plants profitability, and none of the effects were found to be significant. When the independent variables are analyzed in combina-

Table 11. Materials cost analysis: The affect of year

	ERP	ERP II	APS	EDI	OP	OS	OP, OS	APS, OP, & OS	ERP, OP, & OS	ERP II, OP, & OS	EDI, OP, & OS	ERP, APS, OP, & OS	ERP, EDI, OP, & OS	ERP II, EDI, OP, & OS	ERP, EDI, APS, OP, & OS	ERP, & OP	ERP, EDI, APS, & OP
Int.	<.0001	<.0001	<.0001	<.0001	<.0001	<.0001	<.0001	<.0001	<.0001	<.0001	<.0001	<.0001	<.0001	0.0066	<.0001	<.0001	<.0001
2003	0.2861	0.2875	0.3043	0.3681	0.3033	0.3014	0.2939	0.3919	0.2927	0.3073	0.3746	0.3064	0.4065	0.3558	0.6586	0.3537	0.6269
2004	0.2890	0.2687	0.3076	0.4413	0.3053	0.3164	0.3144	0.3615	0.4275	0.2418	0.4310	0.4134	0.6763	0.4000	0.9693	0.4367	0.8896
2005	0.7264	0.7827	0.7543	0.8384	0.7582	0.7369	0.6731	0.5166	0.7509	0.7064	0.6176	0.6450	0.7251	0.6850	0.7730	0.7637	0.8480
2006	0.0636	0.0705	0.0674	0.1175	0.0663	0.0596	0.0569	0.0830	0.0428	0.0590	0.0857	0.0621	0.0663	0.1019	0.2317	0.0649	0.2071
2007	.	.	.	.	.	.	.	.	.	.	.	.	.	.	.	.	.

tions, along with their interactions, several models showed one or more IT systems to be significant or marginally significant. In the APS|OP|OS model, the APS system was marginally significant at the 0.05 level, and tended to lower material costs. In both the ERP|OP|OS and ERP|EDI|OP|OS models, the ERP|OP interaction was found to be marginally significant and significant respectively. In the case of the ERP|OP|OS model's interaction, the net effect was a tendency to increase material costs, while the net effect of the interaction in the ERP|EDI|OP|OS model was to lower material costs. With the ERP|EDI|APS|OP|OS model, both the ERP|OP and the EDI|APS interactions were found to be significant at the 0.05 level, and while the net effect of the ERP|OP interaction was to increase material costs, the EDI|APS interaction tended to decrease material costs.

When the non-significant variables and interactions were removed from the ERP|EDI|APS|OP|OS model, both ERP|OP and the EDI|APS interactions remained marginally significant and significant respectively, the EDI main variable became significant at the 0.05 level. Then net estimated effect of the ERP|EDI|APS|OP model was to decrease material costs. Furthermore, in each multi-variable model where one or more variable and/or interactions where

Significant, the net effect was to decrease materials costs. Based upon these results, we would have to conclude that ERP, APS, and OP systems have the potential to improve material costs. Due to this conclusion being based upon the interactive affects, there does not excess strong conclusive evident to support the failing of the null hypothesis. The full statistical output can be found in Table A4 of Appendix A.

Overhead Costs

In the MPI survey, the overhead costs were reported as a percentage of the cost of goods sold.

The hypotheses testing the performance metric of overhead costs are as follow:

Table 12. Overhead cost analysis: The affect of year

	ERP	ERP II	APS	EDI	OP	OS	OP, OS	APS, OP, & OS	ERP, OP, & OS	ERP_II, OP, & OS	EDI, OP, & OS	ERP, APS, OP, & OS	ERP, EDI, OP, & OS	ERP, EDI, APS, OP, & OS	ERP_II, EDI, OP, & OS	ERP, & OP	APS, & OP	ERP, APS, & OP	ERP, APS, OP, & ERP*OP (only)
Int.	<.0001	<.0001	<.0001	<.0001	<.0001	<.0001	<.0001	<.0001	<.0001	<.0001	<.0001	<.0001	<.0001	<.0001	0.0066	<.0001	<.0001	<.0001	<.0001
2003	0.9892	0.9357	0.9590	0.9027	0.9351	0.9331	0.9975	0.8340	0.9503	0.9552	0.8721	0.9213	0.8494	0.7353	0.9020	0.8729	0.7332	0.7323	0.8798
2004	.09279	0.9893	0.9966	0.9248	0.9696	0.9594	0.9856	0.8986	0.79991	0.9316	0.8301	0.8316	0.5971	0.4934	0.8141	0.7801	0.8819	0.7861	0.7741
2005	0.2700	0.2991	0.2857	0.3120	0.2876	0.2843	0.1819	0.1096	0.1940	0.1839	0.1796	0.1411	0.2203	0.2000	0.1904	0.2805	0.1618	0.1755	0.2803
2006	0.2562	0.2831	0.2695	0.3206	0.2849	0.2605	0.2101	0.2580	0.2004	0.2093	0.3324	0.2315	0.2932	0.4549	0.3489	0.2631	0.2520	0.2357	0.2583
2007																			

H5: Information Technology system will not improve the plant's overhead costs.

H5$_a$: Enterprise Resource Planning systems will increase the plant's overhead costs.

H5$_b$: Enterprise Resource Planning II systems will increase the plant's overhead costs.

H5$_c$: Electronic Data Interchange systems will increase the plant's overhead costs.

H5$_d$: Forecasting/Demand Management systems will increase the plant's overhead costs.

H5$_e$: Online Purchasing systems will increase the plant's overhead costs.

H5$_f$: Online Selling systems will increase the plant's overhead costs.

As can be seen in Table 12, the intercept (coincides with year 2007), was strongly significant at the 0.05 level in all the analysis. In none of the models were any of the other years significant.

In the analysis of the single main effect variables, none were found to be significant, and their estimated effects were minor. When the variables were analyzed in combinations, along with their interactions, OP and APS were found to be marginally significant at the 0.05 level in two models, and OP was significant in one model. In several models the interactions between ERP and OP, and APS and OP were found to be significant and marginally significant. In a model of just these variables (ERP|APS|OP), only OP was found to be significant, and the interaction between APS and OP was found marginally significant. The net effect of all of the multi-variable models was to increase overhead costs. Reducing the model to only APS|OP, only the interaction effect was significant, with a net estimated effect of a minor increase in overhead costs. There does not excess strong conclusive evident to support the failing of the null hypothesis. The full statistical output can be found in Table A5 of Appendix A.

Table 13. Breakout of NAICS Industry Group 311 – Food manufacturers and processors

4 Digit NAICS Codes			2003	2004	2005	2006	2007
3111 - Animal Food Mfg	Supplier Integration	None	0	1/50%	1/100%	1/33%	0
		Some	1/100%	1/50%	0	2/67%	0
		Extensive	0	0	0	0	0
	Customer Integration	None	0	0	0	0	0
		Some	1/100%	0	1/100%	2/67%	0
		Extensive	0	2/100%	0	0	0
3112 - Grain & Oilseed Milling	Supplier Integration	None	0	0	0	0	0
		Some	1/100%	3/100%	0	1/100%	2/100%
		Extensive	0	0	0	0	0
	Customer Integration	None	0	0	0	1/100%	0
		Some	1/100%	2/100%	0	0	2/100%
		Extensive	0	1/100%	0	0	0
3113 - Sugar & Confectionery Product Mfg	Supplier Integration	None	0	0	1/100%	0	0
		Some	2/67%	1/50%	0	0	1/100%
		Extensive	1/33%	1/50%	0	0	0
	Customer Integration	None	0	0	0	0	0
		Some	2/67%	2/100%	1/100%	0	0
		Extensive	1/33%	0	0	0	1/100%
3114 - Fruit & Vegetable Preserving & Specialty Food Mfg	Supplier Integration	None	1/50%	0	0	2/67%	0
		Some	1/50%	3/75%	1/100%	1/33%	1/33%
		Extensive	0	1/25%	0	0	2/67%
	Customer Integration	None	0	1/25%	0	2/67%	0
		Some	2/100%	2/50%	1/100%	1/33%	3/100%
		Extensive	0	1/25%	0	0	0
3115 - Dairy Product Mfg	Supplier Integration	None	2/29%	0	1/33%	0	1/50%
		Some	2/29%	0	2/67%	4/80%	0
		Extensive	3/42%	0	0	1/20%	1/50%
	Customer Integration	None	2/29%	0	2/67%	1/20%	0
		Some	3/43%	0	1/33%	4/80%	2/100%
		Extensive	2/28%	0	0	0	0
3116 - Animal Slaughtering & Processing	Supplier Integration	None	0	1/25%	2/50%	1/25%	2/100%
		Some	0	2/50%	1/25%	2/50%	0
		Extensive	2/100%	1/25%	1/25%	1/25%	0
	Customer Integration	None	0	2/40%	2/50%	2/50%	0
		Some	0	3/60%	2/50%	2/50%	2/100%
		Extensive	2/100%	0	0	0	0

continued on following page

Table 13. continued

3117 - Seafood Product Preparation & Packaging	Supplier Integration	None	0	0	0	2/100%	0
		Some	0	0	0	0	0
		Extensive	0	0	0	0	0
	Customer Integration	None	0	0	0	1/50%	0
		Some	0	0	0	1/50%	0
		Extensive	0	0	0	0	0
3118 - Bakeries & Tortilla Mfg	Supplier Integration	None	0	0	1/33%	1/25%	0
		Some	4/100%	0	2/67%	3/75%	0
		Extensive	0	0	0	0	0
	Customer Integration	None	0	0	0	0	0
		Some	4/100%	0	3/100%	4/100%	0
		Extensive	0	0	0	0	0
3119 - Other Food Mfg	Supplier Integration	None	4/67%	1/17%	0	1/20%	2/29%
		Some	2/33%	3/50%	0	4/80%	4/57%
		Extensive	0	2/33%	0	0	1/14%
	Customer Integration	None	4/66%	0	0	2/40%	0
		Some	1/17%	3/50%	0	3/60%	6/86%
		Extensive	1/17%	3/50%	0	0	1/14%
Code not disclosed by respondents	Supplier Integration	None	1/7%	0	0	0	0
		Some	8/65%	8/73%	3/100%	2/100%	1/100%
		Extensive	4/31%	3/27%	0	0	1/100%
	Customer Integration	None	3/23%	1/9%	1/50%	0	0
		Some	10/77%	8/73%	1/50%	2/100%	1/100%
		Extensive	0	2/18%	0	0	0

Source: MPI Census of US Manufacturers Survey

Degree of Supplier and Customer Integration

The trend in most industries today is to use IT systems not only to improve the efficiency of internal operations, but to also improve external efficiency through closer integration with customers and suppliers. Table 13, shows the degree to which the US food manufacturers have integrated with their supply chain (self reported).

When supplier and customer integration was analyzed with respect to profitability, cost of goods sold, labor costs, material costs, and overhead costs, only supplier integration was found to be significant at the 0.05 level, and then only when associated with labor costs. The full statistical output can be found in Table A6 of Appendix A.

CONCLUSION

Our study has shown that although there is significant usage of information technologies in the downstream portion of the food manufacturing supply chains (similar to the beef industry), these systems are not significantly contributing to improvement in plant performance. The systems that seem to be making the most contributions are enterprise resource planning systems, forecasting/demand management systems, electronic data interchange systems, and online purchasing systems; and these contributions are mixed and inconclusive. There is also indication that extensive supplier integration helps to reduce labor costs.

Theory would indicate that all of these systems should improve plant performance. ERP systems are used to improve the collection and dissemination of information, and improve the coordination of planning and production activities, both inside the plant and across the supply chain. EDI systems typically improve the timeliness to communications between plants. Forecasting and demand management systems can improve the effectiveness of planning by providing increased accuracy in forecasted demands. Online purchasing systems are expected to reduce search costs in the procurement process. Given this, the food industry should be able to better coordinate activities all along their respective supply chains; and many areas of the food industry have made significant progress such as in the poultry and pork industries. From our results it is indeterminate as to how much information technologies are adding to these industries performance.

Though online technologies are starting to being used by upstream participants in the beef industry's supply chain, they have yet to make any significant impact. Clearly, the use of internet technologies is in its infancy within this industry and most supply chain participants have not placed an adequate degree of their effort to this new medium. As of yet, information technologies do not seem to be supplying the aid needed for improvements to occur.

REFERENCES

Bardhan, I., Whitaker, J., & Mithas, S. (2006). Information technology, production process outsourcing, and manufacturing plant performance. *Journal of Management Information Systems*, *23*(2), 13–40. doi:10.2753/MIS0742-1222230202

Chandra, C., & Kumar, S. (2000). Supply chain management in theory and practice: A passing fad or a fundamental change. *Industrial Management & Data Systems*, *100*(3), 100–113. doi:10.1108/02635570010286168

Chandrashekar, A., & Schary, P. B. (1999). Toward the virtual supply chain: The convergence of IT and organization. *International Journal of Logistics Management*, *10*(2), 27–39. doi:10.1108/09574099910805978

Choi, B., Tsai, N., & Jones, T. (2008). Building enterprise network infrastructure for a supermarket store chain. *Journal of Cases on Information Technology*, 31–46.

Cooper, M. C., Lambert, D. M., & Pagh, J. D. (1997). Supply chain management: More than new name for logistics. *International Journal of Logistics Management*, *8*(1), 1–14. doi:10.1108/09574099710805556

Croxton, K. L., Garcia-Dastugue, S. J., Lambert, D. M., & Rodgers, D. S. (2001). The supply chain management processes. *International Journal of Logistics Management*, *12*(2), 13–36. doi:10.1108/09574090110806271

Euclides, F. K. (2004). Supply chain approach to sustainable beef production from a Brazilian perspective. *Livestock Production Science*, *90*(1), 53–61. doi:10.1016/j.livprodsci.2004.07.006

Fearne, A. (1998). The evolution of partnerships in the meat supply chain: Insights from the British beef industry. *Supply Chain Management, Bradford*, *3*(4), 214. doi:10.1108/13598549810244296

Fisher, M. F. (1997). What is the right supply chain for your product? A simple framework can help you figure out the answer. *Harvard Business Review*, (March-April): 105–116.

Frasquet, M., Cervera, A., & Gil, I. (2008). The impact of IT and customer orientation on building trust and commitment in the supply chain. *International Review of Retail, Distribution and Consumer Research*, *18*(3), 343. doi:10.1080/09593960802114164

García-Arca, J., & Carlos Prado-Prado, J. (2007). The implementation of new technologies through a participative approach. *Creativity and Innovation Management*, *16*(4), 386. doi:10.1111/j.1467-8691.2007.00450.x

Hughes, D. (1994). *Breaking with tradition: Building partnerships and alliances in the European food industry*. Ashford: Wye College Press.

Lambert, D. M., Cooper, M. C., & Pagh, J. D. (1998). Supply chain management: Implementation issues and research opportunities. *International Journal of Logistics Management*, *9*(2), 1–19. doi:10.1108/09574099810805807

Langley, C. J., & Holcomb, M. C. (1992). Creating logistics customer value. *Journal of Business Logistics*, *13*(2), 1–27.

Lawrence, C. (2006). Friend or foe. *Farmers Weekly*, *144*(25), 18–19.

Levy, M., & Grewal, D. (2000). Overview of the issues of supply chain management in a networked economy. *Journal of Retailing*, *76*(4), 415–429. doi:10.1016/S0022-4359(00)00043-9

Lewis, I., & Talalayevsky, A. (1997). Logistics and information technology: A coordination perspective. *Journal of Business Logistics*, *18*(1), 141–157.

Lewis, I., & Talalayevsky, A. (2004). Improving the interorganizational supply chain through optimization of information flows. *Journal of Enterprise Information Management*, *17*(3), 229–237. doi:10.1108/17410390410531470

Mentzer, J. T., DeWitt, W., Keebler, J. S., Min, S., Nix, N. W., Smith, C. D., & Zacharia, Z. G. (2001). Defining supply chain management. *Journal of Business Logistics*, *22*(2), 1–25.

Mighell, R. L., & Jones, L. A. (1963). Vertical coordination in agriculture. *USDA-ERS Agricultural Economics Report*, 19.

Min, S., & Mentzer, J. T. (2000). The role of marketing in supply chain management. *International Journal of Physical Distribution & Logistics Management*, *30*(9), 765–787. doi:10.1108/09600030010351462

Moberg, C. R., Seph, T. W., & Freese, T. L. (2003). SCM: making the vision a reality. *Supply Chain Management Review*, *7*(5), 34–39.

Mohtadi, H. (2008). Information sharing in food supply chains. *Canadian Journal of Agricultural Economics*, *56*(2), 163.

Narayanan, V. G., & Raman, A. (2004). Aligning incentives in supply chains. *Harvard Business School Publishing, Article # R0411F, November*.

Neureuther, B. D., & Kenyon, G. N. (2008). The impact of information technologies on the US beef industry's supply chain. *International Journal of Information Systems and Supply Chain Management*, *1*(1), 48–65.

Nitschke, T., & O'Keefe, M. (1997). Managing the linkage with primary producers: experiences in the Australian grain industry. *Supply Chain Management, Bradford*, *2*(1), 4. doi:10.1108/13598549710156295

Peypoch, R. (1998). The case for electronic business communities. *Business Horizons, 4*(6), 17–20. doi:10.1016/S0007-6813(98)90073-8

Romeo, P. (2006). Buyers embrace more sophisticated supply-purchasing procedures. *Nations Restaurant News, 40*(21), 92–93.

Salin, V. (2000). Information technology and cattle-beef supply chains. *American Journal of Agricultural Economics, 82*(5), 1105–1111. doi:10.1111/0002-9092.00107

Siegel, J. G., & Shim, J. K. (1991). *Financial Management*. Hauppauge, NY: Barron's Business Library.

Williams, J. R., Haka, S. F., Bettner, M. S., & Carcello, J. V. (2008). *Financial Accounting* (13th ed.). New York: McGraw-Hill Publishing.

Wise, R., & Morrison, D. (2000). Beyond the exchange: The future of B2B. *Harvard Business Review, 78*(6), 86–96.

Yao, Y., Palmer, J., & Dresner, M. (2007). An interorganizational perspective on the use of electronically-enabled supply chains. *Decision Support Systems, 43*(3), 884. doi:10.1016/j. dss.2007.01.002

APPENDIX A

Table A1. Profitability analysis: The affect of IT systems

Independent variables	Estimate	Std Error	DF	T Value	Pr > |t|
ERP	-0.04408	0.1008	73.8	-0.44	0.6633
ERP II	-0.1964	0.2208	74	-0.89	0.3766
APS	-0.2190	0.08525	73.7	-2.57	**0.0122**
EDI	-0.04701	0.08271	70.1	-0.57	0.5716
OP	-0.08234	0.08793	73.2	-0.94	0.3521
OS	0.09916	0.1077	71.3	0.92	0.3605
OP	-0.2265	0.2172	70.5	-1.04	0.3006
OS	0.1246	0.1488	71.7	0.84	0.4052
OP*OS	0.1106	0.2422	71.5	0.46	0.6494
APS	-0.2278	0.2504	68.5	-0.91	0.3663
OP	-0.4060	0.3167	67.9	-1.28	0.2042
OS	0.1403	0.2480	65.7	0.57	0.5736
APS*OP	0.2610	0.2284	68.3	1.14	0.2571
APS*OS	-0.1507	0.3282	67.9	-0.46	0.6477
OP*OS	0.2021	0.2687	69	0.75	0.4546
ERP	0.07428	0.3174	66.4	0.23	0.8158
OP	-0.1728	0.3455	68.8	-0.50	0.6186
OS	0.1732	0.3453	68.8	0.50	0.6175
ERP*OP	-0.06699	0.2597	68.2	-0.26	0.7972
ERP*OS	-0.05670	0.4016	67.7	-0.14	0.8881
OP*OS	0.1050	0.2616	69	0.40	0.6893
ERP_II	-0.1155	0.2824	70	-0.41	0.6838
OP	-0.1541	0.5156	69.8	-0.30	0.7659
OS	0.1111	0.1549	69.9	0.72	0.4758
ERP_II*OP	-0.07462	0.4676	69.9	-0.16	0.8737
ERP_II *OS	0	.	.	.	.
OP*OS	0.1225	0.2483	69.6	0.49	0.6232
EDI	0.1087	0.2475	66.1	0.44	0.6620
OP	-0.1395	0.3542	68.7	-0.39	0.6949
OS	0.1383	0.1944	69	0.71	0.4794
EDI*OP	-0.1517	0.2319	68.8	-0.65	0.5153
EDI*OS	-0.01482	0.3272	65.5	-0.05	0.9640
OP*OS	0.084336	0.3205	67.7	0.26	0.7932
ERP	0.1570	0.3384	62.6	0.46	0.6443
APS	-0.2186	0.3054	63.9	-0.72	0.4769
OP	-0.2723	0.3937	64.2	-0.69	0.4916
OS	0.1433	0.3732	64.7	0.38	0.7022
ERP*APS	-0.05608	0.2165	64.8	-0.26	0.7965
ERP*OP	-0.1682	0.2735	64.1	-0.62	0.5394
APS*OP	0.2919	0.2395	64.3	1.22	0.2275
ERP*OS	0.008183	0.4051	64.3	0.02	0.9839
APS*OS	-0.1467	0.3419	63.7	-0.43	0.6692
OP*OS	0.1699	0.2824	65	0.60	0.5495

Independent variables	Estimate	Std Error	DF	T Value	Pr > |t|
ERP	0.004063	0.3525	64.3	0.01	0.9908
EDI	0.2026	0.3614	63.5	0.56	0.5771
OP	-0.02497	0.4779	64.9	-0.05	0.9585
OS	0.06975	0.3854	64.9	0.18	0.8569
ERP*EDI	-0.09972	0.2433	61.9	-0.41	0.6833
ERP*OP	-0.1087	0.2754	63.8	-0.39	0.6944
EDI*OP	-0.1472	0.2485	65	-0.59	0.5559
ERP*OS	0.09852	0.4493	64.7	0.22	0.8271
EDI*OS	-0.02136	0.3635	65	-0.06	0.9533
OP*OS	0.04420	0.3469	65	0.13	0.8990
ERP_II	-0.1648	0.4036	65.2	-0.41	0.6843
EDI	-0.03890	0.6360	65.4	-0.06	0.9514
OP	0.07648	0.5887	65	0.10	0.9175
OS	0.1243	0.2020	66	0.62	0.5403
ERP_II*EDI	0.1470	0.5887	65.2	0.25	0.8036
ERP_II*OP	-0.2027	0.5821	65.5	-0.35	0.7289
EDI*OP	-0.1687	0.2523	66	-0.67	0.5061
ERP_II*OS	0	.	.	.	.
EDI*OS	-0.00320	0.3436	64.8	-0.01	0.9926
OP*OS	0.08325	0.3352	65.7	0.25	0.8047
ERP	0.07175	0.3720	58.6	0.19	0.8477
EDI	0.07970	0.4071	60	0.20	0.8454
APS	-0.2664	0.3157	58.8	-0.84	0.4022
OP	0.09587	0.4797	59.8	0.20	0.8423
OS	-0.1024	0.4026	59.7	-0.25	0.8001
ERP*EDI	-0.08229	0.2572	58.8	-0.32	0.7502
ERP*APS	-0.07622	0.2469	60	-0.31	0.7586
EDI*APS	0.1830	0.2181	59.8	0.84	0.4049
ERP*OP	-0.3578	0.3025	58.8	-1.18	0.2417
<u>EDI*OP</u>	-0.4888	0.2762	58.1	-1.77	**<u>0.0821</u>**
<u>APS*OP</u>	0.5253	0.2775	57.3	1.89	**<u>0.0634</u>**
ERP*OS	0.3271	0.4593	59.9	0.71	0.4791
EDI*OS	0.3217	0.3718	59.3	0.87	0.3904
APS*OS	-0.3917	0.3707	58.9	-1.06	0.2949
OP*OS	0.01421	0.3452	60	0.04	0.9673
EDI	0.2286	0.1554	69.4	1.47	0.1459
<u>APS</u>	-0.4073	0.1518	69.8	-2.68	**<u>0.0091</u>**
OP	-0.1112	0.1505	68.1	-0.74	0.4627
EDI*OP	-0.2747	0.1845	69.9	-1.49	0.1410
APS*OP	0.2883	0.1922	69.1	1.50	0.1381

Table A2. Cost of goods sold analysis: The affect of IT systems

Independent variables	Estimate	Std Error	DF	T Value	Pr > |t|
ERP	-0.03383	0.08187	78.7	-0.41	0.6806
ERP II	0.02797	0.1861	78.9	0.15	0.8809
<u>APS</u>	0.1559	0.07082	78.6	2.20	**<u>0.0307</u>**
EDI	0.02496	0.06777	78.2	0.37	0.7137
<u>OP</u>	0.1385	0.07071	78.1	1.96	**<u>0.0538</u>**
OS	0.03759	0.09045	76.1	0.42	0.6789
OP	0.1666	0.1819	75.4	0.92	0.3627
OS	-0.03042	0.1231	76.5	-0.25	0.8055
OP*OS	-0.01969	0.2018	76.4	-0.10	0.9225

Independent variables	Estimate	Std Error	DF	T Value	Pr > |t|
APS	0.1412	0.2103	73.1	0.67	0.5039
OP	0.3835	0.2633	72.4	1.46	0.1497
OS	-0.09771	0.2080	70	-0.47	0.6399
APS*OP	-0.2746	0.1870	72.5	-1.47	0.1464
APS*OS	0.1921	0.2719	71.2	0.71	0.4821
OP*OS	-0.1144	0.2226	73.8	-0.51	0.6087
ERP	0.2149	0.2617	71.5	0.82	0.4143
OP	0.03495	0.2833	74	0.12	0.9022
OS	0.2446	0.2847	74	0.86	0.3930
ERP*OP	0.09571	0.2104	73.6	0.45	0.6505
ERP*OS	-0.3537	0.3288	73.3	-1.08	0.2856
OP*OS	0.03850	0.2151	74	0.18	0.8584
ERP_II	-0.06000	0.2352	75	-0.26	0.7994
OP	0.07903	0.4315	74.7	0.18	0.8552
OS	-0.03791	0.1279	74.8	-0.30	0.7678
ERP_II*OP	0.08707	0.3908	75	0.22	0.8243
ERP_II *OS	0	.	.	.	.
OP*OS	-0.01115	0.2068	74.5	-0.05	0.9572
EDI	-0.1434	0.2064	68.6	-0.69	0.4894
OP	0.2238	0.2934	72	0.76	0.4481
OS	-0.07583	0.1594	73.9	-0.48	0.6356
EDI*OP	0.03140	0.1898	72.9	0.17	0.8690
EDI*OS	0.1221	0.2698	65.8	0.45	0.6522
OP*OS	-0.09098	0.2677	70.9	-0.34	0.7349
ERP	0.1380	0.2751	67.6	0.50	0.6175
APS	0.03413	0.2508	69.2	0.14	0.8922
OP	0.2194	0.3172	69.9	0.69	0.4915
OS	0.1911	0.3064	69.7	0.62	0.5348
ERP*APS	0.1071	0.1720	69	0.62	0.5356
ERP*OP	0.1775	0.2197	69.7	0.81	0.4218
APS*OP	-0.3197	0.1951	69	-1.64	0.1059
ERP*OS	-0.4408	0.3303	69.3	-1.33	0.1864
APS*OS	0.2786	0.2801	68.2	0.99	0.3235
OP*OS	-0.06376	0.2291	70	-0.28	0.7816
ERP	0.3274	0.2874	70	1.14	0.2585
EDI	-0.2426	0.2981	70	-0.81	0.4185
OP	0.07252	0.3916	70	0.19	0.8536
OS	0.2773	0.3147	70	0.88	0.3813
ERP*EDI	0.006467	0.1957	70	0.03	0.9737
ERP*OP	0.09460	0.2242	70	0.42	0.6743
EDI*OP	0.08743	0.2014	70	0.43	0.6656
ERP*OS	-0.4836	0.3644	70	-1.33	0.1888
EDI*OS	0.1842	0.2960	70	0.62	0.5357
OP*OS	-0.03802	0.2851	70	-0.13	0.8943
ERP_II	-0.03065	0.3374	70	-0.09	0.9279
EDI	-0.06192	0.5334	70.4	-0.12	0.9079
OP	0.06137	0.6156	70.6	0.10	0.9209
OS	-0.07921	0.1653	70.9	-0.48	0.6333
ERP_II*EDI	-0.08228	0.4939	70.1	-0.17	0.8682
ERP_II*OP	0.1432	0.4873	70.8	0.29	0.7697
EDI*OP	0.05124	0.2072	70.9	0.25	0.8053
ERP_II*OS	0	.	.	.	.
EDI*OS	0.1035	0.2842	66.9	0.36	0.7170
OP*OS	-0.06821	0.2806	69.8	-0.24	0.8086

Independent variables	Estimate	Std Error	DF	T Value	Pr > |t|
ERP	0.2706	0.3001	65	0.90	0.3707
EDI	-0.1562	0.3324	65	-0.47	0.6400
APS	0.02328	0.2600	65	0.09	0.9289
OP	0.06416	0.3921	65	0.16	0.8705
OS	0.3097	0.3304	65	0.94	0.3520
ERP*EDI	-0.04410	0.2078	65	-0.21	0.8326
ERP*APS	0.1378	0.1977	65	0.70	0.4882
EDI*APS	-0.08646	0.1789	65	-0.48	0.6304
ERP*OP	0.2879	0.2470	65	1.17	0.2480
EDI*OP	0.3706	0.2188	65	1.69	**0.0951**
APS*OP	-0.4957	0.2226	65	-2.23	**0.0294**
ERP*OS	-0.7007	0.3739	65	-1.87	**0.0654**
EDI*OS	-0.09088	0.2987	65	-0.30	0.7619
APS*OS	0.4655	0.3000	65	1.55	0.1256
OP*OS	-0.02326	0.2835	65	-0.08	0.9349
ERP	0.2321	0.2538	71.2	0.91	0.3634
EDI	-0.2009	0.1323	70.4	-1.52	0.1334
APS	0.3229	0.1286	71.8	2.51	**0.0143**
OP	0.1757	0.1305	70.3	1.35	0.1824
OS	0.2927	0.2487	72	1.18	0.2432
EDI*OP	0.2320	0.1611	71.8	1.44	0.1542
APS*OP	-0.2567	0.1620	71	-1.59	0.1153
ERP*OS	-0.3469	0.2682	71.7	-1.29	0.2001

Table A3. Labor costs analysis: The affect of IT systems

Independent variables	Estimate	Std Error	DF	T Value	Pr > |t|
ERP	-0.04177	0.07445	82.8	-0.56	0.5763
ERP II	-0.03467	0.1822	83.4	-0.19	0.8496
APS	-0.01728	0.06716	82.5	-0.26	0.7976
EDI	0.1164	0.06444	84.9	1.81	**0.0743**
OP	0.08786	0.06660	83.5	1.32	0.1907
OS	0.086667	0.08145	83.3	1.06	0.2904
OP	0.2056	0.1623	79.8	1.27	0.2090
OS	0.1179	0.1133	82.8	1.04	0.3012
OP*OS	-0.1708	0.1821	81.2	-0.94	0.3513
APS	-0.08895	0.1907	77.5	-0.47	0.6423
OP	0.1664	0.2482	76.9	0.67	0.5044
OS	0.09276	0.1821	77	0.51	0.6119
APS*OP	0.07357	0.1821	79.3	0.40	0.6873
APS*OS	0.006739	0.2464	77.5	0.03	0.9783
OP*OS	-0.1581	0.2141	78.7	-0.74	0.4625
ERP	-0.2789	0.1910	78.2	-1.46	0.1482
OP	0.2353	0.2159	78.7	1.09	0.2792
OS	-0.09793	0.1981	78.1	-0.49	0.6225
ERP*OP	-0.01486	0.1723	77.8	-0.09	0.9315
ERP*OS	0.2949	0.2248	77.8	1.31	0.1933
OP*OS	-0.1930	0.1838	78.1	-1.05	0.2971
ERP_II	-0.1835	0.2324	81.1	-0.79	0.4322
OP	-0.2251	0.4219	80.4	-0.53	0.5951
OS	0.09270	0.1176	81.7	0.79	0.4326
ERP_II*OP	0.4253	0.3848	79.5	1.11	0.2724
ERP_II *OS	0	.	.	.	.
OP*OS	-0.1394	0.1859	80	-0.75	0.4554

Independent variables	Estimate	Std Error	DF	T Value	Pr > |t|
EDI	-0.05233	0.1809	78.8	-0.29	0.7732
OP	0.3894	0.2567	77.9	1.52	0.1334
OS	0.01328	0.1455	80.4	0.09	0.9275
EDI*OP	-0.1572	0.1737	80	-0.91	0.3681
EDI*OS	0.3003	0.2392	80.1	1.26	0.2129
OP*OS	-0.3253	0.2336	78.2	-1.39	0.1677
ERP	-0.2809	0.2234	75.2	-1.26	0.2125
APS	-0.00076	0.2354	74.4	-0.00	0.9974
OP	0.1726	0.2782	73.5	0.62	0.5369
OS	-0.07173	0.2263	72.4	-0.32	0.7521
ERP*APS	0.009815	0.1647	72.4	0.06	0.9526
ERP*OP	-0.04244	0.1959	74.8	-0.22	0.8291
APS*OP	0.08906	0.1918	75.5	0.46	0.6438
ERP*OS	0.3215	0.2438	74.7	1.32	0.1913
APS*OS	-0.1036	0.2615	73.7	-0.40	0.6931
OP*OS	-0.1439	0.2167	74.5	-0.66	0.5088
ERP	-0.2592	0.2190	75.8	-1.18	0.2402
EDI	0.04328	0.2458	74	0.18	0.8607
OP	0.3953	0.3080	72.7	1.28	0.2035
OS	-0.1522	0.2093	74.4	-0.73	0.4695
ERP*EDI	0.005100	0.1650	75.4	0.03	0.9754
ERP*OP	-0.06188	0.1785	73.7	-0.35	0.7298
EDI*OP	-0.1521	0.1788	75.6	-0.85	0.3975
ERP*OS	0.2886	0.2377	74.6	1.21	0.2284
EDI*OS	0.1951	0.2602	75.3	0.75	0.4557
OP*OS	-0.2918	0.2437	72.9	-1.20	0.2350
ERP_II	-0.1147	0.3225	74.9	-0.36	0.7231
EDI	-0.01117	0.5035	75.5	-0.02	0.9824
OP	-0.05457	0.5744	75.8	-0.10	0.9246
OS	-0.00205	0.1499	77.7	-0.01	0.9891
ERP_II*EDI	-0.04404	0.4708	75.5	-0.09	0.9257
ERP_II*OP	0.4203	0.4664	75.9	0.90	0.3704
EDI*OP	-0.1354	0.1854	76.5	-0.73	0.4673
ERP_II*OS	0	.	.	.	.
EDI*OS	0.2851	0.2486	76.7	1.15	0.2550
OP*OS	-0.2882	0.2432	75.7	-1.18	0.2398
ERP	-0.2554	0.2471	71.5	-1.03	0.3048
EDI	0.08521	0.2861	70.7	0.30	0.7667
APS	-0.01871	0.2464	69.6	-0.08	0.9397
OP	0.3459	0.3418	68.4	1.01	0.3151
OS	-0.1209	0.2352	67.6	-0.51	0.6088
ERP*EDI	0.005548	0.1797	71	0.03	0.9755
ERP*APS	0.03975	0.1790	68.7	0.22	0.8250
EDI*APS	-0.05808	0.1624	68.3	-0.36	0.7218
ERP*OP	-0.1367	0.2025	70.1	-0.67	0.5020
EDI*OP	-0.1847	0.1929	69.3	-0.96	0.3417
APS*OP	0.1644	0.2011	68.9	0.82	0.4164
ERP*OS	0.3389	0.2565	70.2	1.32	0.1907
EDI*OS	0.2490	0.2735	70.2	0.91	0.3656
APS*OS	-0.1958	0.2678	68.6	-0.73	0.4671
OP*OS	-0.2381	0.2622	68.8	-0.91	0.3672
ERP	-0.08213	0.1381	80.3	-0.61	0.5427
EDI	0.1826	0.1299	79.1	1.41	0.1638
APS	-0.05115	0.09648	80.4	-0.53	0.5975
OP	0.04613	0.1381	80.3	0.33	0.7392
EDI*APS	-0.06328	0.1506	77.7	-0.42	0.6758
ERP*OP	0.03711	0.1601	79.8	0.23	0.8173

Table A4. Materials cost analysis: The affect of IT systems

Independent variables	Estimate	Std Error	DF	T Value	Pr > |t|
ERP	1.2982	4.5767	81.6	0.28	0.7774
ERP II	-6.9982	11.1476	81.7	-0.63	0.5319
APS	-0.03197	4.1207	81.1	-0.01	0.9938
EDI	-5.4114	3.9962	83.6	-1.35	0.1793
OP	-0.6819	4.1241	82	-0.17	0.8691
OS	-4.0100	5.0122	82	-0.80	0.4260
OP	5.3271	10.0661	78.2	0.53	0.5982
OS	-2.1301	7.0580	81.8	-0.30	0.7636
OP*OS	-5.7381	11.3138	79.8	-0.51	0.6134
APS	-20.6672	11.4593	75.3	-1.80	**_0.0753_**
OP	1.3727	14.8918	74.8	0.09	0.9268
OS	-13.3626	10.9302	74.9	-1.22	0.2253
APS*OP	11.5069	10.9873	77.2	1.05	0.2982
APS*OS	14.7924	14.8063	75.5	1.00	0.3210
OP*OS	-8.2236	12.9018	76.7	-0.64	0.5258
ERP	-3.2205	11.7611	76.4	-0.27	0.7850
OP	-10.8010	13.3030	76.6	-0.81	0.4193
OS	4.3852	12.1979	76.4	0.36	0.7202
ERP*OP	19.2928	10.5974	75.8	1.82	**_0.0726_**
ERP*OS	-10.6567	13.8286	75.9	-0.77	0.4433
OP*OS	-3.2791	11.3179	76.4	-0.29	0.7728
ERP_II	3.1517	14.3885	79.7	0.22	0.8272
OP	36.3789	26.0736	78.5	1.40	0.1669
OS	-1.5934	7.2926	80.8	-0.22	0.8276
ERP_II*OP	-30.8304	23.7488	77.6	-1.30	0.1981
ERP_II *OS	0	.	.	.	.
OP*OS	-6.8113	11.4823	78.4	-0.59	0.5548
EDI	-5.2038	11.2229	77.1	-0.46	0.6442
OP	-6.0425	15.9080	76.4	-0.38	0.7051
OS	1.6442	9.0536	79.3	0.18	0.8564
EDI*OP	14.7491	10.8019	78.8	1.37	0.1760
EDI*OS	-12.6998	14.8697	78.6	-0.85	0.3957
OP*OS	1.6894	14.4799	76.6	0.12	0.9074
ERP	7.5316	13.3927	73	0.56	0.5756
APS	-17.7583	14.0816	72.3	-1.26	0.2113
OP	-9.2544	16.6018	71.2	-0.56	0.5790
OS	-3.8362	13.4757	70.5	-0.28	0.7767
ERP*APS	-5.6148	9.8106	70.5	-0.57	0.5689
ERP*OP	18.0601	11.7272	72.3	1.54	0.1279
APS*OP	6.5864	11.5104	73.4	0.57	0.5689
ERP*OS	-18.0016	14.5892	72.3	-1.23	0.2212
APS*OS	20.0076	15.6194	71.7	1.28	0.2043
OP*OS	-8.1815	12.9701	72.5	-0.63	0.5302

Independent variables	Estimate	Std Error	DF	T Value	Pr > |t|
ERP	-7.1907	13.3087	73.8	-0.54	0.5906
EDI	-9.1337	14.8702	72	-0.61	0.5410
OP	-23.0055	18.5845	70.6	-1.24	0.2199
OS	8.7510	12.6746	72.4	0.69	0.4921
ERP*EDI	6.7398	10.0172	73.4	0.67	0.5032
ERP*OP	22.1118	10.7876	71.4	2.05	**0.0441**
EDI*OP	12.6900	10.8577	73.6	1.17	0.2463
ERP*OS	-10.1775	14.3896	72.2	-0.71	0.4817
EDI*OS	-14.7075	15.7805	72.9	-0.93	0.3544
OP*OS	4.0395	14.7108	70.9	0.27	0.7844
ERP_II	10.7788	19.6156	72.4	0.55	0.5844
EDI	20.5959	30.6654	73.1	0.67	0.5039
OP	4.3024	35.0181	73.6	0.12	0.9026
OS	1.5946	9.1934	76.1	0.17	0.8628
ERP_II*EDI	-26.3569	28.6864	73.3	-0.92	0.3612
ERP_II*OP	-12.3279	28.4378	73.7	-0.43	0.6659
EDI*OP	17.1335	11.3242	74.6	1.51	0.1345
ERP_II*OS	0	.	.	.	.
EDI*OS	-15.1123	15.1864	74.3	-1.00	0.3229
OP*OS	3.0767	14.8223	73.4	0.21	0.8361
ERP	4.9319	14.1374	68	0.35	0.7283
EDI	-24.2474	16.3181	67.8	-1.49	0.1419
APS	-16.1550	13.9729	66.5	-1.16	0.2517
OP	-20.9702	19.2684	65.1	-1.09	0.2805
OS	-1.9146	13.2362	64.9	-0.14	0.8854
ERP*EDI	8.4878	10.2572	67.9	0.83	0.4109
ERP*APS	-14.2506	10.1213	66	-1.41	0.1638
EDI*APS	18.5009	9.1697	65.7	2.02	**0.0477**
ERP*OP	26.0717	11.4863	66.3	2.27	**0.0265**
EDI*OP	10.2030	10.9260	66.3	0.93	0.3538
APS*OP	0.9023	11.3613	65.6	0.08	0.9369
ERP*OS	-19.2928	14.5525	64.9	-1.33	0.1895
EDI*OS	-14.0404	15.5170	66.4	-0.90	0.3688
APS*OS	25.1224	15.1246	65.7	1.66	0.1015
OP*OS	-1.2920	14.8086	65.5	-0,09	0.9307
ERP	-10.6682	7.9718	77.2	-1.34	0.1847
EDI	-21.7784	7.6739	76	-2.84	**0.0058**
APS	-3.5862	5.7303	77.5	-0.63	0.5333
OP	-13.2467	8.1905	77.1	-1.62	0.1099
EDI*APS	18.4487	8.8590	75.1	2.08	**0.0407**
ERP*OP	18.6798	9.4700	76.3	1.97	**0.0522**

Table A5. Overhead cost analysis: The affect of IT systems

Independent variables	Estimate	Std Error	DF	T Value	Pr > |t|
ERP	-0.03181	0.06491	81.9	-0.49	0.6254
ERP II	0.01526	0.1586	44.7	0.10	0.9236
APS	-0.02607	0.05842	81.5	-0.45	0.6566
EDI	0.01985	0.05715	84.2	0.35	0.7292
OP	-0.02898	0.05838	82.3	-0.50	0.6209
OS	0.04740	0.07118	82.4	0.67	0.5073
OP	-0.2355	0.1412	78.5	-1.67	**0.0993**
OS	-0.01588	0.09863	82.4	-0.16	0.8725
OP*OS	0.2296	0.1585	80.3	1.45	0.1513

Independent variables	Estimate	Std Error	DF	T Value	Pr > |t|
APS	0.2769	0.1601	75.8	1.73	**0.0877**
OP	-0.1420	0.2081	75.2	-0.68	0.4971
OS	0.1304	0.1528	75.3	0.85	0.3960
APS*OP	-0.1942	0.1532	77.9	-1.27	0.2089
APS*OS	-0.1862	0.2068	75.9	-0.90	0.3708
OP*OS	0.2476	0.1800	77.3	1.38	0.1726
ERP	0.1313	0.1614	76.8	0.08	042.59
OP	-0.01505	0.1855	77.2	-0.08	0.9355
OS	-0.02029	0.1701	76.8	-0.12	0.9054
ERP*OP	-0.2690	0.1479	76.2	-1.82	**0.0728**
ERP*OS	0.03213	0.1930	76.2	0.17	0.8682
OP*OS	0.2004	0.1579	76.8	1.27	0.2081
ERP_II	-0.1307	0.2022	80.9	-0.65	0.5199
OP	-0.6543	0.3671	80	-1.78	0.0785
OS	-0.03752	0.1022	81.6	-0.37	0.7146
ERP_II*OP	0.4126	0.3350	78.8	1.23	0.2217
ERP_II *OS	0	.	.	.	.
OP*OS	0.2578	0.1618	79.3	1.59	0.1151
EDI	0.2207	0.1574	77.6	1.40	0.1650
OP	-0.1882	0.2233	76.7	-0.84	0.4019
OS	0.02643	0.1268	79.8	0.21	0.8354
EDI*OP	-0.1775	0.1513	79.3	-1.17	0.2443
EDI*OS	-0.06334	0.2083	79.2	-0.30	0.7619
OP*OS	0.2419	0.2032	76.9	1.19	0.2374
ERP	0.01686	0.1877	73.8	0.09	0.9286
APS	0.2260	0.1975	72.9	1.14	0.2563
OP	0.003729	0.2331	71.8	0.02	0.9873
OS	0.07117	0.1894	70.8	0.38	0.7082
ERP*APS	0.04136	0.1379	70.8	0.30	0.7651
ERP*OP	-0.2325	0.1645	73.2	-1.41	0.1617
APS*OP	-0.1355	0.1612	74.2	-0.84	0.4034
ERP*OS	0.1055	0.2046	73.1	0.52	0.6076
APS*OS	-0.2078	0.2192	72.2	-0.95	0.3465
OP*OS	0.2397	0.1819	73.1	1.32	0.1917
ERP	0.1021	0.1876	74.1	0.54	0.5877
EDI	0.2854	0.2098	72.1	1.36	0.1780
OP	0.004327	0.2624	70.5	0.02	0.9869
OS	-0.03841	0.1788	72.6	-0.21	0.8305
ERP*EDI	-0.1008	0.1412	73.7	-0.71	0.4776
ERP*OP	-0.2655	0.1522	71.5	-1.74	**0.0854**
EDI*OP	-0.1419	0.1530	73.9	-0.93	0.3567
ERP*OS	0.09583	0.2030	72.4	0.47	0.6383
EDI*OS	-0.04252	0.2225	73.2	-0.19	0.8490
OP*OS	0.2198	0.2077	70.9	1.06	0.2935
ERP_II	-0.2772	0.2779	73.1	-1.00	0.3214
EDI	-0.2004	0.4341	73.9	-.046	0.6457
OP	-0.2789	0.4954	74.4	-0.56	0.5751
OS	0.008037	0.1296	77	0.06	0.9507
ERP_II*EDI	0.4225	0.4060	74	1.04	0.3014
ERP_II*OP	0.1223	0.4023	74.5	0.30	0.7620
EDI*OP	-0.2143	0.1600	75.4	-1.34	0.1845
ERP_II*OS	0	.	.	.	.
EDI*OS	-0.02290	0.2146	75.4	-0.11	0.9153
OP*OS	0.2325	0.2097	74.2	1.11	0.2713

Independent variables	Estimate	Std Error	DF	T Value	Pr > |t|
ERP	-0.00994	0.2080	69.4	-0.05	0.9620
EDI	0.3418	0.2403	68.9	1.42	0.1593
APS	0.1687	0.2062	67.4	0.82	0.4161
OP	0.01890	0.2849	65.8	0.07	0.9473
OS	0.05847	0.1958	65.4	0.30	0.7661
ERP*EDI	-0.1174	0.1510	69.1	-0.78	0.4397
ERP*APS	0.1149	0.1495	66.7	0.77	0.4449
EDI*APS	-0.07485	0.1355	66.3	-0.55	0.5825
ERP*OP	-0.2858	0.1695	67.4	-1.69	**0.0964**
EDI*OP	-0.1168	0.1613	67.2	-0.72	0.4713
APS*OP	-0.07810	0.1678	66.4	-0.47	0.6432
ERP*OS	0.1771	0.2147	67.5	0.83	0.4123
EDI*OS	-0.02841	0.2290	67.5	-0.12	0.9016
APS*OS	-0.2430	0.2234	66.4	-1.09	0.2808
OP*OS	0.2674	0.2188	66.3	1.22	0.2260
ERP	0.1529	0.1117	80.3	1.37	0.1748
OP	0.1676	0.1150	79.7	1.46	0.1489
ERP*OP	-0.2646	0.1336	79.1	-1.98	**0.0512**
ERP	0.1090	0.1196	80.1	0.91	0.3649
APS	0.1159	0.1062	80.9	1.09	0.2785
OP	0.2573	0.1261	77.5	2.04	**0.0447**
ERP*OP	-0.1996	0.1409	78.9	-1.42	0.1604
APS *OP	-0.2216	0.1327	80.3	-1.67	**0.0988**
APS	0.1533	0.09895	81.9	1.55	0.1252
OP	0.1400	0.09592	80.4	1.46	0.1482
APS *OP	-02752	0.1264	81.6	-2.18	**0.0323**

Table A6. Analysis of supplier and customer integration

	Effect	Treatment	Estimate	Error	DF	t Value	Pr > |t|
Profit	Supp_Int	Extensive	0.0243	0.1312	68.1	0.19	0.8536
	Supp_Int	None	-0.1107	0.111	69.3	-1.00	0.3221
	Supp_Int	Some	0	.	.	.	.
	Cust_Int	Extensive	0.02274	0.1441	69.8	0.16	0.8750
	Cust_Int	None	-0.01013	0.1157	69.6	-0.09	0.9304
	Cust_Int	Some	0	.	.	.	.
COGS	Supp_Int	Extensive	-0.03616	0.1026	65.4	-0.35	0.7256
	Supp_Int	None	0.04938	0.09234	74.8	0.53	0.5944
	Supp_Int	Some	0	.	.	.	.
	Cust_Int	Extensive	-0.1042	0.1155	74.8	-0.90	0.3698
	Cust_Int	None	-0.00969	0.09654	74.7	-0.10	0.9204
	Cust_Int	Some	0	.	.	.	.
Labor Costs	Supp_Int	Extensive	0.237	0.09569	80.6	2.48	**0.0153**
	Supp_Int	None	0.07954	0.08608	79	0.92	0.3583
	Supp_Int	Some	0	.	.	.	.
	Cust_Int	Extensive	-0.09909	0.1068	78.4	-0.93	0.3566
	Cust_Int	None	0.05709	0.09082	79.8	0.63	0.5314
	Cust_Int	Some	0	.	.	.	.

	Effect	Treatment	Estimate	Error	DF	t Value	Pr > |t|
Material Costs	Supp_Int	Extensive	-7.648	5.8891	79.4	-1.30	0.1978
	Supp_Int	None	-5.3336	5.2784	77.7	-1.01	0.3154
	Supp_Int	Some	0	.	.	.	.
	Cust_Int	Extensive	6.4419	6.5434	76.7	0.98	0.3280
	Cust_Int	None	-4.8887	5.5779	78.6	-0.88	0.3835
	Cust_Int	Some	0	.	.	.	.
Overhead Costs	Supp_Int	Extensive	-0.02488	0.08512	80	-0.29	0.7708
	Supp_Int	None	0.000133	0.07646	77.8	0.00	0.9986
	Supp_Int	Some	0	.	.	.	.
	Cust_Int	Extensive	-0.04587	0.09486	76.9	-0.48	0.6301
	Cust_Int	None	0.05645	0.08072	78.9	0.70	0.4864
	Cust_Int	Some	0	.	.	.	.

Chapter 8
The Impact of Social, Economic Variables and Logistics Performance on Asian Apparel Exporting Countries

K. F. Au
The Hong Kong Polytechnic University, Hong Kong

Chan M.H. Eve
The Hong Kong Polytechnic University, Hong Kong

ABSTRACT

Endowed with abundant supply of raw materials and low labor cost Asian countries have become the world's largest exporters of apparel products for the past few decades. In 2007, the value of Asian suppliers' total apparel exports to the world amounted to US$ 165 billion which represented 52% of the world's total apparel exports. The gravity trade model is utilized with an exploration at the aggregate level. Analyzing the data for fourteen exporting countries and their sixteen importing partners from 2000 to 2007, the country-specific, economic, social factors, in additional to logistics performance are analyzed statistically to identify the major determinants that have influenced the apparel trading of Asian countries to the EU-15, and American markets. Taking the robustness advantage of the gravity model, the analytical results indicate strong support for the model with parameters including GDP, per capita GDP, population size, female employment, value added factors and logistics performance. All these show statistically significance and positive effects. In contrast, distance, real exchange rates and wages have negative impacts on apparel trading. An important finding is that new variables, namely exporting countries' logistics performance can derive competitive advantage, otherwise, it erects a trade barrier in its own right in apparel exports.

INTRODUCTION

Apparel industry is central to the global economy and has played an especially important role in the export-oriented development of Asia; initially in Hong Kong, South Korea and Taiwan, and more recently, China. Today, this sector still constitutes a substantial source of income and employment for many Asian nations. There is cross-national statisti-

DOI: 10.4018/978-1-60566-974-8.ch008

cal evidence that average incomes in a country are higher when this sector is healthy (Diao and Somwaru, 2001). Global apparel exports amounted to US$309 billion in 2007. Approximately 130 countries produce apparel for export; many are highly dependent on this merchandise export for employment and foreign exchange. Although some 30 nations are significant importers of apparel in reality, apparel suppliers are dependent on two principal import markets; the EU and USA. The EU is the world's largest apparel importer. With its enlargement of member countries to 27, EU accounted for about 48% of world apparel imports, surpassing the USA's share by 17% in 2007. Still, it is important to note that a substantial amount of apparel trade in the world today remains within the industrial core.

Controlling the strongest purchasing power, the EU and USA lead buyers have shaped the geography of global apparel supply significantly over the past few decades. The number of leading global apparel exporting countries has increased sharply between 1980 and 2000. Countries whose apparel exports exceeded US$1 billion in 1980 included only the East Asian NIEs, namely Hong Kong, Taiwan and Korea, along with China and USA. A decade later, the list also included Indonesia, Thailand and Malaysia, India and Pakistan. By 2000, the Philippines, Vietnam, Bangladesh, Sri Lanka and Cambodia joined the rag trade as late comers. Yet there remains a substantial variation in the degree to which apparel is principal export items among the world's 25 largest exporters. As Gereffi and Memedovic (2003) noted: *"In Northeast and Southeast Asia, apparel has declined in importance, except in China where it remains the top export items, and in Indonesia and Vietnam where apparel has climbed to third place."* (p.22) Asian nations are mostly dependent on apparel exports, which often accounts for a significant share of their total industrial goods' exports and hence, export earnings have created a relatively high degree of dependency on this sector.

If one looks at the changing regional patterns for American apparel imports during the last several decades, it is clear that the Northeast Asian countries including Taiwan and South Korea are declining in their importance, South and Southeast Asia, namely India, Pakistan, Bangladesh and Sri Lanka have stabilized, and China has climbed to the first rank. The countries that have been most successful in exporting to USA are those that have developed, or are developing their full-package production capabilities, such as Hong Kong, South Korea and Taiwan in the first instance and China in the latter. On the other side of the globe, EU's apparel imports show a similar pattern, with China and Hong Kong playing the leading role among the East exporters which are capable of providing full-package manufacture.

By virtue of strong demands and high purchasing powers for fashion products at a reasonable price, the EU-27 and USA are the top two dominant apparel importers in the world. In 2007, the value of the world's apparel exports to the EU-27 and USA amounted to US$ 135 billion and US$ 83 billion respectively, which together represented 78 percent of the world's total apparel exports. Specifically, the apparel imports of the EU-15 amounted to US$ 128 billion, accounting for 95 percent of the region's total apparel imports (see Figure 1). In this case, the value of Asian apparel exports to the EU-15 and USA amounted to US$55 billion and US$54 billion respectively, which represented 43 percent and 65 percent of the region in question accordingly (see Figure 2).

The pattern of **Asia's apparel exports** has shown the trajectory of successful growth and become the world's largest exporting region for past decades not only because of their abundant supply of raw materials, technological capability and low production costs but also through adopting the full-package supply model. In 2007, the value of Asian suppliers' total apparel exports to the world amounted to US$ 165 billion which represented 52% of the world's total apparel exports. This vicious circumstance is motivating the

Figure 1. World apparel imported by the EU-27 and USA, 1990-2007. (Value in US$ billion)

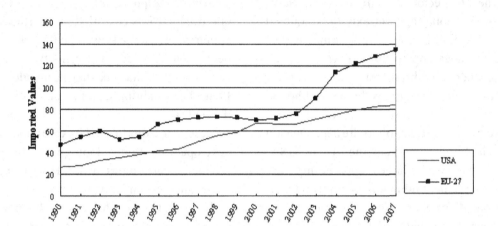

analysis in this paper. The **gravity trade model** is utilized with an exploration at the aggregate level. Analyzing the data for fourteen exporting countries and their sixteen importing partners from 2000 to 2007, the macroeconomic and social factors, in additional to logistics performance are analyzed statistically to identify the major determinants that have influenced the apparel trading of Asian countries to the EU-15 and USA. Apparel industry is examined in the study because of its extensive globalization of production and distribution and the complexity involved in the design of supply chains.

Figure 2. Asian apparel imported by the EU-15 and USA, 1990-2007. (Value in US$ billion)

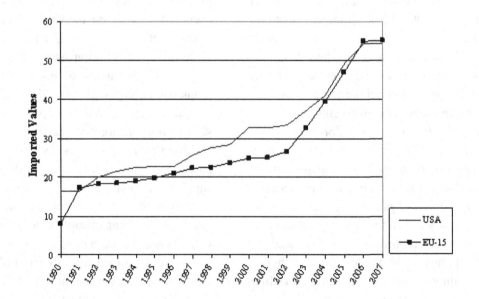

LITERATURE REVIEW

Global Apparel Supply Chains

Globalization of production has made the design and management of **supply chains** in some industries (e.g., apparel, automobiles, and consumer electronics) more important and complicated. Moreover, greater consumer demand for new products and more product varieties have reduced product life sharply. This is particularly evident for fashionable apparel. Fashion retailers need to respond quickly to the latest trend of consumer demand by offering new products in the shortest possible time. Equally, facing a growing competitive market, apparel retailers that offer basic items for the mass market also need to maintain their operations as efficient as possible in order to stay profitable. In response to these demands, apparel suppliers have increasingly employed lean, agile, or a combination of both approaches to manage their supply chains, as shown in some case studies (Bruce, et al. 2004).

Institutional Barriers for Developing the Full-Package Apparel Supply Model

In an effort to develop global lean and agile supply chains, Asian apparel suppliers have to reexamine to what extent their current practices can achieve the expected level of agility and leanness in order to overcome hurdles to develop the full-package supply capability. One important institutional factor is the **logistics performance** of exporting country which determines trade costs in both financial and time aspects. Recent studies of country logistics performance show large between-country and between-region performance variations. For example, Djankov et al. (2006) reported that it takes an average 32 days in South Asia (including Bangladesh, India, Pakistan and Sri Lanka), and only 23 days and 6 days in ASEAN and Singapore respectively to move a 20-foot container of an identical good from a factory in the largest business city to a ship in the most accessible port. This shows that neither having well-established physical infrastructure and good transport services nor being close to the market per se can guarantee quick delivery, as the time required to fulfill customs, administrative, and port requirements to load the cargo onto a ship could be much longer than the time of inland carriage and handling. Nordas et al. (2006) in a case study of Bulgaria's and the Dominican Republic's apparel and textile exports found that buyers are willing to source from producers with higher costs if they can guarantee shorter lead times. Also, improvements in transport, logistics and customs procedures are essential for suppliers to stay competitive in supplying high-value apparel to markets of close proximity with a short lead time, while reducing the cost disadvantage as compared to remote low-cost suppliers. It is likely that long lead time and high variability in lead time which stem from poor logistics performance will erect a non-tariff trade barrier for suppliers, especially those in developing countries, to be integrated in global supply chains.

Recently, the World Bank has conducted a survey study on logistics performance of 150 countries and developed the **Logistics Performance Index (LPI)** and its seven indicators (Arvis et al. 2007):

1. Efficiency of the clearance process by customs and other border agencies.
2. Quality of transport and information technology (IT) infrastructure for logistics.
3. Ease and affordability of arranging international shipments.
4. Competence of the local logistics industry.
5. Ability to track and trace international shipments.
6. Domestic logistics costs.
7. Timeliness of shipments in reaching destination.

Table 1. LPI score and ranking of fourteen Asian exporting countries

Country	World LPI Ranking	The LPI score
Hong Kong, China	8	4.00
Taiwan, China	21	3.64
Republic of Korea	25	3.52
Malaysia	27	3.48
China	30	3.32
Thailand	31	3.31
India	39	3.07
Indonesia	43	3.01
Vietnam	53	2.89
Philippines	65	2.69
Pakistan	68	2.62
Cambodia	81	2.50
Bangladesh	87	2.47
Sri Lanka	92	2.40

Source: The World Bank (Arvis et al., 2007)

Each country's performance in different dimensions was recorded on a 1 to 5 scale (lowest to highest performance). The LPI was aggregated as a weighted average of various logistics performance indicators using the Principal Component Analysis method. The World Bank's survey results showed that high income countries were top performers; however, there were huge differences between countries at other income levels. See Table 1 for the LPI score and ranking of fourteen Asian exporting countries. Also, positive associations between logistics performance and trade performance including growth and competitiveness, export diversification, and trade expansion were found.

As traditional measures of logistics performance such as direct freight costs, average delays, and port efficiency may reflect the overall logistics performance partially, the current study applied gravity model to examine to what extent the logistics performance of Asian countries (reflected by the LPI) and key macroeconomic and social factors influence Asia's apparel exports to the EU and USA.

The Gravity Trade Model

The use of **gravity model** is well-established in international trade literature (Bayoumi & Eichengree, 1995). In its basic form, the gravity model posits that trade between two countries is positively influenced by the economic size of the trading partners and negatively affected by distance, and a bevy of special factors that either enhance or impede trade between countries. Empirically, the framework has been used to evaluate policy issues, such as regional trading agreements (Sharma & Chua, 2000) and multilateral agreements (Subramanian & Wei, 2003), as well as implications of WTO accession for current non-members (Lissovolik & Lissovolik, 2004) and calculation of trade potential (Nilsson, 2000).

While most of the aforementioned policy issues were widely discussed in the literature, the impact of Asian suppliers' growth in apparel industry as seen through the lenses of the gravity model has not been fully explored. In this study there are two novelties. First, few studies have incorporated a measure of country logistics performance as comprehensive as LPI in the gravity model to analyze the apparel trade flow. Second, past gravity research (Batra, 2004; Athukorala, 2007) focused mainly on regional investigations and general commodities, and not specifically on the global apparel trade. Thus, this study contributes to existing literature by filling these gaps, extending a broader analysis on apparel trading and providing an insight into the principal determinants that have stimulated Asia's apparel exports.

ESTIMATION AND VARIABLES

The following gravity equation, typically specified in logarithms, is developed to examine the impact of key macroeconomic and social factors in addition to logistics performance on the Asian apparel export values:

$$\ln(EXP_{ij})_t = \alpha + \beta_1 \ln(GDP_i)_t + \beta_2 \ln(PCGDP_i)_t + \beta_3 \ln(GPD_j)_t + \beta_4 \ln(PCGDP_j)_t + \beta_5 \ln(D_{ij}) +$$

$$\beta_6 \ln(POP_{jt}) + \beta_7 REXRATE_{ijt} + \beta_8 \ln(VALADDED_i)_t + \beta_9 \ln(WAGE_i)_t + \beta_{10} \ln(FEMALE_i)_t + \beta_{11}(LPI_i)_t + U_{ijt}$$

where t (t = 1…8) starting from 2000 to 2007, representing the time when trading transactions took place:

$\ln(EXP_{ij})_t$ = Log of export value of apparel in millions of US dollars from Asian suppliers to the USA, EU-15 and Japan, i denotes Asian suppliers' variables, j represents the import markets;

α = Unobserved effects or fixed effects which do not change over time, and capture all unobserved time-constant factors that affect EXP_{ij};

β = Slope parameter, also known as the partial regression coefficient. It represents the expected increase in the outcome variable for a unit increase in the predictor variable. In this case, the slope coefficient β_1 measures the change in the conditional mean of dependent variable (exported apparel value) per one unit change in independent variable X_1 (GDP), holding the values of the other independent variables $X_2…X_{11}$ constant.

$\ln(GDP_i)_t$ = GDP log of Asian suppliers in millions of US dollars;

$\ln(PCGDP_i)_t$ = Per capita GDP log of Asian suppliers in millions of US dollars;

$\ln(GDP_j)_t$ = GDP log of importers in millions of US dollars;

$\ln(PCGDP_j)_t$ = Per capita GDP log of importers in millions of US dollars;

$\ln(D_{ij})$ = Geographical distance (in km) log between the individual capitals of importers and Asian suppliers;

$\ln(POP_{jt})$ = The population size log of importers;

$REXRATE_{ijt}$ = The real exchange rate of foreign currency per unit in US dollars;

$\ln(VALADDED_i)_t$ = Log of the value added amount in the apparel industry of Asian suppliers;

$\ln(WAGE_j)_t$ = Wage log of suppliers in millions of US dollars;

$\ln(FEMALE_i)$ = Log of the number of women in the work force of Asian suppliers;

$(LPI_i)_t$ = The Logistics Performance Index of Asian suppliers;

U_t = Other omitted influences on exports

The analyses include exports between fourteen Asian apparel exporters and their sixteen importing countries. The dependent variable is the exported apparel value in log form, between pairs of countries. In addition to the LPI, the independent variables include a set of macroeconomic factors: the log exports of country i to country j, the log GDPs of the two countries, log per capita GDPs of the two countries, distance between them, log of population size of importers, real exchange rate, log of value added factors, the number of women in the workforce, and labor costs of the exporters.

Since the economic size of the exporting and importing countries is usually measured by the GDP, the GDPs of importing countries and their apparel exporters are considered to represent the economic masses which impact the apparel exports of the country's economy. Moreover, the GDPs also indicate the supply capabilities of the apparel exporting countries. The estimated coefficients β_1 and β_3 should be positive.

Based on the gravity principle, per capita GDP of the exporting country is used as a proxy of capital intensity. As the apparel industry is a labor-oriented industry, per capita GDP of Asian suppliers is utilized to indicate the impact of the monetary conditions for the workforce in countries with apparel exports. Additionally, the income level or purchasing power of importing countries is represented by per capita GDP. Controlling for GDP, richer countries (in terms of per capita GDP) are likely to demand more choices of differentiated products which may be imported from countries that are specialized in the production of those products. As such, the estimated coefficients β_2 and β_4 are expected to be positive.

The identification of distance effects on international trade has proven to be one of the most robust empirical findings in international trade (Frankel and Rose, 2002). In general, longer distance demands higher trade costs, and thus erecting a trade barrier. The estimated coefficient β_5 should therefore be negative. The population size of the importer's country has a direct and positive relationship with the consumption of manufactured commodities and therefore, to secure a better understanding of this effect on apparel imports, population size of the importer's country is taken into consideration. The real exchange rate is a key factor affecting trade flows. The depreciation (appreciation) of a country's currency against other currencies stimulates (reduces) the country's exports. Thus, the sign of β_7 will depend on the changes of the exporting

countries' currencies against the trading partner countries' currencies.

Apparel production involves a large amount of manual handling. The value added factors refer to the additional value created at a particular stage of the manufacturing process. In modern macroeconomics, this implies adverts which contribute to the factors of production, such as land, labor and capital goods. These enhance the value of a product and correspond to the incomes received by the owners. The factors of production provide "services" which increase the unit price of a product relative to the cost per unit of intermediate inputs used in production. A higher value of materials and supplies added in apparel production should contribute more to the exports. Therefore, the sign of the estimated coefficient β_8 is expected to be positive.

Since trade liberalization has progressed after the completion of the ATC in 2005, price competition among apparel suppliers have become more intense. The level of exporters' worker wages is one of the crucial deciding factors in the entire apparel trade flow. Nearly three quarters of workers working in the global apparel production industry are women. The participation rate of female labor force in developing countries is even higher. As more female workers provide higher production capacity for apparel exports, a positive estimated coefficient β_{10} is expected.

In addition to the above macroeconomic factors, the LPI is added as a key independent variable. Exporting countries sharing similar factor endowments may differ in their logistics performance in terms of customs clearance efficiency, transport and IT infrastructure quality, ease of arranging international shipments, the ability to track and trace shipments, domestic logistics cost, timeliness in reaching destination, and competence of the domestic logistics industry. It is anticipated that exporting countries' logistics performance contributes to their apparel exports. Thus, estimated coefficient β_{11} should be positive.

Data Source

Apparel export values of all exporting economies with the exception of Taiwan, were obtained from the UN COMTRADE, http://comtrade.un.org. The export values of Taiwan were extracted and compiled from the Directorate General of Customs, Ministry of Finance, ROC, http://cus93.trade.gov.tw/english/FSCE/FSC0011E.asp. Data on real GDP, per capita GDP (at constant 1990 prices in US dollars), real exchange rates and population size of countries were secured from the International Financial Statistics (IFS) database. Real GDP and per capita GDP of Taiwan were acquired from the Taiwan Statistical Data Book, Council for Economic Planning and Development, R.O.C. The distance between countries was drawn from Vulcansoft Distance Calculator, http://www.vulcansoft.com/city97.html. The value added amount, number of female workers and labor wages were extracted and complied from the UNIDO industrial statistics dataset. The scores of LPI were obtained from the study of World Bank (Arvis et al., 2007). The data consisted of 224 observations for sixteen importing countries and fourteen Asian exporting countries from 2000-2007[1].

Results of Econometric Estimation and Discussion

The gravity model fits the data well and all estimated coefficients are significant at $p < 0.05$ (see Table 2). As expected, the regression results of Model 1 show that exports increase with the GDP, GDP per capita of the importing and exporting countries, population of the importing countries, the number of female workers, value added factor and the LPI of exporting countries. Exports fall with distance, real exchange rate and labor wage. As a whole, Model 1 accounts for 67% of the variance of apparel export values. On top of the contribution of macroeconomic factors examined in Model 1, the LPI per se explains the extra 9%

of variance of apparel export values, boosting the total adjusted R^2 value to 76% in Model 2.

GDP and Per Capita GDP

The analytical results aligned with other gravity trading model studies of bilateral trade (Glick & Rose, 2002), and showed that the GDPs of importers and exporters positively influenced the apparel trade. This conformed to the theoretical expectation; a higher GDP creates a stronger demand for apparel imports and also a larger supply for exports. The results can be interpreted as a 10% increase in importers' GDPs (all else constant) results a 22.3% increase in their apparel imports, while the same amount of GDP increase for exporters result in an 11.8% increase in their exports. Similar effects are also observed for exporters' and importers' per capita GDPs.

Physical Distance

Consequent to the growing pressure for quick responses, geographic proximity is an important criterion for apparel sourcing. The variable geographical distance (D_{ij}) negatively affects apparel trading, reflecting that an increase in distance and thus logistics costs lead to a reduction in apparel exports. This is in accordance with the common prediction that greater physical distance between bilateral trading destinations erects a barrier for trades (Au & Chan, 2008).

Population

Population size also demonstrates a positive effect on trade flow between countries. As shown in the results, a 10% increase in the population size of importers results in an 18.9% increase in apparel imports. This supports the view that larger population size is associated with greater import value (Chan, Au & Sarkar 2008).

Table 2. Results of two regression models

Dependent Variable: ln(EXP$_{ij}$)	Model 1	Model 2
Independent Variables	Coefficient	Coefficient
Constant	-31.12***	-25.45***
ln(GDP$_i$)	+1.07***	+1.18***
ln(PCGDP$_i$)	+1.59***	+1.76***
Ln(GDP$_j$)	+2.19***	+2.23***
Ln(PCGDP$_j$)	+4.67**	+4.56**
ln(D$_{ij}$)	-1.90***	-1.85***
ln(POP$_j$)	+1.97**	+1.89**
REXRATE$_{ij}$	-1.63**	-1.78**
ln(VALADDED$_i$)	+1.19***	+1.23***
ln(WAGE$_i$)	-0.76**	-0.79**
ln(FEMALE$_i$)	+0.83**	+0.86**
LPI$_i$	-	+4.53***
Adjusted R^2	0.67	0.76

Note: **N=224,** ** Significant at 0.05 level, ***Significant at 0.01 level

Exchange Rates

The exchange rate coefficient is negative, suggesting a depreciation of exporting countries' currencies against those of their partner countries, and thus promoting apparel exports. This confirms the expectation that whenever there is a real depreciation or appreciation of foreign currencies against the American dollar, there will be an increase or decrease in apparel exports (Chan & Au 2007).

Value Added Factors

The variable (VALADDED$_j$) has a positive impact on the apparel export trends of Asian suppliers. The results indicate that with a 10% increase in the 'VALADDED$_j$' of supplier, there would be a 12.3% increase in apparel exports to the trading partners. This demonstrates the importance for apparel suppliers to embark on the route to implement the full-package supply model, offering a range of high value-added services for buyers.

Wages

For the wage variable, the coefficient shows a negative sign for the apparel exports. This implies that exporting countries with lower production costs which result from low labor cost are seen to be attractive supply source for importers. This is particular true for basic apparel items that are sold all year round and that are not highly time sensitive.

Female Workers

The results show that a 10% increase of female workers in the exporting countries results in an 8.6% increase in apparel exports. It is true that apparel industry depends heavily on the supply of female workers in the expansion of production capacity. Unlike other industries that are capital intensive, production of apparel requires lots of manual handling even though use of some advanced machines and equipment can improve productivity.

The LPI

The results in Model 2 show that a 10% improvement in the exporters' LPI increases apparel exports by 45.3%, all else equal. This clearly indicates that an exporting country's logistics performance promotes or hinders its inclusion in global apparel supply chains. The success of transforming from simple assembly model to full-package supply model will not succeed if improvements are to be done only at the firm level. Domestic logistics companies, port operators, transnational logistics service providers, financial institutions, government agencies and electronic commerce service providers all have a role to play to improve the logistics performance of exporting countries in the areas such as transportation and IT infrastructure, customs clearance system, and domestic logistics costs, as shown in the case of Hong Kong (Ho, et al. 2003).

Implication of this study for lead buyers in the EU and USA is that they can keep tracking the changes of key macroeconomic and social factors in addition to exporters' LPI in the (re) design of their apparel supply chains. Apparel suppliers in North Africa and Eastern Europe as well as Mexico that enjoy close proximity to the major markets per se cannot avoid the chance of being delinked from the agile supply chain in the supply of highly time sensitive items, if the logistics performance of the late comers in the same geographical region has improved significantly. Suppliers in Asia may have a chance to expand their supply from basic to fairly time sensitive apparel products, if their countries' logistics performance is elevated. Equally, late comers in Asia may have a chance to participate in global lean apparel supply chains.

CONCLUSION

This empirical study examines to what extent key macroeconomic and social factors, in addition to country logistics performance affect the volume of Asia's apparel exports to the EU and USA. As expected, the econometric results provide strong support for the gravity trading model and show that GDP, per capita GDP, distance, population, exchange rates, value added factor, wages, and the number of female workers are significant factors that influence apparel exports. Worth noting is that exporting countries' logistics performance can confer a competitive advantage and thus also erect a trade barrier in its own right, either enhancing or reducing the chance of being integrated in global apparel supply chains. This is especially true for exporting countries in the same geographical region with similar factors endowment. If trade liberalization continues to solidify, large lead buyers will keep on searching a worldwide basis for the best mix of suppliers to forge their global lean supply chains. Exporting countries' logistics performance may become a key determinant in differentiating the winners from losers in the global apparel industry.

ACKNOWLEDGMENT

The authors would like to acknowledge The Hong Kong Polytechnic University in providing research funding for this study.

REFERENCES

Arvis, J. F., Mustra, M., Panzer, J., Ojala, L., & Naula, T. (2007). Connecting to compete: Trade logistics in the global economy. Washington: World Bank.

Athukorala, P. C. (2007). The rise of China and East Asian export performance: Is the crowding-out fear warranted? Working paper, The Australian National University, 10.

Au, K.F., & Chan, M. H., Eve. (2008). Economic, social and policy determinants of EU-5 and American Apparel imports: A gravity model analysis. *International Journal of Information Systems and Supply Chain Management, 1*(3), 33–48.

Batra, A. (2004). India's global trade potential: The gravity model approach. *ICRIER working paper.* New Delhi: Indian Council for Research on International Economic Relations, 151.

Bayoumi, T., & Eichengreen, B. (1995). Is regionalism simple a diversion? Evidence from the Evolution of the EC and EFTA. *IMF Discussion Paper,* 109.

Bruce, M., Daly, L., & Towers, N. (2004). Lean or agile: A solution for supply chain management in the textiles and clothing industry? *International Journal of Operations & Production Management, 24*(2), 151–170. doi:10.1108/01443570410514867

Chan, M.H., Eve & Au, K.F. (2007). Determinants of China's textiles export: An analysis by gravity model. *Journal of Textile Institute., 98*(5), 463–469.

Chan, M.H., Eve; Au, K.F., & Sarkar, M.K. (2008). Antecedents to India's textile exports: 1985-2005. *International Journal of Indian Culture and Business Management, 1*(3), 265–276. doi:10.1504/IJICBM.2008.017785

Diao, X., & Somwaru, A. (2001). Impact of the MFA phase-out on the world economy: An intertemporal global general equilibrium analysis. *TMD Discussion Paper No.79.* Trade and Macroeconomics Division, International Food Policy Research Institute.

Djankov, S., Freund, C., & Pham, C. S. (2006). Trading on Time. World Bank Policy. *Research working paper 3909.*

Frankel, J., & Rose, A. (2002). An estimate of the effect of common currencies on trade and income. *The Quarterly Journal of Economics, 117*(2), 437–466. doi:10.1162/003355302753650292

Gereffi, G., & Memedovic, O. (2003). *The Global apparel value chain: What prospects for upgrading by developing countries.* United Nations Industrial Development Organization (UNIDO).

Glick, R., & Rose, A. K. (2002). Does a currency union affect trade? The time-series evidence. *European Economic Review, 46*(6), 1125–1151. doi:10.1016/S0014-2921(01)00202-1

Ho, D. C. K., Au, K. F., & Newton, E. (2003). The process and consequences of supply chain virtualization. *Industrial Management & Data Systems, 103*(5-6), 423–433. doi:10.1108/02635570310479990

Lissovolik, B., & Lissovolik, Y. (2004). Russia and the WTO: The "Gravity" of Outsider Status. *Working Paper WP/04/159.* International Monetary Fund.

Nilsson, L. (2002). Trade integration and the EU economic membership criteria. *European Journal of Political Economy, 16,* 807–827. doi:10.1016/S0176-2680(99)00060-9

Nordas, H. K., Pinali, E., & Grosso, M. G. (2006). Logistics and time as a trade barrier. *OECD trade policy working papers, 35.* OECD Publishing.

Subramanian, A., & Wei, S. (2003). The WTO promotes trade, strongly but unevenly. *NBER working paper No. 10024.* Cambridge, MA: NBER.

ENDNOTES

[1] Importers include 16 countries, Belgium, France, Italy, Luxembourg, Netherlands, Germany, Denmark, Ireland, United Kingdom, Greece, Portugal, Spain, Austria, Finland, Sweden and the United States

2   Exporters include 14 Asian countries, Bangladesh, Cambodia, China, Hong Kong, India, Indonesia, Malaysia, Pakistan, Philippines, South Korea, Sri Lanka, Taiwan, Thailand and Vietnam

Chapter 9
A Supplementary Framework for Evaluation of Integrated Logistics Service Provider

Kwok Hung Lau
Royal Melbourne Institute of Technology University, Australia

Wun Leong Ma
Royal Melbourne Institute of Technology University, Australia

ABSTRACT

As a result of globalization, supply chains of many large business organizations nowadays tend to cover wider geographic areas spanning across different countries and continents. The growth in length and complexity gradually replaces the traditional linear supply chains with extended supply networks comprising not only suppliers, manufacturers, distributors, and end customers, but also service providers. With the increasing use of third-party logistics (3PL) providers by international firms seeking integrated logistics services, many global 3PL providers are forming partnerships with large corporations to take care of the latter's logistics operations in different regions. The selection of the right 3PL provider for alliance is therefore paramount to the success of global supply chain management. This chapter investigates the significance of this subject and proposes a supplementary framework for evaluation of 3PL providers as global logistics partners for international firms. Using resource-based view theory and competencies hierarchy as theoretical underpinnings, the framework focuses on the core competencies of 3PL providers and their abilities to attain economies of scale helping users achieve their outsourcing objectives.

INTRODUCTION

Rapid advancements in information and communication technology (ICT) in recent years, coupled with the collapse of entry-to-market and other trading barriers, have changed significantly the way organizations operate in terms of business model and operating scale (Ritchie & Brindley, 2002). Globalization, lead-time reduction, customer orientation, and outsourcing are some major changes contributing to an increasing interest in advanced logistics services and global supply chain management (Hertz & Alfredsson, 2003). Successful global logistics depends heavily on communication and

DOI: 10.4018/978-1-60566-974-8.ch009

Figure 1. A traditional linear supply chain model

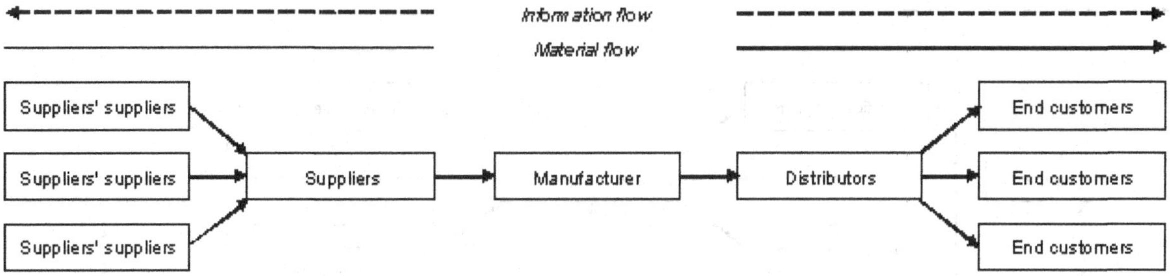

transportation. Improved communication between different business partners through the use and sharing of real-time information facilitates the logistics of production and inventory over wider geographic areas. Efficient transport arrangement, such as volume consolidation and cross docking, makes possible the actual transactions between nodes (Bookbinder, 2005). Owing to the increased levels of resource requirement, complexity, and risk in running global logistics, many firms tend to outsource their logistics operations to third-party logistics (3PL) providers and focus on their core businesses. Successful management of global supply chains therefore requires radical changes in supply chain structure, business processes, and relationships with business partners particularly logistics service providers.

Changes in Supply Chain Structure

Traditionally, supply chain is relatively linear in structure (Figure 1). A typical manufacturing supply chain involves a few tiers of suppliers, the manufacturer (the focal company), a few tiers of distributors (including wholesalers and retailers), and finally the end customers. Materials mainly flow from upstream to downstream (*i.e.*, from suppliers to end customers) with a small reverse flow of returns while information tends to flow in both directions. Transportation is provided either in-house by the various parties separately or outsourced to different 3PL providers (see for example Ballou, 2004; Bowersox, Closs & Cooper,

2002; Chopra & Meindl, 2007; Coyle, Bardi & Langley Jr., 2003; Wisner, Leong & Tan, 2005). With globalization and disintermediation as a result of advancement in ICT, the linear supply chain model and the associated uncoordinated logistics operations can no longer meet the demand of customers for higher efficiency, shorter lead time, and wider geographic coverage. Supply chain tends to become networked (Figure 2) with the focal company as the hub and a major 3PL provider looking after the logistics operations of the whole supply chain for the focal company in different regions (Ritchie & Brindley, 2002; Simchi-Levi, Kaminsky & Simchi-Levi, 2008; Waters, 2003).

Trends Revealed in Global 3PL Surveys

The importance of logistics and supply chain management and the increasing use of 3PL providers are clearly reflected in the latest global 3PL survey conducted by Capgemini, Georgia Institute of Technology, Oracle, and DHL. According to the findings of the 2008 survey, 89% of all 3PL users surveyed (87% from North America and Europe, 90% from Asia Pacific, and 97% from Latin America) agree that 3PL relationships represent a strategic, competitive advantage to their companies. They opine that successful outsourcing with strong client-provider relationship and detailed contract including clear expectations and metrics helps achieve savings in cost and fixed

Figure 2. A networked supply chain model

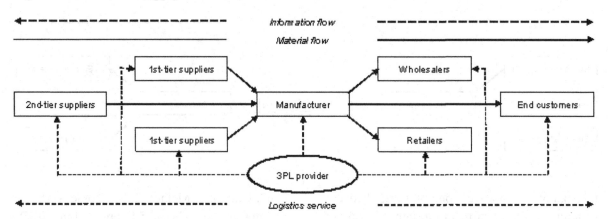

assets and reduce order cycles. 3PLs are also able to deliver better customer service and business process efficiencies (Langley Jr. *et al.*, 2008, p. 4). These findings align with the study of Power, Sharafali & Bhakoo (2007, p. 228) that 3PLs are considered by their customers as providers of means of competing through greater flexibility while enabling better cost management. They see 3PL providers as providing them with a "potential pathway to more innovative business models".

Across all the four regions surveyed in the 2008 global 3PL survey, the most frequently outsourced services include domestic transportation (85%), international transportation (81%), warehousing (72%), customer clearance and brokerage (65%), and forwarding (52%). The survey also reveals a growing trend of outsourcing. The spending in 3PL services (2008 against 2011-2013) is projected to increase by an average of 7% from 49% to 56% in North America, 8% from 61% to 69% in Europe, 7% from 57% to 64% in Asia Pacific, and 11% from 48% to 59% in Latin America. Furthermore, there is strong evidence of 3PL users to rationalize or reduce the number of 3PL providers they used suggesting that 3PL users are seeking integrated logistics services, *i.e.*, services incorporating multiple logistics functions such as warehousing, transportation, and channel assembly offered as a package. On the reasons for using integrated logistics services, 75% of all

respondents consider greater ease of managing outsourced logistics services (*i.e.*, one point of contact) as a major benefit. Integrated logistics is regarded as a way to attain end-to-end account-ability from a 3PL. Other benefits include reduced management time and effort (69%), ability for the company to focus on core business (67%), and improvement of overall logistics efficiency and effectiveness (56%). The 2008 survey reports that 47% of the responding organizations "are moving to rationalize or reduce the number of 3PLs they use" (Langley Jr. *et al.*, 2008, p. 18) in compari-son with 48% and 55% reported in the 2007 and 2006 surveys respectively. The survey organizers consider that this may reflect a continuing trend of consolidation on the side of the 3PL providers (Langley Jr. *et al.*, 2007, p. 15). This finding ties in with the frequent mergers, acquisitions, and consolidations in the 3PL sector in recent years leading to the emergence of "global 3PL provid-ers". Prominent examples include DHL and Exel; Kuehne & Nagel and USCO, UPS and Fritz and Menlo Forwarding, Deutsche Bahn and Bax Global, Uti Worldwide and Standard Corporation, and PWC Logistics and Geo-Logistics (Langley Jr. *et al.*, 2006, p. 16).

Benefits of Logistics Outsourcing

There are many advantages in logistics outsourcing, which refers to the carrying out of a company's logistics activities by a third-party operator. The most common benefits are saving in cost, reduction in risk, increase in capacity, and improvement in service quality. Others include time savings, cash infusion, freeing up in-house staff, focusing on core activities, talent availability, access to specialists, business process re-engineering, greater flexibility, greater productivity, and bigger geographical coverage (Burdon & Bhalla, 2005; Embleton & Wright, 1998; Kakabadse & Kakabadse, 2002; Lau & Zhang, 2006). In theory, logistics outsourcing should enable firms to access their 3PL providers' expertise and specialist skills. It should also bring cost savings to firms through economies of scale achieved by their 3PL providers via transaction bundling and volume consolidation (Beaumont & Sohal, 2004; Bhatnagar, Sohal & Millen., 1999; Rabinovich, Windle, Dresner & Corsi, 1999). In other words, firms are making use of their 3PL providers' core competencies – generally refer to what a company is specialized in or good at (Javidan, 1998; Prahalad & Hamel, 1990) – and cost efficiencies through economies of scale – commonly refer to efficiency gained from increasing scale of operation (Campbell, 1990; Fleischmann, 1993; Jara-Díaz & Basso, 2003) – to achieve logistics outsourcing goals and objectives. This belief is supported by the study of five big European companies by Brandes, Lilliecreutz & Brege (1997) on the reasons and process of outsourcing. Following this argument, core competencies of 3PL providers and their abilities to achieve economies of scale can therefore be regarded as two of the major critical determinants of logistics outsourcing success.

Table 1 lists some of the major objectives of logistics outsourcing and the outcomes expected from the activity. It can be seen that the success of the first objective depends on the 3PL provider's ability to achieve economies of scale for its user while the remaining ones rely on the expertise and capabilities of the 3PL provider. In short, the underlying assumption for successful logistics outsourcing is that the service provider is competent in its business. Providing logistics services should be the core competencies of the 3PL provider that supplement its user's deficiency in this area. This is particularly significant for international firms in managing their global supply chains. Competent 3PL providers are able to pool skilled professionals and other useful resources at low costs and execute the same services repeatedly for their uses over the globe. The generation of cumulative experience through scale and scope economies resulting in better, varied, and faster services at lower costs is essential to efficient global supply chain management. Such accrual of advantages would not have been possible had the clients executed the activities in their own premises (Kedia & Lahiri, 2007).

Structure of the Chapter

In the light of the growing demand for integrated logistics services from international firms, this chapter aims to correlate the different logistics outsourcing relationships with the two major factors of success, namely core competencies and ability to achieve economies of scale. The importance of finding a compatible 3PL provider in the management of a global supply chain is also discussed and a supplementary framework for the selection of integrated logistics service provider is proposed. A longitudinal case study is used to examine the impacts of core competencies and economies of scale (or the absence of them) on logistics outsourcing. The findings provide generic parameters to help develop the supplementary integrated logistics service provider evaluation framework. Section 2 of the chapter reviews the literature in a few areas including the theoretical underpinnings of outsourcing, vertical and hori-

Table 1. Major objectives of logistics outsourcing

Objective of logistics outsourcing	Expected outcome	Relevant studies
To reduce costs of logistics operation	Reduction in capital investment in infrastructure, assets, human resources, and other related costs	Brandes, Lilliecreutz & Brege (1997), Embleton & Wright (1998), Bhatnagar *et al.* (1999), Lankford & Parsa (1999), Vining and Globerman (1999), Kakabadse & Kakabadse (2002), Momme (2002), Beaumont & Sohal (2004), Burdon & Bhalla (2005), Vaidyanathan (2005), Langley Jr. *et al.* (2008), Lau & Zhang (2006), Holcomb & Hitt (2007)
To lower risk	Reduction in risk of inefficient capital investment	Brandes *et al.* (1997), Embleton & Wright (1998), Lankford & Parsa (1999), Kakabadse & Kakabadse (2002), Beaumont & Sohal (2004), Burdon & Bhalla (2005), Lau & Zhang (2006)
To reduce management time and resources for logistics operation	Release of management to focus on core business, reduction of human resources, and related administrative costs	Stank & Daugherty (1997), Embleton & Wright (1998), Beaumont & Sohal (2004), Burdon & Bhalla (2005), Lau & Zhang (2006)
To enhance reliability of delivery	Provision of on-time delivery and accurate order fulfillment to customers	Lankford & Parsa (1999), Burdon & Bhalla (2005), Vaidyanathan (2005)
To improve quality of customer service	Provision of better and higher quality of customer service than what was provided prior to outsourcing	Momme (2002), Langley Jr. *et al.* (2008)
To access best practices in logistics operation	Use of best practices and latest technologies in carrying out the outsourced activities	Embleton & Wright (1998), Razzaque & Sheng (1998)
To enhance flexibility to changes initiated by changing customer demand and market condition	Provision of flexible service for varying scale of operation and change management capability to meet the need of customers	Embleton & Wright (1998), Wadhwa & Ravindran (2007)
To achieve innovation and continuous improvement in logistics operation	Availability of information technologies to enable coordination, synchronization and optimization of logistics operations	Linder, Cole & Jacobson (2002), Kedia & Lahiri (2007)

zontal logistics alliances, international outsourcing partnerships, and strategic development of 3PL providers, as well as the latest studies in the evaluation of 3PL providers. Section 3 describes the methodology employed for the research. A summary of the findings from the case study, a thorough analysis of the observations, and a discussion of the implications are provided in Sections 4 to 6. Section 7 proposes a supplementary evaluation framework that builds upon the works of previous research and the current case study. It is hoped that the proposed framework can assist international firms in making better logistics outsourcing decisions through proper assessment of core competencies of the potential 3PL providers and their abilities to achieve economies of scale. The chapter concludes in Section 8 with a discussion on the limitation of the study and the direction for further research.

BACKGROUND LITERATURE

Theoretical Underpinnings of Outsourcing

In studying outsourcing and 3PL practices in supply chain management, a number of contemporary theories have been applied. The most common ones include the principal-agent theory (PAT), transaction cost analysis (TCA), the network theory (NT), and the resource-based view (RBV) theory

(Halldórsson, 2007; McIvor, 2008b). Based on the separation of ownership and control of activities between the principal and the agent, PAT looks at the various agency problems, such as asymmetric information and conflicting objectives, arising from the separation and aims to design a contract that can mitigate potential agency problems. The focus is to develop the most efficient contract including the right mix of behavioural and outcome-based incentives to motivate the agent to act in the interest of the principal (Eienshardt, 1989; Logan, 2000). TCA specifies the conditions under which a firm should manage an economic exchange internally within its boundary or externally through inter-organizational arrangement. It focuses on minimizing the total transaction costs of producing and distributing a particular good or service. These costs are determined by frequency, specificity, uncertainty, limited rationality, and opportunistic behavior involved in the transactions (Williamson, 1975, 1985, 1996). The analytical framework helps determine a firm's boundary and accounts for the efficiency seeking behavior of the firm through inter-organizational arrangements governed by contracts (Baiman & Rajan, 2002; Maltz, 1993). NT is based on the view that performance of a firm depends on how efficiently a network of business partners, direct and indirect, cooperates. It focuses on reciprocity in cooperative relationships which combine resources of organizations to achieve more advantages than through individual efforts (Haakansson, 1987; Haakansson & Snehota, 1995; Oliver, 1990). Under this theory, a network is in a constant state of movement and change and the links between organizations are developed on the basis of mutual trust through exchange processes (*e.g.*, information, goods and services) and adaptation processes (*e.g.*, personal, technical, and administrative elements) (Johanson & Mattsson, 1987). RBV sees the firm as a bundle of resources and assets and emphasizes the use of rare, valuable, in-imitable and un-substitutable resources to gain sustainable competitive advantage (Barney, 1991; Conner, 1991; Grant, 1991;

Wernerfelt, 1984). Resources include tangible physical assets, intangible information and knowledge, and capabilities that are built upon effective use of tangible and intangible resources, repeated and refined practices, and accumulated experiences. Capabilities are more difficult to imitate or substitute and therefore add greater value to the firm (Collis 1994; Reed & DeFillippi, 1990). PAT and TCA are often used to account for the make-or-buy decision in supply chains focusing on contractual arrangement (see for example Baiman & Rajan, 2002; Bensaou, 1999) whereas NT and RBV are more employed to explain partnerships and alliances in logistics emphasizing on effective use of resources and capabilities to develop supply chain competences (Eisenhardt & Martin, 2000; Harland & Knight, 2001).

Integrated Logistics Services

As a result of globalization, the international market for logistics and transport services becomes larger and complex. International firms rely more and more on 3PL providers for logistics solutions. This trend has already been identified in the 2006 global 3PL survey and reaffirm in the 2008 survey. The findings reveal that 3PL users are sometimes frustrated with apparent differences in doing business with specific 3PL providers from one region to another. The use of a "global 3PL provider" not only rids the user of the management headache but also enables the user to capture local benefits such as low labour costs so as to help reduce the net landed cost of its products (Langley Jr. *et al.*, 2006, p. 16; 2008, pp. 16-17). Consequently, collaboration between 3PL users and providers has become more and more important. Many 3PL providers desire to move their customers from a conventional customer-supplier relationship to a true "partnership" (Langley Jr. *et al.*, 2006, p. 5). In the 2007 survey, the topic of collaboration between 3PL users and providers is explored in depth covering the benefits, the model to be used, and the elements of successful collaboration (Langley Jr.

et al., 2007, pp. 18-25). The importance of 3PL-customer relationship is again highlighted in the 2008 survey and the willingness of collaboration between 3PLs and users is considered paramount to outsourcing success. "Openness to collaboration and use of integration-enabling technology by 3PLs are essential elements to successful use of 3PL systems and services integration" (Langley Jr. *et al.*, 2008, p. 5).

In Europe, similar emphasis on integrated logistics services and good 3PL-customer relationship is also observed. Taking the definition by the European Commission (2001), 3PL is defined as "activities carried out by an external company on behalf of a shipper [or client] and [they] consist of at least the provision of management of multiple logistics services. These activities are offered in an integrated way, not on a stand-alone basis. The co-operation between shipper and the external company is an intended continuous relationship [lasting for at least one year]" (as cited in Carbone & Stone, 2005, p. 496). For a global supply chain, the major 3PL provider can take over the entire logistics management as well as operations from its user. These include management, analysis, and design of activities associated with transport and warehousing (*e.g.*, inventory management), information related activities (*e.g.*, tracking and tracing), as well as value-added activities (*e.g.*, secondary assembly of products and supply chain management) (Laarhoven, van Berglund & Peters, 2000). In fact, as the 2008 global 3PL survey reveals (Langley Jr. *et al.*, 2008, p. 16), there is a growing trend of 3PL integration or vertical logistics alliances in which the 3PL provider and the user maintain a long-term formal or informal relationship to render all or a considerable number of logistics activities. The 3PL provider sees itself as a long-term partner in this arrangement to provide a comprehensive range of services to the user (Bagchi & Virum 1998). A vertical alliance includes planning and overseeing the inbound and outbound freight flows in the nodes of the logistics network. In the alliance, the 3PL

provider looks for improvements to the service levels, inventories management, and order processing for the user company (Peters, Cooper, Lieb & Randall, 1998).

Horizontal and Vertical Alliances

To acquire the necessary capabilities and a global presence required for vertical alliances, many 3PL providers pursue horizontal alliances through horizontal cooperation, merges and acquisitions. Horizontal alliance can be a means to spread costs and risks and to increase the scope of services. This practice is attractive when costs of developing new services and solutions for complex problems facing customers in dynamic markets are too high for a single 3PL provider (Carbone & Stone 2005). Horizontal cooperation is defined by the European Commission (2001) as concerted practices between companies operating at the same levels in the market. Short-term horizontal alliances can be formed between 3PLs, information technology (IT) consultants, and software vendors. The search for higher capability of offering "global consulting" in supply chain management is seen by some as evidence of evolution from 3PL to 4PL – a term coined by Accenture to refer to "a supply chain integrator that assembles and manages the multiple resources, capabilities, and technology of its own organization with those of complementary service providers to deliver a comprehensive supply chain solution" (as cited in Carbone & Stone, 2005, p. 506). Permanent horizontal alliances through merges and acquisitions enable 3PL provider to have wider geographic coverage and control of major traffic flows through the creation of efficient transport chains. The alliances also provide sufficient size to cope with high investment cost in physical infrastructure and ITC for efficient operation. Economies of scale are also permitted through business process re-engineering and entry into new market segments. Through the acquisition of specialist capabilities, especially higher value-added services, strategic and operational synergies can also be achieved (Plehwe & Bohle, 1998).

With closer cooperation between 3PL provider and the user, the role of 3PL provider also changes from provision of standard logistics services to development of customer solutions. Based on the balance between general problem solving capability (GPSC) and the degree of customer adaptation (DOCA), Hertz and Alfredsson (2003, p. 141) propose four different development strategies for 3PL providers as follows:

- *Standard 3PL provider* (relatively high GPSC and relatively high DOCA): The 3PL provider offers a highly standardized modular system to customers with relatively simple combination of standardized services such as warehousing, distribution, pick and pack, *etc.*
- *Service developer* (high GPSC and relatively high DOCA): The 3PL provider offers an advanced modular system of a large variety of services such as specific packaging, cross-docking, track and trace, and special security system, *etc.*, and a common IT-system used for all customers.
- *Customer adapter* (relatively high GPSC and high DOCA): The 3PL provider offers totally dedicated solutions involving the basic services for each customer. For example, the service provider might take over the customer's warehouses and logistics activities totally. The 3PL provider is seen as a part of the customer organization.
- *Customer developer* (high GPSC and high DOCA): The 3PL provider develops advanced customer solutions for each customer by handling the entire logistics operations. Value-adding services and enhancement of knowledge are common and the role of the 3PL provider is more like a consultant.

In vertical alliances, the 3PL provider acts as a customer developer involving a high integration with the user often in the form of taking over its whole logistics operations. Its role is a logistics integrator to offer integrated logistics solutions to the user and share the risks and rewards of the logistics management with the user.

3PL-Customer Relationships

Similarly, Kedia & Lahiri (2007) also look at international outsourcing of service (IOS) as a form of partnership that can be classified into three different types: *tactical*, *strategic*, and *transformational*. With the increase of value proposition from low to high to highest and the involvement of provider from arm's length to deep to intense, the IOS partnership moves from tactical to strategic to transformational. Tactical IOS partnership is basically transaction oriented aiming at cost reduction. Involvement of the service provider is rule-based and contract-oriented. Strategic IOS partnership emphasizes on value enhancement required to enable a company to remain locally responsive as well as globally integrative. It is usually achieved through building long-term relationships with a few best-in-class integrated service providers that possess cumulative experiences and scope of organizational learning for their users. In vertical alliances, a transformational IOS partnership is the ultimate goal. From the user's point of view, the partnership helps the user share its risk with the provider because of the reduced need for capital expenditure on infrastructure and manpower development. It also enhances the user's flexibility as the provider's logistical competencies assist in providing faster response in a globalized business environment. Finally, transformational IOS partnership provides opportunities for the user to redefine its businesses through transformation (*i.e.*, changes of business model) or business process re-engineering (*i.e.*, changes of practice). Transformational IOS partnership provides opportunities to enhance the user's overall competitiveness through paradigm shift and is therefore wider in scope than mere business process reengineering, which is mainly to improve efficiency of certain logistic activity. The success of the relationship depends on the trustworthiness of partners and the culture distance between the two parties. Study by Tian, Lai & Daniel (2008) suggests that user's satisfaction with prior interactions with the service provider, the reputation, relationship-specific investment, and information sharing of the 3PL provider are key determinants of the user's level of trust towards the 3PL provider. This trust may facilitate loyalty behaviour towards the service provider.

3PL Provider Selection

As vertical alliance impacts significantly on successful global supply chain management, the selection of the right 3PL provider is of utmost importance. Studies in this regard are quite abundant (see for example Beaumont & Sohal, 2004; Bhatnagar, Sohal & Millen, 1999; Boyson, Corsi, Dresner & Rabinovich, 1999; Langley Jr. *et al.*, 2008; Lynch, 2000; McIvor, 2008a; Razzaque & Sheng, 1998; Stock, Greis & Kasarda., 1998). Jharkharia & Shankar (2007) reviewed the literature and summarized some of the most commonly used criteria for the selection of 3PL provider as follows: compatibility with the users, cost of service, quality of service, reputation of the company, long-term relationship, performance measurement, quality of management, information sharing and mutual trust, operational performance, IT capability, size and quality of fixed assets, delivery performance, financial performance, market share, geographical spread and range of services provided, and flexibility in operations and delivery. Among these criteria, many are related to the core competencies of the 3PL provider as well as its ability to achieve economies of scale and pass the cost savings back to the user.

In the light of the above review, this research aims to investigate how core competencies of 3PL providers and their abilities to achieve economies of scale determine the type of partnerships they can enter with their users and how the two factors contribute to the success of logistics outsourcing.

METHODOLOGY

This research is founded on a longitudinal case study of the outsourcing experiences of a global company focusing on the service providers' core competencies and abilities to achieve economies of scale. In general, case studies are less vigorous than empirical studies. Furthermore, because of the use of small sample, the case study approach also faces a limitation in generalizing the findings to reflect the situation of the whole industry. Nevertheless, the approach is suitable for exploratory and explanatory research like the one described in this chapter to provide a preliminary in-depth investigation of a problem (Benbasat, Goldstein & Mead, 1987; Walsham, 1995; Yin, 1994). The intention is not to generalize the findings but to use them to better understand the crux of a problem and to propose recommendations for solution as well as directions for further research.

A Case Study

The global company in the case study provides information services to its clients all over the world. As its core activity is information gathering and dissemination, it relies on outsourcing to handle its non-core activities such as logistics operations. Between 1989 and 1999, the company changed three 3PL providers. The purpose of the case study is to unearth the reasons for the repeated outsourcing failures and investigate how they can be attributed to lack of core competencies and inabilities to achieve economies of scale. Through the logistics manager of the company who oversaw the entire outsourcing process and managed the three 3PL providers during the period,

Table 2. Source and usage of information in the case study

Source of information	Usage of information in the case study
User company's logistics outsourcing analysis reports	To identify the logistics activities outsourced, the expectations of the user company from the 3PL providers, and the performance metrics employed in monitoring the logistics services provided.
Proposals submitted by the 3PL providers for bidding the logistics outsourcing contracts	To understand the capabilities of the 3PL providers in providing the required logistics services, the cost figures and other statistics provided by the 3PL providers for evaluation, the track records and the reputations of the 3PL providers in the industry.
User company's evaluation reports for the selected 3PL providers	To understand why the 3PL providers were selected and determine if the user company had performed the standard evaluation procedures properly.
Performance records of the 3PL providers during their respective contract periods	To examine the performances of the 3PL providers against the expected targets and identify the problem areas and their causes.
Performance evaluation reports at the end of the contract periods	To review the user company's overall comments on the performance of the 3PL providers during their respective contract periods and understand the reasons for the termination of the contracts.

detailed first-hand information about the case was collected for analysis which helps determine if core competencies of the 3PL providers and any achievement of economies of scale existed. Table 2 shows the source and the usage of information in the case study.

For reason of commercial confidentiality, pseudonymous names have been used. The parties involved in this case include the user company X and its three logistics service providers (A, B, and C) which were freight forwarders before they became 3PL providers. All the three logistics service providers in this case study were international companies with global presence and local offices in Singapore (Table 3). As leading international information service provider supply-ing news and financial information to its clients worldwide, X installed computers and terminals at its clients' premises to provide the subscribed data and information. With regional headquarters set up in Singapore, X had outsourced its logistics operations to freight forwarders since 1989. In the 1980s, outsourcing practice in Singapore was still at its infancy. Many 3PL providers were actually freight forwarding companies. The services that X outsourced include warehousing, inbound and outbound logistics, inventory management, local transportation, international freight delivery, and regional distribution of subscriber equipment.

X awarded the logistics service contracts to the 3PL providers on a "2+1"-year basis, *i.e.*, two years initially with a scope for extending

Table 3. Profiles of the 3PL providers in the case study

3PL name	Country based	Contract period	Specialization	Service provided to X
A	UK public-listed company	1989 – 1995	International airfreight forwarding and local transportation	- Day-to-day management of X's logistics activities including warehousing, inbound and outbound logistics, local transportation, international airfreight forwarding, and inventory management - Order processing and customer service
B	US public-listed company	1995 – 1997	International freight forwarding and heavy weight movement	Same as above
C	Singapore-based private company	1997 – 1999	International air and sea freight forwarding	Same as above

to another year. The contract required the 3PL provider to manage all the logistics operations of X including the provision of warehouse space, facilities, manpower, equipment and tools necessary for the activities. The service was charged at a fixed price (*i.e.*, a lump sum) and a variable price scheme according to the type of service and activity performed. X hoped that it could reduce its investment in resources and achieve flexibility through logistics outsourcing. It expected the 3PL provider to deliver the subscriber equipment from the point of receipt to its clients in the most efficient and economic manner. In other words, X expected the 3PL provider to achieve economies of scale for its logistics operations and reduce its logistics expenditure.

Basis of Comparison

To facilitate analysis, an ideal situation of integrated logistics outsourcing, *i.e.*, the 3PL provider being a customer developer (Hertz & Alfredsson, 2003) and the outsourcing relationship being transformational (Kedia & Lahiri 2007), is used as a basis for comparison to gauge the performance of the three 3PL providers in the case. It is assumed that logistics functions such as transportation, inventory management, capacity planning, *etc.* should be coordinated and managed by the 3PL provider with logistical competency. Information and material flows should be streamlined and integrated by the 3PL provider to achieve economies of scale through consolidation of transactional and physical movement activities. Furthermore, the 3PL providers should be able to develop unique customer solutions and redefine business processes for its user through transformation or business process re-engineering thereby help its user gain efficiency and cost effectiveness. Through the comparison, it can be established whether core competencies of the 3PL providers and their abilities to achieve economies of scale for user existed.

FINDINGS

Problems with the 3PL Providers

Analysis of the case reveals that the three 3PL providers failed to bring efficiency gains to X as expected despite of a full outsourcing of logistics operations. Problems with the 3PL providers as listed in Table 4 show that they did not operate, coordinate, or manage X's logistics activities as customer developers. Their IOS relationships with X were mainly tactical. Apart from C, the other two 3PL providers did not provide complete centralized coordination and management of logistics activities for X leading to duplicated effort and wasteful operation on some occasions. The lack of logistics information systems and other IT support from the 3PL providers also prohibited them from integrating and streamlining the material and information flows of X to achieve higher efficiency. These outcomes can be attributed to a few common practices. First, all the three 3PL providers did not invest adequately in resources to develop their capabilities and competencies. They did not possess their own warehouses to achieve economies of scale or logistics information systems to enable better planning, coordination, and management of logistics activities for X. Second, the quality of their staff was less than satisfactory (*e.g.*, untrained staff) and their management of X's logistics operations was ineffective (*e.g.*, no quality or ISO9000 compliant process). Finally, they provided little or no IT support to manage X's supply chain to maintain efficient information flow or to coordinate material flow.

The lack of own warehouses and the reliance on leased facilities have limited the capabilities of the three 3PL providers to offer cost benefits to X through economies of scale. Since X spent a significant portion of its logistics cost in warehousing and related activities, its objective to reduce cost and to gain considerable savings through outsourcing was not realized basically. Apart from some bulk freight rate savings obtained through

Table 4. Problems with the 3PL providers in the case study

Area	Problems with A	Problems with B	Problems with C
Warehousing	• Did not possess own warehouse. Used leased private warehouse for X with no sharing of warehouse transaction cost to achieve economies of scale. • Cost of usage all charged to X and not shared among other customers. Did not achieve economies of scale. • Did not possess own WMS to optimize warehouse operation.	• Did not possess own warehouse. Used private warehouse especially leased for X (*i.e.*, subcontracting). • X solely funded the leased warehousing and the related services. No consolidation of cargo with other customers of B or sharing of fixed cost to achieve economies of usage.	• Did not possess own warehouse. Used private warehouse especially leased for X (*i.e.*, subcontracting). • Cost of usage all charged to X and not shared among other customers. Did not achieve economies of scale.
Staffing	• No pooling of staff from other business units to share the fixed staff cost of providing service to X. Temporary staff members were recruited to provide the manpower resources at the leased warehouse for X. • Inexperienced warehouse operation staff. X had to provide training to the staff of A to use its MRP II system. • Staff lacked basic logistics knowledge. X had to provide on-the-job training to the staff of A which had no in-house training program of its own. • High staff turnover rate (>40%).	• B's logistics team for X comprised full-time and part-time staff with a 40% turnover that seriously affected service continuity and performance (*e.g.*, 20% variance was found in annual stocktake). • X had to provide training to the staff of B to use its MRP II system. • Much time was spent in re-training new comers and handing over job duties as a result of frequent staff changes.	• Staff either pooled from internal units or through external recruitment. However, there was no sharing of staff cost. • X had to provide on-the-job trainings on inventory management and order processing to the logistics team members of C. • High staff turnover of 50% occurred mainly at the supervisor level. Poor staff stability seriously affected day-to-day operation. Unsatisfactory performance and low customer service level were reported throughout the contract period (*e.g.*, 10% variance was found in annual stocktake).
Transportation	• Did not possess own vehicle fleet. Used subcontractors for delivery service. Little control and no economies of scale were achieved. • Did not possess own TMS for efficient scheduling and route planning. • Poor tracking system (used telephone only). Failed to provide a high level of on-time delivery service to customers as required by X.	• Used a combination of own and leased vehicle fleets. Economies of scale were achieved through consolidation of cargos for X and other customers of B. However, the benefit gained was not passed back to X as cost savings. • Did not posses own TMS for efficient scheduling and route planning. • No monitoring of performance of subcontractors to ensure they worked up to the service level required by X.	• Possessed own transport fleet and full-time staff to handle all transport activities with a dedicated team to serve X. However, capacity was not fully utilized and economies of scale were not achieved. • Possessed own TMS with GPS technology to track and trace its transport fleet resulting in faster turnaround time.
Management	• Not able to provide one-stop solution to client's problem. • Vertical control in each department created unnecessary delays in communication and action. • Lack of unity of control. Fragmented management of inventory and distribution resulted in duplicated effort and wasteful operation.	• No major problems identified.	• No major problems identified.
IT support	• Service not provided.	• B possessed own team of IT professionals but failed to develop a logistics information system to integrate with X's legacy system for end-to-end supply chain management as stated in its proposal submitted to X. • Technical complexity, prohibitive cost, and inadequate number of participating customers for cost sharing were the main causes of the failure.	• Did not possess own IT staff but hired external consultants for any IT system project. • In the proposal submitted for bidding the outsourcing contract, C proposed to provide a low cost IT solution to replace X's own MRP II system but the project had never taken off.

volume consolidation, the major benefit X enjoyed in the logistics outsourcing was a reduction in staff cost. However, the savings were offset by the poor and unsatisfactory service performance of the 3PL providers manifested by their high staff turnovers, incompetent management, and inefficient services.

ANALYSIS

Common Issues Identified

X's case unfolds the following common issues with the three 3PL providers which suggest that they did not actually possess core competencies in all the services they provided and they were not able to achieve economies of scale as expected:

- Performance of the 3PL providers was good in international freight forwarding but only average or even poor in other logistics activities. Apart from freight forwarding, the three 3PL providers acted more like a resource provider than an integrated logistics service provider with little capability to add value to their user's supply chain. They were more like generalists providing little specialist skills or specialized equipment or systems for the outsourced services.
- Workers of the three 3PL providers were incompetent due to poor training and high turnover rate. Many of them lacked the basic knowledge or skills to perform their jobs well. The main role of the three 3PL providers in most activities was to supply manpower resources. As a result, the three 3PL providers failed to reduce the management responsibility and time of their user because of ineffective communication and lack of problem-solving and decision-making skills.
- Owing to the lump sum payment arrangement for warehousing service, there was

no cost benefit arising from economies of scale through the sharing of use of facilities. In general, the services were not provided across the whole customer bases of the 3PL providers and were charged at fixed price rather than on a cost-sharing basis.
- The three 3PL providers were generally weak in IT capability to provide support to X. Their scale of operation and financial strength did not permit the provision and sharing of such service across all their users.

Roots of the Problems

The above issues are all related to the amount of resources invested by the 3PL providers, the capabilities of utilizing their resources, the competencies in providing efficient logistics services, and the abilities to bring cost savings to their users through increasing scale of operation and size of customer base. They boil down to the 3PL providers' core competencies and abilities to achieve economies of scale. The findings of the case study suggest that the 3PL providers did not have the necessary resources and capabilities to offer different logistics services. According to the RBV theory, valuable resources and un-substitutable capabilities are pre-requisites of competencies enabling a firm to achieve sustainable competitive advantage (Barney, 1991; Conner, 1991; Grant, 1991; Wernerfelt, 1984). Among others, they are the key determinants of outsourcing success. The findings also reveal that although the three 3PL providers in the case study were experts in the freight forwarding business, they were not necessarily competent in all the logistics activities they performed. Core competencies developed in one area as a result of long establishment, large investment, accumulated skills, and cumulative experience did not automatically translate into core competencies in other areas of logistics operation. To the 3PL providers, core activities might be the businesses they could do best or make the greatest profit. To their users, however, the 3PL providers' core competencies should be their unique expertise and experiences that could assist their users in conducting the outsourced logistics activities in the most efficient and cost effective manner. This mismatch became the root of the disappointment and the cause of the repeated outsourcing failures in the case of X.

The issues identified above are not necessarily specific to the case of X or a particular industry. In fact, the lack of resources, capabilities, or core competencies are common weaknesses of many companies to various extents. From a 3PL user's perspective, however, the success of logistics outsourcing hinges on the condition that the 3PL provider will not be plagued by these problems. A logical conclusion is that these generic issues have to be thoroughly addressed in the selection of integrated logistics providers.

DISCUSSION

Inadequacy in the 3PL Provider Selection Process

X's case reveals the significance of examining the core competencies of the potential 3PL providers and their abilities in achieving economies of scale before making the final outsourcing decision. To a large extent, X should be responsible for its logistics outsourcing failures. The company had an obligation to understand what core competencies of the 3PL providers were required in order to achieve its outsourcing objectives. It should also have established that the selected 3PL providers actually possessed the required competencies prior to signing the contracts. X might understand well its own logistics costs and level of customer service required. However, evidence suggests that it had not fully examined the 3PL providers' capabilities and core competencies before requesting proposals. X selected its 3PL providers

on the basis of price, range of services offered, and technical competency to provide facilities, equipment, and tools necessary for the running of its logistics operations. Using the Request for Proposal (RFP) approach, X aimed to shop for the best 3PL providers among its freight forwarders hoping that the 3PL providers could take over a wide range of its logistics functions at lower costs. However, most of the outsourcing benefits that X hoped for did not materialize because of a sharp disparity between X's expectation and the actual performance of each of the three 3PL providers.

In outsourcing its logistics functions, X did have followed closely the standard procedures of outsourcing as outlined in Figure 3. The company conducted its competence analysis and mapping of activities properly (Stages 1 to 3) before requesting proposals from the 3PL providers (Stage 4). It also developed its own set of performance measures and cost parameters to evaluate the performance of the 3PL providers (Stages 5 to 7). The repeated termination of logistics outsourcing contracts (Stage 8) therefore suggests that simply following the standard procedures might not be adequate. More detailed guidelines would be required for the most critical stage (Stage 4) in which the eligible 3PL providers are evaluated and the most compatible one is selected.

Despite the fact that core competencies and ability to achieve economies of scale are critical to the success of logistics outsourcing, there are few studies in the literature on the selection of 3PL providers focusing on what the core competencies of 3PL providers are and how they can achieve economies of scale in practice for the benefit of their users. For example, Arnold (2000) proposes an outsourcing model with design alternatives for manufacturing firms combining transaction cost economics with a core competency approach. His main objective, however, is to develop a "de-materialized company" (p. 28) for optimizing outsourcing design and management. Similarly, Hafeez, Zhang & Malak (2002) provide a structured framework for determining

Figure 3. Standard procedures of the logistics outsourcing process

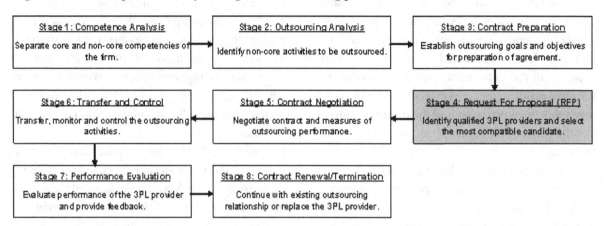

the key capabilities of a firm using the analytic hierarchy process. Nevertheless, the framework is used mainly for identifying competency gaps within the firm with a view that the result might facilitate the making of outsourcing decisions.

Momme (2002) proposes a framework for outsourcing manufacturing in which competence analysis is the first of the six phases outlined. However, the analysis focuses more on identifying the client's own core activities than that of the supplier's. It appears that there is little attempt to explore the core competencies of the supplier, which are supposed to complement the client's non-core business skills. Also, the issue of economies of scale has not been addressed in the proposed framework. It has yet to be proven that economies of scale achieved by the supplier, if any, would bring cost savings to its client. Similarly, Vaidyanathan (2005) recommends a framework to establish a set of criteria for the selection of 3PL provider using IT as the focus to peruse the core functionalities of 3PL provider such as inventory management, transportation, and warehousing. Nonetheless, core competencies and economies of scale are again not at the centre of discussion. In view of the above inadequacy, this chapter attempts to fulfil the existing gap by proposing a supplementary evaluation framework for the selection of 3PL provider focusing on the

two foregoing critical factors. Likewise, McIvor (2008a) proposes a practical framework for managers to identify suitable outsourcing strategies for their business processes taking into account relative capabilities, contribution to competitive advantage, and opportunism potential. The framework provides a mechanism for understanding which process should be kept internal and which should be outsourced based on both organizational capability and opportunism considerations. In the same way, Espino-Rodríguez & Rodríguez-Díaz (2008) develop an integrated model for strategic outsourcing analysing the impacts of both relational and internal capabilities on outsourcing. Again, the focuses of analysis in the two studies are more on the user's capabilities than that of the 3PL provider.

PROPOSED FRAMEWORK

Theoretical Basis

X's case reveals that resources and capabilities of the 3PL providers are essential elements of their core competencies in providing logistics services to their users. This finding ties in with the tenet of the RBV theory that valuable resources and un-substitutable capabilities are pre-requisites of sustainable competitive advantage (Barney, 1991; Conner, 1991; Grant, 1991; Wernerfelt, 1984). It also aligns with the competencies hierarchy proposed by Javidan (1998) in which he contends that core competencies of a firm build upon its competencies which, in turn, depend on its capabilities to utilize its resources. Javidan (1998) defines the four levels of his competencies hierarchy as follows (p. 62):

- *Resources* are the inputs into the firm's value chain;
- *Capabilities* refer to the firm's ability to exploit resources;
- *Competency* is a cross-functional integration and co-ordination of capabilities; and
- *Core competencies* are skills and areas of knowledge that are shared across business units and resulted from the integration and harmonization of strategic business unit competencies.

The difficulty in rising from one hierarchy level to another (*i.e.*, *Resources* to *Capabilities* to *Competencies* to *Core Competencies*) increases with the ascent but the value to the firm also inflates in increasing magnitude.

Javidan's (1998) competencies hierarchy is a relatively simple and generic framework used mainly to relate a firm's core competencies to building blocks like resources, capabilities, and competencies. The framework is not especially designed for identification of core competencies by itself. Instead, it is used to show the linkages between the building blocks and the firm's strategic hierarchy comprising functional strategy, business strategy, corporate strategy, and mission statement. Nevertheless, the concept of competencies hierarchy, which is built upon resource-based view and theory (Barney, 1991; Grant, 1991; Peteraf, 1993; Wernerfelt, 1984), does provide a useful reference for an evaluation framework to access the core competencies of 3PL providers. The issues identified in X's case presented in this

chapter help define the dimensions of the array and supply the individual cell of the framework with ingredients.

Development

As X's case reveals, quantity and quality of resources committed by the 3PL providers, capabilities to exploit the resources and directly control the outsourcing operations, and competencies in integrating and coordinating the logistics functions for users are critical determinants of success in maintaining the logistics outsourcing relationship. As such, some of the issues identified in the case study, such as the use of owned or leased assets, full-time to temporary employee ratio, staff turnover and stability, and the use of subcontractor and consultant, *etc.*, can in fact be translated into generic criteria to evaluate and assess the core competencies of 3PL providers in general. Basically, a successful 3PL provider should process certain amount of resources and capabilities in order to attain core competencies in providing logistics services and to transfer cost benefits derived from economies of scale to users. These resources and capabilities include fully controlled assets such as warehouse and transport vehicle fleet, qualified personnel and well-trained staff, specialized handling equipment for service such as warehouse automated storage system, track-and-trace system, *etc.*, and a large customer base with sufficient volume of transactions to enable cost sharing.

Based on the above discussion, this chapter proposes a supplementary 3PL provider core competencies evaluation framework as shown in Figure 4. The framework makes use of the findings of the case study to develop a list of generic evaluation items grouped under "resources", "capabilities" and "competencies" – the building blocks of core competencies – and use them to examine if the 3PL provider's core competencies are present. The "competencies" building block in the proposed evaluation framework is akin to the "competency" building block in Javidan's (1998) competencies hierarchy. While "competency" in Javidan's (1998) hierarchy refers to a cross-functional integration and coordination of capabilities (p. 62), the "competencies" building block in the proposed evaluation framework refers to the availability of integrated processes that reflect the ability of the 3PL provider to make use of its resources and capabilities to develop best-of-class practices. The proposed framework is not meant to replace any existing 3PL provider evaluation models such as the ones proposed by Momme & Hvolby (2002) and Vaidyanathan (2005). In making logistics outsourcing decisions, there are many factors other than core competencies and ability to achieve economies of scale to consider. They include cost, quality, service, performance, strategic fit, compatibility of organization culture, and financial stability, among others (Beaumont & Sohal, 2004; Vaidyanathan, 2005). Therefore, the proposed framework only attempts to supplement the evaluation process upon the completion of the normal assessment procedure at the RFP stage.

Application

In using the proposed supplementary framework to evaluate the available resources of a 3PL provider, it is recommended that staff qualification and training, staff turnover and stability, ratio of full-time to temporary staff, percentage of assets owned or leased, *etc.* should be examined. Similarly, to evaluate the service provider's capabilities, it is necessary to consider whether the 3PL provider has IT capabilities developed in-house or by consultants, whether logistics is truly its core business or just the main source of revenue, and whether the 3PL provider is a recognized leader in the industry, *etc.* To evaluate the 3PL provider's competencies, its ability to achieve economies of scale and to pass the benefits back to its users, the presence of quality assurance procedures, benchmarking, dedicated management team for client to coordinate activities, the capability to manage

its subcontractors and use their competences as leverage, and the availability of flexible price model, *etc.* are some of the criteria.

Presence of quality processes and dedicated management team enable the 3PL provider to deliver high level of service to the user's customers. The use of subcontractors can provide the 3PL provider with greater flexibility in transport management and capacity planning. Nevertheless, effective use of subcontractors' core competencies as a leverage to build up the 3PL's own core competencies hinges on a good management of these subcontractors. Scale of operation and size of customer base usually affect a 3PL provider's ability to help its user to cut cost through economies of scale. Although cost savings can be achieved through multiple offering of services to different users, order consolidation hence volume discount, and sharing of usage of resources and assets, users will not be benefited if the costs of usage of facilities are not shared across the 3PL provider's customer base. Therefore, the availability of variable price model allowing the spreading of fixed costs across multiple users forms another evaluation criterion under the proposed framework.

Benefits

It is believed that a categorical item-by-item evaluation (*i.e.*, checking against pre-determined parameters) using the proposed framework should help identify the 3PL provider as a resource owner or a resource provider, a specialist or a generalist, and a problem solver or only a process provider. This will enable the 3PL user firm to better understand what outsourcing relationship (*i.e.*, tactical, strategic, or transformational) should be developed and what role the 3PL provider could play in the outsourced logistics activities (*i.e.*, a standard 3PL provider, a service developer, a customer adaptor, or a customer developer). The categorization also helps determine the strengths and weaknesses of the 3PL provider in terms of its investment in resources and innovation, proven

Figure 4. A proposed supplementary framework for 3PL provider evaluation

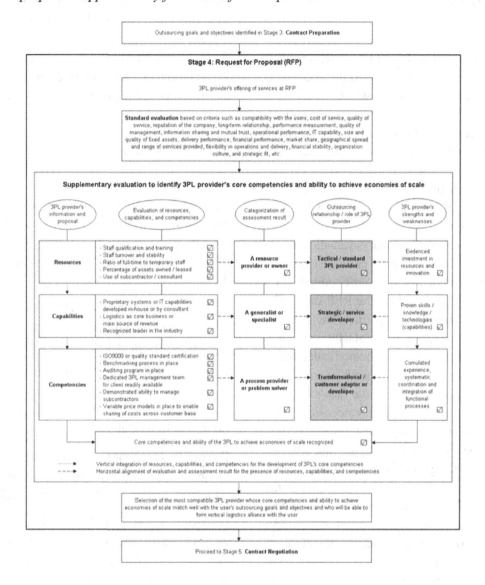

skills and knowledge, and ability to coordinate and integrate logistics processes. This will facilitate the 3PL user firm in checking whether the 3PL provider has the capabilities and competencies to actually meet its user's logistics outsourcing needs, as well as the cumulative experience and scope for organizational learning that are necessary for forming vertical logistics alliance. Despite the fact that logistics is usually not the core business of 3PL user firms, the step-by-step approach proposed in the supplementary framework permits the recogni-

tion of the 3PL provider's core competencies in a more systematic and objective manner. By applying the proposed evaluation framework at the RFP stage together with other evaluation processes to all the eligible 3PL providers, the outsourcing firm would be able to determine which provider could help the company achieve its logistics outsourcing goals and objectives and provide the best scope for long-term transformational IOS partnership through vertical logistics alliance.

CONCLUSION

This chapter argues that "core competencies" and "economies of scale" are two critical factors, among others, that contribute to the success or failure of logistics outsourcing which is paramount to modern-day global supply chain management. Core competencies of a 3PL provider build on the amount of resources it possesses, its capabilities to fully exploit these resources, and its competencies in utilizing the capabilities to provide efficient and cost effective integrated logistics services to users.

The proposed supplementary evaluation framework presented in this chapter can assist logistics outsourcing firms to assess the core competencies of eligible 3PL providers at the RFP stage. The framework is meant to supplement the standard evaluation process instead of replacing any procedure. It provides a systematic method to determine if core competencies of a 3PL provider are present and whether they match with the firm's logistics outsourcing needs. Through a categorical item-by-item evaluation process, the framework could assist outsourcing firms in determining what logistics outsourcing relationship should be formed and what role the 3PL provider could play in the partnership. The evaluation would not only help determine whether the 3PL provider could achieve the logistics outsourcing goals and objectives of its user but also reveal if there is scope for vertical logistics alliance that is critical to successful global supply chain management.

As this study involves only one case with three 3PL providers to identify generic issues in logistics outsourcing, the findings might not be totally comprehensive although they have helped establish essential parameters for the proposed evaluation framework. To fully investigate the impact of core competencies and economies of scale on outsourcing success, more studies are needed to explore the current practices of 3PL providers in different industries and regions for comparison. This might be incorporated into annual global outsourcing surveys like the one currently conducted by Capgemini, Georgia Institute of Technology, Oracle, and DHL (Langley Jr. *et al.*, 2008). The findings should be useful in improving or refining the proposed evaluation framework to extend its applicability to the practitioner community.

REFERENCES

Arnold, U. (2000). New dimensions of outsourcing: a combination of transaction cost economics and the core competencies concept. *European Journal of Purchasing & Supply Management*, *6*(1), 23–29. doi:10.1016/S0969-7012(99)00028-3

Bagchi, P. K., & Virum, H. (1998). Logistical alliances: trends and prospects in integrated Europe. *Journal of Business Logistics*, *19*(1), 191–213.

Baiman, S., & Rajan, M. V. (2002). Incentive issues in inter-firm relationships. *Accounting, Organizations and Society*, *27*(3), 213–238. doi:10.1016/S0361-3682(00)00017-9

Ballou, R. H. (2004). *Business logistics/supply chain management: A balanced approach.* (5th ed.). New Jersey: Pearson, Prentice Hall.

Barney, J. B. (1991). Firm resources and sustained competitive advantage. *Journal of Management*, *17*(1), 99–120. doi:10.1177/014920639101700108

Beaumont, N., & Sohal, A. (2004). Outsourcing in Australia. *International Journal of Operations & Production Management*, *24*(7), 688–700. doi:10.1108/01443570410541993

Benbasat, I., Goldstein, D. K., & Mead, M. (1987). The case study research strategy in studies of information systems. *MIS Quarterly*, *11*(4), 369–386. doi:10.2307/248684

Bensaou, M. (1999). Portfolios of buyer-supplier relationships. *Sloan Management Review, 40*(4), 35–44.

Bhatnagar, R., Sohal, A. S., & Millen, R. (1999). Third party logistics services: A Singapore perspective. *International Journal of Physical Distribution & Logistics Management, 29*(9), 569–587. doi:10.1108/09600039910287529

Bookbinder, J. H. (2005). Global logistics. [Editorial]. *Transportation Research Part E, Logistics and Transportation Review, 41*(6), 461–466. doi:10.1016/j.tre.2005.07.001

Bowersox, D. J., Closs, D. J., & Cooper, M. B. (2002). *Supply chain logistics management.* Boston: McGraw Hill.

Boyson, S., Corsi, T., Dresner, M., & Rabinovich, E. (1999). Managing third party logistics relationships: what does it take. *Journal of Business Logistics, 20*(1), 73–100.

Brandes, H., Lilliecreutz, J., & Brege, S. (1997). Outsourcing – success or failure?: Findings from five case studies. *European Journal of Purchasing & Supply Management, 3*(2), 63–75. doi:10.1016/S0969-7012(97)00001-4

Burdon, S., & Bhalla, A. (2005). Lessons from the untold success story: Outsourcing engineering and facilities management. *European Management, 23*(5), 576–582. doi:10.1016/j.emj.2005.09.012

Campbell, J. F. (1990). Freight consolidation and routing with transport economies of scale. *Transportation Research Part B: Methodological, 24*(5), 345–361. doi:10.1016/0191-2615(90)90008-M

Carbone, V., & Stone, M. A. (2005). Growth and relational strategies used by the European logistics service providers: Rationale and outcomes. *Transportation Research Part E, Logistics and Transportation Review, 41*(6), 495–510. doi:10.1016/j.tre.2005.06.001

Chopra, S., & Meindl, P. (2007). *Supply chain management: Strategy, planning, & operation.* (3rd ed.). New Jersey: Pearson, Prentice Hall.

Collis, D. (1994). Research note: How valuable are organisational capabilities. *Strategic Management Journal, 15*(8), 143–152. doi:10.1002/smj.4250150910

Conner, K. R. (1991). A historical comparison of resource-based theory and five schools of thought within industrial organization economics: do we have a new theory of the firm? *Journal of Management, 17*(1), 121–154. doi:10.1177/014920639101700109

Coyle, J. J., Bardi, E. J., & Langley, C. J., Jr. (2003). *The management of business logistics: A supply chain perspective.* (7th ed.). Ohio: South-Western, Thomson.

Eisenhardt, K. M. (1989). Building theories from case study research. *Academy of Management Review, 14*(4), 535–550. doi:10.2307/258557

Eisenhardt, K. M., & Martin, J. A. (2000). Dynamic capabilities: what are they? *Strategic Management Journal, 21*(10/11), 1105–1121. doi:10.1002/1097-0266(200010/11)21:10/11<1105::AID-SMJ133>3.0.CO;2-E

Embleton, P. R., & Wright, P. C. (1998). A practical guide to successful outsourcing. *Empowerment in Organizations, 6*(3), 94–106. doi:10.1108/14634449810210832

Espino-Rodríguez, T. F., & Rodríguez-Díaz, M. (2008). Effects of internal and relational capabilities on outsourcing: An integrated model. *Industrial Management & Data Systems, 108*(3), 328–345. doi:10.1108/02635570810858750

European Commission (2001). *Protrans: analysis of European logistics regions.* Deliverable No. 2, November, Competitive and Sustainable Growth Programme of the 5th Framework programme.

Fleischmann, B. (1993). Designing distribution systems with transport economies of scale. *European Journal of Operational Research, 70*(1), 31–42. doi:10.1016/0377-2217(93)90230-K

Grant, R. M. (1991). The resource-based theory of competitive advantage: Implications for strategy formulation. *California Management Review, 33*(3), 114–135.

Haakansson, H. (1987). *Industrial technological development: A network approach*. London: Croom Helm.

Haakansson, H., & Snehota, I. (1995). *Developing Relationships in Business Networks*. London: Routledge.

Hafeez, K., Zhang, Y., & Malak, N. (2002). Determining key capabilities of a firm using analytic hierarchy process. *International Journal of Production Economics, 76*(1), 39–51. doi:10.1016/S0925-5273(01)00141-4

Halldórsson, A. (2007). Complementary theories to supply chain management. *Supply Chain Management: An International Journal, 12*(4), 284–296. doi:10.1108/13598540710759808

Harland, C. M., & Knight, L. A. (2001). Supply network strategy: role and competence requirements. *International Journal of Operations & Production Management, 21*(4), 476–489. doi:10.1108/01443570110381381

Hertz, S., & Alfredsson, M. (2003). Strategic development of third party logistics providers. *Industrial Marketing Management, 32*(2), 139–149. doi:10.1016/S0019-8501(02)00228-6

Holcomb, T. R., & Hitt, M. A. (2007). Toward a model of strategic outsourcing. *Journal of Operations Management, 25*(2), 464–481. doi:10.1016/j.jom.2006.05.003

Jara-Díaz, S. R., & Basso, L. J. (2003). Transport cost functions, network expansion and economies of scope. *Transportation Research Part E, Logistics and Transportation Review, 39*(4), 271–288. doi:10.1016/S1366-5545(03)00002-4

Javidan, M. (1998). Core competence: What does it mean in practice? *Long Range Planning, 31*(1), 60–71. doi:10.1016/S0024-6301(97)00091-5

Jharkharia, S., & Shankar, R. (2007). Selection of logistics service provider: An analytic network process (ANP) approach. *Omega, 35*(3), 274–289. doi:10.1016/j.omega.2005.06.005

Johanson, J., & Mattsson, L. G. (1987). Inter-organizational relations in industrial systems: a network approach compared with the transaction cost approach. *International Journal of Operations & Production Management, 17*(1), 34–48.

Kakabadse, A., & Kakabadse, N. (2002). Trends in outsourcing: contrasting USA and Europe. *European Management Journal, 20*(2), 189–198. doi:10.1016/S0263-2373(02)00029-4

Kedia, B. L., & Lahiri, S. (2007). International outsourcing of services: A partnership model. *Journal of International Management, 13*(1), 22–37. doi:10.1016/j.intman.2006.09.006

Laarhoven, P., van Berglund, M., & Peters, M. (2000). Third-party logistics in Europe – five years later. *International Journal of Physical Distribution and Logistics Management, 30*(5), 425–442. doi:10.1108/09600030010336216

Langley, C. J., Jr., Morton, J., Wereldsma, D., Swaminathan, S., Murphy, J., Deakins, T. A., et al. (2008). *2008 Third-Party Logistics: Results and Findings of the 13th Annual Study*. Capgemini, Georgia Institute of Technology, Oracle, and DHL.

Langley, C. J., Jr., van Dort, E., Morton, J., Hoemmken, S., Goh, A., Zabawa, M., et al. (2007). *2007 Third-Party Logistics: Results and Findings of the 12th Annual Study*. Capgemini, Georgia Institute of Technology, SAP, and DHL.

Langley, C. J., Jr., van Dort, E., Ross, T., Topp, U., Allen, G. R., & Sykes, S. R. (2006). *2006 Third-Party Logistics: Results and Findings of the 11th Annual Study*. Capgemini, Georgia Institute of Technology, SAP, and DHL.

Lankford, W. M., & Parsa, F. (1999). Outsourcing: A primer. *Management Decision, 37*(4), 310–316. doi:10.1108/00251749910269357

Lau, K. H., & Zhang, J. (2006). Drivers and obstacles of outsourcing practices in China. *International Journal of Physical Distribution & Logistics Management, 36*(10), 776–792. doi:10.1108/09600030610714599

Linder, J. C., Cole, M. I., & Jacobson, A. L. (2002). Business transformation through outsourcing. *Strategy and Leadership, 30*(4), 23–28. doi:10.1108/10878570210435342

Logan, M. S. (2000). Using agency theory to design successful outsourcing relationships. *International Journal of Logistics Management, 11*(2), 21–32. doi:10.1108/09574090010806137

Lynch, C. F. (2000). *Logistics Outsourcing: A Management Guide*. Illinois: Council of Logistics Management Publications.

Maltz, A. (1993). Private fleet use: a transaction cost model. *Transportation Journal, 32*(3), 46–53.

McIvor, R. (2008a). What is the right outsourcing strategy for your process? *European Management, 26*(1), 24–34. doi:10.1016/j.emj.2007.08.008

McIvor, R. (2008b). How the transaction cost and the resource-based theories of the firm inform outsourcing evaluation. *Journal of Operations Management*. doi:.doi:10.1016/j.jom.2008.03.004

Momme, J. (2002). Framework for outsourcing manufacturing: strategic and operational implications. *Computers in Industry, 49*(1), 59–75. doi:10.1016/S0166-3615(02)00059-3

Momme, J., & Hvolby, H. H. (2002). An outsourcing framework: action research in the heavy industry sector. *European Journal of Purchasing and Supply Management, 8*(4), 185–196. doi:10.1016/S0969-7012(02)00003-5

Oliver, C. (1990). Determinants of inter-organizational relationships: integration and future directions. *Academy of Management Review, 15*(2), 241–265. doi:10.2307/258156

Peteraf, M. (1993). The cornerstones of competitive advantage: a resource-based view. *Strategic Management Journal, 14*, 179–192. doi:10.1002/smj.4250140303

Peters, M., Cooper, J., Lieb, R. C., & Randall, H. L. (1998). The third-party logistics industry in Europe: provider perspectives on the industry's current status and future prospects. *International Journal of Logistics: Research and Application, 1*(1), 9–25. doi:10.1080/13675569808962035

Plehwe, D., & Bohle, D. (1998). *Uberlegungen zum forschungsfeld transnationale organisation in Europa*. B-Social Science Research Center, Berlin.

Power, D., Sharafali, M., & Bhakoo, V. (2007). Adding value through outsourcing: Contribution of 3PL services to customer performance. *Management Research News, 30*(3), 228–235. doi:10.1108/01409170710733296

Prahalad, C. K., & Hamel, G. (1990). The core competence of the corporation. *Harvard Business Review, 68*(3), 79–91.

Rabinovich, E., Windle, R., Dresner, M., & Corsi, T. (1999). Outsourcing of integrated logistics functions: An examination of industry practices. *International Journal of Physical Distribution & Logistics Management, 29*(6), 353–373. doi:10.1108/09600039910283587

Razzaque, M. A., & Sheng, C. C. (1998). Outsourcing of logistics functions: a literature survey. *International Journal of Physical Distribution & Logistics Management, 28*(2), 89–107. doi:10.1108/09600039810221667

Reed, R., & DeFillippi, R. J. (1990). Causal ambiguity, barriers to imitation and sustainable competitive advantage. *Academy of Management Review, 15*(1), 88–102. doi:10.2307/258107

Ritchie, B., & Brindley, C. (2002). Reassessing the management of the global supply chain. *Integrated Manufacturing Systems, 13*(2), 110–116. doi:10.1108/09576060210415446

Simchi-Levi, D., Kaminsky, P., & Simchi-Levi, E. (2008). *Designing & Managing the Supply Chain: Concepts, Strategies & Case Studies.* (3rd ed.). New York: Irwin McGraw Hill.

Stank, T. P., & Daugherty, P. J. (1997). The impact of operating environment on the formation of co-operative logistics relationships. *Transportation Research Part E, Logistics and Transportation Review, 33*(1), 53–65. doi:10.1016/S1366-5545(96)00005-1

Stock, G. N., Greis, N. P., & Kasarda, J. D. (1998). Logistics, strategy, and structure: a conceptual framework. *International Journal of Production Management, 18*(1), 37–52. doi:10.1108/01443579810192772

Tian, Y., Lai, F., & Daniel, F. (2008). An examination of the nature of trust in logistics outsourcing relationship: empirical evidence from China. *Industrial Management & Data Systems, 108*(3), 346–367. doi:10.1108/02635570810858769

Vaidyanathan, G. (2005). A framework for evaluating third-party logistics. *Communications of the ACM, 48*(1), 89–94. doi:10.1145/1039539.1039544

Vining, A., & Globerman, S. (1999). A conceptual framework for understanding the outsourcing decision. *European Management Journal, 17*(6), 645–654. doi:10.1016/S0263-2373(99)00055-9

Wadhwa, V., & Ravindran, A. R. (2007). Vendor selection in outsourcing. *Computers & Operations Research, 34*(12), 3725–3727. doi:10.1016/j.cor.2006.01.009

Walsham, G. (1995). Interpretive case studies in IS research: nature and method. *European Journal of Information Systems, 4*(1), 74–81. doi:10.1057/ejis.1995.9

Waters, D. (2003). *Logistics: An Introduction to Supply Chain Management.* New York: Palgrave Macmillan.

Wernerfelt, B. (1984). A resource-based view of the firm. *Strategic Management Journal, 5*(2), 171–180. doi:10.1002/smj.4250050207

Williamson, O. E. (1975). Markets *and Hierarchies: Analysis and Antitrust Implications.* London: The Free Press.

Williamson, O. E. (1985). *The Economic Institutions of Capitalism: Firms, Markets, Relational Contracting.* New York: The Free Press.

Williamson, O. E. (1996). *The Mechanisms of Governance.* Oxford: Oxford University Press.

Wisner, J. D., Leong, G. K., & Tan, K. C. (2005). *Principles of Supply Chain Management: A Balanced Approach.* Ohio: South-Western, Thomson.

Yin, R. K. (1994). *Case Study Research: Design and Methods.* (2nd ed.). London: Sage Publications.

Chapter 10
The Construction of Green Supply Chain Management System

Heekyung An
Shimadzu Corporation, Japan

ABSTRACT

Considering the implications of EU environmental laws such as REACH (registration, evaluation, authorization, and restriction of chemicals) and EuP (directive on eco-design of energy-using products) as well as RoHS (restrictions of the use of certain hazardous substances in electrical and electronic equipment) Directive, they have been acquired to advance GSCM (green supply chain management) more and more. The aim of this article is to introduce the construction of GSCM system that improves collaborative relationships between an EEE manufacturer and its suppliers. The study is conducted in three steps. Firstly, the four elements, which are necessities to form collaborative relationships between an EEE manufacturer and its suppliers, are described. Secondly, the condition and construction of GSCM system including the four elements is proposed. Finally, we presented the method that the GSCM system is constructed as a practicable tool in the initial stage by a case study held in Shimadzu Corporation.

INTRODUCTION

The RoHS (restrictions of the use of certain hazardous substances in electrical and electronic equipment) has driven the implementation and development of GSCM (green supply chain management) for Japanese EEE manufacturers who produce EEE products that are exported to the EU market. The EEE manufacturers have pressed their parts suppliers to participate in various activities for compliance with the directive and for meeting the demands of EU market. The three common environmental activities are; (1) obtaining certification of EMS (environmental management system), (2) sharing knowledge of substances presence in EEE parts, and (3) warranting RoHS substances not included in EEE parts. However, the activities are likely to have been promoted without suppliers' sufficient acknowledgement and abilities. Moreover, many Japanese parts suppliers do not directly face with EU market. It is necessary that the demands of an EEE manufacturer to its suppliers should be balanced with suppliers' capacities for an effective advancement of the GSCM. The suppliers' capacities for complying with EEE manufacturer's demand depends on their acknowledgement on RoHS directive and environmental problems, financial status, technical and human resources. Therefore, the EEE manufacturers have been faced with the fact that they must form collaborative relationships between the EEE manufacturer and the parts supplier to improve GSCM performance.

This research presents the construction of GSCM system to promote collaborative relationships between an EEE manufacturer and its parts suppliers. The GSCM system is also a standard to organize and systemically operate environmental activities. In this article, we described the construction of the GSCM system including the four elements to form collaboration and introduced the method to apply the GSCM at the initial stage in the case study of Shimadzu Corporation.

THE FOUR ELEMENTS FOR FORMING COLLABORATIVE RELATIONSHIPS

To correspond to environmental problems related to end products, EEE manufacturers implement GSCM for the next three stages. To improve environmental problems related to the product, EEE manufacturers set the GSCM policy and purpose as the first stage. Then EEE manufacturers set the environmental requirement based on the GSCM policy and purpose as a second stage. As the third stage, EEE manufacturers promote the supplier's cooperation to cope with the environmental requirement in the GSCM implementation. Here, to promote the cooperation of the supplier in the GSCM implementation, EEE manufacturers need to share the GSCM policy and purpose with parts suppliers in the second stage. Moreover, EEE manufacturers are requested to advance joint action with the supplier up to the second stage and the third stage. To advance sharing the GSCM policy and purpose and joint action, EEE manufacturers should share the knowledge and information with supplier. Activities for supplier support have to be implemented to effectively advance the sharing of GSCM policy and purpose, and its joint action. Therefore, we suggest four elements to form and develop collaborative relationships between an

Figure. 1. Elements for forming collaborative relationships

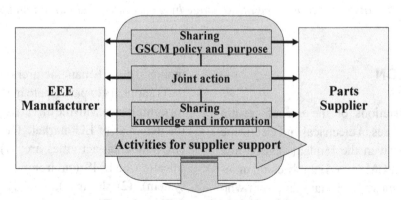

240

EEE manufacturer and its parts suppliers. The four elements are: (1) sharing GSCM policy and purpose, (2) joint action, (3) sharing knowledge and information, and (4) activities for supplier support.

Sharing GSCM Policy and Purpose

Sahay (2003) described that building up mutual trust was indispensable in the collaborative relationships between the organizations. He said that the mutual trust between organizations is improved when they shared policy and purpose to advance some business activities. For acquiring competing domination in the market, manufacturers who produce end products have to promptly correspond to the trend of the market that is affected by environmental regulation. The manufacturers have to set up "GSCM policy and purpose" to comply with the change of new environmental regulations and the market (Kovács, 2005; Marianne, 2004). This necessitates the sharing of the GSCM policy and purpose with their suppliers who produce parts composing end products. Parts suppliers have to be provided with information and knowledge about environmental regulations and market trends to understand the background of the GSCM policy and purpose by buyers who are end-product manufacturers. After the necessity of measures promotion consents, the supplier can accept the GSCM policy and the purpose. After the suppliers recognized the necessity for accepting the GSCM policy and purpose, the GSCM policy and purpose are included in the policy of production and environmental activity of suppliers. The suppliers will then advance their production and business activities with the ability to adapt and cope with the market demands and regulations.

Joint Action

The joint action is a necessity for improving collaborative relationships between a manufacturer and its suppliers in the GSCM implementation (Purba, 2004; Sahay, 2003; Thomas & Oliver, 1991; Ypatia, Katerina, & George, 2006). Danny, Priscila, and Geoffrey (2006) pointed out that the GSCM implementation without joint action is likely to lead formation of adversarial relationships between a manufacturer and its suppliers. They introduced that joint action should be consisted of joint planning and joint doing. Tage (2000) described that joint action was operated through the process of joint planning, joint doing and joint monitoring. The joint monitoring checks the status of implementing joint action. In this study, joint reviewing is included in the process of the joint action. Joint reviewing is a necessity for applying the result of joint monitoring to improve continuous performance of the whole joint action. Therefore, the joint action is implemented through a continuous cycle process of joint planning, joint doing, joint monitoring and joint reviewing.

Sharing Knowledge and Information

Louise and Stuart (2001) identified the uncertainties on environmental aspect, the method of improving environmental performance, the capacity of resource or technology for advancing environmental activities in GSCM implementation. Many suppliers have a lack of information about what kind of hazardous substances are in their products, whether such substances restricted by RoHS are in their products or not, because of uncertainty on environmental aspect. They do not have any idea how to solve or improve the environmental problem even though they understand the environmental aspect in their production and business due to the uncertainty on the method of improving environmental performance and the capacity of resource or technology for advancing environmental activities. The uncertainty between a manufacturer and its suppliers has to be lessened to improve the mutual trusts among organizations and to promote the formation of collaborative relationships between them. Sharing knowledge and information is an essential element to decrease the uncertainty between a manufacturer and its suppliers. EEE manufacturer should share knowledge and information for GSCM implementation with its suppliers to lessen various uncertainties which are obstacles in GSCM implementation (Robert & Shelby, 1994).

In this research, sharing knowledge and information between an EEE manufacturer and its supplier for GSCM implementation are classified into sharing knowledge and information: (1) for sharing GSCM policy and purpose, (2) for process of joint planning, (3) process of joint doing and joint monitoring, and (4) process of joint reviewing.

Activities for Supplier Support

Many suppliers have suffered from the difficulties coping with environmental requirement from manufacturers because of lack of environmental knowledge, environmental consideration, and financial or technological resources (Richard & Jon, 1996; Ypatia et al., 2006). The problem in these suppliers causes the supplier's cooperation in the GSCM implementation to be obstructed. In this research, therefore, activity for supporting suppliers by manufacturers who try to improve GSCM performance is classified into three; (1) providing knowledge and information on the trend of environmental regulations and the market, (2) technical assistance, and (3) providing human and financial resources.

THE CONSTRUCTION OF GSCM SYSTEM

Requirement for Systematic Management

Systematic management for GSCM implementation means that a manufacturer works together with its suppliers to advance the activities for GSCM on a standardized tool in this study. The standardized tool is based on the concept of PDCA cycle, which flows the four-step process of "plan," "do," "check," and "act" to improve GSCM performance continuously. The details of

each process have to be documented or recorded in order to share and confirm the process and the result of GSCM implementation.

Application of Environmental Management System Standard

ISO 14001, which is the international standard of environmental management system satisfies the two requirements of systematic management operated by PDCA cycle and documentation. It has become as one of the worldwide accredited EMS certification of organizations because "it is intended to apply to all types and sizes of organization and to accommodate diverse geographical, cultural and social conditions." According to the ISO Survey 2006, the cases of organization obtaining the certification of ISO 14001 have totaled to 129,199 in December 2006. And there is a continuous increase in acquisition counts all over the world. The widely used ISO 14001 was applied to the construction of GSCM system used by both manufacturer and supplier in this study (International Organization for Standardization, 2006).

Comparison of the Requirements for GSCM System and ISO 14001 Standard

The GSCM system includes four elements for forming collaborative relationships between a manufacturer and its suppliers, and two requirements for systematic system.

PDCA Cycle and Documentation--ISO 14001 is a standard based on the concept of improving management performance continuously by PDCA cycle. It is described that ISO 14001 is to cycle the processes of "plan," "do," "check," and "act" in annex A.1. "Environmental management system requirements" of ISO 14001 include "Documentation" (4.4.4. of ISO 14001) and "control of documents" (4.4.5. of ISO 14001). Organization shall report and document the main elements of the environmental management system and their interaction, and reference to related documents

(4.4.4 of ISO 14001). The documents have to be controlled and maintained for implementation of environmental management system (4.4.5. of ISO 14001).

The four elements for forming collaborative relation--Environmental policy shall be defined by top management, and then documented, implemented and maintained within the defined scope of its environmental management system (4.2 of ISO14001; 2004). The environmental policy is communicated and shared among all members from the top management to the bottom management related to the construction and operation of EMS. The environmental policy which is described in ISO 14001 corresponds to "GSCM policy and purpose." "Joint action" is a significant element for forming collaborative relationships among all person or organization related to some common activities. The processes of joint action are joint planning, joint doing, joint monitoring and joint reviewing. The four processes correspond to the processes of EMS described in ISO 14001. "Joint planning," "joint doing," "joint monitoring," and "joint reviewing" correspond to "planning," "implementation and operation," "checking," and "management review," respectively. "Sharing knowledge and information" is an essential element to implement effectively the EMS. All workers for EMS implementation have to share knowledge and information to advance the environmental activities. Sharing knowledge and information is described in "communication" (4.4.3 of ISO 14001:2004). "The organization shall ensure that any person performing tasks for it or on its behalf has the potential to cause a significant environmental impact identified by the organization and is competent on the basis of appropriate education, training or experience" as described in 4.4.2 of ISO 14001. As activities of education and training are to support members in charge of EMS, and program of education and training is to support suppliers in charge of GSCM (Japanese Standards Association, 2004).

Composition of GSCM System

The previous paragraphs describe the ISO 14001 standard including the four elements for forming collaborative relationships and the requirement for systematic management. Moreover, the ISO 14001 standard is the prevailing international standard of environmental management system in the world, and an applicable tool for any kind of organization. For these reasons, the contents and composition of ISO 14001 are applied to the composition of GSCM system in this study. The GSCM system shall then be an applicable tool for any suppliers. The GSCM system consists of "definition," "GSCM policy and purpose," "scope and application object," "joint planning," "joint doing," "joint monitoring," and "joint reviewing." Moreover, this system intends to implement and operate GSCM through the continuous cycle process of "joint planning," "joint doing," "joint monitoring," and "joint reviewing."

1. **Scope and application object:** For the purpose of complying with environmental regulations or market demands, and strengthening competitiveness, the GSCM system is applied as a management tool for the supply chain. "The cooperation for GSCM system" means an organization in which a manufacturer and its suppliers are combined to implement GSCM. The cooperation for the GSCM system is composed of a "leader of GSCM system" and the "cooperators of GSCM system." The leader of GSCM system shall establish the GSCM policy and purpose and share it with the cooperators of GSCM system. In this research, an EEE manufacturer is regarded as the leader of GSCM system.

2. **Joint planning:** The joint planning based on GSCM policy and purpose is implemented in the processes of listing up GSCM aspects, evaluation of GSCM aspects, specifying remarkable GSCM aspects, setting up goals,

and GSCM program. Firstly, a leader of GSCM system lists up GSCM aspects that seem to be related to the achievement of GSCM policy and purpose. Secondly, the leader of GSCM system evaluates whether the GSCM aspects have an important influence on the achievement of GSCM policy and purpose or not, and then specifies remarkable GSCM aspects. The remarkable GSCM aspects shall be announced to and understood by the cooperators of GSCM system. Thirdly, the GSCM goals are set up to improve the remarkable GSCM aspects. The GSCM goals are set up for long-term achievement. The GSCM specific goals are for short terms. These goals are expressed numerically as much as possible for the quantitative evaluation, and documented to be maintained and controlled. Furthermore, the goals shall be set up as practicable as possible through evaluating the capability of cooperators of GSCM system to achieve such goals. Finally, the GSCM program should be settled to achieve the GSCM goals and specific goals.

THE MEASUREMENT SURVEY FOR UNDERSTANDING THE SITUATION OF COOPERATORS

It is significant that joint planning is practically established to achieve the GSCM goals and improve the GSCM performance. Understanding the situations such as how much capacity cooperators have for complying with GSCM system is needed to set up GSCM goals and GSCM program in the stage of joint planning. The measurement survey for understanding the situation of cooperators (MSUS) is to be carried out in the stage of joint planning, and then the result of MSUS is to be reflected for setting the GSCM goals, GSCM specific goal and then overall GSCM program. Therefore, MSUS is presented as a method for constructing practical GSCM system in this chapter. The MSUS was conducted for Shimadzu Cooperation Assembly that is organized by Shimadzu Corporation itself and its 115 suppliers providing EEE parts to Shimadzu Cooperation from the period of August 29, 2006 to October 1, 2006. Shimadzu Corporation and 115 suppliers correspond to "leader of GSCM system" and "cooperators of GSCM system," respectively. The method of MSUS was through the development of questionnaire for the 115 "cooperators of the GSCM system." The respondents were 63 among 115. The questionnaire aimed to grasp the conditions of GSCM policy and purpose shared with supplier, and the GSCM aspect as understood by the suppliers. Furthermore, the questionnaire also tried to estimate the practicality of the GSCM goals and to set up a practical GSCM program.

The Situation of Sharing "GSCM Policy and Purpose" and "GSCM Aspect"

Table 1 shows the situation of "GSCM policy and purpose" expressed in number of notified

Table 1. The situation of sharing GSCM policy and purpose

The situation of sharing GSCM policy and purpose	Answered cooperators
Notified	53
Not notified	2
No memory	8
Total	63

"cooperators of the GSCM system." (i.e., 53 among 63 companies). On the other hand, eight cooperators answered they have no experience or any sort of idea whether they have been informed about the "GSCM policy and purpose." Moreover, two cooperators answered that the explanation of "GSCM policy and purpose" had not been informed to them. From this result, it is clear that there are cooperators who lack understanding of the "GSCM policy and purpose." The cooperators who do not understand the "GSCM policy and purpose" need to be provided with information and knowledge and repeatedly done by the leader of GSCM system to achieve the GSCM goals.

Shimadzu Corporation who is the leader of GSCM system in this study has set up the "obtaining certification of EMS" for its suppliers as a GSCM aspect. Table 2 shows the situation whether cooperators have recognized "obtaining certification of EMS" as a GSCM aspect. Twenty cooperators have not recognized "obtaining certification

of EMS" as a GSCM aspect. Therefore, the leader of GSCM system needs to help the cooperators to understand the GSCM aspect by sharing information or supporting their programs.

Estimating Practicable GSCM Goal and Specific Goal

Figure 2 shows the condition of the cooperators who have obtained or planned for obtaining certification of EMS. Thirty three cooperators among 62 have already got EMS certification. The cooperators operating EMS have to be further trained and supported to advance the activities based on EMS by the leader of GSCM system. The GSCM goal and specific goal for "obtaining certification of EMS" are targeting 29 cooperators who have not yet obtained the certification of EMS. Seven cooperators answered that they had planned to get the certification within 1 year. One cooperator answered that it has a plan to

Table 2. The situation of sharing GSCM aspect

The situaion of sharing GSCM aspect	Cooperators
Notified	42
Not notified	20
Total	62

Figure 2. The situation of obtaining certification of EMS

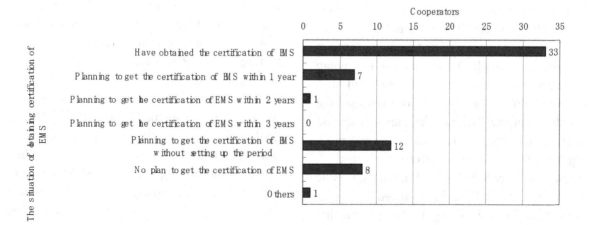

obtain the certification within 2 years. Twelve cooperators have a plan to obtain the certification in the future, although they did not make sure the period for obtaining the certification. However, eight cooperators answered that they did not have any plan to get the certification of EMS. From the results, we can consider the setting up the GSCM goal to be in the span of three years and specific goal for one year. Among the 29 cooperators who have not obtained the certification of EMS, 20 cooperators have positively thought about operating EMS and obtaining the certification. Although 12 cooperators have not yet determined the period of acquiring the certification of EMS, they are likely to introduce and implement EMS to their companies within three years through the leader's supports. The result therefore provides the standard to set up practicable GSCM goals and GSCM program.

Grasping the Point of Setting up GSCM Program

MSUS aims to have understood the situation of the support service to cooperators by the leader of GSCM system for setting up practical GSCM program. GSCM program is to schedule process and selecting method for achieving GSCM goals. This article is only limited to presenting the selection method for supporting the cooperators. Figure 3 shows the supporting method that helps cooperators to understand what EMS is and how EMS is implemented or operated. The methods are "holding seminar," "dispatching the specialist and the person in charge" and "guiding through mailing and e-mail. The selection of more than one answer to these survey questions had been allowed in this case study. The answered results of "holding seminar," "dispatching the specialist and the person in charge" and "guiding through mailing and e-mail" were respectively 31, 15, and 12. These results are based on the limited knowledge of the respondents. Here, it is assumed that "holding seminar" is easily recognized as a supporting

method by the cooperators. "Holding seminar" has a merit of the leader of GSCM system being the educator and trainer and positively influences many cooperators at the same time. On the other hands, 11 cooperators answered that they have no experience or knowledge whatsoever about the need of support by leader and its continuous support from the leader of GSCM system.

CONCLUSION

The application of GSCM system was presented in this article to improve the effectiveness of GSCM implementation and operation. The GSCM system consists of four elements and two conditions. The elements are sharing GSCM policy and purpose, joint action, sharing knowledge and information, and the activities for supplier support. All these are aim to improve the collaborative relationships between a manufacturer and its suppliers. The two conditions are the "application of PDCA cycle" and the documentation to systematically advance the GSCM implementation. These identified elements and conditions must be integrated within the worldwide-applied ISO 14001 for the construction of GSCM system, since the ISO 14001 is the most applicable EMS for any organization. Here, the ISO 14001-based GSCM system is assumed to be used by any supplier. The main processes of the GSCM system are composed of the "GSCM policy and purpose," "joint planning," "joint doing," "joint monitoring," and "joint reviewing." Balancing the four elements for forming collaborative relationships and documentation operates the processes that are based on PDCA cycle. However, the GSCM system needs to be planned as a practical system in the initial stage of the construction. Therefore, we considered the method for establishing GSCM goals and program in the process of "joint planning." The measurement survey for understanding the situation of cooperators (MSUS) was presented as a simple and useful method for setting up practicable GSCM goals and program. The

MSUS has to be further developed and utilized for a continuous and practical operation of the GSCM in the future.

REFERENCES

Aref, A. H., Marilyn, M. H., & Joseph, S. (2005). Performance measurement for green supply chain management. *Benchmarking: An international Journal, 12*(4), 330-352.

Danny, P. C., Priscila, B. O., & Geoffrey, H. (2006). Coordination collaborative joint efforts with suppliers: The effects of trust, transaction specific investment and information network in the Dutch flower industry. *Supply Chain Management: An International Journal, 11*(3), 216-224

European Union. (2003). Directive 2002/95/EC of the European Parliament and of the Council of 27 January 2003. *Official Journal of the European Union.*

International Organization for Standardization. (2006). *The ISO survey-2006*, 9-25.

Japanese Standards Association. (2004). Environmental management systems-Requirements with guidance for use. *ISO 14001:2004*, 1-18

Kovács, G. (2005). Supply chain collaboration for sustainability. *Business Strategy and the Environment Conference Proceeding 2005.*

Louise, C., & Stuart, H. L. (2001). Managing the environmental adaptation process in supplier-customer relationships. *Business Strategy and the Environment, 10*, 225-237

Marianne, F., & Michael, S. J. (2004). Organizing environmental supply chain management-experience from a sector with frequent product shift and complex product chains: The case of the Danish Textile Sector. *Greener Management International, 45*, 43-62

Purba, R. (2004). Greening production: A South-East Asian experience. *International Journal of Operations & Production Management, 24*(3), 289-320

Richard, L., & Jon, H. (1996). The environment as a supply chain management issue. *British Journal of Management, 7*, 45-62

Robert, M. M., & Shelby, D. H. (1994). The commitment-trust theory of relationship marketing. *Journal of Marketing, 58*, 20-38

Sahay, B. S. (2003). Understanding trust in supply chain relationships. *Industrial Management & Data Systems, 103*(8), 553-563

Tage, S. L. (2000). European logistics beyond 2000. *International Journal of Physical Distribution & Logistics Management, 30*(5), 377-387

Thomas, R., & Oliver, N. (1991). Components supplier patterns in the UK Motor Industry. *OMEGA, 19*(6), 609-616

Ypatia, T., Katerina, G., & George, T. (2006). Supplier management and its relationship to buyers. *International Journal of Production Economics, 101*, 99-108

This work was previously published in the International Journal of Information Systems and Supply Chain Management, Vol. 1, Issue 3, edited by J. Wang, pp. 70-79, copyright 2008 by IGI Publishing (an imprint of IGI Global).

Chapter 11
The Factors Influence Suppliers Satisfaction of Green Supply Chain Management Systems in Taiwan

Hsiu-Chia Ko
National Sun Yat-Sen University, Taiwan

Fan-Chuan Tseng
National Sun Yat-Sen University, Taiwan

Chun-Po Yin
National Sun Yat-Sen University, Taiwan

Li-Chun Huang
National Sun Yat-Sen University, Taiwan

ABSTRACT

This study investigated user satisfaction when a new interorganizational information system (green supply chain management system; GSCMS) was introduced to a supplier by a leader in the Taiwan electronic industry. GSCMS providers, according to the requirements of the supplier network leader, trained the representatives of suppliers. All suppliers of two sample vendors (manufacturers of electronic products) were surveyed. Five putative influencing factors were considered: perceived usefulness, perceived ease of use, training, computer anxiety, and computer self-efficacy. We find four factors significantly affect user satisfaction. The results show that the training provided by focal vendors will influence the satisfaction of users. Next, the anxiety and uncertainty experienced by users decreases when they acquire more knowledge about the operation of the new GSCMS. Finally, user satisfaction can be increased by designing the functions and interfaces of a GSCMS in accordance with the user perceptions of usefulness and ease of use, moreover, implications and suggestions are also discussed.

INTRODUCTION

European Union (EU) RoHS Directive relates to restrictions of the use of certain hazardous substances in electrical and electronic equipment, and states that from July 1, 2006, all electrical and electronic products imported into the EU must be proved not to contain six certain hazardous substances. The Ministry of Economic Affairs of Taiwan assesses that around 44 types of Taiwanese electrical and electronic products (which are exported to the EU) will be impacted by these restrictions. The directive will directly influence over 30,000 companies and annual trade of around NT$ 250 billion in Taiwan (i.e., 2.45% of the GDP), and indirectly influence over NT$ 400 billion annually (Epoch Times International, 2005). In order to facilitate the export of products to Europe, Taiwanese companies that export electrical and electronic products have embarked on implementing green supply chain management systems (GSCMSs) in order to conform to the new requirements.

Park and Krishnan (2005) point out that effective supply chain management can lower development and procurement costs, spur innovation, increase flexibility, and speed up product development. The function of a GSCMS is to ensure that all electrical and electronic products will conform to the relevant environmental controls before they are exported. The implementation of GSCMS by Taiwanese companies that export electrical and electronic products is therefore expected to be an important and necessary weapon to maintain their global competitiveness.

Generally, an electronic product was composed of a large number of raw materials that provided by many different suppliers, the formats of substances examination reports of each raw material may also be different. In the past, to obtain a substances report of an electronic product, manufactures (dominant network vendors) have to contact each raw material supplier individually and ask them to deliver their substance examina-

tion reports. Then, the focal vendors integrate all substance examination report of each raw material into a substance report of an electronic product manually. The whole process is complex, time-consuming, and easy to make mistakes to endanger the results. Besides, if there were any tiny changes on substance examination reports, the whole process will be run again.

GSCMS is a Web-based interface, which integrates with the bill of material (BOM) of dominant network vendor. This means that the GSCMS could easy obtain all the raw materials of an electronic product from the BOM. The vendors will set up an account and a password for each supplier that enables them to access the GSCMS. Once the supplier login the GSCMS, they will see a list of all raw material and requirements that they have to provide the substance examination reports and relevant information. The suppliers can upload or manage their substance examination reports online immediately. Besides, they can also search and trace all the substance examination reports status confirmed by the vendor. As long as the substance examination reports are in the valid period, they can be repeatedly used. Furthermore, GSCMS also save every substances examination reports, suppliers can download their former reports, and modify the formats to fit with other dominant network vendors' requirements. After all the substance examination reports of each raw material are entered by their supplier, the vendors can calculate the substance of their electronic products easily and accurately.

Dominant network leaders can use their superior bargaining power in an interorganizational information system to increase their competitive advantage as well as to secure supplier benefits by streamlining interorganizational processes. In Taiwan, a GSCMS is mainly constructed by focal vendors in the electrical and electronic industry, with suppliers generally not being invited to participate in its design and development. Thus, introducing a GSCMS into the supplier network will inevitably cause changes in organizational culture and in the behaviors of managers and data processing users at both the dominant network leaders and supplier sites (Soumi, 1994).

There is literature on supply chain management suggesting that a collaborative relationship is beneficial to achieving long-term competitive advantages (Faisal, Banwet, & Shankar, 2006; Hsu, 2005; Olorunniwo & Hartfield, 2001). Thus, implementing an effective win-win GSCMS requires both dominant network vendors and suppliers to accept and be satisfied with the system. The purpose of this study was to elucidate the satisfaction of suppliers who employ an interorganizational GSCMS under pressure from focal vendors. The influencing factors examined were perceived usefulness, perceived ease of use, training, computer anxiety, and computer self-efficacy. We chose two dominant network vendors (manufacturers of electronic products) and their suppliers' representatives as our research samples. The survey approach and statistical analyses were applied in this study.

The remainder of this article is structured as follows. Section 2 discusses the key factors that may affect user satisfaction with a supplier, and then describes the research model. Section 3 delineates the processes used for data collection, selection, and analysis. Section 4 presents and discusses the results from the study, and finally conclusions are drawn and suggestions for further research are presented in Section 5.

MODEL FACTORS

User satisfaction is an important indicator of the success of an information system. DeLone and McLean (1992) evaluate this through six indicators: the quality of the system, the quality of the information, the system usage, user satisfaction, individual influences, and organizational influences. In 2003 DeLone and McLean reviewed the successful information system models that were implemented during the intervening decade, and

reasserted that successful information systems are those that promote user working performance and efficiency.

The parameters used to directly evaluate the success of information systems include the promotion of cost-effectiveness, productivity, accuracy of decision-making, and competitive advantage. However, at the time of the present study, the application of GSCMSs was still in its infancy, and data related to these parameters were difficult to acquire; thus, user satisfaction was chosen as an index to evaluate the success of a GSCMS. Indeed, this is consistent with many studies assessing the success of information systems based on user satisfaction (Igbaria, 1992; Ives, Olson, & Baroudi, 1983; Lee, 1995; Palvia, 1996; Whitten, 2004).

Acceptance behavior is considered to be influenced by a variety of factors, including individual differences, social influences, beliefs and attitudes, situational influences, and managerial interventions (Agarwal, 2000). The subjects in the present study were GSCMS representatives of suppliers, with the focus on the individual user level. Individual user's differences may influence user evaluations of a GSCMS in this environment. Moreover, because the GSCMS was in the introductory stage, system characteristics such as functions and interfaces had significant effects on user satisfaction. Training performances was another possible influencing factor due to the users having been trained by the GSCMS software provider. This study therefore investigated the factors influencing user satisfaction in three dimensions: system, individual differences, and training. The system dimension includes the perceived ease of use and perceived usefulness, and the factors of individual differences include computer self-efficacy and computer anxiety.

Perceived Usefulness and Perceived Ease Of Use

At the time of this study, the application of GSC-MSs was still in its infancy in Taiwan. At such an early stage, the most important question is what will affect user acceptance of the new type of system. The technology acceptance model (TAM) is frequently applied to predict user acceptance of new systems, where the perceived usefulness is defined as the beliefs of individuals that using a particular technology will enhance their working performance and efficiency (Davis, 1989). Hsu and Chiu (2004) believe that perceived usefulness is a critical factor to determining user satisfaction, because users can evaluate a new system directly after they have applied it. Hsu and Chiu also show that there is a positive relationship between the perceived usefulness and satisfaction of users with electronic information services. Zviran, Pliskin, and Levin (2005) demonstrates the presence of a strong positive correlation between perceived usefulness and user satisfaction, implying that perceived usefulness is one of the critical factors affecting user satisfaction with an electronic data processing system. Moreover, Bhattacherjee (2001) uses expectation confirmation theory to explore the relationship between user perceptions and satisfaction with online bank services, and declares that user satisfaction is influenced by user expectation and perceived usefulness after applying a new system.

GSCMSs represent new integrated systems for examining products that are being employed by suppliers. Before applying such a system, suppliers may assess its usefulness based on the existing processes used to examine products, with this being evaluated after the suppliers have actually used the new system. We believe the evaluation of the usefulness of a new GSCMS will affect user satisfaction. Thus, the first hypothesis is proposed as follows:

H1: *Perceived usefulness is positively related to user satisfaction with a GSCMS.*

In the TAM theory of Davis, perceived ease of use is defined as how little effort it required to use a particular system. Igbaria, Guimaraes, and Davis (1995) believe that the ease of use of an information system determines the user acceptance. Moreover, Mahmood, Burn, Gemoets, and Jacquez (2000) assert from a meta-analysis that the user perception of the value of an information system is positively correlated with its ability to support decision-making. Furthermore, Adamson and Shine (2003) point out that in a mandatory environment, perceived ease of use is the most important factor affecting user satisfaction.

The bargaining power is asymmetric when implementing a GSCMS, in that it is higher for focal vendors than for suppliers. Moreover, a GSCMS is only constructed by focal vendors; that is, without the participation of suppliers. The suppliers can only participate in transactions with focal vendors by adopting a GSCMS, and thus face a mandatory environment in such trading. From the research results mentioned above we can infer that in a mandatory environment, perceived ease of use will be one of the key factors influencing user satisfaction of suppliers who use a GSCMS. This leads to the following second hypothesis:

H2: *Perceived ease of use is positively related to user satisfaction with a GSCMS.*

Training

Amoako-Gyampha and Salam (2004) describe training as the transfer of knowledge about the basic framework and the skills needed to operate the information system to users. The aim of training is to facilitate the correct and smooth operation of an information system by its users. Training has been validated as an essential factor influencing the successful implementation of an information system (Saga & Zmud, 1994; Webster, 1998). The user satisfaction index of Bailey and Pearson (1983) evaluates user satisfaction with an electronic data processing information system, and Palvia (1996) asserts that in small companies training is a significant factor affecting user satisfaction.

Training helps users to familiarize themselves with the system (Saga & Zmud, 1994). In this study, the GSCMS was a new system for those suppliers who did not have the opportunity to participate in its development. Hence, the provision of sufficient training programs by focal vendors to users before implementing a GSCMS might reduce user resistance and increase user satisfaction. The third hypothesis is therefore stated as follows:

H3: *Training is positively related to user satisfaction with a GSCMS.*

Computer Anxiety

Individuals experience anxiety when one or more of their values are threatened, since such values form the foundation of their existence (May, 1996). When faced with a new information system, uncertainty regarding the cost, individual performance, and/or organizational effectiveness may induce anxiety in individuals. Fagan, Neill, and Wooldridge (2003-04) argue that anxiety is an unpleasant emotional reaction experienced by individuals in threatening situations, and the use of a computer appears to provide a fertile environment for such reactions. Heinssen, Glass, and Knight (1987) indicate that computer anxiety is an affective state where an individual feels fear and apprehension about interacting with the computer, and also anticipates negative outcomes from the interaction. Thus, there is a negative relationship between computer anxiety and utilization (Harrison & Rainer, 1996). The fourth hypothesis is thus as follows:

H4: *Computer anxiety is negatively related to user satisfaction with a GSCMS.*

Computer Self-Efficacy

The notion of self-efficacy comes from cognitive psychology, and refers to the perceived ability of an individual to perform a given task, which further affects behaviors and decisions (Bandura, 1986, 1997). When individuals believe that they are able to successfully perform a task, they tend to be satisfied with the outcome of their behavior (Bandura, 1986, 1997; Hsu & Chiu, 2004). Compeau and Higgins (1995) extend the concept of self-efficacy to the field of information technology, and propose the concept of computer self-efficacy that refers to individuals believing they are able to use computers effectively in any situation (Compeau & Higgins, 1995; Marakas, Yi, & Johnson, 1998; Venkatesh, Morris, Davis, & Davis, 2003).

Several studies have revealed that the confidence of individuals in using computers to perform specific tasks influences their acceptance of an information system. For example, Wu (1999) found that the computer self-efficacy and satisfaction with their computer ability were related in students after they had learnt about operating computers. Henry and Stone (1994) assert that computer self-efficacy affects user satisfaction in the use of medical information systems, and Henry and Stone (1995) demonstrate that computer self-efficacy is positively related to performance satisfaction. Hsu, Chiu, and Fu (2004) described how satisfaction with the utilization of the Web, Web self-efficacy, and user expectations determine the continuation of Web usage. Accordingly, computer self-efficacy is also regarded as an important factor for the evaluation of user satisfaction with a GSCMS. Therefore, the fifth hypothesis is as follows:

H5: *Computer self-efficacy is positively related to user satisfaction with a GSCMS.*

RESEARCH METHODOLOGY

Research Model

Drawing on the related concepts of user satisfaction discussed above, we proposed the research model shown in Figure 1 to identify the factors that affect user satisfaction with a GSCMS. The definitions and sources of the six constructs contained in the model are summarized in Table 1.

Instrument

The survey questionnaire contained three parts: (1) general demographic questions, (2) perceptual scales of each construct in the research model, and (3) one open-ended question. The demographic questions were used to collect information about the respondent's sex, age, level of education, working experience, previous experiences of using computers and the Internet, and similar experiences of applying other information systems. In the final part of survey, the respondent was free to write down any ideas about the GSCMS.

To investigate the factors that may affect supplier satisfaction with a GSCMS, the respondents were asked to indicate their degree of agreement with 42 statements, and the user satisfaction was measured by 4 items (see Table 3). The six constructs other than computer self-efficacy were scored on a 7-point Likert scale ranging from strongly disagree (=1) to strongly agree (=7). Computer self-efficacy was measured on a percentage scale comprising 10 increments, ranging from 0% (not at all confident) to 100% (totally confident). The different measurement

scale of computer self-efficacy was due to follow its original development format.

Data Collection and Sample Analysis

The sample vendors of this study were two manufacturers of electronic products. The survey was conducted after two GSCMS training programs were run in 2005. The GSCMS adopted by both vendors were the same systems that implemented by a software Corporation. This Corporation is the market leader of GSCMS and holds 55% market share in Taiwan. Thus, it could be a case in point for this investigation. The paper-based questionnaires were distributed to 229 representatives of the suppliers, with the 164 returned questionnaires being examined by 4 researchers. Fourteen questionnaires were discarded due to the presence of many missing values, and hence 150 completed questionnaires were used in statistical analyses, representing a response rate of 65.5%.

Table 2 lists the demographic statistics of the sample. Among the 150 respondents, most of them ($n = 104$, 71.3%) were between 21 and 35 years old. The majority ($n = 124$, 84.9%) were educated to the associate's or baccalaureate degree level, and had worked for 1–3 years ($n = 118$, 69.4%). Most of them ($n = 131$, 87.1%) had used computers for at least 5 years, and had at least 5 years of experience using the Internet ($n = 116$, 76.8%).

Figure 1. Factors affecting user satisfaction with a green supply chain management system, with the associated hypothesis numbers

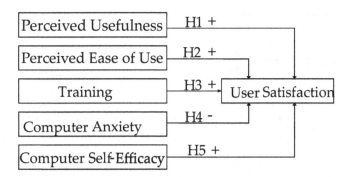

Table 1. Constructs, definitions, and sources

Construct	Definition	Sources
User Satisfaction	Users believe that an information system is able to fulfill their requirements.	Ives et al., 1983; DeLone and McLean, 1992
Perceived Usefulness	Users believe that using the system would enhance their working performance.	Davis, 1989
Perceived Ease of Use	Users believe that using the system would be free of effort.	Davis, 1989
Training	Instructing users to operate the information system correctly and smoothly.	Nelson and Cheney, 1987
Computer Anxiety	Users fear negative outcomes from using computers.	Heinssen et al., 1987; Fagan et al., 2003-04
Computer Self- Efficacy	Users believe that they are able to handle a computer well in any situation.	Compeau and Higgins, 1995; Marakas et al., 1998; Venkatesh et al., 2003

Table 2. Demographic characteristics of the samples (some frequencies do not sum to 150 due to missing data)

Characteristic	Category	Frequency	Percentage (%)
	21–30	62	42.5
	31–35	42	28.8
Age (years)	36–40	19	13.0
	41–45	16	11.0
	>45	7	4.8
	High school diploma	20	13.7
Level of education	Associate's degree	71	48.6
	Baccalaureate degree	53	36.3
	Master's degree	3	2.1
	1	28	19.0
	2	43	29.3
Working experience (years)	3	31	21.1
	4	17	11.6
	5	8	5.4
	6	20	13.6
	<3	8	5.4
	3, 4	11	7.5
Experience of computer use (years)	5–7	27	18.4
	8–10	42	28.6
	>10	59	40.1

continued on following page

Table 2. continued

Characteristic	Category	Frequency	Percentage (%)
Experience of Internet use (years)	<1	2	1.4
	1, 2	7	4.8
	3, 4	25	17.0
	5–7	44	29.9
	8–10	43	29.3
	>10	25	17.0
Experience of using a similar system (years)	Never	68	46.3
	<1	29	19.7
	1, 2	28	19.0
	3, 4	9	6.1
	5–7	3	2.0
	>8	1	0.7
Position	Manager	18	14.17
	Auxiliary Manager	7	5.51
	Chief of Section	17	13.39
	Sales	37	29.13
	Engineer	8	6.30
	Quality Assurance Staff	7	5.51
	Employee	33	25.98

About half of the users had never used a similar information system previously ($n = 68$, 46.3%). In spite of our samples are representatives of suppliers, it is notable that among our samples, about 33% (managers, auxiliary managers and chief of section) were staffs of management level, and 1/3 (quality assurance staffs and employee) were the potential system users. The combination of our research samples was suitable for representing the suppliers' attitude toward the system usage.

DATA ANALYSIS AND DISCUSSION

Construct Validity and Reliability

First, an exploratory factor analysis was used to examine the construct validity. Principal components analysis with varimax rotation revealed that all items loaded on their expected constructs greater than the threshold loading of 0.45 for more than 150 samples (Hair, Anderson, Tatham, & Black, 1998). Cronbach's alpha coefficient was assessed to examine the internal consistency of the items in each construct, and exceeded the threshold of 0.6 recommended by Nunnally and Bernstein (1994) for all six constructs. As indicated in Table 3, all constructs in the model exhibited adequate construct validity and reliability.

We also examine the discriminant validity by comparing the square root of the AVEs (Average Variance Extracted) and the interconstruct correlations which indicates that more variance is shared between the construct and its indicators than with other constructs (Fornell & Larcker, 1981). Table 4 shows that the square roots of all the

Table 3. Reliability, descriptive statistics, and factor loadings

Construct (Sources) (Cronbach's alpha)	Measure	Mean	SD	Factor loading
Perceived Usefulness (Davis, 1989) (0.970)	Using the GSCMS in my job will help me to perform tasks quickly.	4.787	1.207	0.813
	Using the GSCMS will improve my working performance.	4.737	1.173	0.846
	Using the GSCMS in my job will increase productivity.	4.660	1.169	0.880
	Using the GSCMS will enhance my effectiveness in the job.	4.691	1.170	0.894
	Using the GSCMS will assist me to handle my job easily.	4.740	1.184	0.865
	The GSCMS is useful to my job.	4.927	1.136	0.810
Perceived Ease of Use (Davis, 1989) (0.956)	I believe learning how to operate the GSCMS will be easy for me.	4.739	1.028	0.846
	I can operate the GSCMS easily to complete my job.	4.620	1.054	0.879
	Interfaces of the GSCMS are clear and understandable.	4.704	1.067	0.825
	I can use the GSCMS skillfully.	4.507	1.035	0.859
	It is easy for me to become a skillful GSCMS user.	4.844	2.622	0.42
	I consider the GSCMS to be easy to operate.	4.676	1.020	0.812
Training (Amoako-Gyampah & Salam, 2004) (0.931)	The GSCMS training is comprehensive.	4.777	1.073	0.829
	My understanding of the GSCMS improved after receiving training.	4.765	1.083	0.821
	Training assists me to adopt the GSCMS with confidence.	4.698	1.041	0.753
	The length of training is adequate, and includes a detailed introduction to the GSCMS.	4.537	1.162	0.817
	Program instructors have sufficient knowledge to help me to understand the GSCMS.	4.805	1.109	0.816
Computer Anxiety (Heinssen et al., 1987) (0.950)	I am anxious about using computers.	2.704	1.432	0.909
	I am afraid that the computer will destroy my data if I press the wrong key.	2.822	1.409	0.897
	My fear of making irrecoverable mistakes makes me hesitant to use a computer.	2.510	1.423	0.945
	Computers scare me.	2.308	1.415	0.916
Computer Self-Efficacy (Venkatesh et al., 2003) (0.879)	I believe I can use the GSCMS to complete my job even without any instructions.	5.514	1.806	0.701
	With help, I can use the GSCMS to complete my job even when I encounter difficulties.	7.141	1.845	0.869
	I believe I can complete my job by using the GSCMS if I have sufficient time.	7.490	1.686	0.881
	I can complete my job by using the GSCMS if it contained a help systems.	7.280	1.755	0.875

continued on following page

Table 3. continued

Construct (Sources) (Cronbach's alpha)	Measure	Mean	SD	Factor loading
	I am satisfied with the information that I receive from the GSCMS.	4.587	0.936	0.672
User Satisfaction (Wixom & Todd, 2005; Palvia, 1996) (0.879)	I consider the GSCMS a success.	4.615	0.948	0.660
	I am satisfied with the GSCMS.	4.608	0.997	0.651
	I consider that the GSCMS fulfills my expectations.	4.538	0.988	0.633

Table 4. The square root of AVE values

Construct	Training	PU	PEOU	CA	CSE	SA
Training	**0.8857**					
PU	0.6032	**0.9333**				
PEOU	0.4989	0.5307	**0.8496**			
CA	-0.1334	-0.1357	-0.1472	**0.8373**		
CSE	0.1428	0.2218	0.2353	-0.3258	**0.8550**	
SA	0.7304	0.6920	0.5312	0.0109	0.1795	**0.9615**

Note:
1. *PU=Perceived Usefulness, PEOU=Perceived Ease of Use, CA=Computer Anxiety, SA=User Satisfaction*
2. *The diagonal elements (in bold) represent the square root of AVE.*

AVEs (i.e., the numbers on the diagonal) are greater than the correlations among constructs (i.e., the off-diagonal numbers), indicating satisfactory discriminant validity of all the constructs.

Hypothesis Testing

Multivariate regression analysis with the stepwise method was used to validate the hypothesized relationships among the research constructs. User satisfaction was set as the dependent variable, and the independent variables were perceived usefulness, perceived ease of use, training, computer self-efficacy, and computer anxiety. Multicollinearity was examined in the regression analysis using the variance inflation factor, which was below the common cutoff threshold of 10 (Hair et

al., 1998) for all constructs, indicating the absence of significant multicollinearity.

Four factors, perceived usefulness (H1), perceived ease of use (H2), training (H3), and computer anxiety (H4) were significant ($P < 0.05$), indicating that they affected user satisfaction with the GSCMS. Training explained most variance (53.03%) of user satisfaction, next perceived usefulness explained 9.75% variance, and computer anxiety was negative effect that accounted 1.51% variance, finally perceived ease of use accounted 0.85% variance. However, computer self-efficacy (H5) was not significantly related to user satisfaction. A total of 65.14% of the variance (adjusted R^2) was accounted for user satisfaction. The hypothesis testing results were summarized in Table 5. The analysis results will be discussed in next section.

Table 5. Results from regression testing

Independent Variable	Dependent Variable (Satisfaction)			
	Standardized Coefficient (Beta)	Significance	Variance Inflation Factor	Correlation
H1: Perceived Usefulness	0.326	0.000 *	1.770	Yes
H2: Perceived Ease of Use	0.127	0.035 *	1.505	Yes
H3: Training	0.468	0.000 *	1.693	Yes
H4: Computer Anxiety	−0.141	0.005 *	1.029	Yes
H5: Computer Self-Efficacy	0.057	0.277	1.180	No
R^2		0.661		
Adjusted R^2		0.651		

Note: *P < 0.05, indicating correlated factors

CONCLUSION AND DISCUSSIONS

This study reveals that perceived usefulness, perceived ease of use, training, and computer anxiety significantly affect user satisfaction with a GSCMS, with training being the most significant factor. GSCMSs are a new type of system for suppliers and not participating in their development. Thus, appropriate training programs can familiarize users with the functions and interface of a GSCMS so as to facilitate their operation of the system. This would also decrease the user perceptions of uncertainty when they encounter a new GSCMS, and lead to positive evaluations of the new system. The investigation by Yasin and Quigley (1994) into the viewpoints of chief executive officers on the effectiveness of information systems revealed that training decreases their anxiety about using information technology and helps them to understand the restrictions and potentiality of information technology. Moreover, William and David (1995) asserted that the training is strongly positively correlated with user satisfaction.

The EU RoHS Directive forces suppliers to search for a suitable new system that helps them to immediately conform to the regulations. The functions and interfaces of such a supply chain management system are expected to operate effectively and efficiently so as to meet the requirements of focal vendors. The results in perceived usefulness and perceived ease of use significantly influences user performance and satisfaction. As discussed earlier, the TAM has been widely and successfully adopted to predict the acceptance and usage of information systems. For example, Lin and Wu (2004) apply the TAM to the influence of end-user computing on small and medium enterprises in Taiwan. Haines and Andrew (1997) employ perceived usefulness and perceived ease of use in an exploration of the factors underpinning successful human resource management systems. Our research results similarly demonstrate the importance of user perceptions of usefulness and ease of use.

The results also show that computer anxiety is one of the significant factors affecting user satisfaction that employ a GSCMS. When adopting a new system, users will encounter both managerial and procedural changes. People instinctively tend to resist changes due to the associated anxiety. However, in our study we found that the level of suppliers had an average under 2.822 on the 7-point scale. The association between computer anxiety and user satisfaction shows that a lower computer anxiety brings higher supplier satisfaction.

Previous studies have found that computer self-efficacy is positively related to user satisfaction (e.g., Fagan et al., 2003-04), whereas in the present study we found no such relationship. According to Bandura (1997), self-efficacy improves after a new technology has actually been used, even when the users initially doubt their own ability to do this. Guskey and Tschannen-Moran (1988) also suggest that the introduction of a new technology can initially have a negative impact on users, but that their self-efficacy will improve gradually as they become accustomed to the new technology. Although computer self-efficacy did not have a significant effect on user satisfaction in our study, it is thought to affect user satisfaction after sufficient training and practical operation.

The EU is one of the most powerful economic entities in the world, and is also the main export area for Taiwan. Ever-increasing eco-awareness will mean that strict restrictions such as the RoHS Directive will increase the importance of GSCMSs in assisting suppliers. The results from this study also show that training is the most significant factor influencing supplier satisfaction with a GSCMS. Therefore, both the focal vendors and the system designers should provide training that is sufficient to increase user satisfaction of suppliers. Moreover, the results indicate that usefulness and ease of use are fundamental to the success of a system, and hence system designers must understand user requirements and the practical problems that they will encounter. With regard to computer anxiety, previous studies have indicated that people who are familiar with computers show more confidence and feel less anxiety when using computers (Coffin & MacIntyre, 1999; Loyd & Gressard, 1984;). Hence, this study argues that training is essential in order to decrease computer anxiety and promote satisfaction with a GSCMS amongst representatives of suppliers.

Finally, the use of GSCMSs is still in its infancy in Taiwan. The problems or the implications that

may occur after their adoption for suppliers are not addressed in present research. Future studies should aim to develop managerial and practical solutions to all the related problems. Besides, the condition and structure of industry in Taiwan may be specific to our study, and it should be careful to generalize the research results to other countries.

REFERENCES

Adamson, I., & Shine, J. (2003). Extending the new technology acceptance model to measure the end user information systems satisfaction in a mandatory environment: A bank's treasury. *Technology Analysis and Strategic Management, 15*(4), 441-455.

Agarwal, R. (2000). Individual acceptance of information technologies. In R. W. Zmud (Ed.), *Framing the domain of IT management* (pp. 85-104). Pinnaflex, Ohio.

Amoako-Gyampah, K., & Salam, A. F. (2004). An extension of the technology acceptance model in an ERP implementation environment. *Information and Management, 41*(6), 731-745.

Bailey, J., & Pearson, S. W. (1983). Development of a tool for measuring and analyzing computer user satisfaction. *Management Science, 29*(5), 530-545.

Bandura, A. (1986). *Social foundations of thought and action: A social cognitive theory.* Englewood, Cliffs NJ: Prentice-Hall.

Bandura, A. (1997). *Self-efficacy: The exercise of control.* New York: Freeman.

Bhattacherjee, A. (2001). Understanding information systems continuance: An expectation-confirmation model. *MIS Quarterly, 27*(3), 351-370.

Coffin, R. J., & MacIntyre, P. D. (1999). Motivational influences on computer-related affective states. *Computers in Human Behavior, 15*(5), 549-569.

Compeau, D. R., & Higgins, C. A. (1995). Application of social cognitive theory to training for computer skills. *Information Systems Research, 6*(2), 118-143.

Davis, F. D. (1989). Perceived usefulness, perceived ease of use, and user acceptance of information technology. *MIS Quarterly, 13*(3), 319-340.

DeLone, W. H., & McLean, E. R. (2003). The DeLone and McLean model of information systems success: A ten-year update. *Journal of Management Information Systems, 19*(4), 9-30.

DeLone, W. H., & McLean, E. R. (1992). Information systems success: The quest for the dependent variable. *Information Systems, 3*(1), 1, 60-95.

Epoch Times International (2005). *RoHS's influences on the promotion of electrical and electronic enterprises in Taiwan.* Retrieved July 30, 2007, from http://www.epochtw.com/5/5/23/2824.htm, Accessed July 11, 2006.

Fagan, M. H., Neill, S., & Wooldridge, B. R. (2003-04). An empirical investigation into the relationship between computer self-efficacy, anxiety, experience, support and usage. *The Journal of Computer Information Systems, 44*(2), 95-110.

Faisal, M. N., Banwet, D. K., & Shankar, R. (2006). Mapping supply chains on risk and customer sensitivity dimensions. *Industrial Management and Data Systems, 106*(6), 878-895.

Fornell, C., & Larcker, F. (1981). Evaluating structural equation models with unobservable variables and measurement error. *Journal of Marketing Research, 18*(1), 39-50.

Guskey, T. (1988). Teacher efficacy, self-concept, and attitudes toward the implementation of instructional innovation. *Teaching and Teacher Education, 4*(1), 63-69.

Haines, V. Y., & Andre, P. (1997). Conditions for successful human resource information systems. *Human Resource Management, 36*(2), 261-275.

Hair, J. F., Anderson, R. E., Tatham, R. L., & Black, W. C. (1998). *Multivariate data analysis* (5th ed.). Prentice-Hall.

Harrison, A. W., & Rainer, R. K. (1996). A general measure of user computer satisfaction. *Computers in Human Behavior, 12*(1), 79-92.

Heinssen, R. K., Glass, C. R., & Knight, L. A. (1987). Assessing computer anxiety: Development and validation of the computer anxiety rating scale. *Computers and Human Behavior, 3*(1), 49-59.

Henry, J. W., & Stone, R. W. (1994). A structural equation model of end-user satisfaction with a computer-based medical information system. *Information Resources Management Journal, 7*(3), 21–33.

Henry, J. W., & Stone, R. W. (1995). Computer self-efficacy and outcome expectancy: The effects on the end-user's job satisfaction. *Computer Personnel, 16*, 15–34.

Hsu, L-L. (2005). SCM system effects on performance for interaction between supplierss and buyers. *Industrial Management and Data Systems, 105*(7), 857-875.

Hsu, M., Chiu, C., & Fu, T. (2004). Determinants of continued use of the www: an integration of two theoretical models. *Industrial Management and Data Systems, 104*(9), 766-775.

Hsu, M. H., & Chiu, C. M. (2004). Predicting electronic service continuance with a decomposed theory of planned behaviour. *Behaviour and Information Technology, 23*(5), 359-373.

Igbaria, M. (1992). An examination of microcomputer usage in Taiwan. *Information and Management, 22*(1), 19-28.

Igbaria, M., Guimaraes, T., & Davis, G. B. (1995). Testing the determinants of microcomputer usage via a structural equation model. *Journal of Management Information Systems, 11*(4), 87-114.

Ives, B., Olson, M. H., & Baroudi, J. J. (1983). The measurement of user information satisfaction. *Communications of the ACM, 26*(1), 785-793.

Lee, S. M., Kim, Y. R., & Lee, J. (1995). An empirical study of the relationships among end-user information systems acceptance training, and effectiveness. *Journal of Management Information Systems, 12*(2), 189-202.

Loyd, C. P., & Gressard, B. H. (1984). Reliability and factorial validity of computer attitude scales. *Education and Psychological Measurement, 44*(2), 501–505.

Mahmood, M. A., Burn, J. M., Gemoets, L. A., & Jacquez, C. (2003). Variables affecting information technology end-user satisfaction: A meta-analysis of the empirical literature. *International Journal of Human-Computer Studies, 52*(4), 751-771.

Marakas, G. M., Yi, M. Y., & Johnson, R. D. (1998). The multilevel and multifaceted character of computer self-efficacy: Toward clarification of the construct and an integrative framework for research. *Information Systems Research, 9*(2), 126-163.

May, R. (1996). *The meaning of anxiety.* New York: Norton and Company.

Olorunniwo, F., & Hartfield, T. (2001). Strategic partnering when the supply base is limited: A case study. *Industrial Management and Data Systems, 101*(1), 47-52.

Palvia, P. C. (1996). A model and instrument for measuring small business user satisfaction with information technology. *Information and Management, 31*(3), 151-163.

Park, D., & Krishnan, H. A. (2005). Gender differences in supply chain management practices. *Internal Journal Management and Enterprise Development, 2*(1), 27-37.

Saga, V. L., & Zmud, R. W. (1994). The nature and determinants of IT acceptance, routinization, and infusion. In L. Levine (Ed.), *Diffusion transfer and implementation of information technology* (pp. 67-86). Amsterdam: Elsevier Science.

Venkatesh, V., Morris, M. G., Davis, G. B., & Davis, F. D. (2003). User acceptance of information technology: Toward a unified view. *MIS Quarterly, 27*(3), 425-478.

Webster, J. (1998). Desktop videoconferencing: Experiences of complete users, wary users, and non-users. *MIS Quarterly, 22*(3), 257-286.

Whitten, D. (2004). User information satisfaction scale reduction: Application in an IT outsourcing environment. *Journal of Computer Information Systems, 45*(2), 17-26.

William, L., Gardner III, & David, B. G. (1995). Information system training, usage, and satisfaction and exploratory of the hospital industry. *Management Communication Quarterly, 9*(1), 78-114.

Wu, W. H. (1999). *A study of learner self-regulation in computer skill training: An application of social cognitive theory.* Unpublished doctoral dissertation of University of National Sun Yat-Sen in Taiwan.

Yasin, M. M., & Quigley, J. V. (1994). The utility of information systems: Views of CEOs and information system executives. *Industrial Management and Data Systems, 94*(5), 25-29.

Zviran, M., Pliskin, N., & Levin, R. (2005). Measuring user satisfaction and perceived usefulness in the ERP context. *Journal of Computer Information Systems, 45*(3), 43-52.

This work was previously published in the International Journal of Information Systems and Supply Chain Management, Vol. 1, Issue 1, edited by J. Wang, pp. 66-79, copyright 2008 by IGI Publishing (an imprint of IGI Global).

Chapter 12
Cooperative Pricing Under Forecasting Sharing in the Manufacturer–E–Retailer Supply Chain

Ruiliang Yan
Virginia State University, USA

Sanjoy Ghose
University of Wisconsin - Milwaukee, USA

ABSTRACT

With the rapid development of the Internet, many retailers and individuals nowadays use this technology to engage in direct e-retailing sales. In this article, we investigate the value of demand-forecast information sharing in a manufacturer-e-retailer supply chain. The value of market information depends not only on its accuracy, but also on the e-retailer's market power and the product's Web compatibility. We develop a theoretical approach to examine the value of information sharing for the manufacturer and the e-retailer first, and then we further check to see how information sharing is moderated by the e-retailer's market share and the product's e-market-base demand. Our results suggest that under some conditions, both the manufacturer and the e-retailer can be better off from information sharing. Especially when the e-retailer's market share is larger and the product's e-market-base demand is higher, information sharing is more valuable for the supply chain players. Using our analysis findings, we indicate marketing strategies that the manufacturer and the e-retailer may want to adopt.

INTRODUCTION

The surge in the growth of information systems over the past two decades has significantly reshaped supply chain management and given businesses an unprecedented marketing opportunity. In the United States, business-to-consumer (B2C) sales over the Internet are increasing at an unprecedented rate. The Census Bureau of the Department of Commerce estimated that retail e-commerce sales for the first quarter of 2006 were $25.2 billion, a 7% increase from the first quarter of 2005. In the same period, the total retail sales increased by only 3.2% and retail sales over the Internet for the whole year of 2005 totaled $87.7 billion. The growth rate is going to increase even further in the near future. As a result, the growth of the Internet has made it attractive for many retailers or individuals to engage in e-commerce sales, especially for those products that are more suitable for selling through the e-market (W. Y. Chiang, Chhajed, & Hess, 2003).

The significant benefit of information systems is to let firms share information (i.e., demand-forecast information, sales trends and data, etc.) quickly and conveniently so that market information can be more accurate and efficient in a supply chain. Information sharing can effectively improve the efficiency of supply chain management. The manufacturer and the retailer can use the information systems to respond to customer demand more quickly and improve the accuracy of demand forecasts by information sharing. There is obviously no doubt that a good information base helps decision making. But can information sharing within a supply chain increase the profits of both the manufacturer and the retailer?

In our research, we focus on the value of demand-forecast information sharing in a supply chain consisting of a manufacturer and an e-retailer (e-commerce retailer). We use a game theoretical model to specifically study the following questions. Under what conditions can both the manufacturer and the e-retailer benefit from information sharing? Under what condition is only one player better off and the other worse off from information sharing? When the market share of the e-retailer or the e-market-base demand of the product category is larger, what is the value of information sharing? Based on our results, we suggest marketing strategies for the supply chain players (the manufacturer and the e-retailer) to adopt. Findings from our research should be of value when the manufacturer and the e-retailer make plans on how to improve market information accuracy, which can then be transmitted to their profits.

The rest of our article is organized as follows. The second section provides a summary of the relevant literature. Then, the third section presents our modeling framework, while the section after that analyzes the cases of no information sharing and information sharing for the manufacturer and the e-retailer under the Stackelberg game. The fifth section studies the value of information sharing for the manufacturer and the e-retailer and how the value of information sharing is further moderated by the market share of the online retailer and the e-market-demand base of the product category. We present our numerical analysis next, and conclusions and managerial implications are presented in the final section. All relevant proofs are given in the appendices for clarity of exposition.

LITERATURE REVIEW

Given the increasing importance of information, researchers have looked at the subject of information from a variety of perspectives. Raju and Roy (2000) provide a good summary of this by discussing the studies done by, among others, Hilton (1981), Vives (1984), Morrison and Schmittlein (1991), Blattberg and Hoch (1990), Padmanabhan and Rao (1993), Day (1990), Glazer (1991), Sarvary and Parker (1997). Raju and Roy themselves examined the impact of market information on firm performance. Their results showed that information is always more valuable in more competitive industries and for larger firms. Gavirneni, Kapuscinski, and Tayur (1999) studied partial and complete shared information on inventory policies between a supplier and a retailer, and they estimated the savings of the supplier and addressed when information sharing was more valuable. Bourland, Powell, and Pyke (1996) showed that both the manufacturer and the retailer would profit from information sharing when their ordering cycles were significantly out of phase. Gavirneni, Kapuscinski and Tayur (1999) studied partial and complete shared information of inventory policies between a supplier and a retailer; they estimated the savings of the supplier due to information sharing and indicated when information sharing was more valuable. Cachon and Fisher (2000) investigated the value of information sharing between one supplier and multiple identical retailers. They found that information sharing led to savings due to lead time and batch size reduction. Lee, So, and Tang (2000) looked at the value of information sharing in a two-level supply chain and found that information sharing can provide significant inventory reduction and cost savings. Corbett, Zhou, and Tang (2004) found that it is better for the supplier to offer a two-part contract to the buyer once there is full information sharing. Cheng and Wu (2005) researched the impact of information sharing in a two-level supply chain with multiple retailers. They showed that the manufacturer always benefits from information sharing. Huang, Chu, and Lee (2006) examined strategic information sharing in a supply chain. They showed that reducing the cost of sharing information and increasing the profit margin of either the retailer or the vendor will facilitate information sharing. Li and Lin (2006) discussed information sharing and information quality in supply chain management. They showed that trust and shared vision between supply chain partners have a positive influence on information sharing and information quality, but supplier uncertainty has a negative influence.

W. K. Chiang and Feng (2007) found that the manufacturer benefits more from information sharing than retailers when supply uncertainty and demand volatility are present.

However, so far, most research on information sharing has focused solely on inventory and logistics and did not consider the important effects of the e-retailer's market power and the product category on the value of information sharing. Our article addresses this limitation and fills a conceptual and practical gap for a structured analysis of the current state of knowledge regarding the value of information sharing between the manufacturer and the e-retailer. Our objective is mainly to show the strategic value of information sharing for the supply chain players when the market power of the e-retailer is larger and the product category is more compatible with the e-market. In the business market, the supply chain consisting of Amazon.com and its manufacturers is a typical example for our research.

MODEL FRAMEWORK

In this section, we consider a simple supply chain made up of one manufacturer and one e-retailer. We assume that the manufacturer is the Stackelberg leader and the e-retailer is the follower. We also assume that both the manufacturer and the retailer choose their optimal decision variables to optimize their profits (both the manufacturer and the retailer are risk neutral). To derive the optimal decisions, we use the Bayesian-Nash equilibrium (Harsanyi, 1968), each player's strategy is a best response to its conjecture about the behavior of the rival, and the conjectures are right in the equilibrium.

In the Stackelberg competition model, the manufacturer acting as market leader moves first and sets its wholesale price to optimize its own profit. Subsequently, the e-retailer acts as the market follower and sets a price to maximize its profit. The demand is uncertain. Each supply chain player (the manufacturer and the e-retailer) obtains a forecast about the base level of demand and uses this forecast in setting its price.

Specifically, we assume that the e-retailer has some market power and has a downward-sloping demand function given by

$$d = \theta\,(\lambda\,a - bp), \qquad (1)$$

where $0 < \theta < 1$ and θ is the market share accounted for by the e-retailer and represents its market power in the retailing market. In other words, the larger θ is, the more powerful the e-retailer is. For example, since the market share of Amazon.com is larger than the market share of Overstock.com, it is more powerful than Overstock.com. The variable a is the primary demand, and λ is the product's Web fit, where $0 < \lambda \leq 1$ (Kacen, Hess, & Chiang, 2002). Products that are perfectly suitable for selling through the e-market have product Web fit equal to one (e.g., books, CDs, music, airline tickets, etc.) and those that are less suitable for selling through the e-market have lower product Web fit (e.g., food, vegetables,

etc.). Thus, $\lambda\,a$ represents the product's e-market-base demand. It is obvious that when the value of the product's Web fit is larger, the product's e-market-base demand is greater. The variable p is the retail price charged by the e-retailer and b is the price sensitivity of the retailer's market demand to its retail price. An information forecast diagram is shown in Figure 1.

In order to capture uncertainty in demand due to evolving market conditions, we assume like Raju and Roy (2000) that the market-base demand of a product in the e-market, a, is a random variable, where $a = \overline{a} + e$, and e is normally distributed with mean zero and variance σ_0^2, that is, $\mathrm{var}(a - \overline{a}) = \sigma_0^2$. We confine the demand uncertainty to an additive intercept term. We also assume that the market shares do not change randomly and the coefficients do not change over time. In other words, the slope parameters are stable and known (Malueg & Tsutsui, 1996). Each supply chain player gives a forecast about a. The manufacturer's forecast of a is f_1, and the e-retailer's forecast is f_2. We assume that:

Figure 1. The information forecast diagram

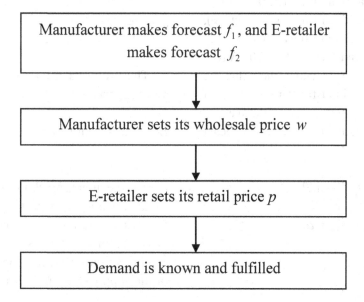

265

$$f_1 = a + \varepsilon_1, \quad (2)$$

$$f_2 = a + \varepsilon_2, \quad (3)$$

where ε_1 and ε_2 are normally distributed, independent of the base level of demand a, with mean zero and variance σ_1^2 and σ_2^2, respectively. The precision of forecast (or forecasting error) is given as σ_i^2. A higher (lower) variance implies a less (more) accurate forecast. The forecast errors ε_1 and ε_2 could be correlated. The extent of correlation (ρ) depends on the data and methodology used by the supply chain players in their forecasting process. Similar data and information resources will result in higher correlation between forecasts. Therefore, we further assume that the forecast errors ε_1 and ε_2 follow a bivariate normal distribution. The covariance matrix of forecast errors is represented by

$$\Sigma \begin{bmatrix} \sigma_1^2 & \rho\sigma_1\sigma_2 \\ \rho\sigma_1\sigma_2 & \sigma_2^2 \end{bmatrix}.$$

We assume that the covariance is not greater than the variance, that is, $\rho\sigma_1\sigma_2 \leq \sigma_1^2$ and $\rho\sigma_1\sigma_2 \leq \sigma_2^2$. All parameters of the model, except the forecasts, are common knowledge to the supply chain players.

Under the normality assumption (as well as the generalized linear information structure), conditional expectations are linear. We use the results from Cyert and DeGroot (1970), Vives (1984), and Winkler (1981), which show that the expected value of the industry demand given a forecast f_i is a convex combination of the average demand (the prior), $\bar{a}$, and the observed forecast f_i. Specifically, we have

$$E(a \mid f_i) = (1 - t_i)\bar{a} + t_i f_i, i = 1, 2, \quad (4)$$

$$E(a \mid f_1, f_2) = I\bar{a} + Jf_1 + Kf_2 = a_s, \quad (5)$$

where

$$I = \frac{(1-\rho^2)\sigma_1^2\sigma_2^2}{(1-\rho^2)\sigma_1^2\sigma_2^2 + \sigma_0^2(\sigma_1^2 + \sigma_2^2 - 2\rho\sigma_1\sigma_2)},$$

$$J = \frac{\sigma_0^2(\sigma_2^2 - \rho\sigma_1\sigma_2)}{(1-\rho^2)\sigma_1^2\sigma_2^2 + \sigma_0^2(\sigma_1^2 + \sigma_2^2 - 2\rho\sigma_1\sigma_2)},$$

$$K = \frac{\sigma_0^2(\sigma_1^2 - \rho\sigma_1\sigma_2)}{(1-\rho^2)\sigma_1^2\sigma_2^2 + \sigma_0^2(\sigma_1^2 + \sigma_2^2 - 2\rho\sigma_1\sigma_2)},$$

and

$$t_i = \frac{\sigma_0^2}{\sigma_i^2 + \sigma_0^2}, i = 1, 2.$$

The variable t_i is referred to as the forecast accuracy parameter and it is inversely proportional to the error variance σ_i^2. As σ_i^2 changes from 0 to ∞, the forecast goes from being perfectly informative to being not informative at all as t_i changes from 1 to 0.

As σ_0^2 is the variance of the random demand intercept, the conditional expectation of one player's forecast given the other player's forecast can be expressed as follows:

$$E(f_j \mid f_i) = (1 - d_i)\bar{a} + d_i f_i, i = 1, 2; j = 3 - i, \quad (6)$$

where

$$d_i = \frac{\sigma_0^2 + \rho\sigma_1\sigma_2}{\sigma_0^2 + \sigma_i^2}, i = 1, 2.$$

The proposed information model structure also suggests that

$$E[(f_j - a)^2] = E[(e + \varepsilon_i)^2] = \sigma_0^2 + \sigma_i^2, i = 1, 2. \quad (7)$$

The manufacturer chooses its wholesale price to maximize its own expected profit and the retailer updates its retail price to maximize its expected profit. Optimal decisions about pricing would be conditional on the forecast (the private information of the supply chain player) and known demand function parameters. Thus, the demands and the resulting profits would also be conditional on the forecasts and other known parameters. In the next section, we model a Stackelberg-type game played by the supply chain players where they make the decisions sequentially and find optimal solutions to the model.

ANALYSIS

The standard Stackelberg game model is a model of duopoly in economics. In game theory terms, the players of this game are a leader and a follower and they compete with each other. The leader moves first, choosing a price to maximize its profit. The follower observers the leader's choice and then picks a price to maximize its profit. However, in this article, just as Jeuland and Shugan (1983), W. Y. Chiang et al. (2003), and Raju and Zhang (2005) did in their research, we modify this standard Stackelberg game model and provide a nonstandard application for our research so that we can make use of it in a supply chain context. Therefore, the manufacturer and the retailer make decisions sequentially in this game. The retailer (market follower) maximizes its profits given its forecast and the manufacturer's wholesale price (market leader). The manufacturer then incorporates this best-response retail price of the retailer in its expected profit function, and given its own forecast, chooses a wholesale price to maximize its profit. For this type of game, we develop optimal policies under two scenarios: (a) when forecast information is not shared between the manufacturer and the retailer, and (b) when the forecast information is shared between the manufacturer and the retailer. We then compare these results to derive the value of information sharing for the supply chain players.

No Information Sharing

In this case, we assume that the manufacturer and the e-retailer maximize their respective expected profits by choosing optimal pricing policies. Thus, the expected profit, conditional on their respective forecasts, can be expressed as follows:

$$E[\pi_1^N \,|f_1] = E[\theta(w-c)\,(\lambda a - bp)\,|f_1] \qquad (8)$$

$$E[\pi_2^N \,|f_2] = E[\theta(p-w)\,(\lambda a - bp)\,|f_2], \qquad (9)$$

where c is the product unit cost and w is the manufacturer's whole price. The variables π_1^N and π_2^N denote the manufacturer's profit and the e-retailer's profit under no information sharing, respectively. Since the manufacturer is the Stackelberg leader and the retailer is the follower, we derive the optimal values, which are summarized in Theorem 1. Proof is given in Appendix 1.

Theorem 1: *The Bayesian Stackelberg equilibrium pricing structures in the non-information-sharing setting are given by*

$$w^N = \frac{\lambda a_{rS} + bc}{2b}$$

$$p^N = \frac{\lambda(2a_S + a_{rS}) + bc}{4b}.$$

The corresponding expected profits are given as

$$E[\pi_1^N] = \frac{\theta\,(\lambda(2a_S - a_{rS}) - bc)(\,\lambda a_{rS} - bc)}{8b}$$

$$E[\pi_2^N] = \frac{\theta\,(\lambda(2a_S - a_{rS}) - bc)^2}{16b},$$

where $a_S = \bar{I}a + Jf_1 + Kf_2$, $a_{rS} = \bar{I}a + Jf_1 + Kf_2((1 - d_1)\bar{a}\ d_1f_1)$.

From the results in Theorem 1, it is shown that the optimal wholesale price for the manufacturer is obtained by using only the manufacturer's forecast. The e-retailer, on the other hand, has knowledge of the manufacturer's forecast before making its price decisions. The results in Theorem 1 show that the manufacturer's wholesale price is increasing with f_1 and the e-retailer's retail price is increasing with f_1 and f_2. This means that the more optimistic the manufacturer or the e-retailer feels about the product's e-market-base demand, the higher a price it will set. Next, we compare these optimal strategies with those using another case in which the manufacturer and the e-retailer share their forecast information with each other.

Information Sharing

In this situation, the manufacturer and the e-retailer share the forecasts with each other before marking their respective optimal decisions. Thus, the expected profits of the supply chain players are

$$E[\pi_1^S \,|f_1,f_2] = E[\theta(w-c)\,(\lambda a - bp)\,|f_1,f_2] \tag{10}$$

$$E[\pi_2^S \,|f_1,f_2] = E[\theta(w-c)\,(\lambda a - bp)\,|f_1,f_2], \tag{11}$$

where π_1^S and π_2^S denote the manufacturer profit and the e-retailer profit, respectively, under information sharing with each other. We derive the optimal Stackelberg values, which are summarized in Theorem 2. Proof is given in Appendix 2.

Theorem 2: *The Bayesian Stackelberg equilibrium pricing structures in the information-sharing setting are given by*

$$w^S = \frac{\lambda a_S + bc}{2b}$$

$$p^S = \frac{3\lambda a_S + bc}{4b}.$$

The corresponding expected profits are given as

$$E[\pi_1^S] = \frac{\theta\,(\lambda a_S - bc)^2}{8b}$$

$$E[\pi_2^S] = \frac{\theta\,(\lambda a_S - bc)^2}{16b}.$$

The results in Theorem 2 also show that under the information-sharing setting, if the manufacturer or the e-retailer is more optimistic about the product's e-market-base demand, higher prices will be set.

VALUE OF INFORMATION SHARING

In order to examine how information sharing affects the profits of the manufacturer and the e-retailer, we compare each player's expected profit without information sharing in Theorem 1 with their expected profits with information sharing in Theorem 2. Then we obtain

$$E[\pi_1^S] - E[\pi_1^N] = \frac{\theta\lambda^2 (a_S - a_{rS})^2}{8b} > 0 \tag{12}$$

$$E[\pi_2^S] - E[\pi_2^N] = \frac{\theta\lambda(\,\lambda(3a_S - a_{rS}) - 2bc)(a_{rS} - a_S)}{16b}. \tag{13}$$

Equations 12 and 13 show that when $a_S = a_{rS}$, the Nash equilibrium of this Bayesian game (i.e., any given game with incomplete information is equivalent to a certain game with complete information; Harsanyi, 1968) is reached. In other words, when the manufacturer's expectation of the e-retailer's forecast is equal to the e-retailer's actual forecast, the Nash equilibrium can be reached.

Furthermore, from Equations 12 and 13, we can derive Proposition 1 as follows.

Proposition 1: *The manufacturer always benefits from information sharing. However, the e-retailer only benefits from information sharing under the condition of*

$$(a_{rS} - a_S)(\lambda(3\,a_S - a_{rS}) - 2bc) > 0. \tag{14}$$

Proposition 1 shows some important implications. The value of information sharing to the manufacturer is intuitive. The rationale is that under information sharing, the manufacturer acting as leader has the e-retailer's forecast information, thus the manufacturer can benefit from the additional information to make an optimal wholesale pricing policy. Therefore, the manufacturer should actively cooperate with the e-retailer to pursue information sharing under any circumstances, even if the manufacturer needs to make some side payment to the e-retailer in order to motivate the e-retailer to share the forecasts. Our result in Proposition 1 is consistent with results of a prior study (W. K. Chiang & Feng, 2007).

However, our Proposition 1 also suggests that the e-retailer might not profit from information sharing. The rationale is that the manufacturer uses the information strategically to maximize its own profit. Equation 14 shows that a_{rS} must be larger than a_S or $E[f_2|f_1] > f_2$, then the information sharing equilibrium can be reached. In other words, the manufacturer's expectation of the e-retailer's forecast must be higher than the e-retailer's actual forecast. The rationale is that under Equation 14, the manufacturer overestimates the e-retailer's forecast and would like to set a higher wholesale price in the non-information-sharing setting. The e-retailer, in turn, then will set a higher retail price resulting from a higher wholesale price charged, which thus leads to decreased demand at the e-retailer. This will lead to decreased profits for both the manufacturer and the e-retailer. Therefore, when the e-retailer shares forecasts with the manufacturer, the manufacturer's expectation of the retailer's forecast reduces, which leads to reduced charge on the wholesale price. The e-retailer then profits from the reduced wholesale price. Thus, under Equation 14, the e-retailer would always like to share its forecast with the manufacturer without any side payment. However, when the manufacturer's expectation of the e-retailer's forecast is lower than the e-retailer's actual forecast or $E[f_2|f_1] < f_2$, the manufacturer will set a lower wholesale price in the non-information-sharing case. If the e-retailer shares its forecast with the manufacturer, the manufacturer would charge a higher wholesale price, which then in turn decreases the e-retailer profit.

Effect of E-Retailer's Market Share on the Value of Information Sharing

Furthermore, in order to examine the effect of an e-retailer's market share on the contribution of information sharing for each player, we differentiate $\partial(E[\pi_i^S] - E[\pi_i^N])$ ($i = 1, 2$) with respect to θ.

$$\frac{\partial(E[\pi_i^S] - E[\pi_i^N])}{\partial\theta}$$

($i = 1, 2$) is the impact of a change in the e-retailer's market share on the value of information sharing for each player. Therefore, from our analysis, we come up with Proposition 2 as follows.

Proposition 2: *When Equation 14 is satisfied, the value of information sharing for each supply chain player increases with the e-retailer's market share, θ.*

Proof. Proof is given in Appendix 3

Proposition 2 shows that when Equation 14 is satisfied, both supply chain players (the manufacturer and the e-retailer) benefit more from information sharing when the e-retailer's market share is larger. The rationale is intuitive that larger market share contributes more to the firm's profit, and thus information sharing is more valuable to both the manufacturer and the e-retailer when θ is larger.

Effect of Product Web Fit on the Value of Information Sharing

To investigate how product Web fit affects the worth of information sharing for each player, we differentiate $\partial(E[\pi_i^S] - E[\pi_i^N])$ ($i = 1, 2$) with respect to λ and obtain Proposition 3.

Proposition 3: *When Equation 14 is satisfied, the value of information sharing for each player increases with the product Web fit* λ.

Proof. Proof is given in Appendix 4.

Proposition 3 shows the important implication that information sharing is more valuable to supply chain players when the product is more compatible with the e-market.

NUMERICAL ANALYSIS

While our findings in the propositions can be derived analytically, the analytical expressions are too complex to provide meaningful insight. Thus, we now present numerical analysis to illustrate the magnitude of manufacturer and e-retailer profits under the cases of no information sharing and information sharing, and the impact of key parameters on the profits of the manufacturer and e-retailer as well as on the value of information sharing. In our simulation, we use the following parameter values: $b = 1$, $c = 10$, $\lambda = 0.8$, $\sigma_0 = 10$, and $\rho = 0.1$. We vary the values of θ, $\bar{a}$, σ_1, and σ_2 using the following data ranges.

$\theta \in \{0, 0.1, 0.2, 0.3, 0.4, 0.5, 0.6, 0.7, 0.8, 0.9, 1.0\}$

$\bar{a} \in \{100, 200, 300, 400, 500, 600, 700, 800, 900, 1000\}$

$\sigma_1 \in \{1, 2, 3, 4, 5, 6, 7, 8, 9, 10\}$

$\sigma_2 \in \{1, 2, 3, 4, 5, 6, 7, 8, 9, 10\}$

When each set of parameters is analyzed, we assume that information sharing occurs only under Equation 14.

Effect of E-Retailer's Market Share, θ

The impacts of the e-retailer's market share on the profits of the manufacturer and the e-retailer are shown in Figure 2. Since the manufacturer acts as the Stackelberg leader, its profit is always higher than the e-retailer's profit in this supply chain. Figure 2 shows that both the manufacturer and the e-retailer benefit from information sharing. Especially for the e-retailer, information sharing is more valuable (the gap between the *information sharing* curve and *no information sharing* curve is larger) when the e-retailer's market share is larger.

Effect of Product's E-Market-Base Demand, $\lambda\bar{a}$

The impacts of the product's e-market-base demand on the profits of the manufacturer and the e-retailer are shown in Figure 3. We saw in Figure 2 that the manufacturer profit is higher than the e-retailer's profit, and both the manufacturer and the e-retailer benefit from information sharing. These results hold in Figure 3 as well and the reasons are the same. Furthermore, Figure 3 shows that to the e-retailer, information sharing is more valuable (the gap between the *information sharing* curve and *no information sharing* curve is larger) when the product's e-market-base demand is larger.

Effect of Manufacturer Forecasting Accuracy, σ_1

The impacts of the manufacturer forecasting accuracy on each supply chain player's profit are shown in Figure 4. The manufacturer's profit is also higher than that of the e-retailer for all values of σ_1, the standard deviation of forecast error. The

Figure 2. Impact of e-retailer's market share on supply chain players' profits

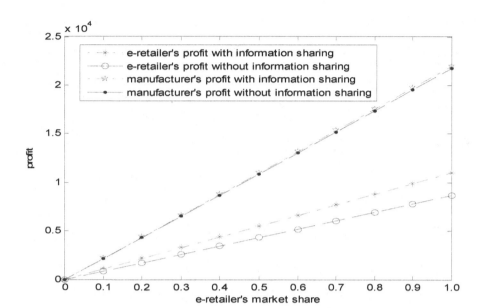

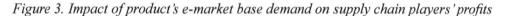

Figure 3. Impact of product's e-market base demand on supply chain players' profits

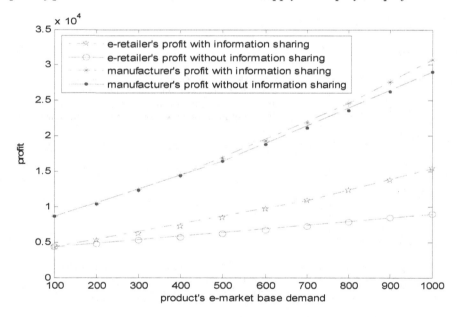

reason is similar to that discussed under "Effect of E-Retailer's Market Share, θ."

In Figure 4, we also observe that the profits as well as the value of information sharing (the difference between profits in the information-sharing case and non-information-sharing case)

increase for the manufacturer and the e-retailer as the forecast accuracy increases. This is to be expected because an improvement in forecast accuracy would reward the cooperation of both supply chain players. Particularly, the e-retailer can profit more from the information sharing.

Figure 4. Impact of manufacturer's forecasting accuracy on supply chain players' profits

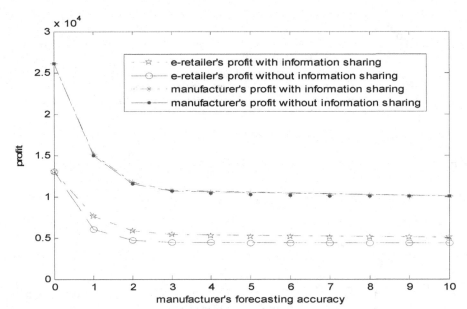

Figure 5. Impact of e-retailer's forecasting accuracy on supply chain players' profits

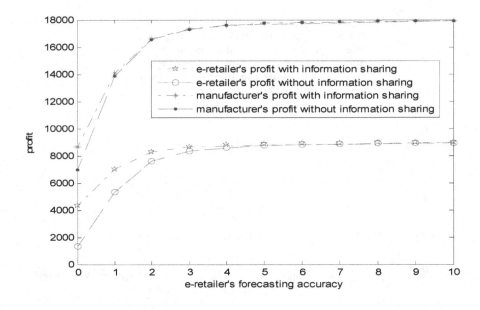

Effect of E-Retailer Forecasting Accuracy, σ_2

Figure 5 summarizes the impacts of σ_2, the e-retailer forecasting accuracy, on the performance of each supply chain player. While the profits of the manufacturer and the e-retailer increase, the value of information sharing decreases for both the manufacturer and the e-retailer when σ_2 increases. We also observe that information sharing becomes less valuable for both the manufacturer and the e-retailer when the e-retailer's forecast becomes inaccurate.

This is to be expected because a higher σ_2 reduces the e-retailer's forecasting accuracy.

CONCLUSION AND MANAGERIAL IMPLICATIONS

In this research, we investigate the value of information sharing in a simple manufacturer-e-retailer supply chain. We show that information sharing has a strategic impact on the manufacturer and the e-retailer. While the manufacturer always benefits from an information-sharing strategy, the e-retailer can be better off only when the manufacturer's expectation of the e-retailer's forecast is higher than the e-retailer's actual forecast. Thus, information sharing may occur under some limited conditions. If the manufacturer and e-retailer share the forecasts of information (when the manufacturer's expectation of the e-retailer's forecast is higher than the e-retailer's actual forecast), both can benefit from information sharing; when the e-retailer's market share is larger and the product's e-market-base demand is higher, they will profit even more. Our numerical analysis further shows that information sharing is very valuable to both the manufacturer and the e-retailer when the manufacturer's expectation of the e-retailer's forecast is higher than the e-retailer's actual forecast. The e-retailer always benefits more from information sharing when the accuracies of both the manufacturer and the e-retailer forecasts are high.

Possible future work extending from the present article can be accomplished in various ways. First, our analysis is based on a single-period model; therefore, for future potential research, it is a good idea to investigate how the sharing of information might work in a multiperiod environment. Second, in this research we assume that there is no cost of getting information. Thus, this research can also be extended to include other variables, such as information cost, in order to continue studying the influence and impacts of external factors relative to information accuracy. In the future, researchers can also use empirical data analysis to investigate the information-sharing model. Next, we summarize the managerial implications of our research.

In today's business environment, retailers and individuals are increasingly using the Internet to sell directly to customers. The rise of this e-commerce phenomenon provides a motivation for retailers to better understand the sales and profit implications of this new system. Since e-retailing is booming, it is managerially important to develop a mechanism for improving the accuracy of market information. This is an intuition-based conclusion. In our article, we use mathematical models to show that this intuition can be made objectively by using a demand-forecast information-sharing strategy (supply chain players share their forecasts with each other). We prove that by strategically employing such a strategy, both the manufacturer and the e-retailer can effectively improve their individual profits, especially when the e-retailer's market share is large (e.g., Amazon.com, Overstock.com, etc.) and the product's e-market-base demand (e.g., music, books, airline tickets, cell phones, etc.) is high. This finding is of immense managerial significance since both the manufacturer and the e-retailer, knowing that their profits would be enhanced, would feel the natural urge to improve the forecast accuracy by cooperatively sharing their demand forecasts. Thus, entities such as Amazon.com, Overstock.com, and other large e-retailers may want to actively pursue information sharing with their manufacturers, especially when the product category is more compatible with the e-retailing market.

REFERENCES

Blattberg, R. C., & Hoch, S. J. (1990). Database models and managerial intuition: 50% model + 50% manager. *Management Science, 36*(8), 887-899.

Bourland, K. E., Powell, S. G., & Pyke, D. F. (1996). Exploiting timely demand information to reduce inventories. *European Journal of Operational Research, 92*, 239-253.

Cachon, G., & Fisher, M. (2000). Supply chain inventory management and the value of shared information. *Management Science, 46*(8), 1032-1048.

Cheng, T. E. C., & Wu, Y. N. (2005). The impact of information sharing in a two-level supply chain with multiple retailers. *The Journal of the Operational Research Society, 56*(10), 1159.

Chiang, W. K., & Feng, Y. (2007). The value of information sharing in the presence of supply uncertainty and demand volatility. *International Journal of Production Research, 45*(6), 1429.

Chiang, W. Y., Chhajed, D., & Hess, J. D. (2003). Direct marketing, indirect profits: A strategic analysis of dual-channel supply chain design. *Management Science, 49*(1), 20.

Corbett, C. J., Zhou, D. M., & Tang, C. S. (2004). Designing supply contracts: Contract type and information asymmetry. *Management Science, 50*(4), 550-559.

Cyert, R. M., & DeGroot, M. H. (1970). Bayesian analysis and duopoly theory. *Journal of Political Economics, 78*(5), 1168-1184.

Day, G. S. (1990). *Market driven strategy: Processes for creating value.* New York: The Free Press.

Gavirneni, S., Kapuscinski, R., & Tayur, S. (1999). Value of information in capacitated supply chains. *Management Science, 45*(1), 16-24.

Glazer, R. (1991). Marketing in an information-intensive environment: Strategic implications of knowledge as an asset. *Journal of Marketing, 55*(10), 1-19.

Harsanyi, J. (1967). Games with incomplete information played by Bayesian players: Part I. The basic model. *Management Science, 14*(3), 159-182.

Harsanyi, J. (1968). Games with incomplete information played by Bayesian players: Part II. Bayesian equilibrium points. *Management Science, 14*(5), 320-334.

Hilton, R. W. (1981). The determinants of information value: Synthesizing some general results. *Management Science, 27*(1), 57-64.

Hung, W., Chu, J., & Lee, C. C. (2006). Strategic information sharing in a supply chain. *European Journal of Operational Research, 174*(3), 1567.

Jeuland, A. P., & Shugan, S. M. (1983). Managing channel profits. *Marketing Science, 2*(3), 239-272.

Kacen, J., Hess, J., & Chiang, W. K. (2002). *Bricks or clicks? Consumer attitudes toward traditional stores and online stores* (Working paper). Champaign, IL: University of Illinois.

Lee, H., So, V. K., & Tang, C. (2000). The value of information sharing in a two-level supply chain. *Management Science, 46*(5), 626-643.

Li, S. H., & Lin, B. S. (2006). Accessing information sharing and information quality in supply chain management. *Decision Support Systems, 42*(3), 1641.

Malueg, D. A., & Tsutsui, S. O. (1996). Duopoly information exchange: The case of unknown slope. *International Journal of Industrial Organization, 14*, 119-136.

McGee, J., & Prusak, L. (1993). *Managing information strategically.* Toronto, Canada: John Wiley Sons.

Morrison, D. G., & Schmittlein, D. C. (1991). How many forecasters do you really have? Mahalanobis provides the intuition for the surprising Clemen and Winkler result. *Operation Research, 39*(5), 519-523.

Padmanabhan, V., & Rao, R. C. (1993). Warranty policy and extended service contracts: Theory and application to automobiles. *Marketing Science, 12*(6), 230-247.

Raju, J. S., & Roy, A. (2000). Market information and firm performance. *Management Science, 46*(8), 1075-1084.

Raju, J. S., & Zhang, J. Z. (2005). Channel coordination in the presence of a dominant retailer. *Marketing Science, 24*(2), 254-304.

Sarvary, M., & Parker, P. M. (1997). Marketing information: A competitive analysis. *Marketing Science, 16*(1), 24-38.

Vives, X. (1984). Duopoly information equilibrium: Cournot and Bertrand. *Journal of Economic Theory, 34*, 71-94.

Winkler, R. (1981). Combining probability distributions from dependent information sources. *Management Science, 27*(4), 479-488.

APPENDIX 1

When there is no information sharing between the manufacturer and the e-retailer,

$$E[\pi_1^S | f_1] = E[\theta(w - c)(\lambda a - bp) | f_1]$$

$$E[\pi_2^S | f_2] = E[\theta(w - c)(\lambda a - bp) | f_2].$$

The conditional expectations and variances (Winkler, 1981) are shown below.

$$E(a | f_i) = (1 - t_i)\bar{a} + t_i f_i, i = 1, 2,$$

$$E(f_j | f_i) = (1 - d_i)\bar{a} + d_i f_i, i = 1, 2; j = 3 - i,$$

$$E(a | f_1, f_2) = I\bar{a} + Jf_1 + Kf_2, \text{ and}$$

$$E[(f_i - \bar{a})^2] = E[(e - \varepsilon_i)^2] = \sigma_0^2 + \sigma_i^2, i = 1, 2,$$

where

$$t_i = \frac{\sigma_0^2}{\sigma_i^2 + \sigma_0^2},$$

$$d_i = \frac{\sigma_0^2 + \rho\sigma_1\sigma_2}{\sigma_0^2 + \sigma_i^2}, i = 1, 2,$$

$$0 \le \rho\sigma_1\sigma_2 \le \sigma_i^2,$$

$$I = \frac{(1 - \rho^2)\sigma_1^2\sigma_2^2}{(1 - \rho^2)\sigma_1^2\sigma_2^2 + \sigma_0^2(\sigma_1^2 + \sigma_2^2 - 2\rho\sigma_1\sigma_2)},$$

$$J = \frac{\sigma_0^2(\sigma_2^2 - \rho\sigma_1\sigma_2)}{(1 - \rho^2)\sigma_1^2\sigma_2^2 + \sigma_0^2(\sigma_1^2 + \sigma_2^2 - 2\rho\sigma_1\sigma_2)}, \text{ and}$$

$$K = \frac{\sigma_0^2(\sigma_1^2 - \rho\sigma_1\sigma_2)}{(1 - \rho^2)\sigma_1^2\sigma_2^2 + \sigma_0^2(\sigma_1^2 + \sigma_2^2 - 2\rho\sigma_1\sigma_2)}.$$

In the Stackelberg game, the retailer can infer the manufacturer's forecast from the manufacturer's wholesale price even if there is no explicit information-sharing arrangement between the manufacturer and the retailer. Therefore, the retailer has the manufacturer's forecast information before it can set its optimal retail price, but the manufacturer does not have the same advantage. So, based on the above analysis, we first find the e-retailer's price,

$$\frac{\partial(E[\pi_2^N | f_1, f_2])}{\partial p} = 0.$$

Then we obtain $p = \dfrac{\lambda E(a \mid f_1, f_2) + bw}{2b}$,

substituting $p = \dfrac{\lambda E(a \mid f_1, f_2) + bw}{2b}$ into $E[\pi_1^N \mid f_1] = E[\theta(w - c)\,(\lambda a - bp) \mid f_1)]$ and letting

$$\frac{\partial(E[\pi_1^N \mid f_1])}{\partial w} = 0.$$

After some computation, we then obtain all of the results summarized in Theorem 1.

APPENDIX 2

When there is information sharing between the manufacturer and the e-retailer,

$$E[\pi_1^S \mid f_1, f_2] = E[\theta(p - w)\,(\lambda a - bp) \mid f_1, f_2]$$

$$E[\pi_2^S \mid f_1, f_2] = E[\theta(p - w)\,(\lambda a - bp) \mid f_1, f_2].$$

Similarly, we find the e-retailer's price first,

$$\frac{\partial(E[\pi_2^S \mid f_1, f_2])}{\partial p} = 0$$

then we obtain

$$p = \frac{\lambda E(a \mid f_1, f_2) + bw}{2b}$$

substituting

$$p = \frac{\lambda E(a \mid f_1, f_2) + bw}{2b}$$

into

$$E[\pi_2^S \mid f_1, f_2] = E[\theta(p - w)\,(\lambda a - bp) \mid f_1, f_2]$$

and letting

$$\frac{\partial(E[\pi_1^S \mid f_1, f_2])}{\partial w} = 0.$$

After some computation, we then obtain all of the results summarized in Theorem 2.

APPENDIX 3

When $(a_{rS} - a_S)(\lambda (3a_S - a_{rS}) - 2bc) > 0$

and

$$E[\pi_1^S] - E[\pi_1^N] = \frac{\theta\lambda(\lambda(3a_S - a_{rS}) - 2bc)(a_{rS} - a_S)}{16b} > 0$$

then

$$\frac{\partial(E[\pi_1^S] - E[\pi_1^N])}{\partial\theta} = \frac{\lambda(\lambda(3a_S - a_{rS}) - 2bc)(a_{rS} - a_S)}{16b} > 0$$

and

$$\frac{\partial(E[\pi_2^S] - E[\pi_2^N])}{\partial\theta} = \frac{\lambda^2(a_S - a_{rS})^2}{8} > 0$$

Therefore, Proposition 2 is proven.

APPENDIX 4

When $(a_{rS} - a_S)(\lambda (3a_S - a_{rS}) - 2bc) > 0$ and

$$E[\pi_1^S] - E[\pi_1^N] = \frac{\theta\lambda(\lambda(3a_S - a_{rS}) - 2bc)(a_{rS} - a_S)}{16b} > 0$$

then

$$\frac{\partial(E[\pi_1^S] - E[\pi_1^N])}{\partial\lambda} > 0$$

and

$$\frac{\partial(E[\pi_2^S] - E[\pi_2^N])}{\partial\lambda} > 0$$

Therefore, Proposition 3 is proven.

This work was previously published in the International Journal of Information Systems and Supply Chain Management, Vol. 1, Issue 2, edited by J. Wang, pp. 1-18, copyright 2008 by IGI Publishing (an imprint of IGI Global).

Chapter 13
Designing a Dynamic Buyer–Supplier Coordination Model in Electronic Markets Using Stochastic Petri Nets

Iraj Mahdavi
Mazandaran University of Science and Technology, Iran

Shima Mohebbi
K.N.Toosi University of Technology, Iran

Namjae Cho
Hanyang University, Korea

Mohammad Mahdi Paydar
Mazandaran University of Science and Technology, Iran

Nezam Mahdavi-Amiri
Sharif University of Technology, Iran

ABSTRACT

Functional relationship between supplier and buyer in an open market place leads to investigate the role of both quantifiable and non-quantifiable parameters in coordination mechanism with the aim of achieving higher performance in supply chain activities. Here, we develop a supply chain model and a new agent to analyze and simulate the players' behavior in the network. A cooperative game theory framework is utilized between buyer and supplier in order to increase the supply chain performance. The study is supported by presenting SC Net Optimizer as a tool for implementing the proposed coordination mechanism and evaluates the performance of the chain by simulation using stochastic Petri nets (SPNs). The model provides a more realistic optimization process by taking into consideration the dynamic information flow in an uncertainty environment.

INTRODUCTION

Globalization of market competition, reducing gap between products in terms of quality and performance are compelling the researchers to rethink about ways to manage business operations more efficiently and effectively (Sarmah, Acharya, & Goy, 2006). Electronic market has added a new dimension to the investigation of the business relationship. Electronic markets are defined as a network information system that serves as enabling infrastructure for buyers and sellers to exchange information, transact, and perform other related activities (Lancastre & Lages, 2006). The benefits of e-environments motivate the researchers to align and coordinate the business processes and activities of the net members dynamically as well as to improve the overall performance of supply chain strategies.

A supply chain can be viewed as a network with the entities possibly owned by owners in geographically diverse locations. Supply chain management (SCM) benefits from a variety of concepts that were developed in several different disciplines as marketing, information systems, economics, system dynamics, logistics, operational management, and operations research. In the literature, supply chains are usually described as multi-echelon inventory systems. However, most existing models can only describe a restricted class of supply chains with simplifications (Chen, Lionel, Chu, & Labadi, 2005). For instance, most multi-echelon inventory models don't explicitly take account of transportation operations and capacity constraints in supply chain by simply assuming a constant lead time between any two adjacent stocking locations (Tayur, Ganeshan, & Magazine, 1998). These models lack flexibility and generality in describing real-life supply chains. The coordination, however, is quite difficult because of the inherent complexity and uncertainty of the supply chains.

Here, we view the supply chain as a discrete event dynamic system (DEDS) and the research is geared towards providing the mathematical model that can describe material, information, and financial flows of a decentralized supply chain in an integrated way. This provides a tool, which can help industrial practitioners to model, evaluate performance, and optimize operational policies of their supply chains. In the next section, we provide a brief literature review about coordination mechanism.

The rest of this article is organized as follows: In background, the literature on coordination mechanism in both centralized and decentralized supply chain, game theory, agent, and simulation-based approaches in supply chain is reviewed. In the next section, system architecture, detailed mechanisms of the model and supply network strategy are presented. The scenario statement of small supply network section describes the details of implementing the simulation and develops the scenario design. Moreover, some discussions are provided for performance criteria of supply chain. Finally, the conclusions and some guidelines for future research are presented.

BACKGROUND

Coordination Mechanism

Several strategies such as credit option, buy/back return policies, quantity flexibility, and commitment of purchase quantity are used to align the business process and activities of diverse members of supply chains in terms of cost, response time, timely supply, and customer service (Sarmah et al., 2006). They particularly investigate SC coordination models that have used quantity discount as a coordination tool under deterministic environment, which has received much attention in production/operation management.

Supply chain coordination is concerned with the development and implementation of such strategies. There is no universal coordination strategy that will be efficient and effective for all supply chains as the performance of coordination strategy in SC characteristics is dependent. Totally, if the coordination is weak or does not exist at all, a conflict of objectives appears among different participants, who try to maximize personal profits. Besides, all the relevant information for some reason can be unreachable to chain participants, or the information can get deformed in non-linear activities of some parts of chain leading to irregular comprehension. All these lead to the bullwhip effect resulting from information disorder within a supply chain. Different chain phases have different calculations of demand quantity, and thus the longer the chain between the retailer and wholesaler the bigger the demand variation.

The advent of new information systems and technologies (IS and IT) such as electronic data interchange (EDI), Internet, intranet, and extranet, in particular, and inter-organizational communication and coordination mechanisms cast unprecedented opportunities for the integration of supply chains (Mahdavi et al., 2007). Thus, dynamic and timely information flow in an uncertain environment play important roles in coordination mechanisms. The interested reader may refer to Pant, Sethi, and Bhandari (2003) to have better understanding of creation and implementation of e-supply chain systems. The authors draw on research in the areas such as Web-based information systems and inter-organizational information systems. Averbakh and Xue (2007) also pointed to supply chain scheduling problems in off-line environment and proposed online environment, with unknown future.

An interesting development in the field of e-SCM is exploiting the benefits offered by co-ordination mechanism on functional relationship between buyer and supplier. The buyers in an electronic market are faced with supplier selection. Moreover, the presence of multiple suppliers will require the buyer to set-up a competitive mechanism for capacity allocation among the selected suppliers (Hazra & Mahadevan, 2006). In this case, a collaborative strategy that can allocate the benefits of coordination among the supply chain members should be applied to align the objectives of coordination. Such a system is regarded as a decentralized supply chain system.

Three dimensions are introduced by Li and Wang (2007) on which the operational activities of a supply chain can be coordinated in order to maximize system profits. First, order quantities that optimize individual performance are often not able to optimize system performance. There is a vast literature on discount policies that suppliers can use to entice buyers to increase their order quantities so as to improve profits (Wang, 2005). Second, orders can be synchronized to reduce system inventory. If the buyers are coordinated to place orders at the same point in time, the supplier may adopt a lot-for-lot policy and carry no inventory. If the buyers aren't coordinated on the timing of their orders, the supplier inventory replenishment cost is double of that under the lot-for-lot policy (Wang, Chay, & Wu, 2006). Finally, accurate, timely, and easily accessible information can improve decisions. In the context of SCM, a supplier is able to match inventory supply better with demand when information is available on the buyers' inventory status. Although, the benefits of information depends on how it is used.

In the next section, we review the concept of centralized and decentralized supply chains as well as the role of supply chain coordination.

Centralized / Decentralized Supply Chain

A centralized supply chain system is viewed as an entity that aims to optimize system performance. Various production/inventory policies have been developed to optimize the performance of a centralized supply chain system. There are two main categories in centralized supply nets: (1) deterministic systems, and (2) stochastic systems.

The objective of a deterministic system is to develop a production/inventory policy to minimize system cost. It is typically assumed that demand occurs at a buyer/retailer side continuously at a constant rate. Early studies have focused on the existence and development of optimal policies. However, such policies are usually difficult to implement. A comprehensive review of such models can be seen in Li et al. (2007).

In reality, a stochastic model that specifies demand as a stochastic process is often more accurate than its deterministic counterpart (Zheng, 1992). However, a barrier to the application of a stochastic model is that the optimal policy does not have a simple structure. This implies that appropriate coordination mechanisms are especially necessary (Li et al., 2007). Moreover, information sharing contributes another dimension to coordination when demand is stochastic. A decentralized supply chain differs from a centralized system in that members act independently to optimize their individual performance. Although more and more firms have realized that collaboration with their supply chain partners can significantly improve their profits, the centralization of inventory and production decisions for a decentralized SC is often unrealistic (Li et al., 2007). Therefore, the challenge is to devise coordination mechanisms that are not only able to coordinate the activities but also to align the objectives of independent supply chain members (Chen, Drezner, Ryan, & Simchi-Levi, 2000).

Cheung and Lee (2002) discuss the value of sharing information about the retailers' inventory positions, which could be used to coordinate shipments from the supplier to enjoy economies of scale in shipments, and for eventual unloading of the shipments to retailers to rebalance their stocking positions. In view of previous studies, for a decentralized supply chain system with members belonging to different firms a coordination mechanism should include at least three components: (i) an operational plan to coordinate the decisions and activities of supply chain members, (ii) a structure to share information among the members, and (iii) an incentive scheme to allocate the benefits

of coordination so as to entice the cooperation of all members (Li et al., 2007).

Here, we introduce the concept of dynamic information flow in a decentralized supply chain. An agent is designed to analyze and simulate the players' behaviors in an SC network. A cooperative game theory framework is also utilized between the actors in order to increase the supply chain performance.

Game Theory

Traditional research in operation management focused on providing tools in order to analyze the corresponding problems. The tools relied largely upon dynamic programming and other optimization techniques. In the past several years, SCM has evolved to recognize that a business process consisting of several decentralized firms and operational decisions of these different entities impact one another's profit and thus the profit of the whole SC (Nagarajan & Sosˇic´, 2008). In a decentralized supply chain where the members belong to two different firms, the method of bargaining and negotiation solution, which is dynamic in nature may result in a better coordination in SC as compared to the static coordination solution in a centralized supply chain. To effectively model and analyze decision-making in such multi-person situation where the outcome depends on the choice made by every party, game theory is a natural choice (Nagarajan et al., 2008). More comprehensive literature review on game theory for supply chain agents can be found in Nagarajan et al. (2008).

There is a broad division of game theory into two approaches: (1) cooperative, and (2) non-cooperative. In a non-cooperative game, the intention of the players is to maximize their individual gain, while in a cooperative game both buyer/seller would consider maximizing the system profit.

Different types of game models have different solution concepts. The bargaining game in a cooperative game theory addresses the problems in which a group of two or more agents are faced with a set of feasible outcomes, any one of which will be the result if it is specified by a unanimous agreement of all participants. In the event that no unanimous agreement is reached, a given disagreement outcome is the result.

In the Stackelberge game, the player who holds a more powerful position is called the leader and the other player who reacts to the leader's decision is called the follower and the solution obtained to this game is the Stackelberg solution (Sarmah et al., 2006). When two players negotiate, it is reasonable to expect that the player with the higher bargaining power receives a larger share of the pie than his weaker counterpart

Our model of supply chain is composed of three main players: (1) supplier/seller, (2) buyer/customer, and (3) control/optimization service agent. The word supplier/seller is used to represent the upstream member in the supply chain who sells the items to the buyers. An agent facilitates the communication between customers and suppliers and allows us to design, simulate, and analyze our collaborative strategies.

Agent-Based Supply Chain Management

In general, global optimization is a central issue for system modeling approaches. The main interest of managers is to ensure that the overall cost is reduced and operations among various systems are integrated through coordination (Fazel Zarandi et al., 2007). In a decentralized supply chain, where the members belong to two different firms, the method of bargaining and negotiating solution, which is dynamic in nature, may result in a better coordination in SC as compared to the static coordination solution in a centralized supply chain. To effectively model and analyze decision-making in such a multi-person situation, where the outcome depends on the choice made by every party, dynamic information sharing is

a natural choice. Lately, Internet-based technologies such as Web services have been emerging. However, despite the merits of these technologies, there exist some limitations in flexibility and dynamic coordination of distributed participants in supply chains. The agent-based systems are alternative technologies for SCM because of certain features such as distribution, collaboration, autonomy, and intelligence (Fox, Barbucean, & Teigen, 2000). According to Wooldridge (2002) and García-Sánchez et al. (2005), agents make the second-generation e-commerce systems possible, in which many aspects of a customer's buying behavior is automated. A comprehensive review of agent-based approaches in supply chain can be found in Parunak (1999).

Simulation and Petri Nets in Supply Chain Management

Supply chain experts have also taken various complementary perspectives when investigating coordination and information sharing within a supply chain. One useful tool for evaluating the performance and achieving more visibility of complex systems is simulation-based approach. Simulation-based approaches allow dynamic modeling of firm behaviors with varying degrees of constraints and policies as well as show the visibility and efficiency of various strategies and stochastic events. Since contemporary manufacturing enterprises are more strongly coupled in terms of material, information and service flows, there exists a strong urge for process oriented approach to address the issues of integrated modeling and analysis. Petri nets are a powerful tool for modeling and analysis of discrete event systems such as manufacturing systems (Wang, 1998). Since from a high level of abstraction supply chains are also discrete event systems, it is possible to develop a Petri net for modeling and analysis of supply chains (Chen et al., 2005). The advantages of Petri nets have been identified and comparisons have been made with other models by several researchers (Li & Zhou, 2004; Lin, Shan, Liu, Qu, & Ren, 2005), etc. For more details on PN, readers are referred to Jensen (1997).

Although the literature of Petri nets is comprehensive, very little work applied Petri nets to modeling of supply chains. Supply chains are modeled by use of colored Petri nets, where each supply chain entity is modeled by a block with action, resource and control as a subnet of a colored Petri net model (Chen et al., 2005). Supply chains are also modeled using generalized stochastic Petri nets (GSPNs) (Viswanadhm & Raghavan, 2000). PNs have well-developed formalisms and semantics that can model systems with interacting concurrent components. In any net, there are two basic elements: Nodes and links. A PN has two types of nodes: Places and transitions. Places are used to represent resources such as storage spaces or states of processes. Transitions are used to indicate actions or operations. A PN employs directed arcs to connect from places to transitions or vice versa. The dynamic feature of a PN is achieved by tokens, which can represent customer requests. An arbitrary distribution of tokens on the places is called a marking. Each marking corresponds to a state of the modeled system. The execution of the PN is regulated by the number and distributions of tokens and changes the system state.

A Stochastic Petri Net (SPN) consists of (1) a finite set of places, P, (2) a finite set of transitions, T, and (3) input and output arcs connecting places to transitions. However, the transition times must either be deterministic or follow exponential distributions (Lee, Huang, Liu, & Xu, 2006). Since the interval time of requests and inventory replenishments have mostly exponential distributions, we run the simulation through a SPN. In the next section, we introduce a coordination mechanism among buyers and sellers in an e-market. The proposed solution approach combines operation research methodologies and what-if simulation approaches in an agent-based system.

THE PROPOSED COORDINATION MODEL AND SIMULATION ALGORITHM

Assume that suppliers are located in different nations with a vast network of clearing and forward agents. The integration of these geographically separated supplier locations and the fulfillment of demands of different customer centers are a big challenge. Indeed, consider a family of products that a buyer would like to procure from an electronic market for which there are some pre-qualified suppliers available to supply as per specification. The information for a rough-cut capacity planning will be carried out at different supplier locations based on actual shift time, total actual time available during the planning period, and the average break-down by supplier-agent interaction. We assume the inventory system of supplier with periodic review (s, S) policy where the inventory replenishment decisions are based on position. The agent mediates the interaction between buyers and suppliers in an electronic marketplace. It computes the optimum quantities of transactional commodities for both buyer and seller by considering the whole SC profit under game theory framework. It also evaluates the performance of the current system in terms of inventory level and service level for buyers.

Transaction Agent for Control and Optimization

In agent-based supply chain management section, we described the roles of agents in coordination and information sharing in supply networks. This section presents the functionality of the transaction agent (TA) as well as its architecture in our model. It plays the most important role in our proposed supply chain system as it handles all computational processes used to coordinate and evaluate the network.

Agent Architecture

The major components and functions of an agent are as follows:

a. Offered prices of buyers, quantitative and qualitative attributes related to customers' evaluation (Table 1).
b. Desired prices of suppliers based on capacity and inventory carrying cost, quantitative and qualitative attributes related to suppliers' perception (Table 1).
c. Preprocessing and building customer profiles and computing the optimum solution with no cooperation in SC net.
d. Preprocessing and building supplier is profile and computing the optimum solution in order to satisfy relevant demand and capacity.
e. Preprocessing, building and applying the model in a cooperative game theory framework.

The overall architecture of agent is presented in Figure 1. The proposed model, after a contact made by the agent, using simulation module and coordination mechanism, determines the optimum quantities of transactional commodities for both buyers and sellers in market with the aim of minimizing the total system cost as well as evaluating the performance of current status. The simulation module increases the clarity of market status and allows both buyers and sellers to evaluate and

Table 1. Quantitative and qualitative attributes corresponding to buyer and seller

	Buyer	Seller
Quantitative Attribute	Lead Time, Transportation Cost, ...	Sales Volume, Capacity, Product Life Cycle,...
Qualitative Attribute	Service Level, Aesthetics, Management,...	Customer Satisfaction, Technological Standard, Geographical Benefit,...

Figure 1. Agent's architecture

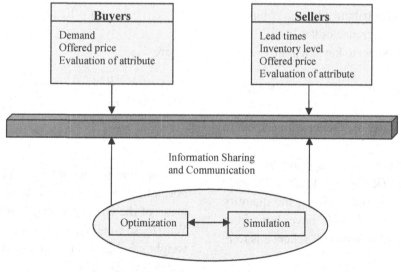

adopt their strategies in the uncertain environment. The agent then delivers the message back to buyers and sellers. In the next section, we will illustrate the ways of acquiring of rich and accurate profiles in an electronic supply chain system. Managers are required neither to understand the entire coordination mechanism supported by the agent, nor to identify the demand function.

Analytical Modeling

Here, we discuss the analytical approach used in this article. First, we state the overall procedures and strategy. Then, these procedures are applied to the SC problem. The notations to be used in the proposed model are presented next.

Notations:

b_i: The ith number of customers/buyers for $i = 1,2,...,m$.

s_j: The jth number of suppliers/sellers for $j = 1,2,...,k$.

k_d: The key attributes of the dth aspect of customers' perception for $d = 1,2,...,n$.

c^d_{ij}: The preference value of ith customer on j^{th} supplier for key attribute d.

s^d_{ij}: The preference value of jth supplier on i^{th} customer for key attribute d.

BP^i_{dr}: The relative preference of key attribute d with respect to key attribute r for the ith buyer.

SP^j_{dr}: The relative preference of key attribute d with respect to key attribute r for the jth supplier.

a_{ij}: The final priority of ith buyer with respect to j^{th} seller.

β_{ij}: The final priority of jth seller with respect to i^{th} buyer.

p^b_{ij}: The offered price of ith buyer for j^{th} seller.

p^s_{ij}: The offered price of jth seller for i^{th} buyer.

X_{ij}: The decision variable giving the quantity of commodities which i^{th} buyer buys from j^{th} seller (or equivalently, j^{th} seller sells to i^{th} buyer).

Buyer's Profile

The agent receives all the necessary information about the quantitative and qualitative attributes related to each product from m customers electronically. Then the agent decides on n key attributes for all aspects of customers' perceptions. Then, a vector of comprehensive key attribute is created as $CK = \{k_1, k_2,..., k_n\}$. For each key attribute d, the agent also designs a customer-key attributes incidence matrix as

$$CKIM^d = \left[C^d_{ij} \right]$$

where C^d_{ij} represents the preference value of ith customer for j^{th} supplier ($i = 1,2,...,m$ and $j = 1,2,...,k$) corresponding to key attribute d. The scale of preferences is categorized in Figure 2.

To normalize the preferences, we divide each component of the $CKIM^d$ in to the sum of its corresponding column. Each value within the normalized matrix indicates the relative weight a customer associates with a supplier on a special key attribute of a product. We can also calculate the weight of each attribute as a priority of corresponding key attribute for each buyer's view using the following formula:

$$W^i = \left[v^i_d \right]_{n \times 1}, \quad i = 1,...,m, \tag{1}$$

where,

$$v^i_d = \left(\sum_{r=1}^{n} \left(\frac{BP^i_{dr}}{\sum_{l=1}^{n} BP^i_{lr}} \right) / n \right), d = 1,...n. \tag{2}$$

Note that v^i_d according to (2) represents the normalized weight of key attribute d using the mean of the corresponding relative preferences. With these weights, we can calculate the average weight of $CKIM^d$ matrixes to obtain the buyer profile matrix as below:

Figure 2. The scale for preferences

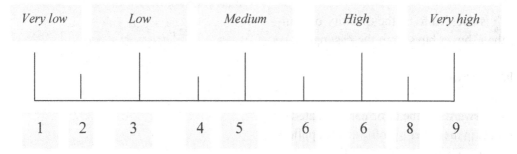

$$MCKIM = \begin{bmatrix} a_{11} & \cdot & \cdot & a_{1k} \\ a_{21} & \cdot & \cdot & a_{2k} \\ \cdot & \cdot & \cdot & \cdot \\ \cdot & \cdot & \cdot & \cdot \\ a_{m1} & \cdot & \cdot & a_{mk} \end{bmatrix}$$

where,

$$a_{ij} = \sum_{d=1}^{n} C_{ij}^{d} W_{d}^{i}.$$

We observe that the value calculated for a_{ij} as above represents the final priority level of ith customer on j^{th} supplier.

It is evident that, based on the association between the elements of the final priority matrix *(MCKIM)* and cost elements, the lower the weight corresponding to a buyer associated with a supplier, the higher the costs will be. Hence, we modify the elements of MCKIM as:

$$(MCKIM)' = \left[a'_{ij} \right]_{m \times k}$$

so that $a'_{ij} = 1 - a_{ij}$ for all entities of the corresponding matrix. This modification produces a matrix with each component representing the non-desirability of buying from a supplier for an individual buyer.

The agent also constitutes the buyer's price matrix separately as follows:

$$P^b = \begin{bmatrix} p_{11}^{b} & \cdot & \cdot & p_{1k}^{b} \\ \cdot & \cdot & \cdot & \cdot \\ \cdot & \cdot & \cdot & \cdot \\ p_{m1}^{b} & \cdot & \cdot & p_{mk}^{b} \end{bmatrix}$$

The prices should be adjusted ultimately to reflect non-quantifiable factors. Thus, in order to obtain the interaction between price and relevant attributes matrices, independent multiplication as a relative matching method can be applied as follows:

$$PA^b = [T^b_{ij}]$$

where,

$$T_{ij}^{b} = p_{ij}^{b} \times a'_{ij} \quad \begin{array}{l} \forall i = 1,...,m \\ \forall j = 1,...,k. \end{array} \quad (3)$$

Therefore, the PA^b matrix introduces the buyers' priorities of matching between prices and attributes in an electronic supply chain environment.

Finally, we can use this matrix in the following model to obtain optimal solution for buyers with no cooperation within the SC network:

$$Min\ P^b\ (X) = \sum_{i} \sum_{j} (T_{ij}^{b} \times X_{ij})$$

$$(4)$$

s. t.

demand and supply are satisfied

where, X_{ij} is decided to be the quantity of commodity the ith buyer buys from the jth supplier.

Supplier's Profile

The agent forwards all the information related to each product in the buyer's profile to all suppliers electronically. Then agent obtains the value of each supplier on key attributes of customers. After obtaining all the information from the supplier's side, a supplier-key attribute incidence matrix is created. The agent the designs the supplier-key attribute incidence matrix as $SKIM^d = [S^d_{ij}]$, where each S^d_{ij} represents the preference value of the jth supplier on the ith buyer $(j = 1,2,...,k$ and $i = 1,2,...,m)$ corresponding to key attribute d. This value indicates the priority level of suppliers on buyers to satisfy the specific attribute of customers.

To normalize the preferences, we divide each component of the $SKIM^d$ in to the sum of its corresponding column. Each value within the normalized indicates the relative weight a customer associates with a supplier on a special key attribute of a product. We can also calculate the weight of each attribute as a priority of corresponding key attribute for each supplier's view using the following formula:

$$W^j = \left[v^j_d \right]_{n \times 1}, \quad j = 1,...k \qquad (5)$$

where

$$v^j_d = (\sum_{r=1}^{n} (\frac{SP^j_{dr}}{\sum_{l=1}^{n} SP^j_{lr}})/n), d=1,...,n \qquad (6)$$

Note that v^j_d according to (6) represents the normalized weight of key attribute d using the mean of its corresponding relative preferences. With these weights we can calculate the weight

mean of $SKIM^d$ matrix to obtain the supplier profile matrix as below:

$$MSKIM = \begin{bmatrix} \beta_{11} & . & . & \beta_{1k} \\ \beta_{21} & . & . & \beta_{2k} \\ . & . & . & . \\ . & . & . & . \\ \beta_{m1} & . & . & \beta_{mk} \end{bmatrix}$$

where,

$$\beta_{ij} = \sum_{d=1}^{n} S^d_{ij} W^j_d$$

We observe that the value calculated for β_{ij} as above.

It is evident that, based on the association between the elements of final priority matrix and price elements, the higher the weight corresponding to a supplier associated with a buyer, the higher the revenues will be. Hence, we modify the elements of $MSKIM$ as:

$$(MSKIM)' = \left[\beta'_{ij} \right]_{m \times k}$$

with $\beta'_{ij} = 1+\beta_{ij}$ for all entities of the corresponding matrix. The agent also constitutes the offered price matrix of jth seller to i^{th} buyer as follows:

$$P^S = \begin{bmatrix} p^S_{11} & . & . & p^S_{1k} \\ . & . & . & . \\ . & . & . & . \\ p^S_{m1} & . & . & p^S_{mk} \end{bmatrix}$$

The adjusted prices of suppliers can then be calculated as:

$$PA^s = [T^s_{ij}]$$

where,

$$T_{ij}^S = p_{ij}^S \times \beta_{ij}' \qquad \begin{array}{l} \forall i = 1, ..., m \\ \forall j = 1, ..., k. \end{array} \qquad (7)$$

The PA^s matrix introduces the priorities of matching between prices and attributes in an electronic supply chain environment. Using this matrix in the following model, the optimal solution for suppliers with no cooperation within the SC network will be obtained.

$$Max \ P^s(X) = \sum_i \sum_j (T_{ij}^S \times X_{ij}) \qquad (8)$$

s.t.

demand and supply are satisfied

where, X_{ij} is decided to be the quantity of commodity the jth supplier sells to the ith buyer.

Supply Chain Optimal Solution

In a non-cooperative game, the individual players independently, the intention of each player is to maximize his individual gain. On the other hand, in a cooperative game both buyer and supplier would consider maximizing the system profit subject to each buyer's total annual cost at cooperation being at least equal to the one at non-cooperation. This is due to the reality that the optimal solutions with no cooperation are ideal ones. Thus, in order to make the transaction practical, a compromised combined weighted objective should be optimized. Thus, the objective function for this cooperative game from the general model can be written as:

$$Max \ Z = -\lambda * P^b(X) + (1-\lambda) * P^s(X)$$

s.t.

$$P^b(X) \geq p^*(b)$$

$$P^s(X) \leq p^*(s)$$

and demand and supply are satisfied,

where $p^*(b)$ and $p^*(s)$ represent the optimal values of the buyer and supplier objective functions

before cooperation, respectively.

The value of λ is set to varies between 0 and 1, depending upon the bargaining power of the suppliers and the buyers. Solving this linear model, the optimal values of transactional commodities for both buyers and sellers in the market will be obtained minimize the total system cost while coordinating among players.

In the next section, the simulation approach interacting with the coordinated optimization process will be described. We intend to show that Petri nets can serve as a simulation tool for studying the bullwhip effect and especially for experimenting on how different replenishment strategies would affect the parameters of certain players and of the entire supply chain.

Simulation and Performance Evaluation

As described in transaction agent for control and optimization, the agent after the optimization process evaluates the performance of the network by simulation using SPN and sends the results to buyers and suppliers according to their access levels. The input data for simulation would be based on historical data in buyers and suppliers profiles. Here, the profiles are constructed through random numbers generation. The following section describes the simulation algorithm of trading strategy in the network.

Supply Chain Strategy

In the computational simulation of trading strategy between suppliers and buyers, the simulation algorithm has four main stages: *initialization, identification, adaptation, and updating.* Briefly, initialization starts with opening the market structure and gives the initial valuations of the agent. In the identification stage, each player then infers a model representing how the system is behaving and identifies the partner that will most probably be offered for trading in the next round (i.e., each player selects which plants are likely to be traded). In adaptation, each player computes the set of partners he or she will attempt to buy and sell given the inferred model (i.e., the set of partners most likely to be traded) in order to simplify the coordination problem. Then, at least two of the players trade a plant. Finally, in the updating stage the algorithm updates the state of the model (i.e., it recalculates the capacities owned by each player) and the respective cost structures.

In what follows, we apply our proposed methodology to a small network with two suppliers. Then, *SC Net Optimizer* as a simulation and analysis tool is presented. It supports the data acquisition in supply chain and reports the optimal solution in SC as well as evaluates the performance of the currents status of the market in terms of inventory levels for suppliers and service levels.

SCENARIO STATEMENT OF SMALL SUPPLY NETWORK

Consider a scenario in which the sellers sell a product (electronic connector). The manufacturer

needs three raw materials to produce the connector: Flat, rod, and screw. At the manufacturer's site, rods of aluminum are cut into shafts with a given length, flat is bored and ground. Each finished product is then produced by assembling a shaft, a flat and two screws. The product will be packaged in seller site and delivered to customers (Chen et al., 2005).

Figure 3 shows the Petri net model of the SC. The interpretation of the places and the transitions in the model are given by Table 2 and Table 3, respectively, where the D(T) in Table 2 denotes the mean firing delay (in days) of transition T. In the model, there are three types of flows: Material flow, information flow and financial flow. The material flow is represented by timed transitions t_1 and t_2 (inventory replenishments of suppliers), t_3 (delivery preparation) and their associated places and arcs. The information flow is represented by immediate transitions t_4, t_6, t_7, t_9, t_{11}, t_{12}, and their associated places and arcs. The financial flow is represented by timed transition t_{10} and its associated places and arcs. For the sake of simplicity, we assume that supply net is composed of two different suppliers. We also consider the inventory system of suppliers with the periodic review (s, S) policy in which S refers to the desired maximum

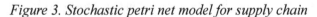

Figure 3. Stochastic petri net model for supply chain

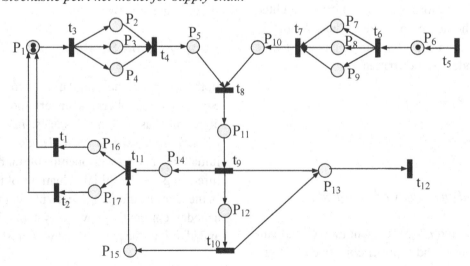

level of inventory and s is the maximum inventory in reorder point. That is, the order will be released if the on hand inventory is equal or less than s. The inventory carrying cost for each part of the family is deterministic for suppliers and is based on historical data.

We have chosen Java platform to design the application of the simulator called *SC Net Optimizer*. The data storage is done by MYSQL and through a control-filter that rejects faulty measurements. It is assumed that the firing time of buyer's demand follows an exponential distribution with mean value 0.0355 where it can be obtained from historical data. The demands will be filled if there is a sufficient on-hand inventory. Otherwise, the demand will be removed. The inventory policy parameters of two suppliers are taken as ($S_1=5000$, $s_1=2000$) and ($S_2=5500$, $s_2=2300$) arbitrarily. For financial flow, buyers pay to suppliers within a given time period after receiving the finished products. The preference values in buyer and seller profiles are generated randomly in terms of an introduced comparison scale. We run the model under this strategy that buyer has more bargaining power than supplier by taking $\lambda=0.6$ in SC model. Figures 4 and 5 illustrate the layout

of related knowledge definition for buyer/supplier profiles and optimal solution.

Due to stochastic nature of the model, multiple replication of simulation over a long time horizon should be performed to obtain a reliable estimation of the performance indices. For the industrial case, the number of replications is taken to be N=25 and the simulation horizon is taken to be $T=T_0+10T_0$ time units with $T_0=200$ (Chen et al., 2005). In this study, we have shown the model with 10 successive iterations for a single period. The final result of simulation for SC optimal solution and remainder stocks diagram for each supplier are given in Figure 6.

DISCUSSIONS

The buyer company enters its demand and selects the desired comprehensive attributes in order to prioritize the suppliers (Figure 4). Then, the buyer is asked to enter the suggested price for each seller. The agent forwards this information to the seller profile and sellers enter their supplies and own preference values for corresponding attributes (Figure 5). The optimal solutions or weight values

Table 2. Interpretation of transistions

T	Description	D(T)
t1	Inventory replenishment of seller 1	5
t2	Inventory replenishment of seller 2	2
t3	Start of delivery preparation	-
t4	Seller profile	-
t5	Demand	0.0355
t6	Start of order placement	-
t7	Buyer profile	-
t8	Loading of solutions on input buffer	-
t9	Start of loading information flow	-
t10	Payment from buyer to seller	1
t11	Loading sales information for seller	-
t12	Loading sales information for buyer	-

Table 3. Interpretation of places

P1	Record of available inventory of stocks
P2	Record of offered price (seller)
P3	Record of quantitative attributes (seller)
P4	Record of qualitative attributes (seller)
P5	Minimization of corresponding model
P6	Pending customer orders
P7	Record of offered price (buyer)
P8	Record of quantitative attributes (buyer)
P9	Record of qualitative attributes (buyer)
P10	Minimization of corresponding model
P11	Minimization of cooperative model
P12	Final stocks order in delivering preparation
P13	Updated buyers profile in SC network
P14	Updated sellers profile in SC network
P15	Record of financial flows
P16	Record of remainder stocks (seller 1)
P17	Record of remainder stocks (seller 2)

Figure 4. User interface for buyer profile in the sc net optimizer

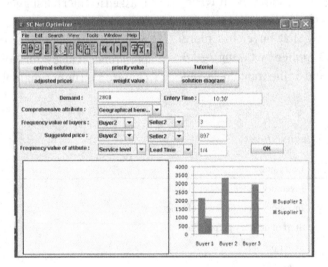

can be observed by selecting the menu or hitting the related buttons for both buyers and sellers.

As shown in Figure 4, the optimal solution for buyer 1 in the network, for instance, is to deal with both sellers whereas this is in conflict with sellers' optimal solution. These locally optimal solutions can lead to disturbing to the stability of the network since there is no cooperation among the entities. Thus, a coordination mechanism is required to facilitate the transactional relationship and also build a structure to share the information such that the benefits are allocated to all member of the network. Comparing the reported outcomes of the suggested coordination mechanism (Figure 6)

Figure 5. User interface for seller profile in the SC net optimizer

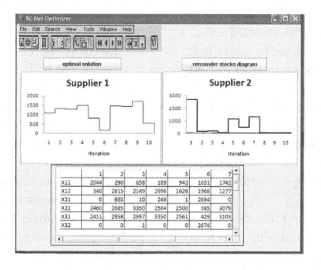

Figure 6. The SC optimal solution

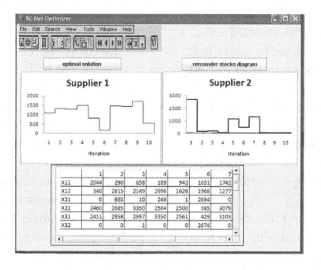

with the individual optimal solutions, clarifies the role of real-time information flow and negotiation results in the profit of the whole supply network. The remaining stock diagrams in SC profile provide opportunities for the suppliers to evaluate their strategies for inventory management.

Overall, we have shown through the use of a small network that the present approach is a useful tool to solve and evaluate SC network problems. This optimization is centered on the negotiation among buyers and sellers. Clearly, the optimal

values of the SC profile will depend on the price matrix in buyer and seller profiles. These are controllable parameters that one encounters in the decision making process while negotiating in a supply chain.

Inventory systems form another important component of supply chains and inventory management plays a key role in SCM. Inventory management addresses two fundamental issues: When a stock should replenish its inventory and how much should be ordered for each replenishment. The performance criteria of the supply chain can include average inventory level and also the service level for each stock, where the service level is defined as the probability that the customer's orders are filled on time. The first criterion is easy to obtain since it corresponds to the average number of tokens in the discrete place representing the stock. For the evaluation of service level, we need to know the total time that the discrete place has no token while the place representing customer orders is not empty in each simulation. Our SC net simulator provides the graphical results for average inventory level and also the visibility of orders for determining inventory policy.

The point estimation of each performance index and the standard error of estimation obtained by the simulation can be calculated. Given the point estimation and the standard error, a confidence interval for each performance index can be calculated for any given level of confidence under the condition of the independence of replications (Chen et al., 2005). A 100(1-α)% confidence interval for performance index θ, based on t-distribution, is given as

$$\overline{\theta} - t_{\alpha/2,N-1}S/\sqrt{N} \leq \theta \leq \overline{\theta} + t_{\alpha/2,N-1}S/\sqrt{N}$$

where $\overline{\theta}$ and S are the point estimation and the standard error of the estimation of θ, respectively, N is the number of independent replications, and $t_{\alpha/2,N-1}$ is the 100(1-$\alpha/2$) percentage point of a t-distribution with $N-1$ degrees of freedom.

CONCLUSION

The advent of Internet-based marketplaces motivate the researchers to investigate the conceptual buyer/supplier coordination models to save the system costs and ultimately improve the performance of the supply chain. A coordination mechanism for decentralized supply chain whereby members are separate economic entities has to include a collaborative strategy to optimize system per-

formance and provide an incentive scheme to distribute the benefits of coordination so as to entice cooperation. Moreover, the coordination of a supply chain also requires that accurate and timely information about members' operational decisions and activities be shared among all in order to reduce uncertainties.

We developed an agent-based framework to facilitate collaboration and information sharing in the environment with high supply and demand uncertainties. Due to the complexities of supply chain systems, we have introduced the concept of dynamic supply chain information flow. An agent is designed to analyze and simulate the players' behaviors in the SC network. Coordination is made to control inventory at different echelons and minimize the total cost of the SC by sharing information. Consequently, optimization can be achieved more effectively and the bullwhip effect is reduced. The basic information is considered in the form of a customer-key attribute incidence matrix to obtain a real-time customer profile. The supplier profile is designed to analyze the possibility of interaction between two main actors in SC, suppliers and buyers. The interaction between the suggested price and comprehensive attributes in each profile is computationally derived to produce a more realistic model. In order to improve the SC performance, these profiles are applied under a cooperative game theory framework to give rise to the SC optimal solutions.

Finally, we defined a scenario to run the proposed model. The study was supported by presenting *SC Net Optimizer* as a tool for implementing the proposed coordination mechanism and evaluating the performance of the chain by simulation using stochastic Petri nets (SPNs). This approach presents a great potential to resolve several problems in real-world SC systems such as evaluation of inventory policies while the parameters are stochastic in nature. The use of our model for an extensive empirical analysis on Web pages as well as extension of the supply chain coordination model and sensitivity analysis performance are interesting areas of further research. Moreover, the interval time of demand was assumed to have an exponential distribution. This assumption could be relaxed to consider any general distribution for further research.

ACKNOWLEDGMENT

The first and fourth authors acknowledge Mazandaran University of Science and Technology, the second author thanks K.N.Toosi University of Technology, and the fifth author thanks Sharif University of Technology for supporting this study. The authors are also grateful to the anonymous referees for their valuable comments and suggestions resulting in an improved presentation.

REFERENCES

Averbakh, I., & Xue, Z. (2007). Online supply chain scheduling problems with preemption. *European Journal of Operational Research, 181*(1), 500-504.

Chen, H., Lionel, A., Chu, F., & Labadi, K., (2005). Modeling and performance evaluation of supply chains using batch deterministic and stochastic Petri nets. *IEEE transactions automation science and engineering, 2*(2), 132-144.

Chen, F., Drezner, Z., Ryan, J. K., Simchi-Levi, D. (2000). Quantifying the bullwhip effect in a simple supply chain: The impact of forecasting lead time and information. *Management Science, 46*(3), 436-4.

Cheung, K., Lee, H., (2002). The inventory benefit of shipment coordination and stock rebalancing in a supply chain. *Management Science, 48*(2), 300-306.

Fox, M. S., Barbucean, M., & Teigen, R. (2000). Agent-oriented supply chain management. *International Journal of Flexible Manufacturing Systems, 12*(2), 165-188.

Hazra, J., & Mahadevan, B. (2006). Impact of supply base heterogeneity in electronic markets. *European Journal of Operational Research, 174*, 1580-1594.

Jensen, K. (1997). Colored PN: Basic concepts, analysis methods and practical use; monographs in theoretical computer science. Springer-Verlag, 2nd corrected printing.

Lancastre, A., & Lages, L.F. (2006). The relationship between buyer and a B2B e-marketplace: Cooperation determinants in an electronic market context. *Industrial Marketing Management, 35*, 774 - 789.

Lee, C., Huang, H. C., Liu, B., & Xu, Z. (2006). Development of timed color Petri net simulation models for air cargo terminal operations. *Computers and Industrial Engineering, 51*, 102-110.

Li, X., & Wang, Q., (2007). Coordination mechanisms of supply chain systems. *European Journal of Operational Research, 179*, 1-16.

Li, Z. W., & Zhou, M. C. (2004). Elementary siphons of Petri nets and their application to deadlock prevention in flexible manufacturing systems. *IEEE Transactions on Systems, Man and Cybernetics*, Part A, *34*(1), 38-51.

Lin, C., Shan, Z., Liu, T., Qu, Y., & Ren, F. (2005). Modeling and inference of extended interval temporal logic for nondeterministic intervals. *IEEE Transactions on Systems, Man and Cybernetics*, Part A, *35*(5), 682–696.

Mahdavi, I., Cho, N., & Mohebbi, S., (2007). A fuzzy-based analytical model of dynamic information flow in e-SCM. *Contemporary Management Research, 3*(4), 287-298.

Nagarajan, M., & Sosˇicˊ, G., (2008). Game-theoretic analysis of cooperation among supply chain agents: Review and extensions. *European Journal of Operational Research, 187*(3), 719-745

Pant, S., Sethi, R., & Bhandari, M. (2003). Making sense of the e-supply chain landscape: An implementation framework. *International Journal of Information Management, 23*, 201-221.

Parunak, H. V. D. (1999). *Multi-agent systems: A modern approach to distributed artificial intelligence*. Cambridge, MA: The MIT Press.

Sarmah, S. P., Acharya, D., & Goyal, S. K. (2006). Buyer vendor coordination models in supply chain management. *European Journal of Operational Research, 175*, 1-15.

Tayur, S. H., Ganeshan, R., & Magazine, M. J. (1998). *Quantitative models for supply chain management*. Norwell, MA: Kluwer.

Viswanadhm, N., & Raghavan, N. R. S. (2000).

Performance analysis and design of supply chains: A Petri net approach. *Journal of Operation Research Society, 51*(10), 1158-1169.

Wang, J. (1998). *Timed Petri nets: Theory and application*. Norwell, MA: Kluwer.

Wang, Q. (2005). Discount pricing policies and the coordination of decentralized distribution systems. *Decision Sciences, 36*(4), 627-646.

Wang, Q., Chay, Y., & Wu, Z. (2006). A simple coordination strategy for a decentralized supply chain. Working Paper, Nanyang Business School, Nanyang Technological University, Singapore.

Wooldridge, M. (2002). *An introduction to multi-agent systems*. New York: Wiley.

Zheng, Y. (1992). On properties of stochastic inventory systems. *Management Science, 38*(1), 87-103.

This work was previously published in the International Journal of Information Systems and Supply Chain Management, Vol. 1, Issue 3, edited by J. Wang, pp. 1-20, copyright 2008 by IGI Publishing (an imprint of IGI Global).

Chapter 14
Strategic Management of International Subcontracting:
A Transaction Cost Perspective

Yue Wang
University of New South Wales, Australia

ABSTRACT

Research on international subcontracting has been policy-oriented and industry-focused. There is a lack of understanding of the phenomenon from strategic management and international business perspectives. This article conceptualizes international subcontracting as a type of relational contract formed by buyers and suppliers from different countries, aiming to facilitate the sourcing of products or components with buyer-specific requirements. It builds a transaction cost model for studying the strategic choice of international subcontracting as an intermediate governance structure, sitting between arm's length outsourcing arrangement and vertically integrated multinational enterprises (MNEs). A set of propositions are developed to aid future empirical research and to provide managers with some guidelines for organizing supply chain across borders. The model also allows managers to examine the complex nature of a range of subcontracting relationships and identify the specific mechanisms that can be used to preserve and manage the dyadic principal-subcontractor exchanges.

INTRODUCTION

International subcontracting is an important phenomenon in international business (IB) studies (Casson, 1990) and has been an effective means of accelerating industrial development since 1960s, fostering the specialization among countries that reflects comparative advantages (Germidis, 1980).

Through such measures as the establishment of free trade zones, developing countries encourage local firms to undertake subcontracting jobs for foreign firms to earn hard currency and to accumulate technological know-how (Hamada, 1974). Firms from developed countries are frequently attracted into subcontracting arrangements to exploit low labour and production costs in developing countries. The studies of international subcontracting are mainly policy-oriented (Cohen, 1975; Riedel, 1975; Sengenberger & Pyke, 1991) and geography or industry-focused (Kashyap, 1992; Lawson, 1992; Rogerson, 1995). Few have examined why firms from developed countries choose to use subcontracting arrangements in the first place. Moreover, despite some classifications of international subcontracting activities according to functional or market criteria (Gereffi, 1993; Holmes, 1986), the nature of subcontracting relationships remains unexplored due to the lack of theoretical underpinning of international subcontracting as a form of international business organization. Grounded on transaction cost theory (Buckley & Casson, 1976; Hennart, 1982; Rugman, 1981; Williamson, 1975, 1979, 1985), this article aims to provide a firm-level analytical framework for analysing the subcontracting choice and the nature of subcontracting relationships, complementing the existing literature's emphasis on studying international subcontracting as a macro-economic phenomenon. The framework will also aid managers in choosing strategically between outsourcing, subcontracting, and vertical integration when organizing their supply chain.

Although "transaction costs differ depending on both the nature of the transaction and on the way that it is organized" (Coase, 1937, p. 386), transaction cost economics (TCE) as formally developed by Williamson (1975, 1979) is not mainly concerned with the transaction itself, but with the contractual arrangements (the ways) through which transactions are organized (Cheung, 1983). Contractual or institutional arrangements, normally referred to as governance structures, are "the institutional matrix within which transactions are negotiated and executed" (Williamson, 1979, p. 239). Drawing upon the legal concept of generic contracting forms (Macneil, 1974, 1978) and relating them to the nature of transactions, Williamson (1979) matched the transactions to the contracts. By so doing, he provided a framework 'to assess the efficacy of alternative means of contracting'

(Williamson, 1990, p. 8) and illustrated which governance structure (including the firm, the mark and intermediate contracts) has the lowest cost under given circumstances.

Despite the criticisms (some are highly theoretical and sometimes obscure or even mistaken on what they are criticising) (e.g., Conner & Prahalad, 1996; Ghoshal & Moran, 1996), empirical studies show Williamson-type of transaction cost-comparative contracting approach has more predictive power than other major IB theories such as resource-based view (RBV) in informing the choice between different forms of governance structures for organising firm interdependence (e.g., Hennart, 1991; Reddy, Osborn, & Hennart, 2002). Much of the RBV (Barney, 1991; Peteraf, 1993; Wernerfelt, 1984) and its closely-related competence perspective (Foss, 1996; Knudsen, 1995) entail ex post rationalizations for success and has been remiss in predictive respects (Williamson, 1999). This article therefore employs TCE as an analytical framework for examining the choice of international subcontracting.

THE CONCEPT OF INTERNATIONAL SUBCONTRACTING

There is a great deal of ambiguity on the definition of subcontracting in the existing literature (Hovi, 1994). However, there are some essential features about the international subcontracting as a form of investment. First, international subcontracting involves two independent units located in different countries, reflecting a type of cross-border inter-firm relationship. But the fact that a firm is legally independent does not necessarily mean that it will be economically independent. The relationship between subcontracting parties is defined as "quasi-integration," in which subcontractors from less developed countries are often dependent on principals from developed countries, where the demand of subcontracting is derived (Germidis, 1980). Second, in a subcontracting arrangement, the subcontractor provides the principal with products or services on agreed terms and conditions set by the principal, where certain business activities such as marketing or product design may not be carried out by the subcontractor (Halbach, 1989). The goods produced are required to conform to specifications intended for a definite principal, making it impossible or very difficult to sell them to other customers (Germidis, 1980). Third, the principal usually provides specialised physical equipment and/or ongoing technical assistance to the subcontractor to assure product specifications and quality (Sharpston, 1977). The enforcement mechanisms are usually between principals and subcontractors themselves and no third party oversees the execution of the contract. The bond linking them together is thus out of market (Germidis, 1980). Consequently, a significant level of transaction-specific investment has to be undertaken both by subcontractors to meet the specifications set by principals and by principals to ensure the performance of subcontractors. These basic characteristics reveal that the nature of international subcontracting conforms to Williamson's (1979, 1985) notion of a relational contract with a bilateral governance structure. Casson (1987) identified subcontracting as a distinctive type of intermediate contractual arrangement, an alternative to the vertically integrated multinational enterprises (MNEs).

The lack of a clear definition of subcontracting in the existing literature is due to the lack of theoretical underpinning. Based on the essential features identified above and in line with Williamson-type of transaction costs-comparative institutional framework, this paper defines international subcontracting as a type of long-term relational contract between buyers and suppliers in different countries that aims to facilitate the sourcing of products or components with buyer-specific requirements. This definition distinguishes international subcontracting from common arm's length industrial outsourcing and in-house supply within an MNE's network, providing the basis for conducting an analysis of

the choice of international subcontracting over its alternatives and for developing some testable propositions regarding such a choice.

THE CHOICE OF INTERNATIONAL SUBCONTRACTING

The previous conceptualization allows us to examine the choice of international subcontracting as an intermediate relational contract, lying between arm's length outsourcing arrangement and internalised MNEs, and to develop some testable propositions based on the comparison between international subcontracting and its market and hierarchy alternatives.

The Choice of Subcontracting over Outsourcing

In transaction cost framework, the choice of a relational contracting form is made when transactions between buyers and suppliers are characterised by mixed asset specificity, recurrent exchange and a low degree of uncertainty (Williamson, 1979, 1985). Central to the framework is the concept of asset specificity (Williamson, 1975). Also labelled transaction/relationship-specific assets or dedicated assets (e.g., Dyer, 1997; Dyer & Singh, 1998; Dyer & Nobeoka, 2000), asset-specificity refers to durable human and physical investments undertaken to support particular transactions (Williamson, 1985) and cannot be redeployed to another transaction without some loss in the productivity of the asset or some increase in the costs in adapting the asset in the new transaction (Besanko, Dranove, & Shanley, 2004). In a buyer-supplier exchange relationship, relationship-specific investments are nonfungible signals of commitment that create economic losses if the relationship is prematurely terminated (Jap & Anderson, 2003). The requirement for transaction or relationship-specific investments creates potential costs in the market execution of transactions. When the asset specificity feature involved in transactions is low, buyers and suppliers keep their relationship at arm's length.

A common industrial outsourcing activity refers to such market-based transaction of standard products or components which involve little transaction-specific investment. In outsourcing, both buyers and suppliers capitalise on their comparative advantages of trading and realising economies of specialization (Sharpston, 1977). While outsourcing may involve a long-term relationship between buyers and suppliers, it does not require the support of long-term contract. The products and components in common outsourcing activities are non-specific and there are many buyers and sellers. Some buyers and suppliers may be engaged in the trading of standard goods for a long time. But they are not bonded by contracts requirement and each side can switch to other trading parties easily due to the low asset specificity in their trading relationship.

When products or components contain some degree of product specifications and are not "off the shelf," they can no longer be bought on the spot market. Buyers look for long-term contractual arrangements to assure the supply of the specialised inputs and products. As previously defined, subcontracting is a kind of long-term contract that aims to facilitate the sourcing of products or components with buyer-specific requirements. This clarification is important because the term "subcontracting" is often misunderstood as an exclusive portrait of buyer-supplier relationship and therefore the distinction between common outsourcing and subcontracting is blurred (Wang, 2007). As such, asset specificity is an important reason for making long-term contracts (Kay, 1995), explaining the choice of subcontracting over outsourcing. To protect themselves from exposure to transaction costs arising from making asset-specific investments, both parties involved in subcontracting relations have incentives to form a long-term relational contract. Thus, we suggest:

Proposition 1: *International subcontracting is chosen over outsourcing when there is a high level of asset-specificity in the purchasing/supplying transaction.*

The Choice of Subcontracting over Vertical Integration

The economic rationale of international subcontracting is to realise economies of specialization through externalising non-core production activities to achieve cost advantage (Sharpston, 1977). But firms can acquire existing low-cost suppliers in developing countries as their subsidiaries or set up plants in low-cost regions and relocate non-core activities to the new ventures. On the other hand, if the aim is to access technology expertise or other proprietary know-how held by suppliers, the buyer firm could still acquire them through equity integration with suppliers. Therefore, other than achieving production cost economies and acquiring complementary assets, there must be additional reasons for firms to choose subcontracting rather than vertical integration through acquisitions or greenfield.

Engaging vertical integration through acquisition to exploit low production costs or to access complementary assets overseas would entail significant transaction and information costs, which justify the choice of subcontracting. First, the desired assets of the acquied firm are hard to disentangle from the non-desired ones, which impose a high cost on acquiring suppliers (Hennart, 1988). Under this circumstance, purchasing the target overseas firm would force the buyer to enter unrelated fields or to expand suddenly in size, with the attendant management problems (Hennart, 1991). This cost is particularly high for firms that rely mostly on cost rather than differentation to survive. Thus, we suggest:

Proposition 2: *International subcontracting is chosen over acquisition of overseas suppliers when* the desired assets of the acquied firm are hard to disentangle from the non-desired ones.

Second, management costs after the acquistion make subcontracting preferrable. Acquisition of a foreign supplier means the buyer also takes over an existing labor force and a well-established administrative structure. Considerable difficulties might be expected by the buyer in managing the foreign supplier firm that has cultivated its own organizational routines and corporate culture, in addition to the national culture distance (Hennart & Park, 1993). Hence, a subcontracting arrangement may be desirable as it avoids the post-acquisition management costs by leaving the management of supplier firm to the overseas subcontractor itself. Thus:

Proposition 3: *International subcontracting is chosen over acquisition of overseas suppliers when the post-acquisition management costs are expected to be high.*

Third, information costs in assessing the value of the target firm inhibit the acquisition (Hennart & Park., 1993). Buyers may not acquire overseas suppliers for the purpose of establishing low-cost supply bases but for the potential gain from complementary assets held by suppliers. But it may be difficult to assess the true value of these complementary assets due to the intrinsic bounded rationality constraint and the expectation that overseas suppliers may opportunistically exaggerate the value of their assets. A subcontracting arrangement retains the possibility for principals to gather information on the value of overseas subcontractors' complementary assets without financial exposure in an equity relationship, and may be used as a transitional arrangement for future acquisition of the overseas supplier. Hence, we propose:

Proposition 4: *International subcontracting is chosen over acquisition of overseas suppliers*

when the pre-acquisition costs in assessing the value of the target firm are high.

Fourth, high exit barriers in an equity relationship may jepodize the flexibility valued by the firms. In contrast, a subcontracting arrangement allows the buyers to rescind the contractual relationship with suppliers at a relatively low exit cost. In addition, impediments to acquistions arising from governmental and institutional barriers are not uncommon. Many developing countries discourage and restrict the foreign equity control of local companies while the pervasive anti-trust legislation in developed countries also acts against acquisitions (Wang, 2007). We therefore suggest:

Proposition 5: *International subcontracting is chosen over acquisition of overseas suppliers when there are institutional barriers to acquisition*

When making the choice between subcontracting and building new plants (greenfield) in low-cost countries, the following factors need to be considered. First, relocating low value-added operations to newly established greenfield plants may achieve a similar level of cost reduction in labor and other production factors. But relocation to another country through greenfields requires additional knowledge in managing labor and production in an unfamilar environment, and becoming acquainted with the specific local cultures and environment is a time-consuming process (Bell, 1996). Greenfield investments may be necessary for companies that aim to develop foreign markets for their products, but not for firms that simply seek a low cost supply base overseas. When the cost of learning cannot be recovered quickly, a subcontracting arrangement rather than a greenfied will be sufficient to achieve the objective of cost reduction.

Second, even when the buyer firm plans to develop the foreign market in the future, subcontracting may still be a preferred entry mode as it allows the firm to acquire knowledge of local market before the subcontracting arrangement is replaced by a wholly-owned subsidiary (Kogut, 1988). In this case, the choice of subcontracting economises on the cost of acquiring local knowledge, allowing the prospective entrant to test the potential of the local market while exploiting the foreign country as a low cost supply base in the mean time. Hence:

Proposition 6: *International subcontracting is chosen over greenfield when there are sigificant costs involved in learning how to operate greenfield plants overseas*

THE RANGE OF SUBCONTRACTING RELATIONSHIP

Transaction-specific investments bond principals and subcontractors in a relational long term supply arrangement, but it also leaves room for parties to bargain, shirk, or break the relationship for short-term gains (Williamson, 1985). The so-called hold-up problem often arises when one party in an exchange relationship commits transaction-specific or relationship-specific investments (Wathne & Heide, 2000). The asymmetric investments in specific assets allow a firm to behave opportunistically to increase its short-term, unilateral gains in a dyadic channel relationship (Brown, Dev, & Lee, 2000). In a subcontracting relationship, whether and how to preserve the contractual arrangement is primarily a matter of the nature of the relationship between the principal and the subcontractor concerned.

There is a whole range of international subcontracting relationships in terms of the degree of interdependence and bargaining power between principals and subcontractors. The perceived dependence and bargaining power are the function of the combination of many factors, including the degree of asset-specific investments, frequency of transactions and uncertainty (Williamson, 1979, 1985). Variations along those transactional dimensions determine the degree of interdependence and

bargaining power between subcontracting parties, which in turn constitute a variety of subcontracting relationships. This section not only examines a range of subcontracting relationships but also their corresponding governance mechanisms. In studying how firms mitigate opportunism in marketing channels, Brown et al. (2000) identified three specific mechanisms: (1) ownership, (2) investment in transaction-specific assets, and (3) development of relational exchange norms such as role integrity, flexibility, and long-term orientation. As ownership does not apply to the governance of subcontracting relationship, which is essentially a commercial exchange, we focus on the efficacy of the other two mechanisms in preserving and managing subcontracting relationships.

First, a loose subcontracting relationship denotes a low interdependence degree between principals and subcontractors, the switching cost for both parties is low as neither side makes significant asset-specific investments. The principal does not rely on a particular subcontractor or subcontractors for supply and the subcontractor also has a broad customer base. The principal only need to provide minimal technical assistance to the subcontractor and the subcontractor does not need sophisticated machinery and skills to perform subcontracting jobs. The frequency of orders has little impact on the relationship since both sides are loosely tied to each other and the exit costs are low for both sides when facing market demand fluctuations. Examples abound in commercial subcontracting (Gereffi, 1993). In this case, neither the principal nor the subcontractor has strong incentive to maintain a long-term association with each other. Consequently, neither investment in transaction-specific assets nor development of relational exchange norms will be necessary.

Second, a subcontractor is more dependent when the principal has stronger bargaining power. This occurs when asset-specific investments made by the parties are asymmetric. The buyer commitments are usually confined to specific physical capital, including specific dies, moulds and tooling for the manufacture of a contracted product (Nishiguchi, 1994). The subcontractor, on the other hand, has to invest in special-purpose equipment, employ skilled workers and engineers who are devoted to customer-specific operation; expand production capacity to meet the principal's requirement. The industry structure is such that many suppliers from developing countries are competing for relatively few buyers from developed countries. It is difficult for a subcontractor to diversify its customer-base and its sales revenue. To secure long-term orders from the principal, the subcontractor has to invest a greater degree of specific assets, which in turn leave them vulnerable to the potential hold-up by the principal. However, such an unbalanced subcontracting relationship may not be unstable. Although buyers from developed countries have much leverage among many suppliers in developing countries, stable long-term relationships with their suppliers can enhance performance certainty by reducing the costs in seeking suitable overseas suppliers, in drawing up multiple contracts, and in monitoring multiple suppliers in different countries. All of these benefits would be lost in a frequent shift of suppliers. Opportunism by one party can erode the long-term gains potentially accruing to both parties in a dyadic buyer-supplier relationship (Brown et al., 2000). These are also the reasons why arm's length outsourcing may involve a long-term relationship. But the higher degree of asset specificity points to a more inter-locked pattern of relationship in subcontracting than in outsourcing. Both the principal and the subcontractor have incentives to maintain the long-term relationships. Consequently, both sides may invest in transaction-specific assets and develop relational exchange norms in order to consolidate the relationship.

Third, situations where a principal is more dependent on a subcontractor are less common. They happen when the overseas subcontractor holds know-how crucial to the principal's production cycle. Some once-off and occasional large purchasing orders that involve sophisticated work such as in aerospace (Esposito & Storto, 1994) and shipbuilding industries (Smitka, 1991) might qualify as examples, since they require highly specialized expertise and more importantly there are more buyers than suppliers in the global market. Subcontractors enjoy stronger bargaining power when they are not merely producing certain products or components, but serve as intermediates for transferring knowledge of the local market to foreign buyer firms. In this case, a local subcontractor's bargaining power stem not from the transaction characteristics, but from the foreign buyer's strategic purpose in developing the local market with the help of the local supplier (Wang, 2007). Nevertheless, the subcontractor may be unaware of the principal's strategic motive and fail to materialise its power advantage in dealing with the foreign principal firm.

Fourth, when the principal and the subcontractor are mutually and heavily dependent on each other, the demand for equal collaboration is high. Subcontracting of this type requires highly specialized investments from both sides and the relationship is balanced (Wang, 2007). In such a subcontracting relationship, the principal typically contracts out the assembly of a final product. The principal commitments contain a high degree of asset specificity since complete assembly requires the highest integration of contract-specific physical facilities, including dedicated assembly lines, tooling and testing equipment (Nishiguchi, 1994). Moreover, the principal will incur human asset-specific investments in the form of managerial training and technical assistance to the overseas subcontractor to attain the production specifications (Sharpston, 1977). For subcontractors, end-product assembly for a particular overseas buyer will require specific investments both in human capital (e.g., employ highly skilled workers or provide special training) and in physical assets (e.g., purchase specialised machinery and equipment).

Therefore, principals and subcontractors commit a similar level of asset-specific investments, which support an equal collaborative relationship characterised by common interest, mutual obligations, and trust (Morris & Imrie, 1992; Smitka, 1991). Under this circumstance, the principal and the subcontractor rely on both mechanisms to govern their ongoing exchanges and mitigate opportunism: investments in transaction-specific assets that create a mutual hold-up situation and development of shared relational exchange norms such as role integrity and harmonious conflict resolution (Brown et al., 2000).

CONCLUSION

International subcontracting is often studied as an important instrument for industrial development at the policy level. Few studies have looked at the phenomenon from international business and strategic management perspectives. In line with Williamson-type of transaction cost-comparative contracting approach, the article defines international subcontracting as a type of long-term relational contract between buyers and suppliers in different countries, aiming to facilitate the sourcing of products or components with buyer-specific requirements. Building rigorously on the transaction cost theory, the paper develops an analytical framework to investigate the choice of international subcontracting over its market (arm's length outsourcing) and hierarchy alternatives (vertical integrated MNEs).

The comparison between subcontracting and its alternatives provides both prescriptive and pridictive value for international managers who face the strategic choice between outsourcing, subcontracting and vertical integration when organizing the supply chain across national borders. Table 1 summarizes the major transaction characteristics, advantages, and distantages of the different forms of supply chain organization.

Based on the framework, we developed a set of testable propositions that can be used not only for future empirical research but also to aid managers in making strategic choice between outsourcing, long term subcontracting, and vertical integration (Greenfield or acquisition) for organizing supply chain across borders. For example, we suggest that international subcontracting should be chosen over outsourcing when there is a higher level of asset-specificity in the purchasing/supplying transaction. It should be chosen over greenfield when there are sigificant costs involved in learning how to operate greenfield plants overseas. When choosing between international subcontracting and acquisition of overseas suppliers, managers

Table 1. Outsourcing, subcontracting, and vertical integration

	Transaction characteristics	Advantages	Disadvantages	When to use it
Outsourcing	Arm's length contract	Better for realizing economies of specialization and comparative advantages	Unstable exchange relationship due to low switching costs	Most suitable for facilitating trading of standard goods and services
Subcontracting	Relational contract with bi-lateral governance	Stable long-term relationship between particular buyers (principals) and suppliers (subcontractors)	High switching costs to alternative trading partners due to higher degree of asset-specific investments	Most suitable for facilitating purchasing and supplying of goods and services containing some degree of asset-specific investments
Vertical integration	Relational contract with unified governance	Complete hierarchical control over the supply of goods and services within the boundary of the firm	High agency costs in incentivising and managing in-house suppliers	Most suitable for organizing purchasing and supplying of highly idiosyncratic goods and services

should consider a range of factors, including how difficult it is to disentangle the desired assets of the acquied firm from the non-desired ones, how costly it is to assess the true market value of the acquisition targets ex ante and in managing the acquired firms ex post.

The framework also allows us to examine the specific nature of a range of subcontracting relationships. We identify four types of subcontracting relationships in terms of the degree of interdependence and bargaining power between principals and subcontractors. We demonstrate how the variations along transactional dimensions, especially asset-specific investments by the principal and the subcontractor, shape the different dyadic exchange relationship. We also argue that the two major governance mechanisms, investments in transaction-specific assets and development of relational exchange norms, have different efficacy in preserving and managing a range of subcontracting relationships. The paper thus offers a conceptually coherent foundation for researchers and managers to analyse international subcontracting as a form of international business organization at the firm level, complementing the existing literature's emphasis on studying the topic as a macro-economic phenomenon.

REFERENCES

Barney, J. B. (1991). Firm resources and sustained competitive advantage. *Journal of Management, 17*(1), 99-120.

Bell, J. (1996). *Single or joint venture: A comprehensive approach to foreign entry mode choice.* Aldershot: Avebury.

Besanko, D., Dranove, D., & Shanley, M. (2004). *Economics of strategy* (3rd ed.). New York: John Wiley & Sons.

Brown, J. R., Dev, C. S., & Lee, D. J. (2000). Managing marketing channel opportunism: The efficacy of alternative governance mechanism. *Journal of Marketing, 64*, 51-65.

Buckley, P. J., & Casson, M. (1976). The future of the multinational enterprise. London: Macmillan.

Casson, M. (1990). *Enterprise and competitiveness: A system view of international business.* Oxford: Clarendon Press.

Casson, M. (1987). *The firm and the market.* Oxford: Basil Blackwell.

Cheung, S. N. S. (1983). The contractual nature of the firm. *Journal of Law and Economics, 16*, 1-21.

Coase, R. H. (1937). The nature of the firm. *Economica, 4*, 386-405.

Cohen, B. (1975). *Multinational firms and Asian exports.* New Haven, CT: Yale University Press.

Conner, K. R., & Prahalad, C. K. (1996). A resource-based theory of the firm: Knowledge versus opportunism. *Organization Science, 7*(5), 477-501.

Dyer, J. (1997). Effective interfirm collaboration: How firms minimize transaction costs and maximize transaction value. *Strategic Management Journal, 18*, 535-556.

Dyer, J., & Nobeoka, K. (2000). Creating and managing a high performance knowledge-sharing network: The Toyota case. *Strategic Management Journal, 21*, 345-367.

Dyer, J., & Singh, H. (1998). The relational view: Cooperative strategy and sources of interorganizational competitive advantage. *Academy of Management Review, 23*(4), 660-679.

Esposito, E., & Storto, C. L. (1994). Qualitative and structural changes of the subcontracting firms: A micro-analytical approach to the study of inter-firm relationships. In J. M. Veciana (Ed.), *SMEs: Internationalisation, networks, and strategy* (pp.345-358). Aldershot: Avebury.

Foss, N. J. (1996). Introduction: The emerging competence perspective. In N. J. Foss & C. Knudsen (Eds.), *Towards a competence theory of the firm* (pp.1-12). London: Routledge.

Gereffi, G. (1993). International subcontracting and global capitalism: Reshaping the Pacific Rim. In R. A. Palat (Ed.), *Pacific-Asia and the future of the World System* (pp. 67-82), Westport: Greenwood Press.

Germidis, D. (1980). *International subcontracting: A new form of investment*. Paris: OECD.

Ghoshal, S., & Moran, P. (1996). Bad for practice: A critique of the transaction cost framework. *Academy of Management Journal, 21*(1), 13-47.

Halbach, A. J. (1989). *Multinational enterprises and subcontracting in the third world: A study of inter-industry linkages*. Geneva: International Labour Office.

Hamada, K. (1974). An economic analysis of the duty free zone. *Journal of International Economics, 4*(3), 225-241.

Hennart, J. F. (1991). The transaction cost theory of joint ventures: An empirical study of Japanese subsidiaries in the United States. *Management Science, 37*(4), 483-497.

Hennart, J. F. (1988). A transaction cost theory of equity joint ventures. *Strategic Management Journal, 9*(4), 361-374.

Hennart, J. F. (1982). *A theory of multinational enterprise*. Ann Arbor, MI: University of Michigan Press.

Hennart, J. F., & Park, Y. R. (1993). Greenfield vs. acquisitions: The strategy of Japanese investors in the United States. *Management Science, 39*(9), 1054-1070.

Holmes, J. (1986). The organization and locational structure of production subcontracting. In A. J. Scott, & M. Storper (Eds.), *Production, work, and territory: The geographical anatomy of industrial capitalism* (pp. 80-106), Boston: Allen & Unwin.

Hovi, N. (1994). Internationalising subcontractors: Is co-operation an alternative? In J. M. Veciana (Ed), *SMEs: Internationalisation, networks, and strategy* (pp. 359-379), Aldershot: Avebury.

Jap, S. D., & Anderson, E. (2003). Safeguarding interorganizational performance and continuity under ex post opportunism. *Management Science, 49*(12), 1684-1701.

Kashyap, S. P. (1992). *Recent developments in the small enterprises sector in India: Economic and social aspects*. Geneva: International Institute for Labour Studies.

Kay, N. M. (1995). *Why firms succeed*. New York: Oxford University Press.

Kogut, B. (1988). Joint ventures: Theoretical and empirical perspectives. *Strategic Management Journal, 9*, 319-332.

Knudsen, C. (1995). Theories of the firm, strategic management, and leadership. In C. A. Montgomery (Ed.), *Resource-based and evolutionary theories of the firm: Towards a synthesis* (pp. 179-218). Boston: Kluwer Academic Publishers.

Lawson, V. (1992). Industrial subcontracting and employment forms in Latin America: A framework for contextual analysis. *Progress in Human Geography, 16*, 1-23.

Macneil, I. R. (1978). Contracts: Adjustment of long term economic relations under classical, neo-classical and relational contract law. *Northwestern University Law Review, 72*, 854-905.

Macneil, I. R. (1974). The many futures of contract. *Southern California Law Review, 47*, 691-738.

Morris, J., & Imrie, R. (1992). *Transforming buyer-supplier relations: Japanese-style industrial practices in western context*. London: Macmillan.

Nishiguchi, T. (1994). *Strategic industrial sourcing: The Japanese advantage.* New York: Oxford University Press.

Peteraf, M. A. (1993). The cornerstone of competitive advantages: A resource-based view. *Strategic Management Journal, 14,* 179-191.

Reddy, S. B., Osborn, R. N., & Hennart, J. F. (2002). The prevalence of equity and non-equity cross-border linkages: Japanese investments and alliances in the United States. *Organization Studies, 23*(5), 759-780.

Riedel, J. (1975). The nature and determinants of export-oriented direct foreign investment in a developing country: A case study of Taiwan. *Weltirtschaftliches Archiv, 3*(3), 505-528.

Rogerson, C. M. (1995). Looking to the Pacific Rim: Production subcontracting and small-scale industry in South Africa. *International Small Business Journal, 13*(3), 65-79.

Rugman, A. M. (1981). *Inside the multinationals: The economics of internal markets.* New York: Columbia University Press.

Sengenberger, W., & Pkye, F. (1991). Small firm industrial districts and local economic regeneration: Research and policy issues. *Labour and Society, 16,* 1-24.

Sharpston, M. (1977). International subcontracting. *Oxford Economic Papers, 27,* 94-135.

Smitka, M. J. (1991). *Competitive ties: Subcontracting in Japanese automotive industry.* New York: Columbia University Press.

Wang, Y. (2007). To internationally subcontract or not. *Monash Business Review, 3*(1), 48-49.

Wathne, K. H., & Heide, J. B. (2000). Opportunism in interfirm relationships: Forms, outcomes, and solutions. *Journal of Marketing, 64,* 36-51.

Wernerfelt, B. (1984). A resource-based view of the firm. *Strategic Management Journal, 5,* 171-180.

Williamson, O. E. (1999). Strategy research: Governance and competence perspectives. *Strategic Management Journal, 20*(12), 1087-1108.

Williamson, O. E. (1990). The firm as a nexus of treaties: An introduction. In M. Aoki, B. Gustafsson, & O. E. Williamson (Eds.), *The firm as a nexus of treaties* (pp. 1-25), London: Sage.

Williamson, O. E. (1985). *The economic institutions of capitalism.* New York: Free Press.

Williamson, O. E. (1979). Transaction cost economics: The governance of contractual relations. *The Journal of Law and Economics, 12*(2), 233-262.

Williamson, O. E. (1975). *Markets and hierarchies: Analysis and antitrust implications.* New York: Free Press.

This work was previously published in the International Journal of Information Systems and Supply Chain Management, Vol. 1, Issue 3, edited by J. Wang, pp. 21-32, copyright 2008 by IGI Publishing (an imprint of IGI Global).

Chapter 15
The Strategic Implications of E–Network Integration and Transformation Paths for Synchronizing Supply Chains

Minjoon Jun
New Mexico State University, USA

Shaohan Cai
Carleton University, Canada

DaeSoo Kim
Korea University Business School, Korea

ABSTRACT

Streamlining information flows across the physical supply chain is crucial for successful supply chain management. This study examines different structures of e-networks (i.e., virtual supply chains linked via electronic information and communication technologies) and their maximum capabilities to gain e-network benefits. Further, this research explores four levels of e-network integration based on a 2x2 e-network technology and transaction integration matrix. Of the four levels, an e-network with high e-technology/high e-transaction integration appears to be most desirable for the companies that aspire to achieve the maximum benefits from their IT investments. Finally, this study identifies three alternative transformation paths toward a powerful high e-technology/high e-transaction integration network and discusses strategic implications of selecting those paths, in terms of e-network structures, availability of financial and technical resources, supply chain members' collaborative planning, e-security mechanisms, and supply chain size.

INTRODUCTION

As competition in the marketplace has increasingly intensified during the past decade, the strategic significance of close collaboration among supply chain members has dramatically increased. This advanced importance of collaborative chain activities is primarily attributable to the change of competitive scenes from a firm vs. a firm to a supply chain vs. a supply chain (Li, Rao, Ragu-Nathan, & Ragu-Nathan, 2005). A supply chain can be defined as encompassing all activities associated with the flow and transformation of goods from the raw material stage through to the end user, as well as the associated information flows (Handfield & Nicholas, 1999).

As this definition implies, a high level of information sharing and collaboration among chain members is an important prerequisite to achieving high performance of the entire supply chain (Li, Ragu-Nathan, Ragu-Nathan, & Rao, 2006; Monczka, Peterson, & Handfield, 1998; Sahin & Robinson, 2005). Many researchers have emphasized this crucial role of inter-organizational information transactions in supply chain management (SCM). They consistently argue that streamlining information flows across the entire chain is one of the critical success factors for gaining maximum SCM benefits, such as lowering product costs, reducing product development cycle time, and increasing responsiveness to customers' changing preferences (e.g., Christiaanse & Kumar, 2000; Cooper & Tracey, 2005; van Hoek, 2001).

However, in reality, lack of information sharing due to inadequate information systems and lack of trust among chain members appear to be serious obstacles to obtaining such SCM benefits (Cooper & Tracey, 2005; Wisner & Tan, 2000). Therefore, to survive in today's fierce competition between supply chains in global markets, the effective use of newly emerged information technologies has already become an important concern for managers who aspire to use an SCM approach as a strategic competitive weapon (Chopra, 2003;

Elmuti, 2002). Those information technologies include the Internet, intranet, extranet, wireless technologies like radio frequency identification (RFID), and information integration systems such as enterprise resource planning (ERP), product lifecycle management (PLM), supply chain planning (SCP), supply chain execution (SCE), customer relationship management (CRM), supplier relationship management (SRM), and business process management (BPM).

However, despite the prominent importance of information systems and their integration across the supply chain, most of the previous studies have addressed this issue in the context of a dyadic relationship (e.g., a buyer and a supplier), rather than from the vantage point of an entire supply chain with multiple layers (e.g., a buyer, a buyer's buyer, and a supplier, a supplier's supplier) (Christiaanse & Kumar, 2000). More specifically, relatively little research has addressed such an important issue as "what types of, and in what way, electronic chains (e-networks) should be adopted and implemented to support all the intra- and inter-organizational activities across the supply chain, where the e-network refers to a non-physical, virtual supply chain linked by electronic information and communication technologies?"

Therefore, this study aims at expanding the body of knowledge on e-networks established in the physical supply chain by addressing the following five questions:

1. What types of e-networks exist in practice and what are their key characteristics?
2. What potential benefits can be obtained by an effective e-network management?
3. What measurement schemes can be employed to assess and categorize the various levels of e-network integration?
4. What are the strategic implications of various e-network integration levels and e-network types in gaining e-network benefits?
5. What transformation strategies and their related factors need to be considered in

transforming an existing e-network into the most desirable one, which enables chain members to effectively achieve their common SCM goals?

The present study contributes to the literature in three ways. First, this study develops a classification scheme to better represent and understand the diverse and complex nature of e-network structures and their maximum capabilities to gain e-network benefits. Second, this article proposes a 2x2 e-network technology and transaction integration matrix to categorize various levels of e-network integration, and to identify the most desirable level of integration for achieving the maximum benefits from IT investments. Finally, this study introduces three alternative e-network transformation paths toward a powerful high e-technology/high e-transaction integration network and discusses the managerial implications related to those paths.

E-NETWORK TYPES AND POTENTIAL BENEFITS

Kumar and van Dissel (1996), from an interdependence view of organizations, have classified electronic data interchange (EDI)-based interorganizational information systems (IOSs) into three categories: value/supply-chain IOS (enabling sequential transactions among chain members), pooled information resource IOS (sharing common IS/IT resources), and networked IOS (sharing data and supporting collaborative work among members). Building on Kumar and van Dissel's (1996) work, the present study developed a four-type e-network classification scheme to better represent current IOS environments, where Web-based technologies are widely utilized for data sharing and information transmissions. These four types are tree, hub, net, and hybrid e-networks (see Figure 1).

Figure 1. Classification of e-network structures

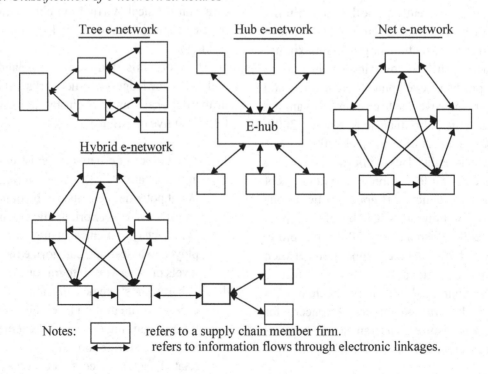

Notes: refers to a supply chain member firm.
refers to information flows through electronic linkages.

Tree E-Network

The "tree" e-network, similar to Kumar and van Dissel's (1996) value/supply chain IOS, is very close to a typical, physical supply chain in its shape, which has one or more suppliers or buyers in each of its multi-tier stages. This e-network structure usually takes a linear form of electronic linkages, reflecting sequential supplier-buyer relationships from end suppliers to end customers. Currently, it is commonly found in most industries, including basic apparel, book publishing, computer, and food and beverage.

Hub E-Network

Similar to the pooled information resource IOS, the "hub" e-network, often called "e-hub" or "e-marketplace," is centered on a platform through which both suppliers and buyers are linked to make transactions and/or simultaneously exchange necessary data and information such as order status, shipment schedules, inventory levels, and CAD/CAM data with one another (Kaplan & Sawhney, 2000; Sharifi, Kehoe, & Hopkins, 2006; Zeng & Pathak, 2003). This nonlinear intermediary, often called infomediary, is further classified into vertical and horizontal exchanges, aggregation, and auction and reverse auction hubs (Kaplan & Sawhney, 2000; Zeng & Pathak, 2003). Vertical exchange hubs (e.g., eSteel.com, PaperExchange. com, FloraFlex.com) provide deep domain-specific content and relationships, typically by automating and hosting procurement process for an industry-specific vertical market, while horizontal exchange hubs (e.g., SupplyCore.com, Employease.com, Citadon.com) focus on providing the same functions, such as procurement, benefit administration, and project management, or automating the same business process scalable across multiple vertical markets (Jennings, 1999; Kaplan & Sawhney, 2000).

Next, aggregators serve as hubs in one-way B2C networks (e.g., AOL, Yahoo!, Tavelocity. com, Buy.com) to function as one-stop shopping places for smaller purchasers or operate as hubs in two-way B2B networks (e.g., PlasticsNet.com) that mediate between buyers and sellers and create benefits for both sides with domain expertise. Finally, auction (e.g., eBay, FreeMarkets) or reverse auction (e.g., uBid, Priceline.com) hubs create value by spatial matching of buyers and sellers for a specific bid event for unique non-standard or perishable products. Recently, more companies act as reverse auction hubs, but not as intermediaries, by increasingly sharing material specifications with suppliers, selecting and pre-qualifying them, and running bidding events (e.g., GE's Source-Bid Events). Furthermore, some hubs in the automotive, consumer packaged goods (CPG), logistics service, and business solution system industries (e.g., Transora.com, Transplace. com, mySAP.com) are providing some or all of the aforementioned services.

Net E-Network

The "net" e-network, similar to the networked IOS, refers to the structure in which chain members have direct electronic linkages with one another in a networked supply chain (or a supply network) (Kehoe & Boughton, 2001). For example, in the construction industry, each firm involved in a specific construction project needs to have a direct access to other participants, even though they may not have an explicit or a direct contracting relationship (Cheng, Li, Love, & Irani, 2001). Although these virtual nonlinear net e-networks are rarely found in practice, this type of e-network is increasingly emerging in some industries as evidenced by the interviews of managers in electronic, mechanics, and paper industries (Kemppainen & Vepsalainen, 2003).

Hybrid E-Network

The "hybrid" e-network takes a combined form of the previously mentioned e-network structures, for example, a tree-hub e-network or a tree-net e-network. In practice, many large-sized firms, such as Ford, GM, GE, and Cisco, often employ this complex type of e-networks for managing their supply chains.

Potential E-Network Benefits and E-Network Type

A review of the relevant literature (e.g., Bauer, Poirier, Lapide, & Bermudez, 2001; Edwards, Peters, & Sharman, 2001; Heinrich, 2003; Hendon,

Nath, & Hendon, 1998; Iacovou, Benbasat, & Dexter, 1995; Jennings, 1999; Kaplan & Sawhney, 2000; Ovalle & Marquez, 2003; Phan & Stata, 2002; Poirier & Bauer, 2001; Sharifi et al., 2006; Turban, Lee, King, & Turban, 2000) has revealed a variety of potential e-network benefits and varying degrees of the benefits that can be realized by each e-network type. Figure 2 summarizes the key points of benefits and capabilities.

There are three categories of potential e-network benefits: informational, operational, and strategic. First, informational benefits pertain to

Figure 2. E-network benefits and maximum potential gains by e-network type

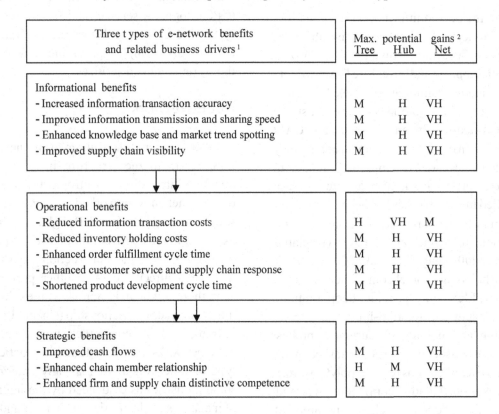

Three types of e-network benefits and related business drivers [1]	Max. potential gains [2]		
	Tree	Hub	Net
Informational benefits			
- Increased information transaction accuracy	M	H	VH
- Improved information transmission and sharing speed	M	H	VH
- Enhanced knowledge base and market trend spotting	M	H	VH
- Improved supply chain visibility	M	H	VH
Operational benefits			
- Reduced information transaction costs	H	VH	M
- Reduced inventory holding costs	M	H	VH
- Enhanced order fulfillment cycle time	M	H	VH
- Enhanced customer service and supply chain response	M	H	VH
- Shortened product development cycle time	M	H	VH
Strategic benefits			
- Improved cash flows	M	H	VH
- Enhanced chain member relationship	H	M	VH
- Enhanced firm and supply chain distinctive competence	M	H	VH

Notes:

1. Three types of e-network benefits and their related business drivers are partly adapted and compiled from Bauer et al. (2001), Edward et al. (2001), Heinrich (2003), Hendon et al. (1998), Iacovou et al. (1995), Jennings (Jennings, 1999), Kaplan and Sawhney (2000), Phan and Stata (Li et al., 2006; Monczka et al., 1998; , 2002), Ovalle and Marquez (2003), Poirier and Bauer (2001), Sharifi(2006), and Turban et al. (2000).

2. Maximum potential gains by e-network type: M = Moderate, H = High, VH = Very High.

the effects of e-networks on intra- and inter-organizational information transactions: increased information transaction accuracy, improved information transmission and sharing speed, enhanced market knowledge base and trend spotting, and improved supply chain visibility (Iacovou et al., 1995; Ovalle & Marquez, 2003; Sharifi et al., 2006; Turban et al., 2000). Second, operational benefits refer to the impacts of e-networks on the efficiency of the intra- and inter-organizational business processes: reduced information transaction costs and inventory holding costs, enhanced order fulfillment cycle time, customer service and supply chain response time, and shortened product development cycle time (Hendon et al., 1998; Iacovou et al., 1995; Sharifi et al., 2006). Finally, strategic benefits relate to the effects of e-networks on the competitive position of the entire supply chain in the marketplace: improved cash flows, enhanced chain member relationships, and enhanced distinctive competence of member firms and the entire supply chain (Edwards et al., 2001; Iacovou et al., 1995; Phan & Stata, 2002).

It should be noted that the informational benefits achieved by a highly effective e-network can help chain members obtain a wide range of operational and, in turn, strategic benefits. For example, accurate real-time information transactions across the e-network can enable members to reduce their inventory holding costs and improve their customer service, which in turn could improve their cash flows and enhance distinctive competence of the supply chain as a whole. Moreover, in principle, the net and hub e-networks have a greater potential in gaining maximum e-network benefits than the tree e-network, because the net and hub e-networks enable their members to communicate simultaneously with one another through direct connections (net type) or indirect connections via a platform (hub type), rather than transferring necessary information in a sequential fashion (tree type).

The overall magnitude of informational, operational, and strategic benefits that can be obtained tends to increase as the e-network structure changes from tree to hub to net. However, compared to tree e-networks, hub and net e-networks might have some constraints in gaining substantial cost savings on information transactions as one of the key informational benefits and improving chain partner long-term relationships as one of the key strategic benefits, because of the inherent nature of the hub and net e-networks—that is, multilateral and simultaneous communications among chain members and low switching costs to reconfigure the e-network after changing some of its partner firms. Furthermore, the actual realization of e-network benefits across the supply chain, in reality, is still highly dependent upon the chain members' planning and execution of their e-network efforts. It should also be noted that the aforementioned operational and strategic benefits could also be achieved by other initiatives, such as eliminating non-value-added activities across the supply chain and carefully selecting and retaining competent chain members.

E-NETWORK INTEGRATION MEASUREMENT FRAMEWORK

Successful e-network implementation — seamlessly automating the information transaction processes across organizational boundaries via information and communication technologies—helps all of the chain members achieve maximum e-network benefits and in turn can enhance their competitiveness. Specifically, the types and magnitude of e-network benefits that a supply chain obtains can be primarily determined by how well an e-network is integrated among members. In addition, different e-network structures and supply chain sizes may moderate the effects of e-network integration levels on the e-network benefits that are actually realized.

Measurements of E-Network Integration

Prior studies have proposed various measurements to assess the integration level of inter- and intra-organizational electronic communication. In the context of EDI, Premkumar and Ramamurthy (1995) suggest three key dimensions of EDI utilization: extent of adaptation (the extent of using EDI for generating purchasing order and sales invoice for trading partners), internal diffusion (extent to which EDI is integrated to systems such as shipping/distribution and inventory control), and external connectivity (the extent to which customers are linked by EDI, and the amount of transactions conducted through EDI). Similarly, Massetti and Zmud (1996) propose a four-facet measurement of EDI usage. They are: (1) volume, which represents the extent to which an organization's document exchanges are handled through EDI connections; (2) diversity, which refers to the number of distinct document types that an organization handles via EDI; (3) depth, which refers to the degree of electronic consolidation that has been established between the business processes of two or more trading partners; and (4) breadth, which represents the extent to which an organization has established EDI connections with external organizations such as suppliers, customers, government agencies, and financial institutions.

Later, Shore and Venkatachalam (2003) attempted to measure supply chain information sharing capability in terms of information technology infrastructure (infrastructure capability) and capability of communication collaboration activities (collaboration capability). Recently, in the context of Internet communication, Cai, Jun, and Yang (2006) measured inter-organizational Internet communication in terms of frequency, diversity, and formality dimensions.

It should be noted that all the dimensions identified by the aforementioned studies could be broadly categorized into two groups: e-technology integration (the extent to which electronic linkages are established among chain members) and e-transaction integration (the extent to which electronic linkages are utilized to share information by chain members). Considering the characteristics of the two groups of integration, the following two dimensions of e-network integration are proposed in this study: *e-network information technology (e-technology) integration* and *e-network information transaction (e-transaction) integration*.

The *e-technology* integration dimension, similar to Shore and Venkatachalam's (2003) concept of infrastructure capability, measures the extent to which business processes are electronically consolidated via ICT within and between members in a supply chain. The degree of e-technology integration is heavily influenced by the chain members' willingness to participate in the e-network integration efforts, as well as the connectivity and compatibility of their IS infrastructure (Byrd & Turner, 2001). Connectivity (or breadth) refers to the ability of chain members' IS infrastructure to link to any other IS within and between organizations (adapted from Duncan, 1995; Massetti & Zmud, 1996). On the other hand, compatibility (or depth) means the ability of chain members' IS infrastructure to automatically exchange and handle any type of information (e.g., text, video, image, and audio) across any technology components (regardless of manufacturer, make, or type) in the chain (adapted from Duncan, 1995; Massetti & Zmud, 1996). Thus, high e-technology integration refers to the ideal situation where all chain members' information systems are not only linked internally and externally across the chain (high connectivity), but also able to automatically share information among themselves (high compatibility). Conversely, low e-technology integration pertains to situations where most chain members' ISs are not linked either internally or externally across the chain (low connectivity) and/or are unable to automatically share information among themselves (low compatibility).

The *e-transaction* integration dimension, similar to Shore and Venkatachalam's (2003) concept of collaboration capability, represents the extent to how much (volume) and what types of documents (diversity) are transmitted via electronic linkages among members within a supply chain (adapted from Massetti & Zmud, 1996). The chain-wide electronic transaction volume can be determined by dividing the total number of documents transmitted through *electronic linkages* in a given time period within a supply chain by the total number of documents transmitted through electronic linkages or other communication means such as mail in the same time period within the supply chain. The chain-wide electronic transaction diversity can be measured by the total number of different document types transmitted through electronic linkages in a given time period within a supply chain. Consequently, the e-transaction integration should reach a certain level for individual members to benefit from their IT investments. This constraint often makes some chain members reluctant to participate in the chain-wide efforts of tightening e-technology integration. Many firms in the consumer packaged goods industry often face this economic feasibility constraint in adopting collaborative planning, forecasting, and replenishment (CPFR) practices.

However, it should be noted that there are some differences between the present study's two measurements and Shore and Venkatachalam's (2003) counterparts. First, while Shore and Venkatachalam's (2003) information technology infrastructure dimension focuses on assessing downstream *individual* suppliers' integration capabilities, the present study's e-technology integration dimension concentrates on measuring both upstream buyers' and downstream suppliers' IS integration (i.e., dual-direction communication). Next, while Shore and Venkatachalam's (2003) collaboration capability dimension focuses on assessing suppliers' ability and willingness to share a variety of information with buyers, the present study's e-transaction integration dimension concentrates

on measuring the extent of actual information sharing between upstream buyers and downstream suppliers throughout the supply chain.

E-Network Technology-Transaction Integration Matrix

Based on the two dimensions of e-network integration discussed earlier, the authors developed a 2x2 matrix with vertical and horizontal axes representing the high–low levels of e-technology integration and e-transaction integration, respectively. Figure 3 presents four groups of e-networks classified by the two e-network integration dimensions. The four groups are: powerful e-networks (high e-technology/high e-transaction integration), inefficient e-networks (low e-technology/high e-transaction integration), ineffective e-networks (high e-technology/low e-transaction integration), and impotent e-networks (low e-technology/low e-transaction integration).

Powerful E-Network: High E-Technology / High E-Transaction Integration

In the high e-technology and high e-transaction e-network, a variety and large volume of information is transmitted between members through highly automated (or high-depth) electronic linkages like computer system-to-computer system connections. For example, the members of this powerful e-network can communicate real-time information with one another through SCM solution systems or other inter-organizational systems that are integrated with their respective internal ERP systems, thereby ensuring the visibility or transparency of supply chain business processes. A typical example would be the Cisco Systems' virtual manufacturing system. The system included 37 factories, which are linked to Cisco via the Internet. Approximately 80% of Cisco's purchase orders were automatically released via

Figure 3. E-network technology-transaction integration matrix and transformation paths

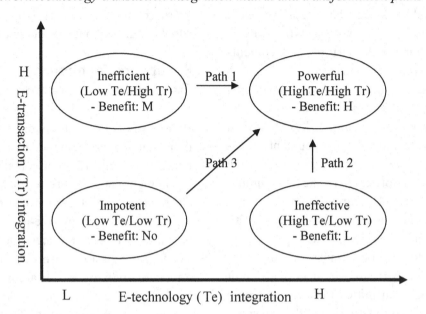

the Internet to its members. By using this virtual system, Cisco's partners manufactured all the components, performed 90% of the subassembly work, and conducted 55% of the final assembly. Furthermore, the system allowed Cisco to speed time-to-market of its products through collaboration with its suppliers and customers (Ansley, 2000). In other words, through the virtual manufacturing system, Cisco was able to create the right design in a shorter time frame by sharing information seamlessly with its partners in the process of new product development, including prototyping, design change, and quality testing.

The potential benefits that can be realized by this powerful e-network are not greatly affected by e-network type. In the case of advanced hub and net e-networks, the highly automated and integrated electronic linkages enable their members to perform simultaneous, real-time communications with one another directly (net e-networks) or indirectly through a platform (hub e-networks). Even in the less advanced tree e-network, the information and data sent by one member can be rapidly transmitted throughout

the e-network without any interruption, because the fully integrated electronic linkages within and between members can automatically handle and deliver electronic documents in a sequential order across the e-network. Therefore, this powerful e-network can eliminate or significantly reduce labors needed for intra- and inter-organizational information exchanges, resulting in eliminating keyed-in errors, lowering information transaction costs, increasing information sharing, and making timely information available to all participants.

In addition, the powerful e-network can help members to eliminate or substantially mitigate so-called "bullwhip effects" in a supply chain. The bullwhip effects can occur when the members make ordering decisions based on the orders only from the next downstream member rather than all the chain members (Lee, Padmanabhan, & Whang, 1997). In this case, each member tends to overestimate the demand of its products to ensure on-time delivery, and order raw materials and components based on the inflated forecasting. The overestimated order variability is then amplified across the supply chain, resulting in high inventory, poor customer service, lost revenues, misguided capacity plans, ineffective transportation, and missed production schedules (Lee et al., 1997). Therefore, in order to reduce the bullwhip effects and improve the total supply chain performance, the extent of information sharing needs to increase in a supply chain (Yu, Yan, & Cheng, 2001). All firms within such a powerful e-network are most likely to achieve a wide range of informational, operational, and strategic e-network benefits to the maximum. Further, the high level of information transactions across the chain can warrant its partners' IT investments.

Inefficient E-Network: Low E-Technology / High E-Transaction Integration

In the low e-technology and high e-transaction integration e-network, active information transactions occur between members, mostly through inefficient low-depth electronic linkages, such as file-to-file connections (e.g., e-mail exchanges between trading partners), since many members have not yet integrated their own internal IS with an IOS, such as Web-EDI, extranets, and SCM solution systems. Some chain partners may not even have any electronic connections with other members, and may rely on traditional communication media like fax and phone for their inter-firm communication needs.

Therefore, this type of e-network usually employs numerous employees to manually handle a large volume and variety of information transmission; such human intervention may result in slow and inaccurate information transactions and/or less information sharing between members. Consequently, those firms are likely to incur "opportunity costs" and fail to gain the maximum potential of IT benefits by additional investment on their IS infrastructure.

One typical example of such inefficient network could be found in the case of one of the Komatsu America Corp.-Peoria Manufacturing

Operations (KAC-PMO). The company is a world-leading producer of special, heavy mining equipment, which has approximately 350 direct materials suppliers. Although KAC-PMO had its own ERP system in place and made various types of data, such as sales forecasts and an e-catalog electronically available to its key suppliers through the system, both the company and its suppliers had to utilize mostly traditional communication channels to exchange information, because there was a lack of fully integrated IOSs between them (Versendaal & Brinkkemper, 2003). According to Versendaal and Brinkkemper (2003):

[KAC-PMO's] forecast reports and purchase orders were printed and faxed to suppliers. Suppliers keyed-in order data when receiving a purchase order fax. Suppliers provided [order] fulfillment dates to KAC-PMO on paper or by phone. KAC-PMO entered promise dates of supplier fulfillment manually. Purchase order change proposals needed to be approved manually. (p. 44)

Later, under the heavy pressure of the needs to share a large amount of information with its key suppliers more frequently, KAC-PMO decided to implement an electronic trading exchange system, which enables the company to connect with most of its suppliers electronically.

It is worth noting that when some members form a hub or net e-network in a small segment of this inefficient e-network, the negative impacts of the overall low e-technology integration on the speed, accuracy, and timeliness of information transmission may be restricted only to the remainder of the members linked by low-depth electronic connections. On the other hand, if this inefficient e-network takes the form of a tree e-network and thus all information transmission across the e-network should be performed in a sequential fashion, most of the supply chain members will gain very limited informational benefits because of some "bottleneck" members, which inadvertently make delays or errors in transferring information through their low-depth electronic connections, requiring frequent human interventions.

Ineffective E-Network: High E-Technology / Low E-Transaction Integration

Even though most members in the high e-technology and low e-transaction integration e-network adopt modern IT, they use their highly integrated electronic linkages just to transmit a small volume and few types of documents. Thus, such under-utilization of the e-network causes those firms to incur "out-of-pocket costs" and achieve only minimal benefits from their IT investments.

The high e-technology/low e-transaction integration e-network can often be found in a small supply chain or a partial segment of a large supply chain, where a focal company has a dominant position and coerces other members to adopt intra- and inter-organizational IS. In this case, the coerced members tend to be reluctant to share their critical information with the focal company because they fear that the dominant firm would exploit the information to its own advantage, resulting in an ineffective e-network. Mostly, this phenomenon is due to the lack of trust, collaboration, and win-win thinking.

The failure of Covisint, a hub e-network in the automotive industry, represents a good example of the gloomy future of the ineffective e-network that fails to transform itself into the powerful e-network and justify its huge IT investment. As a joint venture of Ford, General Motors, and DaimlerChrysler, Covisint promised to bring more suppliers to the table of the OEM giants, lower the cost of transactions, open up the market for suppliers, and create visibility in the chain (Campbell, 2004).

However, while the suppliers of the big three were pushed to adopt Covisint, mistrust between the vehicle manufacturers and their suppliers resulted in the resistance from the suppliers (Koch, 2002). Particularly, the major first tier suppliers

were reluctant to utilize Covisint since they wanted to maintain their own data and subcontractors separately from the system (Rosenberg, 2003). Furthermore, many suppliers viewed such a network as a 'competitive-edge equalizer'. That is, if all parties are using the same technology and process, it is impossible for an individual supplier to build competitive advantage (Campbell, 2004). Thus, although 11,000 auto parts suppliers utilized the Covisint in some fashion, they only occupied 10-15% of the exchange's revenue, and the big three automotive makers accounted for the majority of the revenue. This fact implies that the Covisint (high e-technology integration) was severely underutilized (low e-transaction integration) by the downstream chain members. Eventually, the Covisint was sold to other firms in early 2004.

Impotent E-Network: Low E-Technology / Low E-Transaction Integration

In the low e-technology and low e-transaction integration e-network, most of the information exchanges between members are handled through low-depth electronic linkages and/or traditional communication media. This rather disintegrated e-network with a low volume and few types of document exchange usually slows down the pace of manufacturing processes across the supply chain, resulting in losses of its competitive edge against competitors.

Such a low e-technology/low e-transaction integration e-network can be observed in a large supply chain, where little or no chain-wide effort has been exerted to build highly integrated communication networks between members. For example, before Hewlett-Packard adopted the SCM software for its supply chain, its chain members had been using various applications with different sophistication levels, ranging from complex ERP programs to simple spreadsheets. Thus, sharing information among the chain members had been limited to passing data only to their adjacent members, and the speed of communication across the supply chain had been very slow. Consequently, this impotent e-network had slowed down the pace of the chain-wide manufacturing process and negatively affected the cash flows of all the chain members (eCompany Now Staff, 2000). In addition, the impotent e-network can often exist in a traditional EDI environment, where a dominant firm in an asymmetric relationship forces its weak trading partner to adopt EDI systems and the reluctant EDI adopters are inclined to use non-integrated, PC-based standalone EDI systems due to the lack of financial and technical resources.

STRATEGIC IMPLICATIONS OF E-NETWORK TRANSFORMATION PATHS

Of the aforementioned four groups of e-network integration, the high e-technology/high e-transaction e-network ideally provides maximum IT benefits to its members and can contribute to the sustainable competitiveness of the entire supply chain. Hence, it can be recommended that firms with e-networks falling into the other three groups (low e-technology/high e-transaction, high e-technology/low e-transaction, and low e-technology/low e-transaction) should consider transforming their e-networks into a powerful e-network (high e-technology/high e-transaction). The following section discusses three alternative transformation paths toward the powerful e-network and strategic considerations involving the transformation process.

Path 1: From Low E-Technology / High E-Transaction to High E-Technology / High E-Transaction

According to the case reported by Kok et al. (2005), Philip Semiconductors (PS) followed Path 1 in its transformation from an inefficient e-network (low e-technology/high e-transaction integration) to a powerful e-network (high e-technology/high e-transaction integration). Before 1999, Philip Semiconductors had a decentralized short-term planning process, which was disconnected from its medium-term planning. All the members of PS's supply chain, including contract manufacturers and customers, had independent weekly planning cycles based on orders from the immediate downstream member (i.e., tree e-network, low e-technology/high e-transaction). These independent processes caused long information latency and strong information distortion by poor visibility of material availability and local optimization, resulting in high bullwhip effects across the supply chain.

Later, PS implemented the collaborative planning process, which calculates the synchronized plan that determines and transmits all orders to be released at all links in the supply chain via a tightly integrated e-network system with a central (or shared) database (i.e., hub e-network; high e-transaction/high e-technology). The e-hub has enabled PS's chain members to virtually guarantee quantities and delivery time, thereby mitigating dramatically the influence of bullwhip effects and saving around US$5 million each year.

When members in an inefficient low e-technology/high e-transaction e-network attempt to fully integrate their ISs across the chain, it is recommended that they pay particular attention to the following three important issues: acquiring needed financial and technical resources, planning collectively for seeking the best software solutions, and adopting Internet-related technologies as communication channels.

First, some members in an inefficient low e-technology/high e-transaction e-network, mostly small firms, may not have sufficient financial and technical resources for integrating ISs internal and external to them. It is thus essential for a focal company to assist its partners in solving diverse and complex problems associated with IS integration.

Second, all members should take a collective planning approach to seeking optimal software solutions for the entire chain, which can avoid or significantly mitigate the adverse impacts by the lack of IS connectivity and compatibility on chain-wide information flows and ultimately reduce total e-network costs. For example, in today's chemical industry, many firms with ERP systems have been experiencing difficulties in connecting their ISs with those of other members, since they purchased the systems from various ERP vendors (e.g., SAP, Oracle) which have set their own standards (Roberts, 2000). Under such circumstances, only collective planning processes can yield a unified software solution to the various connectivity and compatibility problems. Of the three e-network structures, the net e-network is more likely to experience such problems than the tree or hub e-networks, since each member of the net e-network should establish its direct electronic linkages with the rest.

Finally, as argued by Horvath (2001), it is important for the e-network with a low e-technology integration to have the capability of open and low-cost connectivity through broadband Internet connections or virtual private networks. This capability enables small chain members to access a collaborative e-network infrastructure without a major investment in proprietary technology, thereby leading to a high level of e-network integration. In addition, third-party software and systems support for supply chain applications may play a key role in integrating small chain partners into a powerful e-network (Green, 2001; Horvath, 2001).

Path 2: From High E-Technology / Low E-Transaction to High E-Technology / High E-Transaction

Westerman and Cotteleer (1999) report the case of Tektronix Inc., a manufacturer of electronic tools and devices, which has migrated from an ineffective EDI-based net e-network (high e-technology/low e-transaction) to a powerful Internet-based hub e-network (high e-technology/ low e-transaction) by following Path 2. In 1992, the company operated seven separate data centers, which were decentralized and segregated by divisions. It had over 460 legacy systems just in the United States, none of which was standardized for global operation. Moreover, each of the company's manufacturers had its own communication protocol. In order to coordinate among these manufacturers, the company had to install multiple lines and protocol converters around its global network. As a result, although the connection between these divisions and manufacturers could be regarded as a high level of integration, the performance of the overall network was still suffering. Due to the sub-optimization of the network by the different divisions, the company could not obtain real-time information of inventory and performance, and could not effectively manage customer account and credit on a global basis. Therefore, the volume and diversity of documents transmitted electronically across the entire supply chain was limited.

To overcome the ineffective use of the information systems, the company initiated a project of network restructure. By 1994, all the members in the network switched from EDI- to Internet-based systems. The company also consolidated its multiple data centers into a single one. A global ERP system was also implemented to integrate all of its business divisions together. With such an Internet-based, fully integrated hub network and improved information flow, the company was able to achieve good inventory visibility, reduce credit approval cycle time, and make better decisions.

The ineffective high e-technology/low e-transaction e-network has technologically the greatest potential to be transformed into a powerful high e-technology/high e-transaction e-network by rapidly increasing the variety and volume of information that transmitted through its already established electronic networks. One major reason for the low information transmission is that the e-network has been optimized only for its certain segment(s), rather than for the entire e-network. This sub-optimized information network discourages members from increasing document variety and volume transmitted throughout the e-network, resulting in an ineffective e-network. Hence, to optimize and standardize IS infrastructure, members should not only adopt advanced electronic linkages, but also exert collective e-network planning efforts.

Another key reason for the e-network underutilization is related to potential security risks and trust issues. There exist various types of potential security threats to the e-network: destruction or unauthorized use of information/resources; corruption or modification of information/resources; theft, removal, or loss of information/resources; and deception via presentation of false data (Kolluru & Meredith, 2001). Because of such potential security risks and lack of mutual trust, many members might have intentionally restricted the use of their electronic linkages to exchanging just a few routine documents, and avoided adopting advanced applications that enable them to share confidential information, such as CAD/CAM, capacity, and demand data, which are essential for gaining operational and strategic e-network benefits.

Therefore, to utilize their integrated ISs to the full extent, various security technologies, such as authentication, access control, and auditing processes, are needed to ensure the confidentiality of members' critical information. In addition, it is necessary to establish legal and contractual mechanisms that regulate member behaviors and specify policies regarding the deviations from the contract terms. In an effort to establish effective security measures, all members should participate in the process of designing and implementing both technical mechanisms and legal agreements, thereby enhancing mutual trust among them. Over time, however, trust and cooperation need to be generated as a result of

a series of interactions between chain members (Chopra & Meindl, 2004).

Path 3: From Low E-Technology / Low E-Transaction to High E-Technology / High E-Transaction

Liu, Zhang, and Hu (2005) report a case of one large Chinese motorcycle corporation, Nanjing Jin Chen Motorcycle, and its suppliers, which have implemented an inter-enterprise supply chain management system to move from an impotent e-network (low e-technology/low e-transaction) to a powerful e-network (high e-technology/low e-transaction), following Path 3. Before the implementation of the e-network, the company and its suppliers generally did not have efficient internally integrated information systems in place, not to mention IOSs (i.e., low e-technology/low e-transaction).

To enhance the work flows between the supply chain members, the motorcycle company initiated a project to integrate its business processes with those of its suppliers through an Internet-based IOS, which allows them to share and exchange information smoothly and quickly. Each of the supply chain members is provided with a work-flow support supply chain management system, which comes with an integrated interface that enables seamless information exchange between the supply chain members. The implementation of the systems enables the company and its suppliers to share a variety of real-time information, such as statistical data, manufacturing plan, and inventory information (i.e., high e-technology/low e-transaction).

The impotent low e-technology/low e-transaction e-network is most likely to face the obstacles that both high e-technology/low e-transaction and low e-technology/high e-transaction e-networks often encounter during their transformation process towards a high e-technology/high e-transaction e-network. Thus, members of the impotent e-network should pay attention to the suggestions offered in the two previous sub-sections to increase the levels of both e-technology and e-transaction integration. Further, they may also need to address the following two issues involving the issue of supply chain size.

First, it is conceivable that members of certain segments within a large-scale supply chain have engaged in a so-called "market exchange" relationship. This type of business relationship can be easily observed in the e-marketplace, where firms neither exchange much information with one another nor develop specialized assets to work together (Bensaou, 1999). Since firms in such a relationship, if necessary, want to switch their trading partners at a low cost with minimal damage, they are not strongly motivated to invest substantial funds on the projects for inter-organizational IT integration, thereby resulting in a low e-technology/low e-transaction e-network.

To solve the e-network problems originating from the different types of business relationships among chain members, leading firms in a large-scale supply chain may need to consider a hybrid e-network that consists of multiple e-network structures and/or various levels of electronic linkages. For example, a focal company and its key chain members can establish a private e-hub that allows a large volume of information exchange and close coordination of inter-firm operations. In addition, an e-marketplace, like eSteel.com, can be offered to the firms in the "market exchange" relationship to negotiate, buy, and sell products over the Internet without heavy capital investment in their IS infrastructure.

Next, when multiple focal companies coexist in a large-scale supply chain, and each of those firms has electronic linkages with its close trading partners (e.g., first-tier suppliers or buyers), chain members will encounter various problems arising from the software incompatibility between sub-chains in their endeavor to increase e-technology and e-transaction integration simultaneously (Raupp & Schober, 2000). Thus, these focal companies are well-advised to work together to address

such an issue and adopt a common standard and/or flexible technologies such as those enabled by XML (extensible markup language) which allow data exchange between different applications for their e-network (Meehan, 2001). Further, a recent RFID initiative by Wal-Mart with its key chain members could be considered a next-generation level of e-technology and e-transaction integration that enables all the chain members to achieve not only informational and operational benefits, but strategic benefits of their e-network.

CONCLUSION AND MANAGERIAL IMPLICATIONS

In recent years, an increasing number of companies have adopted supply chain management (SCM) as a key driver for delivering increased value to customers by focusing on their core competencies, outsourcing non-critical and/or non-competency activities to their upstream suppliers and downstream customers, and integrating all chain members to act as a single entity (Chandrashekar & Schary, 1999). Accordingly, to coordinate and synchronize various business activities at all levels across the supply chain, an effective e-network, along with its associated business process reengineering, should be adopted and implemented (Elmuti, 2002; Kehoe & Boughton, 2001).

In theory, an e-network with high e-technology/high e-transaction integration appears to be the most desirable for the companies that aspire to achieve the maximum benefits from their IT investment and in turn enhance their competitiveness in the marketplace. This fully integrated e-network makes it possible to timely exchange diverse information and data and offer real-time high visibility to all chain partners, thereby eliminating the bullwhip effect across the supply chain. At the same time, the high level of information exchange in such an e-network warrants members' IT investment. In practice, however, such an e-network is not always desirable and feasible. The varying degrees of members' IS infrastructure, competitive pressure in the marketplace, and more importantly, various types of inter-organizational relationships collectively and substantially affect the magnitude of e-network technology and transaction integration.

For example, some firms adopting a total SCM approach may seek to fully integrate chain members' IS for streamlining and synchronizing information flows across the supply chain. However, as time passes, these firms may recognize the need to disintegrate and reconfigure their entire supply chain to sustain their competitive advantages by eliminating non-value-added activities and incompetent chain members, and by utilizing distinctive competence of new members (Markus, 2000). In this case, those firms would have improved their performance by pursuing a "quick integration/ quick disintegration" IS strategy to quickly adapt themselves to changing business environments (Christiaanse & Kumar, 2000; Markus, 2000). Fortunately, the enhanced modularity (which is defined as the ability of the IS infrastructure to add, modify, and remove any software or data components with ease and with no major overall effect; see Duncan, 1995) of current ERP systems (which are mainly used as a means to integrate a firm's internal functions) and the increasing availability of the Internet (which is increasingly used as a major communication channel between firms) enable companies to adopt such a flexible and dynamic e-network strategy.

Next, managers should clearly understand key characteristics of three types of e-networks in terms of information flows control. While the information transmitted across a tree e-network could be easily intercepted or manipulated by any chain members because of its sequential nature of information flows, such a security problem can be eliminated or substantially mitigated in a net e-network, since all members can directly communicate with one another simultaneously. However, in the net e-network, conflicts concerning

the ownership of information and accountability of its transactions may arise frequently, since a focal company has almost no control over the information exchange between other chain members (Kumar & van Dissel, 1996). In the case of a hub e-network, a focal company can use the e-hub to monitor all the information transmitted through a central platform. This may pose a threat to other members in that the focal company may exploit the collected information through the platform to seek its own interests rather than those of all chain participants. Another point that should be considered by managers in the adoption of high e-technology/high e-transaction e-networks is that establishing new electronic networks often entails redesigning physical supply networks and restructuring business processes internal and external to all chain members (Barratt, 2004).

Finally, it is often more difficult to manage highly automated electronic linkages in a large supply chain than a small counterpart. As argued by Raupp and Schober (2000), members in a small supply chain are likely to share common norms and attitudes, thereby enhancing their supply chain cohesion and ensuring efficient collaboration. Therefore, to establish a high e-technology/high e-transaction e-network in a small supply chain, the chain members can rely on implicit contractual arrangements to coordinate and regulate their interactions and information sharing through the e-network. In contrast, a large supply chain has such a complex e-network that there is always a probability that some members will have their direct or indirect competitors in the same chain. Consequently, these firms are often reluctant to release their sensitive information to others in the chain. Thus, to maintain a high e-technology/ high e-transaction e-network, members should establish tight security mechanisms, mutual trust among members, and right alignment of roles and responsibilities toward common SCM goals, thereby preventing opportunistic behaviors of any member.

Future research, as an extension of the current study, should empirically examine the five research questions mentioned in the introduction section based on the proposed 2x2 e-network technology and transaction integration matrix, and the topology of e-networks. Since the study will explore a relatively new research area, the study of cases is deemed appropriate (Yin, 1994). For this study, multiple data collection methods, such as interviews and on-site observations, should be employed to triangulate the information collected. Interviewees are composed of top managers including IT and SCM directors from focal companies as well as their chain members, who are in charge of the design and/or implementation of e-networks. Several rounds of interviews need to be conducted with each of the interviewees through site visits or telephone calls. The collected data need to be coded and analyzed by following the procedure suggested by Miles and Huberman (1994): conducting within-case analysis (e.g., identifying each participant company's e-network transformation path) and then cross-case analysis (e.g., comparing and contrasting the e-network transformation paths adopted by different participant companies).

REFERENCES

Ansley, M. (2000). Virtual manufacturing. *CMA Management, 74*(1), 31-35.

Barratt, M. (2004). Understanding the meaning of collaboration in the supply chain. *Supply Chain Management: An International Journal, 9*(1), 30-42.

Bauer, M.J., Poirier, C.C., Lapide, L., & Bermudez, J. (2001). *E-Business: The Strategic Impact on Supply Chain and Logistics.* Oak Brook, IL: Council of Logistics Management.

Bensaou, B.M. (1999). Portfolios of buyer-supplier relationships. *Sloan Management Review, 40*(4), 35-44.

Byrd, T.A., & Turner, D.E. (2001). An exploratory analysis of the value of the skills of IT personnel: Their relationship to IS infrastructure and competitive advantage. *Decision Sciences, 32*(1), 21-54.

Cai, S., Jun, M., & Yang, Z. (2006). The impact of interorganizational Internet communication on purchasing performance: A study of Chinese manufacturing firms. *Journal of Supply Chain Management, 42*(3), 16-29.

Campbell, A. (2004). Online supply chain solutions. *Supply Chain Europe, 13*(4), 54-55.

Chandrashekar, A., & Schary, P.B. (1999). Toward the virtual supply chain: The convergence of IT and organization. *International Journal of Logistics Management, 10*(2), 27-39.

Cheng, E.W.L., Li, H., Love, P.E.D., & Irani, Z. (2001). An e-business model to support supply chain activities in construction. *Logistics Information Management, 14*(1/2), 68-77.

Chopra, S. (2003). What will drive the enterprise software shakeout? *Supply Chain Management Review, 7*(1), 50-56.

Chopra, S., & Meindl, P. (2004). *Supply chain management: Strategy, planning, and operation* (2nd ed.). Upper Saddle River, NJ: Pearson Prentice Hall.

Christiaanse, E., & Kumar, K. (2000). ICT-enabled coordination of dynamic supply webs. *International Journal of Physical Distribution & Logistics Management, 30*(3/4), 268-285.

Cooper, D.P., & Tracey, M. (2005). Supply chain integration via information technology: Strategic implications and future trends. *International Journal of Integrated Supply Management, 1*(3), 237-257.

Duncan, N.B. (1995). Capturing flexibility of information technology infrastructure: A study of resource characteristics and their measure. *Journal of Management Information Systems, 12*(2), 37-57.

eCompany Now Staff. (2000). *Supply-chain software: Hewlett-Packard.* Retrieved May 4,

2003, from *http://www.business2.com/articles/mag/0,1640,8619,00.html*

Edwards, P., Peters, M., & Sharman, G. (2001). The effectiveness of information systems in supporting the extended supply chain. *Journal of Business Logistics, 22*(1), 1-27.

Elmuti, D. (2002). The perceived impact of supply chain management on organizational effectiveness. *Journal of Supply Chain Management, 38*(3), 49-57.

Green, F.B. (2001). Managing the unmanageable: Integrating the supply chain with new developments in software. *Supply Chain Management, 6*(5), 208-211.

Handfield, R.B., & Nicholas, E.L. (1999). *Introduction to supply chain management.* Upper Saddle River, NJ: Prentice Hall.

Heinrich, C. (2003). *Adapt or die: Transforming your supply chain into an adaptive business network.* Hoboken, NJ: John Wiley & Sons.

Hendon, R.A., Nath, R., & Hendon, D.W. (1998). The strategic and tactical value of electronic data interchange for marketing firms. *Mid-Atlantic Journal of Business, 34*(1), 53-73.

Horvath, L. (2001). Collaboration: The key to value creation in supply chain management. *Supply Chain Management: An International Journal, 6*(5), 205-207.

Iacovou, C.L., Benbasat, I., & Dexter, A.S. (1995). Electronic data interchange and small organizations: Adoption and impact of technology. *MIS Quarterly, 19*(4), 465-485.

Jennings, D. (1999). *Online B2B exchanges: The new economics of market.* New York: Deloitte Consulting.

Kaplan, S., & Sawhney, M. (2000). E-hubs: The new B2B marketplaces. *Harvard Business Review, 78*(3), 97-103.

Kehoe, D.F., & Boughton, N.J. (2001). New paradigms in planning and control across manufacturing supply chains: The utilization of Internet technologies. *International Journal of Operations & Production Management, 21*(5/6), 582-593.

Kemppainen, K., & Vepsalainen, A.P.J. (2003). Trends in industrial supply chains and networks. *International Journal of Physical Distribution & Logistics Management, 33*(8), 701-719.

Koch, C. (2002). Interview: Covisint's last chance. *CIO, 16*(5), 1.

Kok, T.D., Janssen, F., Doremalen, J.V., Wachem, E.V., Clerkx, M., & Peeters, W. (2005). Philips electronics synchronizes its supply chain to end bullwhip effect. *Interface, 35*(1), 37-48.

Kolluru, R., & Meredith, P.H. (2001). Security and trust management in supply chains. *Information Management, 9*(5), 233-236.

Kumar, K., & van Dissel, H.G. (1996). Sustainable collaboration: Managing conflict and cooperation in interorganizational systems. *MIS Quarterly, 20*(3), 279-300.

Lee, H.L., Padmanabhan, V., & Whang, S. (1997). The bullwhip effect in supply chains. *Sloan Management Review,* (Spring), 93-102.

Li, S., Ragu-Nathan, B., Ragu-Nathan, T.S., & Rao, S.S. (2006). The impact of supply chain management practices on competitive advantage and organizational performance. *Omega, 34*(2), 107-124.

Li, S., Rao, S.S., Ragu-Nathan, T.S., & Ragu-Nathan, B. (2005). Development and validation of a measurement instrument for studying supply chain management practices. *Journal of Operations Management, 23*(6), 618-641.

Liu, J., Zhang, S., & Hu, J. (2005). A case study of an inter-enterprise work flow-support supply chain system. *Information & Management, 42*(3), 441-454.

Markus, M.L. (2000). Paradigm shifts—e-business and business/systems integration. *Communication for Association for Information Systems, 4*(10). Retrieved February 23, 2003, from *http://web. bentley.edu/empl/m/lmarkus/Markus_Web_Documents_(pdf)/Paradigm_Shifts.pdf*

Massetti, B., & Zmud, R.W. (1996). Measuring the extent of EDI usage in complex organizations: Strategies and illustrative examples. *MIS Quarterly, 20*(3), 331-345.

Meehan, M. (2001). Covisint exchange vows it will support ebXML. *Computerworld, 35*(23), 16.

Miles, M.B., & Huberman, A.M. (1994). *Qualitative data analysis: Grounded theory procedures and techniques.* London: Sage.

Monczka, R.M., Peterson, K.J., & Handfield, R.B. (1998). Success factors in strategic supplier alliances: The buying company perspective. *Decision Science, 29*(3), 553-573.

Ovalle, O.R., & Marquez, A.C. (2003). The effectiveness of using e-collaboration tools in the supply chain: An assessment study with system dynamic. *Journal of Purchasing and Supply Management, 9*(4), 151-163.

Phan, D.D., & Stata, N.M. (2002). E-business success at Intel: An organization ecology and resources dependence perspective. *Industrial Management & Data Systems, 102*(4), 211-217.

Poirier, C.C., & Bauer, M.J. (2001). *E-supply chain: Using the Internet to revolutionize your business.* San Francisco: Berrett-Koehler.

Premkumar, G., & Ramamurthy, K. (1995). The role of interorganizational and organizational factors on the decision mode for adoption of interorganizational systems. *Decision Sciences, 26*(3), 303-337.

Raupp, M., & Schober, F. (2000). Why buyer-supplier chains differ: A strategic framework for electronic network organizations. *Proceedings of the 33rd Annual Hawaii International Conference on Systems Sciences* (HICSS), Maui, HI.

Roberts, M. (2000). The dawn of next-generation digital supply chains. *Chemical Week,* (July 26), 8-10.

Rosenberg, A. (2003). *Focus on collaboration: Collaborative B2B.* Retrieved September 26, 2007, from *http://www.basex.com/press.nsf/0/CD3491C3C2D8 D85256D0D001CC5D8?OpenDocument*

Sahin, F., & Robinson, E.P. (2005). Information sharing and coordination in make-to-order supply chains. *Journal of Operations Management, 23*(6), 579-598.

Sharifi, H., Kehoe, D.F., & Hopkins, J. (2006). A classification and selection model of e-marketplaces for better alignment of supply chains. *Journal of Enterprise Information Management, 19*(5), 483-503.

Shore, B., & Venkatachalam, A.R. (2003). Evaluating the information sharing capabilities of supply chain partners: A fuzzy logic model. *International Journal of Physical Distribution & Logistics Management, 33*(9), 804-824.

Turban, E., Lee, J., King, D., & Turban, E. (2000). *Electronic commerce: A managerial perspective.* Upper Saddle River, NJ: Prentice Hall.

van Hoek, R. (2001). E-supply chains-virtually non-existing. *Supply Chain Management, 6*(1), 21-28.

Versendaal, J., & Brinkkemper, S. (2003). Benefits and success factors of buyer-owned electronic trading exchanges: Procurement at Komatsu America corporation. *Journal of Information Technology Cases and Applications, 5*(4), 39-52.

Westerman, G., & Cotteleer, M.J. (1999). *Tektronix, Inc.: Global ERP implementation.* Boston: Harvard Business School Press.

Wisner, J.D., & Tan, K.C. (2000). Supply chain management and its impact on purchasing. *Journal of Supply Chain Management, 36*(4), 33-42.

Yin, R.K. (1994). *Case study research: Design and methods.* Thousand Oaks, CA: Sage.

Yu, Z., Yan, H., & Cheng, E.T.C. (2001). Benefits of information sharing with supply chain partnerships. *Industrial Management & Data Systems, 101*(3), 114-119.

Zeng, A.Z., & Pathak, B.K. (2003). Achieving information integration in supply chain management through B2B e-hubs: Concepts and analyses. *Industrial Management & Data Systems, 103*(9), 657-665.

This work was previously published in the International Journal of Information Systems and Supply Chain Management, Vol. 1, Issue 4, edited by J. Wang, pp. 39-59, copyright 2008 by IGI Publishing (an imprint of IGI Global).

Chapter 16
A Strategic Framework for Managing Failure in JIT Supply Chains

Jaydeep Balakrishnan
University of Calgary, Canada

Frances Bowen
University of Calgary, Canada

Astrid L.H. Eckstein
Canada

ABSTRACT

Supply chains can be disrupted at both local and global levels. Just-In-Time (JIT) companies should be particularly interested in managing supply chain failure risk as they often have very little inventory to buffer themselves when their upstream supply chain fails. We develop previous research further and present a strategic framework to manage supply chain failure in JIT supply chains. We identify two dimensions along which the risks of failure can be categorized: location and unpredictability. We go on to identify strategies which companies can use either before (proactive) or after (reactive) the failure to manage supply chain failure. We support our framework with examples of actual responses to supply chain failures in JIT companies. It is also hoped that our strategic framework will be validated empirically in the future leading to specific guidance for managers.

INTRODUCTION

Just-in-time (JIT) manufacturing, with its focus on continuous improvement through waste reduction and problem solving, has been widely hailed as a philosophy that improves organizational performance. JIT principles include only having required inventory; improving quality; trimming lead time by reducing setup time, queue length, and lot sizes; and reducing costs in the process (Cox & Blackstone, 2002). The philosophy offers organizations some significant cost and quality benefits (e.g., Funk, 1995; Duguay, Landry, & Pasin, 1997; Claycomb, Germain, & Droge, 1999), so it is not surprising that large numbers of organizations around the world have implemented or are in the process of implementing JIT manufacturing.

However, there are several disadvantages and implementation difficulties associated with JIT (Im, Hartman, & Bondi, 1994; Inman & Mehra, 1989), including supply chain failure (Altenburg, Griscom, Hart, Smith, & Wohler, 1999; Zsidisin, Ragatz, & Melnyk, 2005; Kleindorfer & Saad, 2005; Craighead, Blackhurst, Rungtusanatham, & Handfield, 2007). The risk of supply chain failure refers to the combination of the probability that an element of the supply chain will fail, and the magnitude of the disruption caused by the failure throughout the remainder of the chain. A recent McKinsey survey found that managers face increasing supply chain risk (Krishnan & Shulman, 2007). Understanding supply chain failure is particularly important for JIT organizations because companies using JIT are especially susceptible to failures in their upstream supply chain as they have limited inventory to protect them if the parts do not arrive on time.

Tang (2006) categorizes supply chain risk as operational or disruptional. Operational risk refers to inherent uncertainties such as uncertain customer demand, uncertain supply, and uncertain cost. Disruption risks relate to natural and man-made disasters or economic crises. This article focuses on the disruptional risk aspect of JIT supply chains since, as Tang points out, the impact of disruptional risk is far greater than that of operational risk.

We begin by briefly outlining research on risk within supply chains, and on the particular challenges facing managers within JIT supply chains. We then go on to develop two dimensions of supply chain failure based on our inference from industry practice reported in the literature: (1) the location, and (2) the unpredictability of the supply chain failure (or unpredictability in recovering from failure). While others have focused on dimensions of supply chain failure such as controllability of the risk or severity of impact, we extend these treatments by emphasizing the location of the supply chain failure: whether the risk of supply chain failure is internal to the firm, external to the firm but internal to the supply chain, or whether it is systemic within an industry/region external to the supply chain. We illustrate the framework by categorizing some of the proactive and reactive processes used by companies to mitigate JIT supply chain failure. We conclude with a discussion of the implications of our framework for research on supply chain failure and JIT, and for practitioners. Our location-based view provides managers with an additional lens with which to view JIT supply chain risk, and an organizing framework to generate potential strategic risk management options.

It is hoped that this exploratory framework will lead to future studies using empirical approaches such as case-based research to validate the proposed framework. Case-based research (Miles & Huberman, 1994; Yin, 1994) can be used to explore in depth the use of different risk management approaches, among others. This type of in-depth research will allow the development of specific guidelines that managers can use to address supply chain risk within the enterprise.

SUPPLY CHAIN FAILURE AND JIT SYSTEMS

Sudden or catastrophic supply chain failure in JIT environments can have serious organizational impacts. The most common response has been to reduce or stop production until systems were operational again. The September 11, 2001 (9/11) terrorist attacks which delayed goods flowing between the United States and Canada, (Keenan, 2001), the 1995 stoppage of commercial traffic on the Rhine River in Germany due to flooding, the August 2003 power outage in the Northeastern and Midwest United States and Ontario, Canada, and the aftermath of the Kobe earthquake are examples.

Mitchell (1995) would categorize these examples as "performance loss" or "time loss" due to supply chain failure. However, the impact of supply chain failure does not end with merely immediate performance and time losses; they can extend to "financial loss" due to lost orders or the operational cost of remedying the failure, "physical loss" of facilities or supplies in cases of fire or flood, and even to "social loss" of the firm's reputation for reliability or "psychological loss" due to the stress of coping with the failure or damage to the organization's self-perception. It is therefore crucial that we better understand supply chain failure, and develop robust supply chain mechanisms and structures to cope with actual or potential failure.

Research on the supply chain design implications of following a JIT manufacturing strategy has tended to focus on "single sourcing, close supplier location, long-term relationships, schedule coordination and sharing, frequent deliveries of small lot sizes and stable supply-chain pipelines" (Das & Handfield, 1997, p. 246). Technical modeling on, for example, lead time uncertainty (e.g., Schwartz & Weng, 2000) has been complemented by survey-based research on the perceived cost reductions from implementing JIT purchasing and logistics (e.g., Dong, Carter, & Dresner, 2001). While some

of these studies make passing reference to the risk of supply chain failure, research on JIT supply chains has contradictory messages on managing such risk. On the one hand, some JIT supply chain characteristics such as schedule coordination and long-term relationships encourage repeated interactions, trust, and increased information sharing, hence decreasing the likelihood of supply chain failure over time. On the other, increased strategic risk, or over-reliance on a single or limited number of suppliers (Sadgrove, 1996), can magnify the impact or outcome of any potential upstream supply chain failure since the JIT firm may have fewer alternative sourcing options.

Thus managerial recommendations for designing supply chains to handle failures are often complex or even contradictory. Mechanisms and structures to manage supply chain failure differ in their scope and timing. To take some examples from a recent list by Elkins, Handfield, Blackhurst, and Craighead (2005), some design strategies are implemented within a focal organization (e.g., training employees, including expected costs of failures in the total cost equation), some are implemented across the entire supply chain (e.g., enhancing system-wide visibility and supply chain intelligence by using near-real-time databases), and others require the involvement of supply chain members within particular industries or regions (e.g., gathering intelligence and monitoring critical supply-base locations). Similarly, some strategies are implemented before a failure (e.g., creating early warning systems to discover critical events outside normal planning parameters), and others are designed in response to a failure (e.g., conducting a detailed incident report and analysis following a major disruption). Further complicating the intervention suggestions is that some risks are much more unpredictable than others, and so need relatively more or less intensive monitoring and management.

Given the complexity of supply chain risk, many authors have developed two-dimensional frameworks for risk management. For example

Meitz and Castleman (1975), Kraljic (1983), and Sheffi and Rice (2005) incorporate the probability that an element of the supply chain will fail and the magnitude of the disruption caused by the failure throughout the remainder of the chain as dimensions. Chopra and Sodhi (2004) examine 'level of risk' and 'cost of mitigating reserve' as dimensions in order to suggest risk mitigation strategies. Cavinato (2004) examines risk on the 'risk/uniqueness' and 'value/profit potential' dimensions. Kleindorfer and Saad (2005) examine supply chain risk management from a 'cost of disruption' vs. 'cost of risk mitigation' perspective. Thus the various two-dimensional frameworks have proved useful lenses for managers attempting to manage supply chain risk.

Recent treatments of supply risk also recognize the importance of both the source and outcome of the risk of failure (Zsidisin, 2003), and explicitly recognize that the source of supply chain failure can occur further away than the immediate buyer-supplier dyad (Zsidisin, 2003b; Spekman & Davis, 2004). Natural disasters, strikes, or fires can affect not only the first tier, but also second- or third-tier suppliers that are integrated within the JIT manufacturing system. Supply chain failures arising from apparently remote disruptions can have significant impact on an integrated supply chain, particularly within an increasingly uncertain, post-9/11 global environment (Spekman & Davis, 2004; Barry, 2004). Our framework will assist decision makers to develop appropriate responses to apparently distant supply failure risks by focusing on the location of the risk.

An important aspect of managing supply chain failure is to understand how and why supply chain disruptions occur. Chopra and Sodhi (2004) emphasize the importance of understanding the drivers of risk (labor disputes, inadequate capacity, and weather are some examples) and categorize them to help develop effective risk mitigation strategies. Kleindorfer and Saad (2005) suggest 10 principles to help understand and mitigate supply chain failure. Craighead et al. (2007) identify network density, network complexity, and node criticality as drivers of supply chain failure risk, and recovery and warning as drivers of supply chain failure mitigation.

While these are useful starting points for understanding the risk of failure in JIT systems, a framework is needed which helps managers deal with the complexity of risks arising in distant supply locations both before (proactive) and after (reactive) the failure. The research in *proactive* planning in supply chain disruption risk has paid insufficient attention to risk mitigation strategies based on location of the risk (i.e., whether the disruption risk is internal to the firm, external to the firm but internal to the supply chain, or external to the supply chain). This is an important oversight in our current understanding of the proactive management of supply chain failure since risks internal to the firm may be most controllable while disruption risk external to the supply chain may be least controllable. While focusing on the location of supply chain failure, our framework echoes previous research, which includes the unpredictability of the risk. We suggest that the proactive approach to JIT supply chain risk mitigation can be understood better if analyzed on the 'location of failure' and 'unpredictability of failure' dimensions.

In addition, while many articles discuss avoidance of disruption by upfront planning, only a few (Lee, 2004; Sinha et al., 2004; Zsidisin, Melnyk, & Ragatz, 2005a; Zsidisin, Ragatz, & Melnyk 2005b; Tang, 2006; Craighead et al., 2007) discuss *reactive* recovery in the case of supply chain failure. Since supply chain failures will take place occasionally even with the best of proactive planning, we should also address the reactive management of supply chain failure. We suggest that the recovery from JIT supply chain failure (reactive approach) can be usefully analyzed along the same two dimensions of location and unpredictability.

LOCATION AND UNPREDICTABILITY AS DIMENSIONS OF SUPPLY CHAIN FAILURE

While the risk of supply chain failure is influenced by many factors, we focus on two primary dimensions: location and unpredictability. To consider location first, supply chain failures may be classified as: internal to the organization, external to the firm but internal to the supply chain, or external to the supply chain. Internal organizational failures include strikes or chaos arising from internal reorganization. It is important to note that a focal firm's internal failures could affect other supply chain members (for the other members the risk is external to the firm but internal to supply chain situation). Conversely, suppliers might suffer performance loss due to their own internal reorganization or financial difficulties, but this could affect the focal firm and so is categorized as external to the firm but internal to the supply chain. External to supply chain failures are generally due to acts of God such as weather or natural disasters, or acts of human aggression such as terrorism, sabotage, or arson (though these could apply to the other two categories also).

Location as a dimension of supply chain failure is related with controllability to the extent that failures arising further from the firm are less controllable than the focal firm. The advantage of location over controllability is that if managers can understand the location of a given risk, then they are better equipped to find a proactive plan or reactive response based on the location. Highly uncontrollable risks have the implication of managerial impotence. However, as we argue below, risks in distant locations encourage managers to think of mitigation actions matched with the location.

Our second dimension, unpredictability, captures the extent to which the probabilities of a failure and its impacts are ambiguous. This extends from traditional notions of risk (where probabilities and variables are known) and uncertainty

(where variables are known, but probabilities are not), to an extreme form of unpredictability where neither the variables nor probabilities associated with supply chain failures are known (Hall & Vredenburg, 2005). Thus highly predictable failures can be understood with traditional risk measurement and management techniques, whereas highly unpredictable failures can usually only be identified after the fact.

The location of supply chain failure is often correlated with unpredictability of occurrence (or the unpredictability of recovering from a failure), since in general, the nearer the failure is to the focal organization, the more information the focal firm may have of the variables or probabilities of failure. Usually, an organization has little visibility of external failures even though it still has to deal with the failure. Sometimes, there may be an indication that the failure will occur such as in the case of an impending hurricane, but at other times there may be no warning. However, even some potential failures internal to the firm are unpredictable, and other external failures may be predictable. Therefore our framework maps location against unpredictability in an orthogonal two-dimensional space, including the entire conceptual set of failures from internal to external and from high predictability to low.

Examples of external failures which have high unpredictability include natural disasters, which can have very far-ranging effects, like floods and earthquakes. In these instances, an entire geographic locale is affected, usually including transportation arteries and local suppliers. Major parts of the global supply chain can be affected for all companies, whether JIT or not, such as with the 1995 earthquake in Kobe, Japan (Forman, Williams, & Sapsford, 1995), the ice storm and resulting power outage of 1998 that produced chaotic conditions in eastern Canada (Chipello, 1998), the 9/11 terrorist attack (Ip, 2001), and the SARS epidemic in Asia (Young, 2003).

Supply chain failure internal to the chain can arise due to actions taken or occurring within the supply chain. Consequently, for the most part they have at least some predictability and can be prevented by better supply chain practices. However, when the supply chain fails due to a strike at the logistics provider, for example, the effect can often be widespread. In the United States, the United Parcel Service (UPS) strike greatly affected its customers, especially those who used UPS as their sole "rush goods" transporter. During the strike, because UPS handled such a large portion of the U.S. market (63% of all rapid deliveries and 80% of all ground deliveries), other companies like Federal Express and the U.S. Postal Service were not able to pick up all the slack. The competition also placed a number of restrictions on customers due to increased volume (Coleman & Jennings, 1998). Nonetheless, since everyone in the U.S. was dealing with the impact of the strike, customers had to be more understanding. Another example of a high-impact strike is when the major trade unions strike, such as the 2002 longshoremen strike on the U.S. West Coast (Cavinato, 2004).

Examples of predictable failures within the firm would be reorganization, including mergers and acquisitions, plant expansions, major supply chain software installations, and the like. When Union Pacific acquired Southern Pacific Rail Corporation, poor integration of the scheduling systems resulted in more than 10,000 rail cars a day stalled due to a shortage of locomotives, crew members, and track space. Union Pacific's customers, whether JIT or not, had to work around the supply chain failure (WSJ, 1997). Problems with an Enterprise Resource System (ERP) software installation resulted in shipment delays and incomplete order shipments at the Hershey Company (Stedman, 1999). While the company kept producing, the software implementation glitches resulted in chocolate piling up in warehouses instead of being shipped.

A less predictable failure within the supply chain would be if a supplier goes bankrupt or encounters financial difficulties, which can result in the work being stopped quickly. This can be a

particularly serious failure, since there is a focus on single sourcing and small lot deliveries in JIT. Land Rover in the UK faced this difficulty when its only chassis supplier UPF-Thomson faced financial difficulties in 2001 (Meczes, 2004).

Sometimes, what starts as an internal failure can have far-ranging effects. Natural disasters can impact locally, as when a fire guts a building, though the impact may be significant when that building houses the sole supply for another organization, as in the case of a lightning-bolt-based fire at a Philips semiconductor plant that supplied Nokia and Ericsson (Latour, 2001) and at Aisin, a supplier of Toyota (Reitman, 1997).

Thus location and unpredictability of failure appear to be dimensions that warrant investigation. In the following sections we elaborate on the strategic issues in the proactive and reactive management of supply chain failure in JIT systems. As mentioned earlier it is hoped that this discussion will lead to future empirical research into this topic, leading to more specific management suggestions.

PROACTIVE MANAGEMENT OF SUPPLY CHAIN FAILURE

How can firms anticipate, avoid, or minimize supply chain failure before it occurs? In Figure 1 we map proactive risk mitigation strategies in our location/unpredictability framework (see Kelindorfer & Saad, 2004; Chopra & Sodhi, 2004; Lee, 2004; Johnson, 2001; Sinha et al., 2001). Based on examples of strategies and tactics that firms have adopted, and suggestions of strategies from the literature, we derive three main proactive options for firms along the shaded arrow depending on the location and unpredictability of the failure. These range from: (1) designing a robust internal structure and system, through (2) designing a robust external structure and system, to (3) measuring and monitoring risks in the external environment.

Figure 1. Proactive management of supply chain failure

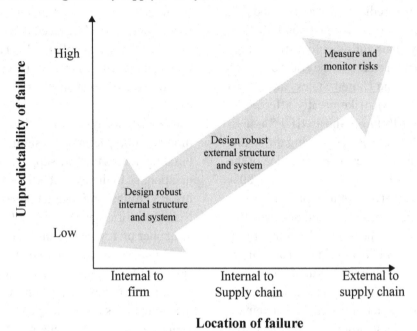

Location of failure

Robust Internal Structures and Systems

To manage highly predictable (i.e., low unpredictability) and internal potential failures, firms *design robust internal structures and systems.* For example, when companies believe that a supply chain failure may be coming, they may have a policy of stockpiling parts; that is, they implement failure anticipation inventory (Chopra & Sodhi, 2004; Sheffi & Rice, 2005). When GM speculated that its unions might go on strike, it tried to prevent supply chain failure; it stockpiled in advance, had contingency plans, and maintained backup data from the suppliers on the components of their products (Becker, 1998).

Another aspect of internal system design is business continuity planning (Zsidisin, Ragatz, & Melnyk, 2005; Zsidisin, Melnyk, & Ragatz, 2005; Sinha et al., 2004; Kleindorfer & Saad, 2004; Chopra & Sodhi, 2004). Steps such as risk analysis, contingency plans, logic charts and tabletop exercises, and failure modes and effect analysis

(FMEA) would be useful in planning to deal with supply chain failure. This type of system planning becomes even more important when the company knows that the probability of a failure occurring may be higher than usual. For example, locations that suffer snowstorms, hurricanes, and the like with known probabilities can plan for disaster recovery within certain tolerances. Internally, if a strike is expected or if a labor contract is coming up for renewal, the company can choose to make "just in case" plans.

Lee (2004) emphasizes the great importance of agility, adaptability, and alignment in building robust supply chains (he calls it the Triple-A supply chain). Honda is a leader in flexible assembly plants, producing more than one model on the same line, and the same model at more than one plant. The Honda plant in Ontario, Canada, can build the Odyssey van and two types of SUVs on the same assembly line, while the Honda plant in Alabama can also produce the Odyssey (Keenan, 2003). While this increases Honda's flexibility from a competitive viewpoint, it also protects against supply chain failures. In case of a supply chain failure in Ontario, production at Alabama could be ramped up. Similarly Toyota is following a strategy of spreading out the location of its plants in North America to reduce what it teams as "geographic risk" (Shirouzu, 2005).

Another strategy is to minimize variability, that is, increase the ability to manage the process consistently. An example of variability would be the breakdown in machinery that might delay a shipment. Variance reduction and process improvement allow the organization to become better at supply chain management, which can result in fewer supply chain failures. If waste and variability can be removed (the JIT philosophy), the chain becomes more robust and it becomes easier to prevent problems from occurring. For example, the JIT practice of small batch sizes and reduced lead times helps reduce variability, or risk, in supply (Lee, Padmanabhan, & Whang, 1997). This could help avoid spikes in the supply chain that often creates a domino effect leading to supply chain failure.

Reducing the size of the product line through rationalization and the use of modularity will help duplicate production capacity (Kleindorfer & Saad, 2004; Chopra & Sodhi, 2004). This will allow production shifts in the case of supply chain failures. For instance, in 1999 Unilever made plans to trim away 1,000 of its 1,600 brands to focus on global/regional brands instead of local/national brands. The primary focus would become 400 brands that account for almost 90% of its annual revenue (Beck, 1999). Part of the rationale was to simplify the supply chain, which should make it more robust. When there are fewer products, it is also easier to duplicate production. Producing the same product at multiple locations allows the company to shift production when the supply chain fails at one facility. Even if a product is not duplicated, standardized components (modular design) and processes make it easier to locate an alternate source when the chain fails, as compared to totally customized components. An auto manufacturer

was caught short recently because it failed to do this. It had a single supplier for rubber radiator gaskets that used unique machinery to produce these gaskets. When a fire destroyed the gasket supplier's machines, the only option left was to remanufacture the machines with much cost and time delay, as no alternative supplier could be found due to the uniqueness of the machines (Martha & Subbakrishna, 2002). In contrast, Toyota made use of the Aisin fire to improve its system by launching a project to increase parts standardization. In the case of the Philips fire, among its customers, Nokia was able to recover more quickly since it could find alternate sources of supply because its phone was more modularly designed than that of another customer, Ericsson (Tang, 2006).

Firms can also design their internal systems to manage product design and product portfolio for supply chain robustness. Innovative product manufacturers often use flexibility or postponement to deal with rapid changes in demand (Lee, 2004). Dell is able to circumvent the negative effects of components partially, by offering promotions and price discounts for other products for which components are available. Thus operations continue as normally as possible and the standardized modular components are being used rather than being left to accumulate dust and cost in inventory.

Other aspects of internal system design can include analyzing risk early in the product lifecycle. Teradyne Inc. incorporates supply chain analysis at the product design stage (Atkinson, 2003). The company tries to identify potential failures early in product design. The goal is to create a product sourcing plan that becomes a roadmap that anticipates and generates mitigation plans for every risk identified. Risks could relate to technology, suppliers, and parts. Naturally, suppliers should be involved in the product design stage to maximize the flexibility in the design for supply chain robustness (i.e., *external structure and system,* which is discussed later).

Designing a robust internal system can be helped by a formalized process (Hauser, 2003). Companies can seek to optimize supply chain performance by analyzing supply chain risk and making sound business decisions based on this analysis. This helps companies identify, quantify, and prioritize risks (sometimes hidden) in their supply chain and take proactive action to mitigate these risks. Hauser's model involves the following steps: (1) identifying risks, (2) understanding which risks can lead to significant supply chain disruption, (3) quantifying the economic impact, (4) determining the organization's desired risk profile, (5) conducting simulations and identifying key performance measures, (6) developing risk mitigation initiatives along with timing and sequences, and (7) measuring and monitoring performance. A similar process is used in business continuity planning (Barnes, 2001; Zsidisin, Ragatz, & Melnyk, 2005; Zsidisin, Melnyk, & Ragatz, 2005). A utility in the Midwestern United States was able to recover from the effects of a very major storm much better than other utilities in the same area because it had a plan in place that outlined what suppliers were to do in the event of a storm. While other utilities struggled to get power back to customers within four weeks, this utility was able to get power back to all its customers within two weeks. Other strategies to prevent supply chain failure could involve carrying critical parts at strategic locations (Atkinson, 2003; Aichlmayr, 2001).

Robust External Structures and Systems

The best defense when risk of failure is outside the firm but in the supply chain, and the risk is fairly predictable, is to *design robust external structures and systems* (Johnson, 2001; Kleindorfer & Saad, 2004; Chopra & Sodhi, 2004). This might include alternate sources of supply and distribution. A comparison of Japanese and American auto manufacturers in 1990 showed that while Japanese companies in Japan had about a third of the suppliers per assembly plant compared to their American counterparts, they only had 12% of their parts single-sourced compared to 69% for the Americans (Womack, Jones, & Roos, 1990, p. 157). This is confirmed by a study by Shin, Collier, and Wilson (2001) that found that dual or multiple sourcing was common. Increased globalization in the logistics industry and information technology is making it more feasible to find alternate sources of supply; not only are there more logistics providers, these providers are also global. This increases the chances of locating a supplier worldwide who is able to supply the affected facility.

Craighead et al. (2007) discuss the effect of supply chain density, supply chain complexity, and node criticality on the possibility of disruptions. Thus when one designs the supply chain structure, these factors must be analyzed in order to come up with a resilient design. Sinha et al. (2004) and Tang (2006) address external supply chain structure from a risk perspective.

Another example of a robust structure is the use of collaborative planning, forecasting, and replenishment (CPFR), which these days involves supply chain management (SCM) software and can help avoid problems (Tang, 2006). Greater visibility in the supply chain can be a successful mechanism to prevent disruptions (Christopher & Lee, 2001). If a supplier or one of its partners goes through a merger, acquisition, plant expansion, or software installation, operational planning with the supplier is critical. Texas Instruments uses CPFR to manage items on a JIT basis (Roberts, 2004). If disruptions do occur, real-time information available in SCM software also allows quick what-if analysis. This will help the organization make alternate plans to combat the disruption, whether it is alternate suppliers, routes, or logistics providers. Technologies like Internet marketplaces allow for quick identification of alternate sources of supply, while technologies such as Geographical Positioning Systems (GPSs) and Radio Frequency

Identification (RFID) will allow companies to monitor the location of inventory within the supply chain, an important requirement in a JIT system where there is no excess inventory.

It is important to select supply chain partners carefully and strategically when structuring the supply chain based on their capability (Johnson, 2001). The partners in the supply chain, whether suppliers or customers, will have an impact on the chain. When their part of the chain fails, the whole supply chain is affected. Thus, the primary selection criteria should be their capability to maintain supply and their ability to respond in case of supply chain failure. For instance, it is important to examine a potential supplier's financial viability. In addition their plans in case of supply chain disruption should be examined. The example of the utility in the Midwest is a good illustration of this. When power fails, manufacturing will be significantly affected. Thus even the capability of utility partners within the supply chain is important.

Measurement and Monitoring

Prescription from the literature is weakest on how to deal with highly unpredictable events, especially those events external to the supply chain. Perhaps the best solution for highly unpredictable failures is consistent *measurement and monitoring*. Authors such as Hauser (2001), Zsidisin, Ellram, Cater, and Cavinato (2004), and Sinha (2004) include monitoring as part of their risk management process. In highly unpredictable situations this takes on added importance since it is difficult to plan ahead for something that is not known. Such monitoring can include early warning systems to discover internal system operations that exceed normal planning parameters (for internal to the firm); screening and regularly monitoring current suppliers for possible supply chain risks (for external to the firm, but internal to the supply chain situations); and scanning the external environment possibly through the use of

scenario analysis (for external to the supply chain situations). The most recent literature in this area has begun to develop prescriptions on how to manage highly unpredictable failures (e.g., Rice & Caniato, 2003; Zsidisin, Ragatz, & Melnyk, 2005; Zsidisin, Melnyk, & Ragatz, 2005; Sinha et al., 2004; Craighead et al., 2007). The emphasis in these prescriptions is on upfront planning and monitoring so that the firm is in a good position to improvise if the unpredictable does occur. For example, one company seeing the potential for disruption in the supply chain leased additional transportation equipment, just in case (Craighead et al., 2007). While the inability to predict or take proactive action may be frustrating, it is important to note that highly unpredictable failures such as weather, acts of war, and other natural causes are likely to be more widespread with wide-ranging effects. So partners in the supply chain as well as customers themselves may be affected and are more likely to be understanding. In this situation the focus moves to reactive options in the post-failure stage outlined below, where it is important to be able to respond quickly to restore the supply chain.

Planning and buffering can be useful in managing failure. Though it is easier to buffer when the unpredictability is low, it has been used in highly unpredictable situations if the situation warrants it. During the Y2K warnings, the Cap Gemini Group commissioned a survey; it found that about 40% of the U.S. companies surveyed planned to stockpile inventory. Xerox Corp. built up a month's supply of raw materials (about four times the usual amount) and made sure suppliers were Y2K compliant (Aeppel, 1999). Similarly, when Toyota expects major demand changes within the year, it knows that its supply chain needs to be more responsive than usual. It sets the load of the machine at half of its future capacity; each worker operates several machines. This gives the capacity flexibility and buffer.

REACTIVE MANAGEMENT OF SUPPLY CHAIN FAILURE

What can companies do in the immediate aftermath of the failure to mitigate the damage? We suggest that it should vary according to the location and unpredictability of the recovery from failure (see Figure 2). The two core strategies suggested are communication and improvisation. Companies can also use a combination of these two core strategies.

The appropriateness of each strategy depends on the location of the failure. In Figure 2 as the location of the failure moves closer to being internal to the supply chain and unpredictability is lower, customers may feel that the failure could have been predicted and so be less forgiving. Thus they would expect the company experiencing the failure to act quickly to fix the problem (an 'improvisation imperative'). On the other hand for failures that are more external to supply chain and are more unpredictable, customers would be more willing to accept slower improvisation, but will expect communication on progress toward normalization (a 'communication imperative').

Consider two examples of internal failure discussed earlier. In the case of failure due to new software implementation, customers might expect that those problems were predictable (as there are many cases of firms experiencing this type of disruption). So they expect the company to have done some proactive planning to prevent such failures and to have recovery plans. In this situation, firms need to improvise quickly to fix the software problem. On the other hand if the failure was due to a factory fire resulting from a freak lightning strike, customers may be more forgiving and be satisfied with immediate communication and later improvisation.

The Communication Imperative

A example of the *communication* imperative situation due to freak events was experienced by Mitel Corp. (a semiconductor manufacturer) in 1998 during the ice storm. Mitel had to rent

Figure 2. Reactive management of supply chain failure

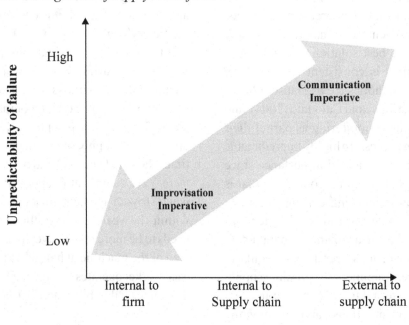

generators to produce electricity; even so, it could not recover lost time, as it was a 24-hour-a-day operation. So, Mitel communicated with its customers daily on the telephone to update them on the situation, and rescheduled production and shipment carefully to satisfy their customers as much as possible (Chipello, 1998). Kleindorfer and Saad (2004) and Craighead et al. (2007) also emphasize communication and information sharing in these circumstances.

Communicating with downstream customers helps alleviate the customer's anxieties, and they may be more likely to be willing to accept delays. If there is no communication, then their supply chain could also be severely disrupted, giving rise to strained relationships with their customers. Customers understand that supply chains do not always run smoothly and thus are going to be more forgiving if they are kept informed rather than if they are left in the dark. This communication strategy is particularly effective when the failure has its origins external to the supply chain. Customers may be more understanding if the whole system is down due to events external to the supply chain such as a flood, earthquake, or Teamsters Union strike, since many companies in the industry would be affected.

The Improvisation Imperative

As mentioned, when the failure is more predictable, the core strategy is to *improvise*. This relates to the business continuity planning (BCP) process discussed in Zsidisin, Ragatz, and Melnyk as well as Zsidisin, Melnyk, and Ragatz (2005, 2005). Sometimes companies will find room for additional capacity through improvement within the current system (*internal improvisation*). Tri-City Heat Treat Co. is a tier-two automobile supplier of heat-treated wheel nuts. To satisfy its customers' needs, it agreed to increase production, but the ordered equipment became delayed. Tri-City did its best to cope; besides asking customers with less pressing orders to wait, it worked round the

clock to generate ideas to increase capacity. It used process improvement to eliminate gaps in a production line, turning the batch process into a continuous process (Petzinger, 1995). Similarly, Nishin Kogyo, a minor supplier of valves to Toyota, found a way to increase its efficiency permanently by 30% during the Toyota-Aisin crisis (Reitman, 1997).

Alternatively, companies can increase capacity by increasing labor hours (a type of *internal improvisation*). Many JIT plants tend to have excess capacity (Knod & Schonberger, 2001; Korgoankar, 1992), which allows time for activities such as maintenance, process improvement, and employee training. So if a crisis hits, it is possible to use this as a temporary alternate source to make the required parts or to increase production after the failure is rectified. This can be done by using a third shift, by working overtime, or by hiring temporary workers.

Another option to improvise internally is to not waste existing capacity. Such improvisation might include producing incomplete units. For example, when Johnson Controls went through a strike, it produced seats with management and temporary workers to maintain production. Multifunctional workers also help manage supply chain failure since production may be shifted to other products when one product's supply chain has failed. Demand shifts from one model to another can be influenced through the use of promotions and price incentives, as was done by Dell during a parts shortage (Martha & Subbakrishna, 2002).

Alternately a firm can *improvise externally* around the failure. One way to do this is to find an alternate source of supply and delivery. Although this may be more costly than the normal source, it still can be less expensive than the chain not functioning. This may include shifting sourcing locations, finding alternate routes, and using alternate modes of transportation (Aichlmayer, 2001). Naturally, this would have to involve the cooperation of the logistics provider. After the Kobe earthquake, some companies considered altering their supply routes. Nissan Motor Co. and others investigated costly new alternate routes to avoid supply bottlenecks. Seven-Eleven Japan Co. considered using helicopters to supply convenience stores in the region (Shirouzu, Williams, Sapsford, & Reitman, 1995). If the failure is likely to delay the shipment enough that it will miss a crucial deadline, one may have to find faster alternatives. For example, when a shipment of Sony PlayStations being transported by sea got delayed at the Suez Canal, the company chartered Russian cargo aircraft in order to deliver to customers on time for the crucial Christmas season (Maitland, 2005).

EXTENSIONS AND CONCLUSION

In the past two decades many organizations have embraced JIT and faced challenges of operations protection during supply chain failure since there is little inventory buffer. We presented an organizing framework for some of the structural designs and mechanisms that companies have used to prevent supply chain failure, and to mitigate the effects when the supply chain has broken. We have illustrated that many successful strategies and tactics used by firms, together with several risk mitigation strategies from the literature, can be usefully mapped on a two-dimensional framework anchored on the location and unpredictability of the failure. Since companies plan to persist with JIT even with the possibility of supply chain failure, we hope that our framework will be useful in positioning risks of failure and mitigation options.

While we have initially separated proactive from reactive responses, these may be dynamically connected over time. Firms may learn based on reactive experience. Gulliver (1987) discusses British Petroleum's appraisal of the management of the completed projects so that the lessons can be applied to future projects. The same principle could be applied in the case of supply chain failure. Through reactive improvisation, firms could learn which types of improvisation were effective, and use this to improve the proactive tactics in the future.

Similarly, it is important to note that the ability to reactively manage the supply chain failure is contingent on proactive planning. For example the ability to rely on suppliers to improvise depends on the relationships built within the supply chain. If the company's supply chain structure was not built on long-term strategic relationships, the ability to rely on suppliers to react may be diminished. Within the company, the ability to improvise may be improved by ensuring that employees are trained in process improvement and critical analysis skills, and if crisis planning is done up front.

Even after the fire at the Aisin plant, Toyota plans to keep its policy of single-source suppliers for certain parts despite the dependency, or strategic risk, to which this exposes them. However, the company is building fail-safe mechanisms such as improving the ability of the supplier to shift production to another site if a disaster strikes (Reitman, 1997). Hajime Ohba, general manager of the Toyota Supplier Support Center in Kentucky, publicly responded with Toyota's rationale for JIT after the fire. He said that a better solution is to keep the company's resources at a consistently low cost level, and then rely on the cooperative relationships in the supply network if anything does go wrong (Ohba, 1997). In fact JIT also helps maintain supply chain flexibility when deployed properly. Toyota believes that small lot production allows for flexibility to meet changes in demand, regardless of the cause. This flexibility develops the capability of the supplier to rapidly respond to any crisis (Ohba, 1997).

The evidence points to the fact that over the long term, the benefits of reduced waste and variability through JIT more than offset the disadvantages of being caught without inventory in the unlikely event of a supply chain failure. Accordingly, consultants such as Mercer Management Consulting still advise clients to carry on with JIT since it is estimated that in the auto industry alone, companies are saving $1 billion in carrying costs due to JIT policies (Aichlmayer, 2001). What is required is to make the appropriate adjustments for any unreliability in supply that cannot be avoided. Even from an insurance perspective, implementing JIT systems can have benefits. While some premiums may increase due to increased risks such as that of non-conformance in a supply contract and the increase in road accidents due to more frequent deliveries, the philosophy of focusing on perfection can reduce the premiums related to the risk of product liability and warranty claims (McGillivray, 2000). Also the lack of inventory means lower losses in the case of disasters such as fires.

Given the fact that JIT is likely to be a popular philosophy in the foreseeable future, it is important to provide guidance to organizations using JIT to manage the risk of failure in their supply chains effectively. The proposed framework should help companies manage the risk in JIT-based supply chains. We suggest that managing supply chain failure within JIT systems involves a two-pronged approach. Before the event, JIT involves making the production system as foolproof as possible and forming close relationships with capable suppliers. We have argued that a variety of structures and mechanisms can be used to mitigate the low-to-medium unpredictability events at the firm, supply chain, and external locations. However, some highly unpredictable events can occur despite a well-functioning JIT system. Before the event, firms can monitor and measure events in their internal system, supply chain, and external environment. After a failure occurs the options are more limited to a combination of improvisation and communication with the supply chain. In the ideal case, a well-designed JIT supply chain can use its high visibility, communication, and group problem-solving approach to cooperate to quickly find solutions to supply chain failure. In this article we have illustrated the framework

using company experiences and previous supply chain risk research. Further research could attempt empirical validation of the proposed framework.

In the meantime, we hope that our strategic framework encourages managers to consider the location and unpredictability of supply chain failure as they devise strategies to cope with this crucial decision arena in JIT systems. We also hope that researchers will explore the framework using empirical research to validate it, and provide specific guidance to managers regarding the management of location and unpredictability issues in JIT supply chain failure.

REFERENCES

Aeppel, T. (2003). Inventories may bloat as year 2000 nears: Companies to stockpile in case supply chain snaps. *Wall Street Journal*, (February 9), A2.

Aichlmayer, M. (2001). The future of JIT—time will tell. *Transportation and Distribution, 42*(12), 18-22.

Altenburg, K., Griscom, D., Hart, J., Smith, F., & Wohler, G. (1999). Just-in-time logistics support for the automobile industry. *Production and Inventory Management Journal, 40*(2), 59-66.

Atkinson, W. (2003). Riding out global challenges. *Purchasing, 132*(14), 43.

Barnes, J.C. (2001). *A guide to business continuity planning.* New York: John Wiley & Sons.

Barry, J. (2004). Supply chain risk in an uncertain global supply chain environment. *International Journal of Physical Distribution and Logistics Management, 34*(9), 695-697.

Beck, E. (1999). Unilever to cut more than 1,000 brands. *Wall Street Journal*, (September 22), A17.

Becker, J. (1998). GM strike inflicts supply chain pain. *Modern Purchasing, 40*(8), 9-10.

Cavinato, J.L. (2004). Supply chain logistics risk. *International Journal of Physical Distribution and Logistics Management, 34,* 383-387.

Chipello, C.P. (1998). Canadian ice storm provided stern test of popular just-in-time method. *Wall Street Journal,* (January 26), A2.

Chopra, S., & Sodhi, M.S. (2004). Managing risk to avoid supply-chain breakdown. *MIT Sloan Management Reivew, 46*(1), 53-61.

Christopher, M., & Lee, H. (2004). Mitigating supply chain risk through improved confidence. *International Journal of Physical Distribution and Logistics Management, 34*(5), 388-396.

Claycomb, C., Germain, R., & Droge, C. (1999). Total system JIT outcomes: Inventory, organization and financial effects. *International Journal of Physical Distribution and Logistics Management, 29*(10), 612-624.

Coleman, B.J., & Jennings, K.M. (1998). The UPS strike: Lessons for just-in-timers. *Production and Inventory Management Journal, 39*(4), 63-67.

Cox, J.F. III, & Blackstone, J.H. Jr. (Eds.). (2002). *APICS dictionary.* Alexandria, VA: APICS—The Educational Society for Resource Management.

Craighead, C.W., Blackhurst, J., Rungtusanatham, M.J., & Handfield, R.B. (2007). The severity of supply chain disruptions: Design characteristics and mitigation capabilities, *Decision Sciences, 38*(1), 131-156.

Das, A., & Handfield, R.B. (1997). Just-in-time and logistics in global sourcing: An empirical review. *International Journal of Physical Distribution and Logistics Management, 27*(2/4), 244-252.

Dong, Y., Carter, C.R., & Dresner, M.E. (2001). JIT purchasing and performance: An exploratory analysis of buyer and supplier perspectives. *Journal of Operations Management, 19*(4), 471-484.

Duguay, C.R., Landry, A., & Pasin, F. (1997). From mass production to flexible/agile production. *International Journal of Operations and Production Management, 17*(11/12), 1183-1195.

Elkins, D., Handfield, R.B., Blackhurst, J., & Craighead, C.W. (2005). 18 ways to guard against disruption. *Supply Chain Management Review, 9*(1), 46-53.

Forman, C., Williams, M., & Sapsford, J. (1995). Shaken giant: Quake's aftershocks will rattle segments of Japan's economy. *Wall Street Journal,* (January 18), A1.

Funk, J.L. (1995). Just-in-time manufacturing & logistical complexity: A contingency model. *International Journal of Operations and Production Management, 15*(5), 60-71.

Gulliver, F.R. (1987). Post-project appraisals pay. *Harvard Business Review,* (March).

Hall, J., & Vredenburg, H. (2005). Managing stakeholder ambiguity. *Sloan Management Review, 47*(1), 11-13.

Hauser, L.M. (2003). Risk-adjusted supply chain management. *Supply Chain Management Review, 7*(6), 64-71.

Im, J.H., Hartman, S.J., & Bondi, P.J. (1994). How do JIT systems affect human resource management? *Production and Inventory Management Journal, 35*(1), 1-4.

Inman, R.A., & Mehra, S. (1989). Potential union conflict in JIT implementation? *Production and Inventory Management Journal, 30*(4), 19-21.

Ip, G. (2001). Risky business: As security worries intensify, companies see efficiencies erode. *Wall Street Journal,* (October 24), A1.

Johnson, M.E. (2001). Learning from toys: Lessons in managing supply chain risk from the toy industry. *California Management Review, 43*(2), 106-123.

Keenan, G. (2001). Slowdown at border shuts plants. *The Globe and Mail,* (September 12), B4.

Keenan, G. (2003). Chrysler future lies in flexibility. *The Globe and Mail,* (May 24), B3.

Kleindorfer, P.R. & Saad G.H. (2005). Managing disruption risks in supply chains. *Production and Operations Management, 14*(1), 53-68.

Knod, E.M., & Schonberger, R.J. (2001). *Operations management—meeting customers' demands.* New York: McGraw-Hill.

Korgaonker, M.G. (1992). *Just in time manufacturing.* Ahmedabad, India: Macmillan India.

Kraljic, P. (1983). Purchasing must become supply chain management. *Harvard Business Review,* (September-October), 109-117.

Krishnan, M., & Shulman J. (2007). Reducing supply chain risk. *The McKinsey Quarterly,* (1). Retrieved April 7, 2007, from http://www.mckinseyquarterly.com

Latour, A. (2001, January 29). Trial by fire: A blaze in Albuquerque sets off major crisis for cell-phone giants—Nokia handles supply shock with aplomb as Ericsson of Sweden gets burned—was Sisu the difference? *Wall Street Journal,* p A1.

Lee, H. (2004). The triple-a supply chain. *Harvard Business Review,* (October).

Lee, H.L., Padmanabhan, V., & Whang, S. (1997). The bullwhip effect in supply chains. *Sloan Management Review, 38*(3), 93-102.

Maitland, A. (2005). Make sure you have your Christmas stock in. *Financial Times,* (December 19), 12.

Martha, J., & Subbakrishna, S. (2002). Targeting a just-in-time supply chain for the inevitable next disaster. *Supply Chain Management Review, 6*(5), 18-23.

McGillivray, G. (2000). Commercial risk under JIT. *Canadian Underwriter, 67*(1), 26-28.

Meczes, R. (2004). It'll never happen to us. *Motor Transport,* (June 10), 14.

Meitz, A.A., & Castleman, B.B. (1975). How to cope with supply shortages. *Harvard Business Review, 53*(1), 91.

Miles, M.B., & Huberman, A.M. (1994). *Qualitative data analysis: An expanded sourcebook.* Thousand Oaks, CA: Sage.

Mitchell, V.-W. (1995). Organizational risk perception and reduction: A literature review. *British Journal of Management,* (6), 115-133.

Ohba, H. (1997). Letters to the editor: Toyota's solution to supply problems. *Wall Street Journal,* (March 7), A15.

Petzinger, T. Jr. (1995). Damewood Brothers are racing to beat the just-in-time system. *Wall Street Journal,* (June 30), B1.

Reitman, V. (1997). To the rescue: Toyota's fast rebound after fire at supplier shows why it is tough. *Wall Street Journal,* (May 8), A1.

Rice, J.B., & Caniato, F. (2003). Building a secure and resilient supply chain. *Supply Chain Management Review, 7*(5), 22-30.

Roberts, B. (2004). Double trouble. *Electronic Business, 30*(5), 62-67.

Sadgrove, K. (1996). *The complete guide to business risk management.* Aldershot, UK: Gower.

Schwartz, L.B., & Weng, Z.K. (2000). The design of a JIT supply chain: The effect of lead time uncertainty on safety stock. *Journal of Business Logistics, 21*(2), 231-252.

Sheffi, Y. & Rice, J.B. Jr. (2005). A supply chain view of the resilient enterprise. *MIT Sloan Management Review, 47*(1), 41-48.

Shin, H., Collier, D., & Wilson, D. (2001). Supply management orientation and supplier/buyer performance. *Journal of Operations Management, 18*, 317-222.

Shirouzu, N. (2005). Toyota, lured by incentives, picks Canadian site for its next plant. *Wall Street Journal,* (June 27), B6.

Shirouzu, N., Williams, M., Sapsford, J., & Reitman, V. (1995). Kobe's rebuilding may take longer than expected as damage toll mounts. *Wall Street Journal,* (January 19), A3.

Sinha, P.R., Whitman, L.E., & Malzahn, D. (2004). Methodology to mitigate supplier risk in an aerospace supply chain. *Supply Chain Management, 9*(2), 154-168.

Spekman, R.E., & Davis, E.W. (2004). Risky business: Expanding the discussion on risk and the extended enterprise. *International Journal of Physical Distribution and Logistics Management, 34*(5), 414-433.

Stedman, C. (1999). Failed ERP gamble haunts Hershey. *Computerworld, 33*(4), 89.

Tang, C.S. (2006). Perspectives in supply chain risk management. *International Journal of Production Economics, 103*(2), 451-488.

Womack, J.P., Jones D.T., & Roos, D. (1990). *The machine that changed the world.* New York: Rawson.

WSJ. (1997). Union Pacific faces claims over delays. *Wall Street Journal,* (October 10), A3.

Yin, R.K. (1994, June 25). *Case study research: Design and methods.* Thousand Oaks, CA: Sage.

Young, D. (2003). SARS could hurt Christmas. *The Globe and Mail,* (June 25). B9.

Zsidisin, G.A. (2003). A grounded definition of supply risk. *Journal of Purchasing and Supply Management,* (9), 217-224.

Zsidisin, G.A. (2003b). Managerial perceptions of supply risk. *Journal of Supply Chain Management,* (Winter), 14-25.

Zsidisin, G.A., Ellram, L.M., Cater, J.R., & Cavinato, J.L. (2004). An analysis of supply risk assessment techniques. *International Journal of Physical Distribution and Logistics Management, 34*(5), 397-413.

Zsidisin, G.A., Melnyk, S.A., & Ragatz, G.L. (2005b). An institutional theory perspective of business continuity planning for purchasing and supply management. *International Journal of Production Research, 43*(16), 3401-3420.

Zsidisin, G.A., Ragatz, G.L., & Melnyk, S.A. (2005a). The dark side of supply chain management. *Supply Chain Management Review,* (March), 46-52.

This work was previously published in the International Journal of Information Systems and Supply Chain Management, Vol. 1, Issue 4, edited by J. Wang, pp. 20-38, copyright 2008 by IGI Publishing (an imprint of IGI Global).

Chapter 17
A Nelder and Mead Methodology for Solving Small Fixed–Charge Transportation Problems

G. Kannan
National Institute of Technology, India

P. Senthil
National Institute of Technology, India

P. Sasikumar
National Institute of Technology, India

V.P. Vinay
National Institute of Technology, India

ABSTRACT

The term 'supply chain management' has become common in the business world, which can be understood from the positive results of research in the area, particularly in supply chain optimization. Transportation is a frontier in achieving the objectives of the supply chain. Thrust is also given to optimization problems in transportation. The fixed-charge transportation problem is an extension of the transportation problem that includes a fixed cost, along with a variable cost that is proportional to the amount shipped. This article approaches the problem with another meta-heuristics known as the Nelder and Mead methodology to save the computational time with little iteration and obtain better results with the help of a program in C++.

INTRODUCTION

The series of companies (actors) that interact for the production and delivery of goods and service is called a supply chain. The actors are connected through the flow of products, the flow of information, and the flow of money. A definition is given by Simchi-Levi, Kaminsky, and Simchi Levi (2000) for supply chain; they state that supply chains are flexible, dynamic, and complex networks of organizations. The reason for the existence of supply chains is that there are very few companies that can produce end products for end customers from raw materials on their own, without the assistance of other organizations. The company that produces the raw material is often not the same company that sells the end products to the end customers. In order to provide end products to the end customers, a network of actors is involved in activities (such as purchasing, transforming, and distribution) to produce products and/or services. All of these actors add value to the end product (Lummus, 1999). These companies that interact to produce end products, and to contribute to the value of end products, are called supply chain companies. Supply chain management covers all material management activities including inventory receipts, shipments, moves, and counts within a client and its organizations and to suppliers and customers. From this description, the image of a supply chain in general is obtained.

In the automotive world many lessons were understood from the Japanese approaches. The just-in-time (JIT) revolution pointed out that purchasing is a key issue, which involves far more than simply negotiating deals with and managing supply from direct suppliers. Ford, GM, and other western car manufacturers saw many differences in the approach adopted by their counterparts in Japan. The differences were the approaches like the idea of 'partnership sourcing', where the car manufacturers and suppliers worked together to attack quality and cost issues, and then shared the benefits. This was in marked contrast to the established western approach where cost reductions were negotiated (or, more accurately, imposed) and the suppliers then worked alone to try to retain some measure of profit from the deal. The lesson from the Japanese companies was that if the suppliers have problems, then it is not only they who suffer.

The other key point that purchasing professionals learned from Japan was that their success was dependent not only on dealings with their direct suppliers, but with the companies further down the procurement cycle who supplied the suppliers. The companies supplying the direct suppliers with components did not have the same purchasing power in the raw materials market as the direct suppliers themselves. This led to the direct suppliers assisting their suppliers in dealings with providers of, for example, metals, plastics, and electronic components.

This evolved into the various forms of suppliers called Tier 1, Tier 2, and Tier 3 suppliers, as shown in Figure 1. So the Japanese concept finally made it very clear that the manufacturers must manage and think of every link in a chain. The managers always wish to optimize the resources as the primary objective. Optimization problems are ubiquitous in the mathematical modeling of real-world systems and cover a very broad range of applications. So the proposed optimization model in this work proves to be of practical significance and may play a key role in the real-life business needs of decision making of the managers.

Optimization modeling requires appropriate time. The general procedure that can be used in the process cycle of modeling is to: (1) describe the problem, (2) prescribe a solution, and (3) control the problem by assessing/updating the optimal solution continuously, while changing the parameters and structure of the problem. Clearly, there are always feedback loops among these general steps. The diagrammatic representation of the process cycle in optimization is depicted in Figure 2.

Figure 1. A diagrammatic representation of a supply chain (Lambert, Cooper, & Pagh, 1998)

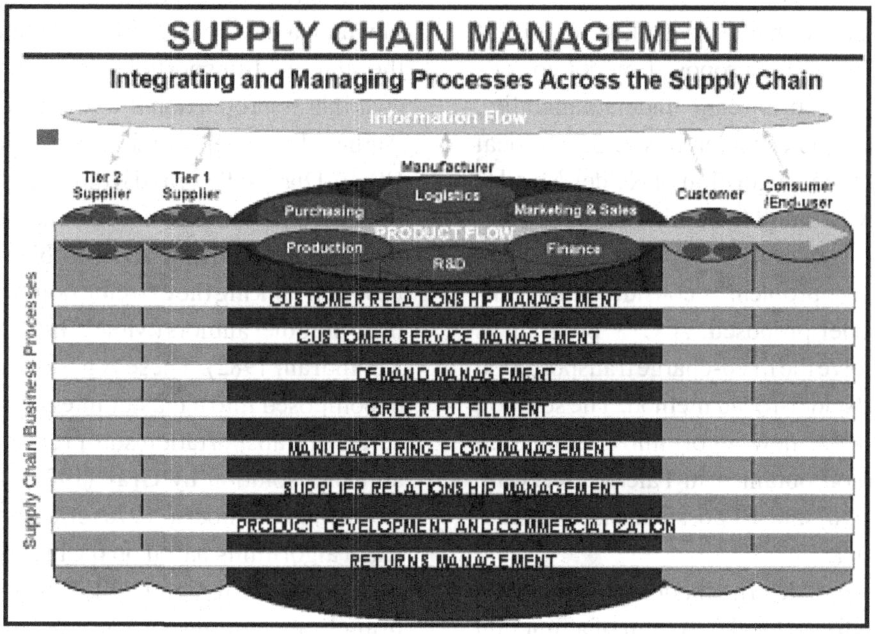

SUPPLY CHAIN MANAGEMENT

Integrating and Managing Processes Across the Supply Chain

Figure 2. Stages of optimization

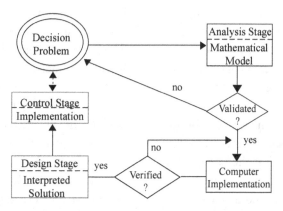

Describe the Problem, Prescribe a Solution, Update the Solution

The various classifications of optimization problems are: (1) Mathematical Programming, (2) Convex Program, (3) Data Envelopment Analysis, (4) Dynamic Programming, (5) Separable Program, (6) Geometric Program, (7) Fractional Program, (8) Heuristic Optimization, (9) Global Optimization, and (10) Meta-Heuristics. Most meta-heuristics have been created for solving discrete combinatorial optimization problems. Practical applications in engineering, however, usually require techniques that handle continuous variables, or miscellaneous continuous and discrete variables. As a consequence, a large research effort has focused on fitting several well-known meta-heuristics, like simulated annealing (SA), tabu search (TS), genetic algorithms (GA), Nelder and Mead method, and ant colony optimization (ACO), to the continuous cases.

As stated above that every link is important in a supply chain, this proposed model considers a single echelon for easy understandability, and computation is considered where in a local search optimization algorithm of Nelder-Mead is applied to solve a small fixed-charge transportation problem.

A sample test problem is considered for validating the model proposed. A C++ program is developed to solve the fixed-charge transportation problem with Nelder-Mead method. The solution obtained with the new algorithm is compared with the solution obtained in Palekar, Karwan, and Zionts (1990) and all possible case of transportation model.

The Nelder and Mead methodology is a simplex method for finding a local optimum of a function of several variables. The method proceeds by comparing the functional values as the vertices of a triangle, rejecting the worst, selecting the best, and changing the triangle vertices. The search continues until functional value satisfies, as explained in the problem section of this article. It is found to be very effective and computationally compact.

The rest of the article is arranged in the following manner. The literature survey is discussed in the next section. The problem is then described, with the solution methodology proposed. The article concludes with results and discussion.

LITERATURE REVIEW

Currently, there is intensive research work being carried out in supply chain management. Quite a large number of publications have appeared on the subject matter, particularly on supply chain optimization problems. In this section, a synopsis of the contributions that are important to this work is presented.

The fixed-charge transportation problem is an extension of the classical transportation problem, in which a fixed cost is incurred, independent of the amount transported, along with a variable cost that is proportional to the amount shipped. Authors like Cooper and Drebes (1967), Drenzler (1969), Diaby (1991), and Kuhn and Baumol (1962) have used well-known heuristic approaches for the fixed-charge transportation problem. Techniques based on ranking the extreme points were adopted by some other authors (Murty, 1968; Sadagopan & Ravindran, 1982). These types of problems were decomposed into a master integer program and a series of transportation sub-programs to provide an exact solution by Gray (1971). Palekar et al. (1990) and Steinberg (1970) attempted to provide exact algorithms based on the branch-and-bound method. Schaffer and O'Leary (1989) used a branch-and-bound procedure, incorporating penalties into the procedure to improve the solution to the fixed-charge transportation problem. Hultberg and Cardoso (1997) considered the teacher assignment problem as a special case of the fixed-charge transportation problem and solved it with a branch-and-bound algorithm.

Gen, Kumar, and Kim (2005) proposed the use of a hybrid genetic algorithm to solve the network design problem inherent in the fixed-charge transportation problem. Haq and Kannan (2006) proposed the development integrated supplier selection multi-echelon distribution inventory model (MEDIM) in a built-to-order supply chain environment using fuzzy analytical hierarchy process (FAHP) and a genetic algorithm. Adlakha and Kowalski (2003) and Sandrock (1988) presented a simple heuristic algorithm for the solution of a small fixed-charge problem. And Sun, Aronson, McKeown, and Drinka (1998) developed a tabu search approach for the fixed-charge transportation problem which requires the same amount of computational time, but solutions as good as other heuristic approaches. For larger problems and for problems with higher fixed relative to variable costs, the tabu search procedure was 3-4 times faster than the heuristic.

Adlakha, Kowalski, Vemuganti, and Lev (2007) developed a simple heuristic algorithm to the address the more-for-less phenomenon in a distribution model for the fixed-charge transportation problem. Yang and Liu (2007) investigated the fixed-charge solid transportation problem under a fuzzy environment and tried to solve the models with the help of a hybrid intelligent algorithm designed based on the fuzzy simulation technique and tabu search algorithm. Jo, Li, and Gen (2007) solved a nonlinear fixed-charge transportation problem by spanning a tree-based genetic algorithm. And Kannan, Kumar, and Vinay (2008) provided comments and suggestions to the nonlinear fixed-charge transportation problem of Jo et al. (2007).

The Nelder-Mead method (also called the simplex, or downhill simplex method) is a commonly used nonlinear optimization algorithm (Nelder & Mead, 1965) and is a numerical method for minimizing an objective function in a many-dimensional space. No literature is found that uses this simplex method to solve the fixed-charge transportation problem. This work attempts to solve the fixed-charge transportation problem with the help of the local search method of Nelder and Mead methodology and hence forth proposes a new model.

PROBLEM DESCRIPTION

The objective function of our fixed-cost transport model is to get the optimal distribution routes between manufacturing units and customers in case of single echelon. A single-echelon supply chain has only one link with two entities—that is, it lets us consider a manufacturer and an end customer—as depicted in Figure 3.

The mathematical model of the single echelon fixed-cost problem under consideration is formulated as:

Minimize

$$Z = \sum_{i=1}^{p} \sum_{j=1}^{q} \left(C_{ij} X_{ij} + F_{ij} Y_{ij} \right) \tag{1}$$

Subjected to

$$\sum_{j=1}^{q} X_{ij} \leq S_i \quad (i = 1, 2, 3, ..., p)$$

(Plant supply capacity constraint) (2)

$$\sum_{i=1}^{p} X_{ij} = D_j \quad (j = 1, 2, 3, ..., q)$$

(Demand constraint) (3)

Table 1. Test problem for single echelon

		Customer "j"			
		1	2	3	S_i
Plant "i"	1	F_{ij}=200 C_{ij}=1	800 1	800 1	800
	2	400 6	1200 4	600 1	600
	3	100 1	600 7	600 1	600
D_j		200	900	900	

Figure 3. Single-echelon supply chain

Manufacturing plant (Supply)		Customer (Demand)

Table 2. General illustration of allocation of units in sequence without violating constraints

		Customer "j"			S_i
		1	2	3	
Plant "i"	1	Cell 1	Cell 2	Cell 3	800
	2	Cell 4	Cell 5	Cell 6	600
	3	Cell 7	Cell 8	Cell 9	600
D_j		200	900	900	

Table 3. Illustration of allocation of units in sequence without violating constraints

		Customer "j"			S_i
		1	2	3	
Plant "i"	1	0	0	800	800
	2	200	400	0	600
	3	0	500	100	600
D_j		200	900	900	

Table 4. Result of single echelon

		Customer "j"			S_i
		1	2	3	
Plant "i"	1	0	800	0	800
	2	0	0	600	600
	3	200	100	300	600
D_j		200	900	900	

$X_{ij} \geq 0$

$$Y_{ij} = \begin{cases} 1, & \text{if } X_{ij} > 0 \\ 0, & \text{otherwise} \end{cases}$$

(Non-negative constraints)   (4)

where

X_{ij} = No. of quantity transported from plant (i) to customer (j)

C_{ij} = Cost of transportation between plant (i) and customer (j)

F_{ij} = Fixed transportation cost between plant (i) and customer (j)

Solution Methodology Adopted

All possible allocations of units in sequence without violating constraints is done, and the procedure is followed until total costs for N! combinations are found out, where N is the product between the number of customers and the number of manufacturing plants. The values of total cost are sorted out, and least total cost and its corresponding distribution are displayed by a C++ program. The program gets inputs like fixed and variable cost for each route (*Fij & Cij*), demand of customers (*Dj*), and capacity of manufacturing units (*S$_I$*). N is calculated as:

N = number of customers X number of manufacturing units   (5)

In the case considered, N = 3x3 = 9. All possible combinations of N (i.e., take the first order 324561879) are found by using permute function. The units are allocated for each cell in the sequence of combinational order (i.e., 324561879) without violating demand and supply constraints:

Order –324561879

The total transportation cost is found for the allocated table using formula 4.1:

$$Z = \sum_{i=1}^{p} \sum_{j=1}^{q} \left(C_{ij} X_{ij} + F_{ij} Y_{ij} \right)$$

Substituting the values in the above equation, we obtain:

$$Z = 0 + 0 + ((800 \times 1) + 800) + ((200 \times 6) + 400)) + ((400 \times 4) + 1200)) + 0 + 0 + ((500 \times 7) + 600)) + ((100 \times 1) + 600))$$
$$= 10,800 \text{ units}$$

The procedure is followed until total costs for N! combinations are found out (i.e., 9!). Values of total cost are sorted out, and least total cost and its corresponding distribution are displayed. The minimum total cost is 5,300 units.

Nelder and Mead Method

A simplex method for finding a local minimum of a function of several variables has been devised by Nelder and Mead (1965). For two variables, a simplex is a triangle, and the method is a pattern search that compares function values at the three vertices of triangle. The worst vertex, where $f(x, y)$ is largest, is rejected and replaced with a new vertex. A new triangle is formed and the search is continued. The process generates a sequence of triangles (which might have different shapes), for which the function values at the vertices get smaller and smaller. The size of the triangles is reduced and the coordinates of the minimum point are found. The algorithm is stated using the term *simplex* (a generalized triangle in *N* dimensions) and will find the minimum of a function of *N variables*. It is effective and computationally compact. The flow chart for the Nelder and Mead method is given in Figure 4.

Initial Triangle BGW

Let $f(x, y)$ be the function that is to be minimized. To start, we are given three vertices of a triangle: $V_k = (x_k, y_k)$, $k = 1, 2, 3$. The function $f(x, y)$ is then evaluated at each of the three points: $z_k = f(x_k, y_k)$ for $k = 1, 2, 3$. The subscripts are then reordered so that $z1 \leq z2 \leq z3$. We use the notation, $B = (x_1, y_1)$, $G = (x_2, y_2)$, and $W = (x_3, y_3)$, to help remember that B is the best vertex, G is good (next to best), and W is the worst vertex.

Midpoint of the Good Side

The construction process uses the midpoint of the line segment joining B and G. It is found by averaging the coordinates:

$$M = (B+G) \backslash 2$$
$$= ((X1+X2)\backslash 2, (Y1+Y2)\backslash 2) \qquad (6)$$

Reflection Using the Point R

The function decreases as we move along the side of the triangle from W to B, and it decreases as we move along the side from W to G. Hence it is feasible that $f(x, y)$ takes on smaller values at points that lie away from W on the opposite side of the line between B and G. We choose a test point R (as shown in Figure 5) that is obtained by "reflecting" the triangle through the side BG. To determine R, we first find the midpoint M of the side BG. Then draw the line segment from W to M and call its length d. This last segment is extended a distance d through M to locate the point R. The vector formula for R is:

$$R = M + (M - W) = 2M - W \qquad (7)$$

The notations used (Luersen & Riche, 2004) in the algorithm are explained below:

Pi: Simplex point

Fi: Objective function value at Pi

Ph: Simplex point where the objective function assumes its highest value

Ps: Simplex point where the objective function assumes its second highest value

Pl: Simplex point where the objective function assumes its lowest value

Pm: centroid simplex point (not considering Ph)

r: reflection coefficient = 1

β: contraction coefficient = 1/2

α: expansion coefficient = 2

Figure 4. Flow chart for Nelder and Mead method (Luersen & Riche, 2004)

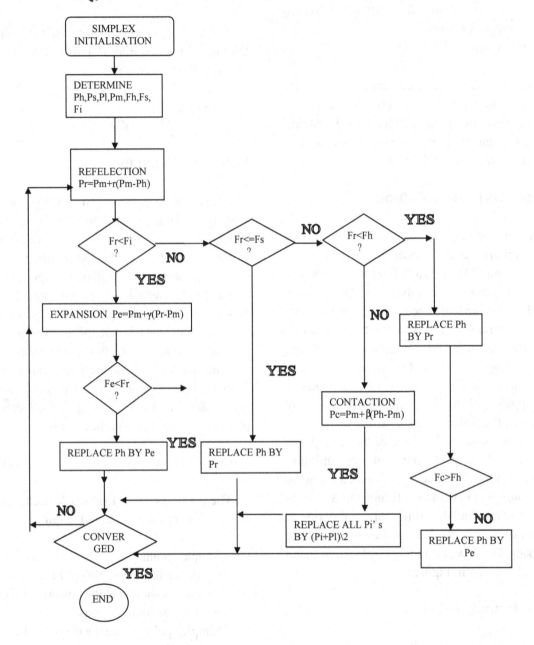

Expansion Using the Point E

If the function value at R is smaller than the function value at W, then we have moved in the correct direction toward the minimum. Perhaps the minimum is just a bit farther than the point R. So we extend the line segment through M and R to the point E. This forms an expanded triangle BGE as shown in Figure 6. The point E is found by moving an additional distance d along the line joining M and R. If the function value at E is less than the function value at R, then we have found a better vertex than R. The vector formula for E is:

Figure 5. Reflection of worst point

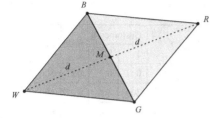

Figure 6. Expansion of worst point

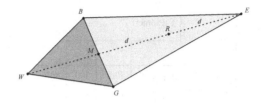

Figure 7. Contraction of worst point

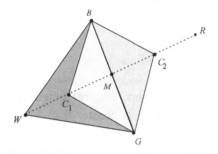

Figure 8. Shrinking of triangle towards optimal point

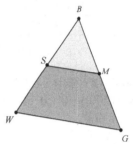

$$E = R + (R - M) = 2R - M \qquad (8)$$

Contraction Using the Point C

If the function values at R and W are the same, another point must be tested. Perhaps the function is smaller at M, but we cannot replace W with M because we must have a triangle. Consider the two midpoints $C1$ and $C2$ of the line segments WM and MR, respectively (see Figure 7). The point with the smaller function value is called C, and the new triangle is BGC. Note: the choice between $C1$ and $C2$ might seem inappropriate for the two-dimensional case, but it is important in higher dimensions.

Shrink Toward B

If the function value at C is not less than the value at W, the points G and W must be shrunk toward B (see Figure 8). The point G is replaced with M, and W is replaced with S, which is the midpoint of the line segment joining B with W.

Application of the Methodology to the Problem

The code in C++ is written for the solving the problem with Nelder and Mead. The same test problem is selected for applying the proposed method of Nelder and Mead for solving. The written program gets inputs like fixed and variable cost for each route (*Fij & Cij*), demand of customers(*Dj*), and capacity of manufacturing units (S_I). As previously noted, N is calculated:

N = number of customers X number of manufacturing units

N = 3x3 = 9 (9)

N Random sequences are found out (i.e., first order –324561879), and the total transportation cost is found for the allocated table using formula 1:

$$Z = \sum_{i=1}^{p} \sum_{j=1}^{q} \left(C_{ij} X_{ij} + F_{ij} Y_{ij} \right)$$

Table 5. Test problem

		Customer "j"			Si
		1	2	3	
plant "i"	1	Fij=200 Cij=1	800 1	800 1	800
	2	400 6	1200 4	600 1	600
	3	100 1	600 7	600 1	600
Dj		200	900	900	

Table 6. Illustration of calculation of total costs for N+ 1 point

		Customer "j"			Si
		1	2	3	
Plant "i"	1	0	0	800	800
	2	200	400	0	600
	3	0	500	100	600
Dj		200	900	900	

$Z = 0 + 0 + ((800*1) + 800) + ((200*6) + 400)) + ((400*4) + 1200)) + 0 + 0 + ((500*7) + 600)) + ((100*1) + 600))$

$=10,800$

The (N+1)th total cost is found out from well-known transport methods—that is, the least cost method and north west corner method. The best of these two is taken as the N+1th total cost. The total cost = 5,300 = N+1th total cost. This is done for quicker convergence. N+1 total costs are sorted. The centroid of points leaving the worst point is then calculated:

$$Pm = (1/N)\sum_{i=0}^{n-1} X_i \qquad (10)$$

Similarly the worst point (max cost) is reflected by:

Pr=Pm +r (Pm-Ph)   (11)

The reflected point is checked with all other points. If it is better (least value) than all other points, expansion is performed and worst point is replaced by expansion point:

Pe=Pm +γ (Pr-Pm)   (12)

In first iteration, the reflected point is 6555.554688, which is greater than 5,300 (best point). So the result is not satisfied and the program checks next condition. If the reflected point is better than the worst point, the worst point is replaced by the reflected point. The reflected point 6555.554688 is less than the worst point (10,800) and hence satisfied. So 10,800 is replaced by 6555.554688. If the reflected point is worse even than the worst point, contraction is performed and the worst point is replaced by the contraction point using the formula:

Pc=Pm+β(Ph-Pm)   (13)

The above procedure is repeated until initial simplex is converged.

RESULT AND DISCUSSION

The data available from Palekar et al. (1990) is used for validating the model proposed in this article. The meta-heuristic approach (algorithm) used in this article is a Nelder and Mead algorithm; it is used to optimize the model thus constructed and generate a near optimal\optimal minimum total cost.

Table 7. Parameter comparison with Palekar's method

Parameters Considered for Evaluation	Proposed Nelder and Mead Model	Palekar et al. (1990) Model
Minimum cost	5,300	5,600
Number of iterations	3	18

Table 8. Comparison of parameters with all possible case transportation models

Parameters Considered for Evaluation	Proposed Nelder and Mead Model	All Possible Case Transportation Models
Minimum cost	5,300	5,300
Number of iterations	3	9!

The first set of data considered for validation of the proposed model was taken from Palekar et al. (1990). In this case the model proposed in this work generated a solution that performed better (in that total cost was lesser as compared to their solution). The proposed model converged upon the optimal solution at the third iteration itself. The computational efficiency of the model proposed in Palekar et al (1990) was not known.

The next comparison is with all possible case transportation models that arrive at an optimal cost from all possible combinations of N! times. The optimal cost of 5,300 was obtained after N! iterations (i.e., 9!), but the result obtained is the most optimal one because it checks all possible ways of allocation of units for transportation.

As can be seen from Table 8 and 9, the model proposed in this work performs better on almost all accounts as compared to the methods available above.

REFERENCES

Adlakha, V., & Kowalski, K. (2003). A simple algorithm for solving small fixed charge transportation problems. *Omega: International Journal of Management Science, 31,* 105-111.

Adlakha, V., Kowalski, K., Vemuganti, R.R., & Lev, B. (2007). More-for less algorithm for fixed charge transportation problems. *Omega, International Journal of Management Science, 35,* 116-127.

Cooper, L., & Drebes, C. (1967). An approximate algorithm for the fixed charge problem. *Naval Research Logistics Quarterly, 14,* 101-113.

Diaby, M. (1991). Successive linear approximation procedure for generalized fixed-charge transportation problems. *Journal of Operational Research Society, 42,* 991-1001.

Drenzler, D.R. (1969). An approximate method for the fixed charge problem. *Naval Research Logistics Quarterly, 16,* 411-416.

Gen, M., Kumar, A., & Kim, J.R. (2005). Recent network design techniques using evolutionary algorithms. *International Journal of Production Economics, 98*(2), 251-261.

Gray, P. (1971). Exact solution of the fixed-charge transportation problem. *Operations Research, 19,* 1529-38.

Haq, A.N., & Kannan, G. (2006). Design of an integrated supplier selection and multi-echelon distribution inventory model in a built- to order supply chain environment. *International Journal of Production Research, 44*(10), 1963-1985.

Hultberg, T.H., & Cardoso, D.M. (1997). The teacher assignment problem: A special case of the fixed charge transportation problem. *European Journal of Operational Research, 101*(3), 463-473.

Jo, J.B., Li, Y., & Gen, M. (2007). Nonlinear fixed charge transportation problem by spanning tree-based genetic algorithm. *Computers & Industrial Engineering, 53*(2), 290-298.

Kannan, G., Kumar, P.S., & Vinay, V.P. (2008). Comments on the erratum to nonlinear fixed charge transportation problem by spanning tree-based genetic algorithm. *Computers & Industrial Engineering.*

Kuhn, H.W., & Baumol, W.J. (1962). An approximation algorithm for the fixed charge transportation problem. *Naval Research Logistics Quarterly, 9,* 1-15.

Lambert, D.M., Cooper, M.C., & Pagh, J.D. (1998). Supply chain management: Implementation issues and research opportunities. *International Journal of Logistics Management, 9*(2), 1-20.

Luersen, M.A., & Riche, R.L. (2004). Globalized Nelder–Mead method for engineering optimization. *Computers and Structures, 82,* 2251-2260.

Lummus, R. (1999). Defining supply chain management: A historical perspective and practical guidelines. *Industrial Management and Data Systems, 99*(1), 11-17.

Murty, K.G. (1968). Solving the fixed charge problem by ranking the extreme points. *Operations Research, 16,* 268-279.

Nelder, J.A., & Mead, R. (1965). A simplex for function minimization. *Computer Journal, 7,* 308-313.

Palekar, U.S., Karwan, M.H., & Zionts, S. (1990). A branch-and- bound method for the fixed charge transportation problem. *Management Science, 36,* 1092-105.

Sadagopan, S., & Ravindran, A. (1982). A vertex ranking algorithm for the fixed-charge transportation problem. *Journal of Optimization Theory Applications, 37,* 221-230.

Sandrock, K. (1988). A simple algorithm for solving small fixed- charge transportation problems. *Journal of Operations Research Society, 39,* 467-475.

Schaffer, J.R., & O'Leary, D.E. (1989). Use of penalties in a branch and bound procedure for the fixed charge transportation problem. *European Journal of Operational Research, 43,* 305-312.

Simchi Levi, D., Kaminsky, P., & Simchi Levi, E. (2000). *Designing and managing the supply chain.* New York: McGraw-Hill.

Steinberg, D.I. (1970) The fixed charge problem. *Naval Research Logistics Quarterly, 17,* 217-235.

Sun, M., Aronson, J.E., McKeown, P.G., & Drinka, D. (1998). A tabu search heuristic procedure for the fixed charge transportation problem. *European Journal of Operational Research, 106*(2-3), 441-456.

Yang, L., & Liu, L. (2007). Fuzzy fixed charge solid transportation problem and algorithm. *Applied Soft Computing, 7*(3), 879-889.

Compilation of References

Abel, P. (2004). *RFID benefits*. Paper presented at Productivity Conference Nashville, TN, p. 20, Retrieved from http://www.fmi.org/events/productivity/2004/Prod_CDROM/presentations/ RFID_benefits.pdf

Adamson, I., & Shine, J. (2003). Extending the new technology acceptance model to measure the end user information systems satisfaction in a mandatory environment: A bank's treasury. *Technology Analysis and Strategic Management, 15*(4), 441-455.

Adlakha, V., & Kowalski, K. (2003). A simple algorithm for solving small fixed charge transportation problems. *Omega: International Journal of Management Science, 31,* 105-111.

Adlakha, V., Kowalski, K., Vemuganti, R.R., & Lev, B. (2007). More-for less algorithm for fixed charge transportation problems. *Omega, International Journal of Management Science, 35,* 116-127.

Aeppel, T. (2003). Inventories may bloat as year 2000 nears: Companies to stockpile in case supply chain snaps. *Wall Street Journal,* (February 9), A2.

Agarwal, R. (2000). Individual acceptance of information technologies. In R. W. Zmud (Ed.), *Framing the domain of IT management* (pp. 85-104). Pinnaflex, Ohio.

Aichlmayer, M. (2001). The future of JIT☐time will tell. *Transportation and Distribution, 42*(12), 18-22.

Al-Ali, A. S. A., Sajwani, F., Al-Muhairi, A., & Shahenn, E. (2007). Assessing the feasibility of using rfid technology in airports. In *1st Annual RFID Eurasia, Istanbul, Turkey.*

Alien (2005). *Alien Technology Corporation announces 12.9 cent RFID Labels*. Retrieved from Available at URL: http://www.isminfo.com/RFID/PDFs/2005_09_13_Alien.pdf

Altenburg, K., Griscom, D., Hart, J., Smith, F., & Wohler, G. (1999). Just-in-time logistics support for the automobile industry. *Production and Inventory Management Journal, 40*(2), 59-66.

Amoako-Gyampah, K., & Salam, A. F. (2004). An extension of the technology acceptance model in an ERP implementation environment. *Information and Management, 41*(6), 731-745.

Angeles, R. (2005). RFID technologies: Supply-chain applications and implementation issues. *Information Systems Management, 22,* 51–65. doi:10.1201/1078/449 12.22.1.20051201/85739.7

Angeles, R. (2007). An empirical study of the anticipated consumer response to RFID product item tagging. *Industrial Management & Data Systems, 107,* 461-483.

Ansley, M. (2000). Virtual manufacturing. *CMA Management, 74*(1), 31-35.

Aref, A. H., Marilyn, M. H., & Joseph, S. (2005). Performance measurement for green supply chain management. *Benchmarking: An international Journal, 12*(4), 330-352.

Arnold, U. (2000). New dimensions of outsourcing: a combination of transaction cost economics and the core competencies concept. *European Journal of Purchasing & Supply Management, 6*(1), 23–29. doi:10.1016/S0969-7012(99)00028-3

Arumugam, A. K., Doufexi, A., Nix, A. R., & Fletcher, P. N. (2003). An investigation of the coexistence of 802.11g WLAN and high data rate Bluetooth enabled consumer electronic devices in indoor home and office environments. *IEEE Transactions on Consumer Electronics, 49*(3), 587-596.

Asif, Z., & Mandviwalla, M. (2005). Integrating the supply chain with RFID: A technical and business analysis. *Communications of the Association for Information Systems, 15,* 393-427.

Atkinson, W. (2003). Riding out global challenges. *Purchasing, 132*(14), 43.

Atock, C. (2003). Where is my stuff? *Manufacturing Engineering, 82*(2), 24–27. doi:10.1049/me:20030202

Auramo, J., Kauremaa, J., & Tanskanen, K. (2005). Benefits of IT in supply chain management: an explorative study of progressive companies. *International Journal of Physical Distribution & Logistics Management, 53*(2), 82–100. doi:10.1108/09600030510590282

Averbakh, I., & Xue, Z. (2007). Online supply chain scheduling problems with preemption. *European Journal of Operational Research, 181*(1), 500-504.

Avery, (2005). *Avery Dennison offers GEN 2 RFID inlays at lowest price industry.* Press Release. Retrieved from http://www.rfid.averydennison.com/pages/news/pdf/091905.pdf

Ayoade, J. (2006). Security implications in RFID and authentication processing framework. *Computers & Security, 25,* 207-212.

Bagchi, P. K., & Virum, H. (1998). Logistical alliances: trends and prospects in integrated Europe. *Journal of Business Logistics, 19*(1), 191–213.

Bagchi, S., Buckley, S., Ettl, E., & Lin, G. (1998). Experience using the IBM supply chain simulator. In D.J.Medeires, E.F.Watson, J.S.Carson, & M.S.Manivannan (Eds.), *Proceedings of the 1998 Winter Simulation Conference* (pp. 1387-1394).

Bailey, J., & Pearson, S. W. (1983). Development of a tool for measuring and analyzing computer user satisfaction. *Management Science, 29*(5), 530-545.

Baiman, S., & Rajan, M. V. (2002). Incentive issues in inter-firm relationships. *Accounting, Organizations and Society, 27*(3), 213–238. doi:10.1016/S0361-3682(00)00017-9

Baines, T., Whitney, D., & Fine, C. (1999). Manufacturing technology sourcing practices in the USA. *International Journal of Production Research, 37*(4), 939–956. doi:10.1080/002075499191616

Baker, G. P., & Hubbard, T. N. (2003). Make versus buy in trucking: Asset ownership, job design, and information. *The American Economic Review, 93*(3), 551–572. doi:10.1257/000282803322156981

Balakrishnan, R., & Sivaramakrishnan, K. (2001). Sequential solutions to capacity-planning and pricing decisions. *Contemporary Accounting Research, 18*(1), 1–26. doi:10.1506/Y6TG-1KQ9-12GV-L5YY

Balakrishnan, S. (1994). The dynamics of make-or-buy decisions. *European Journal of Operational Research, 74,* 552–571. doi:10.1016/0377-2217(94)90231-3

Ball, M. O., Chen, C.-Y., & Zhao, Z.-Y. (2004). Available to promise. In D. Simchi-Levi, D. Wu, & Z.M. Shen (Eds.), *Handbook of Quantitative Analysis: Modeling in an-e-business era* (pp. 446-483). Kluwer.

Ballou, R. H. (2004). *Business logistics/supply chain management: A balanced approach.* (5th ed.). New Jersey: Pearson, Prentice Hall.

Bandura, A. (1986). *Social foundations of thought and action: A social cognitive theory.* Englewood, Cliffs NJ: Prentice-Hall.

Bandura, A. (1997). *Self-efficacy: The exercise of control.* New York: Freeman.

Banker, R. D., Hwang, I., & Mishra, B. K. (2002). Product costing and pricing under long term capacity commitment. *Journal of Management Accounting, 14,* 79–97. doi:10.2308/jmar.2002.14.1.79

Bardhan, I., Whitaker, J., & Mithas, S. (2006). Information technology, production process outsourcing, and manufacturing plant performance. *Journal of Management Information Systems, 23*(2), 13–40. doi:10.2753/MIS0742-1222230202

Barnes, J.C. (2001). *A guide to business continuity planning.* New York: John Wiley & Sons.

Barney, J. B. (1991). Firm resources and sustained competitive advantage. *Journal of Management, 17*(1), 99–120. doi:10.1177/014920639101700108

Barratt, M. (2004). Understanding the meaning of collaboration in the supply chain. *Supply Chain Management: An International Journal, 9*(1), 30-42.

Barratt, M., & Rosdahl, K. (2002). Exploring business-to-business market sites. *European Journal of Purchasing & Supply Management, 8*(2), 111–122. doi:10.1016/S0969-7012(01)00010-7

Barry, J. (2004). Supply chain risk in an uncertain global supply chain environment. *International Journal of Physical Distribution and Logistics Management, 34*(9), 695-697.

Bassett, R. (1991). Make-or-buy decisions. *Management Accounting,* November, 58-59.

Bauer, M.J., Poirier, C.C., Lapide, L., & Bermudez, J. (2001). *E-Business: The Strategic Impact on Supply Chain and Logistics.* Oak Brook, IL: Council of Logistics Management.

Beaumont, N., & Sohal, A. (2004). Outsourcing in Australia. *International Journal of Operations & Production Management, 24*(7), 688–700. doi:10.1108/01443570410541993

Beck, E. (1999). Unilever to cut more than 1,000 brands. *Wall Street Journal,* (September 22), A17.

Becker, J. (1998). GM strike inflicts supply chain pain. *Modern Purchasing, 40*(8), 9-10.

Bell, J. (1996). *Single or joint venture: A comprehensive approach to foreign entry mode choice.* Aldershot: Avebury.

Ben-Arieh, D. (2000). Cost estimation system for machined parts. *International Journal of Production Research, 38*(17), 4481–4494. doi:10.1080/00207540050205244

Benbasat, I., Goldstein, D. K., & Mead, M. (1987). The case study research strategy in studies of information systems. *MIS Quarterly, 11*(4), 369–386. doi:10.2307/248684

Bensaou, B.M. (1999). Portfolios of buyer-supplier relationships. *Sloan Management Review, 40*(4), 35-44.

Berman, O., & Ashrafi, N. (1993). Optimization models for reliability of modular software systems. *IEEE Transactions on Software Engineering, 19*(11), 1119–1123. doi:10.1109/32.256858

Besanko, D., Dranove, D., & Shanley, M. (2004). *Economics of strategy* (3rd ed.). New York: John Wiley & Sons.

Bhatnagar, R., Sohal, A. S., & Millen, R. (1999). Third party logistics services: A Singapore perspective. *International Journal of Physical Distribution & Logistics Management, 29*(9), 569–587. doi:10.1108/09600039910287529

Bhattacherjee, A. (2001). Understanding information systems continuance: An expectation-confirmation model. *MIS Quarterly, 27*(3), 351-370.

Bhuptani, M., & Moradpour, S. (2005). *RFID field guide: Deploying radio frequency identification systems.* New York: Prentice Hall.

Black, J. A., & Boal, K. B. (1994). Strategic resources: traits, configurations, and paths to sustainable competitive advantage. *Strategic Management Journal, 15,* 131–148.

Blattberg, R. C., & Hoch, S. J. (1990). Database models and managerial intuition: 50% model + 50% manager. *Management Science, 36*(8), 887-899.

Bode, J. (2000). Neural networks for cost estimation: simulations and pilot application. *International Journal of Production Research, 38*(6), 1231–1254. doi:10.1080/002075400188825

Boer, L. D., Harink, J., & Heijboer, G. (2002). A conceptual model for assessing the impact of electronic procurement. *European Journal of Purchasing & Supply Management, 8,* 25–33. doi:10.1016/S0969-7012(01)00015-6

Bookbinder, J. H. (2005). Global logistics. [Editorial]. *Transportation Research Part E, Logistics and Transportation Review, 41*(6), 461–466. doi:10.1016/j.tre.2005.07.001

Bourland, K. E., Powell, S. G., & Pyke, D. F. (1996). Exploiting timely demand information to reduce inventories. *European Journal of Operational Research, 92,* 239-253.

Bowersox, D. J., Closs, D. J., & Cooper, M. B. (2002). *Supply chain logistics management.* Boston: McGraw Hill.

Boyson, S., Corsi, T., Dresner, M., & Rabinovich, E. (1999). Managing third party logistics relationships: what does it take. *Journal of Business Logistics, 20*(1), 73–100.

Brandes, H., Lilliecreutz, J., & Brege, S. (1997). Outsourcing – success or failure?: Findings from five case studies. *European Journal of Purchasing & Supply Management, 3*(2), 63–75. doi:10.1016/S0969-7012(97)00001-4

Brown, I., & Russell, J. (2007). Radio frequency identification technology: An exploratory study on adoption in the South African retail sector. *International Journal of Information Management.*

Brown, J. R., Dev, C. S., & Lee, D. J. (2000). Managing marketing channel opportunism: The efficacy of alternative governance mechanism. *Journal of Marketing, 64,* 51-65.

Brown, K. L., Inman, A., & Calloway, J. A. (2001). Measuring the effect of inventory inaccuracy in MRP inventory and delivery performance. *Production Planning and Control, 12*(1), 46–57. doi:10.1080/09537280150203979

Buckley, P. J., & Casson, M. (1976). The future of the multinational enterprise. London: Macmillan.

Burdon, S., & Bhalla, A. (2005). Lessons from the untold success story: Outsourcing engineering and facilities management. *European Management, 23*(5), 576–582. doi:10.1016/j.emj.2005.09.012

Businessweek. (2007, April 25). *Asia RFID market need gov't boost.* Retrieved from *http://www.businessweek. com/globalbiz/content/apr2007/gb20070425_369568. htm?chan=search*

Byrd, T. A., & Turner, D. E. (2001). An exploratory analysis of the value of the skills of IT personnel: Their relationship to IS infrastructure and competitive advantage. *Decision Sciences, 32*(1), 21-54.

Cachon, G., & Fisher, M. (2000). Supply chain inventory management and the value of shared information. *Management Science, 46*(8), 1032-1048.

Cagliano, R., Caniato, F., & Spina, G. (2005). E-business strategy: How companies are shaping their supply chain through the internet. *International Journal of Operations & Production Management, 25*(12), 1309–1327. doi:10.1108/01443570510633675

Cai, S., Jun, M., & Yang, Z. (2006). The impact of interorganizational Internet communication on purchasing performance: A study of Chinese manufacturing firms. *Journal of Supply Chain Management, 42*(3), 16-29.

Campbell, A. (2004). Online supply chain solutions. *Supply Chain Europe, 13*(4), 54-55.

Campbell, J. F. (1990). Freight consolidation and routing with transport economies of scale. *Transportation Research Part B: Methodological, 24*(5), 345–361. doi:10.1016/0191-2615(90)90008-M

Carbone, V., & Stone, M. A. (2005). Growth and relational strategies used by the European logistics service providers: Rationale and outcomes. *Transportation Research Part E, Logistics and Transportation Review, 41*(6), 495–510. doi:10.1016/j.tre.2005.06.001

Casson, M. (1987). *The firm and the market.* Oxford: Basil Blackwell.

Casson, M. (1990). *Enterprise and competitiveness: A system view of international business.* Oxford: Clarendon Press.

Cavinato, J.L. (2004). Supply chain logistics risk. *International Journal of Physical Distribution and Logistics Management, 34,* 383-387.

Chandra, C., & Kumar, S. (2000). Supply chain management in theory and practice: A passing fad or a fundamental change. *Industrial Management & Data Systems, 100*(3), 100–113. doi:10.1108/02635570010286168

Chandrashekar, A., & Schary, P. B. (1999). Toward the virtual supply chain: The convergence of IT and organization. *International Journal of Logistics Management, 10*(2), 27–39. doi:10.1108/09574099910805978

Chao, C.-C., Yang, J.-M., & Jen, W.-Y. (2007). Determining technology trends and forecasts of RFID by a historical review and bibliometric analysis from 1991 to 2005. *Technovation, 27,* 268–279. doi:10.1016/j.technovation.2006.09.003

Chen, C.-Y., Zhao, Z.-Y., & Ball, M. O. (2002). A model for batch advanced available-to-promise. *Production and Operations Management, 11*(4), 424–440.

Chen, F., Drezner, Z., Ryan, J. K., Simchi-Levi, D. (2000). Quantifying the bullwhip effect in a simple supply chain: The impact of forecasting lead time and information. *Management Science, 46*(3), 436-4.

Chen, H., Lionel, A., Chu, F., & Labadi, K., (2005). Modeling and performance evaluation of supply chains using batch deterministic and stochastic Petri nets. *IEEE transactions automation science and engineering, 2*(2), 132-144.

Chen, J.L., Chen, M.C., Chen, C.W., & Chang, Y.C. (2007). Architecture design and performance evaluation of RFID object tracking systems. *Computer Communications.*

Cheng, E.W.L., Li, H., Love, P.E.D., & Irani, Z. (2001). An e-business model to support supply chain activities in construction. *Logistics Information Management, 14*(1/2), 68-77.

Cheng, T. E. C., & Wu, Y. N. (2005). The impact of information sharing in a two-level supply chain with multiple retailers. *The Journal of the Operational Research Society, 56*(10), 1159.

Cheung, K., Lee, H., (2002). The inventory benefit of shipment coordination and stock rebalancing in a supply chain. *Management Science, 48*(2), 300-306.

Cheung, S. N. S. (1983). The contractual nature of the firm. *Journal of Law and Economics, 16,* 1-21.

Chiang, W. K., & Feng, Y. (2007). The value of information sharing in the presence of supply uncertainty and demand volatility. *International Journal of Production Research, 45*(6), 1429.

Chiang, W. Y., Chhajed, D., & Hess, J. D. (2003). Direct marketing, indirect profits: A strategic analysis of dual-channel supply chain design. *Management Science, 49*(1), 20.

Chipello, C.P. (1998). Canadian ice storm provided stern test of popular just-in-time method. *Wall Street Journal,* (January 26), A2.

Cho, D., & Lee, D. (1998). A new paradigm in strategy theory: 'ser-M'. *Monash Mt. Eliza Business Review, 1*(2), 82–97.

Choi, B., Tsai, N., & Jones, T. (2008). Building enterprise network infrastructure for a supermarket store chain. *Journal of Cases on Information Technology,* 31–46.

Chopra, S. (2003). What will drive the enterprise software shakeout? *Supply Chain Management Review, 7*(1), 50-56.

Chopra, S., & Meindl, P. (2007). *Supply chain management: Strategy, planning, & operation.* (3rd ed.). New Jersey: Pearson, Prentice Hall.

Chopra, S., & Sodhi, M.S. (2004). Managing risk to avoid supply-chain breakdown. *MIT Sloan Management Reivew, 46*(1), 53-61.

Chow, H.K.H., Choy, K.L., & Lee, W.B. (2007). A dynamic logistics process knowledge-based system: an RFID multi-agent approach. *Knowledge Based Systems, 20,* 357-372.

Chow, H.K.H., Choy, K.L., Lee, W.B., & Lau, K.C. (2006). Design of a RFID case-based resource management system for warehouse operations. *Expert System with Applications, 30,* 561-576.

Christakos, G., Bogaert, P., & Serre, M. (2002). *Temporal GIS: Advanced functions for field-based applications.* Berlin, Germany: Springer.

Christiaanse, E., & Kumar, K. (2000). ICT-enabled coordination of dynamic supply webs. *International Journal of Physical Distribution & Logistics Management, 30*(3/4), 268-285.

Christopher, M., & Lee, H. (2004). Mitigating supply chain risk through improved confidence. *International Journal of Physical Distribution and Logistics Management, 34*(5), 388-396.

Claycomb, C., Germain, R., & Droge, C. (1999). Total system JIT outcomes: Inventory, organization and financial effects. *International Journal of Physical Distribution and Logistics Management, 29*(10), 612-624.

Clemen, R. T., & Reilly, T. (2004). *Making hard decisions with DecisionTools* (1st ed.). Duxbury Press.

Clemons, E. K., & Michael, M. C. (1991). Sustaining IT advantage: the role of structural differences. *MIS Quarterly, 15*(3), 275–293. doi:10.2307/249639

Coase, R. H. (1937). The nature of the firm. *Economica, 4,* 386-405.

Cochran, E. B. (1976). Using regression techniques in cost analysis - Part 1. *International Journal of Production Research, 14*(4), 465–487. doi:10.1080/00207547608956619

Cochran, E. B. (1976). Using regression techniques in cost analysis - Part 2. *International Journal of Production Research, 14*(4), 489–511. doi:10.1080/00207547608956620

Cockcroft, S. (1997). A taxonomy of spatial data integrity Constraints. *GeoInformatica, 1*(4), 327-343.

Coffin, R. J., & MacIntyre, P. D. (1999). Motivational influences on computer-related affective states. *Computers in Human Behavior, 15*(5), 549-569.

Cohen, B. (1975). *Multinational firms and Asian exports.* New Haven, CT: Yale University Press.

Coleman, B.J., & Jennings, K.M. (1998). The UPS strike: Lessons for just-in-timers. *Production and Inventory Management Journal, 39*(4), 63-67.

Collins, J. (2004, August 23). *Sybase initiates RFID solution.* Retrieved from *http://www.rfidjournal.com/article/articleview/1093/1/1/*

Collis, D. (1994). Research note: How valuable are organisational capabilities. *Strategic Management Journal, 15*(8), 143–152. doi:10.1002/smj.4250150910

Compeau, D. R., & Higgins, C. A. (1995). Application of social cognitive theory to training for computer skills. *Information Systems Research, 6*(2), 118-143.

Conner, K. R. (1991). A historical comparison of resource-based theory and five schools of thought within industrial organization economics: do we have a new theory of the firm? *Journal of Management, 17*(1), 121–154. doi:10.1177/014920639101700109

Conner, K. R., & Prahalad, C. K. (1996). A resource-based theory of the firm: Knowledge versus opportunism. *Organization Science, 7*(5), 477-501.

Connolly, C. (2007). Sensor trends in processing and packaging of food and pharmaceuticals. *Sensor Review, 27,* 103-108.

Cooper, D.P., & Tracey, M. (2005). Supply chain integration via information technology: Strategic implications and future trends. *International Journal of Integrated Supply Management, 1*(3), 237-257.

Cooper, L., & Drebes, C. (1967). An approximate algorithm for the fixed charge problem. *Naval Research Logistics Quarterly, 14,* 101-113.

Cooper, M. C., Lambert, D. M., & Pagh, J. D. (1997). Supply chain management: More than new name for logistics. *International Journal of Logistics Management, 8*(1), 1–14. doi:10.1108/09574099710805556

Cooper, R. (1988). The rise of activity-based costing - Part 2: What is an activity-based costing? *Journal of Cost Management, 7*(4), 41–48.

Corbett, C. J., Zhou, D. M., & Tang, C. S. (2004). Designing supply contracts: Contract type and information asymmetry. *Management Science, 50*(4), 550-559.

Cox, J.F. III, & Blackstone, J.H. Jr. (Eds.). (2002). *APICS dictionary.* Alexandria, VA: APICS. The Educational Society for Resource Management.

Coyle, J. J., Bardi, E. J., & Langley, C. J., Jr. (2003). *The management of business logistics: A supply chain perspective.* (7th ed.). Ohio: South-Western, Thomson.

Craighead, C.W., Blackhurst, J., Rungtusanatham, M.J., & Handfield, R.B. (2007). The severity of supply chain disruptions: Design characteristics and mitigation capabilities, *Decision Sciences, 38*(1), 131-156.

Croom, S. (2000). The impact of web-based procurement on the management of operating resources supply. *Journal of Supply Chain Management, 35*(1), 4–10. doi:10.1111/j.1745-493X.2000.tb00065.x

Crosetto, M., & Tarantola, S. (2001). Uncertainty and sensitivity analysis: Tools for GIS-based model implementation. *International Journal of Geographical Information Science, 15*(5), 415-437.

Croxton, K. L., Garcia-Dastugue, S. J., Lambert, D. M., & Rodgers, D. S. (2001). The supply chain management processes. *International Journal of Logistics Management, 12*(2), 13–36. doi:10.1108/09574090110806271

Cyert, R. M., & DeGroot, M. H. (1970). Bayesian analysis and duopoly theory. *Journal of Political Economics, 78*(5), 1168-1184.

Danny, P. C., Priscila, B. O., & Geoffrey, H. (2006). Coordination collaborative joint efforts with suppliers: The effects of trust, transaction specific investment and information network in the Dutch flower industry. *Supply Chain Management: An International Journal, 11*(3), 216-224

Das, A., & Handfield, R.B. (1997). Just-in-time and logistics in global sourcing: An empirical review. *International Journal of Physical Distribution and Logistics Management, 27*(2/4), 244-252.

Davis, F. D. (1989). Perceived usefulness, perceived ease of use, and user acceptance of information technology. *MIS Quarterly, 13*(3), 319-340.

Day, G. S. (1990). *Market driven strategy: Processes for creating value.* New York: The Free Press.

Dean, E. B. (1989). Parametric cost estimating: A design function. *The Thirty-third Annual Meeting of the American Association of Cost Engineers*, San Diego, CA.

Dehning, B., Richardson, V. J., & Zmud, R. W. (2007). The financial performance effects of IT-based supply chain management systems in manufacturing firms. *Journal of Operations Management, 25*, 806–824. doi:10.1016/j.jom.2006.09.001

DeHoratius, N., & Raman, A. (2008). Inventory record inaccuracy: An empirical analysis. *Management Science, 54*(4), 627–641. doi:10.1287/mnsc.1070.0789

Delen, D., Hardgrave, B. C., & Sharda, R. (2007). RFID for better supply-chain management through enhanced information visibility. *Production and Operations Management, 16*(5), 613–624.

Deloitte, (2005). Chips with everything. *Deloitte Consulting Consumer Business.* Retrieved from http://www.ebusinessassociation.org/ssi/events/presentations/Chips%20with%20everything.pdf

DeLone, W. H., & McLean, E. R. (1992). Information systems success: The quest for the dependent variable. *Information Systems, 3*(1), 1, 60-95.

DeLone, W. H., & McLean, E. R. (2003). The DeLone and McLean model of information systems success: A ten-year update. *Journal of Management Information Systems, 19*(4), 9-30.

Diaby, M. (1991). Successive linear approximation procedure for generalized fixed-charge transportation problems. *Journal of Operational Research Society, 42*, 991-1001.

Dierickx, I., & Cool, K. (1989). Asset stock accumulation and sustainability of competitive advantage. *Management Science, 35*(12), 1504–1513. doi:10.1287/mnsc.35.12.1504

Dobson, T., & Todd, E. (2006). Radio frequency identification technology. *Computer Law & Security Report, 22*, 313-315.

Dodd, C. A., Clarke, I., & Kirkup, M. H. (1998). Camera observations of customer behavior in fashion retailing: Methodological propositions. *International Journal of Retail & Distribution Management, 26*(8), 311-317.

Dong, Y., Carter, C.R., & Dresner, M.E. (2001). JIT purchasing and performance: An exploratory analysis of buyer and supplier perspectives. *Journal of Operations Management, 19*(4), 471-484.

Donovan, R. J., Rossiter, J. R., Marcoolyn, G., & Nesdale, A. (1994). Store atmosphere and purchasing behavior. *Journal of Retailing, 70*(3), 283-294.

Downs, P. E., & Haynes, J. B. (1984). Examining retail image before and after a repositioning strategy. *Journal of the Academy of Marketing Science, 12*, 1-24.

Drenzler, D. R. (1969). An approximate method for the fixed charge problem. *Naval Research Logistics Quarterly, 16*, 411-416.

Duguay, C. R., Landry, A., & Pasin, F. (1997). From mass production to flexible/agile production. *International Journal of Operations and Production Management, 17*(11/12), 1183-1195.

Duncan, N. B. (1995). Capturing flexibility of information technology infrastructure: A study of resource characteristics and their measure. *Journal of Management Information Systems, 12*(2), 37-57.

Dyer, J. (1997). Effective interfirm collaboration: How firms minimize transaction costs and maximize transaction value. *Strategic Management Journal, 18*, 535-556.

Dyer, J., & Nobeoka, K. (2000). Creating and managing a high performance knowledge-sharing network: The Toyota case. *Strategic Management Journal, 21*, 345-367.

Dyer, J., & Singh, H. (1998). The relational view: Cooperative strategy and sources of interorganizational competitive advantage. *Academy of Management Review, 23*(4), 660-679.

eCompany Now Staff. (2000). *Supply-chain software: Hewlett-Packard.* Retrieved May 4, 2003, from *http://www.business2.com/articles/mag/0,1640,8619,00.html*

Edwards, P., Peters, M., & Sharman, G. (2001). The effectiveness of information systems in supporting the extended supply chain. *Journal of Business Logistics, 22*(1), 1-27.

Eisenhardt, K. M. (1989). Building theories from case study research. *Academy of Management Review, 14*(4), 535–550. doi:10.2307/258557

Eisenhardt, K. M., & Martin, J. A. (2000). Dynamic capabilities: what are they? *Strategic Management Journal, 21*(10/11), 1105–1121. doi:10.1002/1097-0266(200010/11)21:10/11<1105::AID-SMJ133>3.0.CO;2-E

Eklin, M., Arzi, Y. & Shtub, A. (2008). A comparative study of rough-cut cost estimation in a finite-capacity stochastic environment. *Accepted for publication in the International Journal of Revenue Management.*

Eklin, M., Arzi, Y., & Shtub, A. (2008). Rough-cut cost estimation in a capacitated environment. *International Journal of Information Systems and Supply Chain Management, 1*(2), 19–39.

Eklin, M., Arzi, Y., & Shtub, A. (2009). Model for cost estimation in a finite-capacity stochastic environment based on shop floor optimization combined with simulation. *European Journal of Operational Research, 194*(1), 294–306. doi:10.1016/j.ejor.2007.11.048

Elkins, D., Handfield, R. B., Blackhurst, J., & Craighead, C. W. (2005). 18 ways to guard against disruption. *Supply Chain Management Review, 9*(1), 46-53.

Ellinger, A. E., Lynch, D. F., & Hensen, J. D. (2002). Firm size, web site content, and financial performance in the transportation industry. *Industrial Marketing Management, 32*(3), 177–185. doi:10.1016/S0019-8501(02)00261-4

Ellis, G. (1992). Make-or-buy: A simpler approach. *Management Accounting*, June, 22-23.

Ellis, G. (1993). Solving make-or-buy problems with linear programming. *Management Accounting*, November, 52-53.

Elmuti, D. (2002). The perceived impact of supply chain management on organizational effectiveness. *Journal of Supply Chain Management, 38*(3), 49-57.

Embleton, P. R., & Wright, P. C. (1998). A practical guide to successful outsourcing. *Empowerment in Organizations, 6*(3), 94–106. doi:10.1108/14634449810210832

Emiliani, M. L., & Stec, D. F. (2002). Realizing savings from online reserve auctions. *An International Journal of Supply Chain Management, 7*(1), 12–23. doi:10.1108/13598540210414355

Epoch Times International (2005). *RoHS's influences on the promotion of electrical and electronic enterprises in Taiwan.* Retrieved July 30, 2007, from http://www.epochtw.com/5/5/23/2824.htm, Accessed July 11, 2006.

Ervolina, T., & Dietrich, B. (2001). Moving toward dynamic available to promise in supply chain management: Status and future research. In S. Gass, & A. Jones (Eds.). Preprints produced by R. H. Smith School of Business, U. of MD and Manufacturing Eng. Lab., NIST.

Espino-Rodríguez, T. F., & Rodríguez-Díaz, M. (2008). Effects of internal and relational capabilities on outsourcing: An integrated model. *Industrial Management & Data Systems, 108*(3), 328–345. doi:10.1108/02635570810858750

Esposito, E., & Storto, C. L. (1994). Qualitative and structural changes of the subcontracting firms: A micro-analytical approach to the study of inter-firm relationships. In J. M. Veciana (Ed.), *SMEs: Internationalisation, networks, and strategy* (pp.345-358). Aldershot: Avebury.

Essig, M., & Arnold, U. (2001). Electronic procurement in supply chain management: an information economics-based analysis of electronic markets. *The Journal of Supply Chain Management, 37*(4), 43–49. doi:10.1111/j.1745-493X.2001.tb00112.x

Euclides, F. K. (2004). Supply chain approach to sustainable beef production from a Brazilian perspective. *Livestock Production Science, 90*(1), 53–61. doi:10.1016/j.livprodsci.2004.07.006

European Commission (2001). *Protrans: analysis of European logistics regions.* Deliverable No. 2, November, Competitive and Sustainable Growth Programme of the 5th Framework programme.

European Union. (2003). Directive 2002/95/EC of the European Parliament and of the Council of 27 January 2003. *Official Journal of the European Union.*

Evans, N.D. (2004, June 28). *Planning for RFID data.* Retrieved from *http://www.rfidjournal.com/article/articleview/1004/1/82/*

Fagan, M. H., Neill, S., & Wooldridge, B. R. (2003-04). An empirical investigation into the relationship between computer self-efficacy, anxiety, experience, support and usage. *The Journal of Computer Information Systems, 44*(2), 95-110.

Faisal, M. N., Banwet, D. K., & Shankar, R. (2006). Mapping supply chains on risk and customer sensitivity dimensions. *Industrial Management and Data Systems, 106*(6), 878-895.

Falco, M., Nenni, M. E., & Schiraldi, M. M. (2001). Development of a product-costing model oriented to productive capacity analysis. *The 4th SMESME International Conference,* Alborg, Denmark (pp. 180-187).

Fearne, A. (1998). The evolution of partnerships in the meat supply chain: Insights from the British beef industry. *Supply Chain Management, Bradford, 3*(4), 214. doi:10.1108/13598549810244296

Feldman, P., & Shtub, A. (2006). A model for cost estimation in a finite-capacity environment. *International Journal of Production Research, 44*(2), 305–327. doi:10.1080/00207540500227646

Fischer, G., & Ostwald, J. (2001). Knowledge management: Problems, promises, realities, and challenges. *IEEE Intelligent Systems, 16*(1), 60-72.

Fisher, M. F. (1997). What is the right supply chain for your product? A simple framework can help you figure out the answer. *Harvard Business Review,* (March-April): 105–116.

Fleisch, E., & Tellkamp, C. (2005). Inventory inaccuracy and supply chain performance: a simulation study of a retail supply chain. *International Journal of Production Economics, 95*(3), 373–385. doi:10.1016/j.ijpe.2004.02.003

Fleischmann, B. (1993). Designing distribution systems with transport economies of scale. *European Journal of Operational Research, 70*(1), 31–42. doi:10.1016/0377-2217(93)90230-K

Folinas, D. (2006). Traceability data management for food chains. *British Food Journal, 108,* 622-633.

Fontanella, J. (2004). Finding the ROI in RFID. *Supply Chain Management Review, 8*(1), 13–14.

Forman, C., Williams, M., & Sapsford, J. (1995). Shaken giant: Quake's aftershocks will rattle segments of Japan's economy. *Wall Street Journal,* (January 18), A1.

Fornell, C., & Larcker, F. (1981). Evaluating structural equation models with unobservable variables and measurement error. *Journal of Marketing Research, 18*(1), 39-50.

Foss, N. J. (1996). Introduction: The emerging competence perspective. In N. J. Foss & C. Knudsen (Eds.), *Towards a competence theory of the firm* (pp.1-12). London: Routledge.

Fowler, K. (2004). Build versus buy. *IEEE Instrumentation & Measurement Magazine, 7*(3), 67–73. doi:10.1109/MIM.2004.1337916

Fox, M. S., Barbucean, M., & Teigen, R. (2000). Agent-oriented supply chain management. *International Journal of Flexible Manufacturing Systems, 12*(2), 165-188.

Frasquet, M., Cervera, A., & Gil, I. (2008). The impact of IT and customer orientation on building trust and commitment in the supply chain. *International Review of Retail, Distribution and Consumer Research, 18*(3), 343. doi:10.1080/09593960802114164

Frohlich, M. T., & Westbrook, R. (2002). Demand chain management in manufacturing and services: web-based integration, drivers and performance. *Journal of Operations Management, 20*(6), 729–745. doi:10.1016/S0272-6963(02)00037-2

Funk, J.L. (1995). Just-in-time manufacturing & logistical complexity: A contingency model. *International Journal of Operations and Production Management, 15*(5), 60-71.

Ganesh, J. (2004). Managing customer preferences in a multi-channel environment using Web services. *International Journal of Retail & Distribution Management, 32*(2/3), 140-146.

García-Arca, J., & Carlos Prado-Prado, J. (2007). The implementation of new technologies through a participative approach. *Creativity and Innovation Management, 16*(4), 386. doi:10.1111/j.1467-8691.2007.00450.x

Gavirneni, S., Kapuscinski, R., & Tayur, S. (1999). Value of information in capacitated supply chains. *Management Science, 45*(1), 16-24.

Geiger, T. S., & Dilts, D. M. (1996). Automated design-to-cost: Integrated costing into the design decision. *Computer Aided Design, 28,* 423–438. doi:10.1016/0010-4485(94)00030-1

Gen, M., Kumar, A., & Kim, J.R. (2005). Recent network design techniques using evolutionary algorithms. *International Journal of Production Economics, 98*(2), 251-261.

Gereffi, G. (1993). International subcontracting and global capitalism: Reshaping the Pacific Rim. In R. A. Palat (Ed.), *Pacific-Asia and the future of the World System* (pp. 67-82), Westport: Greenwood Press.

Germidis, D. (1980). *International subcontracting: A new form of investment.* Paris: OECD.

Ghoshal, S., & Moran, P. (1996). Bad for practice: A critique of the transaction cost framework. *Academy of Management Journal, 21*(1), 13-47.

Glazer, R. (1991). Marketing in an information-intensive environment: Strategic implications of knowledge as an asset. *Journal of Marketing, 55*(10), 1-19.

GMA. (2004). A balanced perspective: EPC/RFID Implementation in the CPG Industry. *Grocery Manufacturers of America.* Retrieved from http://www.gmabrands.com/publications/docs/2005/BalancedPerspective.pdf

Goyal, K., & Krishna, D. (2005). *RFID middleware integration to the entire supply chain.* RFID Journal White Paper.

Grant, R. M. (1991). The resource-based theory of competitive advantage: Implications for strategy formulation. *California Management Review, 33*(3), 114–135.

Gray, P. (1971). Exact solution of the fixed-charge transportation problem. *Operations Research, 19,* 1529-38.

Green, F.B. (2001). Managing the unmanageable: Integrating the supply chain with new developments in software. *Supply Chain Management, 6*(5), 208-211.

Gruen, T. W., Corsten, D. S., & Bharadwaj, S. (2002). *Retail out of stocks: A worldwide examination of extent, causes, and consumer responses.* Washington, D.C.: Grocery Manufacturers of America. Retrieved from http://www.gmabrands.com/publications/docs/RetOOS.pdf

Gulliver, F.R. (1987). Post-project appraisals pay. *Harvard Business Review,* (March).

Gunasekaran, A., Marri, H. B., & Yusuf, Y. Y. (1999). Application of activity-based costing: Some case experiences. *Managerial Auditing Journal, 14*(6), 286–293. doi:10.1108/02686909910280217

Guskey, T. (1988). Teacher efficacy, self-concept, and attitudes toward the implementation of instructional innovation. *Teaching and Teacher Education, 4*(1), 63-69.

Haakansson, H. (1987). *Industrial technological development: A network approach.* London: Croom Helm.

Haakansson, H., & Snehota, I. (1995). *Developing Relationships in Business Networks.* London: Routledge.

Hafeez, K., Zhang, Y., & Malak, N. (2002). Determining key capabilities of a firm using analytic hierarchy process. *International Journal of Production Economics, 76*(1), 39–51. doi:10.1016/S0925-5273(01)00141-4

Haines, V. Y., & Andre, P. (1997). Conditions for successful human resource information systems. *Human Resource Management, 36*(2), 261-275.

Hair, J. F., Anderson, R. E., Tatham, R. L., & Black, W. C. (1998). *Multivariate data analysis* (5th ed.). Prentice-Hall.

Halbach, A. J. (1989). *Multinational enterprises and subcontracting in the third world: A study of inter-industry linkages.* Geneva: International Labour Office.

Hall, J., & Vredenburg, H. (2005). Managing stakeholder ambiguity. *Sloan Management Review, 47*(1), 11-13.

Halldórsson, A. (2007). Complementary theories to supply chain management. *Supply Chain Manage-ment: An International Journal, 12*(4), 284–296. doi:10.1108/13598540710759808

Hamada, K. (1974). An economic analysis of the duty free zone. *Journal of International Economics, 4*(3), 225-241.

Handfield, R.B., & Nicholas, E.L. (1999). *Introduction to supply chain management.* Upper Saddle River, NJ: Prentice Hall.

Haq, A.N., & Kannan, G. (2006). Design of an integrated supplier selection and multi-echelon distribution inventory model in a built- to order supply chain environment. *International Journal of Production Research, 44*(10), 1963-1985.

Hardgrave, B., Waller, M., & Miller, R. (2005). *Does RFID Reduce Out of Stocks?* Sam Walton School of Business, RFID Research Center, University of Arkansas, Fayetteville, AR.

Harland, C. M., & Knight, L. A. (2001). Supply network strategy: role and competence requirements. *International Journal of Operations & Production Management, 21*(4), 476–489. doi:10.1108/01443570110381381

Harrison, A. W., & Rainer, R. K. (1996). A general measure of user computer satisfaction. *Computers in Human Behavior, 12*(1), 79-92.

Harrison, M., McFarlane, D., Parlikad, A.K., & Wong, C.Y. (2005). *Information management in the product lifecycle: the role of networked RFID.* Auto-ID Center White Paper.

Harsanyi, J. (1967). Games with incomplete information played by Bayesian players: Part I. The basic model. *Management Science, 14*(3), 159-182.

Harsanyi, J. (1968). Games with incomplete information played by Bayesian players: Part II. Bayesian equilibrium points. *Management Science, 14*(5), 320-334.

Harsh, M. F. (1993). *the impact of activity based costing on managerial decisions: an empirical analysis.* Ph.D. Dissertation, Virginia Polytechnic Institute & State University, Blacksburg, VA, USA.

Hauser, L.M. (2003). Risk-adjusted supply chain management. *Supply Chain Management Review, 7*(6), 64-71.

Hazra, J., & Mahadevan, B. (2006). Impact of supply base heterogeneity in electronic markets. *European Journal of Operational Research, 174*, 1580-1594.

Heinrich, C. (2003). *Adapt or die: Transforming your supply chain into an adaptive business network.* Hoboken, NJ: John Wiley & Sons.

Heinssen, R. K., Glass, C. R., & Knight, L. A. (1987). Assessing computer anxiety: Development and validation of the computer anxiety rating scale. *Computers and Human Behavior, 3*(1), 49-59.

Helander, M. E., Zhao, M., & Ohlsson, N. (1998). Planning models for software reliability and cost. *IEEE Transactions on Software Engineering, 24*(6), 420–434. doi:10.1109/32.689400

Hendon, R.A., Nath, R., & Hendon, D.W. (1998). The strategic and tactical value of electronic data interchange for marketing firms. *Mid-Atlantic Journal of Business, 34*(1), 53-73.

Hennart, J. F. (1982). *A theory of multinational enterprise.* Ann Arbor, MI: University of Michigan Press.

Hennart, J. F. (1988). A transaction cost theory of equity joint ventures. *Strategic Management Journal, 9*(4), 361-374.

Hennart, J. F. (1991). The transaction cost theory of joint ventures: An empirical study of Japanese subsidiaries in the United States. *Management Science, 37*(4), 483-497.

Hennart, J. F., & Park, Y. R. (1993). Greenfield vs. acquisitions: The strategy of Japanese investors in the United States. *Management Science, 39*(9), 1054-1070.

Henry, J. W., & Stone, R. W. (1994). A structural equation model of end-user satisfaction with a computer-based medical information system. *Information Resources Management Journal, 7*(3), 21–33.

Henry, J. W., & Stone, R. W. (1995). Computer self-efficacy and outcome expectancy: The effects on the end-user's job satisfaction. *Computer Personnel, 16*, 15–34.

Hertz, S., & Alfredsson, M. (2003). Strategic development of third party logistics providers. *Industrial Marketing Management, 32*(2), 139–149. doi:10.1016/S0019-8501(02)00228-6

Hieta, S. (1998). Supply chain simulation with LOGSIM-Simulator. In D.J.Medeires, E. F. Watson, J.S. Carson, & M.S. Manivannan. In *Proceedings of the 1998 Winter Simulation Conference* (pp. 323-326).

Hilton, R. W. (1981). The determinants of information value: Synthesizing some general results. *Management Science, 27*(1), 57-64.

Holcomb, T. R., & Hitt, M. A. (2007). Toward a model of strategic outsourcing. *Journal of Operations Management, 25*(2), 464–481. doi:10.1016/j.jom.2006.05.003

Holmes, J. (1986). The organization and locational structure of production subcontracting. In A. J. Scott, & M. Storper (Eds.), *Production, work, and territory: The geographical anatomy of industrial capitalism* (pp. 80-106), Boston: Allen & Unwin.

Horvath, L. (2001). Collaboration: The key to value creation in supply chain management. *Supply Chain Management: An International Journal, 6*(5), 205-207.

Hossain, M. M., & Prybutok, V. R. (2008). Consumer acceptance of RFID technology: An exploratory study. *IEEE Transactions on Engineering Management, 55*(2), 316–328. doi:10.1109/TEM.2008.919728

Hou, J.-L., & Huang, C.-H. (2006). Quantitative performance evaluation of RFID applications in the supply chain of the printing industry. *Industrial Management & Data Systems, 106*(1), 96–120. doi:10.1108/02635570610641013

Hovi, N. (1994). Internationalising subcontractors: Is co-operation an alternative? In J. M. Veciana (Ed), *SMEs: Internationalisation, networks, and strategy* (pp. 359-379), Aldershot: Avebury.

Hsu, L.-L. (2005). SCM system effects on performance for interaction between supplierss and buyers. *Industrial Management and Data Systems, 105*(7), 857-875.

Hsu, M. H., & Chiu, C. M. (2004). Predicting electronic service continuance with a decomposed theory of planned behaviour. *Behaviour and Information Technology, 23*(5), 359-373.

Hsu, M., Chiu, C., & Fu, T. (2004). Determinants of continued use of the www: an integration of two theoretical models. *Industrial Management and Data Systems, 104*(9), 766-775.

Huang, G.Q., Zhang, Y.F., & Jiang, P.Y. (2007). RFID-based wireless manufacturing for walking-worker assembly islands with fixed-position layouts. *Robotics and Computer-Integrated Manufacturing, 23,* 469-477.

Huber, N., & Michael, K. (2007). Vendor perceptions of how RFID can minimize product shrinkage in the retail supply chain. In *1st Annual RFID Eurasia, Istanbul, Turkey.*

Hughes, D. (1994). *Breaking with tradition: Building partnerships and alliances in the European food industry.* Ashford: Wye College Press.

Hui, M. K., & Bateson, J. E. (1991). Perceived control and consumer choice on the service experience. *Journal of Consumer Research, 18,* 174-185.

Hultberg, T.H., & Cardoso, D.M. (1997). The teacher assignment problem: A special case of the fixed charge transportation problem. *European Journal of Operational Research, 101*(3), 463-473.

Hung, W., Chu, J., & Lee, C. C. (2006). Strategic information sharing in a supply chain. *European Journal of Operational Research, 174*(3), 1567.

Iacovou, C.L., Benbasat, I., & Dexter, A.S. (1995). Electronic data interchange and small organizations: Adoption and impact of technology. *MIS Quarterly, 19*(4), 465-485.

Igbaria, M. (1992). An examination of microcomputer usage in Taiwan. *Information and Management, 22*(1), 19-28.

Igbaria, M., Guimaraes, T., & Davis, G. B. (1995). Testing the determinants of microcomputer usage via a structural equation model. *Journal of Management Information Systems, 11*(4), 87-114.

Iglehart, D. L., & Morey, R. C. (1972). Inventory systems with imperfect asset information. *Management Science, 18*(8), 388–394. doi:10.1287/mnsc.18.8.B388

Im, J.H., Hartman, S.J., & Bondi, P.J. (1994). How do JIT systems affect human resource management? *Production and Inventory Management Journal, 35*(1), 1-4.

Inman, R.A., & Mehra, S. (1989). Potential union conflict in JIT implementation? *Production and Inventory Management Journal, 30*(4), 19-21.

Intel (2004, September). *EPC-RFID solutions that power the high-resolution supply chain.* Retrieved from http://www.intel.com/business/bss/solutions/blueprints /pdf/oatsystems.pdf

International Organization for Standardization. (2006). *The ISO survey-2006,* 9-25.

Ip, G. (2001). Risky business: As security worries intensify, companies see efficiencies erode. *Wall Street Journal,* (October 24), A1.

Ives, B., Olson, M. H., & Baroudi, J. J. (1983). The measurement of user information satisfaction. *Communications of the ACM, 26*(1), 785-793.

Jahan-Shahi, H., Shayan, E., & Masood, S. H. (2001). Multivalued fuzzy sets in cost/time estimation of flat plate processing. *International Journal of Advanced Manufacturing Technology, 17,* 751–759. doi:10.1007/s001700170121

Janz, B.D., Pitts, M.G., & Otondo, R.F. (2005). Information systems and health care II: Back to the future with RFID: Lessons learned: some old, some new. *Communications of the Association for Information Systems, 15,* 132-148.

Jap, S. D., & Anderson, E. (2003). Safeguarding interorganizational performance and continuity under ex post opportunism. *Management Science, 49*(12), 1684-1701.

Japanese Standards Association. (2004). Environmental management systems-Requirements with guidance for use. *ISO 14001:2004*, 1-18

Jara-Díaz, S. R., & Basso, L. J. (2003). Transport cost functions, network expansion and economies of scope. *Transportation Research Part E, Logistics and Transportation Review, 39*(4), 271–288. doi:10.1016/S1366-5545(03)00002-4

Javidan, M. (1998). Core competence: What does it mean in practice? *Long Range Planning, 31*(1), 60–71. doi:10.1016/S0024-6301(97)00091-5

Jennings, D. (1999). *Online B2B exchanges: The new economics of market.* New York: Deloitte Consulting.

Jensen, K. (1997). Colored PN: Basic concepts, analysis methods and practical use; monographs in theoretical computer science. Springer-Verlag, 2nd corrected printing.

Jeuland, A. P., & Shugan, S. M. (1983). Managing channel profits. *Marketing Science, 2*(3), 239-272.

Jharkharia, S., & Shankar, R. (2007). Selection of logistics service provider: An analytic network process (ANP) approach. *Omega, 35*(3), 274–289. doi:10.1016/j.omega.2005.06.005

Jo, J.B., Li, Y., & Gen, M. (2007). Nonlinear fixed charge transportation problem by spanning tree-based genetic algorithm. *Computers & Industrial Engineering, 53*(2), 290-298.

Johanson, J., & Mattsson, L. G. (1987). Inter-organizational relations in industrial systems: a network approach compared with the transaction cost approach. *International Journal of Operations & Production Management, 17*(1), 34–48.

Johnson, M. (1999). From understanding consumer behavior to testing category strategies. *Journal of the Market Research Society, 41*(3), 259-288.

Johnson, M.E. (2001). Learning from toys: Lessons in managing supply chain risk from the toy industry. *California Management Review, 43*(2), 106-123.

Johnson, R. G. (2001). *United States Imagery and Geospatial Information Service geospatial transition plan.* Bethesda, MD: National Imagery and Mapping Agency.

Jones, P., Clarke-Hill, C., Comfort, D., Hillier, D., & Shears, P. (2005). Radio frequency identification and food retailing in the UK. *British Food Journal, 107,* 356-360.

Jones, P., Clarke-Hill, C., Hillier, D., Shears, P., & Comfort, D. (2004). Radio frequency identification in retailing and privacy and public policy issues. *Management Research News, 27,* 46-56.

Jones, P., Clarke-Hill, C., Shears, P., Comfort, D., & Hillier, D. (2004). Radio frequency identification in the UK: Opportunities and challenges. *International Journal of Retail & Distribution Management, 32*(3), 164-171.

Juban, R. L., & Wyld, D. C. (2004). Would you like chips with that? Consumer perspectives of RFID. *Management Research News, 27*(11/12), 29-44.

Juels, A. (2006). RFID security and privacy: A research survey. *IEEE Journal on Selected Areas in Communications, 24*(2), 381–394. doi:10.1109/JSAC.2005.861395

Jung, J. Y. (2002). Manufacturing cost estimation for machined parts based on manufacturing features. *Journal of Intelligent Manufacturing, 13*(4), 227–238. doi:10.1023/A:1016092808320

Kacen, J., Hess, J., & Chiang, W. K. (2002). *Bricks or clicks? Consumer attitudes toward traditional stores and online stores* (Working paper). Champaign, IL: University of Illinois.

Kakabadse, A., & Kakabadse, N. (2002). Trends in outsourcing: contrasting USA and Europe. *European Management Journal, 20*(2), 189–198. doi:10.1016/S0263-2373(02)00029-4

Kang, Y., & Gershwin, S. (2004). *Information inaccuracy in inventory systems stock loss and stockout.* Joint MIT/INFORMS Symposium.

Kang, Y., & Koh, R. (2002). *Applications Research.* Research Report, Auto-ID Center, MIT.

Kannan, G., Kumar, P.S., & Vinay, V.P. (2008). Comments on the erratum to nonlinear fixed charge transportation problem by spanning tree-based genetic algorithm. *Computers & Industrial Engineering.*

Kanters, R.H.L. (2007). *Data management risks of radio frequency identification (RFID).* Unpublished Masters Thesis, Tiburg University, The Netherlands.

Kaplan, S., & Sawhney, M. (2000). E-hubs: The new B2B marketplaces. *Harvard Business Review, 78*(3), 97-103.

Kashyap, S. P. (1992). *Recent developments in the small enterprises sector in India: Economic and social aspects.* Geneva: International Institute for Labour Studies.

Kasturi, R. (2005). *Tapping the RFID data flood.* Retrieved from *http://www.intelligententerprise.com/showArticle.jhtml?articleID=163100818*

Kay, N. M. (1995). *Why firms succeed.* New York: Oxford University Press.

Kedia, B. L., & Lahiri, S. (2007). International outsourcing of services: A partnership model. *Journal of International Management, 13*(1), 22–37. doi:10.1016/j.intman.2006.09.006

Keen, P. (1993). Information technology and the management difference: A fusion map. *IBM Systems Journal, 32,* 17–39.

Keenan, G. (2001). Slowdown at border shuts plants. *The Globe and Mail,* (September 12), B4.

Keenan, G. (2003). Chrysler future lies in flexibility. *The Globe and Mail,* (May 24), B3.

Kehoe, D.F., & Boughton, N.J. (2001). New paradigms in planning and control across manufacturing supply chains: The utilization of Internet technologies. *International Journal of Operations & Production Management, 21*(5/6), 582-593.

Kelepouris, T. (2007). RFID-enabled traceability in the food supply chain. *Industrial Management & Data Systems, 107,* 183-200.

Kempfer, L.M. (2007). A dollop of RFID. *Material Handling Management, 62,* 40-41.

Kemppainen, K., & Vepsalainen, A.P.J. (2003). Trends in industrial supply chains and networks. *International Journal of Physical Distribution & Logistics Management, 33*(8), 701-719.

Kirkup, M., & Carrigan, M. (2000). Video surveillance research in retailing: Ethical issues. *International Journal of Retail & Distribution Management, 28*(11), 470-480.

Kleindorfer, P.R. & Saad G.H. (2005). Managing disruption risks in supply chains. *Production and Operations Management, 14*(1), 53-68.

Kleist, R.A., Chapman, T.A., Sakai, D.A., & Jarvis, B.S. (2004). *RFID labeling: Smart labeling concepts & applications for the consumer packaged goods supply chain.* Printronix.

Knod, E.M., & Schonberger, R.J. (2001). *Operations management: meeting customers' demands.* New York: McGraw-Hill.

Knudsen, C. (1995). Theories of the firm, strategic management, and leadership. In C. A. Montgomery (Ed.), *Resource-based and evolutionary theories of the firm: Towards a synthesis* (pp. 179-218). Boston: Kluwer Academic Publishers.

Koch, C. (2002). Interview: Covisint's last chance. *CIO, 16*(5), 1.

Kogut, B. (1988). Joint ventures: Theoretical and empirical perspectives. *Strategic Management Journal, 9,* 319-332.

Köhne, F., Totz, C., & Wehmeyer, K. (2005). Consumer preferences for location-based service attributes: A conjoint analysis. *International Journal of Management and Decision Making, 6*(1), 16-32.

Kok, A. G., Donselaar, K. H., & Woensel, T. (2008). A break-even analysis of RFID technology for inventory sensitive to shrinkage. *International Journal of Production Economics, 112*(2), 521–531. doi:10.1016/j.ijpe.2007.05.005

Kok, T.D., Janssen, F., Doremalen, J.V., Wachem, E.V., Clerkx, M., & Peeters, W. (2005). Philips electronics synchronizes its supply chain to end bullwhip effect. *Interface, 35*(1), 37-48.

Kolluru, R., & Meredith, P.H. (2001). Security and trust management in supply chains. *Information Management, 9*(5), 233-236.

Korgaonker, M.G. (1992). *Just in time manufacturing.* Ahmedabad, India: Macmillan India.

Koroneos, G. (2004). FDA opens door to RFID packaging. *Pharmaceutical Technology, 28*(12), 17.

Kovács, G. (2005). Supply chain collaboration for sustainability. *Business Strategy and the Environment Conference Proceeding 2005.*

Krajewski, L. J., King, B. E., Ritzman, L. P., & Wong, D. S. (1987). Kanban, MRP, and shaping the manufacturing environment. *Management Science, 33*(1), 39–57. doi:10.1287/mnsc.33.1.39

Kraljic, P. (1983). Purchasing must become supply chain management. *Harvard Business Review,* (September-October), 109-117.

Krishnan, M., & Shulman J. (2007). Reducing supply chain risk. *The McKinsey Quarterly,* (1). Retrieved April 7, 2007, from http://www.mckinseyquarterly.com

Kuhn, H.W., & Baumol, W.J. (1962). An approximation algorithm for the fixed charge transportation problem. *Naval Research Logistics Quarterly, 9,* 1-15.

Kumar, K., & van Dissel, H.G. (1996). Sustainable collaboration: Managing conflict and cooperation in interorganizational systems. *MIS Quarterly, 20*(3), 279-300.

Kurokawa, S. (1997). Make-or-buy decisions in R&D: Small technology based firms in the United States and Japan. *IEEE Transactions on Engineering Management, 44*(2), 124–134. doi:10.1109/17.584921

Laarhoven, P., van Berglund, M., & Peters, M. (2000). Third-party logistics in Europe – five years later. *International Journal of Physical Distribution and Logistics Management, 30*(5), 425–442. doi:10.1108/09600030010336216

Lambert, D.M., Cooper, M.C., & Pagh, J.D. (1998). Supply chain management: Implementation issues and research opportunities. *International Journal of Logistics Management, 9*(2), 1–19. doi:10.1108/09574099810805807

Lancastre, A., & Lages, L.F. (2006). The relationship between buyer and a B2B e-marketplace: Cooperation determinants in an electronic market context. *Industrial Marketing Management, 35,* 774 - 789.

Langley, C. J., & Holcomb, M. C. (1992). Creating logistics customer value. *Journal of Business Logistics, 13*(2), 1–27.

Langley, C. J., Jr., Morton, J., Wereldsma, D., Swaminathan, S., Murphy, J., Deakins, T. A., et al. (2008). *2008 Third-Party Logistics: Results and Findings of the 13th Annual Study.* Capgemini, Georgia Institute of Technology, Oracle, and DHL.

Langley, C. J., Jr., van Dort, E., Morton, J., Hoemmken, S., Goh, A., Zabawa, M., et al. (2007). *2007 Third-Party Logistics: Results and Findings of the 12th Annual Study.* Capgemini, Georgia Institute of Technology, SAP, and DHL.

Langley, C. J., Jr., van Dort, E., Ross, T., Topp, U., Allen, G. R., & Sykes, S. R. (2006). *2006 Third-Party Logistics: Results and Findings of the 11th Annual Study.* Capgemini, Georgia Institute of Technology, SAP, and DHL.

Lankford, W. M., & Parsa, F. (1999). Outsourcing: A primer. *Management Decision, 37*(4), 310–316. doi:10.1108/00251749910269357

Lapide, L. (2004). RFID: What's in it for the forecaster? *The Journal of Business Forecasting Methods & Systems, 23*(2), 16–20.

Laran (2005). *A basic introduction to RFID and its use in the supply chain* [White paper]. Retrieved from http://admin.laranrfid.com/media/files/WhitePaperRFID.pdf

Larson, J. S., Bradlow, E. T., & Fader, P. S. (2005). An exploratory look at supermarket shopping paths. *International Journal of Research in Marketing, 22*(4), 395-414.

Latour, A. (2001, January 29). Trial by fire: A blaze in Albuquerque sets off major crisis for cell-phone giants—Nokia handles supply shock with aplomb as Ericsson of Sweden gets burned—was Sisu the difference? *Wall Street Journal,* p A1.

Lau, K. H., & Zhang, J. (2006). Drivers and obstacles of outsourcing practices in China. *International Journal of Physical Distribution & Logistics Management, 36*(10), 776–792. doi:10.1108/09600030610714599

Law, A. M., & Kelton, W. D. (2000). *Simulation modelling and analysis* (3rd ed.). McGraw Hill Higher Education.

Lawrence, C. (2006). Friend or foe. *Farmers Weekly, 144*(25), 18–19.

Lawson, V. (1992). Industrial subcontracting and employment forms in Latin America: A framework for contextual analysis. *Progress in Human Geography, 16,* 1-23.

Lee, C., Huang, H. C., Liu, B., & Xu, Z. (2006). Development of timed color Petri net simulation models for air cargo terminal operations. *Computers and Industrial Engineering, 51,* 102-110.

Lee, H. (2004). The triple-a supply chain. *Harvard Business Review,* (October).

Lee, H. L. (2002). Aligning supply chain strategies with product uncertainties. *California Management Review, 44*(3), 105–119.

Lee, H., & Ozer, O. (2007). Unlocking the value of RFID. *Production and Operations Management, 16*(1), 40–64.

Lee, H., So, V. K., & Tang, C. (2000). The value of information sharing in a two-level supply chain. *Management Science, 46*(5), 626-643.

Lee, H.L., Padmanabhan, V., & Whang, S. (1997). The bullwhip effect in supply chains. *Sloan Management Review, 38*(3), 93-102.

Lee, S. M., Kim, Y. R., & Lee, J. (1995). An empirical study of the relationships among end-user information systems acceptance training, and effectiveness. *Journal of Management Information Systems, 12*(2), 189-202.

Lee, Y. M., Cheng, F., & Leung, Y. (2004). Exploring the impact of RFID on supply chain dynamics. In R.G.Ingalls, M.D. Rossetti, J.S. Smith, & B. A. Peters (Eds.), *Proceedings of the 2004 Winter Simulation Conference.* Retrieved from http://www.informs-sim. org/wsc04papers/147.pdf

Lee, Y. M., Cheng, F., & Leung, Y. (2009). A quantitative view on how RFID can improve inventory management in a supply chain. *International Journal of Logistics: Research and Applications, 12*(1), 23–43. doi:10.1080/13675560802141788

Levy, H., & Sarnat, M. (1976). The make-or-buy decision. *Journal of General Management, 4*(1), 46–50.

Levy, M., & Grewal, D. (2000). Overview of the issues of supply chain management in a networked economy. *Journal of Retailing, 76*(4), 415–429. doi:10.1016/S0022-4359(00)00043-9

Lewis, I., & Talalayevsky, A. (1997). Logistics and information technology: A coordination perspective. *Journal of Business Logistics, 18*(1), 141–157.

Lewis, I., & Talalayevsky, A. (2004). Improving the inter-organizational supply chain through optimization of information flows. *Journal of Enterprise Information Management, 17*(3), 229–237. doi:10.1108/17410390410531470

Li, S. H., & Lin, B. S. (2006). Accessing information sharing and information quality in supply chain management. *Decision Support Systems, 42*(3), 1641.

Li, S., Ragu-Nathan, B., Ragu-Nathan, T.S., & Rao, S.S. (2006). The impact of supply chain management practices on competitive advantage and organizational performance. *Omega, 34*(2), 107-124.

Li, S., Rao, S.S., Ragu-Nathan, T.S., & Ragu-Nathan, B. (2005). Development and validation of a measurement instrument for studying supply chain management practices. *Journal of Operations Management, 23*(6), 618-641.

Li, S., Visich, F.K., Khumawala, B.M., & Zhang, C. (2006). Radio frequency identification technology: Applications, technical challenges and strategies. *Sensor Review, 26,* 193-202.

Li, X., & Wang, Q., (2007). Coordination mechanisms of supply chain systems. *European Journal of Operational Research, 179,* 1-16.

Li, Z. W., & Zhou, M. C. (2004). Elementary siphons of Petri nets and their application to deadlock prevention in flexible manufacturing systems. *IEEE Transactions on Systems, Man and Cybernetics*, Part A, *34*(1), 38-51.

Liggett, H. R., Trevino, J., & Lavelle, J. P. (1992). Activity-based cost management systems in an advanced manufacturing environment. In H. R. Parsaei (Ed.), *Economic and financial justification of advanced manufacturing technologies.* New York: Elsevier Science Publishers.

Lin, C., Shan, Z., Liu, T., Qu, Y., & Ren, F. (2005). Modeling and inference of extended interval temporal logic for nondeterministic intervals. *IEEE Transactions on Systems, Man and Cybernetics*, Part A, *35*(5), 682–696.

Lin, K., & Lin, C. (2007). Evaluating the decision to adopt RFID systems using analytic hierarchy process. *Journal of American Academy of Business, 11,* 72-78.

Lin, P.P., & Brown, K.F. (2006). Radio frequency identification and how to capitalize on it. *The CPA Journal, 76,* 34-37.

Lin, Z. C., & Chang, D. Y. (2002). Cost-tolerance analysis model based on a neural networks method. *International Journal of Production Research, 40*(6), 1429–1452. doi:10.1080/00207540110116282

Linder, J. C., Cole, M. I., & Jacobson, A. L. (2002). Business transformation through outsourcing. *Strategy and Leadership, 30*(4), 23–28. doi:10.1108/10878570210435342

Liu, J., Zhang, S., & Hu, J. (2005). A case study of an inter-enterprise work flow-support supply chain system. *Information & Management, 42*(3), 441-454.

Logan, M. S. (2000). Using agency theory to design successful outsourcing relationships. *International Journal of Logistics Management, 11*(2), 21–32. doi:10.1108/09574090010806137

Louise, C., & Stuart, H. L. (2001). Managing the environmental adaptation process in supplier-customer relationships. *Business Strategy and the Environment, 10,* 225-237

Loyd, C. P., & Gressard, B. H. (1984). Reliability and factorial validity of computer attitude scales. *Education and Psychological Measurement, 44*(2), 501–505.

Luersen, M.A., & Riche, R.L. (2004). Globalized Nelder–Mead method for engineering optimization. *Computers and Structures, 82,* 2251-2260.

Lummus, R. (1999). Defining supply chain management: A historical perspective and practical guidelines. *Industrial Management and Data Systems, 99*(1), 11-17.

Lynagh, P. M., Murphy, P. R., Poist, R. F., & Grazer, W. F. (2001). Web-based informational practices of logistics service providers: An empirical assessment. *Transportation Journal, 40,* 34–45.

Lynch, C. F. (2000). *Logistics Outsourcing: A Management Guide.* Illinois: Council of Logistics Management Publications.

Macneil, I. R. (1974). The many futures of contract. *Southern California Law Review, 47,* 691-738.

Macneil, I. R. (1978). Contracts: Adjustment of long term economic relations under classical, neoclassical and relational contract law. *Northwestern University Law Review, 72,* 854-905.

Mahdavi, I., Cho, N., & Mohebbi, S., (2007). A fuzzy-based analytical model of dynamic information flow in e-SCM. *Contemporary Management Research, 3*(4), 287-298.

Mahmood, M. A., Burn, J. M., Gemoets, L. A., & Jacquez, C. (2003). Variables affecting information technology end-user satisfaction: A meta-analysis of the empirical literature. *International Journal of Human-Computer Studies, 52*(4), 751-771.

Maitland, A. (2005). Make sure you have your Christmas stock in. *Financial Times,* (December 19), 12.

Maltz, A. (1993). Private fleet use: a transaction cost model. *Transportation Journal, 32*(3), 46–53.

Malueg, D. A., & Tsutsui, S. O. (1996). Duopoly information exchange: The case of unknown slope. *International Journal of Industrial Organization, 14*, 119-136.

Marakas, G. M., Yi, M. Y., & Johnson, R. D. (1998). The multilevel and multifaceted character of computer self-efficacy: Toward clarification of the construct and an integrative framework for research. *Information Systems Research, 9*(2), 126-163.

Marcial, G.G. (2007, May 28). *VeriChip is I.D.'d as a winner.* Retrieved from *http://www.businessweek.com/magazine/content/07_22/b4036093.htm?chan=search*

Marianne, F., & Michael, S. J. (2004). Organizing environmental supply chain management-experience from a sector with frequent product shift and complex product chains: The case of the Danish Textile Sector. *Greener Management International, 45*, 43-62

Markus, M.L. (2000). Paradigm shifts□e-business and business/systems integration. *Communication for Association for Information Systems, 4*(10). Retrieved February 23, 2003, from *http://web.bentley.edu/empl/m/lmarkus/Markus_Web_Documents_(pdf)/Paradigm_Shifts.pdf*

Martha, J., & Subbakrishna, S. (2002). Targeting a just-in-time supply chain for the inevitable next disaster. *Supply Chain Management Review, 6*(5), 18-23.

Martikainen, O. E. (2006). Complementarities creating substitutes: Possible paths towards 3G, WLAN/WiMAX and ad hoc networks. *Info, 8*(4), 21-32.

Mason, A.K. & Kahn, D.J. (1997). Estimating costs with fuzzy logic. *Association for the Advancement of Cost Engineering International Transactions*, EST.03.1-EST.03.6

Massetti, B., & Zmud, R.W. (1996). Measuring the extent of EDI usage in complex organizations: Strategies and illustrative examples. *MIS Quarterly, 20*(3), 331-345.

May, R. (1996). *The meaning of anxiety.* New York: Norton and Company.

McClelland, M. (1992). Using simulation to facilitate analysis of manufacturing strategy. *Journal of Business Logistics, 13*(1), 215–237.

McGee, J., & Prusak, L. (1993). *Managing information strategically.* Toronto, Canada: John Wiley Sons.

McGillivray, G. (2000). Commercial risk under JIT. *Canadian Underwriter, 67*(1), 26-28.

McIvor, R. (2008). How the transaction cost and the resource-based theories of the firm inform outsourcing evaluation. *Journal of Operations Management.* doi:. doi:10.1016/j.jom.2008.03.004

McIvor, R. (2008). What is the right outsourcing strategy for your process? *European Management, 26*(1), 24–34. doi:10.1016/j.emj.2007.08.008

McIvor, R.T., Humphreys, P.K. & McAleer, W.E. (1997). A strategic model for the formulation of an effective make-or-buy decision. *Management Decision, 32*)), 169-178.

McMeekin, T.A., Baranyi, J., Bowman, J., Dalgaard, P., Kirk, M., Ross, T., Schmid, S., & Zwietering, M.H. (2006). Information systems in food safety management. *International Journal of Food Microbiology, 112*, 181-194.

Meczes, R. (2004). It'll never happen to us. *Motor Transport*, (June 10), 14.

Meehan, M. (2001). Covisint exchange vows it will support ebXML. *Computerworld, 35*(23), 16.

Meeks, W.L., & Dasgupta, S. (2004). Geospatial information utility: An estimation of the relevance of geospatial information to users. *Decision Support Systems, 38*(1), 47-63.

Meijboom, B. R. (1986). A two-level planning procedure with respect to make-or-buy decisions, including cost allocations. *European Journal of Operational Research, 23*, 301–309. doi:10.1016/0377-2217(86)90296-1

Meitz, A.A., & Castleman, B.B. (1975). How to cope with supply shortages. *Harvard Business Review, 53*(1), 91.

Mentzer, J. T., DeWitt, W., Keebler, J. S., Min, S., Nix, N. W., Smith, C. D., & Zacharia, Z. G. (2001). Defining supply chain management. *Journal of Business Logistics, 22*(2), 1–25.

Michael, K., & McCathie, L. (2005). The pros and cons of RFID in supply chain management. In *Proceedings of the Fourth International Conference on Mobile Business, July 11 - 13, 2005, Sydney Australia, Session 11D*.

Mighell, R. L., & Jones, L. A. (1963). Vertical coordination in agriculture. *USDA-ERS Agricultural Economics Report, 19*.

Miles, M.B., & Huberman, A.M. (1994). *Qualitative data analysis: An expanded sourcebook*. Thousand Oaks, CA: Sage.

Miles, M.B., & Huberman, A.M. (1994). *Qualitative data analysis: Grounded theory procedures and techniques*. London: Sage.

Min, S., & Mentzer, J. T. (2000). The role of marketing in supply chain management. *International Journal of Physical Distribution & Logistics Management, 30*(9), 765–787. doi:10.1108/09600030010351462

Mitchell, V.-W. (1995). Organizational risk perception and reduction: A literature review. *British Journal of Management, (6)*, 115-133.

Moberg, C. R., Seph, T. W., & Freese, T. L. (2003). SCM: making the vision a reality. *Supply Chain Management Review, 7*(5), 34–39.

Mohtadi, H. (2008). Information sharing in food supply chains. *Canadian Journal of Agricultural Economics, 56*(2), 163.

Momme, J. (2002). Framework for outsourcing manufacturing: strategic and operational implications. *Computers in Industry, 49*(1), 59–75. doi:10.1016/S0166-3615(02)00059-3

Momme, J., & Hvolby, H. H. (2002). An outsourcing framework: action research in the heavy industry sector. *European Journal of Purchasing and Supply Management, 8*(4), 185–196. doi:10.1016/S0969-7012(02)00003-5

Monczka, R.M., Peterson, K.J., & Handfield, R.B. (1998). Success factors in strategic supplier alliances: The buying company perspective. *Decision Science, 29*(3), 553-573.

Morris, J., & Imrie, R. (1992). *Transforming buyer-supplier relations: Japanese-style industrial practices in western context*. London: Macmillan.

Morrison, D. G., & Schmittlein, D. C. (1991). How many forecasters do you really have? Mahalanobis provides the intuition for the surprising Clemen and Winkler result. *Operation Research, 39*(5), 519-523.

Moses, S., Grand, H., Gruenwald, L., & Pulat, S. (2004). Real-time due-date promising by build-to-order environments. *International Journal of Production Research, 42*, 4353–4375. doi:10.1080/00207540410001716462

Murty, K.G. (1968). Solving the fixed charge problem by ranking the extreme points. *Operations Research, 16*, 268-279.

Nagarajan, M., & Sos˘ic´, G., (2008). Game-theoretic analysis of cooperation among supply chain agents: Review and extensions. *European Journal of Operational Research, 187*(3), 719-745

Narayanan, V. G., & Raman, A. (2004). Aligning incentives in supply chains. *Harvard Business School Publishing, Article # R0411F, Novembe*r.

Nelder, J.A., & Mead, R. (1965). A simplex for function minimization. *Computer Journal, 7*, 308-313.

Neureuther, B. D., & Kenyon, G. N. (2008). The impact of information technologies on the US beef industry's supply chain. *International Journal of Information Systems and Supply Chain Management, 1*(1), 48–65.

Newman, A. J., Yu, D. K. C., & Oulton, D. P. (2002). New insights into retail space and format planning from customer-tracking data. *Journal of Retailing and Consumer Services, 9*, 253-258.

Ngai, E. W. T., Cheng, T. C. E., Lai, K., Chai, P. Y. F., Choi, Y. S., & Sin, R. K. Y. (2007). Development of an RFID-based Traceability System. *Production and Operations Management, 16*(5), 554–568.

Ngai, E.W.T., Cheng, T.C.E., Au, S., & Lai, K. (2007). Mobile commerce integrated with RFID technology in a container depot. *Decision Support Systems, 43*, 62-76.

Nishiguchi, T. (1994). *Strategic industrial sourcing: The Japanese advantage.* New York: Oxford University Press.

Nitschke, T., & O'Keefe, M. (1997). Managing the linkage with primary producers: experiences in the Australian grain industry. *Supply Chain Management, Bradford, 2*(1), 4. doi:10.1108/13598549710156295

Novin, A. M. (1992). Applying overhead: How to find the right bases and rates. *Management Accounting, 3,* 40–43.

O'Connor, M.C. (2004, November 30). *RFID users want clear data.* Retrieved from *www.rfidjournal.com/article/articleview/1232/1/1/*

O'Connor, M.C. (2006). *Warehouse management systems that handle RFID data.* Retrieved from *http://www.rfidjournal.com/magazine/article/2259*

O'Connor, M.C. (2006, August 18). *Apparel & footwear summit attracts wide audience.* Retrieved from *http://www.rfidjournal.com/article/articleview/2599/1/1/*

O'Connor, M.C. (2007, January 8). *Michelin shrinks its e-tire pressure monitor.* Retrieved from *http://www.rfidjournal.com/article/articleview/2950/1/1/*

O'Guin, M. C. (1991). *The complete guide to activity-based costing.* New Jersey: Prentice Hall.

Ohba, H. (1997). Letters to the editor: Toyota's solution to supply problems. *Wall Street Journal,* (March 7), A15.

Oliver, C. (1990). Determinants of inter-organizational relationships: integration and future directions. *Academy of Management Review, 15*(2), 241–265. doi:10.2307/258156

Olorunniwo, F., & Hartfield, T. (2001). Strategic partnering when the supply base is limited: A case study. *Industrial Management and Data Systems, 101*(1), 47-52.

Ovalle, O.R., & Marquez, A.C. (2003). The effectiveness of using e-collaboration tools in the supply chain: An assessment study with system dynamic. *Journal of Purchasing and Supply Management, 9*(4), 151-163.

Padillo-Perez, J. M., & Diaby, M. (1999). A multiple-criteria decision methodology for the make-or-buy problem. *International Journal of Production Research, 37*(14), 3203–3229. doi:10.1080/002075499190248

Padmanabhan, V., & Rao, R. C. (1993). Warranty policy and extended service contracts: Theory and application to automobiles. *Marketing Science, 12*(6), 230-247.

Pagarkar, M., Natesan, M., & Prakash, B. (2005). *RFID in integrated order management systems: RFID, VMI and CPFR in integrated order management systems for retail supply chains.* RFID Journal White Paper.

Palekar, U.S., Karwan, M.H., & Zionts, S. (1990). A branch-and-bound method for the fixed charge transportation problem. *Management Science, 36,* 1092-105.

Palmer, M. (2004, February 2). *Build an effective RFID architecture.* Retrieved from *http://www.rfidjournal.com/article/articleview/781/1/82/*

Palvia, P. C. (1996). A model and instrument for measuring small business user satisfaction with information technology. *Information and Management, 31*(3), 151-163.

Pan, Y., & Shi, L. (2004). Stochastic on-line model for shipment date quoting with on-line delivery gurantees. In R. G. Ingalls, M.D. Rossetti, J.S. Smith, & B.A. Peters (Eds.), *Proceedings of the 2004 Winter Simulation Conference.*

Pant, S., Sethi, R., & Bhandari, M. (2003). Making sense of the e-supply chain landscape: An implementation framework. *International Journal of Information Management, 23,* 201-221.

Park, C. W., Iyer, E. S., & Smith, D. C. (1989). The effects of situational factors on in-store grocery shopping behavior: The role of store environment and time available for shopping. *The Journal of Consumer Research, 15*(4), 422-433.

Park, D., & Krishnan, H. A. (2005). Gender differences in supply chain management practices. *Internal Journal Management and Enterprise Development, 2*(1), 27-37.

Parlikad, A.K., & McFarlane, D. (2007). RFID-based product information in end-of-life decision making. *Control Engineering Practice*.

Parunak, H. V. D. (1999). *Multi-agent systems: A modern approach to distributed artificial intelligence*. Cambridge, MA: The MIT Press.

Peteraf, M. A. (1993). The cornerstones of competitive advantage: A resource-based view. *Strategic Management Journal, 14*, 179–191. doi:10.1002/smj.4250140303

Peters, M., Cooper, J., Lieb, R. C., & Randall, H. L. (1998). The third-party logistics industry in Europe: provider perspectives on the industry's current status and future prospects. *International Journal of Logistics: Research and Application, 1*(1), 9–25. doi:10.1080/13675569808962035

Petzinger, T. Jr. (1995). Damewood Brothers are racing to beat the just-in-time system. *Wall Street Journal,* (June 30), B1.

Peypoch, R. (1998). The case for electronic business communities. *Business Horizons, 4*(6), 17–20. doi:10.1016/S0007-6813(98)90073-8

Phan, D.D., & Stata, N.M. (2002). E-business success at Intel: An organization ecology and resources dependence perspective. *Industrial Management & Data Systems, 102*(4), 211-217.

Philips. (2004). Item-Level visibility in the pharmaceutical supply chain: A comparison of HF and UHF RFID technologies. Philips Semiconductors TAGSYS Texas Instruments Inc, July 2004 [White paper]. Retrieved from http://www.ti.com/rfid/docs/manuals/whtPapers/jointPharma.pdf

Phillips, H. C., & Bradlow, R. P. (1991). Camera tracking: A new tool for market research and retail management. *Management Research News, 14*(4/5), 20-22.

Plehwe, D., & Bohle, D. (1998). *Uberlegungen zum forschungsfeld transnationale organisation in Europa*. B-Social Science Research Center, Berlin.

Poirier, C.C., & Bauer, M.J. (2001). *E-supply chain: Using the Internet to revolutionize your business*. San Francisco: Berrett-Koehler.

Poppo, L. (1998). Testing alternatives theories of the firm: Transaction cost, knowledge based and measurement explanations for make-or-buy decision in information services. *Strategic Management Journal, 19*(9), 853–877. doi:10.1002/(SICI)1097-0266(199809)19:9<853::AID-SMJ977>3.0.CO;2-B

Powell, T. C., & Dent-Micallef, A. (1997). Information technology as competitive advantage: the role of human, business, and technology resources. *Strategic Management Journal, 18*(5), 375–405. doi:10.1002/(SICI)1097-0266(199705)18:5<375::AID-SMJ876>3.0.CO;2-7

Power, D. (2005). Determinants of business-to-business e-commerce implementation and performance: A structural model. *Supply Chain Management, 10*(2), 96–113. doi:10.1108/13598540510589179

Power, D., Sharafali, M., & Bhakoo, V. (2007). Adding value through outsourcing: Contribution of 3PL services to customer performance. *Management Research News, 30*(3), 228–235. doi:10.1108/01409170710733296

Prahalad, C. K., & Hamel, G. (1990). The core competence of the corporation. *Harvard Business Review, 68*(3), 79–91.

Prater, E., Frazier, G., & Reyes, P. (2005). Future impacts of RFID on e-supply chains in grocery retailing. *Supply Chain Management, 10*(2), 134–145. doi:10.1108/13598540510589205

Premkumar, G., & Ramamurthy, K. (1995). The role of interorganizational and organizational factors on the decision mode for adoption of interorganizational systems. *Decision Sciences, 26*(3), 303-337.

Purba, R. (2004). Greening production: A South-East Asian experience. *International Journal of Operations & Production Management, 24*(3), 289-320

Qiu, R.G. (2007). RFID-enabled automation in support of factory integration. *Robotics and Computer-Integrated Manufacturing*.

Rabinovich, E., Windle, R., Dresner, M., & Corsi, T. (1999). Outsourcing of integrated logistics functions: An examination of industry practices. *International Journal of Physical Distribution & Logistics Management, 29*(6), 353–373. doi:10.1108/09600039910283587

Rad, P. F., & Cioffi, D. F. (2004). Work and resource breakdown structures for formalized bottom-up estimating. *Coastal Engineering, 46*(2), 31–37.

Rafanelli, M. (2003). *Multidimensional databases: Problems and solutions.* London: Idea Group Publishing.

Rahman, Z. (2003). Internet-based supply chain management: using the Internet to revolutionize your business. *International Journal of Information Management, 23,* 493–505. doi:10.1016/j.ijinfomgt.2003.09.004

Raju, J. S., & Roy, A. (2000). Market information and firm performance. *Management Science, 46*(8), 1075-1084.

Raju, J. S., & Zhang, J. Z. (2005). Channel coordination in the presence of a dominant retailer. *Marketing Science, 24*(2), 254-304.

Ranky, P.G. (2006). An introduction to radio frequency identification (RFID) methods and solutions. *Assembly Automation, 26,* 28-33.

Rao, B. (1999). The Internet and the revolution in distribution: A cross-industry examination. *Technology in Society, 21,* 287–306. doi:10.1016/S0160-791X(99)00018-4

Raunick, D. A., & Fisher, A. G. (1972). A probabilistic make-buy model. *Journal of Purchasing, 8*(1), 63–80.

Raupp, M., & Schober, F. (2000). Why buyer-supplier chains differ: A strategic framework for electronic network organizations. *Proceedings of the 33rd Annual Hawaii International Conference on Systems Sciences* (HICSS), Maui, HI.

Razzaque, M. A., & Sheng, C. C. (1998). Outsourcing of logistics functions: a literature survey. *International Journal of Physical Distribution & Logistics Management, 28*(2), 89–107. doi:10.1108/09600039810221667

Reddy, S. B., Osborn, R. N., & Hennart, J. F. (2002). The prevalence of equity and non-equity cross-border linkages: Japanese investments and alliances in the United States. *Organization Studies, 23*(5), 759-780.

Reed, R., & DeFillippi, R. J. (1990). Causal ambiguity, barriers to imitation and sustainable competitive advantage. *Academy of Management Review, 15*(1), 88–102. doi:10.2307/258107

Regattieri, A., Gamberi, M., & Manzini, R. (2007). Traceability of food products: General framework and experimental evidence. *Journal of Food Engineering, 81,* 347-356.

Reid, A.S. (2007). Is society smart enough to deal with smart cards? *Computer Law & Security Report, 23,* 53-61.

Reiman, M. I., & Wein, L. M. (1999). Heavy traffic analysis of polling systems in tandem. *Operations Research, 47*(4), 524–534. doi:10.1287/opre.47.4.524

Reitman, V. (1997). To the rescue: Toyota's fast rebound after fire at supplier shows why it is tough. *Wall Street Journal,* (May 8), A1.

RFID Journal (2003, November 14). *Report: RFID benefits not equal.* Retrieved from http://www.rfidjournal.com/article/articleview/651/1/26/

RFID Journal. (2002, June 24). *Learning from Prada.* Retrieved from *http://www.rfidjournal.com/article/view/425*

RFID Journal. (2002, October 24). *CD tracking project deemed a hit.* Retrieved from *http://www.rfidjournal.com/article/articleview/98/1/1/*

RFID Journal. (2003, September 22). *Tesco deploys class 1 EPC tags.* Retrieved from *http://www.rfidjournal.com/article/articleview/587/1/1/*

RFID Journal. (2007, February). *EPC/RFID data sharing: Enter a new era of supply chain collaboration between retailers and suppliers.* Retrieved from *http://www.rfidjournal.com/whitepapers/download/209*

Rice, J.B., & Caniato, F. (2003). Building a secure and resilient supply chain. *Supply Chain Management Review, 7*(5), 22-30.

Richard, L., & Jon, H. (1996). The environment as a supply chain management issue. *British Journal of Management, 7,* 45-62

Rieback, M. R., Crispo, B., & Tanenbaum, A. S. (2006). Is your cat infected with a computer virus? *Fourth Annual IEEE International Conference on Pervasive Computing and Communications, Pisa, Italy.*

Riedel, J. (1975). The nature and determinants of export-oriented direct foreign investment in a developing country: A case study of Taiwan. *Weltirtschaftliches Archiv, 3*(3), 505-528.

Ritchie, B., & Brindley, C. (2002). Reassessing the management of the global supply chain. *Integrated Manufacturing Systems, 13*(2), 110–116. doi:10.1108/09576060210415446

Rivera, N., Mountain, R., Assumpcao, L., Williams, A. A., Cooper, A. B., Lewis, D. L., et al. (2008). *ASSIST - Automated System for Surgical Instrument and Sponge Tracking.* 2008 IEEE International Conference on RFID, Las Vegas, Nevada.

Robert, M. M., & Shelby, D. H. (1994). The commitment-trust theory of relationship marketing. *Journal of Marketing, 58,* 20-38

Roberti, M. (2004, April 30). *Wal-Mart begins RFID rollout.* Retrieved from *http://www.rfidjournal.com/article/articleview/926/1/1*

Roberti, M. (2005, October 31). *The serendipity effect.* Retrieved from *http://www.rfidjournal.com/article/articleview/1960/1/2/*

Roberti, M. (2005, October, 17). *Target, Wal-Mart share EPC data.* Retrieved from *http://www.rfidjournal.com/article/articleview/1928/1/1/*

Roberts, B. (2004). Double trouble. *Electronic Business, 30*(5), 62-67.

Roberts, M. (2000). The dawn of next-generation digital supply chains. *Chemical Week,* (July 26), 8-10.

Roberts, S. M., Jones, J. P., & Frohling, O. (2005). NGOs and the globalization of managerialism: A research framework. *33*(11), 1845-1864.

Robinson, E. P., Sahin, F., & Gao, L. (2005). The impact of e-replenishment strategy on make-to-order supply chain performance. *Decision Sciences, 36*(1), 33–64. doi:10.1111/j.1540-5915.2005.00065.x

Rogerson, C. M. (1995). Looking to the Pacific Rim: Production subcontracting and small-scale industry in South Africa. *International Small Business Journal, 13*(3), 65-79.

Romeo, P. (2006). Buyers embrace more sophisticated supply-purchasing procedures. *Nations Restaurant News, 40*(21), 92–93.

Rosenberg, A. (2003). *Focus on collaboration: Collaborative B2B.* Retrieved September 26, 2007, from *http://www.basex.com/press.nsf/0/CD3491C3C2D8D85256D0D001CC5D8?OpenDocument*

Ross, R. B. (2002). *Regression analysis as a cost estimation model for unexploded ordnance cleanup at former military installations.* Master's thesis. Naval Postgraduate school Monterey CA.

Rugman, A. M. (1981). *Inside the multinationals: The economics of internal markets.* New York: Columbia University Press.

Sadagopan, S., & Ravindran, A. (1982). A vertex ranking algorithm for the fixed-charge transportation problem. *Journal of Optimization Theory Applications, 37,* 221-230.

Sadgrove, K. (1996). *The complete guide to business risk management.* Aldershot, UK: Gower.

Saga, V. L., & Zmud, R. W. (1994). The nature and determinants of IT acceptance, routinization, and infusion. In L. Levine (Ed.), *Diffusion transfer and implementation of information technology* (pp. 67-86). Amsterdam: Elsevier Science.

Sahay, B. S. (2003). Understanding trust in supply chain relationships. *Industrial Management & Data Systems, 103*(8), 553-563

Sahin, F., & Robinson, E.P. (2005). Information sharing and coordination in make-to-order supply chains. *Journal of Operations Management, 23*(6), 579-598.

Salin, V. (2000). Information technology and cattle-beef supply chains. *American Journal of Agricultural Economics, 82*(5), 1105–1111. doi:10.1111/0002-9092.00107

Sandrock, K. (1988). A simple algorithm for solving small fixed-charge transportation problems. *Journal of Operations Research Society, 39,* 467-475.

Sarkis, J., & Sundarraj, R. P. (2000). Factors for strategic evaluation of enterprise information technologies. *International Journal of Physical Distribution & Logistics Management, 30*(3/4), 196–220. doi:10.1108/09600030010325966

Sarma, S. (2004). The RFID advantage. *Express Computer Online Magazine.* Retrieved from http://www.expresscomputeronline.com/20041129/technology06.shtml

Sarmah, S. P., Acharya, D., & Goyal, S. K. (2006). Buyer vendor coordination models in supply chain management. *European Journal of Operational Research, 175,* 1-15.

Sarvary, M., & Parker, P. M. (1997). Marketing information: A competitive analysis. *Marketing Science, 16*(1), 24-38.

Saygin, C. (2007). Adaptive inventory management using RFID data. *International Journal of Advanced Manufacturing Technology, 32,* 1045-1051.

Schaffer, J.R., & O'Leary, D.E. (1989). Use of penalties in a branch and bound procedure for the fixed charge transportation problem. *European Journal of Operational Research, 43,* 305-312.

Schwartz, L.B., & Weng, Z.K. (2000). The design of a JIT supply chain: The effect of lead time uncertainty on safety stock. *Journal of Business Logistics, 21*(2), 231-252.

Sellitto, C., Burgess, S., & Hawking, P. (2007). Information quality attributes associated with RFID-derived benefits in the retail supply chain. *International Journal of Retail & Distribution Management, 35,* 69-87.

Sengenberger, W., & Pkye, F. (1991). Small firm industrial districts and local economic regeneration: Research and policy issues. *Labour and Society, 16,* 1-24.

Shah, S. (2006). *Semantics and Internet of things.* RFID Journal White Paper.

Sharifi, H., Kehoe, D.F., & Hopkins, J. (2006). A classification and selection model of e-marketplaces for better alignment of supply chains. *Journal of Enterprise Information Management, 19*(5), 483-503.

Sharpston, M. (1977). International subcontracting. *Oxford Economic Papers, 27,* 94-135.

Sheffi, Y. & Rice, J.B. Jr. (2005). A supply chain view of the resilient enterprise. *MIT Sloan Management Review, 47*(1), 41-48.

Sheffi, Y. (2004). RFID and the innovation cycle. *The International Journal of Logistics Management, 15*(1), 1–10. doi:10.1108/09574090410700194

Shin, H., Collier, D., & Wilson, D. (2001). Supply management orientation and supplier/buyer performance. *Journal of Operations Management, 18,* 317-222.

Shirouzu, N. (2005). Toyota, lured by incentives, picks Canadian site for its next plant. *Wall Street Journal,* (June 27), B6.

Shirouzu, N., Williams, M., Sapsford, J., & Reitman, V. (1995). Kobe's rebuilding may take longer than expected as damage toll mounts. *Wall Street Journal,* (January 19), A3.

Shore, B., & Venkatachalam, A.R. (2003). Evaluating the information sharing capabilities of supply chain partners: A fuzzy logic model. *International Journal of Physical Distribution & Logistics Management, 33*(9), 804-824.

Shtub, A., & Versano, R. (1999). Estimating the cost of steel pipe bending, a comparison between neural networks and regression analysis. *International Journal of Production Economics, 62,* 201–207. doi:10.1016/S0925-5273(98)00212-6

Siegel, J. G., & Shim, J. K. (1991). *Financial Management.* Hauppauge, NY: Barron's Business Library.

Simchi Levi, D., Kaminsky, P., & Simchi Levi, E. (2000). *Designing and managing the supply chain.* New York: McGraw-Hill.

Simchi-Levi, D., & Simchi-Levi, E. (2000). The dramatic impact of the impact on supply chain strategies. *ASCET* Vol. 2, Montgomery Research Inc.

Simchi-Levi, D., Kaminsky, P., & Simchi-Levi, E. (2008). *Designing & Managing the Supply Chain: Concepts, Strategies & Case Studies.* (3rd ed.). New York: Irwin McGraw Hill.

Sinha, P.R., Whitman, L.E., & Malzahn, D. (2004). Methodology to mitigate supplier risk in an aerospace supply chain. *Supply Chain Management, 9*(2), 154-168.

Sirico, L. (2005, July 7). *The cost of compliance.* Issue #36, July 7, 2005. Retrieved from http://mrrfid.com/index.php?itemid=4

Sirico, L. (2005, August 3). *The cost of compliance II: The Details.* Issue #40. Retrieved from http://mrrfid.com/index.php?itemid=50

Sliwa, C. (2003). RFID tunes into supply chains. *Computerworld, 37*(33), 23–26.

Smith, A. E., & Mason, A. K. (1997). Cost estimation predictive modeling: Regression versus neural network. *The Engineering Economist, 42*(2), 137–161. doi:10.1080/00137919708903174

Smitka, M. J. (1991). *Competitive ties: Subcontracting in Japanese automotive industry.* New York: Columbia University Press.

Soars, B. (2003). What every retailer should know about the way into the shopper's head. *International Journal of Retail and Distribution Management, 31*(12), 628-637.

Soliman, K. S., & Janz, B. D. (2004). An exploratory study to identify the critical factors affecting the decision to establish Internet-based inter-organizational information systems. *Information & Management, 41*, 697–706. doi:10.1016/j.im.2003.06.001

Son, Y. K. (1991). Cost estimation model for advanced manufacturing systems. *International Journal of Production Research, 29*(3), 441–452. doi:10.1080/00207549108930081

Sonmez, R. (2004). Conceptual cost estimation of building projects with regression analysis and neural networks.

Canadian Journal of Civil Engineering, 31(4), 677–683. doi:10.1139/l04-029

Sorensen, H. (2003). The science of shopping. *Marketing Research, 15*(3), 30-35.

Spekman, R. E., & Sweeney, P. J. II. (2006). RFID: from concept to implementation. *International Journal of Physical Distribution & Logistics Management, 36*(10), 736–754. doi:10.1108/09600030610714571

Spekman, R. E., & Sweeney, P. J., II. (2006). RFID: From concept to implementation. *International Journal of Physical Distribution & Logistics Management, 36*(10), 736-754.

Spekman, R.E., & Davis, E.W. (2004). Risky business: Expanding the discussion on risk and the extended enterprise. *International Journal of Physical Distribution and Logistics Management, 34*(5), 414-433.

Spieß, P., Bornhövd, C., Lin, T., Haller, S., & Schaper, J. (2007). Going beyond auto-ID: A service-oriented smart items infrastructure. *Journal of Enterprise Information Management, 20*, 356-370.

Stank, T. P., & Daugherty, P. J. (1997). The impact of operating environment on the formation of cooperative logistics relationships. *Transportation Research Part E, Logistics and Transportation Review, 33*(1), 53–65. doi:10.1016/S1366-5545(96)00005-1

Stedman, C. (1999). Failed ERP gamble haunts Hershey. *Computerworld, 33*(4), 89.

Steinberg, D.I. (1970). The fixed charge problem. *Naval Research Logistics Quarterly, 17*, 217-235.

Stevenson, W. J. (2002). *Operations management* (7th ed.). Irwin/McGraw-Hill.

Stewart, R. D. (1982). *Cost Estimating.* New York: John Wiley & Sons, Inc.

Stock, G. N., Greis, N. P., & Kasarda, J. D. (1998). Logistics, strategy, and structure: a conceptual framework. *International Journal of Production Management, 18*(1), 37–52. doi:10.1108/01443579810192772

Sullivan, W. G. (1992). A new paradigm for engineering economy. *The Engineering Economist, 36*(3), 187–200. doi:10.1080/00137919108903044

Sun, M., Aronson, J.E., McKeown, P.G., & Drinka, D. (1998). A tabu search heuristic procedure for the fixed charge transportation problem. *European Journal of Operational Research, 106*(2-3), 441-456.

Swamy, G., & Sarma, S. (2003, February 1). *Manufacturing cost simulations for low cost RFID systems.* [Auto-ID Center White Paper]. Massachusetts Institute of Technology. Retrieved from http://peumans-pc.stanford.edu/research/monolithic-low-cost-rfid-tags/hidden/mit-autoid-wh017.pdf

Tage, S. L. (2000). European logistics beyond 2000. *International Journal of Physical Distribution & Logistics Management, 30*(5), 377-387

Tang, C.S. (2006). Perspectives in supply chain risk management. *International Journal of Production Economics, 103*(2), 451-488.

Tayur, S. H., Ganeshan, R., & Magazine, M. J. (1998). *Quantitative models for supply chain management.* Norwell, MA: Kluwer.

Tellkamp, C., Angerer, A., Fleisch, E., & Corsten, D. (2005). *From pallet to shelf: Improving data quality in retail supply chains using RFID.* Auto ID Center White Paper.

Ten Brinke, E., Lutters, E., Streppel, T., & Kals, H. J. J. (2000). Variant-based cost estimation based on information management. *International Journal of Production Research, 38*(17), 4467–4479. doi:10.1080/00207540050205235

Terry, L. (2004). Supply chain software gets ready for RFID. *Supply Chain Systems Magazine, 24*(6), 18–20.

The Economist. (2007, June 7). *Radio silence.* Retrieved from *http://www.economist.com/search/displaystory.cfm?story_id=9249278&CFID=15975447&CFTOKEN=95269337#top*

Thomas, R., & Oliver, N. (1991). Components supplier patterns in the UK Motor Industry. *OMEGA, 19*(6), 609-616

Tian, Y., Lai, F., & Daniel, F. (2008). An examination of the nature of trust in logistics outsourcing relationship: empirical evidence from China. *Industrial Management & Data Systems, 108*(3), 346–367. doi:10.1108/02635570810858769

Turban, E., Lee, J., King, D., & Turban, E. (2000). *Electronic commerce: A managerial perspective.* Upper Saddle River, NJ: Prentice Hall.

Turban, E., Mclean, E., Wetherbe, J., Bolloju, N., & Davison, R. (2002). *Information technology management: Transforming business in the digital economy.* New York: John Wiley & Sons.

Twist, D.C. (2005). The impact of radio frequency identification on supply chain facilities. *Journal of Facilities Management, 3*, 226-239.

Underhill, P. (1999). *Why we buy: The science of shopping.* New York: Simon & Schuster.

Vaidyanathan, G. (2005). A framework for evaluating third-party logistics. *Communications of the ACM, 48*(1), 89–94. doi:10.1145/1039539.1039544

van Hoek, R. (2001). E-supply chains-virtually non-existing. *Supply Chain Management, 6*(1), 21-28.

Van Oort, P. A. J., & Bregt, A. K. (2005). Do users ignore spatial data quality? A decision-theoretic perspective. *Risk Analysis, 25*(6), 1599-1610.

Vanderhaegen, M., & Muro, E. (2005). Contribution of a European spatial data infrastructure to the effectiveness of EIA and SEA studies. *Environmental Impact Assessment Review, 25*(2), 123-142.

Venables, M. (2005). RFID - Don't believe the hype. *Manufacturing Engineering, 84*(5), 8–9. doi:10.1049/me:20050502

Venkatesan, R. (1992). Strategic sourcing: to make or not to make. *Harvard Business Review*, (November-December): 98–107.

Venkatesh, V., Morris, M. G., Davis, G. B., & Davis, F. D. (2003). User acceptance of information technology: Toward a unified view. *MIS Quarterly, 27*(3), 425-478.

Venkatraman, N., & Grant, J. H. (1986). Construct measurement in organizational strategy research: A critique and proposal. *Academy of Management Review, 11*(1), 71–87. doi:10.2307/258332

Versendaal, J., & Brinkkemper, S. (2003). Benefits and success factors of buyer-owned electronic trading exchanges: Procurement at Komatsu America corporation. *Journal of Information Technology Cases and Applications, 5*(4), 39-52.

Vijayaraman, B. S., & Osyk, B. A. (2006). An empirical study of RFID in the warehousing industry. *International Journal of Logistics Management, 7*(1), 6–20. doi:10.1108/09574090610663400

Vining, A., & Globerman, S. (1999). A conceptual framework for understanding the outsourcing decision. *European Management Journal, 17*(6), 645–654. doi:10.1016/S0263-2373(99)00055-9

Viswanadhm, N., & Raghavan, N. R. S. (2000). Performance analysis and design of supply chains: A Petri net approach. *Journal of Operation Research Society, 51*(10), 1158-1169.

Vives, X. (1984). Duopoly information equilibrium: Cournot and Bertrand. *Journal of Economic Theory, 34*, 71-94.

Vollmann, T. E., Berry, W. L., & Whybark, D. C. (1984). *Manufacturing planning and control systems*. Homewood, IL: Richard D. Irwin Inc.

Vollmer, D. (2004). RFID from compliance to competitive advantage. *Red Prairie Presentation to Productivity, Dallas, TX*. Retrieved from http://www.fmi.org/events/productivity/2005/exh_ed/presentations/Vollmer.pdf

Vose, D. (2000). *Risk analysis* (2nd ed.). Wiley.

Wade, M., & Hulland, J. (2004). The resource-based view and information systems research: Review, extension, and suggestions for future research. *MIS Quarterly, 28*(1), 107–142.

Wadhwa, V., & Ravindran, A. R. (2007). Vendor selection in outsourcing. *Computers & Operations Research, 34*(12), 3725–3727. doi:10.1016/j.cor.2006.01.009

Wakefield, K. L., & Baker, J. (1998). Excitement at the mall: Determinants and effects on shopping response. *Journal of Retailing, 74*(4), 515-539.

Walsham, G. (1995). Interpretive case studies in IS research: nature and method. *European Journal of Information Systems, 4*(1), 74–81. doi:10.1057/ejis.1995.9

Wamba, S. F., Bedavid, Y., Lefebvre, L. A., & Lefebvre, E. (2006). RFID technology and the EPC network as enablers of mobile business: A case study in a retail supply chain. *International Journal of Networking and Virtual Organizations, 3*(4), 450–462. doi:10.1504/IJNVO.2006.011872

Wang, F., & Liu, P. (2005). *Temporal management of RFID data* (pp. 1128-1139). Siemens Corporate Research.

Wang, J. (1998). *Timed Petri nets: Theory and application*. Norwell, MA: Kluwer.

Wang, Q. (2005). Discount pricing policies and the coordination of decentralized distribution systems. *Decision Sciences, 36*(4), 627-646.

Wang, Q., Chay, Y., & Wu, Z. (2006). A simple coordination strategy for a decentralized supply chain. Working Paper, Nanyang Business School, Nanyang Technological University, Singapore.

Wang, Y. (2007). To internationally subcontract or not. *Monash Business Review, 3*(1), 48-49.

Ward, M. (2007). The price of speed. *National Petroleum News, 99*, 28-32.

Warden, T. (2005). *The RFID software conundrum*. RFID Journal White Paper.

Waters, D. (2003). *Logistics: An Introduction to Supply Chain Management*. New York: Palgrave Macmillan.

Wathne, K. H., & Heide, J. B. (2000). Opportunism in interfirm relationships: Forms, outcomes, and solutions. *Journal of Marketing, 64*, 36-51.

Wayman, W. A. (1995). Inventory accuracy through warehouse control. *Production and Inventory Management Journal, 36*(2), 17–21.

Webster, J. (1998). Desktop videoconferencing: Experiences of complete users, wary users, and non-users. *MIS Quarterly, 22*(3), 257-286.

Welch, J. A., & Nayak, P. R. (1992). Strategic sourcing: A progressive approach to the make-or-buy decision. *Academy of Management Executive, 6*(1), 23–31.

Wernerfelt, B. (1984). A resource-based view of the firm. *Strategic Management Journal, 5*(2), 171–180. doi:10.1002/smj.4250050207

Westerman, G., & Cotteleer, M.J. (1999). *Tektronix, Inc.: Global ERP implementation.* Boston: Harvard Business School Press.

White, A., Johnson, M., & Wilson, H. (2008). RFID in the supply chain: lessons from European early adopters. *International Journal of Physical Distribution & Logistics Management, 38*(2), 88–107. doi:10.1108/09600030810861189

Whitten, D. (2004). User information satisfaction scale reduction: Application in an IT outsourcing environment. *Journal of Computer Information Systems, 45*(2), 17-26.

Willcocks, L. P., & Plant, R. (2003). How corporations e-source: from business technology projects to value networks. *Information Systems Frontiers, 5*(2), 175–193. doi:10.1023/A:1022601607218

William, L., Gardner III, & David, B. G. (1995). Information system training, usage, and satisfaction and exploratory of the hospital industry. *Management Communication Quarterly, 9*(1), 78-114.

Williams, J. R., Haka, S. F., Bettner, M. S., & Carcello, J. V. (2008). *Financial Accounting* (13th ed.). New York: McGraw-Hill Publishing.

Williamson, O. E. (1975). *Markets and hierarchies: Analysis and antitrust implications.* New York: Free Press.

Williamson, O. E. (1979). Transaction cost economics: The governance of contractual relations. *The Journal of Law and Economics, 12*(2), 233-262.

Williamson, O. E. (1985). *The Economic Institutions of Capitalism: Firms, Markets, Relational Contracting.* New York: The Free Press.

Williamson, O. E. (1990). The firm as a nexus of treaties: An introduction. In M. Aoki, B. Gustafsson, & O. E. Williamson (Eds.), *The firm as a nexus of treaties* (pp. 1-25), London: Sage.

Williamson, O. E. (1996). *The Mechanisms of Governance.* Oxford: Oxford University Press.

Williamson, O. E. (1999). Strategy research: Governance and competence perspectives. *Strategic Management Journal, 20*(12), 1087-1108.

Winkler, R. (1981). Combining probability distributions from dependent information sources. *Management Science, 27*(4), 479-488.

Wise, R., & Morrison, D. (2000). Beyond the exchange: The future of B2B. *Harvard Business Review, 78*(6), 86–96.

Wisner, J. D., Leong, G. K., & Tan, K. C. (2005). *Principles of Supply Chain Management: A Balanced Approach.* Ohio: South-Western, Thomson.

Wisner, J.D., & Tan, K.C. (2000). Supply chain management and its impact on purchasing. *Journal of Supply Chain Management, 36*(4), 33-42.

Womack, J.P., Jones D.T., & Roos, D. (1990). *The machine that changed the world.* New York: Rawson.

Wong, K.H.M., Hui, P.C.L., & Chan, A.C.K. (2006). Cryptography and authentication on RFID passive tags for apparel products. *Computers in Industry, 57,* 342-349.

Wooldridge, M. (2002). *An introduction to multi-agent systems.* New York: Wiley.

WSJ. (1997). Union Pacific faces claims over delays. *Wall Street Journal,* (October 10), A3.

Wu, W. H. (1999). *A study of learner self-regulation in computer skill training: An application of social cognitive theory.* Unpublished doctoral dissertation of University of National Sun Yat-Sen in Taiwan.

Wu, Y.-C. J., & Chen, J.-X. (2007). RFID application in a CVS distribution center in Taiwan: A simulation study. *International Journal of Manufacturing Technology and Management, 10*(1), 121–135. doi:10.1504/IJMTM.2007.011405

Yang, L., & Liu, L. (2007). Fuzzy fixed charge solid transportation problem and algorithm. *Applied Soft Computing, 7*(3), 879-889.

Yao, Y., Palmer, J., & Dresner, M. (2007). An interorganizational perspective on the use of electronically-enabled supply chains. *Decision Support Systems, 43*(3), 884. doi:10.1016/j.dss.2007.01.002

Yasin, M. M., & Quigley, J. V. (1994). The utility of information systems: Views of CEOs and information system executives. *Industrial Management and Data Systems, 94*(5), 25-29.

Yee, S.-T. (2002). Establishment of product offering and production leveling principles via supply chain simulation under order-to-delivery environment. In E. Yücesan, C.H. Chen, J.L. Snowdon, & J.M. Charnes (Eds.), *Proceedings of the 2002 Winter Simulation Conference* (pp. 1260-1268).

Yin, R.K. (1994). *Case study research: Design and methods.* Thousand Oaks, CA: Sage.

Young, D. (2003). SARS could hurt Christmas. *The Globe and Mail,* (June 25). B9.

Ypatia, T., Katerina, G., & George, T. (2006). Supplier management and its relationship to buyers. *International Journal of Production Economics, 101*, 99-108

Yu, S.C. (2007). RFID implementation and benefits in libraries. *The Electronic Library, 25,* 54-64.

Yu, Z., Yan, H., & Cheng, E.T.C. (2001). Benefits of information sharing with supply chain partnerships. *Industrial Management & Data Systems, 101*(3), 114-119.

Zeng, A.Z., & Pathak, B.K. (2003). Achieving information integration in supply chain management through B2B e-hubs: Concepts and analyses. *Industrial Management & Data Systems, 103*(9), 657-665.

Zheng, Y. (1992). On properties of stochastic inventory systems. *Management Science, 38*(1), 87-103.

Zsidisin, G.A. (2003). A grounded definition of supply risk. *Journal of Purchasing and Supply Management,* (9), 217-224.

Zsidisin, G.A. (2003b). Managerial perceptions of supply risk. *Journal of Supply Chain Management,* (Winter), 14-25.

Zsidisin, G.A., Ellram, L.M., Cater, J.R., & Cavinato, J.L. (2004). An analysis of supply risk assessment techniques. *International Journal of Physical Distribution and Logistics Management, 34*(5), 397-413.

Zsidisin, G.A., Melnyk, S.A., & Ragatz, G.L. (2005). An institutional theory perspective of business continuity planning for purchasing and supply management. *International Journal of Production Research, 43*(16), 3401-3420.

Zsidisin, G.A., Ragatz, G.L., & Melnyk, S.A. (2005). The dark side of supply chain management. *Supply Chain Management Review,* (March), 46-52.

Zviran, M., Pliskin, N., & Levin, R. (2005). Measuring user satisfaction and perceived usefulness in the ERP context. *Journal of Computer Information Systems, 45*(3), 43-52.

About the Contributors

John Wang is a full professor at Montclair State University. Having received a scholarship award, he came to the USA and completed his PhD in operations research from Temple University. He has published over 100 refereed papers and six books. He has also developed several computer software programs based on his research findings. He is the Editor-in-Chief of International Journal of Operations Research and Information Systems, Int. J. of Information Systems and Supply Chain Management, Int. J. of Applied Management Science, and Int. J. of Information Systems in the Service Sector. He has served as a guest editor and referee for many other highly prestigious journals. He has served as track chair and/or session chairman numerous times on the most prestigious international and national conferences. His long-term research goal is on the synergy of data mining, operations research and cybernetics.

* * *

Yohanan Arzi is the president of the ORT Braude College, Karmiel, Israel, and an associate professor in its department of Industrial Engineering & Management. He holds B.Sc. in Industrial Engineering & Management (1979), M.Sc. (1983) and D.Sc. (1991) in Industrial Engineering from the Technion – Israel Institute of Technology, Haifa, Israel. His main teaching and research interests are in operations management, methods engineering, productivity measurement and technology innovation. He has published in many journals throughout the world and was a consultant to industry and services. Prof. Arzi is a senior member of the IIE (USA) and a member of INFORMS (USA). He is on the editorial board of the IIE Transactions on Operations Engineering, on the management of the Israeli Society of Industrial Engineers in the Association of Engineers in Israel, and on the board of directors of the Standards Institute of Israel.

Kin Fan Au is an Associate Head of the Institute of Textiles and Clothing at the Hong Kong Polytechnic University. He received his Master of Science (Eng) degree from the University of Hong Kong and the Doctor of Philosophy degree from The Hong Kong Polytechnic University. In professional affiliation, Dr Au is fellowship members for the Textile Institute (UK) and the Hong Kong Institution of Textile and Apparel. He published many papers related to world T & C trade and quotas. His current research interests include world T & C trade, competitive studies of the textile and clothing industry, knitting technology and techno-economic issues.

Eve Chan is currently the PhD candidate in the Institute of Textiles and Clothing at The Hong Kong Polytechnic University. She received her Bachelor degree in Textiles and Clothing Marketing

& Merchandising from the Hong Kong Polytechnic University. Before joining the postgraduate study, she has worked in the knitwear marketing sector and later as an engineer in a testing laboratory. She published some papers related to Fashion & Textile International Business. Her current research area is international trade of T & C.

Mark Eklin holds B.Sc. (1997) in Industrial Engineering & Management, M.Sc. (2001) and Ph.D. (2009) in Industrial Engineering from the Technion – Israel Institute of Technology, Haifa, Israel. He has wide professional experience in production management and information systems, as the former Head of Planning Section, and in process analysis and operational research as the current Head of Operations Research Section in an Israeli Governmental Organization.

Agnes Galambosi earned her PhD in Systems and Industrial Engineering from the University of Arizona in Tucson. She currently teaches at the Department of Mechanical Engineering and Engineering Science at the University of North Carolina at Charlotte as well as for the College of Graduate Business and Management at the University of Phoenix, Charlotte campus. Her teaching areas include managerial decision-making, decision analysis in health care, quantitative reasoning in business for MBA students, and computational methods for engineers. Besides investigation of Radio Frequency Identification benefits and risks, her current research interests include areas such as development of educational games and analysis of effective teaching techniques for both online and on ground delivery methods, and application of systems methods to climate change modeling, including impact and risk analysis of global change for policy makers

George Kenyon is an Assistant Professor of Operations Management at Lamar University. He received his B.S. in Technology from the University of Houston in 1982, his M.S. in Management Science from Florida Institute of Technology in 1993, and his Ph.D. in Business Administration from Texas Tech University in 1997. His research interests are in the fields of supply chain management, quality management, and operations management. He has published in Journal of Marketing Channels, Quality Management Journal, International Journal of Production Economics, International Journal of Information Systems and Supply Chain Management, and Journal of Case Studies in Accreditation and Assessment. With fifteen years of industry experience, he has acquired experience in various aspects of engineering including systems testing, systems design, and manufacturing, as well as, business planning and supply chain management. This experience has included companies such as Texas Instruments, Rockwell International, The Boeing Company, Aspen Technologies, and Hewlett Packard. As a consultant, his assignments have included scheduling and planning projects with Gulf States Steel, the Westlake Corporation, Miller Brewing, and Phillips Chemical.

Jay S. Kim is Associate Professor of Operations and Technology Management at Boston University's School of Management, where he teaches courses in operations management, global operations, supply chain management, and competing in China. He was the department chair in 1995-97, and the faculty director of the School's various international programs in 1997-2006. He was the research director of Global Manufacturing Futures Project in 1994-97. Professor Kim's research is focused on developing and implementing global operations and supply chain strategies. Recently, he is investigating strategic challenges in supply chain management faced by multinational corporations as they expand into the emerging economies like China. In addition, he studies closely the development of Chinese economy and industries, and works with senior executives to research the corresponding challenges and opportunities faced by the global socio-economic communities.

Kwok Hung (Charles) Lau is currently a Senior Lecturer of Logistics in the School of Management at the Royal Melbourne Institute of Technology University of Australia. He holds a B. Social Science in Geography and an MBA from the Chinese University of Hong Kong, a M.Sc. in Information Systems from the Hong Kong Polytechnic University, a M. Urban Planning from the University of Melbourne, and a Ph.D. degree in Geocomputation from the Royal Melbourne Institute of Technology University. He has papers published in journals and conference proceedings such as Environment and Planning (Part B), International Journal of Physical Distribution and Logistics Management, International Journal of Information Systems and Supply Chain Management, Australasian Transport Reform Forum, International Conference on City Logistics, and Australian and New Zealand Marketing Academy Conference. His areas of research interest include modelling in logistics, e-supply chain management, and outsourcing.

Yoo-Taek Lee is Assistant Professor of Technology, Operations and Information Management Division at Babson College. He teaches in various programs both graduate and undergraduate level. Prior to joining Babson, Professor Lee taught courses to M.B.A. and undergraduate students on operations management, supply chain management, statistics, and international management at Hult International Business School, Boston University, Northeastern University, and Emmanuel College. Professor Lee's research interests include global supply chain strategies, web-based supply chain management applications, and supplier development strategies from the view of socio-economics. His current work focuses on investigating development strategies of small and medium-sized suppliers in global supply chains and on identifying the role of complementary resources to the implementation of web-based applications in managing supply chains. Prior to his D.B.A. studies, Professor Lee worked at Samsung in Korea. His work experience also includes a research associate appointment at Boston University Asian Management Center and the development and management of executive education programs for Asian companies such as Sanyo, Samsung, LG, Daewoo, SK, and for non-profit organizations including the Federation of Korean Industries and Ministry of Commerce in China. Additionally, he has produced more than 65 company best practice reports of Motorola, IBM, Texas Instruments, GE, Federal Express, Intel, Sun Microsystems, and Toyota.

Young M. Lee is a Research Staff Member in the Mathematical Sciences Department of IBM's T.J. Watson Research Center. Dr. Lee received B.S., M.S., and Ph.D. degrees in chemical engineering from Columbia University. He joined the IBM Research Division in 2002, and has been working in the areas of supply chain simulation and optimization. Prior to joining IBM, he had worked for BASF for 14 years, where he had founded and managed the Mathematical Modeling Group, and led development of numerous optimization and simulation models for various logistics and manufacturing processes. His research interest includes simulation and optimization of supply chain, manufacturing, services, workforce management, business processes and disaster response operations. His email address is <ymlee@us.ibm.com>.

Wun Leong (Edmond) Ma has been working in the logistics industry in Hong Kong and Singapore for more than 20 years occupying managerial positions in supply chain management at many multinational corporations (MNCs). He is currently working in a global petrochemical company managing its logistics outsourcing contracts. His other expertises include provision of trainings to MNC staff for various logistics functions and assurance of compliance with developed country export administration regulations. Edmond received his Master of Business degree in Logistics Management at the Royal Melbourne Institute of Technology University in 2005. His areas of research interest include outsourcing and collaborative planning, forecasting, and replenishment.

Jeffrey G. Miller received his Ph.D. in industrial management from Purdue University and his M.B.A. and B.A. from the University of California at Los Angeles. His industrial experience includes manufacturing and operations positions with Dow Chemical. Before joining the faculty at Boston University in 1981, he taught at the Harvard Business School (1973-81), and Purdue University's Krannert Graduate School of Industrial Administration (1970-73). In 1985-86, he was a Visiting Professor at the Graduate School of Management at Stanford University. At Boston University, Miller founded the Manufacturing Roundtable in 1981 and served as Director until 1989. He founded and directed the Center for Team Learning from 1995-2007. He served as Associate Dean for the School of Management from January 1996- August 2000. He has written numerous articles on operations management and strategy, and five books, including three texts. His most recent books include The Team Learning Assistant, Benchmarking Global Manufacturing, and The American Edge.

Brian D. Neureuther is an Associate Professor of Supply Chain and Operations Management at the State University of New York, College at Plattsburgh. He received his Ph.D. in Production and Operations Management from Texas Tech University, his M.B.A. degree from Wright State University in Dayton, Ohio, with a concentration in management science and his B.A. in mathematics from the State University of New York, College at Geneseo. His research interests include supply chain management, supply chain disruption, information technology in supply chains, simulation for production planning and control, and quality control. He has published over 30 peer reviewed journal articles and his work has appeared in journals such as the Journal of Integrated Design and Process Science, the International Journal of Production Economics, IEEE Transactions on Semiconductor Manufacturing, Production Planning and Control, the International Journal of Information Systems in the Service Sector, the Quality Management Journal, the International Journal of Information Systems and Supply Chain Management, and the Journal of Marketing Channels. He has been guest editor of the Journal of Marketing Channels and is on the editorial advisory board of the International Journal of Information Systems and Supply Management and the Journal of Marketing Channels. He has presented at over 32 international and national conferences on topic ranging from teaching pedagogy to managing supply chain risk and has consulted with companies such as Rider University, Neoteric Hovercraft, EDI Telecommunications, Southwestern Wire Cloth, and the Cleveland County Chamber of Commerce (North Carolina). He is a member of the Production and Operations Management Society, the Institute for Operations Research and Management Science, and APICS, the Society of Operations Management.

Ertunga C. Ozelkan, Ph.D., is an Assistant Professor of Systems Engineering and Engineering Management and the Associate Director of the Center for Lean Logistics and Engineered Systems at the University of North Carolina at Charlotte. Prior to UNC Charlotte, he was teaching at the School of Management at the University of Texas at Dallas. Before joining academia, Dr. Ozelkan worked for i2 Technologies, a leading supply chain software vendor in the capacity of a Customer Service and

Global Curriculum Manager and for Tefen USA, a systems design and industrial engineering consulting firm in the area of productivity improvement for Hitech firms. Dr. Ozelkan holds a Ph.D. degree in Systems and Industrial Engineering from the University of Arizona. He teaches courses on supply chain management, lean systems, decision analysis, design of experiments and systems optimization. His current research interests are the modeling of production planning systems and supply chains, and applications in different industries. Dr. Ozelkan is the recipient of IIE's 2006 Lean Division Excellence in Teaching Award.

Avraham Shtub holds the Stephen and Sharon Seiden Chair in Project Management. He has a B.Sc. from the Technion - Israel Institute of Technology, an MBA from Tel Aviv University and a Ph.D. from the University of Washington. He is the recipient of the Institute of Industrial Engineering 1995 "Book of the Year Award" for his Book "Project Management: Engineering, Technology and Implementation" (co-authored with Jonathan Bard and Shlomo Globerson), Prentice Hall, 1994, the Production Operations Management Society 2000 Wick Skinner Teaching Innovation Achievements Award for his book: "Enterprise Resource Planning (ERP): The Dynamics of Operations Management" and the 2008 Project Management Institute Professional Development Product of the Year Award for the training simulator "Project Team Builder – PTB". His were published in English, Hebrew, Greek and Chinese.

Index